ECONOMETRIC MODELS AND ECONOMIC FORECASTS

ECONOMETRIC MODELS AND ECONOMIC FORECASTS

Robert S. Pindyck

Massachusetts Institute of Technology

Daniel L. Rubinfeld

University of Michigan

McGraw-Hill Book Company

New York   St. Louis   San Francisco   Auckland   Düsseldorf   Johannesburg
Kuala Lumpur   London   Mexico   Montreal   New Delhi   Panama   Paris
São Paulo   Singapore   Sydney   Tokyo   Toronto

ECONOMETRIC MODELS AND ECONOMIC FORECASTS

34567890 KPKP 9876

Library of Congress Cataloging in Publication Data

Pindyck, Robert S
    Econometric models and economic forecasts.

    Includes index.
    1. Business forecasting—Mathematical models. 2. Econometrics.
I. Rubinfeld, Daniel L., joint author. II. Title.
HB3730.P54   338.5′44   75–19473
ISBN 0–07–050095–9

This book was set in Times Roman. The editors were J. S. Dietrich and Annette Hall; the designer was Jo Jones; the production supervisor was Leroy A. Young. The drawings were done by J & R Services, Inc. Kingsport Press, Inc., was printer and binder.

CONTENTS

ACKNOWLEDGMENTS

In the course of writing this book we received a considerable amount of help and encouragement from a number of people. Some of this help involved critical review and assistance in identifying errors, suggestions for general or specific modifications of the manuscript, and advice on presenting difficult material. Authors always depend on assistance of this sort to some extent, but we feel that the help that we received was particularly valuable.

The legion of colleagues and critics that played a role in this book is a large one, but there are some individuals who deserve special thanks. We are indebted to Edwin Kuh of MIT for providing inspiration, encouragement, and advice all along the way. In addition, we received a large number of very helpful comments and suggestions from our colleagues Saul Hymans, Jan Kmenta, Ronald Lee, and Harold Shapiro at the University of Michigan, as well as Robert Engle, Jerry Hausman, Douglas Hibbs, and Ken Wise at MIT. Our friends at other universities also provided substantial criticism on earlier drafts of the manuscript and suggestions that aided us in preparation of the final draft. We wish to thank Vittorio Corbo of Sir George Williams University, David Kendrick of the University of Texas, Patrick Larkey of the University of British Columbia, Charles Manski of Carnegie-Mellon University, Lester Taylor of the University of Arizona, Kent Wall of N.B.E.R., and Maurice Wilkinson of Columbia University for being especially helpful.

The preparation of examples for this book was a rather involved and time-consuming process. The task was made considerably easier by the capable and energetic help of our research assistants Robert Ludwig, Jonathan Shane, Stuart Traver, and Nicholas Vasilatos.

The preparation of the final manuscript and production of the book involved a considerable amount of patience as well as skill. We wish to thank Judith Jackson and Deborah S. Caldwell for their reliability and competence in typing the final manuscript. We also wish to thank the editorial staff of McGraw-Hill for their help in the book's production.

Robert S. Pindyck
Daniel L. Rubinfeld

INTRODUCTION

This book is an introduction to the science and art of building and using models. The science of model building consists of a set of tools, most of them quantitative, which are used to construct and then test mathematical representations of portions of the real world. The development and use of these tools are subsumed under the subject heading of econometrics. While not altogether straightforward, econometrics is a well-defined field and therefore relatively easy to describe in written prose. For this reason, the science of model building will be a primary concern of this book. The art of model building is, unfortunately, much harder to describe in words, since it consists mostly of intuitive judgments that occur during the modeling process. Unfortunately, there are no clear-cut rules as to how these model-building judgments should be made, which makes the art of model building difficult to master. Nonetheless, one of the purposes of this book is to convey the nature of that art to the reader to the extent possible. This will be done in part by examples and by discussions of technique, but also by encouraging the reader to do what is ultimately necessary to master the art, namely, to build models of his/her own.

The book focuses upon models of processes that occur in business, economics, and the social sciences in general. These might include models of aggregate economic activity, the sales of an individual firm, or a political process (e.g., estimating the number of votes that a particular candidate can be expected to receive in an election). Discussions of the purposes of building these models are directed toward forecasting and policy analysis, but the reader should bear in mind the general nature of the content.

As one might expect, there are many types of models that can and often have been used for policy analysis and forecasting. This book does not attempt to cover the entire spectrum of model types and modeling methodologies; rather, it concentrates on those models which fit (and test theoretical relationships against) data. This still leaves a rather wide range of models among which to choose. On one end of this range, one might determine the effect of alternative monetary policies on the behavior of the United States economy by constructing a large, multi-equation econometric model of the economy and then simulating it using different monetary policies. The resulting model would be rather complicated and would presume to explain a complex structure in the real world. On the other end of the range, one might desire to forecast the sales volume of a firm and, believing that those sales follow a strong cyclical pattern, use a time-series model to extrapolate the past behavior of sales.

It is this range of models that is the subject matter of this book. The objective of this book is to give the reader some understanding of the science and art of determining what type of model to build, building the model which is most appropriate, testing the model statistically, and then finally applying the model to practical problems in forecasting and analysis.

1 WHY MODELS?

Many of us often either use or produce forecasts of one sort or another. Few of us recognize, however, that some kind of logical structure, or model, is implicit in every forecast or analysis of a social or a physical system. Consider, for example, a stockbroker who tells you that the Dow Jones Industrial Average will rise next year. The stockbroker might have made this forecast because he/she has seen the Dow Jones average rising during the past few years and feels that whatever it was that made it rise in the past will continue to make it rise in the future. On the other hand, he/she might feel that the Dow Jones Industrial Average will rise next year because of a belief that this variable is linked to a set of economic and political variables through a complex set of relationships. The broker might believe, for example, that the Dow Jones average is related in a certain way to the gross national product and to interest rates, so that given certain other beliefs about the most probable future behavior of these latter variables, he/she would be led to believe that a rise in the Dow Jones average is likely.

If we have to find a word to describe the method by which our stockbroker made this forecast, we would probably say that it was intuitive, although the chain of reasoning differed substantially in the two cases cited above. The stockbroker certainty would not say that the forecast was made by building a model of the Dow Jones average; indeed, no equations were written down, nor was any computer used. Nonetheless, in each case, some *implicit* form of model building was involved. If the stockbroker based the optimistic forecast for the Dow Jones average on past increases, he/she has in effect constructed a *time-series model* which extrapolates past trends into the future. If, instead, the forecast was based on a knowledge of economics, a model would still be implicitly involved—it would be composed of the relationships that were loosely conceived in the stockbroker's mind as a result of past experience.

Thus, even the intuitive forecaster constructs some type of model, even if he/she is not aware of doing so. Of course, it is reasonable to ask why one might want to work with an *explicit* model to produce forecasts. Would it be worth the trouble, for example, for our stockbroker to read this book in order to construct an explicit model, estimate it on the computer, and test it statistically? Our response is that there are several advantages to working with models explicitly. Model building forces the individual to think clearly about and account for all the important interrelationships involved in a problem. The reliance on intuition can be dangerous at times because of the possibility that important relationships will be ignored or improperly used. In addition, it is important that individual relationships be tested or validated in some way or another. Unfortunately, this is not usually done when intuitive forecasts are made. In the process of building a model, however, the individual must test or validate not only the model as a whole, but also the individual relationships that make up the model.

When making a forecast, it is also important to provide a statistical measure of confidence to the user of the forecast, i.e., some measure of how accurate one might expect the forecast to be. The use of purely intuitive methods usually precludes any quantitative measure of confidence in the resulting forecast. The statistical analysis of the individual relationships that make up a model, and of the model as a whole, makes it possible to attach a measure of confidence to the model's forecasts.

Once a model has been constructed and fitted to data, a sensitivity analysis can be used to study many of its properties. In particular, the effects of small changes in individual variables in the model can be evaluated. For example, in the case of a model that describes and predicts interest rates, one could measure the effect on a particular interest rate of a change in the rate of inflation. This type of quantitative sensitivity study, which is important both in understanding and in using the model, can be done only if the model is an explicit one.

2 TYPES OF MODELS

In this book we examine three general classes of models that can be constructed for purposes of forecasting or policy analysis. Each involves a different degree of model complexity and structural explanation, and each presumes a different level of comprehension about the real world processes that one is trying to model. The three classes of models are as follows:

(a) *Time-Series Models* In this class of models we presume to know nothing about the real world causal relationships that affect the variable we are trying to forecast. Instead we examine the past behavior of a time series in order to infer something about its future behavior. The time-series method used to produce a forecast might involve the use of a simple deterministic model such as a linear extrapolation, or the use of a complex stochastic model for adaptive forecasting.

One example of the use of time-series analysis would be the simple extrapolation of a past trend in predicting population growth. Another example would be the development of a complex linear stochastic model for passenger loads on an airline. Models such as this have been developed and used to forecast the demand for airline capacity, seasonal telephone demand, the movement of short-term interest rates, as well as other economic variables. Time-series models are particularly useful when little is known about the underlying process that one is trying to forecast. The limited structure in time-series models makes them most reliable only in the short run, but they are nonetheless rather useful.

(b) *Single-Equation Regression Models* In this class of models the variable under study is explained by a single function (linear or nonlinear) of explanatory variables. The equation will often be time-dependent (i.e., the time index will appear explicitly in the model), so that one can predict the response over time of the variable under study to changes in one or more of the explanatory variables.

An example of a single-equation regression model might be an equation that relates a particular interest rate, such as the 3-month Treasury bill rate, to a set of explanatory variables such as the money supply, the rate of inflation, and the rate of change in the gross national product. Regression models are often used to forecast not only the movement in short- and long-term interest rates, but also many other economic and business variables.

(c)   *Multi–Equation Simulation Models*   In this class of models the variable to be studied may be a function of several explanatory variables, but now these explanatory variables are related to each other as well as to the variable under study through a set of equations. The construction of a simulation model begins with the specification of a set of individual relationships, each of which is fitted to available data. Simulation is the process of solving these equations simultaneously over some range in time.

An example of a multi-equation simulation model would be a complete model of the United States textile industry that contains equations that explain variables such as textile demand, textile production output, employment of production workers in the textile industry, investment in the industry, and textile prices. These variables would be related to each other and to other variables (such as total national income, the Consumer Price Index, interest rates, etc.), through a set of linear or nonlinear equations. Given assumptions about the future behavior of national income, interest rates, etc., one could simulate this model into the future and obtain a forecast for each of the model's variables. A model such as this can be used to analyze the impact on the industry of changes in external economic variables.

Multi-equation simulation models presume to explain a great deal about the structure of the physical process that is being studied. Not only are individual relationships specified, but the model accounts for the interaction of all these interrelationships at the same time. Thus, a five-equation simulation model actually contains more information than the sum of five individual regression equations. The model not only explains the five individual relationships, but it also describes the dynamic structure implied by the simultaneous operation of these relationships.

The choice of the type of model to develop is a difficult one, involving trade-offs among time, energy, costs, and desired forecast precision. The construction of a multi-equation simulation model might require large expenditures of time and money, not only in terms of actual work, but also in terms of computer time. The gains that result from this effort might include the better understanding of the relationships and structure involved as well as the ability to make a better forecast. However, in some cases these gains may be small enough so that they are outweighed by the heavy costs involved. Because the multi-equation model necessitates a good deal of knowledge about the process being studied, the construction of such models may be extremely difficult.

The decision to build a time-series model usually occurs in cases when little or nothing is known about the determinants of the variable being studied, when a large number of data points are available (thus making some kind of inference feasible), and when the model is to be used largely for short-term forecasting. Given some information about the processes involved, however, it may not be obvious whether a time-series model or a single-equation regression model is preferable as a means of forecasting. It may be reasonable for a forecaster to construct both types of models and compare their relative performances.

In the course of this book, we plan not only to describe how each type of model is constructed and used, but also to give some insight into the relative costs and benefits involved. Unfortunately, this can be a rather hard problem, as the choice of model type is often not clear. In any case, it seems natural to include a discussion of all three types of models (single-equation regression, multi-equation simulation, and time series) in the confines of a single book.

3   WHAT THE BOOK CONTAINS

The book is divided into three parts, each concentrating on a different class of models. The most fundamental class of models, discussed in the first part of the book, is the single-equation regression model. The econometric methods developed and used to construct single-equation regression models will, with modification, find application in the construction of multi-equation simulation models as well as time-series models. Thus, Part One of this book presents an introduction to the development and estimation of single-equation econometric models.

Chapter 1 begins with an introduction to the basic concepts of regression analysis. The regression model then is developed in detail, beginning with a two-variable model in Chapter 2 and proceeding to the multiple regression model in Chapter 3. These chapters also develop statistical tests and procedures that can be used to evaluate the properties of a regression model.

The estimation techniques used in simple regression analysis require that certain assumptions be made about both the data and the model. At times, these assumptions break down. Chapters 4 and 5 begin a discussion of what can be done in some of these cases. Chapter 4 deals with heteroscedasticity and serial correlation and includes statistical tests for these problems as well as estimation methods that correct for them. Chapter 5 deals with the problem of correlation between explanatory variables and the implicit error term in the regression model. It concentrates on the development of the instrumental variable and two-stage least-squares estimation techniques.

Chapter 6 discusses the use of a single-equation regression model for forecasting purposes. The chapter discusses not only the methods by which a forecast is produced, but also measures that describe the reliability of a forecast, such as confidence intervals and the error of forecast.

The last two chapters of Part One of the book consider extensions of the regression model. These chapters are somewhat more advanced in nature, and could be skipped by the beginning student. Chapter 7 deals with the problems of specification error, missing observations, the estimation of nonlinear models, distributed lag models, and models which pool cross-section and time-series data. Chapter 8 deals with models in which the variable to be explained is qualitative in nature. These include linear probability models, probit models, and logit models.

The foundation of econometrics of Part One is essential for the development of multi-equation simulation models in Part Two of the book. Part Two begins with a chapter on estimation techniques particular to simultaneous equation models. This includes problems of model identification, as well as techniques such as three-stage least squares. Chapters 10 and 11 discuss the methodology of constructing and using multi-equation simulation models. Chapter 10 is an introduction to simulation models, and includes a discussion of the simulation process, methods of evaluating simulation models, alternative methods of estimating simulation models, and general approaches to model construction. Chapter 11 is more technical in nature and discusses methods of analyzing the dynamic behavior of simulation models, including questions of model stability, dynamic multipliers, and methods of tuning and adjusting simulation models. Chapter 11 concludes with a discussion of sensitivity analysis and stochastic simulation.

Part Two closes with a chapter that presents three detailed examples of the construction and use of simulation models. In the first example, a small but complete model of the United States economy is constructed and used for simple policy analysis. The second example develops an industry market model and shows how it can be used to forecast production and prices. The last example shows how simulation techniques can be useful for financial planning in a corporation.

Part Three of this book is devoted to time-series models, which can be viewed as a special class of single-equation regression models. Thus, the econometric tools developed in Part One of the book will find extensive application in Part Three. Part Three begins with Chapter 13, which introduces the basic properties of random time series, as well as the notion of a time-series model. The chapter discusses the properties of stationary and nonstationary time series, and the calculation and use of the autocorrelation function.

Chapters 14, 15, and 16 develop the methods by which time-series models are specified, estimated, and used for forecasting. Chapter 14 covers linear time-series models in detail, including moving average models, autoregressive models, mixed models, and finally models of nonstationary time series. Chapter 15 develops regression methods that can be used to estimate a time-series model, as well as methods of diagnostic checking that can be used to ascertain how well the estimated model "fits" the data. Chapter 16 deals with the computation of the minimum mean-square-error forecast, forecast error, and forecast confidence intervals.

The last chapter of Part Three is devoted entirely to examples of the construction and use of time-series models. After we review the modeling process, we construct models of several economic variables and use them to produce short-term forecasts. Finally, we demonstrate through examples how models can be constructed that combine time-series with regression analysis.

4 USE OF MATHEMATICAL TOOLS

This book is written on a rather elementary level, and can be understood with only a limited knowledge of calculus and no knowledge of matrix algebra. Mathematical derivations and proofs are generally reserved for appendixes or suppressed entirely. In Part One of the book, the development of the regression model in matrix form is included in the appendixes. Thus most if not all of the book should be accessible to advanced undergraduate students as well as graduate students.

It is desirable that the reader of this book have some background in statistics. Although Appendix 2.1 contains a brief review of probability and statistics, the student with *no* background in statistics may find parts of the book somewhat difficult. Typically, this book would be used in an applied econometrics or business-forecasting course which a student would take after completing an introductory course in statistics.

5 ALTERNATIVE USES OF THE BOOK

The book is intended to have a wide spectrum of uses. Curriculum uses include an undergraduate or introductory graduate course in econometrics and an undergraduate or graduate course in business-forecasting. In addition, this book can be of considerable value as a reference book for people doing statistical analyses of economic and business data, or as a text or reference book for the social scientist or business analyst interested in the application of dynamic simulation models to forecasting or policy analysis.

Coverage in an introductory econometrics or business forecasting course must, of course, be dependent to some extent on the background of the student and the goals of the instructor. Emphasis on the use of econometric techniques for purposes of forecasting with econometric models would provide for one focus, but several alternatives are available. We list several alternative uses of the book below, but stress that the great variety of material leaves a good deal of discretion to the instructor planning a course outline.

I UNDERGRADUATE ECONOMETRICS (one semester)
   (i) *Standard*
      Part One—Chapters 1–6; portions of Chapters 7 and 8 optional
      Part Two—Chapter 9

   (ii) *Simulation emphasis*
      Part One—Chapters 1–6
      Part Two—Chapters 10–12

      Both courses would omit all matrix appendixes.

II FIRST-YEAR GRADUATE ECONOMETRICS
   (i) *One semester*
      Part One—Chapters 1–6; Chapters 7 and 8 optional
      Part Two—Chapters 9–12

      Portions of the above and the appendixes may be optional.

(ii) *Two semesters*
Part One—Chapters 1–8
Part Two—Chapters 9–12
Part Three—Chapters 13–14; portions of Chapters 15–17 optional

Emphasis on either simulation and/or time-series analysis would depend upon the interest of the instructor.

III BUSINESS FORECASTING (graduate or advanced undergraduate)
(i) *One semester*
Part One—Chapter 6 plus review of Chapters 1–5
Part Two—Chapters 10–12
Part Three—Chapters 13–17 (selected portions)

(ii) *Two semesters*
Part One—Chapters 1–6
Part Two—Chapters 9–12
Part Three—Chapters 13–17

IV QUANTITATIVE METHODS FOR POLICY ANALYSIS
(i) *Undergraduate—one semester*
Part One—Chapters 1–6
Part Two—Chapters 10–12

(ii) *Graduate—one semester*
Part One—Chapters 1–6
Part Two—Chapters 9–12

(iii) *Graduate—two semesters*
Part One—Chapters 1–6; Chapters 7 and 8 optional
Part Two—Chapters 9–12
Part Three—Chapters 13–17

The book could also be used for courses in quantitative social science modeling (as taught in departments of sociology or political science). A course in social science modeling that uses this book as a text would probably cover most of Parts One and Two of the book.

6 WHAT DISTINGUISHES THIS BOOK FROM OTHERS?

This book attempts to explain the development and use of quantitative models from a broad perspective. Most textbooks on econometrics develop the single-equation regression model as a self-contained and isolated entity. The reader of such a book often infers that statistical regression models are somehow distinct and independent from other aspects of modeling, such as the analysis of a model's dynamic structure or the use of time-series analysis to forecast one or more exogenous variables in the model. This is certainly not the case, as any practitioner of the art knows. In developing a multi-equation simulation model, for example, one must be knowledgeable not only of regression methods, but also of how a model's dynamic behavior results from the interaction of its individual equations.

This book develops the techniques and methods for the construction of all three types of models. Thus, the reader becomes aware of the use of single-equation econometrics as a modeling form in itself, as a tool that can be used in the development of multi-equation simulation models, and as a statistical basis for the development of stochastic time-series models for forecasting. The reader also becomes aware that there is more than one type of model, and (we hope) gains an understanding of what models are most preferable for a particular purpose.

We believe that this wide breadth of coverage is desirable. The simulation and time-series techniques that make up Parts Two and Three of this book are usually presented only at an advanced level. We feel that a strength of this book is that the coverage is broad and includes these advanced techniques, but is presented on a level that can be understood and appreciated by the beginning student.

ECONOMETRIC MODELS AND ECONOMIC FORECASTS

ONE

SINGLE-EQUATION REGRESSION MODELS

Part One of this book is concerned with the theory and application of econometrics. The different types of models that lend themselves to econometric analysis will be described as we develop materials in the text. We begin our discussion with single-equation regression models, simple in form, but quite powerful in terms of the variety of possible business and economic applications. In these models, one variable under study is assumed to be a linear function of several explanatory variables. Single-equation models are important, not only because they can be useful for testing hypotheses and forecasting, but because they form the groundwork for the analysis of simultaneous-equation models and time-series models. Because most of the econometric techniques discussed in Part One of the book are of use in the remaining two parts, we have chosen to develop these methods extensively in a manner which is accessible to all students.

The first six chapters develop the central framework of single-equation econometrics. In Chapter 1, elementary curve-fitting concepts and the notion of least squares are developed. The two-variable model is used in the second chapter as a means of focusing on the statistical properties which might be desired for regression parameter estimates. Emphasis in the chapter is placed on the notion of hypothesis testing and the problem of measuring goodness of fit of a regression line. The third chapter extends the regression model to the multiple-variable case. The presence of more than one explanatory variable in the regression model leads to additional econometric problems relating to the interaction of these variables. These problems include the interpretation of regression coefficients and multicollinearity. Some additional regression statistics which help with the interaction problem are also discussed. Finally, the application of the multiple regression model with dummy variables and other generalizations are considered.

The estimation techniques used in the first part of the book depend crucially upon several assumptions relating to the form of the data and to the specification of the model itself. Chapters 4 and 5 deal with several of these assumptions. In Chapter 4 we focus on the possible existence of heteroscedasticity and serial correlation, describing tests for their existence as well as corrections when they are present. In Chapter 5 we concern ourselves with the difficulties which arise when one or more of the explanatory variables is correlated with the error term in the regression model. To correct for this difficulty, we introduce the methods of instrumental variables and two-stage least-squares estimation. Because the problems in this chapter are likely to arise when the model being studied is truly simultaneous in nature, Chapter 5 serves as an important introduction to the material in Part Two of the book (Chapter 9, especially).

Chapter 6 deals with the problem of forecasting within the context of a single-equation model. The means of obtaining a forecast and some measure of the reliability of that forecast are discussed in the case when the explanatory variables are known as well as unknown, and in the case when the errors of the regression model are serially correlated. The material in Chapter 6 lays the groundwork for the more advanced analysis of forecasting which appears in Parts Two and Three.

The final two chapters of Part One contain materials of a more advanced nature than the first six chapters. Both chapters deal with extensions of the regression model which can be quite important in applied econometric work, but which can be skipped by the reader wishing to focus on Parts Two and Three of the book. Chapter 7 contains brief discussions of five econometric issues— specification error, missing observations, pooling of cross-section and time-series data, distributed lags, and nonlinear estimation. Any of the five chapter sections may be read independently of the remaining four. Finally, Chapter 8 deals with the estimation of models in which the variable to be studied is qualitative rather than quantitative. The chapter emphasizes the means by which the linear probability, probit, and logit models may be used to study problems involving binary as well as multiple choices. Chapter 8 is self-contained and can be read independently from Chapter 7.

1

In this chapter we begin our discussion of econometrics by concentrating on the development of the two-variable linear regression model. In the first section the notion of curve fitting is discussed with reference to an example based on student grade-point averages. The least-squares criterion for curve fitting is presented and compared with several alternative curve-fitting schemes. In the second section, a detailed derivation of the least-squares estimation procedure is included. The chapter concludes with three elementary applications of the least-squares regression technique.

INTRODUCTION TO THE REGRESSION MODEL

1.1 CURVE FITTING

Data resulting from the measurement of variables may come from any number of sources and in a variety of forms. Data which describe the movement of a variable over time are called *time-series* data, and may be daily, weekly, monthly, quarterly, or annual. Data which describe the activities of individual persons, firms, or other units at a given point in time are called *cross-section* data. A marketing study dealing with family expenditures at a given time is likely to utilize cross-section data. Cross-section data might also be used to examine a group of business accounting statements for the purpose of estimating patterns of behavior among individual firms in an industry.

TABLE 1.1
GRADE-POINT AVERAGE AND FAMILY INCOME

Y (grade-point average)	X (income of parents in $1,000)
4.0	21.0
3.0	15.0
3.5	15.0
2.0	9.0
3.0	12.0
3.5	18.0
2.5	6.0
2.5	12.0

FIGURE 1.1
Scatter diagram.

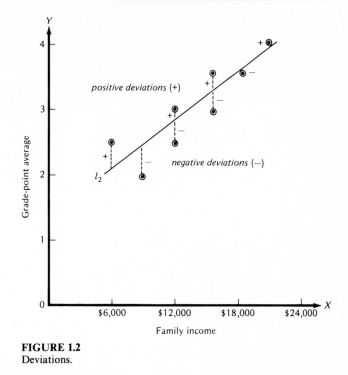

FIGURE 1.2
Deviations.

Let us assume that we are interested in the relationship between two variables X and Y. In order to describe this relationship statistically, we need a set of observations for each variable and a hypothesis setting forth the explicit mathematical form of the relationship between X and Y. The set of observations is called a *sample*.[1] We shall be primarily concerned with the hypothesis that the relationship between X and Y is linear, i.e., that the relationship between X and Y can best be described by a straight line. Given the assumption of linearity, our objective is to specify a rule by which the "best" straight line fitting X and Y is to be determined.

As an example, assume that we wish to test the hypothesis that the grade-point average of a student can be predicted or explained to a large extent by the income of the parents of that student. Eight sample points were obtained (hypothetically) and are described in Table 1.1 and plotted as a scatter diagram in Fig. 1.1. Many straight lines can be chosen to fit the plotted points. One could connect the points from the lowest X value to the highest X value (line l_1), or one could draw a line by eye which appears to fit the full scatter of points (line l_2). A better rule might be to choose a line so that the sum of the distances (positive and negative) from the points on the graph to the line, measured vertically, is zero. (These distances, known as *deviations*, are shown in Fig. 1.2.)

---

[1] The sample data are observations which have been chosen from an underlying *population* which represents the true relationship under study.

This criterion would assure that deviations that are equal in magnitude and equal in sign are given equal importance. Unfortunately, however, this procedure has the undesirable property that deviations which are equal in size but opposite in sign cancel out. We could improve on this method if we were to minimize the absolute value of the deviations of the fitted line from the sample points. Implicit in such a procedure is the judgment that the importance of the deviation is proportional to its magnitude. While the minimization of the sum of absolute deviations is appealing, it does suffer from several disadvantages. First, the procedure is computationally quite difficult to utilize. Second, it is reasonable that large deviations should be treated with relatively greater attention than small deviations. For example, a prediction involving a two-unit error would probably be considered worse than a prediction involving two errors of one unit each.

A procedure does exist which is computationally feasible, which penalizes large errors relatively more than small errors, and which guarantees that half the measured deviations will fall above the fitted line and half will lie below. This procedure is the method of *least squares*. The least-square criterion is as follows: The "*line of best fit*" *is said to be that which minimizes the sum of the squared deviations of the points of the graph from the points of the straight line* (with distances measured vertically). We will see in the next chapter that least squares is also convenient in that it permits statistical testing, but at this point we are concerned solely with describing the procedure itself.

1.2   DERIVATION OF LEAST SQUARES

The purpose of constructing statistical relationships is usually to predict or explain the effects on one variable resulting from changes in one or more predictor or explanatory variables. For the scatter of points in Fig. 1.1 we may write the linear equation $Y = a + bX$, where Y is the *dependent variable* and X the *independent variable*. Because we are trying to explain or predict movements in Y, it is natural to choose as our objective the minimization of the vertical sum of the squared deviations from the fitted line.[2]

The least-squares criterion (using vertical measurements) may be restated formally as follows:

$$\text{Minimize} \sum_{i=1}^{N} (Y_i - \hat{Y}_i)^2 \tag{1.1}$$

---

[2] In general, our decision to write an equation in the form $Y = a + bX$ rather than the reverse form $X = A + BY$ implies that an implicit judgment has been made that movements in the variable Y are "caused" by movements in the variable X and not vice versa. In the grade-point average example, we have assumed implicitly that grade-point average is determined by family income. If we revised our view of causality to one which states that family income is determined by grade-point average, then we would write the equation $X = A + BY$, and our curve-fitting criterion would be adjusted accordingly. Of course, minimizations of the sum of squared vertical and horizontal deviations are not the only least-squares procedures possible. One could minimize the sum of squared deviations measured along any line connecting sample points to the regression line. (An occasional choice is the perpendicular distance.) However, such procedures are more difficult computationally and statistically than the ordinary (vertical-distance) least-squares procedure, and will not be pursued further.

FIGURE 1.3
Fitted values.

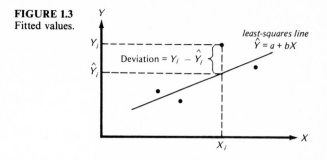

where $\hat{Y}_i = a + bX_i$ is the fitted value of Y corresponding to a particular observation X_i, and N is the number of observations (see Fig. 1.3). The values of a and b are, of course, not known, and must be calculated so as to satisfy the criterion.

The problem is to choose (simultaneously) values for a and b which minimize the expression in Eq. (1.1). This can be done using elementary calculus.[3] We minimize the expression by taking the partial derivatives with respect to a and to b, setting each equal to 0 and solving the resulting pair of simultaneous equations:[4]

$$\frac{\partial}{\partial a} \sum (Y_i - a - bX_i)^2 = -2 \sum (Y_i - a - bX_i) \tag{1.2}$$

$$\frac{\partial}{\partial b} \sum (Y_i - a - bX_i)^2 = -2 \sum X_i(Y_i - a - bX_i) \tag{1.3}$$

Equating these derivatives to zero and dividing by -2, we get

$$\sum (Y_i - a - bX_i) = 0 \tag{1.4}$$

$$\sum X_i(Y_i - a - bX_i) = 0 \tag{1.5}$$

Finally by rewriting Eqs. (1.4) and (1.5), we obtain the pair of simultaneous equations known as the "normal equations":

$$\sum Y_i = aN + b \sum X_i \tag{1.6}$$

$$\sum X_i Y_i = a \sum X_i + b \sum X_i^2 \tag{1.7}$$

---

[3] The reader with limited exposure to the calculus need not be concerned with the details that follow.

[4] An index does not appear in the summation signs, but the index is assumed to range over all observations $1, 2, \ldots, N$.

(Recall that N is the number of observations.) Now we may solve for a and b simultaneously by multiplying (1.6) by $\sum X_i$ and (1.7) by N:

$$\sum X_i \sum Y_i = aN \sum X_i + b(\sum X_i)^2 \tag{1.8}$$

$$N \sum X_i Y_i = aN \sum X_i + bN \sum X_i^2 \tag{1.9}$$

Subtracting (1.8) from (1.9), we get

$$N \sum X_i Y_i - \sum X_i \sum Y_i = b[N \sum X_i^2 - (\sum X_i)^2] \tag{1.10}$$

from which it follows that

$$b = \frac{N \sum X_i Y_i - \sum X_i \sum Y_i}{N \sum X_i^2 - (\sum X_i)^2} \tag{1.11}$$

Given b, we may calculate a from Eq. (1.6):

$$a = \frac{\sum Y_i}{N} - b \frac{\sum X_i}{N} \tag{1.12}$$

Now consider how the formulas in Eqs. (1.11) and (1.12) simplify in the special case when X and Y both have sample means of 0. First, rewriting Eq. (1.12) we notice that

$$a = \overline{Y} - b\overline{X} = 0 \tag{1.13}$$

where $\overline{Y}$ and $\overline{X}$ are the sample means of Y and X, respectively.[5] Thus, when the sample means of X and Y are 0, the intercept of the fitted regression line will be 0. To obtain the corresponding slope estimate in this special case, we divide both the numerator and denominator of Eq. (1.11) by N^2

$$b = \frac{\sum X_i Y_i/N - (\sum X_i/N)(\sum Y_i/N)}{\sum X_i^2/N - (\sum X_i/N)^2}$$

Substituting $\overline{X}$ and $\overline{Y}$,

$$b = \frac{\sum X_i Y_i/N - \overline{X}\,\overline{Y}}{\sum X_i^2/N - \overline{X}^2}$$

But, $\overline{X} = \overline{Y} = 0$ by definition. Therefore,

$$b = \frac{\sum X_i Y_i/N}{\sum X_i^2/N} \tag{1.14}$$

---

[5] The "sample mean" and related notions of probability and statistics are reviewed in Appendix 2.1.

The fact that Eq. (1.14) is less complicated than Eq. (1.11) suggests that it will simplify matters to write the least-squares estimates in terms of variables which are expressed as deviations from their respective sample means, whether those means are zero or not.[6] To do so, we transform the data to deviations form by expressing each observation on X and Y in terms of deviations from their respective means:[7]

$$x_i = X_i - \overline{X}$$

$$y_i = Y_i - \overline{Y}$$

Using this definition, the least-squares slope estimate can be obtained (in the general case) directly from Eq. (1.14), since variables x and y have zero mean.[8]

FIGURE 1.4
Use of deviations form.

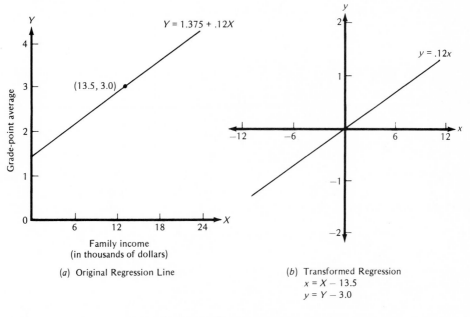

(a) Original Regression Line

(b) Transformed Regression
$x = X - 13.5$
$y = Y - 3.0$

---

[6] The representation of the data in this form is done primarily for expositional purposes. Many of the derivations which appear in ensuing chapters will be greatly simplified if "deviations" data are utilized. This choice of representation involves no loss of generality.

[7] We shall always use small letters in Part One to refer to variables measured as deviations about their means so as not to cause confusion.

[8] $$\bar{x} = \frac{\sum x_i}{N} = \frac{\sum (X_i - \overline{X})}{N} = \frac{\sum X_i}{N} - \overline{X} = \overline{X} - \overline{X} = 0$$

The identical proof holds for $\bar{y}$.

Therefore, we conclude that the least-squares slope estimate is

$$b = \frac{\sum x_i y_i}{\sum x_i^2} \tag{1.15}$$

The transformation of variables into deviations form is depicted graphically in Fig. 1.4. In Fig. 1.4a the regression line is graphed using the original observations, while the deviations form is used in Fig. 1.4b. Notice first that the estimated slopes of both regression lines are identical. This is obvious from Eq. (1.15), since only variables in deviations form enter the calculation. However, the intercept of the regression line in Fig. 1.4b is identically equal to 0. This follows from Eq. (1.13) and the fact that $\overline{X}$ and $\overline{Y}$ are equal to 0 by construction. Thus, if we choose to work with data in deviations form, we transform the origin of the regression line, but we do not alter the slope. Finally, notice that the line in Fig. 1.4b passes through the origin. This is equivalent to the fact that the line in Fig. 1.4a passes through the points of means $(\overline{X}, \overline{Y})$. The proof of this result is left as an exercise for the reader.

Example 1.1   Grade-Point Average

In the grade-point average example described in the text, the least-squares procedure allows us to obtain an intercept of 1.375 and a slope of .12, yielding the line $\hat{Y} = 1.375 + .12X$. The details of the calculations appear in Table 1.2. (The reader should check Fig. 1.1 to see that the resulting equation is quite similar to line l_2, which was determined by careful guesswork.) For any given family income X the regression line allows us to estimate or predict a value for the grade-point average Y. For example, a family income of $12,000 would lead to a predicted grade-point average of $\hat{Y} = 1.375 + .12(12) = 2.815$. While the predicted grade-point average will not necessarily give an accurate guess every time, it will provide a good approximation. For example, we might notice that the two students in the original sample (see Table 1.1) with parents having incomes of $12,000 had grade-point averages of 3.0 and 2.5. The predicted grade-point average happens to lie between the two actual data points.

The slope in the estimated equation tells us that a $1,000 change in family income will lead to an expected change of .12 in grade-point average. The positive value for the slope is consistent with the hypothesis that students with relatively high grade-point averages come from families with relatively high incomes. The intercept of 1.375 tells us that if family income were projected at $0, the best prediction for grade-point average would be 1.375. Since none of the families in our sample had an income near zero, we do not place much confidence in this result.

TABLE 1.2

GRADE-POINT AVERAGE EXAMPLE (CALCULATIONS)

$$\bar{X} = 13.5 \qquad \bar{Y} = 3.0$$

(1) $x_i = X_i - \bar{X}$	(2) $y_i = Y_i - \bar{Y}$	(3) $x_i y_i$	(4) x_i^2
7.5	1.0	7.5	56.25
1.5	.0	.0	2.25
1.5	.5	.75	2.25
−4.5	−1.0	4.5	20.25
−1.5	.0	.0	2.25
4.5	.5	2.25	20.25
−7.5	.5	3.75	56.25
−1.5	.5	.75	2.25
$\sum x_i = 0$	$\sum y_i = 0$	$\sum x_i y_i = 19.50$	$\sum x_i^2 = 162.00$

$$b = \frac{\sum x_i y_i}{\sum x_i^2} = .120$$

$$a = \bar{Y} - b\bar{X} = 1.375$$

$$\hat{Y} = 1.375 + .12X$$

We shall examine the two-variable linear regression model in much greater detail in Chapter 2. However, it will be instructive at this point to make a few specific comments about the least-squares procedure. First, in the model $Y = a + bX$, the slope b is an estimate of dY/dX, the ratio of a change in Y to a change in X. This allows us to interpret the regression slope quite naturally. The interpretation of the intercept, on the other hand, depends on whether sufficient observations near $X = 0$ are available to yield statistically meaningful results. If so, we may interpret the intercept as an estimate of Y when $X = 0$. However, if sufficient observations are not available, then the intercept is simply the height of the least-squares line.

Second, if we had estimated the "wrong" regression, $X = A + BY$, the estimated slope would be[9]

$$B = \frac{\sum x_i y_i}{\sum y_i^2}$$

---

[9] We use the term *wrong regression* under the assumption that we are concerned with the prediction of the Y variable and wish to minimize squared deviation of predicted values $\hat{Y}_i$ from actual values Y_i.

If the estimation processes are to be equivalent, then the wrong regression slope must equal the reciprocal of the original; that is, $B = 1/b$. However, this equality will hold only in the unusual case that $(\sum x_i y_i)^2/(\sum x_i^2 \sum y_i^2) = 1$. The reader should verify that such an occurrence can happen only when *all* the sample points lie on the fitted regression line.

Example 1.2   Clothing Expenditure[10]

Suppose that we wish to study the relationship between expenditures on clothing and total expenditure on consumption goods. More specifically, we wish to see to what extent movements in clothing expenditures can be predicted by movements in overall consumption expenditures. A study of this kind was constructed in France in 1951. Cross-section data were obtained for 112 households of minor officials living in provincial towns. The two variables measured were clothing expenditure Y and total consumption expenditure X. A decision was made to fit the line $Y = a + bX$, since it was believed that individuals choose their clothing expenditures as a direct function of their total chosen outlays. The estimated equation was

$$\hat{Y} = 1.78 + 1.20X$$

On the basis of the positive sign of the slope coefficient, we can conclude that the data are consistent with the hypothesis of a direct relationship between clothing expenditures and total expenditures.

Example 1.3   Stock Prices of Public Utility Companies

As part of a larger corporate finance study, it is hypothesized that the price-earnings multiples for public utilities are influenced by their debt-equity ratios. This is reasonable, since one would expect a higher debt-equity ratio to lead to a more variable earning pattern for a company and that this added risk would lead to a lower stock price and thus a lower price-earnings multiple. The model may be expressed formally as

$$Y = a + bX$$

where Y = price-earnings multiple of company
$\quad\quad X$ = debt-equity ratio of company

---

[10] E. Malinvaud, *Statistical Methods of Econometrics* (Paris: North Holland, 1966), pp. 3–7.

We expect the coefficient b to have a negative value, but have no *a priori* expectation regarding the value of the intercept. Observations were obtained for variables Y and X for a cross section of public utilities (at a fixed point in time). The linear regression result is

$$\hat{Y} = 10.2 - 4.07X$$

The coefficient of -4.07 appears to confirm the stated hypothesis. However, in order to study the validity of the hypothesis in more detail we need to utilize some of the statistical tests which are discussed in the next chapter.

Exercises

1.1 Assume that you are in charge of the central monetary authority in a mythical country. You are given the following historical data on the quantity of money and national income (both in millions of dollars):

Year	Quantity of money	National income
1963	2.0	5.0
1964	2.5	5.5
1965	3.2	6.0
1966	3.6	7.0
1967	3.3	7.2
1968	4.0	7.7
1969	4.2	8.4
1970	4.6	9.0
1971	4.8	9.7
1972	5.0	10.0

(1) Plot these points on a scatter diagram. Then estimate the regression of national income Y on the quantity of money X and plot the line on the scatter diagram.
(2) How do you interpret the intercept and slope of the regression line?
(3) If you had sole control over the money supply and wished to achieve a level of national income of 12.0 in 1973, at what level would you set the money supply? Explain.

1.2 Calculate the regression of income on grade-point average in the example described in the chapter, and compare it with the regression of grade-point average on income. Why are the two results different?

1.3 (1) Assume that least-squares estimates are obtained for the relationship $Y = a + bX$. After the work is completed, it is decided to multiply the units of the X variable by a factor of 10. What will happen to the resulting least-squares slope and intercept?

(2) Generalize the result of (1) by evaluating the effects on the regression of changing the units of X and Y in the following manner:

$$Y^* = c_1 + c_2 Y$$

$$X^* = d_1 + d_2 X$$

What can you conclude?

1.4 What happens to the least-squares intercept and slope estimate when all observations on the independent variable are identical? Can you explain intuitively why this occurs?

1.5 Prove that the estimated regression line passes through the point of means $(\bar{X}, \bar{Y})$. [*Hint:* Show that $\bar{X}$ and $\bar{Y}$ satisfy the equation $Y = a + bX$, where a and b are defined in Eqs. (1.11) and (1.12).]

1.6 How would you interpret the -1.78 value of the intercept in the regression equation of Example 1.2? Explain why the value of the intercept is not likely to be of much practical interest.

2

THE TWO-VARIABLE REGRESSION MODEL

In the first chapter we introduced the process of building and testing models by describing the method of least squares as one of a number of possible means by which a curve may be fitted to data. Our concern was directed toward the algebra of parameter estimation, rather than toward the statistics of model testing. In this chapter we will discuss the statistical testing of the least-squares regression model that contains one dependent and one independent variable. First, we will describe the assumptions underlying the two-variable model, and then we will analyze the statistical properties of the least-squares parameter estimates. We will see that under certain assumptions least-squares estimates are unbiased, consistent, and efficient. The distribution of the estimated parameters will then be used to construct confidence intervals and to test hypotheses about the model. To complete the chapter we will introduce the concept of R-squared, a measure of the goodness of fit of the regression model. We will defer to Chapter 3 a discussion of the regression model with more than two variables.

2.1 THE MODEL

Our objective is to understand the probabilistic nature of the regression model. To do this we expand the analysis to allow for the fact that for a given observed value of X (the independent variable), we may observe many possible values of Y (the dependent variable). As an example consider the consumption pattern of an individual who receives income of $10,000 each year. The portion of this money expended on food is likely to vary each year because of changes in the environment facing the individual. Unless additional knowledge is available we presume that for each observation X (income) observations on Y (food purchases) will differ in a random fashion. To describe this situation formally, we add a random "error" component to the model, writing it as follows:

$$Y_i = \alpha + \beta X_i + \varepsilon_i \tag{2.1}$$

where for each observation Y is a *random variable*, X is fixed (known by the experimenter), and ε is a *random error term*, whose values are based on an underlying probability distribution.[1] Notice that we have switched our notation to utilize Greek letters to represent regression parameters, since our model now contains a random error term.

The error term may arise through the interplay of several forces.[2] First, errors appear because the model is a simplification of reality.[3] We assume, for example, that price is the sole determinant of the demand for a product. In fact, several omitted variables related to demand, such as individual tastes, population, income and weather, may be included in the error term. If these omitted effects are small, then it is reasonable to assume that the error term is random. A second source of error is associated with the collection and measurement of the data. Economic and business data will frequently be difficult to measure. For example, an individual firm may not be willing to relinquish explicit cost data, so that error-free estimates of costs will not be obtained. Given these sources of error, our decision to represent the relationship in Eq. (2.1) as a *stochastic* one should be clear. For every value X there exists a probability distribution of ε, and therefore a probability distribution of the Y's. This is depicted graphically in Fig. 2.1.

We are now in a position to specify fully the two-variable linear regression model by listing its important assumptions.

i The relationship between Y and X is linear as described in Eq. (2.1).
ii The X_i's are nonstochastic variables whose values are fixed.[4]

---

[1] The statistical notions involved here are reviewed in Appendix 2.1.

[2] The error term must be distinguished from the *residual* $(\hat{\varepsilon}_i = Y_i - \hat{Y}_i)$ or deviation of the dependent variable observation from its fitted value. Errors are associated with the true regression model, while residuals arise from the *estimation* process.

[3] We have chosen to postpone a discussion of all sources of error (including specification error) until Chapters 6 and 7.

[4] The assumption that the X's are fixed is equivalent to the assumption that the independent variable in question is perfectly controlled by the researcher who can change its value in accordance with experimental objectives. Such an assumption of nonrandomness in the X variable is highly unrealistic in the study of most business and economic problems. It has been made here solely for expositional purposes. Most of the results of least-squares regression analysis hold under more general assumptions than this, but are substantially more difficult to prove. The fixed X assumption will be relaxed in Chapter 3. Finally, to be complete we should add to our stated assumption a further assumption that the variance of X_i is nonzero, and it is finite for any sample size.

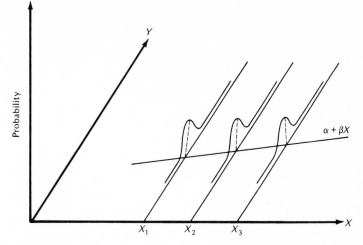

FIGURE 2.1
Two-variable regression model.

iii (*a*) The error term has zero expected value and constant variance for all observations; that is, $E(\varepsilon_i) = 0$ and $E(\varepsilon_i^2) = \sigma^2$.

(*b*) The random variables ε_i are uncorrelated in a statistical sense; i.e., errors corresponding to different observations have zero correlation. Thus, $E(\varepsilon_i \varepsilon_j) = 0$, for $i \neq j$.

This list of assumptions constitutes the *classical linear regression model*.

The assumption that the error term has zero expected value is made in part as a matter of convenience. To see this, assume that the average effect of the omitted errors is equal to α' [that is, $E(\varepsilon_i) = \alpha'$]. Then we may write the two-variable model as

$$Y_i = \alpha + \beta X_i + \varepsilon_i + (\alpha' - \alpha')$$

$$= (\alpha + \alpha') + \beta X_i + (\varepsilon_i - \alpha')$$

$$= \alpha^* + \beta X_i + \varepsilon_i^*$$

where
$$\alpha^* = (\alpha + \alpha')$$
$$\varepsilon_i^* = (\varepsilon_i - \alpha')$$
$$E(\varepsilon_i^*) = E(\varepsilon_i - \alpha') = \alpha' - \alpha' = 0$$

If the error term has a constant variance (as assumed), we call it *homoscedastic*; but if the variance is changing, we call the error *heteroscedastic*. *Heteroscedasticity* (as opposed to *homoscedasticity*) might arise if one is examining a cross section of firms in an industry. There may be reason to believe that error terms associated with very large firms will have greater variance than those

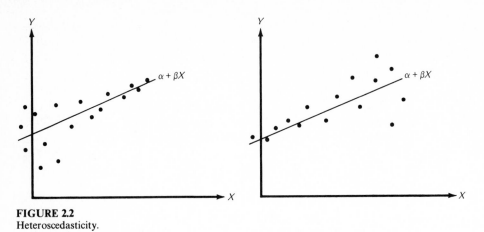

FIGURE 2.2
Heteroscedasticity.

associated with small firms. Figure 2.2 illustrates two cases of heteroscedasticity. In Fig. 2.2*a* the variance of the error term decreases as the value of X increases, while in Fig. 2.2*b* the variance of the errors increases with X.

The assumption that errors corresponding to different observations are uncorrelated is important in both time-series and cross-section studies. When the error terms from different observations are correlated, we say that the error process is *serially correlated* or *autocorrelated*.[5] Figure 2.3 illustrates the cases of negative and positive serial correlation in a time-series study. In this case negative serial correlation means that negative errors in one time period are associated with positive errors in the next, and vice versa. Thus, in Fig. 2.3*a*

FIGURE 2.3
Serial correlation.

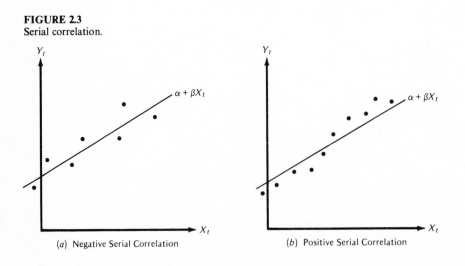

(*a*) Negative Serial Correlation   (*b*) Positive Serial Correlation

---

[5] We shall use the terms *serial correlation* and *autocorrelation* interchangeably in this book.

the data points fluctuate above and below the true regression line with some regularity. When positive serial correlation occurs, on the other hand, a positive error in one period will tend to be associated with a positive error in the next period. Thus, in Fig. 2.3*b* the errors follow a pattern where first they are negative (low values of X), and then they are positive (high values of X).

We should note that as a corollary to assumptions ii and iii(a), we are implicitly assuming that the error term is uncorrelated with the X's. This follows from the assumption that the X's are nonstochastic. Then,

$$E(X_i \varepsilon_i) = X_i E(\varepsilon_i) = 0$$

We shall need this assumption explicitly when we expand our analysis to cover models in which the X's are stochastic, i.e., drawn randomly from a probability distribution. In addition, assumptions iii(a) and iii(b) allow us to conclude that the expected value of the sum of the errors in any sample will be identically zero; that is,

$$E(\sum \varepsilon_i) = \sum E(\varepsilon_i) = 0$$

This result should not be confused with the statement of iii(a), $E(\varepsilon_i) = 0$, which implies that the expected value of error terms associated with a *particular X* will be identically zero for repeated sampling of Y's associated with that X. To obtain the latter result we fix or keep constant each value of X; then we draw samples for the random errors from a population with a known probability distribution. It is the expected value of *each* of these samples of error terms that we assume to be identically zero.[6]

Before we consider the estimation procedure in the stochastic model, two observations are worthy of special note. First, we have described each disturbance, or error term, as having constant variance σ^2. The variance is, of course, an unknown parameter and must be estimated as part of the regression model. Thus, the stochastic regression model described here has three unknown parameters, while the curve-fitting model of Chapter 1 has only two. Second, we have described the assumptions of the model in terms of the error disturbance ε, but we could just as easily have written the assumptions in terms of the probability distribution of the variable Y. In this case the assumptions would appear as follows:

iii (a') The random variable Y has expected value $\alpha + \beta X$ and variance σ^2:

$$[E(Y_i) = E(\alpha + \beta X_i + \varepsilon_i) = \alpha + \beta X_i + E(\varepsilon) = \alpha + \beta X_i]$$

(b') The random variables Y_i are uncorrelated.

---

[6] Another way of saying this is that the probability distribution from which the ε-samples are drawn has a mean of 0. In addition, it is the same probability distribution from which the ε-samples are drawn for all values of X.

2.2   STATISTICAL PROPERTIES OF ESTIMATORS

In order to perform statistical tests on the linear model, we need to specify the probability distribution of the error term. In the *classical normal linear regression model* we assume:

iii (*c*) The error term is normally distributed.

This assumption is important for the statistical testing of the model. If one is willing to believe that the individual errors due to measurement and to omission are small and independent of each other, then the normality assumption is a reasonable one. Given the assumption that the error term ε is normally distributed, it follows that the dependent variable Y is also normally distributed (since Y_i is a linear combination of the ε_i's, each of which is normal).

Now we are in a position to return to the problem of choosing estimated parameters for the stochastic linear regression model. Our goal is to fit an estimated regression line $\hat{Y} = \hat{\alpha} + \hat{\beta}X$ which is in some sense close to the true regression line. We have seen in the last chapter that one procedure is to minimize the sum of the squares of the deviations (measured vertically) of the regression line from the sample points. However, we wish to be able to test how the estimated line differs from the true regression line. To do this we begin by describing some useful statistical properties for any set of estimated parameters. When the introductory discussion is completed we will give close scrutiny to the statistical properties of the least-squares estimators. We shall focus on the properties of the estimator of the parameter β, but the discussion can be applied to all estimated parameters. The material which follows is directly relevant, because the estimated regression parameters are *random variables* with expected values and variances that can be calculated.

To see this point more clearly, recall that we are analyzing a model in which the N values of the independent variable are assumed fixed. If we select a single sample of Y observations associated with the values of the independent variable, we can obtain an "estimate" of the regression slope that is based on the particular observations on Y which happened to occur. If we then replicate or repeat the experiment with the same X values, we obtain a new set of observations on Y (because the ε's will differ in the new sample), and thus, a new estimate of the slope parameter. If we were to draw sufficient samples of the Y variable, we would obtain a distribution of estimates of the parameter β. Since each observed sample of Y produces a specific estimate of β, when we sample Y-values it's equivalent to sampling an estimate of β out of the distribution of sample estimates.

Of course, there will be a distribution of sample estimates associated with every possible technique for estimating β from sample data. However, our objective here is to study the distribution produced by the least-squares estimation procedure (recall from Chapter 1 that $\hat{\beta} = \sum x_i y_i / \sum x_i^2$), in order to evaluate whether least squares is a good procedure for estimating β. It is important to realize that the notation $\hat{\beta}$ often serves a double purpose: $\hat{\beta}$ refers to the slope *estimate* resulting from a specific sample as well as to the *estimator* (associated with the least-squares estimation procedure) that follows a probability distribution.[7]

Lack of Bias

One very desirable property associated with an estimated regression parameter is for the distribution of the estimator to have the parameter as its mean value. Then if we could repeat the experiment many times for new sets of observations on Y, we would be assured of being right on average. We will say that $\hat{\beta}$ is an *unbiased* estimator if the mean or expected value of $\hat{\beta}$ is equal to the true value; that is, $E(\hat{\beta}) = \beta$. The difference between a biased and an unbiased estimator can be seen in Fig. 2.4. The reader should recall that for a sample of size N, $\sum X_i/N$ is an unbiased estimator of the true mean of a population, while $\sum (X_i - \bar{X})^2/(N-1)$ is an unbiased estimator of the true variance of the population.[8] To clarify the exposition we shall define the bias associated with an estimated parameter as follows:

$$\text{Bias} = E(\hat{\beta}) - \beta$$

It is important to realize that while lack of bias in an estimator is a desirable property, lack of bias implies nothing about the dispersion of the estimator about the true parameter. In general, one would like the estimator to be unbiased and also to have a very small dispersion about the mean. This suggests that one should define a second criterion that allows one to choose among alternative unbiased estimators.

FIGURE 2.4
Bias.

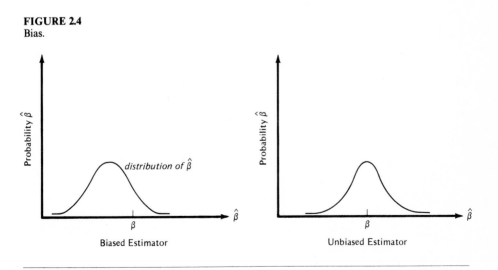

Biased Estimator   Unbiased Estimator

---

[7] We shall show the random nature of the estimated parameters more explicitly in the following section.
[8] See Appendix 2.1 and the suggested references in footnote 25 for details.

Efficiency

We say that $\hat{\beta}$ is an *efficient* unbiased estimator if the variance of $\hat{\beta}$ is smaller than the variance of any other unbiased estimators. In practice it is sometimes difficult to tell whether an estimator is efficient, so that it is natural to describe estimators in terms of their relative efficiency. One estimator is more efficient than another if it has smaller variance. A relatively efficient and a relatively inefficient estimator are shown graphically in Fig. 2.5. Efficiency is a desirable objective because the greater the efficiency associated with an estimation process, the stronger the *statistical* statements that one can make about the estimated parameters. Thus, in the extreme case of an (unbiased) estimator with *zero* variance, we can state with certainty the numerical value of the true regression parameter.

Minimum Mean Square Error

There are many circumstances in which one is forced to trade off bias and variance of estimators. When the goal of a model is to maximize the precision of predictions, for example, an estimator with very low variance and some bias may be more desirable than an unbiased estimator with high variance. One criterion which is useful in this regard is the goal of minimizing *mean square error* defined as follows:

$$\text{Mean square error }(\hat{\beta}) = E(\hat{\beta} - \beta)^2$$

It is not difficult to show that this definition is equivalent to the following:[9]

$$\text{Mean square error} = [\text{Bias }(\hat{\beta})]^2 + \text{Var }(\hat{\beta})$$

FIGURE 2.5
Efficiency.

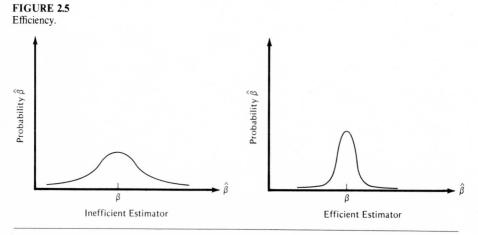

Inefficient Estimator   Efficient Estimator

---

[9] $E(\hat{\beta} - \beta)^2 = E[(\hat{\beta} - \bar{\beta}) + (\bar{\beta} - \beta)]^2$

where $\bar{\beta}$ is the expected value of the estimated regression coefficient.

$= E(\hat{\beta} - \bar{\beta})^2 + [E(\bar{\beta}) - \beta)]^2 + 2(\bar{\beta} - \beta)E(\hat{\beta} - \bar{\beta})$

$= \text{Var }(\hat{\beta}) + [\text{Bias }(\hat{\beta})]^2$ [This follows, since $\bar{\beta} = E(\hat{\beta})$ by definition.]

Thus, the criterion of minimizing mean square error takes into account the variance and the square of the bias of the estimator. When $\hat{\beta}$ is unbiased, the mean square error and variance of $\hat{\beta}$ are equal.

Consistency

To complete our discussion we consider the properties of estimators as the sample size gets very large, i.e., the *asymptotic*, or large-sample, properties. In this respect, we would like our estimator $\hat{\beta}$ to get close in some sense to the true β as the sample size increases; that is, we would like the distribution of $\hat{\beta}$ to converge to β. More specifically, we hope that as the sample size gets infinitely large, the probability that $\hat{\beta}$ will differ from β will get very small. To apply this probabilistic concept to the choice of estimator, we define the probability limit of $\hat{\beta}$ (plim $\hat{\beta}$) as follows: plim $\hat{\beta}$ is equal to β if as N approaches infinity, the probability that $|\beta - \hat{\beta}|$ will be less than any arbitrarily small positive number will approach 1. With this concept it is natural to define the criterion of *consistency* as follows: $\hat{\beta}$ is a *consistent* estimator of β if the *probability limit* of $\hat{\beta}$ is β.[10] Roughly speaking, an estimator is consistent if the probability distribution of the estimator collapses to a single point (the true parameter) as the sample size gets arbitrarily large. This is described graphically in Fig. 2.6.

FIGURE 2.6
Consistency.

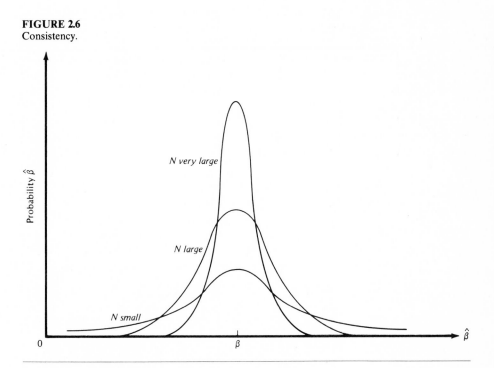

---

[10] Strictly speaking $\hat{\beta}$ converges to β in the probability limit if for any $\delta > 0$,

$$\lim_{N \to \infty} \text{Prob} \left(|\beta - \hat{\beta}| < \delta \right) = 1$$

As a rule, econometricians tend to be more concerned with consistency than with lack of bias as an estimation criterion. A biased yet consistent estimator may not equal the true parameter on average, but it will approximate the true parameter as the sample information grows larger.[11] This is more reassuring from a practical point of view than the alternative of finding a parameter estimate which is unbiased yet which continues to deviate substantially from the true parameter as the sample size gets larger.

It is natural to consider as an alternative criterion to consistency the objective that the *mean square error of the estimator approaches zero as the sample increases.* The mean-square-error criterion implies that the estimator is *unbiased asymptotically* and that its variance goes to zero as the sample size gets very large. It turns out that an estimator with a mean square error that approaches zero will be a consistent estimator, but that the reverse need not be true. In most applications consistent estimators do have mean square errors approaching zero, and the two criteria are used interchangeably.[12]

2.3   BEST LINEAR UNBIASED ESTIMATION

We are now in a position to return to the least-squares estimators described in Chapter 1. Since the least-squares estimators are associated with the stochastic regression model $Y_i = \alpha + \beta X_i + \varepsilon_i$, we have denoted them by $\hat{\alpha}$ and $\hat{\beta}$. The most important justification for the use of least squares is given by the *classical Gauss-Markov theorem*, which states that $\hat{\alpha}$ *and* $\hat{\beta}$ *are the best* (*most efficient*) *linear unbiased estimators of* α *and* β in the sense that they have minimum variance relative to all unbiased estimators. It is important to realize that the Gauss-Markov theorem does not apply to nonlinear estimators.[13] It is possible that a nonlinear estimator might be unbiased and have lower variance than the least-squares linear estimator. More generally, an estimator may be biased and have a lower mean square error than the unbiased estimator. This suggests that there may be circumstances in which one wishes to utilize an objective other than "best, linear unbiased" when selecting an estimation routine. *Robust estimators*, which are biased nonlinear estimators having minimum mean square error, are being seriously studied and appear to have useful applications.

We shall not attempt to prove the Gauss-Markov theorem at this point, but it will be useful to find expressions for the mean and variance of the least-squares estimators.[14] To simplify matters we shall work with the data transformed to appear in the form of deviations about means; i.e., we use $x_i = X_i - \overline{X}$ and $y_i = Y_i - \overline{Y}$. Recall (from Chapter 1) that the true regression line is $E(y_i) = \beta x_i$

---

[11] For example, given a sample of size N, $\sum (X_i - \overline{X})^2/N$ is a biased but consistent estimator of the variance of a population.

[12] See, for example, J. Kmenta, *Elements of Econometrics* (New York: Macmillan, 1971), pp. 162–166.

[13] If $\hat{\beta}$ can be written as $\sum c_i y_i$ where each c_i is a (nonrandom) constant, then $\hat{\beta}$ is said to be linear in y. However, if, for example, $\beta' = \sum c_i \log y_i$, then β' is a nonlinear estimator (in y). Nonlinear estimates may arise from criteria other than the least-squares criterion.

[14] See Appendix 3 for a proof of the Gauss-Markov theorem for the general linear model.

and the estimated slope is

$$\hat{\beta} = (\sum x_i y_i / \sum x_i^2) \qquad (2.2)$$

To simplify the derivation which follows, let

$$c_i = \frac{x_i}{\sum x_i^2}$$

Each c_i is a constant (i.e., nonrandom), since the x's are fixed in the sample. By substituting into (2.2) we get

$$\hat{\beta} = \sum c_i y_i$$

which expresses the estimated slope parameter as a weighted sum of the observations on the dependent variable. We shall use this expression to derive the mean and variance of $\hat{\beta}$ explicitly, but leave to the reader the corresponding derivations relating to $\hat{\alpha}$. (All summations are implicitly assumed to involve observations $i = 1, 2, \ldots, N$.) First,

$$\hat{\beta} = \sum c_i y_i = \sum c_i(\beta x_i + \varepsilon_i) = \sum c_i \beta x_i + \sum c_i \varepsilon_i \qquad (2.3)$$

so that $\qquad E(\hat{\beta}) = \sum c_i \beta x_i + \sum c_i E(\varepsilon_i)$

But $\qquad E(\varepsilon_i) = 0$

Therefore, $\qquad E(\hat{\beta}) = \sum c_i \beta x = \beta \sum c_i x_i = \beta$

(The fact that $\sum c_i x_i = 1$ follows directly from the definition of c_i.)[15] Thus, $\hat{\beta}$ *is an unbiased estimator of* β. Now, consider the variance of $\hat{\beta}$:

$$\text{Var}\,(\hat{\beta}) = E(\hat{\beta} - \beta)^2$$

But, from Eq. (2.3),

$$(\hat{\beta} - \beta) = \sum c_i \beta x_i + \sum c_i \varepsilon_i - \beta$$

$$= (\sum c_i x_i - 1)\beta + \sum c_i \varepsilon_i$$

$$= \sum c_i \varepsilon_i \qquad \text{since } \sum c_i x_i = 1 \text{ from footnote 15}$$

---

[15] $\qquad \sum c_i x_i = \sum \left[\left(\dfrac{x_i}{\sum x_i^2}\right) x_i\right] = \sum \left[\dfrac{x_i^2}{\sum x_i^2}\right] = \dfrac{\sum x_i^2}{\sum x_i^2} = 1$

Therefore, $\quad (\hat{\beta} - \beta)^2 = (\sum c_i \varepsilon_i)^2$

and $\quad \text{Var}(\hat{\beta}) = E[\sum c_i \varepsilon_i]^2$

$$= E[(c_1 \varepsilon_1)^2 + 2(c_1 c_2 \varepsilon_1 \varepsilon_2) + (c_2 \varepsilon_2)^2 + \cdots]$$

But, by assumption the ε_i are uncorrelated; that is, $E(\varepsilon_i \varepsilon_j) = 0$ for $i \neq j$.

Therefore, $\quad \text{Var}(\hat{\beta}) = E(c_1 \varepsilon_1)^2 + E(c_2 \varepsilon_2)^2 + \cdots$

$$= c_1{}^2 E(\varepsilon_1{}^2) + c_2 E(\varepsilon_2{}^2) + \cdots$$

$$= \sum c_i{}^2 E(\varepsilon_i{}^2)$$

$$= \sigma^2 \sum c_i{}^2$$

But $\quad \sum c_i{}^2 = \dfrac{\sum x_i{}^2}{(\sum x_i{}^2)^2} = \dfrac{1}{\sum x_i{}^2}$

Therefore, $\quad \text{Var}(\hat{\beta}) = \sigma^2 / \sum x_i{}^2 \qquad (2.4)$

Using a similar derivation, we find that the mean and variance of the estimator of the intercept term are

$$E(\hat{\alpha}) = \alpha \qquad (2.5)$$

$$\text{Var}(\hat{\alpha}) = \sigma^2 \left[\frac{\sum X_i{}^2}{N \sum (X_i - \bar{X})^2} \right] \qquad (2.6)$$

Finally, consider the covariance between $\hat{\alpha}$ and $\hat{\beta}$. Once again using a similar derivation, we can prove that

$$\text{Cov}(\hat{\alpha}, \hat{\beta}) = \frac{-\bar{X}\sigma^2}{\sum x_i{}^2} \qquad (2.7)$$

Given this information about the means and variances of the least-squares estimators and their covariance, we are ready to discuss statistical testing of the linear model. First, it is important to note that since $\hat{\beta} = \sum c_i y_i$ and the y_i's are normally distributed, *the estimator $\hat{\beta}$ will be normally distributed* (a linear combination of independent normally distributed variables will be normally distributed). Even if the y_i's are not normally distributed, the distribution of $\hat{\beta}$ can be shown to be asymptotically normal (under reasonable conditions) by appeal to the central limit theorem of statistics.[16] Thus, our results will be approximately

---

[16] Roughly speaking, the central limit theorem states that the sample mean of an independently distributed variable will tend toward normality as the sample size gets infinitely large. It applies to $\hat{\beta}$ because $\hat{\beta}$ is a linear combination of the y_i's.

correct for large samples even without the assumption of normality. To sum up our conclusions to this point we may write:

$$\hat{\beta} \sim N \left[\beta, \frac{\sigma^2}{\sum x_i^2} \right] \qquad (2.8)$$

$$\hat{\alpha} \sim N \left[\alpha, \sigma^2 \left(\frac{\sum X_i^2}{N \sum x_i^2} \right) \right] \qquad (2.9)$$

$$\text{Cov} \, (\hat{\alpha}, \hat{\beta}) = -\frac{\bar{X}\sigma^2}{\sum x_i^2} \qquad (2.10)$$

Notice that the variance of $\hat{\beta}$ varies directly with the variance of ε. Thus, other things being equal, we are likely to obtain more precise parameter estimates of the slope when the variance of the error term is small. On the other hand, the variance of $\hat{\beta}$ varies inversely with $\sum x_i^2$. Thus, the larger the variance of X_i, the better you are likely to do in estimating β. Put more simply, when all the sample data on the X's are limited to a small interval, it will be difficult to determine the slope of the regression line accurately.

While the expression for the variance of $\hat{\alpha}$ looks quite complicated, we can note that the expression simplifies to σ^2/N when the mean of X is identically zero. In this case the variance of $\hat{\alpha}$ is at a minimum. This result is not likely to be of much interest in applications, because intercept parameters are usually not of primary concern. Notice also that the sign of the covariance of $\hat{\alpha}$ and $\hat{\beta}$ is opposite in sign to $\bar{X}$. If the mean of X is positive, for example, an overestimate of $\hat{\alpha}$ is likely to be associated with an underestimate of $\hat{\beta}$.

Our analysis is not yet complete, since we need to utilize the sample information to obtain an estimator of the true population variance σ^2. The actual derivation of such an estimator is quite complex and will not be shown here.[17] We will use the following sample estimate of the true variance σ^2:

$$s^2 = \hat{\sigma}^2 = \frac{\sum \hat{\varepsilon}_i^2}{N-2} = \frac{\sum (Y_i - \hat{\alpha} - \hat{\beta} X_i)^2}{N-2} \qquad (2.11)$$

where $\varepsilon_i = Y_i - \hat{Y}_i$ is the regression *residual*. s^2, the *residual variance*, can be shown to be an unbiased as well as consistent estimator of the error variance.[18] The reader might wonder why the *sum of the squared residuals* $\sum \hat{\varepsilon}_i^2$ was divided by $N-2$ in order to get an unbiased estimator of the true variance. The answer lies in the fact that there are N data points in the estimation process, but the estimation of the slope and intercept puts two constraints on the data. This leaves $N-2$ unconstrained observations with which to estimate the residual

---

[17] See Appendix 2.2 for further details.

[18] s is called the *standard error of the regression*. (SER, SE, and SEE are also occasionally used to represent s. The latter is short for standard error of estimate.)

variance. For this reason, the proper divisor of $N - 2$ is referred to as the number of degrees of freedom.

With an estimate of σ^2, we can return to Eqs. (2.8) to (2.10) to obtain sample estimates of the variances associated with the estimated parameters $\hat{\alpha}$ and $\hat{\beta}$ as well as an estimate of the covariance between the two. Each of the three estimates is listed below:

$$s_{\hat{\beta}}^2 = \frac{s^2}{\sum x_i^2} \tag{2.12}$$

$$s_{\hat{\alpha}}^2 = s^2 \left(\frac{\sum X_i^2}{N \sum x_i^2} \right) \tag{2.13}$$

$$\widehat{\text{Cov}}(\hat{\alpha}, \hat{\beta}) = -\frac{\bar{X}s^2}{\sum x_i^2} \tag{2.14}$$

$s_{\hat{\beta}}$ and $s_{\hat{\alpha}}$, the *standard errors* of the estimated coefficients $\hat{\beta}$ and $\hat{\alpha}$, respectively, provide a measure of the dispersion of the estimates (as do the sample estimates of the variances).

2.4   HYPOTHESIS TESTING AND CONFIDENCE INTERVALS

Given the knowledge of the distributions of $\hat{\alpha}$ and $\hat{\beta}$, it is possible to construct confidence intervals and to test hypotheses concerning the estimated parameters.[19] Confidence intervals, or *interval estimates*, provide a range of values which are likely to contain the true regression parameters. With every confidence interval we associate a *level of statistical significance*. Given the level of significance, the confidence intervals are constructed so that the probability that the interval contains the true regression parameter is 1 minus the level of significance. Confidence intervals are particularly useful for testing statistical hypotheses about the estimated regression parameters. The most common test relates to the *null hypothesis*. In general a null hypothesis is a statement or hypothesis that assumes that a certain effect is not present. Because researchers hope to accept the model, the null hypothesis is often constructed so as to make its rejection possible. As an example, consider an attempt to explain aggregate consumption expenditures C in terms of aggregate disposable income DI. A reasonable specification of the model might be that $E(C) = \alpha + \beta(DI)$. We would expect that consumption and disposable income are positively related so that β should be positive. However, to test the validity of the model we set up the null hypothesis that β equals 0. We hope to reject the null hypothesis by obtaining a value of $\hat{\beta}$ which

---

[19] The discussion which follows presupposes that the reader has some knowledge of basic statistics. including hypothesis testing, confidence intervals, and the t distribution. The student whose background in statistics is limited may wish to read Appendix 2.1 before proceeding further.

is sufficiently greater than 0 as to cast significant doubt on the hypothesis that β equals 0. Assume, for example, that $\hat{\beta}$ is estimated to be .9. If we choose a level of significance of 10 percent, the 90 percent confidence interval for β might be

$$.6 < \beta < 1.2$$

This means that the probability that β is within the range (.6, 1.2) is .90. In addition it means that we may reject the null hypothesis that β equals 0 with greater than 90 percent confidence.

One of our prime objectives in econometrics is to analyze data in a manner that permits us to test and evaluate our models. In practice a researcher may have several plausible models among which to choose, and although the choice will depend partly on the purpose of the model, it will also depend on empirical information (i.e., the data). The simultaneous comparison of many models is methodologically difficult. Usually we examine models sequentially, attempting to validate each model as it is brought under study. This means that each model must be specified in a form which yields empirically testable hypotheses. If the data are inconsistent with the model, the model is rejected and an alternative is considered. If the data are consistent with the model, the model is implicitly accepted—until new testable hypotheses or new data are available. Thus, hypothesis testing pertains to a *single* model, and will result in model rejection or model acceptance.

In hypothesis testing a rule for acceptance and rejection must be chosen before the data are examined. One frequently used rule involves the 5 percent level of significance, which sets up a criterion that the rejection of the null hypothesis when it is in fact true should occur less than 5 percent of the time. The choice of significance level is arbitrary and depends in practice on the types of conclusions to be reached from the model. It is important to realize, however, that hypothesis testing in classical econometrics deals almost solely with the problem of incorrectly rejecting a true hypothesis. Because of the nature of testable hypotheses which are specified, alternative hypotheses are most frequently ill-defined, making it impossible to judge the number of times one will accept the null hypothesis when it is in fact false. For this reason, in applied work we tend to distinguish between rejection of a null hypothesis and its acceptance. Thus, we will often state that a null hypothesis has been rejected at a 5 percent level of significance, while leaving implicit the acceptance of the alternative hypothesis.

For example, with our consumption model we tested the null hypothesis that β equals 0. Based on our estimated slope parameter we rejected the null hypothesis in favor of the alternative hypothesis that the slope is nonzero. However, we could have chosen to begin our analysis with a more specific alternative hypothesis, e.g., that the slope parameter is positive. This would slightly alter the statistical testing involved and would add additional information if the null hypothesis were rejected.

It is standard practice in applied econometric work to examine carefully the test statistics and the standard errors of the coefficients. When rejection of the null hypothesis is valid, the model is usually accepted, at least until further information to the contrary becomes available. The level of significance necessary for model acceptance varies substantially among researchers and among the type of model being investigated. For example, a model estimated with a large number of observations may allow one to reject null hypotheses of zero coefficients for many explanatory variables. Rather than use a strict 5 percent significance test, we may rank order the test statistics, omitting variables from the model that are associated with the lowest test statistics.

The statistical test for rejecting the null hypothesis associated with a regression coefficient is usually based upon the t distribution. The t distribution is relevant because for statistical testing we need to utilize a sample estimate of the error variance rather than its true value. To use the t distribution to construct 95 percent confidence intervals for the estimated parameters, we first standardize the estimated regression parameter, say $\hat{\beta}$, by subtracting its true value and dividing by the estimate of its standard error [see Eq. (2.12)]:

$$t_{N-2} = \frac{\hat{\beta} - \beta}{s_{\hat{\beta}}} = \frac{\hat{\beta} - \beta}{s/\sqrt{\sum x_i^2}} \tag{2.15}$$

The standardized variable t_{N-2} will follow the t distribution with $N-2$ degrees of freedom (see Appendix 2.1 for details). Now, we select an appropriate value t_c, called the *critical value*, which assures that 2.5 percent of the t distribution lies in each of its tails; that is,

$$\text{Prob}\,(-t_c < t_{N-2} < t_c) = .95 \tag{2.16}$$

where Prob denotes probability. The critical value of the distribution varies with the number of degrees of freedom, but will equal 1.96 when the number of observations is large.

Now, by substituting from (2.15) we obtain the following:

$$\text{Prob}\left(-t_c < \frac{\hat{\beta} - \beta}{s/\sqrt{\sum x_i^2}} < t_c\right) = .95 \tag{2.17}$$

The critical value of the t statistic in Eq. (2.15) will be central to our decision of whether or not to reject null hypotheses concerning specific values of the true slope parameter β. However, it is of more immediate importance to rewrite Eq. (2.17) slightly to obtain

$$\text{Prob}\left(\hat{\beta} - t_c \frac{s}{\sqrt{\sum x_i^2}} < \beta < \hat{\beta} + t_c \frac{s}{\sqrt{\sum x_i^2}}\right) = .95 \tag{2.18}$$

from which we obtain a 95 percent confidence interval for β equal to

$$\hat{\beta} \pm t_c \frac{s}{\sqrt{\sum x_i^2}} = \hat{\beta} \pm t_c s_{\hat{\beta}} \qquad (2.19)$$

Using a similar procedure, we obtain a 95 percent confidence interval for α:

$$\hat{\alpha} \pm t_c s_{\hat{\alpha}} = \hat{\alpha} \pm t_c s \frac{\sqrt{\sum X_i^2}}{\sqrt{N \sum x_i^2}} \qquad (2.20)$$

Of course, it is possible to determine confidence intervals for any level of significance, as long as the critical value of the t distribution is correctly chosen. Confidence intervals for the unknown parameters provide us with a statistical statement about the range of values likely to contain the true parameter. Thus, Eq. (2.19) tells us that an interval of t_c standard deviations on either side of the estimated slope parameter has a probability of .95 of containing the true parameter. [We know already that if forced to make a single guess as to the true parameter in the correctly specified model $Y = \alpha + \beta X$, we would select the estimated parameter $\hat{\beta}$, because $\hat{\beta}$ is an (efficient) unbiased estimator of β.]

The most usual hypothesis which is tested in the two-variable regression model is that there is no relationship between the variables X and Y. This test is accomplished by considering the following hypotheses:

Null hypothesis: $\beta = 0$

Alternative hypothesis: $\beta \neq 0$

According to the null hypothesis, β equals 0, so that the appropriate test statistic becomes $\hat{\beta}/s_{\hat{\beta}}$. If the ratio of the estimated parameter to its (estimated) standard error is greater than or equal to t_c *in absolute value*, we reject the null hypothesis. Since $t_c = 1.96$ for a large sample size and a 5 percent level of significance, we may often apply the rule of thumb that if the value of the test statistic is greater than 2 in absolute value, we reject the null hypothesis. Another way of looking at this is in terms of the confidence interval about $\hat{\beta}$. If 0 lies within the confidence interval, we cannot reject the null hypothesis, but if it lies outside we do reject it. It is important to stress again that failure to reject the null hypothesis does not necessarily imply its truth. Our hypothesis and confidence interval has been constructed in such a manner that if the null hypothesis is true we will reject it falsely only 5 percent of the time. The testing procedure tells us little about the situation in which we will accept the null hypothesis when it is in fact false. Acceptance of the alternative hypothesis must be done with this in mind.

Example 2.1   Grade-Point Average

Reconsider the grade-point average example from Chapter 1. The estimated relationship between grade-point average Y and family income X was as follows:

$$\hat{Y} = 1.38 + .12X$$

Simple calculations allow one to determine the following relevant statistics:

$$s^2 = .111 \qquad s = .33 \qquad \sum x_i^2 = 162$$

To test the estimated regression parameters, we first select a level of significance —in this case 5 percent. Then we find the critical value of the t distribution (from Table 3 in the end-of-book Appendix) associated with a probability of .025 in each tail and 6 degrees of freedom (recall that there are eight observations and two estimated parameters). In this case

$$t_c \,(5\% \text{ significance}) = 2.447$$

Then, a 95 percent confidence interval for the estimated slope parameter would be

$$\beta = \hat{\beta} \pm t_c \frac{s}{\sqrt{\sum x_i^2}} = .12 \pm \frac{2.45 \times .33}{\sqrt{162}} = .12 \pm .06$$

or $$.06 < \beta < .18$$

In addition,

$$t_6 = \frac{\hat{\beta}}{\sqrt{s^2/\sum x_i^2}} = \frac{.12}{\sqrt{.111/162}} = 4.6$$

We observe that 0 lies *outside* the 95 percent confidence interval for β, allowing us to reject at the 5 percent level of significance the hypothesis that $\beta = 0$. Equivalently, we can observe that the calculated value of t_6 (4.6) is greater than the critical t value of 2.45. Once again we are able to reject the null hypothesis.

Example 2.2   Consumption Expenditures

For illustrative purposes we will consider several attempts to build a two-variable model that explains the dollar value of aggregate consumption expenditures C. As a first attempt we ran a regression in which consumption is the dependent variable and a random time series X is the independent variable.

Data were quarterly from the first quarter of 1958 to the fourth quarter of 1973. The estimated regression is as follows:

$$\hat{C} = 404.32 + 7.57X$$

The standard error of the intercept term is 19.17 and thus the t statistic is $404.32/19.17 = 21.09$. Since the regression involves 64 observations, and 2 estimated parameters, we find (see Table 3 in the end-of-book Appendix) that the critical value of the t distribution at the 5 percent significance level is 2. Thus, we may reject the null hypothesis that the intercept is 0. However, the standard error for the coefficient of X is 36.85, and therefore the t statistic is 0.20. We therefore cannot reject the null hypothesis of a zero slope at the 5 percent (or the 10 percent) level. For this reason, we conclude that consumer spending is not randomly determined, and reject the model in order to search for a better alternative.

A more reasonable choice for an explanatory variable is aggregate disposable income DI. When consumption is regressed on disposable income, the following result is obtained:

$$\hat{C} = -12.73 + .79\text{DI}$$

In this case the intercept is significant at the 5 percent level (with a t statistic of -3.24), but more important the t statistic associated with the coefficient of the disposable income variable is 108.98. Thus, we may reject the null hypothesis of a zero slope in favor of the alternative hypothesis that the slope is nonzero. Rejection of the null hypothesis allows us to accept—at least provisionally—the two-variable regression model. Of course, further research might allow us to find a model of aggregate consumption which is more suitable than the one just described.

2.5   ANALYSIS OF VARIANCE AND CORRELATION

2.5.1   Goodness of Fit

The residuals of a regression can help to provide a useful measure of the extent to which the estimated regression line fits the sample data points. Roughly speaking, a good regression equation is one which helps to explain or account for a large proportion of the variance of Y. Large residuals imply a poor fit, while small residuals imply a good fit. The problem with using the residual (or an estimate of the variance of the error term) as a measure of goodness of fit is that the value of the residual is not unit-free; it depends upon the units of measure of the dependent variable. We would like to find a measure of goodness of fit which is unit-free and for which certain statistical tests can be of value. Intuitively, it seems reasonable that the residual variable divided by the variance of Y will provide the kind of comparison which is sought.

We begin by defining the *variation* of Y about its mean as follows:

$$\text{Variation } (Y) = \sum (Y_i - \overline{Y})^2$$

Our goal is to divide the variation of Y into two distinct parts, the first accounted for by the regression equation and the second associated with the unexplained portion (the error term) of the model. Assume first that the slope of the linear regression model is known to be 0, and we fit a regression estimating only an intercept. Then the best prediction for Y_i associated with any value of X is given by the sample mean of Y:

$$\hat{Y}_i = \hat{\alpha} + 0 \cdot X_i = \hat{\alpha} = \overline{Y}$$

In this special case, we may conclude that the variation of Y measures the square of the difference between the observed values Y_i and the predicted values $\overline{Y}$. More generally, we can improve our predictions by accounting for the fact that the fitted or predicted values of Y_i are dependent upon the observations on X_i; that is,

$$\hat{Y}_i = \hat{\alpha} + \hat{\beta} X_i$$

The additional information will allow us to improve our prediction and to reduce the unexplained portion of the variation in Y. To see this, consider the following identity, which holds for all sample observations:

$$(Y_i - \overline{Y}) = (Y_i - \hat{Y}_i) + (\hat{Y}_i - \overline{Y}) \tag{2.21}$$

FIGURE 2.7
Decomposition of Y_i.

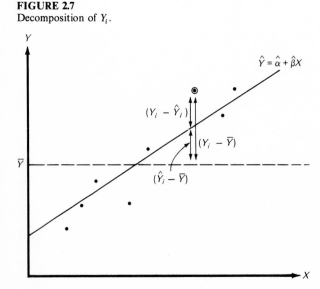

The left-hand term denotes the difference between the sample point and the mean of Y, the middle term the residual, and the right-hand term the difference between the predicted value of Y and the mean of Y. This is depicted graphically in Fig. 2.7.

The analysis to this point depends solely upon one sample point. To expand the analysis to cover all sample points and to measure variation, we square both sides of Eq. (2.21) and then sum over all observations $i = 1, 2, \ldots, N$.

$$\sum (Y_i - \bar{Y})^2 = \sum (Y_i - \hat{Y}_i)^2 + \sum (\hat{Y}_i - \bar{Y})^2 + 2 \sum (Y_i - \hat{Y}_i)(\hat{Y}_i - \bar{Y})^2 \quad (2.22)$$

The last term of the expression can be shown to be identically 0. (The reader should check this by utilizing the fact that $\sum \hat{\varepsilon}_i = 0$ and $\sum \hat{\varepsilon}_i X_i = 0$.) Therefore,

$$\sum (Y_i - \bar{Y})^2 \qquad = \sum (\hat{Y}_i - Y_i)^2 \qquad + \sum (\hat{Y}_i - \bar{Y})^2$$

$\sum (Y_i - \bar{Y})^2$	$= \sum (\hat{Y}_i - Y_i)^2$	$+ \sum (\hat{Y}_i - \bar{Y})^2$
Total variation of Y (or total sum of squares)	Residual variation of Y (or error sum of squares)	Explained variation of Y (or regression sum of squares)
TSS	= ESS	+ RSS (2.23)

To normalize the breakdown of the variation in Y, we divide both sides of the equation by the total sum of squares to get

$$1 = \frac{\text{ESS}}{\text{TSS}} + \frac{\text{RSS}}{\text{TSS}}$$

We define the *R-squared* (R^2) of the regression equation as follows:

$$R^2 = 1 - \frac{\text{ESS}}{\text{TSS}} = \frac{\text{RSS}}{\text{TSS}} \quad (2.24)$$

R^2 is the proportion of the total variation in Y explained by the regression of Y on X. Since the error sum of squares ranges in values between 0 and the total sum of squares, it is easy to see the R^2 ranges in value between 0 and 1. An R^2 of 0 occurs when the linear regression model does nothing to help explain the variation in Y. This might occur, for example, when all sample points lie on the horizontal line $Y = \bar{Y}$, or when the sample points lie on a circle (Fig. 2.8b). An R^2 of 1 can occur only in the case when all sample points lie on the estimated regression line; i.e., the case of a perfect fit (Fig. 2.8a).

It would be useful at this point to relate the notion of R^2 to the regression parameters estimated earlier in this chapter. To do so we write variables measured as deviations from their means, representing them in lowercase letters.

$$y_i = Y_i - \bar{Y} \qquad x_i = X_i - \bar{X}$$

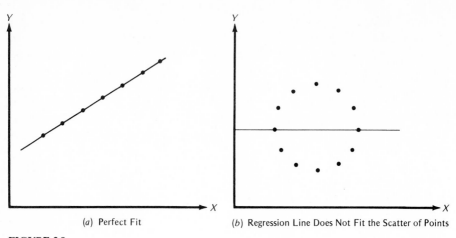

(a) Perfect Fit   (b) Regression Line Does Not Fit the Scatter of Points

FIGURE 2.8
Measuring R-squared.

The predicted values of y_i are

$$\hat{y}_i = \hat{\beta} x_i$$

and each dependent variable observation can be subdivided as follows:

$$y_i = \hat{y}_i + \hat{\varepsilon}_i$$

where $\hat{\varepsilon}_i$ is the regression residual. Then,

$$\sum y_i^2 = \sum \hat{y}_i^2 + \sum \hat{\varepsilon}_i^2 \quad \text{since} \sum \hat{y}_i \hat{\varepsilon}_i = \hat{\beta} \sum x_i \hat{\varepsilon}_i = 0$$

$$= \hat{\beta}^2 \sum x_i^2 + \sum \hat{\varepsilon}_i^2$$

from which it follows that

$$R^2 = \frac{\text{RSS}}{\text{TSS}} = \frac{\sum \hat{y}_i^2}{\sum y_i^2} = \hat{\beta}^2 \frac{\sum x_i^2}{\sum y_i^2}$$

or

$$R^2 = 1 - \frac{\sum \hat{\varepsilon}_i^2}{\sum y_i^2} \tag{2.25}$$

Eq. (2.25) provides a simple formula for calculating R^2.

Note that in the context of our discussion R^2 is only a descriptive statistic. Roughly speaking, we associate a high value of R^2 with a good fit of the regression line, and a low value of R^2 with a poor fit. We must realize, however, that a low value of R^2 can occur for one or several related reasons. In certain cases the X variable may not be a good explanatory variable in the equation.

Even though there is reason to believe that X does help in the prediction of Y, there might remain a good deal of unexplained variation in Y even after the variable X has appeared in the equation. In other words, the explanatory power of X might be poor relative to the total variation in the residual. In time-series studies, for example, one often obtains high values of R^2 simply because any variable growing over time is likely to do a good job of explaining the variation of any other variable growing over time. In cross-section studies, on the other hand, a lower R^2 may occur even if the model is a satisfactory one, because of the large variation across individual units of observation which is inherently present in the data.[20]

It is occasionally useful to summarize the breakdown of the variation in Y in terms of an *analysis of variance*. In such a case, the total unexplained and explained variations in Y are converted to *variances* by dividing by the appropriate number of degrees of freedom.[21] Thus, the variance in Y is the total variation divided by $N - 1$, the explained variance is equal to the explained variation (since the regression involves only 1 degree of freedom above the one used to estimate the mean of Y), and the residual variance is the residual variation divided by $N - 2$.

2.5.2 Correlation

The R^2 is usually of value in analyzing a regression model in which a causal relationship between the dependent variable Y and the independent variable X has been specified. Thus, R^2 is interpreted as more than a measure of correlation among several variables. Regression and correlation techniques differ in that correlation techniques do not involve an implicit assumption of causality, while regression techniques do. We have seen in Chapter 1 that the choice of dependent and independent variables in a regression model is a crucial one. The dependent variable is the variable to be explained or predicted, while the independent variable is the moving force or causal variable. The least-squares technique is appropriate only if the causal structure of the model can be determined before the data are examined. Least-squares regression techniques serve the purpose of *validating* the previously developed model. If a model $Y = \alpha + \beta X$ is specified, one may interpret a significant t statistic on the regression slope parameter as evidence tending to validate the model. On the other hand, an insignificant statistic would lead toward invalidation of the model.

---

[20] This suggests quite properly that R^2 alone may not be a suitable measure of the extent to which a model is satisfactory. A better overall measure might be a statistic which describes the predictive power of the model in the face of new data.

[21] The number of degrees of freedom associated with a calculated statistic is the number of available observations minus the number of constraints placed on the data by the calculation procedure. Thus an estimate of the variation in Y involves $N - 1$ degrees of freedom because one constraint is placed on the data (1 degree of freedom is used up) when deviations are measured about the sample mean which must in itself be calculated. An additional degree of freedom is used up in the calculation of the slope parameter, leaving $N - 2$ degrees of freedom associated with the unexplained variation in the problem.

As an example of correlation without causality, consider a series of observations over time that might have been obtained in a nineteenth-century study of medicine in Africa. One might find a high correlation between the number of doctors present in a region and the prevalence of disease in that same region, but it would be wrong to infer that the presence of doctors is in fact a cause of the spreading disease.

Thus, high correlations do not provide for an inference of causality. One must specify *a priori* (based on previous information) that the number of doctors in a region is a function of the prevalence of disease and test statistically whether such a relationship holds if one is to use regression techniques correctly.

Notice that regression techniques *assume* but do not prove causality. Correlation techniques are often used by researchers to suggest hypotheses or to confirm previously held suspicions. Such procedures are acceptable as long as the researcher is careful not to infer causality directly from the data analysis. There are numerous cases in economics, business, and other fields in which two variables are highly correlated, but both are determined by a third underlying variable. If such is the case, the underlying variable should appear in the regression model as the independent variable.

It is natural to ask what happens to the regression slope parameter when an incorrect causal specification is made. Let us refer back to our discussion at the end of Chapter 1, and compare the slope parameters associated with the following regression models:

i
$$Y = a + bX + e$$

ii
$$X = A + BY + e'$$

The least-squares estimators of b and B are as follows:

$$\hat{b} = \frac{\sum x_i y_i}{\sum x_i^2} \qquad \hat{B} = \frac{\sum x_i y_i}{\sum y_i^2}$$

The two regression slopes will yield identical conclusions about the relationship between movement in X and movement in Y only if $\hat{b} = 1/\hat{B}$ or equivalently if $R^2 = 1$ (see Exercise 2.4). Thus, the choice of specification of the regression model will affect our parameter estimates and our predictions.

2.5.3 Testing the Regression Equation

The procedure of subdividing the variation in Y into two components suggests a statistical test of the existence of a linear relationship between Y and X. Consider the following ratio:

$$F_{1,N-2} = \frac{\text{Explained variance}}{\text{Unexplained variance}} = \frac{\text{RSS}/1}{\text{ESS}/(N-2)} = \frac{\hat{\beta}^2 \sum x_i^2}{s^2}$$

Other things being equal we would expect a strong statistical relationship between X and Y to result in a large ratio of explained to unexplained variance. This test can be applied directly because $F_{1, N-2}$ follows a known distribution (the F distribution) with 1 and $N - 2$ degrees of freedom (see Appendix 2.1). The subscripts on F are used to denote the number of degrees of freedom in the numerator and denominator, respectively. The value of the F statistic will be 0 only when the explained variance in the regression is 0. One would associate a low value with a weak (linear) relationship between X and Y, and a high value with a strong (linear) relationship. Fortunately, the exact numerical distribution of the F statistic is known (see Table 4 of the F distribution in the end-of-book Appendix). For example, one would reject the null hypothesis of no relationship between Y and X at the 5 percent significance level by looking up the appropriate critical value of the F distribution (5 percent significance) with 1 and $N - 2$ degrees of freedom. If the value of $F_{1, N-2}$ calculated from the regression is larger than the critical value, we reject the null hypothesis at the 5 percent level. If the value of $F_{1, N-2}$ is lower than the critical value, we cannot reject the null hypothesis.

A careful reading should lead us to suspect that the F test just described bears a close relationship to the t test associated with the null hypothesis that $\beta = 0$. In fact, we can state quite generally that $F_{1, N-2} = t_{N-2}^2$ for the same level of significance. The F test has been introduced explicitly here because it will be useful for joint tests of hypotheses including a test of the significance of a multiple regression equation. We will make use of the F test for this purpose in Chapter 3.

Example 2.3   Retail Auto Sales

A study was made of the relationship between retail auto sales (dependent variable) and the level of aggregate wages and salaries in the economy (independent variable). One would expect a higher level of wages and salaries to lead to an increase in auto sales. The following is a summary of the regression of retail sales on wages and salaries using monthly time-series data. The equation to be estimated is

$$S = \alpha + \beta W + \varepsilon$$

where S = monthly retail auto sales from January 1963 to April 1970 in *millions* of dollars

W = monthly wages from January 1963 to April 1970 in *billions* of dollars

The fitted regression line is listed below. We have included the t statistics in parentheses below the estimated coefficients. We have placed a "hat" above the dependent variable as a reminder that the equation is used to calculate estimated values of the dependent variable.

$$\hat{S} = 1,767.61 + 7.48W$$
$$(7.4) \qquad (18.5)$$

$$R^2 = .80 \qquad F_{1,\,86} = 344.0$$

The positive constant (representing the intercept term) implies that hypothetically, if there were no wages in a given month, individuals would still purchase automobiles. The coefficient of the wage variable can be interpreted to mean that a \$1 billion increase in wages and salaries will lead to a \$7.48 million increase in auto sales. (The model could be used to predict the future level of auto sales conditional on future salaries.) Notice that the slope coefficient is usually interpreted to measure the change in the dependent variables associated with a *small* change in the independent variable. (In fact in the linear model $\hat{\beta} = \partial S/\partial W$ holds for all changes in W.) The estimated coefficient is not unit-free. Its value is directly related to the units of measurement of the dependent variable S (millions of dollars) and the independent variable W (billions of dollars). In this example we have chosen to write the t statistics, rather than the estimated standard errors, in parentheses. Using the t statistics we can reject the null hypotheses that the intercept and the slope are 0 (taken individually) at the 1 percent as well as the 5 percent level of significance. The R^2 of .80 implies that the regression equation explains 80 percent of the variation in the dependent variable. The $F_{1,\,86}$ value of 344 allows one to reject the null hypothesis that there is no relationship between auto sales and wages and salaries (at the 1 percent level).

If one had reason to believe quite strongly that the graph of auto sales versus wages and salaries should pass through the origin, despite the fact that we have rejected the null hypothesis of a 0 intercept, then it would be natural to run the regression without a constant term (we leave the derivation of the slope estimator as an exercise for the reader). The results for the identical sample are as follows:

$$\hat{S} = 11.71\,W \qquad R^2 = .54$$
$$(10.2)$$

While the t test allows one to reject the null hypothesis, it seems clear that the suppression of the constant term has lowered the explanatory power of the equation.[22] Thus, one will estimate the regression model with an intercept. Only

---

[22] In actuality the R^2 associated with an equation containing no constant term must be interpreted with great care. When the constant is dropped, the derivation in the test must be modified. Of particular importance is the fact that R^2 as defined in Chapter 1 lies within the 0,1 range. In this case, a comparison of the predicted or fitted values of the dependent variables made it clear that the explanatory power of the equation had declined.

if there is strong reason to force the equation through the origin should the intercept be equated to 0.

Example 2.4

In the grade-point average problem (Example 1.1), we calculated the following additional statistics:

$$R^2 = .77 \qquad F_{1, 6} = 21.2$$

The R^2 of .77 allows us to conclude that the family income variable helps to explain 77 percent of the variation in grade-point average for the sample of eight individuals. The F statistic allows us to test the null hypothesis of no relationship between grade-point average and family income. To do so, we use a table of the F distribution to determine the critical value associated with a 5 percent level of significance and 1 and 6 degrees of freedom in the numerator and denominator, respectively. (The 1 degree of freedom is used because the model includes a single explanatory variable, while the 6 degrees of freedom result from the fact that there are eight observations and two parameters to be estimated.) In this case the critical value of F at the 5 percent level is 5.99. Since the calculated F of 21.2 is greater than the critical value, we reject the null hypothesis at the 5 percent level of significance.

Exercises

2.1 Construct 95 percent confidence intervals for the estimated parameters for Exercise 1.1. Can you reject the null hypothesis that $\beta = 0$? $\beta = 1$?
2.2 Discuss the differences in statistical tests associated with the estimated parameters of a regression when:

(1) The error variance is known or not known.
(2) The sample size is finite or infinite.

2.3 Since the standard error of the regression coefficient $\hat{\beta}$ varies inversely with the variance of X, one can improve the significance of the estimated parameter by selecting values of X at the end points of the range of possible values. Explain why this is true, and discuss whether such a procedure is desirable.
2.4 Prove that the estimated slope of the regression of Y on X will equal the reciprocal of the estimated slope of the regression of X on Y only if $R^2 = 1$.
2.5 Can you give an example of an estimator which is asymptotically unbiased, but which is not consistent?

2.6 When the mean of X is identically 0, the covariance between the estimated slope and intercept is 0. Can you explain intuitively why this is true?

2.7 Suppose that you are attempting to build a model that explains aggregate savings behavior as a function of the level of interest rates. Would you rather sample during a period of fluctuating interest rates or a period in which interest rates were relatively constant? Explain.

2.8 Prove that the estimated residuals from the linear regression and the corresponding sample values of X are uncorrelated; that is, $\sum X_i \hat{\varepsilon}_i = 0$. (*Hint:* The problem will be easier if you work with the data in deviations form.)

2.9 Prove that R^2 for the two-variable regression is unchanged if a linear transformation is made on both variables; that is, $Y^* = a_1 + a_2 Y$, $X^* = b_1 + b_2 X$.

2.10 "An R^2 of 1 guarantees a perfect fit, but an R^2 not equal to 1 does not rule out a perfect fit." Can you explain under what conditions this statement is true?

2.11 Return once again to the data in Exercise 1.1. Break down the data into two groups of five observations each, according to the order of magnitude of the independent variable (money supply). In other words the first group should contain the five sample points associated with the five smallest values of the money supply. Calculate the following parameter:

$$B = \frac{\overline{Y}_2 - \overline{Y}_1}{\overline{X}_2 - \overline{X}_1}$$

where the subscript refers to the group number. ($\overline{Y}_2$ is the mean of all Y's in the second group.)

(1) Describe the foregoing process geometrically. In what sense is B an estimated slope parameter?

(2) Compare your estimated parameter to the least-squares slope estimate. Can you prove that B is an unbiased estimator of the true regression slope parameter?

(3) Prove that the variance of the parameter B must be greater than or equal to the variance of the least-squares estimator.

APPENDIX 2.1 / ELEMENTARY STATISTICS—A REVIEW

Random Variables

A *random variable* is a variable that takes on alternative values according to chance. More specifically, a random variable has the property that it assumes different values, each with a probability less than 1. We can also describe a random variable by examining the mechanism which generates its values. This mechanism, called a *probability distribution*, lists all possible outcomes and the probability that each will occur. We might define a random variable as a function that assigns to each outcome of an experiment a real number. For example,

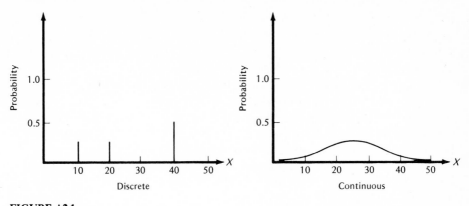

FIGURE A2.1
Probability functions.

assume that we assign a value of 1 to a coin toss of heads and a value of 0 to a toss of tails (if we use a fair coin the probability of heads will be one-half). In this case, we may interpret the value of the coin toss as a random variable. In this particular case the mechanism generating the random variable is the binomial probability distribution.

It is useful to distinguish between *discrete* and *continuous* random variables. A continuous random variable may take on any value on the real number line, while a discrete random variable may take on only a specific number of real values. Figure A2.1 illustrates a discrete as well as a continuous probability function.

Expected Values

The *mean*, or *expected value*, of a random variable is simply a weighted average of the possible outcomes associated with the variable, where the probabilities of the outcomes serve as the appropriate weights. In the discrete case, if the N possible outcomes associated with the random variable X are $X_1, X_2, \ldots, X_N$, then the mean of X would be equal to

$$p_1 X_1 + p_2 X_2 + \cdots + p_N X_N = \sum_{i=1}^{N} p_i X_i = E(X) = \mu_x \qquad \text{(A2.1)}$$

where $\sum p_i = 1$
     p_i = probability that X_i occurs (i.e., the probability that $X = X_i$)
     $E(\ )$ = "expectations operator"[23]

---

[23] We shall use the "expectations operator" frequently in the text. The reader who wishes to refresh his or her memory on the subject should examine any standard introductory statistics book. We shall take as given the following properties of the operation $E(X)$:

1                               $E(aX + b) = aE(X) + b$

2                               $E(aX)^2 = a^2 E(X^2)$

where a and b are constants.

In the case of a continuous random variable we would write

$$\mu_x = E(X) = \int_{-\infty}^{\infty} X p(X) dX$$

Here X is a continuous random variable with probability distribution represented by $p(X)$. If the probability distribution is symmetric, then the mean lies at its center. For this reason, the mean is often taken as a measure of the average or central tendency of the random variable X.

The *variance* is a measure of the spread or dispersion of the variable X around its mean, and is defined as follows:

$$\sigma_x^2 = \sum_{i=1}^{N} p_i[X_i - E(X)]^2 \qquad \text{discrete case} \qquad (A2.2)$$

$$\sigma_x^2 = \int_{-\infty}^{\infty} p(X)[X - E(X)]^2 \, dX \quad \text{continuous case} \qquad (A2.3)$$

The positive square root of the variance is called the *standard deviation*. Both variance and standard deviation are nonnegative, by definition.

Two further definitions will prove to be useful. If we are interested in the relationship between the random variables X and Y, we can derive some useful information by examining their *joint probability distribution*. We define the *covariance* of X and Y as follows:

$$\text{Cov}(X,Y) = \sum_i \sum_j p_{ij}[X_i - E(X)][Y_i - E(Y)] \quad \text{discrete case} \quad (A2.4)$$

where p_{ij} represents the joint probability of X and Y occurring, and

$$\text{Cov}(X,Y) = E\{[X - E(X)][Y - E(Y)]\} \qquad \text{general case} \qquad (A2.5)$$

Finally, we define the *correlation coefficient*:

$$\rho(X,Y) = \frac{\text{Cov}(X,Y)}{\sigma_x \sigma_y} \qquad (A2.6)$$

The covariance is a measure of the linear association between X and Y. If both variables are always above and below their means at the same time, the covariance will be positive. If X is above its mean when Y is below its mean and vice versa, the covariance will be negative (see Fig. A2.2). The value of the covariance is dependent upon the units in which X and Y are measured. The correlation coefficient, on the other hand, is a measure of the association which has been normalized and is "scale-free." It can be shown that the correlation coefficient

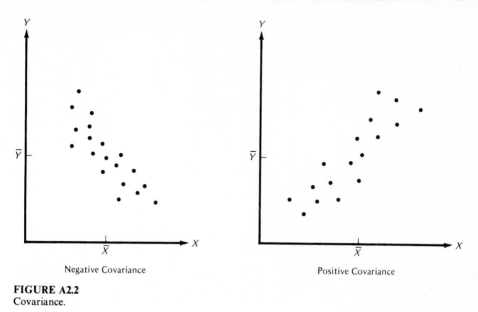

FIGURE A2.2
Covariance.

will always lie between -1 and $+1$. A positive correlation indicates that the variables move in the same direction, while a negative correlation implies that they move in opposite directions. On the other hand, any two variables which are statistically independent will always have a correlation coefficient of 0.

Normal Distribution

In practice we can rarely be sure of the exact form of the probability distribution which underlies the variable X. However, we can describe relevant information about that distribution by calculating the sample mean and variance. Estimates of the mean and variance will vary from sample to sample. For example, assume that an experiment is performed with the tossing of a coin. As before we associate a value of 1 with the occurrence of heads, and a value of 0 with the occurrence of tails. Assume that on 10 tosses of the coin, heads appear 6 times. Then the sample mean is .6. However, the estimator of the mean is a random variable, because 10 additional tosses of the coin might yield a different sample mean.

Now consider the linear regression model, which involves the assumption that there exist true underlying stable values for the parameters. The least-squares procedure yields parameter estimators whose distributions depend upon the distribution of the *unobservable* disturbance, or error term. The most common and useful assumption is that the error is normally distributed, since all knowledge of the distribution is given when we specify its mean and variance. In preparation for the discussion of hypothesis testing and confidence intervals in the text,

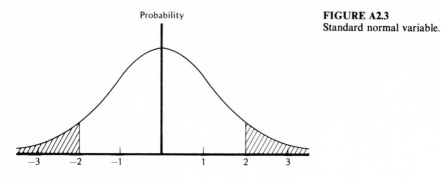

Probability

FIGURE A2.3
Standard normal variable.

we discuss testing procedures that utilize the normal distribution. We assume for the moment that the error variance is known.

Two properties of normally distributed variables are especially useful.

i $\qquad$ $\text{Prob}\,(\mu_x - 2\sigma_x < X_i < \mu_x + 2\sigma_x) \simeq .95$ $\qquad$ (A2.7)

ii $\qquad$ $\text{Prob}\,(\mu_x - 3\sigma_x < X_i < \mu_x + 3\sigma_x) \simeq .99$ $\qquad$ (A2.8)

where μ_x and σ_x are the mean and standard deviation of the normal random variable X. The probability that a single observation of a normally distributed variable X will lie within two standard deviations of its mean is approximately .95. The probability of being within three standard deviations is about .99. Or conversely, the probability that a single observation will be more than two (three) standard deviations away from the mean is .05 (.01). Figure A2.3 contains an illustration of a normal variable with mean 0 and standard deviation 1. The probability that an observation of the random variable X will be in one or the other of the shaded areas is equal to .05.

Hypothesis Testing and Confidence Intervals

Assume for the moment that we know the variance of a random variable X (which is normally distributed), but that the true mean is unknown. It is not surprising that the sample mean $\hat{\mu}_x$ will provide a reasonable guess as to the true value of the mean, but we wish to make statements about the accuracy with which we feel we have estimated the unknown mean value. Confidence statements are difficult to make about individual point estimates such as the sample mean, so we extend our statistical notions to include that of *confidence intervals*. Assume, for example, that we wish to obtain a 95 percent confidence interval about the sample mean (this may be associated with a 5 percent level of significance). We obtain the interval by utilizing the fact that $\hat{\mu}_x$ will be normally distributed with standard deviation $\sigma_x/\sqrt{N}$, where N is the number of observations. In particular, the 95 percent confidence interval will be as follows:

$$\hat{\mu}_x - 2\sigma_x/\sqrt{N} \leq \mu_x \leq \hat{\mu}_x + 2\sigma_x/\sqrt{N} \qquad (A2.9)$$

Suppose, for example, that $N = 100$ and $\sigma_x = 10$. Then $\hat{\mu}_x$ is normally distributed with a standard deviation of 1. If the point estimate of μ_x is $\hat{\mu}_x = 3$, the 95 percent confidence interval will be $1 \leq \mu_x \leq 5$. The 95 percent confidence interval suggests to us that it is very likely that the 1,5 interval will contain the true mean μ_x.

The interpretation of the statement that "with 95 percent confidence $1 \leq \mu_x \leq 5$" is the following: If we could obtain a large number of samples each of size $N = 100$, we would obtain many different point estimates of μ_x. If we calculated the interval $\hat{\mu}_x \pm 2\sigma_x/\sqrt{N}$ corresponding to each sample's estimate of μ_x, we would have a number of interval statements such as

i $\qquad\qquad 1 \leq \mu_x \leq 5 \qquad$ if $\hat{\mu}_x = 3$

ii $\qquad\qquad 1.5 \leq \mu_x \leq 5.5 \qquad$ if $\hat{\mu}_x = 3.5$

iii $\qquad\qquad .7 \leq \mu_x \leq 4.7 \qquad$ if $\hat{\mu}_x = 2.7$

Some of these intervals can be expected to be false, i.e., to exclude the true mean. But over a large number of such calculations, 95 percent of the intervals obtained can be expected to be true, i.e., to contain the true mean.

We are now in a position to utilize the notion of confidence interval to test hypotheses. Consider the null hypothesis that the true mean is equal to zero. For the sample mean of 3 in the above example, we see that the null hypothesis is unlikely to be true, and we reject the null hypothesis (at the 5 percent level of significance) in preference to the alternative—rather vague—hypothesis that the mean is not 0. Note that the null hypothesis has been rejected because it is highly unlikely (although possible) that we would have obtained a sample mean of 3 had the true mean been 0. As a short-cut for testing the null hypothesis that the mean is 0, we can calculate the statistic $\hat{\mu}_x/(\sigma_x/\sqrt{N})$. This statistic will be normally distributed with a variance of 1 and, if the null hypothesis is true, a mean of 0. If the statistic is greater than 2 in absolute value, we can reject the null hypothesis at the 5 percent level, while if it is greater than 3, we can reject it at the 1 percent level (a more powerful statement statistically).

We have, up to this point, assumed that the variance of X was known, but it is more likely (in the context of econometric models especially) that the variance will not be known. We need, therefore, to replace the unknown variance σ_x^2 with the estimated sample variance $\hat{\sigma}_x^2$. (In the text we will be referring to the true error variance as estimated by s^2.) The appropriate test statistic for null hypotheses concerning the mean of X is obtained from the standardized variable obtained by subtracting the true mean from the sample mean and dividing the difference by the sample standard deviation:

$$\frac{\hat{\mu}_x - \mu_x}{\hat{\sigma}_x/\sqrt{N}} \qquad\qquad\qquad \text{(A2.10)}$$

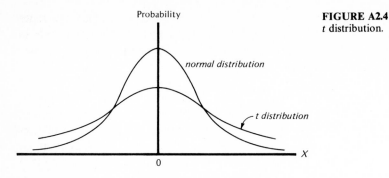

Probability

normal distribution

t distribution

0

X

FIGURE A2.4
t distribution.

When we wish to test the null hypothesis that $\mu_x = 0$, this simplifies to

$$\frac{\hat{\mu}_x}{\hat{\sigma}_x/\sqrt{N}} \tag{A2.11}$$

The distribution of this statistic (known as the Student's t distribution) is closely approximated by the normal distribution when the sample size is relatively large. For small sample sizes the t distribution is flatter than the normal distribution (see Fig. A2.4). But, for N greater than 30, the t and normal distributions are not easily distinguishable.

The t statistic can be utilized to construct confidence intervals in a manner analogous to the normal distribution. A 95 percent confidence interval would be the following:

$$\hat{\mu}_x \pm t_c \hat{\sigma}_x/\sqrt{N} \tag{A2.12}$$

where t_c is the critical value of the t distribution determined from a statistical table based on the number of degrees of freedom in the data and the desired level of significance.[24] The number of degrees of freedom equals the number of data points minus the number of constraints or restrictions placed on the data by the statistical procedure being utilized.

To carry out a test of the hypothesis that the true mean equals a given value μ_x^*, we must first clarify what the alternative hypothesis is. We do this by specifying the null hypothesis $\mu_x = \mu_x^*$ and the alternative hypothesis that $\mu_x \neq \mu_x^*$, as well as a level of significance such as 5 percent or 1 percent. Using the critical value of the t distribution, we calculate the appropriate confidence interval. If the hypothesized mean (μ_x^*) lies outside the confidence interval, we reject the null hypothesis. If it lies inside, we fail to reject. We should note in passing that alternative hypotheses need not be of the two-tailed variety, in which the true

---

[24] The determination of critical values of the t distribution and the appropriate confidence intervals is illustrated in greater detail in the text.

mean may be negative or positive. There are frequent occasions in econometrics when *one-tailed tests* will be desirable. This involves only minor adjustments in the construction of the confidence intervals described previously.

Testing the Linear Regression Model

In the linear regression model we most frequently wish to test the null hypothesis that the slope of the regression line is 0. Since the estimated regression parameters, when standardized, are distributed according to a *t* distribution, we can construct a 95 percent confidence interval. We reject the null hypothesis if 0 lies outside the 95 percent confidence interval about the estimated parameter, and state that the estimated parameter is significant at the 5 percent level. As a rule of thumb we often say that if the calculated value of the *t* distribution (printed out by most computer packages) is greater than 2 in absolute value, we can reject the null hypothesis at the 5 percent level. A more explicit rule would adjust for the fact that the accuracy of the measured standard deviation is dependent upon the number of observations being used.

Chi-Square and *F* Distributions

We have seen that the *t* distribution and occasionally the normal distribution are likely to be useful in performing statistical tests relating to the regression model. To conclude this appendix we should mention two other probability distributions that are of importance in econometric analysis, the chi-square (χ^2) distribution and the *F* distribution. The reader may wish to refer to a statistics textbook for details and clarification.[25]

The chi-square distribution is useful in tests which involve the sum of squares of identically distributed normal variables.[26] The chi-square starts at the origin, is skewed to the right, and has a tail which extends infinitely far to the right (see Fig. A2.5). The exact shape of the distribution depends upon the number of degrees of freedom, with the distribution becoming more and more symmetric as the number of degrees of freedom gets larger. The chi-square distribution can be utilized to perform statistical tests on the sample variance of a data series obtained from a normally distributed population. If there are N observations, then the statistic $(N - 1)s^2/\sigma^2$ will be distributed as chi-square with $N - 1$ degrees of freedom. By examining critical values of the chi-square distribution with the appropriate degrees of freedom, we may decide whether or not to reject the null hypothesis that the variance of the series equals a chosen positive number. We

---

[25] See, for example, A. M. Mood and F. A. Graybill, *Introduction to the Theory of Statistics*, 2d ed. (New York: McGraw-Hill, 1963), and J. E. Freund, *Mathematical Statistics* (Englewood Cliffs, N.J.: Prentice-Hall, 1962).

[26] If X_i is normally and independently distributed with mean 0 and variance σ_x^2, then $\sum_{i=1}^{N} X_i^2$ is distributed as chi-square with N degrees of freedom.

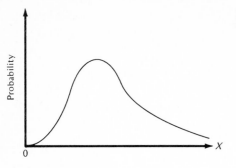

FIGURE A2.5
Chi-square distribution.

will find the chi-square distribution of special use in the time-series portion of the book.

There are likely to be occasions when we wish to test joint hypotheses involving two or more regression parameters. For example, we may wish to test the hypothesis that the regression intercept and slope are both zero against the alternative that one or the other or both are nonzero. The proper test statistic is based on the F distribution, and is characterized by two parameters, the first being associated with the number of estimated parameters in the model and the second with the number of unconstrained degrees of freedom. The F distribution, like the chi-square, has a skewed shape, and ranges in value from 0 to infinity (see Fig. A2.6). In general the F statistic involves the ratio of two independent variances.[27] To avoid difficulties the F statistic is calculated with the larger estimate of variance in the numerator and the smaller estimate in the denominator. The greater the difference between the two variances, the greater the F statistic. Thus, with a sufficiently large value of F we may reject the null hypothesis. In practice, hypothesis testing is accomplished by choosing a level of significance and then looking up the critical value of the F distribution in a standard F table.

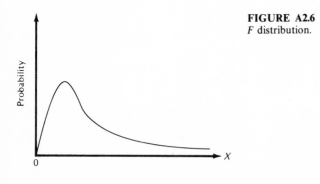

FIGURE A2.6
F distribution.

---

[27] If X_1 and X_2 are independent and distributed as chi-square with N_1 and N_2 degrees of freedom, respectively, then $X_1/N_1 / X_2/N_2$ is distributed according to an F distribution with N_1 and N_2 degrees of freedom.

APPENDIX 2.2 / MAXIMUM-LIKELIHOOD ESTIMATION

A concept frequently utilized in econometrics is that of *maximum likelihood.* Crucial to the concept of maximum likelihood is the fact that different statistical populations generate different samples; any one sample being scrutinized is more likely to have come from some populations rather than from others. For example, if one were sampling coin tosses and a sample mean of .5 were obtained (representing half heads and half tails), it would be clear that the most likely population from which the sample was drawn would be a population with a true mean of .5. Figure A2.7 illustrates a more general case in which a sample $(X_1, X_2, \ldots, X_8)$ is known to be drawn from a normal population with given variance, but unknown mean. Assume that it is known that observations come from either distribution A or distribution B. It should be immediately clear that if the true population were B, then the probability that we would have obtained the sample shown would be quite small. However, if the true population were A, the probability that we would have drawn the sample would be substantially larger. In that sense, the observations "select" the population A as the most likely to have yielded the observed data.

We define the maximum-likelihood estimator of a parameter β as the value of $\hat{\beta}$ which would most likely generate the observed sample observations $Y_1, Y_2, \ldots, Y_N$. In general, if Y_i is normally distributed and each of the Y's is drawn independently, then the maximum-likelihood estimator maximizes

$$p(Y_1)p(Y_2) \cdots p(Y_N)$$

where each p represents a probability associated with the normal distribution.

Before applying our definition directly to the linear regression model, two points should be stressed:

1 The calculated maximum-likelihood estimate is a function of the *particular* sample of Y's chosen. A different sample would result in a different maximum-likelihood estimator.

FIGURE A2.7
Maximum-likelihood estimation.

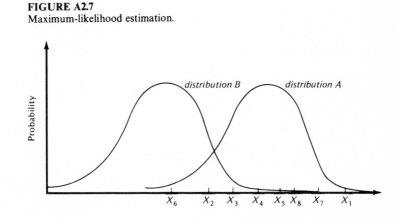

2 $p(Y_1)p(Y_2) \cdots p(Y_N)$ is often referred to as the *likelihood function*. The likelihood function depends not only on the sample values, but also on the unknown parameters of the problem. In describing the likelihood function, we often think of the unknown parameters as varying while the Y's are fixed. This seems reasonable, because finding the maximum-likelihood estimator involves a search over alternative parameter estimators to find those estimators which would be most likely to generate the given sample. For this reason, the likelihood function must be interpreted differently than the joint probability distribution. In the joint probability distribution, the Y's vary and the underlying parameters are fixed.

Now we are in a position to search for the maximum-likelihood estimators of the parameters of the two-variable linear regression model $Y_i = \alpha + \beta X_i + \varepsilon_i$. We know from our initial assumptions that each Y_i is normally distributed with mean $\alpha + \beta X_i$ and variance σ^2. The probability distribution may be written explicitly as follows:[28]

$$p(Y_i) = \frac{1}{\sqrt{2\pi\sigma^2}} \exp\left[-\frac{1}{2\sigma^2}(Y_i - \alpha - \beta X_i)^2\right] \tag{A2.13}$$

where exp denotes the exponential function $[\exp(A) = e^A]$. Then, the likelihood function is

$$L(Y_1, Y_2, \ldots, Y_N, \alpha, \beta, \sigma^2) = p(Y_1)p(Y_2) \cdots p(Y_N)$$

$$= \prod_{i=1}^{N} \left(\frac{1}{\sqrt{2\pi\sigma^2}}\right) \exp\left[-\frac{1}{2\sigma^2}(Y_i - \alpha - \beta X_i)^2\right] \tag{A2.14}$$

where $\prod$ denotes the product of N factors.

We wish to maximize the likelihood function with respect to the parameters α, β, and σ^2. To find the optimum it is necessary to differentiate the likelihood function with respect to each of the three unknown parameters, equate the derivatives to zero, and solve. In fact it is easier to work with the (natural) logarithm of L rather than L itself, an acceptable procedure because L is always nonnegative and the logarithmic function is monotonic; i.e., it preserves ordering. Differentiating (A2.14) partially with respect to α, β, and σ^2 yields the following:

$$\frac{\partial(\log L)}{\partial \alpha} = \frac{1}{\sigma^2}\sum(Y_i - \alpha - \beta X_i) = 0 \tag{A2.15}$$

$$\frac{\partial(\log L)}{\partial \beta} = \frac{1}{\sigma^2}\sum[X_i(Y_i - \alpha - \beta X_i)] = 0 \tag{A2.16}$$

$$\frac{\partial(\log L)}{\partial \sigma^2} = \frac{-N}{2\sigma^2} + \frac{1}{2\sigma^4}\sum(Y_i - \alpha - \beta X_i)^2 = 0 \tag{A2.17}$$

---

[28] See Mood and Graybill, *op. cit.*, for details.

The solution to the Eqs. (A2.15), (A2.16), and (A2.17) yields the following maximum-likelihood estimators:

$$\alpha' = \bar{Y} - \beta'\bar{X}$$

$$\beta' = \frac{\sum (X_i - \bar{X})(Y_i - \bar{Y})}{\sum (X_i - \bar{X})^2}$$

$$\sigma^{2'} = \frac{\sum (Y_i - \alpha' - \beta'X_i)^2}{N}$$

It is now apparent that the maximum-likelihood estimators of α and β are identically equal to the least-squares estimators. It follows therefore that α' and β' are BLUE (best linear unbiased estimators). $\sigma^{2'}$, however, is a biased (although consistent) estimator of σ^2.

3

THE MULTIPLE REGRESSION MODEL

In this chapter we discuss regression models which contain two or more independent variables (in addition to the constant term), i.e., the *multiple* regression model. We begin by describing the assumptions underlying the classical multiple regression model and by showing how the least-squares parameter estimates can be obtained in a model with two explanatory variables. We then discuss the interpretation of regression coefficients and statistics in the multiple regression model. As we will see, problems may arise because of the interaction between the explanatory variables in the regression equation. The problem of multicollinearity, for example (involving highly correlated explanatory variables), can be considerably important in the multiple regression model. We place particular emphasis in this chapter on the various regression statistics which aid in the interpretation of the model, including partial correlation coefficients, beta coefficients, and elasticities. We conclude by discussing the use of dummy variables, which take only specific numerical values. Throughout the chapter examples are used to illustrate the general discussion in the text.

3.1 THE MODEL

We extend the two-variable model by assuming that the dependent variable Y is a linear function of a series of independent variables X_1,

$X_2, \ldots, X_k$, and an error term. This model is a natural extension of the two-variable model, so that it will be unnecessary to derive all our earlier results in full detail.

We write the multiple regression model as follows:

$$Y_i = \beta_1 + \beta_2 X_{2i} + \beta_3 X_{3i} + \cdots + \beta_k X_{ki} + \varepsilon_i \qquad (3.1)$$

Y denotes the dependent variable, the X's denote the independent or explanatory variables, and ε is the error term. X_{2i} represents, for example, the ith observation on explanatory variable X_2. β_1 is the constant term, or intercept, of the equation. It is sometimes helpful to rewrite Eq. (3.1) as follows:

$$Y_i = \beta_1 X_{1i} + \beta_2 X_{2i} + \beta_3 X_{3i} + \cdots + \beta_k X_{ki} + \varepsilon_i \qquad (3.2)$$

where $X_{1i} = 1$ for all observations $i = 1, 2, \ldots, N$. The model in Eq. (3.2) is identical to that of (3.1), but it is more useful for the matrix development of the multiple regression model that is presented in the appendix to this chapter.

The assumptions of the multiple regression model are quite similar to those of the two-variable model:

i The model specification is given by Eq. (3.1).

ii The X's are nonstochastic. In addition, *no exact linear relationship exists among two or more of the independent variables.*

iii (*a*) The error term has 0 expected value and constant variance for all observations.

(*b*) Errors corresponding to different observations are uncorrelated.

(*c*) The error variable is normally distributed.

Assumptions i, ii, and iii, which make up the *classical multiple regression model*, could also be restated in terms of the distribution of the Y's rather than the errors.[1] The only new assumption, concerning the possibility of a linear relationship between the X's, will be discussed when we examine multicollinearity.

For purposes of simplicity we shall often consider a special case of the multiple regression model—the three-variable model:

$$Y_i = \beta_1 + \beta_2 X_{2i} + \beta_3 X_{3i} + \varepsilon_i$$

The least-squares procedure is equivalent to searching for parameter estimates which minimize the residual (or error) sum of squares, defined as follows:

$$\text{ESS} = \sum \hat{\varepsilon}_i^2 = \sum (Y_i - \hat{Y}_i)^2$$

where $\hat{Y}_i = \hat{\beta}_1 + \hat{\beta}_2 X_{2i} + \hat{\beta}_3 X_{3i}$

---

[1] In terms of the Y variable, iii(*a*) and (*c*) are equivalent to the assumption that the Y_i's are independent normally distributed variables with mean $E(Y_i) = \beta_1 + \beta_2 X_{2i} + \beta_3 X_{3i} + \cdots + \beta_k X_{ki}$ and with variance σ^2.

We can minimize ESS by calculating its partial derivatives with respect to the three unknown parameters β_1, β_2, and β_3, equating each to 0 and solving:

$$\frac{\partial ESS}{\partial \beta_1} = 0 \quad \text{or} \quad \sum Y_i = N\beta_1 + \beta_2 \sum X_{2i} + \beta_3 \sum X_{3i} \tag{3.3}$$

$$\frac{\partial ESS}{\partial \beta_2} = 0 \quad \text{or} \quad \sum X_{2i} Y_i = \beta_1 \sum X_{2i} + \beta_2 \sum X_{2i}^2 + \beta_3 \sum X_{2i} X_{3i} \tag{3.4}$$

$$\frac{\partial ESS}{\partial \beta_3} = 0 \quad \text{or} \quad \sum X_{3i} Y_i = \beta_1 \sum X_{3i} + \beta_2 \sum X_{2i} X_{3i} + \beta_3 \sum X_{3i}^2 \tag{3.5}$$

We thus have three equations which can be solved for β_1, β_2, and β_3. A solution will exist unless there are fewer than three observations or there is a linear relationship among the X's, in which case the three equations will not be independent. Assuming that there are more than three observations and the equations are independent, the solution is

$$\hat{\beta}_1 = \bar{Y} - \hat{\beta}_2 \bar{X}_2 - \hat{\beta}_3 \bar{X}_3 \tag{3.6}$$

$$\hat{\beta}_2 = \frac{(\sum x_{2i} y_i)(\sum x_{3i}^2) - (\sum x_{3i} y_i)(\sum x_{2i} x_{3i})}{(\sum x_{2i}^2)(\sum x_{3i}^2) - (\sum x_{2i} x_{3i})^2} \tag{3.7}$$

$$\hat{\beta}_3 = \frac{(\sum x_{3i} y_i)(\sum x_{2i}^2) - (\sum x_{2i} y_i)(\sum x_{2i} x_{3i})}{(\sum x_{2i}^2)(\sum x_{3i}^2) - (\sum x_{2i} x_{3i})^2} \tag{3.8}$$

where $\bar{X}_2 = \sum X_{2i}/N$ $\quad$ $\bar{X}_3 = \sum X_{3i}/N$

3.2 REGRESSION INTERPRETATION AND STATISTICS

Interpretation of regression coefficients requires an expansion of our analysis in the two-variable model. For example, in the three-variable model,

$$Y_i = \beta_1 + \beta_2 X_{2i} + \beta_3 X_{3i} + \varepsilon_i$$

the coefficient β_2 measures the change in Y associated with a unit change in X_2 on the assumption that all other values for the remaining explanatory variables are held constant. Likewise the coefficient β_3 measures the change in Y associated with a unit change in X_3. In both cases the assumption that the values of the remaining explanatory variables are constant is crucial to our interpretation of the coefficients. On the basis of this assumption we call the unknown slope parameters *partial regression coefficients*, since they correspond to the values of the *partial derivatives* of Y with respect to X_2 and X_3.

In order to test the significance of individual regression coefficients, it is natural to ask whether the Gauss-Markov theorem (discussed in Chapter 2) extends to the multiple regression model and whether one can obtain an unbiased estimate of the variance σ^2 as well as information about the distribution of the estimated regression parameters. The derivations of the statistical properties of the multiple regression model are cumbersome without the use of matrix algebra, and so we simply provide a summary of the important results:[2]

i The ordinary least-squares estimator of each coefficient $\beta_j, j = 1, 2, \ldots, k$ is the *best linear unbiased estimator*. When the error term is normally distributed, it is equivalent to the *maximum-likelihood estimator* as well.
ii An unbiased and consistent estimate of σ^2 is provided by

$$s^2 = \frac{\sum \hat{\varepsilon}_i^2}{N - k}$$

iii When the error is normally distributed, t tests can be applied to test the regression coefficients because

$$\frac{\hat{\beta}_j - \beta_j}{s_{\hat{\beta}_j}} \sim t_{N-k} \qquad \text{for } j = 1, 2, \ldots, k$$

In other words, the estimated regression parameters, normalized by subtracting the mean and dividing by the estimated standard error, follow the t distribution with $N - k$ degrees of freedom. Finally, the *standard errors* of each of the coefficients $s_{\hat{\beta}_1}, s_{\hat{\beta}_2}, \ldots, s_{\hat{\beta}_k}$ are derived in the appendix to this chapter because their calculation involves matrix inversion.

3.3 F TESTS, R^2, AND CORRECTED R^2

To extend the notion of R^2 as a measure of goodness of fit to the multiple regression model, we repeat and extend some of the earlier discussion about the decomposition of the variation in the dependent variable Y. Recall that the model with k variables is

$$Y_i = \beta_1 + \beta_2 X_{2i} + \cdots + \beta_k X_{ki} + \varepsilon_i \tag{3.9}$$

We may break down the difference between Y_i and its mean $\overline{Y}_i$ as follows:

$$(Y_i - \overline{Y}) = (Y_i - \hat{Y}_i) + (\hat{Y}_i - \overline{Y}) \tag{3.10}$$

---

[2] The multiple regression model is presented in matrix form in the appendix to this chapter.

Squaring both sides and summing over all observations (1 to N) we obtain[3]

$$\sum (Y_i - \overline{Y})^2 \quad = \sum (Y_i - \hat{Y}_i)^2 \qquad + \sum (\hat{Y}_i - \overline{Y})^2 \qquad (3.11)$$

Variation in Y Residual variation   Explained
variation

or, using the terminology introduced in Chapter 2,

$$\text{TSS} \qquad = \text{ESS} \qquad\qquad + \text{RSS} \qquad\qquad (3.12)$$

Total sum   Residual sum   Regression sum
of squares   of squares   of squares

Then, we define R^2 as follows:

$$R^2 = \frac{\text{RSS}}{\text{TSS}} = \frac{\sum (\hat{Y}_i - \overline{Y})^2}{\sum (Y_i - \overline{Y})^2} = 1 - \frac{\sum \hat{\varepsilon}_i^2}{\sum (Y_i - \overline{Y})^2} \qquad (3.13)$$

R^2 measures the proportion of the variation in Y which is "explained" by the multiple regression equation. R^2 is often informally used as a "goodness of fit" statistic and to compare the validity of regression results under alternative specifications of the independent variables in the model. There are several problems with the use of R^2. In the first place, *all our statistical results follow from the initial assumption that the model has been correctly specified*, and we have no statistical procedure to compare alternative specifications. Second, R^2 is dependent upon the number of independent variables included in the regression model. The addition of more independent variables to the regression equation can never lower R^2 and is likely to raise it (the addition of a new explanatory variable does not alter TSS, but is likely to increase RSS). Thus, one would simply add more variables to an equation if one wished only to maximize R^2. Finally, the interpretation and use of R^2 become difficult when a model is formulated which has a 0 intercept. In such a case the ratio of the regression sum of squares to the total sum of squares need not lie within the (0, 1) range.[4]

---

[3] $\sum (Y_i - \overline{Y})^2 = \sum (Y_i - \hat{Y}_i)^2 + \sum (\hat{Y}_i - \overline{Y})^2 + 2\sum (Y_i - \hat{Y}_i)(\hat{Y}_i - \overline{Y})$. But the last term is identically zero, since

$$\sum (Y_i - \hat{Y}_i)(\hat{Y}_i - \overline{Y}) = \sum \hat{\varepsilon}_i (\hat{Y}_i - \overline{Y}) = \sum \hat{\varepsilon}_i \hat{Y}_i - \sum \hat{\varepsilon}_i \overline{Y}$$

$$= \sum \hat{\varepsilon}_i (\hat{\beta}_1 + \hat{\beta}_2 X_{2i} + \cdots + \hat{\beta}_k X_{ki}) - \overline{Y} \sum \hat{\varepsilon}_i$$

$$= \hat{\beta}_1 \sum \hat{\varepsilon}_i + \hat{\beta}_2 \sum \hat{\varepsilon}_i X_{2i} + \cdots + \hat{\beta}_k \sum \hat{\varepsilon}_i X_{ki} - \overline{Y} \sum \hat{\varepsilon}_i$$

$$= 0 \quad \text{since } \sum \hat{\varepsilon}_i = 0 \text{ and } \sum \hat{\varepsilon}_i X_{ji} = 0 \text{ for } j = 2, 3, \ldots, k.$$

[4] The use of R^2 in a model with zero intercept is discussed in detail in D. Aigner, *Basic Econometrics* (Englewood Cliffs, N.J.: Prentice-Hall, 1971), pp. 85–90.

The difficulty with R^2 as a measure of goodness of fit is that R^2 pertains to explained and unexplained *variation* in Y and therefore does not account for the number of degrees of freedom in the problem. A natural solution is to concern oneself with *variances*, not variations, thus eliminating the dependence of goodness of fit on the number of independent variables in the model. (Recall that variance equals variation divided by degrees of freedom.) We define $\overline{R}^2$, or *corrected R^2*, as follows:

$$\overline{R}^2 = 1 - \frac{\text{Var}(\hat{\varepsilon})}{\text{Var}(Y)}$$

where the sample variances of $\hat{\varepsilon}$ and Y are calculated as follows:

$$\text{Var}(\hat{\varepsilon}) = s^2 = \frac{\sum \hat{\varepsilon}_i^2}{N - k}$$

$$\text{Var}(Y) = \frac{\sum (Y_i - \overline{Y})^2}{N - 1}$$

where k is the number of independent variables. Even though the error sum of squares will decrease (or remain the same) as new explanatory variables are added, the residual variance need not. Notice that both the numerator and denominator in the definition of $\text{Var}(\hat{\varepsilon})$ change when an additional variable is added to the model. In addition, by noting that

$$R^2 = 1 - \frac{s^2}{\text{Var}(Y)} \frac{N - k}{N - 1} \tag{3.14}$$

it is easy to derive a formula[5] for the relationship between R^2 and $\overline{R}^2$:

$$\overline{R}^2 = 1 - (1 - R^2) \frac{N - 1}{N - k} \tag{3.15}$$

Upon examination of Eq. (3.15), it becomes immediately apparent that:

1 If $k = 1$, then $R^2 = \overline{R}^2$.
2 If k is greater than 1, then $R^2 \geq \overline{R}^2$.
3 $\overline{R}^2$ can be negative.

---

[5] From Eq. (3.14) it follows that $1 - R^2 = [s^2/\text{Var}(Y)][(N - k)/(N - 1)]$. But $1 - \overline{R}^2 = s^2/\text{Var}(Y)$. Therefore $1 - R^2 = (1 - \overline{R}^2)[(N - k)/(N - 1)]$. Solving, we get $\overline{R}^2 = 1 - (1 - R^2)[(N - 1)/(N - k)]$.

One should not conclude that the corrected R^2 solves all the difficulties associated with using R^2 as a measure of goodness of fit. The decision about whether or not variables should be included in the model should still depend largely upon *a priori* theoretical considerations. In any case the numerical value of corrected R^2 will be sensitive to the kind of data being used.[6]

The F statistic printed out by most regression programs can be used in the multiple regression model to test the significance of the R^2 statistic. Strictly speaking, the F statistic with $N - 1$ and $T - k$ degrees of freedom allows us to test the hypothesis that *none* of the explanatory variables helps to explain the variation of Y about its mean. In other words, the F statistic tests the joint hypothesis that $\beta_2 = \beta_3 = \cdots = \beta_k = 0$. It can be shown that

$$F_{k-1, N-k} = \frac{R^2}{1 - R^2} \frac{N - k}{k - 1}$$

If the null hypothesis is true, then we would expect R^2, and therefore F, to be close to 0. Thus, we use a high value of the F statistic as a rationale for rejecting the null hypothesis. (See Chapter 2 and Appendix 2.1 for details.) In the two-variable model, for example, the F statistic tests whether the regression line is horizontal. In such a case, $R^2 = 0$ (see Chapter 2) and the regression explains none of the variation in the dependent variable. Notice that we do not test whether the regression passes through the origin ($\beta_1 = 0$)—our objective is simply to see whether we can explain any variation around the mean of Y. As a practical matter, the F test of the significance of a regression equation is of limited use, because it is likely that the F statistic will allow for rejection of the null hypothesis, whether or not the model explains the structure under study. In fact, it is possible for the R^2 to be significant at a given level, even though none of the regression coefficients are found to be significant according to individual t tests.[7] If the value of the F statistic is not significantly different from 0, we must conclude that the explanatory variables do little to explain the variation of Y about its mean.

What if we were to utilize R^2 to compare the validity of alternative regression models when the dependent variable varies from regression to regression? Such a problem occurs frequently in econometric model building when the researcher has little prior information as to what functional form the dependent variable in the model ought to take. Consider the following two models:

---

[6] It is interesting to note that a simple general rule does exist for the individual wishing to maximize corrected R^2. If independent variables are left in the regression equation when their t statistic is greater than 1 and dropped otherwise, then corrected R^2 will be maximized with respect to the set of independent variables under consideration. For details, see P. J. Dhrymes, "On the Game of Maximizing $\bar{R}^2$," *Australian Economic Papers*, vol. 9, December 1970.

[7] This situation might arise, for example, if the independent variables are highly correlated with each other. The result may be high standard errors for the coefficients and low t values; yet the model as a whole might fit the data very well. See section 3.4 for further details relating to the problem of multicollinearity.

I $$Y_i = \beta_1 + \beta_2 X_{2i} + \beta_3 X_{3i} + \varepsilon_i \qquad (3.16)$$

II $$(Y_i - X_{2i}) = \beta_1' + \beta_2' X_{2i} + \beta_3' X_{3i} + \varepsilon_i' \qquad (3.17)$$

Model I differs from II only in that the dependent variables differ. (Y might be total local government expenditures, including federal grants, and X_2 might be grants, making the second dependent variable expenditures paid for by locally raised revenues.) It can be shown (see Exercise 3.1) that:

1 The R^2 and $\bar{R}^2$ measures associated with models 1 and 2 will differ.
2 $\hat{\beta}_1' = \hat{\beta}_1$, $\hat{\beta}_2' = \hat{\beta}_2 - 1$, and $\hat{\beta}_3' = \hat{\beta}_3$.
3 The true errors as well as the least-squares residuals and the residual variance will be identical in the two models.

Thus, both versions of the model provide identical information about the process under study, yet the measures of goodness of fit will vary considerably from one case to the other.

Example 3.1   Auto Sales

In order to predict monthly auto sales using a single-equation model, three explanatory variables are likely to be of value. One would expect that sales would move in the same direction as monthly wages, but that they would be inversely related to the recent price of autos and to the cost of borrowing money to finance the purchase. We therefore use the following data for our model:

   S = monthly retail auto sales (January 1963–April 1974), millions of current dollars
   W = monthly wages (January 1963–April 1974), billions of current dollars
   R = 3-month Treasury bill rate in percentage terms for the same time bounds as above
CPI = monthly Consumer Price Index of new cars (1957–1959 = 100) for the same time bounds as above

The equation to be estimated is

$$S_t = \beta_1 + \beta_2 W_t + \beta_3 R_{t-1} + \beta_4 \text{CPI}_{t-1} + \varepsilon_t$$

where t denotes that the data are measured at time t. Both the interest rate variable and the Consumer Price Index are lagged 1 month in order to account explicitly for the fact that interactions in the economy take time to occur. The regression results (as they may be printed out by a standard computer program) are listed as follows:

Coefficient	Value	Standard error	t statistic
$\hat{\beta}_1$	4,904.0	1,067.0	4.6
$\hat{\beta}_2$	10.3	1.1	9.6
$\hat{\beta}_3$	-140.5	57.3	-2.4
$\hat{\beta}_4$	-35.6	10.6	-3.3

Number of variables = 4 (including the constant)
Number of observations = 88
Degrees of freedom = 84
$R^2 = .849$
$\bar{R}^2 = .842$
$F(3/84) = F_{3,\,84} = 157.8$
Standard error of the regression $(s) = 236.2$
Sum of squared residuals (ESS) = 4.7×10^6

All estimated coefficients are significant at the 5 percent level, since all t statistics are greater than 2 in absolute value and there are 84 degrees of freedom. For this reason, none of the variables should be dropped from the regression. As expected, the monthly wage coefficient is positive. It may be interpreted to mean that an increase of \$1 billion in wages and salaries will lead to a \$10.3 million increase in auto sales, with the effects of all other variables held constant. Also, if the interest rate rises by 1 percentage point, auto sales will drop by \$141 million in the following month. Finally, the estimated price-index coefficient tells us that if the Consumer Price Index for new cars goes up by one point (other things being equal), auto sales will drop by \$36 million.

The R^2 and $\bar{R}^2$ statistics are very close in magnitude as expected, since there are a large number of degrees of freedom in the model. The F statistic with 3 and 84 degrees of freedom is highly significant, allowing us to reject the null hypothesis that all explanatory variable coefficients are jointly 0. Finally, the reader should check that the sum of squared residuals is closely related to the standard error of the regression, since $s^2 = (\text{ESS}/84)$.

Example 3.2   Interest Rate Determination

In this example we build a single-equation model whose purpose is to forecast short-term interest rates. We restrict our attention to the least-squares estimation of the model, although we consider a more sophisticated estimation of this same model in Chapter 4 when we deal with the problem of serially correlated errors. Finally, we use the least-squares model to forecast short-term interest rates in Example 6.2. Throughout our discussion the reader will find it valuable to examine Table 3.1, which summarizes six of the regression results obtained during the process of building the single-equation model. The model is estimated using monthly time-series data running from January of the initial year through

January of the final year of observation. The variables used in the estimation process are as follows:

R = Interest rate on 3-month Treasury bills (dependent variable)
YD = aggregate disposable income, billions of 1958 dollars
M = aggregate money supply (currency plus demand deposits), billions of current dollars
P = Consumer Price Index (1958 = 100)

The symbol Δ is used to denote the process of first-differencing, that is,

$$\Delta YD_t = YD_t - YD_{t-1}$$

The first equation (column I) includes four explanatory variables. Disposable income is expected to have a strong positive effect on interest rates, since increases in disposable income imply increases in the demand for liquid assets. As expected, the YD coefficient is positive and statistically significant (at the 1 percent and 5 percent levels). The change in disposable income is added in an

TABLE 3.1
SELECTED REGRESSION RESULTS

(t statistics are in parentheses)

Independent variables	I	II	III	IV	V	VI
YD_t	.032	.037	.030	.054	.050	.053
	(6.67)	(7.01)	(7.00)	(23.22)	(14.55)	(14.76)
ΔYD_t	−.109	−.172				
	(−.69)	(−1.00)				
$\Delta M_t + \Delta M_{t-1} + \Delta M_{t-2}$	−.197	−.303	−.208	−.305	−.294	−.280
	(−3.36)	(−4.73)	(−3.71)	(−7.38)	(−5.93)	(−6.13)
$\Delta P_t/P_t$	372.922					
	(5.91)					
$\Delta P_t/P_t + \Delta P_{t-1}/P_{t-1}$		249.970	218.17			
		(6.96)	(7.26)			
$\Delta P_t/P_t + \Delta P_{t-1}/P_{t-1} + \Delta P_{t-2}/P_{t-2}$				99.651	41.54	104.37
				(7.83)	(1.89)	(5.23)
Constant	−1.072	−1.086	−.924	−3.750	−3.011	−3.662
	(−1.99)	(−1.85)	(−1.83)	(−14.90)	(−7.87)	(−9.45)
N	157	157	157	181	121	145
R^2	.649	.672	.665	.863	.739	.853
$\bar{R}^2$	.640	.664	.658	.860	.732	.849
Time bounds	1960–73	1960–73	1960–73	1955–70	1958–68	1958–70
(SER)	.816	.788	.794	.524	.509	.552
F	70.29	77.93	101.27	370.93	110.29	271.88

attempt to include (in a detailed manner) the time process involved as interest rates adjust to disposable income changes. Because this variable is statistically insignificant, no serious attempt is made to evaluate the sign of its coefficient. The third variable included in the model is a *moving sum* of *changes* in the money supply. The moving sum (in this case) is a simple sum of money changes over a 3-month time period. It is expected that, other things equal, increases in the average of past changes in the money *supply* will lead to lower interest rates. The results are consistent with this notion, since the regression coefficient is negative and significant at the 5 percent level. Finally, a variable is entered to account for the effect of the rate of change of prices. One would expect (as is borne out) that an increase in the rate of price change will lead to an increase in interest rates. While the results are generally good (three significant t values, and an R^2 of .649), the standard error of the regression is unsatisfactorily high. The standard error of .816 is best interpreted in relation to the mean value of the dependent variable, in this case 3.78. The standard error is approximately 22 percent of the dependent variable mean; from experience we would hope for a *percentage standard error* closer to 10 or 15 percent.

In the second regression equation (column II), the inflation variable is changed from a 1-month rate of change to a 2-month moving-sum rate of change. As in the case of the money supply, it is suspected that inflation affects interest rates with a lag. The results suggest that some improvement has taken place. R^2 has increased (as well as $\bar{R}^2$), as has the F statistic. The fact that the standard error of the equation has decreased is also indicative of a gain in predictive power. In the third regression equation (column III), the previously insignificant ΔYD term is dropped from the equation. This leaves all individual regression coefficients significant and results in a very small increase in the standard error of the regression (since the residual sum of squares is virtually unchanged and the number of degrees of freedom has fallen).

As a final attempt to improve the regression model, the moving-sum rate of inflation variable is increased from a 2- to a 3-month average. The results of the regressions are listed in columns IV, V, and VI—each regression associated with a different set of time bounds. The alteration in the moving-sum inflation term has substantially increased the explanatory power of the equation in all three cases. In regression VI, for example, R^2 has increased to .853, while the standard error of the regression has diminished to .552. This is slightly less than 15 percent of the mean of the dependent variable. At the same time each of the t statistics has increased somewhat in magnitude (in absolute value). For these reasons the final model specification is chosen to be the specification implicit in regressions IV, V, and VI. The specific set of time bounds chosen should depend not upon an analysis of minor changes in regression statistics, but rather upon the specific purposes for which the regression equation is to be utilized. In most actual applications, for example, the model will be estimated using all recent data, so that complete information can be utilized in the forecasting process.

Example 3.3 Consumption Function

Three separate regression equations were used to describe some of the econometric issues involved with the estimation of a simple aggregative consumption function. The three models are as follows (data are quarterly, from 1954–1 to 1971–4, in current dollars):

I $\qquad C_t = \alpha_1 + \beta_1 Y_t + \varepsilon_{1t}$

II $\qquad C_t = \alpha_2 + \beta_2 Y_t + \gamma_2 C_{t-1} + \varepsilon_{2t}$

III $\qquad S_t = \alpha_3 + \beta_3 Y_t + \varepsilon_{3t} \qquad (S_t \equiv Y_t - C_t)$

The regression results are listed in the following table:

	Coefficient	Value	t statistic
Model I	$\hat{\alpha}_1$	14.51	7.03
	$\hat{\beta}_1$	0.88	173.06
	$R^2 = .9977$	ESS $= 966.5$	SER $= 3.72$
Model II	$\hat{\alpha}_2$	5.52	3.06
	$\hat{\beta}_2$	0.31	4.85
	$\hat{\gamma}_2$	0.65	8.78
	$R^2 = .9989$	ESS $= 440.70$	SER $= 2.55$
Model III	$\hat{\alpha}_3$	-14.51	-7.03
	$\hat{\beta}_3$	0.12	24.57
	$R^2 = .8961$	ESS $= 966.5$	SER $= 3.72$

Model I describes the simplest form of the consumption function, in which consumption is determined purely from disposable income Y in the same time period. The coefficient of the disposable income variable measures the marginal propensity to consume. In model II a term is added to include the effect of lagged consumption on present consumption. The term is included to allow for current consumption to be closely dependent upon its own recent behavior as well as on income. The coefficient of the disposable-income term must be interpreted differently in model II than it is in model I. The value of .31 refers to the change in consumption associated with a one-unit change in disposable income, assuming that consumption in the previous period has remained unchanged. The reader should note that the total effect of a change in disposable income on consumption will take place over time and can be measured only by calculating the long-run marginal propensity to consume under the assumption that consumption patterns are equal over time.[8] Solving for $C_t = C_{t-1}$, we find that the long-run marginal propensity to consume implied by model II is $.31/(1 - .65) = .88$.

---

[8] A detailed analysis of model II is presented in Chapter 7 when distributed lags are discussed.

The reader should notice the slight increase in R^2 from model I to model II. R^2 will always increase when additional variables are added to the model, as long as those variables are correlated with the dependent variable and not collinear with the other independent variables. Since the R^2 for the original equation is already quite high, it is tempting to assume that adding additional variables cannot add much to the explanatory power of the model, but the significant t statistic on the lagged consumption term in model II shows that this is not the case.

Model III represents a savings function, not a consumption function, but a quick examination of the regression results shows the two to be quite closely related. This is not surprising, since savings is defined to be the difference between disposable income and consumption for all observations of the data. Notice that the estimated coefficients are very closely related to each other. The intercepts differ only by sign, and the sum of the two slope coefficients is identically 1. The reader can see why this is true by substituting $Y_t - C_t$ for S_t in model III and comparing the results with model I. In addition, the regression sum of squares and standard error of the regressions are identical in both models. In fact, it is not difficult to show that the estimated residuals are identical in both cases. What appears surprising at first is that the R^2 falls substantially when moving from model I to model III. The reason for this drop can be seen by recalling the definition of R^2:

$$R^2 = 1 - \frac{\text{ESS}}{\text{TSS}}$$

Since the estimated residuals are identical in both equations, the error sum of squares is also identical. However, the total sum of squares is different in the two models because the dependent variables are different. The point of this example is that models can be alike in almost all respects (including the ability to forecast or predict) and yet differ substantially in R^2. To depend solely on the use of R^2 as a measure of the explanatory power of a regression equation can be misleading because of the sensitivity of R^2 to the choice of dependent variable. We shall see in Chapter 6 that the standard error of the regression is often more useful as a measure of predictive power of a regression equation than is R^2.

3.4 MULTICOLLINEARITY

One of the assumptions of the classical multiple regression model is that there exists no exact linear relationship between the independent variables in the model. If such a linear relationship does exist, we say that the independent variables are perfectly *collinear*, or that perfect *collinearity* exists. Assume, for example, that the grade-point average model (from Chapter 1) consisted of the following three independent variables:

X_2 = family income, thousands of dollars
X_3 = average hours of study/day
X_4 = average hours of study/week

Variables X_3 and X_4 are collinear because $X_4 = 7X_3$ for *each and every* student being surveyed. If regression results were somehow obtained, it would be impossible to interpret the coefficient of the X_3 variable without simultaneously examining the coefficient of the X_4 variable.[9] Each parameter makes perfect sense if only one of the collinear variables appears in the model. When both appear we are faced with an impossible problem. The coefficient of the X_3 variable is a partial regression coefficient measuring the change in Y associated with a unit change in X_3 *with all other variables constant.* Since it is impossible to keep all other variables constant, we are not able to interpret (or even define) the regression coefficient. The example is so obvious as to suggest that perfect collinearity cannot arise in a realistic setting. There are instances, however, where more complex linear relationships between the independent variables can appear in a model if proper care is not taken. Pure or perfect collinearity is easy to discover, because it will be impossible for the computer (or the individual) to calculate least-squares estimates of the parameters. (With collinearity, the system of normal equations to be solved contains two or more equations which are not independent.) Collinearity presents no particular problem if the linear relationship is known to the researcher. In the grade-point example, one need simply eliminate one of the variables X_3 and X_4 without any loss of predictive or explanatory power.

In practice, we are often faced with the more difficult problem of having independent variables with a high degree of *multicollinearity*. Multicollinearity arises when two or more variables (or combinations of variables) are highly (but not perfectly) correlated with each other. It may be a sample problem, in which case new data may cause the problem to disappear. However, multicollinearity may not be peculiar to a specific sample. In this case the model can be utilized with all its variables, if sufficient care is given to the interpretation of the regression results.

Suppose, for example, that two variables are highly positively correlated (but not perfectly collinear). Then, it will be possible to obtain least-squares estimates of the regression coefficients, but *interpretation* of the coefficients will be quite difficult. The partial regression coefficient of the first of the two highly correlated variables is interpreted to measure the change in Y due to a change in the variable in question, *other things equal.* But, the presence of multicollinearity implies that there will be very little data in the sample to give one confidence about such an interpretation. Any time a given change in one variable occurs, the corresponding observation on its highly correlated partner is likely to change

---

[9] With perfect collinearity, we cannot calculate the least-squares parameter estimates. To see this, reconsider Eqs. (3.3) to (3.5) when X_2 and X_3 are perfectly collinear. In this case, Eqs. (3.4) and (3.5) will not be independent and a solution will not exist.

predictably. Not surprisingly, the distributions of the estimated regression parameters are quite sensitive to multicollinearity. These distributions are sensitive not only to the correlation between independent variables, but also to the magnitude of the standard error of the regression. (Recall that in the two-variable model, the estimated variance of $\hat{\beta}$ is $s^2/\sum x_i{}^2$.) In practice, this sensitivity shows up in the form of very high standard errors for the regression parameter. Frequently, this presents a problem if we believe that one or both of the variables should be in the model, but cannot reject the null hypothesis because of the large estimated standard errors. In such a case, it may be reasonable to drop one of the two variables from the equation and reestimate it.[10]

An often-utilized rule of thumb states that multicollinearity is likely to be a problem if the simple correlation between two variables is larger than the correlation of either or both variables with the dependent variable. Such a rule may be quite reasonable if there are only two independent variables in the model, but can be unreliable in the general case. The principal reason is that simple correlations do not give any information about the possibility of more complicated linear relationships between the independent variables.[11]

Because multicollinearity is dependent directly upon the sample of observations, little can be done to resolve it unless more information about the process in question is available. The easiest way to tell whether multicollinearity is causing problems is to examine the standard errors of the coefficients. If several coefficients have high standard errors and dropping one or more variables from the equation lowers the standard errors of the remaining variables, multicollinearity will usually be the source of the problem. A more sophisticated analysis would take into account the fact that the *covariance* between estimated parameters (as well as the individual standard errors) may be sensitive to multicollinearity. Other things equal, a high degree of collinearity will be associated with a relatively high (in absolute value) covariance between estimated parameters.[12] This suggests that if one estimated parameter $\hat{\beta}_i$ overestimates the true parameter β_i, then a second parameter estimate $\hat{\beta}_j$ is likely to underestimate β_j, and vice versa.[13]

---

[10] As described in Chapter 7 (under the subject of specification error), the gain in the reduction in the standard error of one variable when a second variable is dropped from the equation must be traded off against the possible introduction of bias due to misspecification of the equation. For a more detailed discussion of this issue and some related tests, see C. Toro-Vizcarrondo and T. D. Wallace, "A Test of the Mean Square Error Criterion for Restrictions in Linear Regression," *Journal of the American Statistical Association*, vol. 63, pp. 558–572, 1968, and "Tables for the Mean Square Error Test for Exact Linear Restrictions in Regression," *Journal of the American Statistical Association*, vol. 64, pp. 1649–1663, 1969.

[11] For an additional treatment of tests for multicollinearity see D. E. Farrar and R. R. Glauber, "Multicollinearity in Regression Analysis: The Problem Re-visited," *Review of Economics and Statistics*, vol. 49, pp. 92–107, 1967.

[12] An example of this is given in J. Johnston, *Econometric Methods*, 2d ed. (New York: McGraw-Hill, 1972), pp. 160–163.

[13] One way of improving parameter estimates without the availability of new data involves the use of *ridge regression*. For some details relating to this new estimation process, see B. T. McCallum, "Artificial Orthogonalization in Regression Analysis," *Review of Economics and Statistics*, 52 (1970), pp. 110–113.

3.5 PARTIAL CORRELATION

In the multiple regression model, it is natural to look for an extension of the notion of simple correlation to account for the fact that other variables are kept constant when a given regression parameter is examined. Specifically, we wish to see whether the dependent variable and one independent variable are related after netting out the effect of any other independent variables in the model. To do so, we consider the model

$$Y_i = \beta_1 + \beta_2 X_{2i} + \beta_3 X_{3i} + \varepsilon_i$$

The *partial correlation coefficient* between Y and X_2 must be defined in such a way that it measures the effect of X_2 on Y *which is not accounted for by the other variable in the model.* More specifically, the partial correlation coefficient is calculated by eliminating the linear effect of X_3 on Y (as well as the linear effect of X_3 on X_2) and then running the appropriate regression. The steps are as follows:

1 Run the regression of Y on X_3 and obtain fitted values:

$$\hat{Y} = \hat{\alpha}_1 + \hat{\alpha}_2 X_3$$

2 Run the regression of X_2 on X_3 and obtain fitted values:

$$\hat{X}_2 = \hat{\gamma}_1 + \hat{\gamma}_2 X_3$$

3 Remove the influence of X_3 on both Y and X_2. Let

$$Y^* = Y - \hat{Y} \qquad X_2^* = X_2 - \hat{X}_2$$

4 The partial correlation between X_2 and Y is then the simple correlation between Y^* and X_2^*.

To see why the regression of Y^* on X_2^* gives us our desired partial correlation coefficient, notice that Y^* and X_2^* are both uncorrelated with X_3 by construction.[14] Then, the regression of Y^* on X_2^* relates the part of Y which is uncorrelated with X_3 to the part of X_2 which is uncorrelated with X_3. We shall denote the partial correlation coefficient and simple correlations as follows:

$r_{YX_2 \cdot X_3} =$ partial correlation of Y and X_2 (controlling for X_3)
$r_{YX_2} =$ simple correlation between Y and X_2
$r_{X_2 X_3} =$ simple correlation between X_2 and X_3

---

[14] The fact that Y^* and X_3 (for example) are uncorrelated follows directly from the fact that Y^* represents the residual of the regression of Y on X_3. We have seen in the previous chapter that regression residuals are uncorrelated with explanatory variables.

Given the definition of partial correlation, it is not difficult (although somewhat tedious) to derive the relationship between partial correlation and simple correlation among the relevant variables. We shall state the result without proof, leaving the details to the reader (see Exercise 3.2):

$$r_{YX_2 \cdot X_3} = \frac{r_{YX_2} - r_{YX_3} r_{X_2 X_3}}{\sqrt{1 - r_{X_2 X_3}^2} \sqrt{1 - r_{YX_3}^2}} \tag{3.18}$$

$$r_{YX_3 \cdot X_2} = \frac{r_{YX_3} - r_{YX_2} r_{X_2 X_3}}{\sqrt{1 - r_{X_2 X_3}^2} \sqrt{1 - r_{YX_2}^2}} \tag{3.19}$$

Several observations about partial correlation coefficients can be made directly by examination of Eqs. (3.18) and (3.19). First, partial correlations must range in value from -1 to $+1$ just like simple correlations (recall the derivation of simple correlation). A zero partial correlation between Y and X_2 indicates that there is no linear relationship between Y and X_2 *after the linear effect of X_3 on each has been accounted for*. In such a case we would conclude that X_2 does not have a *direct* effect on Y in the model. In fact, partial correlation coefficients are often used to determine the relative importance of different variables in multiple regression models.

It is interesting to note the relationship between partial correlation and multicollinearity. If X_2 and X_3 are uncorrelated, that is, $r_{X_2 X_3} = 0$, and X_3 and Y are uncorrelated as well ($r_{YX_3} = 0$), then the partial correlation between X_2 and Y reduces to the simple correlation between the two variables. If, on the other hand, X_2 and X_3 are perfectly correlated, that is, $r_{X_2 X_3} = 1$, then the partial correlation cannot be determined.

It is now useful to look at the relationship between partial correlation and R-squared. In the two-variable model it is not difficult to show that it is possible to interpret R^2 as the square of the simple correlation between the dependent and independent variables. It is also possible to interpret the partial correlation between Y and X_2 as measuring the square root of the percentage of variance in Y which is not accounted for by X_3 but which is accounted for by the part of X_2 which is uncorrelated with X_3. Given this fact, it is possible to factor the multiple correlation coefficient into distinct components, each of which serves to explain a proportion of the regression sum of squares in the model. Indeed it is possible to derive the following relationship between multiple and partial correlation (see Exercise 3.2):

$$r_{YX_2 \cdot X_3}^2 = \frac{R^2 - r_{YX_3}^2}{1 - r_{YX_3}^2} \tag{3.20}$$

or
$$1 - R^2 = (1 - r_{YX_3}^2)(1 - r_{YX_2 \cdot X_3}^2) \tag{3.21}$$

The relationships described in Eqs. (3.20) and (3.21) are not easy to interpret.

Equation (3.20) describes the fact (taking square roots of both sides) that the partial correlation coefficient can be determined by taking the square root of the percentage of the variance in Y explained by X_2 (with both variables adjusted to eliminate the effect of X_3).[15]

3.6 BETA COEFFICIENTS AND ELASTICITIES

3.6.1 Beta Coefficients

Beta coefficients are occasionally used to make statements about the relative importance of the independent variables in a multiple regression model. To determine beta coefficients, one simply performs a linear regression in which each variable is "normalized" by subtracting its mean and dividing by its estimated standard deviation. The normalized regression model looks as follows:

$$\frac{Y_i - \overline{Y}}{s_Y} = \beta_2^* \frac{X_{2i} - \overline{X}_2}{s_{X_2}} + \beta_3^* \frac{X_{3i} - \overline{X}_3}{s_{X_3}} + \cdots + \beta_k^* \frac{X_{ki} - \overline{X}_k}{s_{X_k}} + \varepsilon_i \quad (3.22)$$

The beta coefficients bear a close relationship to the estimated coefficients of the original unnormalized multiple regression model. It is not difficult to prove that[16]

$$\hat{\beta}_j^* = \hat{\beta}_j \frac{s_{X_j}}{s_Y} \qquad j = 2, 3, \ldots, k \quad (3.23)$$

In other words, the beta coefficient adjusts the estimated slope parameter by the ratio of the standard deviation of the independent variable to the standard deviation of the dependent variable. A beta coefficient of .7 may be interpreted to mean that a 1 standard deviation change in the independent variable will lead to a .7 standard deviation change in the dependent variable. Both beta coefficients and partial correlation coefficients are connected with the variance of Y, the dependent variable. However, the rescaling associated with the normalized regression makes it possible to compare beta coefficients directly. This cannot be done with the original Y's because the dependent variables are in different units with different variances. It is interesting to note that the beta coefficient of the independent variable in the two-variable model is identically equal to the simple correlation between the two variables (see Exercise 3.10). The beta coefficient of

---

[15] One use of partial correlation is in the *stepwise regression* procedure. For details, see N. Draper and H. Smith, *Applied Regression Analysis* (New York: Wiley, 1966), chap. 6.

[16] Writing Eq. (3.22) in deviations form and Y_i and multiplying both sides by s_Y, we get $y_i = \beta_2^*(s_Y/s_{X_2})x_{2i} + \beta_3^*(s_Y/s_{X_3})x_{3i} + \cdots + \beta_k^*(s_Y/s_{X_k})x_{ki} + \varepsilon_i^*$ from which our result follows directly.

the constant term is undefined since the constant term drops out as a result of the normalization process.[17]

3.6.2 Elasticity

Quite frequently in economics and business one may be interested in interpreting the effect of a percentage change of an independent variable on the dependent variable. The notion of the *elasticity* of a variable is used for this purpose. The elasticity of Y with respect to X_2, for example, may be defined as the percentage change in Y divided by the percentage change in X_2. In general, elasticities are not constant, but change when measured at different points along the regression line. The elasticities which are usually printed out by computer programs are calculated *at the point of the means of each of the independent variables*. For the jth coefficient the elasticity is evaluated as follows:

$$E_j = \hat{\beta}_j \frac{X_j}{Y} \tag{3.24}$$

The values of the elasticity are unbounded and may be positive or negative. Elasticities turn out to be particularly useful because they are unit-free; i.e., their values are independent of the units in which the variables are measured. For example, if $E_j = 2.0$, we can say that about the mean of the variables a 1 percent increase in X_j will lead to a 2 percent increase in Y. If $E_j = -.5$, a 1 percent increase in X_j will lead to a .5 percent decrease in Y. In general, large elasticities imply that the dependent variable is very responsive to changes in the independent variable.

Example 3.4 Sales of Durable Goods

In order to predict the monthly sales of durable goods via a linear regression model, the following data are used:

Dependent variable:

SD = monthly retail sales of durable goods

Independent variables:

DI = retail inventory of department stores in durable goods
IS = inventory sales ratios for all durable goods, retail stores
I = open market rate on prime 4–6 month commercial paper
E = average hourly gross earnings of workers
P = Consumer Price Index for durable goods

---

[17] Beta coefficients, or *standardized regression coefficients*, are discussed in more detail in D. Aigner, *Basic Econometrics* (Englewood Cliffs, N.J.: Prentice-Hall, 1971), pp. 72–80.

The model is specified to be the following:

$$SD_t = \beta_1 + \beta_2\, DI_{t-6} + \beta_3\, IS_{t-1} + \beta_4\, I_{t-1} + \beta_5\, E_{t-1} + \beta_6\, P_{t-1} + \varepsilon_t$$

The regression results are:

Range of data: January 1963 to April 1970

Degrees of freedom: 82 $R^2 = .93$

Standard error of the regression(s) = 263.4 $\bar{R}^2 = .92$

Sum of squared residuals: 5.7×10^6 $F(5/82) = 220.6$

Coefficient	Value	Standard error	t statistic	Mean
$\hat{\beta}_1$	12,091.0	2,321.1	5.2	1.0
$\hat{\beta}_2$	.109	.06	1.8	15,507.9
$\hat{\beta}_3$	−1,690.3	483.6	−3.5	1.96
$\hat{\beta}_4$	−76.2	65.6	−1.2	5.28
$\hat{\beta}_5$	5,585.6	974.4	5.7	2.96
$\hat{\beta}_6$	−175.6	34.4	−5.1	105.1

Coefficient	Partial	Beta	Elasticity
$\hat{\beta}_2$	.19373	.30787	.20864
$\hat{\beta}_3$	−.36010	−.22599	−.40806
$\hat{\beta}_4$	−.12719	−.11866	−.04942
$\hat{\beta}_5$	.53486	1.55429	2.03112
$\hat{\beta}_6$	−.49147	−.67094	−2.26809

Covariance matrix

$\hat{\beta}_1$	5.39×10^6					
$\hat{\beta}_2$	−45.5	.0037				
$\hat{\beta}_3$	$−5.9 \times 10^5$	−4.83	2.3×10^5			
$\hat{\beta}_4$	9.1×10^4	−.056	$−1.4 \times 10^4$	4,307		
$\hat{\beta}_5$	1.04×10^6	−53.3	$−1.4 \times 10^4$	−9,869	9.5×10^5	
$\hat{\beta}_6$	$−6.7 \times 10^4$	1.5	3.05	−531	$−2.3 \times 10^4$	1,181

Correlation matrix

	SD_t	DI_{t-6}	IS_{t-1}	I_{t-1}	E_{t-1}	P_{t-1}
SD_t	1.000					
DI_{t-6}	.943	1.000				
IS_{t-1}	.759	.865	1.000			
I_{t-1}	.831	.910	.860	1.000		
E_{t-1}	.920	.966	.843	.947	1.000	
P_{t-1}	.773	.838	.728	.906	.938	1.000

It is not a coincidence that all independent variables have been chosen to be lagged at least one time period. This accounts for lags in response, while at the same time making the prediction or forecasting problem a much easier one. If one wished to predict monthly retail sales of durable goods at time t, one need simply use the regression equation

$$SD_t = 12,091.0 + .109DI_{t-6} - 1,690.3IS_{t-1} - 76.2I_{t-1}$$

$$+ 5,595.6E_{t-1} - 175.6P_{t-1}$$

To evaluate SD in period $t + 1$, we substitute values for DI given 6 months previously, IS given 1 month previously, etc. If the independent variables were not lagged, some sort of extrapolation process would be needed to forecast their values before a prediction for the dependent variable could be made.[18]

  It is instructive to examine the complete regression output somewhat carefully. Notice that all diagonal elements of the covariance matrix are positive. These are the variances of the estimated coefficients, and are equal to the square of the standard errors of the coefficients. The off-diagonal terms are covariances, which are useful in performing tests which involve combinations of the coefficients of the independent variables. The correlation matrix includes the simple correlation coefficients between all combinations of the dependent and independent variables. As expected, the correlation between each variable and itself is identically equal to 1. All other correlation coefficients are positive and close to 1, which is a typical result when one is working with highly trended time-series data. The high correlations are an indication that multicollinearity may be a problem in the model, but the problem does not seem to be important in light of the significant t statistics associated with the regression results. The column labeled *partial* contains the list of partial correlation coefficients, while the column labeled *beta* includes all the beta coefficients. In this particular example, the independent variable coefficients with the largest t statistics in absolute value also have the largest beta and partial correlation coefficients (this is always true for betas and partial correlations). The beta of 1.55 on lagged earnings can be interpreted to mean that a 1 standard deviation increase in lagged earnings will lead to a 1.55 standard deviation increase in the retail sales of durable goods. The partial correlation coefficient of .53 on the earnings variable, on the other hand, implies that 28 percent ($.53^2$) of the variance of SD not accounted for by the other independent variables is accounted for by earnings. By examining the elasticities, we see that retail sales of durable goods are very sensitive to changes in gross earnings of workers and to the Consumer Price Index for durable goods. If earnings were to rise by 1 percent, then we might

---

[18] This forecasting problem, in the context of a single-equation regression model, is discussed in Chapter 6.

expect retail sales to increase slightly more than 2 percent. On the other hand, if the Consumer Price Index were to rise by 1 percent, retail sales would be expected to fall about 2.3 percent.

3.7   THE GENERAL LINEAR MODEL

We have been dealing with equations which are strictly linear combinations of the X's. Such a restriction in specification is not as limiting as it might seem, because the linear regression model can be applied to a more general class of equations which are still *inherently linear*. Inherently linear models are models which can be expressed in a linear form by a proper transformation of the variables. *Inherently nonlinear* models, on the other hand, cannot be transformed to the linear form. Assume that we begin with a (nonlinear) model represented as

$$Y = F(X_2, X_3, \ldots, X_k, \varepsilon)$$

Then, we can conclude that the model is inherently linear if it can be transformed into the following:

$$f(Y) = \beta_2 \, g_2(X_2, \ldots, X_k) + \cdots + \beta_k \, g_k(X_2, \ldots, X_k) + \varepsilon$$

or $\qquad\qquad Y^* = \beta_2 X_2^* + \beta_3 X_3^* + \cdots + \beta_k X_k^* + \varepsilon \qquad\qquad$ (3.25)

The functions f and g_2 through g_k must be known in order to estimate the coefficients. Notice that the relationship in Eq. (3.25) is inherently linear because it is linear with respect to the coefficients $\beta_2, \beta_3, \ldots, \beta_k$. We shall turn our attention to the estimation of inherently nonlinear models in Chapter 7. For the moment, however, it will be instructive to consider the possibility of finding suitable transformations in special cases. Consider the following econometric models:

I $\qquad\qquad\qquad Y = \beta_1 + \beta_2 X_2 + \beta_3 X_2{}^2 + \varepsilon \qquad\qquad$ (3.26)

II $\qquad\qquad \log Y = \alpha_1 + \alpha_2 \log X_2 + \alpha_3 \log X_3 + \varepsilon \qquad\qquad$ (3.27)

III $\qquad\qquad\qquad Y = \gamma_1 X_2^{\gamma_2} X_3^{\gamma_3} \varepsilon^* \qquad\qquad$ (3.28)

IV $\qquad\qquad\qquad Y = \gamma_1 X_2^{\gamma_2} X_3^{\gamma_3} + \varepsilon' \qquad\qquad$ (3.29)

Model I (the *polynomial model*) provides a means of testing to see whether the relationship between Y and X_2 is nonlinear (although the model itself is linear in the coefficients). Choosing regression parameters is equivalent to finding the best "parabola" which fits the points on a two-dimensional graph of Y and X_2.

The model II is also linear in the parameters and can be utilized if one has reason to believe that variables enter multiplicatively rather than additively into the equation. This can most easily be seen by noticing that model II can be obtained from model III (the *multiplicative model*) by taking the logarithms of both sides. The equivalence of the two models is seen by noting that

$$\alpha_1 = \log \gamma_1 \qquad \alpha_2 = \gamma_2 \qquad \alpha_3 = \gamma_3 \qquad \varepsilon = \log \varepsilon^*$$

Model IV appears to be quite similar to model III but the similarity is deceptive because no transformation of model IV will provide a new model which is linear in the parameters.

The reader should not be lulled into a trap when considering transformations which make models linear in the parameters. Something is often lost in the process. For example, consider the transformation from model II to model III. If we assume that the error process ε is normally distributed, then the error process in model III (ε^*) will not be normal. We usually assume that ε^* follows a distribution whose logarithm is itself normally distributed; i.e., it will be *lognormal*.[19]

To conclude this section, let us consider some additional linear model specifications which are occasionally useful in applied work:

V *Exponential Model*

$$Y = \exp\left(\beta_1 + \beta_2 X_2 + \beta_3 X_3\right) \cdot \varepsilon \tag{3.30}$$

This model can be transformed to

$$\log Y = \beta_1 + \beta_2 X_2 + \beta_3 X_3 + \log \varepsilon$$

VI *Reciprocal Model*

$$Y = \frac{1}{\beta_1 + \beta_2 X_2 + \beta_3 X_3 + \varepsilon} \tag{3.31}$$

This model can be transformed to

$$\frac{1}{Y} = \beta_1 + \beta_2 X_2 + \beta_3 X_3 + \varepsilon$$

VII *Semilog Model*

$$Y = \beta_1 + \beta_2 \log X_2 + \varepsilon \tag{3.32}$$

---

[19] On the other hand, if ε^* is normal, then tests of significance will be invalid when applied to model II, since $\log \varepsilon^*$ will not follow the normal distribution.

In each case, least-squares estimation can be applied directly or to the properly transformed equation to obtain best linear unbiased parameter estimates.

Example 3.5   Estimation of Cost Functions

Nonlinear equations which can be transformed to be linear in the parameters have been used to study cost functions for leather belt shops and for hosiery mills.[20] In the leather belt case, cost records were examined during the period 1935–1938 by 4-week accounting periods. The objective was to see whether or not costs were a nonlinear function of material inputs to the production process. The following regression was run (with all coefficients significant at the 5 percent level):

$$C = -60.178 + .77X + 70.18W$$

where C = total cost, thousands of dollars
$\quad X$ = single-ply equivalent belting, thousands of square feet
$\quad W$ = weight, pounds per square feet

No higher degree term of X was found to be significant, implying that the cost function was essentially linear.

On the other hand, using monthly data (1935–1939) for hosiery mills, a nonlinear relationship between cost and time was found:

$$C = 13.635 + 2.068X + 1.308t - .022t^2$$

where C = total cost, thousands of dollars
$\quad X$ = output, thousands of dozen pairs
$\quad t$ = time, chronological months

3.8   USE OF DUMMY VARIABLES

The variables used in regression equations usually take values over some continuous range. This need not be the case, however, and at times we may wish to use one of more *independent* variables that are restricted to taking on two or more distinct values.[21] For example, we may wish to account for the fact that some individuals go to college and others do not. To do so, we create a dummy variable, which takes on the value 1 if the individual goes to college

---

[20] J. Dean, *Statistical Cost Functions of a Hosiery Mill* (Chicago: University of Chicago Press, 1940), and *The Relation of Cost to Output for a Leather Belt Shop* (New York: National Bureau of Economic Research, 1941), Technical Paper no. 2.

[21] Estimation when the *dependent* variable is a dummy variable is discussed in Chapter 8.

and 0 if not. Dummy variables are particularly useful when dealing with qualitative data. We also show how dummy variables can be utilized in the regression context to account for the fact that observations within a given category are associated with one set of regression parameters, while observations in a second (or third) category are associated with different regression parameters.

Suppose that a firm utilizes two types of production processes to obtain its output. Upon the assumption that the output obtained from each process is normally distributed with different expected values but identical variances, we may represent the production process as a regression equation:

$$Y_i = \beta_1 + \beta_2 X_i + \varepsilon_i \tag{3.33}$$

where Y_i is the output associated with the ith input process and X_i is a dummy variable as follows:

$$X_i \begin{cases} = 1 & \text{if the output was obtained from machine A} \\ = 0 & \text{if the output was obtained from machine B} \end{cases}$$

In this rather simple example, the intercept of the regression line measures the expected output associated with machine B, while the slope measures the difference in output associated with a change from machine B to machine A. This can be seen by taking expected values on both sides of Eq. (3.33) in the case when $X_i = 0$ and when $X_i = 1$:

1 $\qquad\qquad\qquad X_i = 0 \qquad E(Y_i) = \beta_1$

2 $\qquad\qquad\qquad X_i = 1 \qquad E(Y_i) = \beta_1 + \beta_2$

It should be immediately clear that a test of the null hypothesis that $\beta_2 = 0$ provides a test of the hypothesis that there is no difference in the output associated with machines A and B. The reader should check that the actual least-squares estimates of the regression parameters are the mean output associated with machine B and the difference between mean outputs of A and B.

The dummy variable procedure can easily be modified if more than two distinct values are involved. For example, assume that in the above example three different processes may be employed, and one wishes to account for the fact that the output produced by each of the three processes may not be identical. Two dummy variables can be constructed to account for this. (In general, if one needs to differentiate N items, $N - 1$ dummy variables will suffice.) Consider the following model:

$$Y_i = \beta_1 + \beta_2 X_{2i} + \beta_3 X_{3i} + \varepsilon_i \tag{3.34}$$

where $X_{2i} = 1$ if the output was obtained from machine A and 0 otherwise
$\qquad\ \ X_{3i} = 1$ if the output was obtained from machine B and 0 otherwise

Thus, the three production processes are represented by the following combination of values taken by the dummy variables:

	X_2	X_3
Machine A	1	0
Machine B	0	1
Machine C	0	0

By taking expected values for each of these three cases, we can interpret the regression results:

1 $\qquad X_{2i} = 1 \qquad X_{3i} = 0 \qquad E(Y_i) = \beta_1 + \beta_2$

2 $\qquad X_{2i} = 0 \qquad X_{3i} = 1 \qquad E(Y_i) = \beta_1 + \beta_3$

3 $\qquad X_{2i} = 0 \qquad X_{3i} = 0 \qquad E(Y_i) = \beta_1$

The regression intercept represents the expected value of output associated with machine C. The first slope coefficient represents the difference in output associated with a change from machine C to machine A, and the second slope coefficient measures the average change in output associated with a change from machine C to machine B. A test of the null hypothesis that $\beta_2 = 0$ provides a test of the hypothesis that there is no difference between the production process associated with machine A and that associated with machine C, while an analogous test is provided by a t test on the coefficient β_3.

Several comments are worthy of attention before the subject of dummy variables is pursued further.

1 The three alternative production processes were represented by two dummy variables (with the third implicit). Representing such a phenomenon by one variable taking on three values (e.g., machine A = 2, machine B = 1, machine C = 0) is not equivalent to the dummy variable technique unless the differences between outputs associated with the machine C-to-A and machine C-to-B comparisons are identical. In general, there is no reason to make such an assumption.

2 The dummy variable process cannot be represented by three two-way variables X_2, X_3, and X_4, where X_4 takes on the value 1 when machine C is utilized and takes the value 0 otherwise. The introduction of the variable X_4 adds no additional information but does add a nonindependent equation in the derivation of the least-squares estimators. For this reason, it is impossible to obtain least-squares estimates of the regression parameters. This is perhaps best seen by noting the presence of *perfect collinearity* in the model. Collinearity exists because

$$X_{4i} = 1 - X_{2i} - X_{3i} \qquad \text{for each observation } i$$

3 Assume that one wishes to test the null hypothesis that there is no change in output associated with a movement from machine A to machine B. Such a test is provided by an F test of the null hypothesis that the regression coefficients β_2 and β_3 are equal.[22] However, by rewriting the regression equation, the researcher can do the same test using the t statistic provided by the standard regression output. Write the regression model as follows:

$$Y_i = \alpha_1 + \alpha_2 X_{2i} + \alpha_3(X_{3i} + X_{2i}) + \varepsilon_i$$

Then consider the three cases:

I	$X_{2i} = 1$	$X_{3i} = 0$	$E(Y_i) = \alpha_1 + \alpha_2 + \alpha_3$
II	$X_{2i} = 0$	$X_{3i} = 1$	$E(Y_i) = \alpha_1 + \alpha_3$
III	$X_{2i} = 0$	$X_{3i} = 0$	$E(Y_i) = \alpha_1$

A test of the desired hypothesis is then provided by a test of the null hypothesis that $\alpha_2 = 0$.

4 Interpretation of the dummy variable results as described for the models in Eqs. (3.33) and (3.34) involves a description of the difference in effects relative to the intercept term, since the intercept corresponds to the effects of machine C as represented by the excluded category. There is no reason why such a comparison had to be made. In certain cases the researcher may find it valuable to drop the intercept from the regression and use three distinct dummy variables to represent the three machine processes. The regression results will be identical if the proper interpretation is given.

It is now natural to extend the notion of dummy variables to the more general case in which some of the independent variables are continuous while others are dummies. The classic example is the case of the aggregate consumption function, in which rationing, saving campaigns, etc. make wartime consumption behavior different from peacetime behavior. We shall distinguish between five different cases of a simple aggregate consumption function in which we assume that aggregate consumption is determined by aggregate disposable income with no lags involved (this simplification is purely for expositional purposes).

---

[22] For a discussion of such a test see J. Johnston, *Econometric Methods*, 2d ed. (New York: McGraw-Hill, 1972).

Case I

$$C_t = \beta_1 + \beta_2 Y_t + \varepsilon_t \qquad (3.35)$$

This is the case in which peacetime and wartime consumption behavior are assumed to be identical in all respects. There is no need for the use of a dummy variable if one has such knowledge *a priori*.

Case II

$$C_t = \beta_1 + \beta_2 Y_t + \alpha D_t + \varepsilon_t \qquad (3.36)$$

where D_t equals 1 if it is wartime and equals 0 otherwise. Noticing that $E(C_t) = \beta_1 + \beta_2 E(Y_t)$ in peacetime and $(\beta_1 + \alpha) + \beta_2 E(Y_t)$ in wartime, we see that case II corresponds to the assumption that the intercept of the consumption function changes during wartime but the slope parameter stays the same. A test of whether such a change is statistically significant is provided by a test of the null hypothesis that $\alpha = 0$.

Case III

$$C_t = \beta_1 + \beta_2 Y_t + \gamma(D_t Y_t) + \varepsilon_t \qquad (3.37)$$

Noticing that $E(C_t) = \beta_1 + \beta_2 E(Y_t)$ in peacetime and $E(C_t) = \beta_1 + (\beta_2 + \gamma)E(Y_t)$ in wartime, we see that case III corresponds to the assumption that the intercept has remained constant but the slope parameter has changed. In other words, the model in case III assumes that the war brought about a change in the aggregate marginal propensity to consume. A test of whether this change is significant is provided by a test of the null hypothesis that the coefficient of $D_t Y_t$ is 0.

Case IV

$$C_t = \beta_1 + \beta_2 Y_t + \alpha D_t + \gamma(D_t Y_t) + \varepsilon_t \qquad (3.38)$$

This case corresponds to the situation in which both the slope and the intercept are allowed to change. The reader should note, however, that the model has still been expressed as a single equation in which the variance of the error term is assumed to be the same in war and peace years. Least-squares estimation yields *unique* estimates of the standard error of the regression and of the distributions of the estimated regression parameters.

Case V

$$C_t = \beta_1^* + \beta_2^* Y_t + \varepsilon_t^* \qquad \text{war years} \qquad (3.39)$$

$$C_t = \beta_1' + \beta_2' Y_t + \varepsilon_t' \qquad \text{peace years} \qquad (3.40)$$

In this case we have allowed the error variance to vary from war years to peace years. Case V corresponds, of course, to the running of two separate regressions, with two separate estimates of the standard errors of the regression being obtained. The reader can check to see that the estimated regression parameters in case IV and case V are essentially equivalent ($\hat{\beta}'_1 = \hat{\beta}_1$, $\hat{\beta}^*_1 = \hat{\beta}_1 + \hat{\alpha}$, $\hat{\beta}'_2 = \hat{\beta}_2$, $\hat{\beta}^*_2 = \hat{\beta}_2 + \hat{\gamma}$). The choice of model IV or model V depends upon whether the researcher is willing to believe (before examining the data) that the error variance is constant over all model years.[23]

Example 3.6   Labor Force Participation

In a study of labor force participation and unemployment, W. G. Bowen and T. A. Finegan were concerned with the determinants of intercity differences in labor force participation rates for males twenty-five to fifty-four years of age, during the census week of 1950.[24] The variables utilized were:

L = labor force participation rate for males 25–54, percentage
U = unemployment rate, percentage
E = earnings, hundreds of dollars per year
OI = other income, hundreds of dollars per year
S = schooling completed, years
C = color, percentage nonwhite
D = dummy variable, with a 1 assigned to each city in the South and a 0 to all other cities

The regression results for a sample of 78 cities were as follows:

$$L = 94.2 - .24U - .20E - .69(\text{OI}) - .06S + .002C - .80D$$

The dummy variable was significant at the 10 percent level. One can conclude that in 1950 regional differences in customs or mixes of industry did have an effect on labor force participation for prime-age males, with participation being .80 percent lower in the South than in the rest of the nation. The effect measured by the dummy variable appeared *not* to be stable over time because a similar regression model estimated for 1960 yielded an insignificant dummy variable coefficient.

---

[23] It is, of course, possible to test the null hypothesis that the error variance is constant between war and peace years, or more generally to decide when it is reasonable to assume that regression models actually switch from one time period to another. See, for example, R. E. Quandt, "The Estimation of the Parameters of a Linear Regression Obeying Two Separate Regimes," *Journal of the American Statistical Association*, vol. 53, pp. 873–880, 1958, and "Test of the Hypothesis That a Linear Regression System Obeys Two Separate Regimes," *Journal of the American Statistical Association*, vol. 55, pp. 324–330, 1960.

[24] W. G. Bowen and T. A. Finegan, "Labor Force Participation and Unemployment," in Arthur M. Ross (ed.), *Employment Policy and Labor Markets* (Berkeley: University of California Press, 1965), table 4-2.

Example 3.7 Certificates of Deposit

In this example an equation is estimated that predicts the total volume of negotiable certificates of deposit (CD) held by the public on a monthly basis.[25] Our equation is a demand relationship, and one would therefore expect that the dependent variable should depend on total personal wealth and on the interest rate that individuals would receive when part of that wealth is invested in a certificate of deposit. The primary interest rate on certificates of deposit (RCDP) was therefore chosen as an explanatory variable. However, certificates of deposit must compete with other interest-bearing assets, such as Treasury bills and corporate bonds. Thus, the interest rates on Treasury bills (RTB) and corporate bonds (RBaa) are also explanatory variables; when these variables increase, the total demand for certificates of deposit should decrease. These interest rate variables are multiplied by personal income (PI), this last variable serving as a proxy for personal wealth. The difference between the corporate bond interest rate and the interest rate on prime commercial paper (RCP) is also an explanatory variable, and represents the difference between long-term and short-term interest rates—when this difference increases, a long-term investment (such as a certificate of deposit) becomes more attractive. Finally, the lagged dependent variable is also introduced.

It has been shown that the volume of certificates of deposit, as well as many other financial variables, displays a definite seasonal behavior; i.e., there are certain periods during the year when the volume increases and other periods when it decreases, regardless of the behavior of the explanatory variables. For this reason a set of seasonal dummy variables is introduced to explain as much of this seasonal behavior as possible. The seasonal variables (denoted $S3$) take the form of monthly dummy variables multiplied by personal income. Thus, the first seasonal dummy takes on the value 1 when the observation occurs in the month of January and 0 otherwise. The first seasonal variable takes on the value of personal income in the month of January and 0 otherwise. There are a total of 12 seasonal variables in the model, but the constant term has been dropped to eliminate the collinearity problem. The equation was estimated using ordinary least squares and the results are shown below, with t statistics in parentheses.

$$CD_t = .72947CD_{t-1} - .00150RTB_t \cdot PI_t + .00225RCDP_t \cdot PI_t$$
$$(14.61) \phantom{CD_{t-1}} (-2.667) (6.903)$$

$$- .00128RBaa_t \cdot PI_t + .00154(RBaa_t - RCP_t) \cdot PI_t + S3_t$$
$$(-2.453) (2.929)$$

$$R^2 = .9995$$

$$S3_t = \text{seasonal coefficient}_t \cdot PI_t$$

---

[25] This example has been adapted from R. Pindyck and S. Roberts, "Optimal Policies for Monetary Control," *Annals of Economic and Social Measurement*, January 1974.

Seasonal coefficients:

Jan. .01057 (2.886)	May .00952 (2.656)	Sept. .01113 (2.986)
Feb. .00977 (2.768)	June .00971 (2.659)	Oct. .01179 (3.167)
Mar. .00974 (2.279)	July .00163 (3.137)	Nov. .01117 (3.016)
Apr. .00916 (2.607)	Aug. .01208 (3.265)	Dec. .01147 (3.086)

The seasonal coefficients are all significant at the 5 percent level, suggesting that seasonal variations in the volume of certificates of deposit are quite important. The results suggest that August to January are the peak months for public holdings of CDs, while from February to July holdings are relatively lower.

3.9 THE MULTIPLE REGRESSION MODEL WITH STOCHASTIC EXPLANATORY VARIABLES

To this point we have assumed that the independent variables in the multiple regression model were fixed in repeated samples, i.e., nonstochastic. In practice, such an assumption is likely to be unreasonable, given that we infrequently have the opportunity to repeat an experiment a second time. The analysis of economic and social science behavior usually consists of looking at past occurrences, occurrences which are not likely to be repeated. Fortunately for most of the work completed to this point, it is possible to assume that the X's are drawn at random from a probability distribution and still maintain most of the previous results. In this spirit we will make the following assumptions:

i The distribution of each of the explanatory variables is independent of the true regression parameters.
ii Each of the explanatory variables is distributed independently of the true errors in the model.

In interpreting the multiple regression problem, we might think of the set of N observations on Y being drawn simultaneously with the set of N observations on each of the independent variables. In theory many such N observation drawings of Y's and X's could be made. But, it is useful to focus on the estimated parameters associated with a *given* drawing of the X's. Then the previous results for the multiple regression model apply, and we may think of the estimated regression parameters as being estimated *conditional* on the given values of the X's. From this perspective, least-squares estimators will remain unbiased in the sample. In addition, least-squares estimators will be consistent as well as asymptotically efficient estimators of the true regression parameters. Finally, it is possible to prove that the least-squares estimators are the maximum-likelihood estimators of the true regression parameters.

Exercises

3.1 Consider the following two models:

(1) $Y_i = \beta_1 + \beta_2 X_{2i} + \beta_3 X_{3i} + \varepsilon_i$

(2) $(Y_i - X_{2i}) = \beta'_1 + \beta'_2 X_{2i} + \beta'_3 X_{3i} + \varepsilon'_i$

    a. Prove that $\hat{\beta}'_2 = \hat{\beta}_2 - 1 \qquad \hat{\beta}'_1 = \hat{\beta}_1 \qquad \hat{\beta}'_3 = \hat{\beta}_3$
    b. Prove that the least-squares residuals are identical, that is, $\hat{\varepsilon}_i = \hat{\varepsilon}'_i$ for $i = 1, 2, \ldots, N$
    c. Under what conditions will the R^2 associated with model (2) be less than the R^2 associated with model (1)?

3.2 By carefully following the steps in the derivation of the partial correlation coefficients (for the three-variable model) in the text, prove that:

(1)
$$r_{YX_2 \cdot X_3} = \frac{r_{YX_2} - r_{YX_3} r_{X_2 X_3}}{\sqrt{1 - r^2_{X_2 X_3}}\sqrt{1 - r^2_{YX_3}}}$$

(2)
$$r_{YX_2 \cdot X_3} = \sqrt{\frac{R^2 - r^2_{YX_3}}{1 - r^2_{YX_3}}}$$

3.3 Given the model

$$\log Y = \beta_1 + \beta_2 \log X_2 + \beta_3 \log X_3 + \varepsilon$$

prove that the estimated regression coefficients are the elasticities associated with Y and each of the X's and that these elasticities are constant over the regression line.

3.4 "R^2 and $\bar{R}^2$ are two different concepts because the first describes the proportion of explained variation while the second describes the proportion of explained variance." Do you agree or disagree with this statement? Explain.

3.5 Consider the following two experimental procedures:

    a. Run the regression $Y_i = \beta_1 + \beta_2 X_{2i} + \beta_3 X_{3i} + \varepsilon_i$
    b. Run the regression $X_{2i} = \alpha_1 + \alpha_2 X_{3i} + \varepsilon'_i$, calculate the regression residuals $\hat{\varepsilon}'_i$, and finally run the following regression:

$$Y_i = \beta'_1 + \beta'_2 \hat{\varepsilon}_i + \beta'_3 X_{3i} + \varepsilon^*_i$$

Can you prove that $\hat{\beta}'_2 = \hat{\beta}_2$? Can you explain intuitively why this result is true?

3.6 A somewhat naive researcher attempts to estimate an aggregate consumption function for the United States economy by regressing a consumption variable C on disposable income Y and savings S. The model is

$$C = \beta_1 + \beta_2 Y + \beta_3 S + \varepsilon$$

How good a fit is this researcher likely to get when this equation is run? Can you generalize your conclusion? (*Hint:* Notice that $C = Y - S$ identically for all observations.)

3.7 Assume that the sample variances (and standard deviations) of all the variables in a multiple regression model are identically the same. In this case what is the relationship between the estimated beta coefficients and the standard regression parameters?

3.8 "Estimated regression parameters, elasticities, beta coefficients, and partial correlation coefficients will always have the same sign." True or false? Explain.

3.9 Explain the differences between the concepts of simple correlation, partial correlation, and multiple correlation. Why is each useful?

3.10 Show that in the two-variable model the beta coefficient of the independent variable is equal to the simple correlation between the two variables.

APPENDIX 3 / THE MULTIPLE REGRESSION MODEL IN MATRIX FORM

Representation of the Multiple Regression Model

The purpose of this appendix, as well as the appendixes to other chapters, is to present generalizations of important textual items. It would be difficult to accomplish this in a compact form without using matrix algebra. Matrix algebra provides a clear and concise means of describing the techniques of econometrics. We presume that the reader of these appendixes has a prior knowledge of matrix algebra and make no attempt to describe or prove its basic theorems. These materials are clearly presented in other textbooks, which should provide an ample review for the interested reader.[26]

We begin by representing the general linear model in matrix form. Recall from the text that the regression model includes $k + 1$ variables—a dependent variable and k independent variables (including the constant term). Since there are N observations, we may summarize the regression model by writing a series of N equations, as follows:

$$Y_1 = \beta_1 + \beta_2 X_{21} + \beta_3 X_{31} + \cdots + \beta_k X_{k1} + \varepsilon_1$$

$$Y_2 = \beta_1 + \beta_2 X_{22} + \beta_3 X_{32} + \cdots + \beta_k X_{k2} + \varepsilon_2$$

$$\cdots \cdots \cdots \cdots \cdots \cdots \cdots \cdots \cdots \cdots \cdots \cdots \cdots \cdots \cdots \cdots \cdots \cdots \cdots$$

$$Y_N = \beta_1 + \beta_2 X_{2N} + \beta_3 X_{3N} + \cdots + \beta_k X_{kN} + \varepsilon_N$$

$$(A3.1)$$

---

[26] See, for example, J. Johnson, *Econometric Methods*, 2d ed. (New York: McGraw-Hill, 1972), chap. 4; and A. Goldberger, *Econometric Theory* (New York: Wiley, 1964), chap. 2.

The corresponding matrix formulation of the model is:

$$\mathbf{Y} = \mathbf{X}\boldsymbol{\beta} + \boldsymbol{\varepsilon} \tag{A3.2}$$

where

$$\mathbf{Y} = \begin{bmatrix} Y_1 \\ Y_2 \\ \vdots \\ Y_N \end{bmatrix} \quad \mathbf{X} = \begin{bmatrix} 1 & X_{21} & \cdots & X_{k1} \\ 1 & X_{22} & \cdots & X_{k2} \\ \cdots\cdots\cdots\cdots\cdots\cdots \\ 1 & X_{2N} & \cdots & X_{kN} \end{bmatrix}$$

$$\boldsymbol{\beta} = \begin{bmatrix} \beta_1 \\ \beta_2 \\ \vdots \\ \beta_k \end{bmatrix} \quad \boldsymbol{\varepsilon} = \begin{bmatrix} \varepsilon_1 \\ \varepsilon_2 \\ \vdots \\ \varepsilon_N \end{bmatrix} \tag{A3.3}$$

$\mathbf{Y} =$ an $N \times 1$ column vector of dependent variable observations
$\mathbf{X} =$ an $N \times k$ matrix of independent variable observations
$\boldsymbol{\beta} =$ a $k \times 1$ column vector of unknown parameters
$\boldsymbol{\varepsilon} =$ an $N \times 1$ column vector of error observations

In our representation of the matrix $\mathbf{X}$, each component X_{ji} has two subscripts, the first signifying the appropriate column (variable), and the second the appropriate row (observation). Each column of $\mathbf{X}$ represents a vector of N observations on a given variable, with all observations associated with the intercept equal to 1.

The assumptions of the classical linear regression model may be represented as follows:

i The model specification is given by Eq. (A3.1).
ii The elements of $\mathbf{X}$ are fixed and have finite variance. In addition, $\mathbf{X}$ has rank k which is less than the number of observations N.
iii $\boldsymbol{\varepsilon}$ is normally distributed with $E(\boldsymbol{\varepsilon}) = \mathbf{0}$ and $E(\boldsymbol{\varepsilon}\boldsymbol{\varepsilon}') = \sigma^2\mathbf{I}$, where $\mathbf{I}$ is an $N \times N$ identity matrix.

The assumption that $\mathbf{X}$ has rank k guarantees that perfect collinearity will not be present. With perfect collinearity, one of the columns of $\mathbf{X}$ would be a linear combination of the remaining columns and the rank of $\mathbf{X}$ would be less than k. The error assumptions are the strongest possible, since they guarantee the statistical as well as arithmetic properties of the ordinary least-squares estimation process. In addition to normality we assume that each error term has mean 0, all variances are constant, and all covariances are 0. The *variance-covariance matrix* $\sigma^2 \mathbf{I}$ appears as follows:

$$E(\boldsymbol{\varepsilon}\boldsymbol{\varepsilon}') = E\left\{\begin{bmatrix} \varepsilon_1 \\ \varepsilon_2 \\ \vdots \\ \varepsilon_N \end{bmatrix}\begin{bmatrix} \varepsilon_1 & \varepsilon_2 & \cdots & \varepsilon_N \end{bmatrix}\right\} = \begin{bmatrix} E(\varepsilon_1{}^2) & E(\varepsilon_1\varepsilon_2) & \cdots & E(\varepsilon_1\varepsilon_N) \\ E(\varepsilon_2\varepsilon_1) & E(\varepsilon_2{}^2) & \cdots & E(\varepsilon_2\varepsilon_N) \\ \cdots\cdots\cdots\cdots\cdots\cdots\cdots\cdots\cdots \\ E(\varepsilon_N\varepsilon_1) & E(\varepsilon_N\varepsilon_2) & \cdots & E(\varepsilon_N{}^2) \end{bmatrix}$$

$$= \begin{bmatrix} \text{Var}(\varepsilon_1) & \text{Cov}(\varepsilon_1,\varepsilon_2) & \cdots & \text{Cov}(\varepsilon_1,\varepsilon_N) \\ \text{Cov}(\varepsilon_1,\varepsilon_2) & \text{Var}(\varepsilon_2) & \cdots & \text{Cov}(\varepsilon_2,\varepsilon_N) \\ \cdots\cdots\cdots\cdots\cdots\cdots\cdots\cdots\cdots\cdots \\ \text{Cov}(\varepsilon_1,\varepsilon_N) & \text{Cov}(\varepsilon_2,\varepsilon_N) & \cdots & \text{Var}(\varepsilon_N) \end{bmatrix} \qquad (A3.4)$$

where $\boldsymbol{\varepsilon}'$ is the $1 \times N$ vector transpose of $\boldsymbol{\varepsilon}$. If we had chosen to represent assumption iii in terms of the distribution of $\mathbf{Y}$, we would write

iii′ $\mathbf{Y}$ is normally distributed, $E(\mathbf{Y}) = \mathbf{X}\boldsymbol{\beta}$, and $E\{[\mathbf{Y} - E(\mathbf{Y})][\mathbf{Y} - E(\mathbf{Y})]'\} = \sigma^2 \mathbf{I}$.

Least-Squares Estimation

Our objective is to find a vector of parameters $\hat{\boldsymbol{\beta}}$ which minimize the sum of the squared residuals

$$\text{ESS} = \sum_{i=1}^{N} \hat{\varepsilon}_i{}^2 = \hat{\boldsymbol{\varepsilon}}'\hat{\boldsymbol{\varepsilon}} \qquad (A3.5)$$

where $\hat{\boldsymbol{\varepsilon}} = \mathbf{Y} - \hat{\mathbf{Y}}$ $\qquad (A3.6)$

$$\hat{\mathbf{Y}} = \mathbf{X}\hat{\boldsymbol{\beta}} \qquad (A3.7)$$

$\hat{\boldsymbol{\varepsilon}}$ represents the $N \times 1$ vector of regression residuals, while $\hat{\mathbf{Y}}$ represents the $N \times 1$ vector of fitted values for $\mathbf{Y}$. Substituting (A3.6) and (A3.7) into (A3.5), we get

$$\hat{\boldsymbol{\varepsilon}}'\hat{\boldsymbol{\varepsilon}} = (\mathbf{Y} - \mathbf{X}\hat{\boldsymbol{\beta}})'(\mathbf{Y} - \mathbf{X}\hat{\boldsymbol{\beta}})$$

$$= \mathbf{Y}'\mathbf{Y} - \hat{\boldsymbol{\beta}}'\mathbf{X}'\mathbf{Y} - \mathbf{Y}'\mathbf{X}\hat{\boldsymbol{\beta}} + \hat{\boldsymbol{\beta}}'\mathbf{X}'\mathbf{X}\hat{\boldsymbol{\beta}}$$

$$= \mathbf{Y}'\mathbf{Y} - 2\hat{\boldsymbol{\beta}}\mathbf{X}'\mathbf{Y} + \hat{\boldsymbol{\beta}}'\mathbf{X}'\mathbf{X}\hat{\boldsymbol{\beta}}$$

The last step follows because $\hat{\beta}'X'Y$ and $Y'X\hat{\beta}$ are both scalars and are thus equal to their transpose. To determine the least-squares estimators, we minimize by differentiating with respect to $\hat{\beta}$, equating to 0, and solving:

$$\frac{\partial ESS}{\partial \beta} = -2X'Y + 2X'X\hat{\beta} = 0$$

$$\hat{\beta} = (X'X)^{-1}(X'Y) \tag{A3.8}$$

The matrix $X'X$, called the *cross-product matrix*, is guaranteed to have an inverse because our assumption that X has rank k leads directly to the nonsingularity of $X'X$.[27] The reader should check that the matrix generalization of the least-squares estimation process reduces to the results derived in the text for both the two-variable and the three-variable regression models.

One interesting property of the least-squares residuals will be useful in some of the derivations which follow:

$$X'\hat{\varepsilon} = X'(Y - X\hat{\beta}) = X'Y - X'X\beta = 0 \tag{A3.9}$$

This result proves that the sum of the cross-products of the independent variables and the residuals is 0. This is the sample analog of the assumption (since the X's are fixed) that $E(X'\varepsilon) = 0$.

Now consider the properties of the least-squares estimator $\hat{\beta}$. First, we may prove that $\hat{\beta}$ is an unbiased estimator of β:

$$\hat{\beta} = (X'X)^{-1}X'Y = (X'X)^{-1}X'(X\beta + \varepsilon)$$

$$= (X'X)^{-1}(X'X)\beta + (X'X)^{-1}X'\varepsilon$$

$$= \beta + (X'X)^{-1}X'\varepsilon = \beta + A\varepsilon \quad \text{where } A = (X'X)^{-1}X' \tag{A3.10}$$

$$E(\hat{\beta}) = \beta + E(A\varepsilon)$$

$$= \beta + AE(\varepsilon) = \beta$$

since A is fixed in repeated samples.

Looking at Eq. (A3.8), we notice that $A\varepsilon$ represents the regression of ε, the

---

[27] The second-order conditions for the minimization of ESS follow from the fact that $X'X$ is a positive definite matrix.

unknown error term on **X**. As long as the effects of missing variables are randomly distributed, are independent of **X**, and have 0 mean, then the least-squares parameter estimates will be unbiased.

The least-squares estimator will be normally distributed since $\hat{\beta}$ is a linear function of **Y** and **Y** is normally distributed. The properties of the variances of the individual $\hat{\beta}_i$'s and their covariances are determined as follows:

$$\mathbf{V} = E[(\hat{\beta} - \beta)(\hat{\beta} - \beta)']$$

$$= \begin{bmatrix} E(\hat{\beta}_1 - \beta_1)^2 & \cdots & E[(\hat{\beta}_1 - \beta_1)(\hat{\beta}_k - \beta_k)] \\ \cdots\cdots\cdots\cdots\cdots\cdots\cdots\cdots\cdots\cdots\cdots\cdots\cdots \\ E[(\hat{\beta}_k - \beta_k)(\hat{\beta}_1 - \beta_1)] & \cdots & E(\hat{\beta}_k - \beta_k)^2 \end{bmatrix} \quad \text{(A3.11)}$$

$$= \begin{bmatrix} \text{Var}\,(\hat{\beta}_1) & \cdots & \text{Cov}\,(\hat{\beta}_1, \hat{\beta}_k) \\ \cdots\cdots\cdots\cdots\cdots\cdots\cdots\cdots \\ \text{Cov}\,(\hat{\beta}_1, \hat{\beta}_k) & \cdots & \text{Var}\,(\hat{\beta}_k) \end{bmatrix}$$

The diagonal elements of **V** represent the variances of the estimated parameters, while the off-diagonal terms represent the covariances. For purposes of notational simplicity, we shall sometimes write $\mathbf{V} = \text{Var}\,(\hat{\beta})$. Then,

$$\text{Var}\,(\hat{\beta}) = E[(\hat{\beta} - \beta)(\hat{\beta} - \beta)'] = E[(\mathbf{A}\varepsilon)(\mathbf{A}\varepsilon)'] = E[\mathbf{A}\varepsilon\varepsilon'\mathbf{A}']$$

$$= \mathbf{A}E(\varepsilon\varepsilon')\mathbf{A}' = \mathbf{A}(\sigma^2\mathbf{I})\mathbf{A}' = \sigma^2\mathbf{A}\mathbf{A}'$$

since **A** and **A'** are matrices of fixed numbers. But,

$$\mathbf{A}\mathbf{A}' = [(\mathbf{X}'\mathbf{X})^{-1}\mathbf{X}'][(\mathbf{X}'\mathbf{X})^{-1}\mathbf{X}']' = [(\mathbf{X}'\mathbf{X})^{-1}\mathbf{X}'][\mathbf{X}(\mathbf{X}'\mathbf{X})^{-1}]$$

$$= (\mathbf{X}'\mathbf{X})^{-1}(\mathbf{X}'\mathbf{X})(\mathbf{X}'\mathbf{X})^{-1} = (\mathbf{X}'\mathbf{X})^{-1}$$

Therefore,

$$E[(\hat{\beta} - \beta)(\hat{\beta} - \beta)'] = \sigma^2(\mathbf{X}'\mathbf{X})^{-1} \quad \text{(A3.12)}$$

We have already proved that the least-squares estimator is linear and unbiased. In fact, $\hat{\beta}$ is the best linear unbiased estimator of β, in the sense that it has the minimum variance of all unbiased estimators. To complete the proof of the *Gauss-Markov theorem*, we need to show that any other linear estimator **b** has greater variance than $\hat{\beta}$. Recall that $\hat{\beta} = \mathbf{A}\mathbf{Y}$. Without loss of generality, we may write

$$\mathbf{b} = (\mathbf{A} + \mathbf{C})\mathbf{Y}$$

$$= (\mathbf{A} + \mathbf{C})\mathbf{X}\beta + (\mathbf{A} + \mathbf{C})\varepsilon$$

If **b** is unbiased, then

$$E(\mathbf{b}) = (\mathbf{X'X})^{-1}\mathbf{X'X\beta} + \mathbf{CX\beta} = \mathbf{\beta(I + CX)} = \mathbf{\beta} \tag{A3.13}$$

A necessary and sufficient condition for this to hold is for

$$\mathbf{CX = 0}$$

Now examine the matrix Var (**b**). Since $\mathbf{b - \beta} = \mathbf{(A + C)\varepsilon}$,

$$\text{Var } (\mathbf{b}) = E[(\mathbf{b - \beta})(\mathbf{b - \beta})'] = E\{[(\mathbf{A + C})\varepsilon][(\mathbf{A + C})\varepsilon]'\}$$

$$= E[(\mathbf{A + C})\varepsilon\varepsilon'(\mathbf{A + C})']$$

$$= E[\varepsilon\varepsilon'][(\mathbf{A + C})(\mathbf{A + C})']$$

But

$$(\mathbf{A + C})(\mathbf{A + C})' = \mathbf{AA' + CA' + AC' + CC'}$$

$$= (\mathbf{X'X})^{-1}\mathbf{X'X}(\mathbf{X'X})^{-1} + \mathbf{CX}(\mathbf{X'X})^{-1} + (\mathbf{X'X})^{-1}\mathbf{X'C'} + \mathbf{CC'}$$

$$= (\mathbf{X'X})^{-1} + \mathbf{CC'} \qquad \text{since } \mathbf{CX = X'C' = 0}$$

Therefore,

$$\text{Var } (\mathbf{b}) = \sigma^2[(\mathbf{X'X})^{-1} + \mathbf{CC'}] = \text{Var } (\hat{\mathbf{\beta}}) + \sigma^2\mathbf{CC'} \tag{A3.14}$$

We can observe that $\mathbf{CC'}$ is a positive semidefinite matrix. The only case in which the quadratic form associated with this matrix will be 0 is when $\mathbf{C = 0}$ (all elements are 0). When $\mathbf{C = 0}$, our alternative estimator becomes the ordinary least-square estimator $\hat{\mathbf{\beta}}$, and our theorem is proved.

Estimating σ^2, t Tests

In order to calculate the variance-covariance matrix of the estimated parameters, we need to determine an estimate for the scalar σ^2. A natural choice for such an estimator is

$$s^2 = \frac{\hat{\varepsilon}'\hat{\varepsilon}}{N - k} \tag{A3.15}$$

It is tedious, but not difficult, to prove that s^2 provides an unbiased estimator of σ^2. It follows that $s^2(\mathbf{X'X})^{-1}$ yields an unbiased estimator of Var $(\hat{\mathbf{\beta}})$. While normal distribution hypothesis tests are possible when σ^2 is known, we are forced to rely on the use of the t test when s^2 is used to approximate σ^2.

To do so, we use the following statistical results:

1 $\hat{\varepsilon}'\hat{\varepsilon}/\sigma^2$ is distributed as chi-square with $N - k$ degrees of freedom.
2 $(N - k)s^2/\sigma^2$ is distributed as chi-square with $N - k$ degrees of freedom.
3 $(\hat{\beta}_i - \beta_i)$, for $i = 1, 2, \ldots, k$, is normally distributed with mean 0 and variance $\sigma^2 V_i$, where V_i is the ith diagonal element of $(\mathbf{X}'\mathbf{X})^{-1}$.
4 $(N - k)s^2/\sigma^2$ and $\hat{\beta}_i - \beta_i$ are independently distributed.

It follows that

$$t_{N-k} = \frac{\hat{\beta}_i - \beta_i}{s\sqrt{V_i}} \tag{A3.16}$$

is t distributed with $N - k$ degrees of freedom. This allows us to construct confidence intervals for individual regression parameters in a manner analogous to the procedure described in Chapter 2. To test a hypothesis about a particular value of β_i, we substitute that value into Eq. (A3.16). If the t value is great enough in absolute value, we reject the null hypothesis at the appropriately chosen level of confidence. A 95 percent confidence interval for the individual parameter β_i is given by

$$\hat{\beta}_i \pm t_c(s\sqrt{V_i}) \tag{A3.17}$$

where t_c is the critical value of the t distribution associated with a 5 percent level of significance.

R^2, F Test

As in the text, we may break down the total variation of Y into two portions, one representing the explained variation and the second the unexplained. First assume that the Y variable has a 0 mean. In matrix notation, the derivation follows from the fact that we may write the vector $\mathbf{Y}$ as the sum of its predicted values $\hat{\mathbf{Y}} = \mathbf{X}\hat{\boldsymbol{\beta}}$ and the residual vector $\hat{\varepsilon}$:

$$\mathbf{Y} = \mathbf{X}\hat{\boldsymbol{\beta}} + \hat{\varepsilon}$$

Then, $\quad \mathbf{Y}'\mathbf{Y} = (\mathbf{X}\hat{\boldsymbol{\beta}} + \hat{\varepsilon})'(\mathbf{X}\hat{\boldsymbol{\beta}} + \hat{\varepsilon}) = \hat{\boldsymbol{\beta}}\mathbf{X}'\mathbf{X}\hat{\boldsymbol{\beta}} + \hat{\varepsilon}'\mathbf{X}\hat{\boldsymbol{\beta}} + \hat{\boldsymbol{\beta}}'\mathbf{X}'\hat{\varepsilon} + \hat{\varepsilon}'\hat{\varepsilon}$

$$= \hat{\boldsymbol{\beta}}'\mathbf{X}'\mathbf{X}\hat{\boldsymbol{\beta}} + \hat{\varepsilon}'\hat{\varepsilon} \qquad \text{since } \mathbf{X}'\hat{\varepsilon} = \mathbf{0} \text{ and } \hat{\varepsilon}'\mathbf{X} = \mathbf{0} \tag{A3.18}$$

or $\quad$ TSS = RSS + ESS

where TSS = total sum of squares
$\qquad$ RSS = regression (explained) sum of squares
$\qquad$ ESS = residual (unexplained) sum of squares

Then
$$R^2 = 1 - \frac{\text{ESS}}{\text{TSS}} = 1 - \frac{\hat{\epsilon}'\hat{\epsilon}}{\mathbf{Y'Y}} = \frac{\hat{\boldsymbol{\beta}}'\mathbf{X'X}\hat{\boldsymbol{\beta}}}{\mathbf{Y'Y}} \qquad (A3.19)$$

When the dependent variable does not have 0 mean, we must modify our definition of R^2 somewhat. Then $y_i = Y_i - \left(\sum_{i=1}^{N} Y_i\right)\Big/N$, from which it follows that

$$\mathbf{y'y} = \mathbf{Y'Y} - \sum_{i=1}^{N} \left(\frac{Y_i}{N}\right)^2$$

and
$$R^2 = \frac{\text{RSS}}{\text{TSS}} = \frac{\hat{\boldsymbol{\beta}}'\mathbf{X'X}\hat{\boldsymbol{\beta}} - \sum (Y_i/N)^2}{\mathbf{y'y}} \qquad (A3.20)$$

In order to correct for the dependence of goodness of fit on degrees of freedom, we define $\bar{R}^2$, or corrected R^2, as follows:

$$\bar{R}^2 = 1 - \frac{\hat{\epsilon}'\hat{\epsilon}/(N-k)}{\mathbf{y'y}/(N-1)} = 1 - \left(\frac{\hat{\epsilon}'\hat{\epsilon}}{\mathbf{y'y}} \frac{N-1}{N-k}\right) \qquad (A3.21)$$

Now it is appropriate to consider statistical tests on sets of regression coefficients. The most frequently utilized test involves the test of the joint hypothesis that $\beta_2 = \beta_3 = \cdots = \beta_k = 0$. The appropriate F statistic (obeying the F distribution) is

$$F_{k-1, N-k} = \frac{R^2}{1 - R^2} \frac{N-k}{N-1}$$

Other tests involving combinations of the regression parameters are sometimes used. Again, assume that Y has a 0 mean. In this case, we may utilize the result that

$$F = \frac{(\hat{\boldsymbol{\beta}} - \boldsymbol{\beta})'\mathbf{X'X}(\hat{\boldsymbol{\beta}} - \boldsymbol{\beta})}{\hat{\epsilon}'\hat{\epsilon}} \frac{N-k}{N-1}$$

is F distributed with $k - 1$ and $N - k$ degrees of freedom. To test joint hypotheses involving the individual regression parameters, we simply substitute the appropriate test values for $\boldsymbol{\beta}$ and evaluate the F statistic. A sufficiently large value of F allows us to reject the null hypothesis.

4

SERIAL CORRELATION AND HETERO-SCEDASTICITY

Having completed a discussion of the classical normal linear regression model, it seems natural to review each of the model's assumptions in turn. Our goal is to determine those situations in which the assumptions are violated and to find estimation procedures which improve upon the ordinary least-squares procedure when such violations occur. The three sets of assumptions are listed below to refresh the memory of the reader:

i The model is specified as follows:

$$Y_i = \beta_1 + \beta_2 X_{2i} + \beta_3 X_{3i} \cdots + \beta_k X_{ki} + \varepsilon_i \quad (4.1)$$

ii The X's have finite mean and variance and are uncorrelated with the errors in the model. No linear relationship exists among two or more of the independent variables.
iii The errors are independently distributed from a normal population with 0 expected value and constant variance.

The assumption that the model is correctly specified as in Eq. (4.1) is an important one. In practice one usually does not have sufficient knowledge to specify accurately the relevant functional form as well as the variables which should appear in the model. We shall delay discussion of this assumption until Chapter 7, where specification error and model construction are explicitly discussed. The problem of collinearity has been detailed in the previous chapter and will not be pursued further here. The problem arising when the X's and the error term are correlated will be treated separately in the following chapter.

The third assumption consists of several important parts. The assumption of normality was discussed in Chapter 2. Even without the normality assumption, it is possible to prove that least-squares regression estimates of the true underlying parameters are unbiased as well as consistent. In fact, least-squares estimates remain best linear unbiased estimates. However, without the normality assumption one cannot use the standard formulas for the t and F distributions to perform statistical tests.[1] Fortunately, the central limit theorem (see Chapter 2) provides a rationale for using standard statistical tests as approximately correct for reasonably large sample sizes.

The assumption that the error term has a 0 expected value is usually not seriously considered by econometricians. The reason is that if the error has a nonzero expected value, the estimated regression slope parameters will remain unchanged, while the intercept will pick up the effect of the nonzero expected value. It will, of course, be impossible to differentiate between the true intercept and the nonzero expected value in the error term, but in most econometric applications the intercept term is not of central concern. The assumption of the independence of the errors will be considered in section 4.2, while section 4.1 will focus on the assumption that the errors have constant variance.

4.1 HETEROSCEDASTICITY

There are occasions in econometric modeling when the assumption of constant error variance, or *homoscedasticity*, will be unreasonable. For example, if one is examining a cross section of firms in one industry, there may be reason to believe that error terms associated with very large firms have larger variances than error terms associated with smaller firms; sales of larger firms might be more volatile than sales of smaller firms. Or consider a cross-section study of family income and expenditures.[2] It seems plausible to expect that low-income individuals would spend at a rather steady rate, while the spending patterns of high-income families would be relatively volatile. The regularity of low-income spending occurs because most expenditures are on the necessities of life, making large fluctuations a physical impossibility. This suggests that in a model where

---

[1] In addition, it is impossible to prove that ordinary least-squares estimates are maximum likelihood, since the maximum-likelihood approach depends critically upon the assumption of normality. However, it is possible to show that, even in small samples, t and F tests are likely to be approximately valid when the error distribution deviates from normality. For details, see, for example, H. Theil, *Principles of Econometrics* (New York: Wiley, 1971), chap. 8.

[2] This example is studied in detail in S. J. Prais and H. S. Houthakker, *The Analysis of Family Budgets* (Cambridge, England: The University Press, 1955).

expenditures are the dependent variable, error variances associated with high-income families would be greater than their low-income counterparts. *Heteroscedasticity*, or unequal variances, does not usually occur in time-series studies, because changes in the dependent variable and changes in one or more of the independent variables are likely to be of the same order of magnitude. For example, in the aggregate consumption function examples of the previous chapter, both consumption and disposable income grow at about the same rate over time.

For a model with heteroscedastic error disturbances we will assume that each error term ε_i is normally distributed with variance σ_i^2, where the variance $[\text{Var}\,(\varepsilon_i) = E(\varepsilon_i^2) = \sigma_i^2]$ is not constant over observations. When heteroscedasticity is present, ordinary least-squares estimation places more weight on the observations which have large error variances than those with small error variances. The implicit weighting of ordinary least squares occurs because the sum of squared residuals associated with large variance error terms is likely to be substantially greater than the sum of squared residuals associated with low variance errors. The regression line will be adjusted in such a way as to minimize the total sum of squared residuals, and this can best be accomplished by guaranteeing a very good fit in the large-variance portion of the data. Because of this implicit weighting, ordinary least-squares parameter estimates are unbiased and consistent, but they are not *efficient*; i.e., the variances of the estimated parameters are not the minimum variances. In addition, the *estimated* variances of the estimated parameters will be biased estimators of the true variance of the estimated parameters.

The fact that the parameter estimates are unbiased can be seen in the context of the two-variable model with variables measured as deviations about their means. Then

$$\hat{\beta} = \frac{\sum x_i y_i}{\sum x_i^2} = \beta + \frac{\sum x_i \varepsilon_i}{\sum x_i^2}$$

and
$$E(\hat{\beta}) = \beta + \frac{E(\sum x_i \varepsilon_i)}{\sum x_i^2} = \beta$$

Notice that variances of the error terms play no role in the proof that least-squares estimates are unbiased.

The difficulty with the variances of the estimated parameters can also be seen in the two-variable case. Then, from Chapter 2 we know that

$$\text{Var}\,(\hat{\beta}) = \frac{\sigma^2}{\sum x_i^2} \tag{4.2}$$

The variance of the error was taken out of the summation sign during the derivation because the variance was assumed constant. However, when heteroscedasticity is present, the variance is not constant and the derivation does not hold.

The result is that the standard formula (4.2) will lead to biased estimates of the variances of each of the estimated parameters. If these biased estimates are used, then statistical tests and confidence intervals will be incorrect.

The inefficiency of the least-squares estimator arises when the variances of the parameter estimates are *correctly* determined. In this case, the variances will be larger than the variances associated with an alternative linear unbiased estimator to be discussed in the following pages.[3]

4.1.1 Corrections for Heteroscedasticity

We discuss the appropriate estimation technique (which is unbiased, consistent, and efficient) in each of three conceptually separate cases. Each case relies to a different degree upon prior and sample information, but all involve relatively simple estimation procedures.

Case I Known Variances

We first assume that sufficient prior knowledge is available so that values for each of the error variances are known; that is, $\text{Var}(\varepsilon_i) = \sigma_i^2$ is known *a priori*. The case of known variances occurs occasionally in econometric work, but is especially important here in illustrating how to correct for heteroscedasticity. The appropriate technique is called *weighted least squares* and is a special case of a more general econometric technique, known as *generalized least squares*. A matrix derivation of the generalized least-squares procedure appears in Appendix 4.

The weighted least-squares estimation procedure, which can be derived from the maximum-likelihood function (see Appendix 2.2), is best illustrated in the two-variable model. The appropriate estimator is obtained by minimizing the expression

$$\sum \left(\frac{Y_i - \hat{\alpha} - \hat{\beta} X_i}{\sigma_i} \right)^2$$

$\hat{\alpha}$ and $\hat{\beta}$ are, of course, the desired parameter estimates. Writing the original variables in deviations form, the original objective is modified to that of minimizing the expression

$$\sum \left(\frac{y_i - \hat{\beta} x_i}{\sigma_i} \right)^2$$

---

[3] For a discussion of the consistency of estimators and further details about efficiency, see J. Kmenta, *Elements of Econometrics* (New York: Macmillan, 1971), section 8-1.

Solving for the least-squares parameter estimates (as in Chapter 1), we find that

$$\hat{\beta} = \frac{\sum x_i y_i/\sigma_i^2}{\sum x_i^2/\sigma_i^2} = \frac{\sum (x_i/\sigma_i)(y_i/\sigma_i)}{\sum (x_i/\sigma_i)^2} = \frac{\sum x_i^* y_i^*}{\sum (x_i^*)^2}$$

where $x_i^* = x_i/\sigma_i \qquad y_i^* = y_i/\sigma_i$

Thus, the desired estimation procedure is accomplished by weighting the original data and then performing ordinary least-squares estimation upon the transformed model.

To utilize weighted least squares, we redefine the variables in the original regression model of Eq. (4.1) as follows:

$$Y_i^* = \frac{Y_i}{\sigma_i} \qquad X_{ji}^* = \frac{X_{ji}}{\sigma_i} \qquad j = 1, 2, \ldots, k \qquad \varepsilon_i^* = \frac{\varepsilon_i}{\sigma_i}$$

In place of the original linear model (4.1) we use the transformed model[4]

$$Y_i^* = \beta_1 X_{1i}^* + \beta_2 X_{2i}^* + \cdots + \beta_k X_{ki}^* + \varepsilon_i^* \qquad (4.3)$$

or equivalently,

$$\frac{Y_i}{\sigma_i} = \beta_1 \frac{1}{\sigma_i} + \beta_2 \frac{X_{2i}}{\sigma_i} + \cdots + \beta_k \frac{X_{ki}}{\sigma_i} + \frac{\varepsilon_i}{\sigma_i}$$

Note that the transformed error term is homoscedastic (has constant variance):[4]

$$\text{Var}\,(\varepsilon_i^*) = \text{Var}\left(\frac{\varepsilon_i}{\sigma_i}\right) = \frac{1}{\sigma_i^2}\,\text{Var}\,(\varepsilon_i) = \frac{\sigma_i^2}{\sigma_i^2} = 1$$

Unfortunately the analysis just completed is limited in its applicability because the individual error variances are not always known. In fact the necessary information for the application of weighted least squares is the *relative* magnitude of the error variances. Such information may be available, particularly in cross-section studies for which substantial prior empirical evidence is available, but there are many situations in which the relative magnitude of the error variances is not known in advance. This suggests that one might consider special cases in which sufficient sample information is available to make reasonable guesses as to the true error variances.

---

[4] In addition, it is worth noting that the transformed equation has no intercept; i.e., the transformed intercept is not constant over time.

Case II Unknown Variances to Be Estimated from the Sample

In most econometric models only one value of the dependent variable is associated with each given set of independent variable observations. In this case, if no prior information is available, it will be impossible to obtain estimates of the variances of the individual error terms. However, if several observations are available (at least two) for each set of observations on the independent variables, then a solution to the problem does exist. Since such a situation occurs infrequently in actual economic and business applications, we shall not describe the proper estimation procedure in detail. Instead, we consider a simple example which makes use of the presence of multiple observations on each dependent variable (associated with *each* set of independent variables).[5]

Example 4.1   Housing Expenditures

In this example we consider a cross-sectional study of annual housing expenditures and annual income of a group of families. The sample consists of 20 observations, divided into four groups of five each. The sample within each group was obtained (hypothetically) by determining housing expenditures of five families with the identical income. The data are listed below:

Group	Housing expenditures, $000					Income, $000
1	1.8	2.0	2.0	2.0	2.1	5.0
2	3.0	3.2	3.5	3.5	3.6	10.0
3	4.2	4.2	4.5	4.8	5.0	15.0
4	4.8	5.0	5.7	6.0	6.2	20.0

The housing expenditure model is hypothesized to be as follows:

$$Y_i = \alpha + \beta X_i + \varepsilon_i$$

where Y_i = housing expenditures
$\quad X_i$ = income

---

[5] For details concerning this procedure see J. Kmenta, *op. cit.*, pp. 264–267.

An ordinary least-squares regression yields the following regression estimates (t statistics are in parentheses):

$$Y_i = 890.0 + .237X_i$$
$$\quad (4.4) \quad\ (15.9)$$

$$R^2 = .93 \qquad F = 252.7$$

A graphical examination of both the data and knowledge of prior expenditure studies suggested that heteroscedasticity is present in the model. (We shall discuss the correct statistical tests later in the chapter.) Given that data are available by *groups* of the dependent variable, correcting for heteroscedasticity using the principles of case II is possible. Independent estimates of the error variances associated *within each group* are approximated by calculating the sample variance of housing expenditures Y. These estimated variances are 9,800; 50,400; 102,400; and 302,400 for groups 1 through 4, respectively. When the corrected case II procedure is utilized, a slightly higher estimate of the income regression coefficient is obtained and all coefficients are significant at the 5 percent level.

Case III Error Variances Vary Directly with an Independent Variable

In cases where the error variance is not known and in which it is impossible to estimate error variances using grouped data, we must search for another source of information. One possibility is the existence of a relationship between the error variances and the values of one of the explanatory variables in the regression model. Specifically we assume that

$$\text{Var}\,(\varepsilon_i) = CX_i{}^2$$

where C = a nonzero constant
$\quad X_i$ = observation on one of the independent variables

This type of information about error variances is likely to occur quite frequently in both macroeconomic and microeconomic empirical studies. For example, in the housing expenditure example described previously it may be reasonable to assume that the error variance is proportional to the square of the income variable. To illustrate the use of weighted least squares in case III, assume (for example) that $\text{Var}\,(\varepsilon_i) = CX_{2i}^2$ in the general linear regression model

$$Y_i = \beta_1 + \beta_2 X_{2i} + \cdots + \beta_k X_{ki} + \varepsilon_i$$

Then, proceeding as in case I, we use weighted least squares as the correct estimation procedure. To do so, we redefine the variables in the above equation as follows (the value of the constant C does not affect the weighted least-squares procedure):

$$Y_i^* = \frac{Y_i}{X_{2i}} \qquad X_{ji}^* = \frac{X_{ji}}{X_{2i}} \qquad j = 1, 2, \dots, k \qquad \varepsilon_i^* = \frac{\varepsilon_i}{X_{2i}}$$

The transformed regression equation is

$$\frac{Y_i}{X_{2i}} = \beta_1 \frac{1}{X_{2i}} + \beta_2 + \beta_3 \frac{X_{3i}}{X_{2i}} + \cdots + \beta_k \frac{X_{ki}}{X_{2i}} + \frac{\varepsilon_i}{X_{2i}} \qquad (4.4)$$

We can see that the transformed error term is homoscedastic, since

$$\text{Var}\,(\varepsilon_i^*) = \text{Var}\left(\frac{\varepsilon_i}{X_{2i}}\right) = \frac{1}{X_{2i}^2}\,\text{Var}\,(\varepsilon_i) = C$$

In this particular case the original intercept term has become a variable term, while the slope parameter associated with the variable X_2 has become the new intercept term. Ordinary least-squares regression estimates of the parameters in Eq. (4.4) will yield the appropriate (efficient) parameter estimates, since the errors in the transformed equation are homoscedastic.[6]

Example 4.2   Housing Expenditures

The housing expenditure model described previously can be estimated with a correction for heteroscedasticity as suggested by case III. The transformed model is as follows:

$$\frac{Y_i}{X_i} = \beta^* + \alpha^* \frac{1}{X_i} + \varepsilon_i^*$$

and the following regression results are obtained:

$$\frac{Y_i}{X_i} = .249 + 752.9 \frac{1}{X_i}$$
$$\quad\;\; (21.3) \quad (7.7)$$

$$R^2 = .76 \qquad F = 58.7$$

Notice that the revised estimate of the regression coefficient associated with income is .249, an increase over the ordinary least-squares estimates. As expected,

---

[6] For additional details see J. Kmenta, *op. cit.*, pp. 257–264.

the correct use of t and F statistics still allows one to conclude that all regression coefficients are significant at the 5 percent level. Note that the R^2 measure associated with the weighted least-squares procedure is lower than the R^2 associated with the unweighted procedure. The decline in R^2 should not be taken as an indication that the heteroscedasticity correction was incorrect, since the weighted least-squares procedure involves the use of a transformed dependent variable.

4.1.2   Tests for Heteroscedasticity

Having discussed modifications of the least-squares procedure in three separate cases, it is natural to consider whether appropriate statistical procedures can be found to test for heteroscedasticity. In each case we wish to find a test of the null hypothesis of *homoscedasticity*, that is, $\sigma_1{}^2 = \sigma_2{}^2 = \sigma_3{}^2 = \cdots = \sigma_N{}^2$, where N is the number of observations. The specific alternative hypothesis against which the null hypothesis is to be tested depends upon the estimation procedure considered to yield the most desirable correction for heteroscedasticity. Recall that two of the three cases of heteroscedasticity involved corrective techniques which were dependent upon the sample data collected. We will therefore discuss two statistical tests, each using the data to test homoscedasticity against an alternative hypothesis of heteroscedasticity. The first test (case II) does not involve a specific assumption about the nature of the heteroscedasticity, but it does depend heavily upon the data being grouped in the appropriate manner. The second test procedure involves a very specific alternative hypothesis, which is consistent with the model described in case III.

Case II   Bartlett's Test[7]

Assume that there are N observations available for a regression model in which the data are associated with G groups, each of which has a distinct set of independent variable observations. Let N_1 be the number of observations associated with the first group, N_2 the number associated with the second group, and in general N_g the number of observations associated with the gth group, $g = 1, 2, \ldots, G$. The assumption of repeated experimental situations may be valid in practice, but even if not, it is possible to make the test an approximate one. The test procedure appears quite complex, but it is quite easy to apply in practice. It involves the calculation of a test statistic (with a known probability distribution) which is based on estimates of the error variances as provided by estimates of the variances of the dependent variable associated with each set of

---

[7] See A. M. Mood, *Introduction to the Theory of Statistics* (New York: McGraw-Hill, 1950), pp. 269–270; or Edward J. Kane, *Economic Statistics and Econometrics* (New York: Harper & Row, 1968), pp. 373–374.

independent variable observations. More specifically, the test procedure is as follows:

1 Estimate $s_g^2 = (1/N_g) \sum_{i=1}^{N_g} (Y_i - \overline{Y})^2$ for each group of observations, $g = 1, 2, \ldots, G$. s_g^2 can be shown[8] to provide a consistent estimate of σ_g^2.

2 Calculate the test statistic S:

$$S = - \frac{N \log \left[\sum_{g=1}^{G} (N_g/N)s_g^2 \right] - \sum_{g=1}^{G} N_g \log s_g^2}{1 + [1/3(G-1)]\left[\sum_{g=1}^{G} (1/N_g) - (1/N) \right]}$$

3 Under the assumption of homoscedasticity, it is possible to show that S will be distributed as a chi-square statistic with $G - 1$ degrees of freedom.[9] Using a chi-square statistical table, we reject the null hypothesis of equal variances in all groups if S is greater than the critical value of the chi-square distribution at the chosen level of significance.

4 If the null hypothesis is rejected, we apply the modification of least squares as described previously.

Example 4.3   Bartlett's Test

Bartlett's test may be applied to the housing expenditure example described in Examples 4.1 and 4.2. Recall that the model is $Y_i = \alpha + \beta X_i$, where Y represents housing expenditure and X represents income. The data are divided into four groups of five observations each. The estimated values of s_g^2 (9,800; 50,400; 102,400; and 302,400) are used in the calculation of the test statistic S, for which a value of 10.7 is obtained. Under the null hypothesis that σ_i^2 is constant, the test statistic S will obey the chi-square distribution with 3 degrees of freedom (the number of groups minus one). At the 5 percent level the critical value of the chi-square distribution is 7.81. Thus, we can reject the null hypothesis of homoscedasticity at the 5 percent level of significance.

---

[8] For further details see Mood, *op. cit.*; and J. B. Ramsey, "Tests for Specification Errors in Classical Linear Least-Squares Regression Analysis," *Journal of the Royal Statistical Society*, ser. B, vol. 31, pp. 350–371, 1969.

[9] See P. G. Hoel, *Introduction to Mathematical Statistics*, 2d ed. (New York: Wiley, 1955), p. 195.

Case III   Goldfeld-Quandt Test[10]

Assume that we are considering a two-variable model and wish to test the null hypothesis of homoscedasticity against the alternative hypothesis that $\sigma_i^2 = CX_i^2$ as described in case III of the previous section. The Goldfeld-Quandt test procedure is quite simple to apply. It involves the calculation of two least-squares regression lines, one using data thought to be associated with low variance errors and the other using data thought to be associated with high variance errors. If the residual variances associated with each regression line are approximately equal, then the homoscedasticity assumption cannot be rejected. However, if the residual variance increases substantially, then it is possible to reject the null hypothesis. The Goldfeld-Quandt test can be carried out in the following manner:

1 Order the data by the magnitude of the independent variable X, which is thought to be related to the error variance.
2 Omit the middle d observations. d might be chosen, for example, to be approximately one-fifth of the total sample size.
3 Fit two separate regressions, the first (indicated by subscript 1) for the portion of the data associated with low values of X, and the second (indicated by subscript 2) associated with high values of X. Each regression will involve $(N - d)/2$ pieces of data and $[(N - d)/2] - 2$ degrees of freedom. d must be small enough so that enough degrees of freedom are available to allow for the proper estimation of each of the separate regressions.
4 Calculate the residual sum of squares associated with each regression—ESS_1, associated with low X's; and ESS_2, associated with high X's. (ESS is described in Chapter 2.)
5 Assuming that the error process is normally distributed (and no serial correlation is present), the statistic ESS_2/ESS_1 will be distributed as an F statistic with $(N - d - 4)/2$ degrees of freedom in both the numerator and the denominator. We can reject the null hypothesis at a chosen level of significance if the calculated statistic is greater than the critical value of the F distribution as determined from an F table.

The Goldfeld-Quandt test can easily be applied to the general linear model by ordering the observations by the magnitude of one of the independent variables. The number of degrees of freedom in the F statistic will be $(N - d - 2k)/2$, where k is the number of independent variables (including a constant term) in the model. The Goldfeld-Quandt test works because it allows for the independent regression estimation of high and low observation data. However, there is an important cost involved. Because no restrictions are made on the regression parameters (as well as the error variances) in each of the two

---

[10] S. M. Goldfeld and R. E. Quandt, "Some Tests for Homoscedasticity," *Journal of the American Statistical Society*, vol. 60, pp. 539–547, 1965. An interesting alternative to the Goldfeld-Quandt test is proposed by H. Glejser, in "A New Test for Heteroscedasticity," *Journal of the American Statistical Association*, vol. 64, pp. 316–323, 1969.

regressions run, statistical power is lost. A more powerful test would take into account the information that the regression parameters are identical for both sets of data and that only the error variance has changed. Finally, the choice of the number of middle observations to eliminate from the test is somewhat arbitrary. If no middle observations are eliminated, the test is still correct, but experience shows that elimination of observations associated with errors of almost equal variance from the test procedure improves the power of the test.[11]

Example 4.4   Goldfeld-Quandt Test

The Goldfeld-Quandt test can be applied to the housing expenditure example used previously. The data are divided into two samples, the first including those with incomes of $5,000 and $10,000 and the second including higher-income families ($15,000 and $20,000). No middle observations are dropped from the sample because a natural break in the data is available without observations being omitted. The output associated with the two separate regression equations is as follows:

I. *Low-Income Families*

$$Y_i = 600.0 + .276X_i$$
$$(3.1) \quad\;\; (11.3)$$

$$R^2 = .94 \qquad ESS_1 = 3.0 \times 10^5$$

II *High-Income Families*

$$Y_i = 1{,}540.0 + .20X_i$$
$$(1.4) \qquad (3.1)$$

$$R^2 = .55 \qquad ESS_2 = 20.2 \times 10^5$$

The F statistic used to test the homoscedasticity assumption is $ESS_2/ESS_1 = 6.7$. Under the null hypothesis this will be distributed as F with 8 degrees of freedom in the numerator and the denominator. Examination of the table of the F distribution shows that the critical value of the F at the 5 percent level of significance is 6.03. We conclude that we can reject the null hypothesis in favor of the alternative hypothesis of heteroscedasticity.

---

[11] See S. M. Goldfeld and R. E. Quandt, *op. cit.*

4.1.3 Examining the Pattern of Regression Residuals

It is often useful to examine a plot of the residuals of a multiple regression estimation procedure in order to search for the presence of heteroscedasticity. One procedure directly available on some multiple regression computer packages is to plot the residuals against the values of the dependent variable or of one of the independent variables. Inspection of the data may then suggest whether the residual variance remains constant over all observations. However, the jump from examination of the residual plot to conclusions about the true error variance is a large one, because the residual variance is a function of the distribution of the independent variables in the model as well as the variance of the true error term. In the two-variable model, for example, we know that $y_i = \beta x_i + \varepsilon_i$, where the observations are measured as deviations about the means. The residuals are defined by the equation $\hat{\varepsilon}_i = y_i - \hat{\beta} x_i$, where $\hat{\beta}$ is the estimated slope parameter. Using these two equations, we may solve for the residual variance in terms of the error variance as follows:

$$\hat{\varepsilon}_i = y_i - \hat{\beta} x_i = (\beta x_i + \varepsilon_i) - \hat{\beta} x_i$$

$$= \varepsilon_i + (\beta - \hat{\beta}) x_i \qquad (4.5)$$

Squaring both sides of Eq. (4.5), summing over all observations, and dividing by $N - 1$, we find

$$\frac{\sum \hat{\varepsilon}_i^2}{N - 1} = \frac{\sum \varepsilon_i^2}{N - 1} + (\beta - \hat{\beta})^2 \frac{\sum x_i^2}{N - 1} + 2(\beta - \hat{\beta}) \frac{\sum x_i \varepsilon_i}{N - 1}$$

Given that the error is uncorrelated with the independent variable x, the last term is 0 and

$$\text{Var}(\hat{\varepsilon}_i) = \text{Var}(\varepsilon_i) + (\beta - \hat{\beta})^2 \text{Var}(x_i) \qquad (4.6)$$

Thus, the appearance of changing variance in the estimated residuals may be caused by either the variance associated with the true error term or the variance associated with the independent variable x. The previously described statistical tests are needed before any definitive conclusion can be reached about the presence of heteroscedasticity.

4.2 SERIAL CORRELATION

The assumption that errors corresponding to different observations are uncorrelated often breaks down in time-series studies, but can be a problem in some cross-section work as well. Recall that when the error terms from different (usually adjacent) time periods (or cross-section observations) are correlated, we say that the error term is autocorrelated or serially correlated. Serial correlation occurs in time-series studies when the errors associated with observations in a given time period carry over into future time periods. For example, if we are predicting the growth of stock dividends, an overestimate in one year is likely to lead to overestimates in succeeding years.

In this section we deal with the problem of *first-order serial correlation*, in which errors in one time period are correlated directly with errors in the ensuing time period.[12] While it is certainly possible that serial correlation can be negative as well as positive, we concern ourselves primarily with the case of positive serial correlation, in which errors in one time period are positively correlated with errors in the next time period. Positive serial correlation frequently occurs in time-series studies, either because of correlation in the measurement error component of the error term, or more likely because of the high degrees of correlation over time present in the cumulative effects of the omitted variables in the regression model.

As a general rule, the presence of serial correlation will not affect the unbiasedness or consistency of the ordinary least-squares regression estimators, but it does affect their efficiency.[13] In the case of positive serial correlation, this loss of efficiency will be masked by the fact that the estimates of the standard errors obtained from the least-squares regression will be smaller than the true standard errors. In other words, the regression estimators will be unbiased, but the standard error of the regression will be biased downward. This will lead to the conclusion that the parameter estimates are more precise than they actually are. There will be a tendency to reject the null hypothesis when, in fact, it should not be rejected. We shall not prove these results in the chapter, but one can obtain an intuitive feeling for why they are true by examining Fig. 4.1a and b.[14]

Both graphs illustrate the presence of positive serial correlation in a model with a single independent explanatory variable. In Fig. 4.1a, the error term associated with the first observation happens to be positive. This leads to a series of error terms, the first four of which are positive and the last two of which are negative. In Fig. 4.1b, the opposite case has occurred, the first four errors being negative, and the last two being positive. In the first case the estimated regression slope is lower than the true slope, while in the second case it is higher. Since both cases are equally likely to occur, it seems reasonable that least-squares slope estimates will be correct on average; i.e., they will be unbiased. However, in both cases, the least-squares regression lines fit the observed sample data points more closely than does the true regression line, which will lead to an R^2 that gives an overly optimistic picture of the success of least-squares regression. More important, however, least squares will lead to an

---

[12] The more general case can be handled with the use of generalized least-squares estimation, as detailed in Appendix 4.

[13] If the model includes a lagged dependent variable, then the problems are much more severe. The lagged dependent variable case will be discussed briefly in section 5.7.

[14] Some of these assertions are proved in Appendix 4.

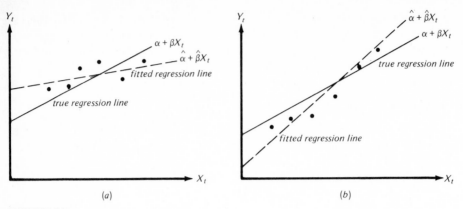

FIGURE 4.1
Positive serial correlation.

estimate of the error variance which is smaller than the true error variance.[15]
Once again the success of the regression procedure will be overstated if the
least-squares estimate of the error variance is used to do statistical tests.

We proceed at this point to discuss several possible solutions to the problem
of serial correlation and then suggest a means by which one might test for the
presence of serial correlation. However, the reader should bear in mind that
both the solutions to the serial correlation problem and the tests themselves
have certain shortcomings. There are cases, for example, when the use of alternative procedures to deal with the serial correlation problem introduces in-
efficiencies which are greater than the inefficiency associated with serial correlation. Thus, judgment must be exercised in the choice of estimation techniques.

4.2.1   Corrections for Serial Correlation

We assume that each of the error terms in a linear regression model is drawn
from a normal population with 0 expected value and constant variance, but
that the errors are not independent over time. Since serial correlation is usually
present in time-series data, we utilize a subscript of t (in place of i) and assume
that the total number of observations is T. The model is as follows:

$$Y_t = \beta_1 + \beta_2 X_{2t} + \beta_3 X_{3t} + \cdots + \beta_k X_{kt} + \varepsilon_t \tag{4.7}$$

$$\varepsilon_t = \rho \varepsilon_{t-1} + v_t \qquad 0 \le \rho < 1 \tag{4.8}$$

where v_t is distributed as $N(0, \sigma_v^2)$ and is independent of other errors over time,
as well as being independent of ε; and ε_t is distributed as $N(0, \sigma_\varepsilon^2)$, but is

---

[15] For a discussion of the lack of bias and consistency of the parameter estimators as well as details
concerning efficiency, see J. Kmenta, *op. cit.*, sec. 8-2.

not independent of other errors over time. The error process as described in Eq. (4.8) is generated by a rule which says that the error in time period t is determined by diminishing the value of the error in the previous period (multiplying by ρ) and then adding the effect of a random variable with 0 expected value. It is the most elementary form of an *autoregressive* error process.[16]

It is easy to check that the effect of an error in any given time period is felt in all future time periods, with a magnitude which diminishes over time. We simply calculate the covariances of ε_t with all previous time periods:

$$\text{Var }(\varepsilon_t) = E(\varepsilon_t{}^2) = E[(\rho\varepsilon_{t-1} + v_t)^2] = E(\rho^2\varepsilon_{t-1}^2 + v_t{}^2 + 2\rho\varepsilon_{t-1}v_t)$$

$$= \rho^2 E(\varepsilon_{t-1}^2) + E(v_t{}^2) \quad \text{since } \varepsilon \text{ and } v \text{ are independent}$$

$$= \rho^2 \text{ Var }(\varepsilon_t) + \text{Var }(v_t) \quad \text{since } \varepsilon \text{ is homoscedastic}$$

Solving,

$$\text{Var }(\varepsilon_t) = \sigma_\varepsilon{}^2 = \frac{\sigma_v{}^2}{1 - \rho^2} \tag{4.9}$$

$$\text{Cov }(\varepsilon_t, \varepsilon_{t-1}) = E(\varepsilon_t \varepsilon_{t-1}) = E[(\rho\varepsilon_{t-1} + v_t)\varepsilon_{t-1}] = E(\rho\varepsilon_{t-1}^2 + v_t\varepsilon_{t-1})$$
$$= \rho E(\varepsilon_{t-1}^2) = \rho \text{ Var }(\varepsilon_t) = \rho\sigma_\varepsilon{}^2 \tag{4.10}$$

Likewise,

$$\text{Cov }(\varepsilon_t, \varepsilon_{t-2}) = E(\varepsilon_t \varepsilon_{t-2}) = \rho^2\sigma_\varepsilon{}^2 \tag{4.11}$$

$$\text{Cov }(\varepsilon_t, \varepsilon_{t-3}) = E(\varepsilon_t \varepsilon_{t-3}) = \rho^3\sigma_\varepsilon{}^2 \tag{4.12}$$

Before proceeding to discuss solutions to the problem of serial correlation, it will be useful to make two further observations (about the error-generating process) which will be of value when explicit estimation techniques are discussed:

1 Some difficulty arises when the error term for the first time period is considered. That error is a function of errors in the previous time period for which no data are available. The result of Eq. (4.9) suggests that we assume that ε_1 is normally distributed with mean 0 and variance $\sigma_v{}^2/(1 - \rho^2)$.

2 A useful formula for the first-order serial correlation coefficient ρ is as follows:

$$\rho = \frac{\text{Cov }(\varepsilon_t, \varepsilon_{t-1})}{\sigma_\varepsilon{}^2} = \frac{\text{Cov }(\varepsilon_t, \varepsilon_{t-1})}{[\text{Var }(\varepsilon_t)]^{1/2}[\text{Var }(\varepsilon_{t-1})]^{1/2}} \tag{4.13}$$

---

[16] We shall consider autoregressive error processes in full generality and in greater detail in Part Three.

since $\sigma_\varepsilon{}^2 = \text{Var}(\varepsilon_t) = \text{Var}(\varepsilon_{t-1})$. Thus, ρ measures the correlation coefficient between errors in time period t and errors in time period $t-1$. When ρ equals 0, no first-order serial correlation is present, while a large value of ρ implies the existence of first-order serial correlation.

If ρ were known, then it would be easy to adjust the ordinary least-squares regression procedure to obtain efficient parameter estimates. The procedure involves the use of *generalized differencing* to alter the linear model into one in which the errors are independent. To describe this procedure, we utilize the fact that the linear model in Eq. (4.7) holds *for all time periods*. In particular,

$$Y_{t-1} = \beta_1 + \beta_2 X_{2t-1} + \cdots + \beta_k X_{kt-1} + \varepsilon_{t-1} \tag{4.14}$$

Multiplying (4.14) by ρ and subtracting from Eq. (4.7), we obtain the desired transformation:

$$Y_t^* = \beta_1(1-\rho) + \beta_2 X_{2t}^* + \cdots + \beta_k X_{kt}^* + v_t \tag{4.15}$$

where $Y_t^* = Y_t - \rho Y_{t-1}$
$X_{2t}^* = X_{2t} - \rho X_{2t-1}$
$X_{kt}^* = X_{kt} - \rho X_{kt-1}$
$v_t = \varepsilon_t - \rho\varepsilon_{t-1}$

are *generalized differences* of Y_t, X_{2t}, ..., X_{kt}, and v_t. By construction the transformed equation has an error process which is independently distributed with 0 mean and constant variance [see Eq. (4.8)]. Thus, ordinary least-squares regression applied to Eq. (4.15) will yield estimates of all the regression parameters. Of course, the intercept of the original model must be calculated from the estimated intercept associated with Eq. (4.15).[17]

We have restricted our discussion of serial correlation to the case in which ρ is strictly less than 1. However, the case in which ρ is identically equal to 1 is of particular interest because it leads to a commonly used estimation procedure.[18]

---

[17] There is only one serious difficulty associated with the generalized differencing process. As described, the transformed equation is defined only for the time period 2, 3, ..., T. Dropping the initial time period from the regression procedure seems plausible, but it results in the loss of important information. A better solution would take the first time period observations into account as follows:

$$Y_1^* = \sqrt{1-\rho^2}\,Y_1 \qquad X_{21}^* = \sqrt{1-\rho^2}\,X_{21} \qquad \cdots \qquad X_{k1}^* = \sqrt{1-\rho^2}\,X_{k1}$$

This transformation works because it adjusts the variance of Y and the X's for the first time period, so that the corresponding error variance is equal to the error variance associated with all other time periods. By construction, $\varepsilon_1^* = (1-\rho)^2\varepsilon_1$ and $\text{Var}(\varepsilon_1^*) = (1-\rho^2)\text{Var}(\varepsilon_1) = \sigma_r{}^2$.

[18] Note, however, that as ρ approaches 1, the error variance in the original equation becomes infinitely large, so that the previous analysis does not follow.

The solution process, known as *first-differencing*, is applied if we estimate the transformed equation (by analogy to the generalized differencing procedure):

$$Y_t^* = \beta_2 X_{2t}^* + \beta_3 X_{3t}^* + \cdots + \beta_k X_{kt}^* + v_t \qquad (4.16)$$

where $Y_t^* = Y_t - Y_{t-1}$
$\quad X_{2t}^* = X_{2t} - X_{2t-1}$
$\quad X_{kt}^* = X_{kt} - X_{kt-1}$
$\quad v_t = \varepsilon_t - \varepsilon_{t-1}$

Note that first-differencing eliminates the need for a constant term in the transformed equation. The intercept of the original equation must be calculated by solving in the original equation when the variables are measured at their respective means.[19] If an intercept term were included, it would pick up the effect of any time trend present in the initial model.

The generalized differencing procedure would be very useful if the value of ρ were known *a priori*. Because this is usually not the case, we examine three alternative procedures for estimating ρ, each of which has certain computational advantages and disadvantages. All three of these procedures yield estimated parameters with the desired properties when the sample size is large, but little is known about their small-sample properties.

I   *The Cochrane-Orcutt Procedure*[20]

This procedure involves a series of iterations, each of which produces a better estimate of ρ than the previous one. It utilizes the notion that ρ is a correlation coefficient associated with errors of adjacent time periods. In the first step, ordinary least squares is used to estimate the original model [Eq. (4.7)]. The residuals from this equation are then used to perform the following regression:

$$\hat{\varepsilon}_t = \rho \hat{\varepsilon}_{t-1} + v_t \qquad (4.17)$$

The estimated value of ρ is used to perform the generalized differencing transformation process, and a new regression is run. The transformed equation is

$$Y_t^* = \beta_1 (1 - \hat{\rho}) + \beta_2 X_{2t}^* + \cdots + \beta_k X_{kt}^* + v_t$$

where $Y_t^* = Y_t - \hat{\rho} Y_{t-1}$
$\quad X_{2t}^* = X_{2t} = \hat{\rho} X_{2t-1}$
$\quad X_{kt}^* = X_{kt} - \hat{\rho} X_{kt-1}$

---

[19] In the two-variable model, for example, $Y_t^* = \beta X_t^*$. To obtain the intercept estimate, we estimate β and then substitute to obtain $\hat{\alpha} = \bar{Y} - \hat{\beta}\bar{X}$.

[20] D. Cochrane and G. H. Orcutt, "Application of Least Squares Regressions to Relationships Containing Autocorrelated Error Terms," *Journal of the American Statistical Association*, vol. 44, pp. 32–61, 1949.

The estimated transformed equation yields parameter values for the original intercept $(\hat{\beta}_1)$ and all the slope parameters $(\hat{\beta}_2, \ldots, \hat{\beta}_k)$. These revised parameter estimates are substituted into the *original* equation, and new regression residuals are obtained. The new estimated residuals are

$$\hat{\hat{\varepsilon}}_t = Y_t - \hat{\beta}_1 - \hat{\beta}_2 X_{2t} - \cdots - \hat{\beta}_k X_{kt}$$

By running the regression

$$\hat{\hat{\varepsilon}}_t = \rho \hat{\hat{\varepsilon}}_{t-1} + v_t$$

these second-round residuals can be used to obtain a new estimate of ρ. The iterative process may be carried on for as many steps as the researcher desires. Standard procedure is to stop the iterations when the new estimates of ρ differ from the old ones by less than .01 or .005, or after 10 or 20 estimates of ρ have been obtained. The specific choice made depends upon the computational costs involved. The primary difficulty with the Cochrane-Orcutt procedure is that there is no guarantee that the final estimate of ρ will be the "optimal" estimate, in the sense of minimizing the sum of squared residuals. The difficulty arises because the iterative technique may lead to a local rather than a global minimum.

II   *The Hildreth-Lu Procedure*[21]

In this procedure, a set of "grid" values are specified for ρ. These are usually spaced values which are to serve as guesses for the value of ρ. If one knew that positive serial correlation were present, one might choose grid values of ρ equal to 0, .1, .2, .3, .4, .5, .6, .7, .8, .9, 1.0. For each value of ρ, the transformed equation

$$Y_t^* = \beta_1(1 - \rho) + \beta_2 X_{2t}^* + \cdots + \beta_k X_{kt}^* + v_t$$

is estimated. The procedure selects the equation with the lowest sum of squared residuals as the best equation. The procedure may be continued with new grid values chosen in the neighborhood of the ρ value that is first selected, until the desired accuracy is attained. In using the Hildreth-Lu procedure, we may choose any limits and any spacing arrangement for the grid values. The technique is practical and, if used with sufficient care, will guarantee that the maximum-likelihood estimate of ρ is approximated. Care should be exercised in the choice of grid values so that the minimum sum of squares obtained is global rather than local.

---

[21] G. Hildreth and J. Y. Lu, "Demand Relations with Autocorrelated Disturbances," *Michigan State University, Agricultural Experiment Station, Technical Bulletin* 276, Nov. 1960.

III   Durbin Procedure[22]

The generalized difference form of the linear model is

$$Y_t - \rho Y_{t-1} = \beta_1(1 - \rho) + \beta_2(X_{2t} - \rho X_{2t-1}) + \cdots + \beta_k(X_{kt} - \rho X_{kt-1}) + v_t$$

$$(4.18)$$

Rewriting this equation slightly, we see that

$$Y_t = \beta_1(1 - \rho) + \rho Y_{t-1} + \beta_2 X_{2t} + \rho\beta_2 X_{2t-1} + \cdots + \beta_k X_{kt} + \rho\beta_k X_{kt-1} + v_t$$

$$(4.19)$$

This suggests that we obtain an estimate for ρ by treating the model in Eq. (4.19) directly as a linear regression model. The estimated coefficient of the Y_{t-1} variable will yield an estimate of ρ which is accurate in large samples, as well as parameter estimates of β_1, β_2, ..., β_k. However, these parameter estimates can be improved if we substitute the estimated serial correlation coefficient $\hat{\rho}$ into the following equation:

$$Y_t - \hat{\rho} Y_{t-1} = \beta_1(1 - \hat{\rho}) + \beta_2(X_{2t} - \hat{\rho}X_{2t-1}) + \cdots + \beta_k(X_{kt} - \hat{\rho}X_{kt-1}) + v_t$$

$$(4.20)$$

Estimation of Eq. (4.20) yields a new, more efficient set of parameter estimates.

4.2.2 Tests for Serial Correlation

Durbin-Watson Test

We shall now consider a test of the null hypothesis that no serial correlation is present ($\rho = 0$). The alternative hypothesis can be that ρ is nonzero, or in the one-tailed case, that ρ is positive (or negative). By far the most popular test for serial correlation is the *Durbin-Watson test*.[23] We concentrate for the remainder of this section on its use and misuse. Alternative parametric and nonparametric tests (which involve no distributional assumptions) are not discussed here.[24]

---

[22] J. Durbin, "Estimation of Parameters in Time-Series Regression Models," *Journal of the Royal Statistical Society*, ser. B, vol. 22, pp. 139–153, 1960.

[23] J. Durbin and G. S. Watson, "Testing for Serial Correlation in Least Squares Regression," *Biometrika*, vol. 38, pp. 159–177, 1951. This test is not directly applicable if the regression does not contain a constant term.

[24] Nonparametric tests are described in S. Siegel, *Nonparametric Statistics for the Behavioral Sciences* (New York: McGraw-Hill, 1956). Other tests are discussed in H. Theil, "The Analysis of Disturbances in Regression Analysis," *Journal of the American Statistical Association*, vol. 60, pp. 1067–1079, 1965.

TABLE 4.1
RANGE OF THE DURBIN-WATSON STATISTIC

Value of DW	Result
$(4 - d_l) < \text{DW} < 4$	Reject the null hypothesis Negative serial correlation is present
$(4 - d_u) < \text{DW} < (4 - d_l)$	Result is indeterminate
$2 < \text{DW} < (4 - d_u)$	Accept the null hypothesis
$d_u < \text{DW} < 2$	Accept the null hypothesis
$d_l < \text{DW} < d_u$	Result is indeterminate
$0 < \text{DW} < d_l$	Reject the null hypothesis Positive serial correlation is present

The Durbin-Watson test involves the calculation of a test statistic based on the residuals from the ordinary least-squares regression procedure. The statistic is defined as follows:

$$\text{DW} = \frac{\sum_{t=2}^{T} (\hat{\varepsilon}_t - \hat{\varepsilon}_{t-1})^2}{\sum_{t=1}^{T} \hat{\varepsilon}_t^2} \tag{4.21}$$

The reader should note that the numerator cannot include a difference for the first observation in the sample, since no earlier observation is available. In addition, if any gaps occur in the data (when observations are missing), the number of entries in the numerator must be further reduced—once for each gap. When successive values of $\hat{\varepsilon}_t$ are close to each other, the DW (Durbin-Watson) will be low, indicating the presence of positive serial correlation. The DW statistic will lie in the $(0, 4)$ range, with a value near 2 indicating no first-order serial correlation.[25] Exact interpretation of the DW statistic is difficult because the sequence of error terms depends not only on the sequence of ε's, but also on the sequence of all the X values. For this reason, most tables include test statistics which vary with the number of independent variables and the number of observations. Two limits are given, usually labeled d_l and d_u. If one is investigating the possibility of positive serial correlation, a value for DW below d_l allows one to reject the null hypothesis of no serial correlation. If DW is greater than d_u, the null hypothesis is retained. The range between d_l and d_u leaves

---

[25] The DW statistic cannot be utilized if the regression equation contains a lagged dependent variable. This matter is pursued further in section 5.7.

us with inconclusive results. For negative serial correlation we simply view matters from the endpoint of 4 instead of the endpoint of 0. The null hypothesis is rejected if the DW statistic is greater than $4 - d_l$, and the hypothesis is accepted if DW is less than $4 - d_u$ and greater than d_u. Within the range between $4 - d_u$ and $4 - d_l$ the test is inconclusive. (See Table 4.1 for a summary of the Durbin-Watson test.)

The region of indeterminacy of the statistical test is due to the fact that the sequence of residuals is influenced by the movement of the independent variables in the regression equation. In this region, it is possible that the seeming correlation of the errors is due to the autocorrelation of the independent variable and not to the serial correlation of the error terms.

We conclude this section by showing the range of the Durbin-Watson statistic and the range of indeterminacy explicitly in a two-variable example (with both variables measured as deviations about means). We assume that

$$y_t = \beta x_t + \varepsilon_t \tag{4.22}$$

$$\varepsilon_t = \rho \varepsilon_{t-1} + v_t \qquad -1 < \rho < 1 \tag{4.23}$$

$$x_t = r x_{t-1} + w_t^* \qquad 0 \le r < 1 \tag{4.24}$$

where w_t^* is a random uncorrelated error term. The third assumption takes account of the fact that the independent variable is likely to be highly autocorrelated in time-series studies. The serial correlation coefficient, r, makes this assumption explicit. Expanding the definition of DW from Eq. (4.21), we find that

$$DW = \frac{\sum\limits_{t=2}^{T} \hat{\varepsilon}_t^{\,2} - 2 \sum\limits_{t=2}^{T} \hat{\varepsilon}_t \hat{\varepsilon}_{t-1} + \sum\limits_{t=2}^{T} \hat{\varepsilon}_{t-1}^{\,2}}{\sum\limits_{t=1}^{T} \hat{\varepsilon}_t^{\,2}}$$

Then, by making several approximations, we can determine that[26]

$$DW \approx 2(1 - \hat{\rho}) \tag{4.25}$$

---

[26] We assume that $\sum\limits_{t=2}^{T} \hat{\varepsilon}_t^{\,2} \simeq \sum\limits_{t=1}^{T} \hat{\varepsilon}_t^{\,2} \simeq \sum\limits_{t=2}^{T} \hat{\varepsilon}_{t-1}^{\,2}$ and $\sum\limits_{t=2}^{T} \hat{\varepsilon}_t \hat{\varepsilon}_{t-1} \simeq \sum\limits_{t=1}^{T} \hat{\varepsilon}_t \hat{\varepsilon}_{t-1}$. Then it follows by direct substitution that

$$DW \simeq 2 - \frac{\sum\limits_{t=1}^{T} \hat{\varepsilon}_t \hat{\varepsilon}_{t-1}}{\sum\limits_{t=1}^{T} \hat{\varepsilon}_t^{\,2}} \simeq 2 - 2 \frac{\text{Cov}\,(\hat{\varepsilon}_t, \hat{\varepsilon}_{t-1})}{\text{Var}\,(\hat{\varepsilon}_t)} \simeq 2 - 2\hat{\rho}$$

It should now be clear that when there is no serial correlation ($\rho = 0$), the Durbin-Watson statistic will be close to 2. Positive serial correlation is clearly associated with DW values below 2, and negative serial correlation with DW values above 2. Now we can take into account the serially correlated nature of the independent variable. From Eq. (4.6) we know that

$$\text{Var}\,(\hat{\varepsilon}_t) = \text{Var}\,(\varepsilon_t) + (\beta - \hat{\beta})^2\,\text{Var}\,(x_t) \tag{4.26}$$

Using a similar procedure, we can show that[27]

$$\text{Cov}\,(\hat{\varepsilon}_t, \hat{\varepsilon}_{t-1}) = \text{Cov}\,(\varepsilon_t, \varepsilon_{t-1}) + (\beta - \hat{\beta})^2\,\text{Cov}\,(x_t, x_{t-1}) \tag{4.27}$$

while Eq. (4.24) allows us to conclude that

$$\text{Cov}\,(x_t, x_{t-1}) = r\,\text{Var}\,(x_t) \tag{4.28}$$

Substituting Eqs. (4.26), (4.27), and (4.28) into Eq. (4.25), we can evaluate the DW statistic in terms of the distribution of the error term and the explanatory variable:[28]

$$\text{DW} \simeq 2 - 2\,\frac{\text{Cov}\,(\varepsilon_t, \varepsilon_{t-1}) + r(\beta - \hat{\beta})^2\,\text{Var}\,(x_t)}{\text{Var}\,(\varepsilon_t) + (\beta - \hat{\beta})^2\,\text{Var}\,(x_t)} \tag{4.29}$$

If the estimated slope parameter is identically equal to the true parameter, then the presence of serial correlation in the X variable is irrelevant to the calculation of the DW statistic. Despite the fact that $\hat{\beta}$ is an unbiased estimator of β, there will be sampling error involved in the estimation process, and so $\hat{\beta}$ will not be identically equal to β. It should be immediately clear from Eq. (4.29) that, other things equal, a higher value of r will lead to a lower value of the Durbin-Watson statistic. In fact, a value of r close to 1 may push the DW statistic close to 0, even though the error terms may be uncorrelated themselves. The reason for the upper and lower limits associated with the DW test now becomes clear. If $r = 1$, the d_l limit is the proper one to apply. Anything below d_l indicates positive serial correlation. If $r = 0$, on the other hand, the d_u limit should be used. Anything above d_u indicates that positive serial correlation cannot be accepted. In working with time series, the X's are likely to be autocorrelated, so that the d_l limit may be the more accurate of the two.

---

[27] From Eq. (4.5) we can write $\hat{\varepsilon}_{t-1} = \varepsilon_{t-1} + (\beta - \hat{\beta})x_{t-1}$. Multiplying this term-by-term by $\hat{\varepsilon}_t = \varepsilon_t + (\beta - \hat{\beta})x_t$, summing over all observations, and eliminating all cross terms, we get the desired results.

[28] Starting with the equation in footnote 26:

$$\text{DW} \simeq 2 - 2\,\frac{\text{Cov}\,(\hat{\varepsilon}_t, \hat{\varepsilon}_{t-1})}{\text{Var}\,(\hat{\varepsilon}_t)}$$

the result follows immediately.

Example 4.5   Bituminous Coal[29]

An attempt was made to explain the demand for bituminous coal (COAL) as a function of the Federal Reserve Board index of iron and steel production (FIS), the Federal Reserve Board index of electrical utility production (FEU), the wholesale price index for coal (PCOAL) and the wholesale price index for natural gas (PGAS). The quantity demanded of bituminous coal has been seasonally adjusted, and the adjusted series was used to perform a linear regression on the explanatory variables listed above. The time series run monthly from January 1965 to December 1972.

The output from the original regression is as follows (with t statistics in parentheses):

$$COAL = 12{,}262 + 92.34FIS + 118.57FEU - 48.90PCOAL + 118.91PGAS$$
$$\quad\;\; (3.51) \quad\;\; (6.46) \quad\quad (7.14) \quad\quad\quad (-3.82) \quad\quad\quad (3.18)$$

$$R^2 = .692 \qquad F(4/91) = 51.0 \qquad DW = .95$$

Although all the t statistics are highly significant, the low DW statistic indicates that serial correlation is present in the estimated residuals.[30] In order to correct for the presence of positive first-order serial correlation, the Hildreth-Lu procedure was applied. A series of regressions was run, each with a different chosen value of ρ. The grid search is described by the following table:

GRID SEARCH

ρ	Sum of squared residuals (ESS)
-1.0	3.8×10^8
$-.8$	3.1×10^8
$-.6$	2.5×10^8
$-.4$	2.0×10^8
$-.2$	1.5×10^8
$.0$	1.2×10^8
$.2$	1.0×10^8
$.4$	9.2×10^7
$.6$	9.0×10^7
$.8$	9.6×10^7
1.0	1.1×10^8

---

[29] This example was constructed by Dynamics Associates, Cambridge, Mass.

[30] The critical values of the DW statistic (at the 5 percent significance level) with 96 observations and 4 independent variables are $d_l = 1.58$ and $d_u = 1.75$.

The final value of ρ chosen was .6, the value associated with the smallest sum of squared residuals of the regressions run. When ρ was assigned the value of .6, the autoregressive transformation performed, and the final regression run, the results were as follows:

$$\text{COAL*} = 16{,}245 + 75.29\text{FIS*} + 100.26\text{FEV*} - 38.98\text{PCOAL*} + 105.99\text{PGAS*}$$
$$\qquad\quad (3.3)\qquad (4.4)\qquad\quad (3.7)\qquad\qquad (-2.0)\qquad\qquad (2.0)$$

where   COAL* = COAL $-$ .6COAL$_{-1}$
$\qquad$ FEV* = FEV $-$ .6FEV$_{-1}$
$\qquad$ PGAS* = PGAS $-$ .6PGAS$_{-1}$
$\qquad$ FIS* = FIS $-$ .6FIS$_{-1}$
$\qquad$ PCOAL* = PCOAL $-$ .6PCOAL
$\qquad$ DW = 2.07

Notice that the DW statistic is substantially higher than in the original regression and that all the estimated regression coefficients continue to be significant at the 5 percent level.

Example 4.6   Interest Rate Determination

In this example we reconsider the attempt (see Example 3.2) to estimate a single-equation model which explains the time path of the 3-month Treasury bill rate (R_t) as a function of aggregate disposable income (YD_t), a 3-month moving sum of changes in the money supply $(\text{MAM} = \Delta M_t + \Delta M_{t-1} + \Delta M_{t-2})$, and a 3-month moving sum of the rate of change of the price level $(\text{MAP} = \Delta P_t/P_t + \Delta P_{t-1}/P_{t-1} + \Delta P_{t-2}/P_{t-2})$. One of the final equations estimated using ordinary least squares is listed below, with t statistics in parentheses:

$$R_t = -3.662 + .053\text{YD}_t - .280\text{MAM}_t + 104.37\text{MAP}_t$$
$$\quad (-9.45)\quad (14.76)\quad (-6.13)\qquad (5.23)$$

$$R^2 = .853 \qquad \bar{R}^2 = .849 \qquad F(3/141) = 271.9 \qquad \text{SER} = .552 \qquad \text{DW} = .24$$

The low Durbin-Watson statistic of .24 strongly suggests the presence of positive first-order serial correlation. This is borne out when we examine a graph of the actual and fitted values of the ordinary least-squares regression in Fig. 4.2. While the R^2 for the equation is reasonably high, the fit, as shown graphically, leaves much to be desired. The existence of serial correlation can be seen graphically by noticing that regression residuals tend to be highly correlated. When the fitted value associated with one observation lies below the true value, it is very likely that neighboring fitted values will do the same. What is especially discouraging from the forecasting perspective is that the last seven fitted or

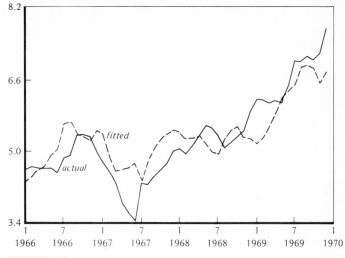

FIGURE 4.2
Interest rate determination. Time bounds: January 1966 to December 1969.

predicted values lie below the actual values. This suggests that unless corrections are made for the presence of serial correlation, forecasts are likely to understate the actual interest-rate time series.

To improve our results, we reestimated the interest rate equation, using the Hildreth-Lu procedure to correct for serial correlation. The results are as follows:

$$R_t^* = -5.155 + .066YD_t^* - .040MAM_t^* + 37.78MAP_t^*$$
$$(-2.70) \quad (4.81) \quad (-1.14) \quad (1.74)$$

where $R_t^* = R_t - .956R_{t-1}$
  $YD_t^* = YD_t - .956YD_{t-1}$
  $MAM_t^* = MAM_t - .956MAM_{t-1}$
  $MAP_t^* = MAP_t - .956MAP_{t-1}$

$R^2 = .177 \quad F(3/174) = 10.1 \quad DW = 1.42$
$\bar{R}^2 = .159 \quad SER = .230 \quad \rho = .956$

All the statistics listed above were obtained from the transformed equation which used the generalized differencing process. The result is that R^2 has fallen, as have the t statistics. However, for our purposes what is important is the ability of the equation to forecast. In fact, the correction for serial correlation substantially improves the fit of the original equation, as seen by examining the plot of fitted and actual values in Fig. 4.3.

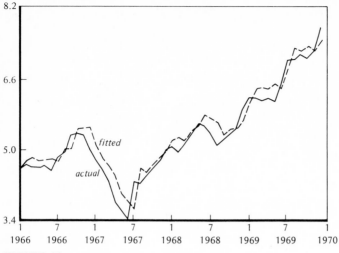

FIGURE 4.3
Interest rate determination (with Hildreth-Lu correction). Time bounds:
January 1966 to December 1969.

Exercises

4.1 Explain intuitively why weighted least squares yields more efficient parameter estimators than ordinary least squares when the error term is known to be heteroscedastic.

4.2 You are estimating a cross-section regression for a sample of 100 cities in the United States in which you hope to explain expenditures on education as a function of the median income in the community, the number of school-age children, and the level of state and federal grants received for educational purposes. Would you expect heteroscedasticity to be a problem in this case? If so, would you use Bartlett's test or the Goldfeld-Quandt test? Why?

4.3 You are estimating the relationship between firm sales and advertising expenditures in an industry. It becomes readily apparent to you that half the firms in the industry are large relative to the other half, and you are concerned about the proper estimation technique in such a situation. Assume that the error variances associated with the large firms are twice the error variances associated with the small firms.

(1) If you used ordinary least squares to estimate the regression of sales on advertising (assuming that advertising is an independent variable, uncorrelated with the error term), would your estimated parameters be unbiased? Consistent? Efficient?

(2) How might you revise the estimation procedure to eliminate or to resolve your difficulties?

(3) Can you test whether the original error variance assumption is valid?

4.4 Why are the errors in cross-section studies unlikely to be serially correlated? Can you give an example in which serial correlation will be present?

4.5 Can ρ take on a value (in absolute value) which is greater than 1? What does this tell you about the stability of the model being studied?

APPENDIX 4 / GENERALIZED LEAST-SQUARES ESTIMATION

In the appendix to Chapter 3 we discussed the matrix generalization of the multiple regression model. Among the assumptions of the "classical" linear model was the assumption that the error term was not autocorrelated and had constant variance. In matrix notation we wrote

$$E(\varepsilon\varepsilon') = \sigma^2 I$$

where I is an $N \times N$ identity matrix

In this appendix we generalize the linear model to apply to cases in which serial correlation and heteroscedasticity are present. We accomplish this by altering our assumption about the variance-covariance matrix of the error terms. We assume that

$$E(\varepsilon\varepsilon') = \sigma^2 \Omega \qquad (A4.1)$$

σ^2 is assumed to be unknown, but Ω is a known $N \times N$ matrix. This is equivalent to the assumption that the elements of Ω are known up to a multiplicative scalar. The only assumption we need to make about the matrix Ω is that it is positive definite.[31] This assumption is quite general, yet necessary for the derivations which follow. The generality of the assumed error structure is evidenced by the fact that heteroscedasticity and first-order serial correlation are special cases.

The most general form of the heteroscedasticity case occurs when the error structure is as follows:

$$\Omega = \begin{bmatrix} \sigma_1^2 & 0 & \cdots & 0 \\ 0 & \sigma_2^2 & \cdots & 0 \\ \cdots\cdots\cdots\cdots\cdots\cdots\cdots \\ 0 & 0 & \cdots & \sigma_N^2 \end{bmatrix}$$

Heteroscedasticity differs from the classical model only in the fact that the error variances differ between observations. All error covariances are assumed

---

[31] A matrix A is positive definite if and only if $x'Ax$ is greater than 0, for all x not equal to 0, where x is an $N \times 1$ vector. See Appendix 3 for references which describe the basic results of matrix algebra.

equal to 0. In the first-order serial correlation example, however, none of the elements of Ω are equal to 0. In this case, the variance-covariance matrix is as follows:

$$\Omega = \sigma^2 \begin{bmatrix} 1 & \rho & \rho^2 & \cdots & \rho^{N-1} \\ \rho & 1 & \rho & \cdots & \rho^{N-2} \\ \rho^2 & \rho & 1 & \cdots & \rho^{N-3} \\ \cdots\cdots\cdots\cdots\cdots\cdots\cdots\cdots\cdots\cdots \\ \rho^{N-1} & \rho^{N-2} & \rho^{N-3} & \cdots & 1 \end{bmatrix}$$

The objective of generalized least-squares estimation is to find parameter estimates for the vector β in the most efficient manner possible, by accounting for the information provided by the knowledge of the form of the matrix Ω. Assuming that all other least-squares assumptions hold, we can get best linear unbiased parameter estimates if we transform the original data set so that the variance-covariance matrix of the transformed errors equals $\sigma^2 I$. Once this is done, application of the Gauss-Markov theorem will give us our desired result. The assumption that Ω is a positive definite matrix is sufficient to guarantee that such a strategy will always succeed. We utilize a basic theorem of matrix algebra which states that there exists a nonsingular $N \times N$ matrix H such that

$$H\Omega H' = I \tag{A4.2}$$

We will find it useful to rewrite (A4.2) in the following form:

$$\Omega = H^{-1}(H')^{-1} = (H'H)^{-1} \tag{A4.3}$$

from which it follows that

$$H'H = \Omega^{-1} \tag{A4.4}$$

We use the matrix H to transform the original model as follows:

$$HY = HX\beta + H\varepsilon \tag{A4.5}$$

or
$$\tilde{Y} = \tilde{X}\beta + \tilde{\varepsilon} \tag{A4.6}$$

where $\tilde{Y} = HY$
$\tilde{X} = HX$
$\tilde{\varepsilon} = H\varepsilon$

The error term $\tilde{\varepsilon}$ is consistent with the classical linear model, since, from Eq. (A4.2),

$$E(\tilde{\varepsilon}\tilde{\varepsilon}') = E(H\varepsilon\varepsilon'H') = \sigma^2 H\Omega H' = \sigma^2 I$$

Since (A4.6) obeys the classical assumptions, we know that the application of ordinary least squares will yield best unbiased parameter estimates. Hence the estimator

$$\tilde{\beta} = (\tilde{X}'\tilde{X})^{-1}\tilde{X}'\tilde{Y} \tag{A4.7}$$

will be efficient.[32]

In terms of our original data, the generalized least-squares estimator $\tilde{\beta}$ is as follows:

$$\tilde{\beta} = [(HX)'(HX)]^{-1}(HX)'(HY) = (X'H'HX)^{-1}X'H'HY$$

$$= (X'\Omega^{-1}X)^{-1}X'\Omega^{-1}Y \tag{A4.8}$$

The variance-covariance matrix of the estimated parameter vector $\tilde{\beta}$ is

$$E[(\tilde{\beta} - \beta)(\tilde{\beta} - \beta)'] = \sigma^2(\tilde{X}'\tilde{X})^{-1} = \sigma^2(X'H'HX)^{-1}$$

$$= \sigma^2(X'\Omega^{-1}X)^{-1} \tag{A4.9}$$

It is worth checking to see that the generalized least-squares results coincide with those of ordinary least squares when $\Omega = \sigma^2 I$. The reader can do so by substituting for Ω in Eqs. (A4.8) and (A4.9) and solving.

In order to apply generalized least-squares (GLS) estimation, we need an estimate of Ω, and in order to perform statistical tests, we need to estimate σ^2. If Ω were known, we could estimate σ^2 from the residuals of the GLS regression. To do so, we utilize our knowledge of the classical linear model, in which an unbiased estimate of σ^2 is given by

$$\hat{\sigma}^2 = \frac{1}{N-k}\tilde{u}'\tilde{u}$$

where $\tilde{u}$ is the vector of GLS residuals in this case. Substituting,

$$\hat{\sigma}^2 = \frac{1}{N-k}(H\hat{\varepsilon})'(H\hat{\varepsilon}) = \frac{1}{N-k}(\hat{\varepsilon}'\Omega^{-1}\hat{\varepsilon})$$

so that an unbiased estimate of $E[(\tilde{\beta} - \beta)(\tilde{\beta} - \beta)']$ is given by

$$\frac{1}{N-k}(\hat{\varepsilon}'\Omega^{-1}\hat{\varepsilon})(X'\Omega^{-1}X)^{-1} \tag{A4.10}$$

---

[32] The Gauss-Markov theorem still applies here because all transformations of the data are *linear*.

If ε is assumed normal, then it is possible to show that $\tilde{\beta}$ is normally distributed. Thus, statistical tests may be applied just as in the case of the classical model.

Our final problem is to find a consistent estimate of Ω. An obvious difficulty arises because Ω is an $N \times N$ matrix with $N(N + 1)/2$ elements. It is impossible to estimate all elements of Ω from only N observations, so that if no other information is available, we must parametrize the form of Ω. The heteroscedasticity and first-order serial correlation assumptions provide two useful ways of parameterizing the model, although numerous alternatives are available.

Once a consistent estimator of Ω is used, our estimator will lose the property of being an unbiased estimator, but will retain an appropriate large-sample property (something close to consistency). If Ω is estimated consistently by a matrix V, then the GLS estimator and its variance-covariance matrix are

$$\hat{\beta} = (X'V^{-1}X)^{-1}X'V^{-1}Y \tag{A4.11}$$

$$E[(\hat{\beta} - \beta)(\hat{\beta} - \beta)'] = \frac{1}{N - k} (\hat{\varepsilon}'V^{-1}\hat{\varepsilon})(X'V^{-1}X)^{-1}$$

$$= \frac{1}{N - k} (\tilde{u}'\tilde{u})(X'V^{-1}X)^{-1} \tag{A4.12}$$

where $\hat{\varepsilon}$ are the ordinary least-squares residuals and $\tilde{u}$ are the generalized least-squares residuals.

In order to complete this appendix, it will be useful to describe the transformation matrix H in both the heteroscedasticity and the first-order serial correlation cases. In the former it is quite easy to choose H so that $H'H = \sigma^2 \Omega$. The reader should check to see that

$$H = \begin{bmatrix} \dfrac{1}{\sigma_1} & 0 & \cdots & 0 \\ 0 & \dfrac{1}{\sigma_2} & \cdots & 0 \\ \cdots\cdots\cdots\cdots\cdots \\ 0 & 0 & \cdots & \dfrac{1}{\sigma_N} \end{bmatrix}$$

is the correct choice. In addition, the reader should check that transforming the data according to the matrix H is equivalent to the weighted least-squares procedure described in the text.

The derivation of $\mathbf{H}$ in the first-order serial correlation case is somewhat more difficult. In this case,

$$\mathbf{H} = \begin{bmatrix} \sqrt{1-\rho^2} & 0 & 0 & \cdots & 0 & 0 \\ -\rho & 1 & 0 & \cdots & 0 & 0 \\ 0 & -\rho & 1 & \cdots & 0 & 0 \\ \cdots\cdots\cdots\cdots\cdots\cdots\cdots\cdots\cdots\cdots\cdots \\ 0 & 0 & 0 & \cdots & 1 & 0 \\ 0 & 0 & 0 & \cdots & -\rho & 1 \end{bmatrix}$$

The fact that $\mathbf{H}$ is the correct choice can be checked by evaluating $(\mathbf{H'H})^{-1} = \mathbf{\Omega}$. The reader should verify that application of the transformation $\mathbf{H}$ to the data is equivalent to using the generalized differencing process and then applying ordinary least squares. In this sense, corrections for serial correlation involve the use of weighted least-squares estimation just as in the heteroscedasticity case.

What if ordinary least-squares estimation is utilized, even when generalized least squares is appropriate? We know, first of all, that if $\mathbf{\Omega}$ is known, OLS and GLS parameter estimates will be unbiased, but OLS parameter estimates will have greater variance than their GLS counterparts. However, it is also true that the OLS estimate of the variance-covariance matrix will be biased. To see this, recall that the OLS variance-covariance matrix is

$$\sigma^2(\mathbf{X'X})^{-1} \tag{A4.13}$$

If the GLS model were in fact correct, the variance-covariance matrix of the parameter vector $\hat{\mathbf{\beta}} = (\mathbf{X'X})^{-1}\mathbf{X'Y}$ would be

$$E[(\hat{\mathbf{\beta}} - \mathbf{\beta})(\hat{\mathbf{\beta}} - \mathbf{\beta})'] = E\{[(\mathbf{X'X})^{-1}\mathbf{X'\varepsilon}][(\mathbf{X'X})^{-1}\mathbf{X'\varepsilon}]'\} \qquad \text{since } \hat{\mathbf{\beta}} = \mathbf{\beta} + (\mathbf{X'X})^{-1}\mathbf{X'\varepsilon}$$

$$= (\mathbf{X'X})^{-1}\mathbf{X'}E[(\mathbf{\varepsilon\varepsilon'})]\mathbf{X}(\mathbf{X'X})^{-1}$$

$$= \sigma^2(\mathbf{X'X})^{-1}\mathbf{X'\Omega X}(\mathbf{X'X})^{-1} \tag{A4.14}$$

The reported variance-covariance matrix in (A4.13) may yield a rather poor estimate of the correct variance-covariance matrix for ordinary least-squares parameter estimates as given by (A4.14).

5

INSTRUMENTAL VARIABLES AND TWO-STAGE LEAST SQUARES

To this point we have assumed that each of the independent variables in the linear regression model was uncorrelated with the true error term. We focus in this chapter on the possible failure of that assumption, placing particular emphasis on problems associated with simultaneous equation models. More generally, we see that there are three instances when independent variables may be correlated with the error term:

1 One or more of the "independent" variables is measured with error.
2 One or more of the "independent" variables is determined in part (through one or more separate equations) by the "dependent" variable.
3 One or more of the "independent" variables is a lagged "dependent" variable in a model in which the error term is serially correlated.

We begin the chapter with the problem of errors in variables. While important in itself, this topic also serves as a useful introduction to the simultaneous equation model. We will see that the ordinary least-squares regression process loses some of its desirable properties when one or more of the right-hand variables in the equation is measured with error. Some of these lost properties can be regained if new variables, called *instruments*, replace the variables measured with error, and a new instrumental variables estimation technique is used to replace ordinary least squares.

While instrumental variables estimation is relevant when dealing with errors in variables, it is even more useful when dealing with estimation problems in the context of simultaneous equation models. For this reason we continue the chapter by introducing the notion of simultaneous equation systems and discuss the identification problem in an intuitive manner. With this necessary background, we return to the estimation problem by describing the technique of two-stage least squares, a frequently used type of instrumental variables estimator. Finally, we conclude the chapter by mentioning the serious difficulties which arise when we attempt to estimate an equation in which a lagged value of the left-hand variable appears as an explanatory variable at the same time that the error process is serially correlated.

5.1 CORRELATION BETWEEN AN INDEPENDENT VARIABLE AND THE ERROR TERM

The difficulties arising when the independent variables and the error are correlated can best be seen by taking a close look at the two-variable model, with both variables measured in deviations form. The least-squares slope estimator is

$$\hat{\beta} = \frac{\sum x_i y_i}{\sum x_i^2} \qquad \text{where } y_i = \beta x_i + \varepsilon_i$$

Substituting and expanding terms, we get

$$\hat{\beta} = \frac{\beta \sum x_i^2 + \sum x_i \varepsilon_i}{\sum x_i^2} = \beta + \frac{\sum x_i \varepsilon_i}{\sum x_i^2} \tag{5.1}$$

The estimator $\hat{\beta}$ has been proved to be an unbiased estimator of β when the X variable observations were assumed to be fixed in repeated samples. The proof depended heavily upon the fact that the expected value of the second term on the right-hand side of Eq. (5.1) was equal to 0. Unfortunately, if we generalize the model to one in which the X's are stochastic in nature, i.e., drawn from a probability distribution, the proof that $\hat{\beta}$ is an unbiased estimator of β does not necessarily follow. To resolve this difficulty, we give up the hope of proving that the expression $\sum x_i \varepsilon_i$ has an expected value of 0 and concentrate instead on its value as the sample size gets arbitrarily large. If we can prove that the expression approaches 0 as the sample size grows, then we can prove the consistency of the estimated parameter.

As a general rule there is no guarantee that X and ε will be uncorrelated, and, therefore, no guarantee that $\hat{\beta}$ will be a consistent estimator of β. To see this, consider the case in which X and ε are known to be positively correlated irrespective of the sample size. A quick examination of Eq. (5.1) makes it apparent that the term on the right-hand side of the equation will be positive and that $\hat{\beta}$ will overestimate the true parameter value no matter what the sample size. Thus, correlation between an independent variable and the error term leads,

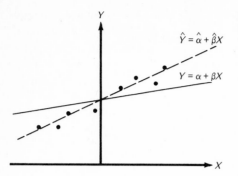

FIGURE 5.1
Correlation of X and ε.

in general, to inconsistent ordinary least-squares parameter estimates. The particular example just used is depicted graphically in Fig. 5.1. The solid line represents the true regression line, while the dotted line represents the ordinary least-squares regression line. In achieving its objective of minimizing the sum of the squares of the estimated residuals, ordinary least squares yields biased and inconsistent estimates of the true regression slope parameter. In this case the slope has been overestimated. (The intercept estimate will be a biased and inconsistent estimator of the true intercept, while the estimate standard error of the regression and the standard errors of the coefficients will also be biased and inconsistent.)

5.2 ERRORS IN VARIABLES

We have assumed that all variables used in the regression calculation procedure were measured without error. In practice, measurement errors (as well as errors in misspecifying the model) are likely to occur, and as we shall see, these errors can substantially alter the properties of the estimated regression parameters. We shall work through the problem of measurement error by considering several increasingly complex cases.

Case I Y Is Measured with Error

Assume that the true regression model (written in deviations form) is as follows:

$$y_i = \beta x_i + \varepsilon_i \tag{5.2}$$

where ε_i represents errors associated with the specification of the model (the effects of omitted variables, etc.). Assume, in addition, that the variable y^*, rather than y, is obtained in the measurement process. We shall assume that

$$y_i^* = y_i + u_i \qquad \text{where Cov } (u_i, x_i) = 0 \tag{5.3}$$

The regression model is estimated with y^* as the dependent variable, with no account made for the fact that y^* is not an accurate measure of y. Adding the measurement error term u_i to each side of Eq. (5.2), we see that this is equivalent to running the regression

$$y_i^* = \beta x_i + (\varepsilon_i + u_i) \tag{5.4}$$

Note that if u_i did not have 0 mean, our estimated regression would need an intercept term. In any case, as long as u_i and x_i are uncorrelated, there is no problem associated with running the regression described in Eq. (5.4). The estimated slope parameter will be unbiased [since $E(u_i x_i) = 0$] and consistent. The only effect of the presence of measurement error in the dependent variable is to increase the error variance. However, the increased error variance will be accounted for in the estimate of s^2, the estimated residual variance, and all statistical tests will apply. (As a general rule, it is impossible to separate out the effects of errors associated with the regression model and measurement error, and no attempt is made to do so.) The situation is not so auspicious, however, when the X variable is also measured with error.

Case II X Is Measured with Error

Assume that $x_i^* = x_i + v_i$, where x_i is the true value and x_i^* is the observed value. The true regression model is

$$y_i = \beta x_i + \varepsilon_i$$

while the actual regression run is

$$y_i = \beta x_i^* + (\varepsilon_i - \beta v_i) = \beta x_i^* + \varepsilon_i^* \tag{5.5}$$

Even if we assume that the measurement error in X is normally distributed with 0 mean, has no serial correlation, and is independent of the error in the true equation, problems arise when using ordinary least squares as a regression technique. This can be most easily seen by noting that the error ε^* and the variable x^* in Eq. (5.5) are correlated (or have a nonzero covariance). In particular,

$$\mathrm{Cov}\,(\varepsilon_i^*, x_i^*) = E[(\varepsilon_i - \beta v_i)(x_i + v_i)] = -\beta \sigma_v^{\,2}$$

Thus, least-squares estimates of the regression parameters will be biased and inconsistent, with the degree of bias and inconsistency being related to the variance of the measurement error.

Case III   X and Y Are Measured with Error[1]

This case contains no new conclusions as compared with the previous case, but it will be instructive to examine it in some detail. The assumptions are as follows:

$$y_i^* = y_i + u_i \qquad u_i \sim N(0, \sigma_u^2)$$

$$x_i^* = x_i + v_i \qquad v_i \sim N(0, \sigma_v^2)$$

$$y_i = \beta x_i$$

u_i and v_i are uncorrelated with each other as well as with x_i, and each error process itself involves no serial correlation. The estimated regression equation will be of the following form:

$$y_i^* = \beta x_i^* + (u_i - \beta v_i) \tag{5.6}$$

Now consider the ordinary least-squares estimator $\hat{\beta}$:

$$\hat{\beta} = \frac{\sum x_i^* y_i^*}{\sum x_i^{*2}} = \frac{\sum (x_i + v_i)(y_i + u_i)}{\sum (x_i + v_i)^2} = \frac{\sum (x_i + v_i)(\beta x_i + u_i)}{\sum (x_i + v_i)^2}$$

$$= \frac{\beta \sum x_i^2 + \beta \sum x_i v_i + \sum x_i u_i + \sum v_i u_i}{\sum x_i^2 + \sum v_i^2 + 2 \sum x_i v_i}$$

$$= \frac{\beta \sum x_i^2}{\sum x_i^2 + \sum v_i^2} = \frac{\beta \, \text{Var}(x)}{\text{Var}(x) + \sigma_v^2} = \frac{\beta}{1 + \sigma_v^2/\text{Var}(x)} \tag{5.7}$$

The derivation just completed suggests, under quite restrictive assumptions, that the presence of measurement error of the type in question will lead to an underestimate of the true regression parameter if ordinary least-squares techniques are utilized. It tells us in addition that if the variance in the error of measurement of X is known, the regression will yield consistent parameter estimates. Unfortunately, it is difficult to imagine much information of this type being available.

As a final item, we should stress that case III has been developed under the assumption that no underlying equation error exists. This is, of course, unlikely to be the case, and makes further pursuit of solutions to the estimation problem in this context undesirable. In particular, we will not discuss the solution to the

---

[1] With no other error in the equation.

errors-in-variables problem in the unlikely situation that the ratio of the measurement error variances is known.[2]

Instrumental Variables Estimation

The problem of errors in measurement of regression variables is quite clearly an important one, and yet econometricians do not have much to offer in the way of useful solutions. As a general rule, we tend to pass over the problem of measurement error, hoping that the errors are small enough so as not to destroy the validity of the estimation procedure. One technique which is available and can solve (in principle) the measurement error problem is the technique of *instrumental variables estimation.*[3] We shall briefly outline the concept of instrumental variables, not so much because it is likely to be useful in the error measurement case, but because it is an important estimation technique when one is dealing with models consisting of systems of simultaneous equations.

The method of instrumental variables involves the search for a new variable Z which is both highly correlated with the independent variable X and at the same time uncorrelated with the error term in the equation (as well as the errors of measurement of both variables). In practice, we are concerned with the consistency of parameter estimates and therefore concentrate on the relationship between the variable Z and the remaining model variables when the sample size gets large. We define the random variable Z to be an *instrument* if:

1 The correlations between Z and ε, u, and v in the equation approach 0 as the sample size gets large.[4]
2 The correlation between Z and X is nonzero as the sample size gets large.

In any given situation it is conceivable that no such instruments will exist or that many instruments will exist. If we are fortunate to be able to choose among several instruments, we simply select the one instrument (or combination of instruments) having the highest correlation with the X variable.

Assuming for the moment that such a variable can be found, we can alter the least-squares regression procedure to obtain estimated parameters which are consistent. Given the nature of the assumptions underlying the choice of instruments, there is unfortunately no guarantee that the estimation process will yield unbiased parameter estimates. To simplify matters, consider case II, in which $y_i = \beta x_i + \varepsilon_i$ and only x is measured with error (as $x^* = x + v$). The correct instrumental variables estimator of the regression slope in the two-variable model is as follows:

$$\beta^* = \frac{\sum y_i z_i}{\sum x_i^* z_i} \tag{5.8}$$

---

[2] This case is discussed in detail in J. Johnston, *Econometric Methods,* 2d ed. (New York: McGraw-Hill, 1972), chap. 6, and in other standard texts. Alternative estimation techniques are discussed in J. Kmenta, *Elements of Econometrics* (New York: Macmillan, 1971), chap. 9.

[3] For a discussion of several alternative estimation procedures, see J. Johnston, *op. cit.,* sec. 9-4.

[4] Technically speaking, we need to refer to the properties of estimators in the probability limit.

The choice of this particular form of estimator is made so that the resulting estimates will be consistent. To see this, we can derive the relationship between the instrumental variables estimator and the true slope parameter in a manner similar to the derivation in Eq. (5.1):

$$\beta^* = \frac{\sum y_i z_i}{\sum x_i^* z_i} = \frac{\beta \sum x_i^* z_i + \sum z_i \varepsilon_i^*}{\sum x_i^* z_i} = \beta + \frac{\sum z_i \varepsilon_i^*}{\sum x_i^* z_i} \tag{5.9}$$

Clearly, the choice of Z as an instrument guarantees that β^* will approach β as the sample size gets large (since $\sum z_i \varepsilon_i^*$ approaches 0), and will therefore be a consistent estimator of β. One might wonder why the variable x_i^* was not replaced by z_i in the denominator of the instrumental variables estimator. The reader should check using the above procedure that the estimator $\beta^{**} = \sum y_i z_i / \sum z_i^2$ does not yield a consistent estimate of β (see Exercise 5.3).

The technique of instrumental variables appears to provide a simple solution to a difficult problem. We have defined an estimation technique which is guaranteed to yield consistent estimates if we can find an appropriate instrument. However, this is likely to be a very difficult problem when errors of measurement are present. The obvious instrument to choose is the true variable, but this is not available or it would have been chosen in the first place. In practice one must search for a suitable *proxy variable* to replace the original. The proxy variable should be highly correlated with the original variable, and uncorrelated with the error in the equation (as the sample size gets large).

To complete this section, it will be useful to list some additional comments relevant to the problem of errors of measurement and to the technique of instrumental variables. First, the ordinary least-squares estimation technique is actually a special case of instrumental variables. This follows by definition, because in the classical regression model X is uncorrelated with the error term and because X is perfectly correlated with itself. Second, if we generalize the measurement error problem to errors in more than one independent variable, then one instrument is needed to "replace" *each* of the designated independent variables. The parameter estimates obtained are, of course, sensitive to the specific choice of instruments made. Finally, we should note that instrumental variables estimation guarantees consistent estimation, but it does not guarantee unbiased estimation. The loss of unbiasedness is not to be taken lightly. In time-series analysis, in particular, the existence of small samples limits the importance of the consistency criterion.

5.3   INTRODUCTION TO SIMULTANEOUS EQUATION MODELS

Quite frequently in business and economic modeling, the process or processes under study can best be represented by a series of simultaneous interdependent equations. The most common examples of such equations are supply-demand models, in which the price of a product is simultaneously determined by the interaction of producers and consumers in a market, and macroeconomic income determination models, in which aggregate consumption and aggregate disposable income are simultaneously determined. We shall use both these models to illustrate the fact that the ordinary least-squares estimation of individual equations in a simultaneous equation model can lead to biased and inconsistent parameter estimates. We shall then discuss in an elementary manner alternative single-equation estimation procedures which yield consistent parameter estimates. More advanced methods of estimating simultaneous equation systems and extensions of the techniques described here will be considered in Chapter 9.

From this point on we shall think of economic and business models as consisting of a series of equations, each equation serving to explain one variable which is determined in the model. For this reason, it will be useful to replace our former notions of independent and dependent variables with some new terminology. Consider a three-equation supply-demand model described as follows:

Supply: $\qquad\qquad Q_t^S = \alpha_1 + \alpha_2 P_t + \alpha_3 P_{t-1} + \varepsilon_t$

Demand: $\qquad\qquad Q_t^D = \beta_1 + \beta_2 P_t + \beta_3 Y_t + u_t \qquad\qquad$ (5.10)

Equilibrium: $\qquad\quad Q_t^D = Q_t^S$

The supply equation, demand equation, and equilibrium condition will determine the market price and the quantity supplied (and demanded) when the market is in equilibrium. For this reason, the variables Q_t^D, Q_t^S, and P_t are often called *endogenous* variables; they are determined within the system of equations. On the other hand, the model contains two variables whose values are not determined directly within the system. These so-called *predetermined variables* help to describe the movement of the endogenous variables within the system. P_{t-1} and Y_t are both predetermined variables in the model summarized in Eq. (5.10). There is, of course, an important difference between the two predetermined variables. The first variable P_{t-1} is in fact determined within the system, but by past values of the variables. Thus, *lagged endogenous* variables are predetermined variables.[5] Finally, the variable Y_t is completely determined outside the model system and is called an *exogenous* variable.

We wish to consider whether bias or inconsistency will be introduced if (for example) the supply equation is estimated using ordinary least squares. In order to simplify matters, we shall rewrite the original model, eliminating the

---

[5] In most of this chapter we shall consider all lagged endogenous variables as predetermined. This assumption is reasonable as long as there is no serial correlation associated with the error term in the equation containing the lagged endogenous equation. We discuss the specific problems associated with serial correlation and lagged endogenous variables in section 5.7. For a more detailed discussion of lags, see section 7.4.

lagged price term from the supply equation and substituting for the equilibrium values of Q_t^S and Q_t^D (represented as Q_t). The theoretically specified *structural model* is as follows:

Supply:
$$Q_t = \alpha_1 + \alpha_2 P_t + \varepsilon_t$$

Demand:
$$Q_t = \beta_1 + \beta_2 P_t + \beta_3 Y_t + u_t$$

(5.11)

To simplify our analysis, we will have occasion to use the model with all variables measured in deviations form, obtained by substituting $q_t = Q_t - \overline{Q}$ and $p_t = P_t - \overline{P}$ into (5.11):

Supply:
$$q_t = \alpha_2 p_t + \varepsilon_t$$

Demand:
$$q_t = \beta_2 p_t + \beta_3 y_t + u_t$$

(5.12)

Our study of the properties of the equation system and derivations which follow will be aided if we solve the equations in (5.12) for each of the endogenous variables as a function solely of the predetermined variables in the model. The so-called *reduced-form* solution is listed below, first in terms of the original variables (5.13) and second when the variables are measured as deviations about their means (5.14).[6]

$$Q_t = \frac{\alpha_2 \beta_1 - \alpha_1 \beta_2}{\alpha_2 - \beta_2} + \frac{\alpha_2 \beta_3}{\alpha_2 - \beta_2} Y_t + \frac{\alpha_2 u_t - \beta_2 \varepsilon_t}{\alpha_2 - \beta_2}$$

$$P_t = \frac{\beta_1 - \alpha_1}{\alpha_2 - \beta_2} + \frac{\beta_3}{\alpha_2 - \beta_2} Y_t + \frac{u_t - \varepsilon_t}{\alpha_2 - \beta_2}$$

(5.13)

$$q_t = \frac{\alpha_2 \beta_3}{\alpha_2 - \beta_2} y_t + \frac{\alpha_2 u_t - \beta_2 \varepsilon_t}{\alpha_2 - \beta_2} = \pi_{12} y_t + v_{1t}$$

$$p_t = \frac{\beta_3}{\alpha_2 - \beta_2} y_t + \frac{u_t - \varepsilon_t}{\alpha_2 - \beta_2} = \pi_{22} y_t + v_{2t}$$

(5.14)

The reader should note that using variables measured in deviations form eliminates the constant term in each of the reduced-form equations, but does not alter the other parameters in any way.

---

[6] To get the reduced form in the latter case, for example, we set the right-hand side of both equations in (5.12) equal; that is, $\alpha_2 p_t + \varepsilon_t = \beta_2 p_t + \beta_3 y_t + u_t$. Solving for p_t, we obtain the second equation in (5.14). Then substituting this equation into $q_t = \alpha_2 p_t + \varepsilon_t$ in (5.12), we get the first equation in (5.14).

Let us assume that we wish to estimate the supply equation in (5.12) using ordinary least squares. The slope parameter estimate would be

$$\hat{\alpha}_2 = \frac{\sum p_t q_t}{\sum p_t^2} \tag{5.15}$$

Substituting for q_t in equation system (5.12), we find that

$$\hat{\alpha}_2 = \frac{\sum p_t(\alpha_2 p_t + \varepsilon_t)}{\sum p_t^2} = \alpha_2 + \frac{\sum p_t \varepsilon_t}{\sum p_t^2} \tag{5.16}$$

If the summation $\sum p_t \varepsilon_t$ on the right-hand side equaled 0 on average, then we would know that ordinary least squares was unbiased. Likewise, if the sum approached 0 as the sample size became large, we would know that ordinary least-squares estimation was consistent. Unfortunately, however, neither of the above is true in general. In simultaneous equation models, where (endogenous) variables in one equation feed back into variables in another equation, the error terms are correlated with the endogenous variables and least squares is both biased and inconsistent. To see the existence of bias, we calculate the expected value of $\sum p_t \varepsilon_t$, while substituting for p_t in the reduced-form equation system (5.14):

$$E(\sum p_t \varepsilon_t) = \frac{\beta_3}{\alpha_2 - \beta_2} E(\sum y_t \varepsilon_t) + \frac{1}{\alpha_2 - \beta_2} E(\sum u_t \varepsilon_t) - \frac{1}{\alpha_2 - \beta_2} E(\sum \varepsilon_t^2)$$

$$= \frac{1}{\alpha_2 - \beta_2} E(\sum u_t \varepsilon_t) - \frac{1}{\alpha_2 - \beta_2} E(\sum \varepsilon_t^2) \qquad \text{since } y_t \text{ is exogenous}$$

$$= \frac{\text{Cov}(u_t, \varepsilon_t) - \text{Var}(\varepsilon_t)}{(\alpha_2 - \beta_2)} \tag{5.17}$$

The expression in Eq. (5.17) will equal 0 only when the errors from the two equations are uncorrelated and there is no error variance in the supply equation, or when the covariance and variance terms just happen to cancel out—both extremely unlikely occurrences. An analogous derivation would yield similar conclusions about the consistency properties of ordinary least squares.

In the case of the supply-demand model, it will not always be possible to predict the direction of bias resulting from the use of least-squares estimation. [The expression in (5.17) may be either positive or negative.] In using least squares to estimate an aggregate consumption function in a simple model of national income determination, however, the direction of bias is known. Written in deviations form, the structural model is as follows:

$$c_t = \beta y_t + \varepsilon_t$$

$$y_t = c_t + i_t + g_t$$

(5.18)

where c = aggregate consumption
i = investment
g = government spending
y = national income
β = the marginal propensity to consume $(0 < \beta < 1)$

i_t and g_t are exogenous variables, and c_t and y_t are endogenous.
  The reduced form of the model is

$$c_t = \frac{\beta}{1-\beta} i_t + \frac{\beta}{1-\beta} g_t + \frac{\varepsilon_t}{1-\beta}$$

(5.19)

$$y_t = \frac{1}{1-\beta} i_t + \frac{1}{1-\beta} g_t + \frac{\varepsilon_t}{1-\beta}$$

Thus, using ordinary least squares,

$$\hat{\beta} = \frac{\sum c_t y_t}{\sum y_t^2} \qquad \text{from Eq. (5.18)}$$

$$= \frac{\sum y_t(\beta y_t + \varepsilon_t)}{\sum y_t^2} = \beta + \frac{\sum y_t \varepsilon_t}{\sum y_t^2}$$

and

$$E(\sum y_t \varepsilon_t) = \frac{1}{1-\beta} [E(\sum i_t \varepsilon_t) + E(\sum g_t \varepsilon_t) + E(\sum \varepsilon_t^2)]$$

$$= \frac{1}{1-\beta} \text{Var}(\varepsilon_t)$$

Here, the direction of bias is clear. Ordinary least squares will overestimate the true value of the marginal propensity to consume.
  Before considering alternative estimation techniques which yield consistent parameter estimates, we should note that the reduced-form equations in (5.19) can be helpful if we wish to predict the long-run effects on C and Y of changes

in government spending and investment. For example, a change in $1 billion of exogenous government spending will lead, in the long run, to a change of $\beta/(1 - \beta)$ billion dollars in aggregate consumption and a change of $1/(1 - \beta)$ billion dollars in disposable income.

5.4 CONSISTENT PARAMETER ESTIMATION

Let us return to the supply-demand example of Eqs. (5.11) and (5.12) and concentrate on the consistent estimation of the *supply parameters*. For convenience, the structural and reduced-form equation systems are reproduced below:

Structural model:

Supply: $\qquad\qquad\qquad q_t = \alpha_2 \, p_t + \varepsilon_t$

$\hspace{9cm}$ (5.12)

Demand: $\qquad\qquad\quad q_t = \beta_2 \, p_t + \beta_3 \, y_t + u_t$

Reduced-form model:

$$q_t = \pi_{12} \, y_t + v_{1t}$$

$\hspace{9cm}$ (5.14)

$$p_t = \pi_{22} \, y_t + v_{2t}$$

The discussion in section 5.2 suggests one approach to the estimation problem— that of instrumental variables. In fact, instrumental variables estimation is quite reasonable in the context of simultaneous equation models, because the predetermined variables in the model serve as excellent instrumental variables. The fact that they are present in the model suggests that they are correlated with the endogenous variables, and the fact that they are predetermined guarantees (by assumption) that they are uncorrelated with the error term. In the supply-demand example the variable y_t would serve as a suitable instrument, yielding the following consistent estimate of the supply slope parameter:

$$\hat{\alpha}_2^* = \frac{\sum y_t \, q_t}{\sum p_t \, y_t}$$

As a rule, the selection of instruments need not be limited to the variables in the model, but such a limitation serves to simplify and regularize the search process.

While the use of instrumental variables is a perfectly appropriate estimation process, we are often faced with the problem of choosing among several available instruments. The choice among available instruments is often arbitrary and such a choice will affect the results of the estimation process. For this reason, we shall examine some alternative single-equation estimation techniques, each implicitly involving different assumptions about instrument choice. As a first step, consider the reduced-form equation system of Eq. (5.14). Since the reduced-form equations contain only exogenous variables on the right-hand side, it is clear that ordinary least squares will estimate the reduced form consistently and with lack of bias. Let us examine these estimated coefficients, $\hat{\pi}_{12}$ and $\hat{\pi}_{22}$, more closely. Notice that π_{12}/π_{22} is identically equal to α_2. This suggests that we can estimate α_2 consistently by solving for the reduced-form equations, estimating them using ordinary least-squares, and then solving to get the estimates of the supply slope parameter, that is, $\hat{\alpha}_2^{**} = \hat{\pi}_{12}/\hat{\pi}_{22}$. In fact, such a procedure is quite legitimate for the supply-demand model and is called *indirect least-squares* estimation. The indirect least-squares estimation process can be used to obtain consistent parameter estimates.[7]

When indirect least-squares estimation is possible and a unique estimate of the structural parameter is available, it is not difficult to show that indirect least-squares estimation is *identical* to instrumental variables estimation with y_t being chosen as the instrument. To see this, substitute for $\hat{\pi}_{12}/\hat{\pi}_{22}$, using our knowledge about ordinary least-squares estimation:

$$\hat{\alpha}_2^{**} = \frac{\hat{\pi}_{12}}{\hat{\pi}_{22}} = \frac{\sum y_t q_t / \sum y_t^2}{\sum p_t y_t / \sum y_t^2}$$

$$= \frac{\sum y_t q_t}{\sum p_t y_t} = \hat{\alpha}_2^*$$

Unfortunately, the example above cannot be generalized. In some cases indirect least squares is not possible, and in other cases it leads to several distinct slope estimates. Consider first the same supply-demand example, but assume that we wish to estimate the slope parameter of the *demand equation*. This would mean using the estimated parameters of the reduced form to obtain an estimate of the parameter β_2. But a brief glance at equation system (5.14) will show that this is impossible; there is no way that the structural parameter can be obtained through estimation of the reduced-form system.[8] On the other hand, consider the supply-demand system when the demand equation has been modified to include a second exogenous variable W for wealth. The structural equations and reduced-form equations are listed below, with all variables measured in deviations form:

Structural model:

$$q_t = \alpha_2 p_t + \varepsilon_t$$

$$q_t = \beta_2 p_t + \beta_3 y_t + \beta_4 w_t + u_t \tag{5.20}$$

---

[7] We cannot prove that indirect least-squares estimates are unbiased. The possible bias is introduced when the ratio of the two unbiased reduced-form estimated parameters is taken.

[8] The problem of structural equation estimation is an important one. We will consider it in greater detail in the next section and in Chapter 9.

Reduced-form model:

$$q_t = \frac{\alpha_2 \beta_3}{\alpha_2 - \beta_2} y_t + \frac{\alpha_2 \beta_4}{\alpha_2 - \beta_2} w_t + \frac{\alpha_2 u_t - \beta_2 \varepsilon_t}{\alpha_2 - \beta_2}$$

$$= \pi_{12} y_t + \pi_{13} w_t + v_{1t}$$

$$p_t = \frac{\beta_3}{\alpha_2 - \beta_2} y_t + \frac{\beta_4}{\alpha_2 - \beta_2} w_t + \frac{u_t - \varepsilon_t}{\alpha_2 - \beta_2}$$

$$= \pi_{22} y_t + \pi_{23} w_t + v_{2t}$$

(5.21)

Once again, the reduced-form equations can be consistently estimated using ordinary least squares. However, we are faced with two choices of supply slope estimators when we attempt to use the indirect least-squares technique. The two estimators are $\hat{\pi}_{12}/\hat{\pi}_{22}$ (as before) and $\hat{\pi}_{13}/\hat{\pi}_{23}$. In general, both estimators will yield consistent estimates of the true parameter, but the estimates will not be identical in each sample. Thus, if we attempt to utilize indirect least squares, we are faced with two choices, either one of which may involve a loss of important information about the model being estimated.

We have seen that indirect least squares is impossible in some cases, yields a unique solution in other cases, and yields a surfeit of possible solutions in still a third case. Each of these three cases is important in its own right. To distinguish conceptually among each of the three cases, we shall pause to consider an important set of problems that arise when one is originally specifying the model to be studied.

5.5 THE IDENTIFICATION PROBLEM[9]

We have just seen that knowledge of the reduced form of a system of equations is not always sufficient to allow us to discern the value of the parameters in the original set of structural equations. The problem of whether we can determine the structural equations, given knowledge of the reduced form, is called the *identification problem*. However, we should note that knowledge of the structural parameters is not absolutely necessary if prediction or forecasting is our primary purpose, because forecasts can be obtained through the reduced-form equations directly.

The consideration of the identification problem comes prior to the consideration of the estimation problem. Once a structural model has been specified, we must check immediately to see whether the equation or equations of interest are identified, i.e., whether we can obtain knowledge of the structural parameters

---

[9] A more extensive discussion of the identification problem appears in section 9.2.

once the reduced form has been estimated. After the identification problem has been explicitly considered, we may then proceed to choose among alternative estimation techniques. As hinted in the previous section, the choice of estimation technique may be quite important in situations in which there is more than one way to estimate the structural parameters, given knowledge of the reduced form.

We shall say that an equation is *unidentified* if there is no way of estimating all the structural parameters from the reduced form. An equation is *identified* if it is possible to obtain values of the parameters from the reduced-form equation system. An equation is *exactly identified* if a unique parameter value exists, and *overidentified* if more than one value is obtainable for some parameters. While we have concentrated on the identification of single equations in a structural system of equations, it is important to realize that within a given structural model, some equations may be identified while others may not. In fact, within a single equation, it is possible that some parameters may be identified, while others may remain unidentified.

Let us continue with our discussion of the identification problem on a more practical level by considering the supply-demand models described previously. Consider first a supply-demand model in which there are no predetermined variables:

Supply: $$Q_t = \alpha_1 + \alpha_2 P_t + \varepsilon_t$$

(5.22)

Demand: $$Q_t = \beta_1 + \beta_2 P_t + u_t$$

We assume that the market is in equilibrium in each time period (we have already eliminated the equilibrium condition by substitution). The key to understanding the identification problem in the context of this model is to focus on the equilibrium condition. At each period of time, there is one value of the price P and one value for the quantity sold Q. In other words, the only data available to the econometrician are the market values (for each period of time) of P and Q. The errors in the equations will make it likely that the values of P and Q obtained will not be identical, but it is likely that all values will lie close to the equilibrium values of P and Q determined by the direct solution of the equations in the model. This situation is depicted in Fig. 5.2. When we try to estimate the separate supply and demand equations using the market data, we obtain meaningless results. There is no way to ascertain the true supply and demand slopes given only the equilibrium data. In fact, the only reason why estimation is possible is because errors appear in both equations.[10]

The model we are describing is one in which both the supply curve and the demand curve are unidentified. Neither equation is identified, because there is no way to obtain the values of the structural parameters (the slopes and

---

[10] For this reason, we expect to obtain low t statistics when estimating unidentified equations.

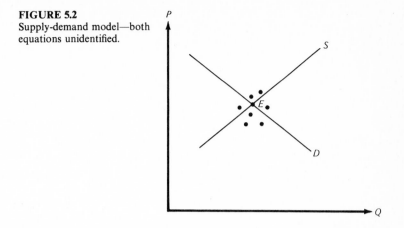

FIGURE 5.2
Supply-demand model—both
equations unidentified.

intercepts of the individual supply and demand curves) from the reduced-form equations. (The reader should check to see that the reduced form is simply the equation describing the point of intersection of the demand and supply curves with errors attached.) It should be apparent from examination of Fig. 5.2 that any pair of demand and supply curves intersecting at point E could just as easily have been the "true" demand and supply curves. In other words, there are an infinite number of structural models (demand and supply curves) which are consistent with the same reduced form (equilibrium value of P and Q). We stress that the problem here does not involve a lack of data. One could have an infinite number of data points for econometric analysis, but the best one could do would be to estimate the equilibrium values of P and Q with great accuracy—the demand and supply curves would still be unidentified.

It should be apparent that identification of equations in a model system necessitates further information of one sort or another. Consider, for example, the supply-demand system of Eq. (5.11) (reproduced here, for convenience):

Supply: $\qquad\qquad\qquad Q_t = \alpha_1 + \alpha_2 P_t + \varepsilon_t$

$\qquad\qquad\qquad\qquad\qquad\qquad\qquad\qquad\qquad\qquad\qquad\qquad$ (5.23)

Demand: $\qquad\qquad\qquad Q_t = \beta_1 + \beta_2 P_t + \beta_3 Y_t + u_t$

Under the assumption that $\beta_3 \neq 0$ and that Y_t does vary substantially over time, we cannot plot one demand curve and one supply curve for all time periods. Because income determines demand and income varies over time, we must account for the fact that the demand curve shifts over time. This situation is depicted in Fig. 5.3.

For each point in time, we obtain a set of values for P and Q, each of which describes the equilibrium (or an approximation thereof) of supply and demand. Because the demand curve shifts over time, the equilibrium values of P and Q also shift over time. It should be clear from Fig. 5.3 that the equilibrium values trace out the path of the underlying supply curve. Thus, the supply curve is

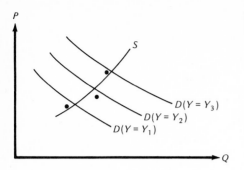

FIGURE 5.3
Supply curve identified.

identified (because the supply parameters can be deduced from the reduced form (the movement of the equilibrium of P and Q). Notice that it is the movement of Y over time that is necessary for the identification of the supply equation. The extent to which Y does move will have an effect on the confidence with which we can estimate the supply curve, but it is simply movement of Y that is important for purposes of identification.

We reiterate that identification is made possible by the existence of prior information about the exogenous variable Y. The supply equation is identified because the exogenous variable Y was excluded from the supply equation; i.e., the coefficient of Y in the supply equation was assumed to be 0. The demand equation is unidentified because prior information is not available which allows for the unique determination of the demand relationship. Were we to consider a model in which the supply relationship is determined by the temperature T in the region and the demand curve is not, then the prior information about the excluded exogenous variable (temperature) in the demand equation would allow the demand curve to be identified.

It is, of course, possible for both the demand and the supply curve to be identified. The following supply-demand model has just this property:

Supply: $Q_t = \alpha_1 + \alpha_2 P_t + \alpha_3 T_t + \varepsilon_t$

Demand: $Q_t = \beta_1 + \beta_2 P_t + \beta_3 Y_t + u_t$

$$(5.24)$$

In this case, it is not easy to depict the supply-demand relationship graphically. It should be clear, however, that if T and Y vary over time (and are not perfectly correlated), then both the demand and supply relationships will shift. The movement of the equilibrium values of P and Q is quite complex, since it results from temperature and income changes, but if sufficient data are available, we can determine the structural values of the demand and supply parameters uniquely. The shifting of the supply curve associated with changes in T helps to plot out the demand curve at the same time that shifts in

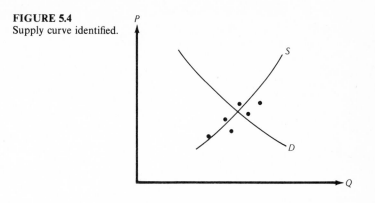

FIGURE 5.4
Supply curve identified.

demand (changes in Y) plot out the supply curve. To reiterate, it is the prior (to estimation) knowledge that certain exogenous variables (known to appear in the structural system) are excluded from individual equations within that system that allows the equations to be identified.

While prior knowledge of the excluded variables in an equation is the most common type of information which allows for identification, it is not the only kind possible. To be more complete, we shall list some examples of the other kinds of prior knowledge which might be sufficient to allow for the identification of the parameters of the supply equation, as in the model of Eq. (5.22):

1 If the slope of the supply curve were known *a priori*, then it would be easy to determine the supply intercept by choosing the straight line with the given slope which best fits the points in Fig. 5.2.
2 If the errors associated with the supply curve are zero (or close to zero relative to demand), then the supply curve can be identified. The (relatively) large variances associated with the demand curve cause the equilibria to shift over time and the supply curve is then traced out. This situation is depicted in Fig. 5.4.

As a final model, reconsider Eq. (5.20), in which the demand curve is a function not only of income, but also of wealth (the two are assumed not to be highly correlated). In this case the demand curve shifts over time due to changes in two variables. The supply equation is overidentified because there are two exogenous variables in the supply-demand system of equations which are excluded from the supply equation.

Our discussion has implicitly involved a search for conditions which are necessary to guarantee the identification of one equation in a two-equation system. The conditions for identification can be generalized in two directions, the first involving a search for necessary and sufficient conditions for identification and the second involving problems which arise when a more complex system is studied. We shall deal in some detail with both these issues when the identification problem is reconsidered in Chapter 9.

5.6 TWO-STAGE LEAST SQUARES

Two-stage least squares (2SLS) provides a very useful estimation procedure for obtaining the values of structural parameters in overidentified equations. Two-stage least-squares estimation utilizes the information available from the specification of an equation system to obtain a unique estimate for each structural parameter. Intuitively speaking, the first stage of 2SLS involves the creation of an instrument, while the second stage involves a variant of instrumental variables estimation. We describe very briefly the workings of two-stage least squares and outline some of its properties.[11]

Consider the supply-demand model described in Eq. (5.20). The structural model and the resulting reduced form are listed as follows (note that we are using deviations form, so that intercepts do not appear explicitly).

Structural model:

Supply: $q_t = \alpha_2 p_t + \varepsilon_t$

(5.25)

Demand: $q_t = \beta_2 p_t + \beta_3 y_t + \beta_4 w_t + u_t$

Reduced form:

$$q_t = \pi_{12} y_t + \pi_{13} w_t + v_{1t}$$

(5.26)

$$p_t = \pi_{22} y_t + \pi_{23} w_t + v_{2t}$$

The supply equation is clearly overidentified, so that neither indirect least squares nor instrumental variables (as described previously) would yield unique parameter estimates. The two-stage least-squares procedure works as follows:

1 In the first stage, the reduced-form equation for p_t is estimated using ordinary least squares. In general, this is accomplished by regressing p_t on all the predetermined variables in the equation system. From the first-stage regression, the fitted values of the dependent variable, $\hat{p}_t$, are determined.[12] The fitted values, $\hat{p}_t$, will by construction be independent of the error terms e_t and u_t (strictly speaking, this independence holds only in large samples, so that we are forced to rely on the consistency property of 2SLS). Thus, the first-stage process allows us to construct a variable which is linearly related to the predetermined model variables (through least-squares estimation) and which is purged of any correlation with the error term in the supply equation. It seems reasonable to view this newly created variable as an instrument to be used in the standard instrumental

---

[11] Two-stage least squares is described in more detail in section 9.3.

[12] From (5.26), $\hat{p}_t = \hat{\pi}_{22} y_t + \hat{\pi}_{23} w_t$, where $\hat{\pi}_{22}$ and $\hat{\pi}_{23}$ are the ordinary least-squares parameter estimates.

variables estimation procedure.[13] In order to obtain more useful results, from a computational point of view, we shall proceed with the second stage of the estimation procedure in a slightly different manner.

2 In the second-stage regression, the supply equation of the structural model is estimated by replacing the variable p_t with the first-stage fitted variable $\hat{p}_t$. The use of ordinary least squares in this second stage will yield a consistent estimate of the supply parameter α_2. If additional predetermined variables appeared in the supply equation, two-stage least squares would also estimate those parameters consistently.

The two-stage least-squares procedure is quite easy to utilize and is frequently employed when overidentified equations are present. By construction, 2SLS eliminates the problem of an oversupply of instruments by using combinations of the predetermined variables to create a new instrument. When an equation is exactly identified, two-stage least-squares estimation is identical to indirect least-squares and instrumental variables estimation. To see this, reexamine the model depicted in Eqs. (5.12) and (5.14). The two-stage least-squares estimation would proceed as follows:

1 Use OLS to estimate the second part of Eq. (5.14). Then calculate the fitted values:

$$\hat{p}_t = \hat{\pi}^*_{22} y_t \qquad \text{when} \quad \hat{\pi}^*_{22} = \frac{\sum p_t y_t}{\sum y_t^2}$$

2 Use OLS to estimate the equation

$$q_t = \alpha_2 \hat{p}_t + \varepsilon_t$$

Then,
$$\hat{\alpha}^{***}_2 = \frac{\sum \hat{p}_t q_t}{\sum \hat{p}_t^2} = \frac{\sum y_t q_t (\sum p_t y_t / \sum y_t^2)}{\sum y_t^2 (\sum p_t y_t / \sum y_t^2)^2}$$

$$= \frac{\sum y_t q_t}{\sum p_t y_t} = \begin{cases} \hat{\alpha}^{**}_2 & \text{using indirect least squares} \\ \hat{\alpha}^{*}_2 & \text{using instrumental variables} \end{cases}$$

Thus, identical parameter estimates will be obtained *if the equation is exactly identified* when two-stage least-squares, indirect least-squares, and instrumental variables estimation techniques are used. In the overidentified case we have seen that the indirect least-squares procedure is no longer valid. However, it is still possible to show that 2SLS and instrumental variables are equivalent

---

[13] It is possible to prove that two-stage least squares is an instrumental variables estimator, whether the equation to be estimated is exactly identified or overidentified. For a proof, see, for example, J. Johnston, *Econometric Methods*, 2d ed. (New York: McGraw-Hill, 1972), sec. 13-2.

estimation procedures on the condition that the first stage of two-stage least squares involves all predetermined variables in the system, and on the condition that the instrument used in the instrumental variables procedure is the fitted value of the first-stage regression, i.e., the regression of the variable correlated with the error term on all predetermined variables in the system.

What happens to 2SLS when the supply equation is not identified, e.g., when the variables y and w appear in the equation? The answer is that 2SLS is impossible when the equation is unidentified. This is quite easy to visualize if one recalls that the fitted-value variable used in the second-stage regression is a weighted average (or linear combination) of the predetermined variables in the system. If the supply equation is unidentified, then no excluded variables exist in that equation. In our example this means that the supply equation includes the variables y and w. When one attempts to regress q_t on $\hat{p}_t$, y_t, and w_t in the second stage, the perfect collinearity between the three regressors will make estimation impossible.

5.7 SERIAL CORRELATION IN THE PRESENCE OF LAGGED DEPENDENT VARIABLES

We have noted in the introduction to this chapter and in section 5.3 that simultaneous equation estimation becomes substantially more difficult when predetermined variables include lagged dependent variables and at the same time the error term is serially correlated. In fact, when serial correlation is present, the notion that lagged endogenous variables are predetermined loses its validity. To see this, consider the simplest possible example of a one-equation model with serially correlated errors. The model is

$$y_t = \beta y_{t-1} + \varepsilon_t \qquad \text{with } \varepsilon_t = \rho \varepsilon_{t-1} + v_t \qquad (5.27)$$

In general, were ordinary least squares used to estimate the slope parameter, inconsistent and biased results would be obtained. Recall that

$$\hat{\beta} = \frac{\sum y_t y_{t-1}}{\sum y_{t-1}^2} = \beta + \frac{\sum y_{t-1} \varepsilon_t}{\sum y_{t-1}^2} = \beta + \frac{\text{Cov}(y_{t-1}, \varepsilon_t)}{\text{Var}(y_{t-1})}$$

But the covariance of y_{t-1} and ε_t is nonzero, since

$$\text{Cov}(y_{t-1}, \varepsilon_t) = E(y_{t-1}\varepsilon_t)$$

$$= E(\beta y_{t-2} + \varepsilon_{t-1})(\rho \varepsilon_{t-1} + v_t)$$

$$= \beta \rho E(\varepsilon_{t-1} y_{t-2}) + \rho E(\varepsilon_{t-1}^2) + \beta E(v_t y_{t-2}) + E(\varepsilon_{t-1} v_t)$$

$$= \beta \rho E(\varepsilon_{t-1} y_{t-2}) + \rho E(\varepsilon_{t-1}^2)$$

But $\qquad E(\varepsilon_{t-1}^2) = E(\varepsilon_t^2) \qquad$ and $\qquad E(\varepsilon_{t-1} y_{t-2}) = E(\varepsilon_t y_{t-1})$

Therefore, $\qquad\qquad E(y_{t-1}\varepsilon_t) = \beta\rho E(y_{t-1}\varepsilon_t) + \rho E(\varepsilon_t^2)$

or $\qquad\qquad\qquad$ Cov $(y_{t-1}, \varepsilon_t) = \dfrac{\rho \text{ Var } (\varepsilon_t)}{1 - \rho\beta}$ $\qquad\qquad$ (5.28)

This covariance will be 0 only when ρ is 0, that is, when there is no serial correlation in the model. Thus, the presence of serial correlation and lagged dependent variables is sufficient to render the ordinary least-squares estimation process biased and inconsistent. Intuitively speaking, the presence of serial correlation and a lagged dependent variable poses a parameter identification problem for the econometrician. If ordinary least squares is used to estimate Eq. (5.27), it will be impossible to tell to what extent the parameter estimate reflects the presence of a nonzero slope and to what extent there is serial correlation in the model.

Correct procedures for the estimation of single-equation models with serially correlated errors and a lagged dependent variable do exist. In general they involve the use of modified instrumental variables or maximum-likelihood techniques.[14] In addition, procedures for simultaneous equation estimation must also be revised when serial correlation and lagged dependent variables exist. In particular, two-stage least-squares estimation must be modified somewhat if consistent parameter estimates are to be obtained.[15]

5.8 EXAMPLES

Example 5.1 Retail Auto Sales

In an attempt to forecast retail auto sales, the following model was specified:

$$A = \beta_1 + \beta_2 W + \beta_3 D + \beta_4 I + \varepsilon$$

where A = retail auto sales, millions of dollars
$\qquad W$ = spendable average weekly earnings
$\qquad D$ = retail sales of durable goods stores, millions of dollars
$\qquad I$ = open market rate of finance company paper placed directly

---

[14] The interested reader should see J. Johnston, *ibid.*, pp. 316–320.
[15] A useful procedure is described by R. C. Fair in "The Estimation of Simultaneous Equation Models with Lagged Endogenous Variables and First Order Serially Correlated Errors," *Econometrica*, May 1970.

One would expect that the coefficients of W and D would be positive, while the coefficient of I would be negative. The ordinary least-squares results are as follows (t statistics in parentheses):

$$A = 502.8 \quad - 15.4W \quad + .73D \quad - 18.3I$$
$$(1.4) \qquad (-2.2) \qquad (19.6) \qquad (-.8)$$

$$R^2 = .97 \quad DW = .80 \quad F = 994 \quad s = 84.5$$

Note that although the R^2 is high, the regression results are questionable. The coefficient of W is negative and significant at the 5 percent level, implying that higher wages are associated with lower sales. The coefficient of I is not significant. In addition, the Durbin-Watson statistic is rather low, implying that serial correlation may be a problem. It is also suspected that the variable D is correlated with the error term. Assuming that the model is correctly specified, the use of two-stage least squares will be appropriate.

The instruments for the first stage of the two-stage process were chosen on the basis of a larger model of auto sales not explicitly described here. The instruments chosen were:

GAS = retail sales of gasoline
 AP = retail sales of apparel
LIQ = retail liquor sales
 FD = retail food sales
DEP = retail department store sales

The results of the first-stage regression are as follows:

$$D = 2519.4 \quad + 1.59DEP \quad - 5.23LIQ \quad + 3.06GAS \quad - .41FD \quad + 9.95AP$$
$$(2.1) \qquad (2.1) \qquad (-1.7) \qquad (2.1) \qquad (-1.1) \qquad (1.0)$$

$$R^2 = .93 \quad DW = 1.15 \quad F = 200 \quad s = 237.7$$

The second stage involved regressing A on I, W, and the fitted values of the first stage of the two-stage procedure (FIT). The second-stage output is as follows:

$$A = -2352.3 \quad + 49.4W \quad + .36FIT \quad - 140.9I$$
$$(-2.6) \qquad (2.6) \qquad (2.9) \qquad (-2.7)$$

$$R^2 = .86 \quad DW = 1.12 \quad F = 154.6 \quad s = 201.8$$

Notice that the results of the two-stage procedure are more meaningful. All the t statistics show high statistical significance, and all the coefficients have the proper signs. The R^2 for the second stage of the two-stage process is lower than the R^2 associated with the ordinary least-squares procedure. This will generally be the case, because the R^2 usually printed by the computer is the R^2

associated solely with the second-stage regression. Another useful measure would be calculated by evaluating the residuals when the estimated coefficients and the original values of A are included in the equation.

Example 5.2 Nondurable Goods Consumption

Assume that as a part of the task of building a large econometric model, one is interested in estimating a single equation in which the dependent variable is the aggregate quarterly expenditures of individuals on nondurable consumption items. A reasonable first choice for a single-equation regression model would be as follows:

$$CN_t = \beta_1 + \beta_2\,YD_t + \beta_3\left(\frac{PCN}{PC}\right)_t + \beta_4\,CN_{t-1} + \varepsilon_t$$

where CN = personal consumption expenditures on nondurable goods in billions
of 1958 dollars (data run quarterly from 1954-1 to 1971-4)
YD = disposable personal income, billions of 1958 dollars
PCN/PC = ratio of the Consumer Price Index for nondurable consumption items to the Consumer Price Index for all items (1957–1959 = 100)

We would expect the coefficients of the YD term and the CN term lagged one period both to be positive and the coefficient of the relative price term to be negative, the latter as a result of the shift into durable consumption likely to follow an increase in the relative price of nondurables. When ordinary least squares was used, the following regression results were obtained:

$$CN_t = 85.49 \quad + .127YD_t \quad -66.7\left(\frac{PCN}{PC}\right)_t + .58CN_{t-1}$$
$$\quad\ (3.9) \qquad\quad (4.8) \qquad\quad (-3.5) \qquad\qquad (6.6)$$

$$R^2 = .998 \quad\quad s = 1.2 \quad\quad DW = 2.03$$

While the results appear quite reasonable, given prior expectations, the nature of the larger econometric model suggests that ordinary least-squares estimation is not appropriate. In particular, the fact that disposable income is determined (in a separate equation) in part by nondurable consumption (one component of disposable income) suggests that simultaneous equation bias may exist. For this reason either two-stage least-squares or instrumental variables estimation ought to be utilized. For pedagogical reasons we shall present the results associated with both estimation techniques.

In the first stage of the two-stage least-squares estimation process, the explanatory variables were obtained by selection from among the right-hand variables appearing in the reduced form of the model system. When large econometric models are estimated, it is frequently impossible to use all reduced-form explanatory variables in the first-stage regression. For purposes of simplicity we have arbitrarily selected a few.[16] The first-stage regression contained YD_t on the left-hand side and YD_{t-1}, CN_{t-1}, and CD_{t-1}, durable goods consumption lagged, on the right-hand side. The results of the first-stage regression will not be printed here in order to save space. The first-stage results are important for our purposes only because they allow us to calculate fitted (or predicted) values for the variable YD. The results of the second-stage regression using those fitted values are as follows:

$$CN_t = 76.07 \quad + .110\hat{Y}D_t \quad - 59.59 \left(\frac{PCN}{PC}\right)_t \quad + .637CN_{t-1}$$
$$ (2.9) \qquad\quad (3.2) \qquad\quad (-2.7) \qquad\qquad\qquad (5.6)$$

$$R^2 = .998 \qquad s = 1.3 \qquad DW = 1.95$$

The results are identical in coefficient sign to the earlier least-squares results, although they differ slightly in terms of order of magnitude.

For purposes of comparison, the instrumental variables estimation technique was used with two different choices of instruments. In the first case, the variable YD_{t-1}, disposable income lagged one quarter, was used as an instrument to replace YD_t. YD lagged should be a good instrument in terms of correlation with YD, but it may be less than desirable if serial correlation is present in the model. In any case, the instrumental variables estimation results are as follows:

$$CN_t = 74.15 \quad + .107YD_t \quad - 58.15 \left(\frac{PCN}{PC}\right)_t \quad + .648CN_{t-1}$$
$$ (3.1) \qquad\quad (3.4) \qquad\quad (-2.8) \qquad\qquad\qquad (6.2)$$

$$R^2 = .998 \qquad s = 1.2 \qquad DW = 2.15$$

The results are quite similar to those obtained by the two-stage least-squares technique, an encouraging result since the choice between instrumental variables and two-stage least squares is often an arbitrary one.

In the second instrumental variables case, the instrument chosen was the set of fitted values obtained from the first stage of the two-stage least-squares results described earlier. The results are as follows:

$$CN_t = 76.07 \quad + .110YD_t \quad - 59.59 \left(\frac{PCN}{PC}\right)_t \quad + .637CN_{t-1}$$
$$ (3.26) \qquad\quad (3.5) \qquad\quad (-2.9) \qquad\qquad\qquad (6.1)$$

$$R^2 = .998 \qquad s = 1.2 \qquad DW = 2.13$$

[16] For a more sophisticated method of variable selection see F. M. Fisher, "Dynamic Structure and Estimation in Economy-wide Econometric Models," in Duesenberry, Fromm, Klein, and Kuh (eds.), *The Brookings Quarterly Econometric Model of the U.S.* (Chicago: Rand McNally, 1965), chap. 15.

Notice that the instrumental variables coefficient estimates are identical to the two-stage least-squares estimates obtained earlier. The two will be identical in the sample as long as all the right-hand exogenous variables in the original equation are among the variables chosen for inclusion in the process of instrument construction, i.e., the first-stage regression. The statistics associated with the parameter estimates are not identical, but this is due to the fact that the 2SLS program prints the outcome of the second-stage regression, while the instrumental variables estimation output uses the parameter estimates and the *original variables* in the calculation of regression residual variance and R^2.

Exercises

5.1 Explain briefly why measurement error in the right-hand variables leads to inconsistent and biased parameter estimates while measurement error in the left-hand variable does not.

5.2 Consider the two-variable regression model. Assume that both variables are measured with error and that the errors of measurement are positively correlated.

(1) Derive (as in the text) the relationship between the ordinary least-squares slope estimate and the true slope parameter.
(2) Can you show in what direction the least-squares estimator will be biased?

5.3 Show in the two-variable model that $\hat{\beta} = \sum y_i z_i / \sum z_i^2$ (where z is an instrument) will not yield a consistent estimate of the true slope parameter. Are there any conditions under which the instrumental variables estimator described will yield a consistent estimate of β?

5.4 Consider the following model (where all errors are uncorrelated over time and homoscedastic):

$$C_t = \alpha_1 + \alpha_2 Y_t + \varepsilon_t$$

$$I_t = \beta_1 + \beta_2 Y_t + \beta_3 Y_{t-1} + u_t$$

$$Y_t = C_t + I_t + G_t$$

(1) Construct the reduced-form system of the model. From the reduced form determine the long-run response of C to a one-unit change in G.
(2) Is the consumption function equation identified? Is it overidentified?
(3) Is the investment equation identified? Overidentified?
(4) What would happen to your estimated marginal propensity to consume if it has been estimated by using ordinary least squares on an equation of the form $C_t = a + b Y_t + \varepsilon_t$?

5.5 Consider the following supply-demand model:

$$Q_t^S = \alpha_1 + \alpha_2 P_t + \varepsilon_t$$

$$Q_t^D = \beta_1 + \beta_2 P_t + \beta_3 Y_t + \beta_4 P_{t-1} + u_t$$

$$Q_t^D = Q_t^S$$

where the ε_t's and u_t's are uncorrelated over time.

(1) Is the supply equation identified? What would happen if the supply equation were estimated using ordinary least squares?
(2) Is the demand equation identified? What would happen if the demand equation were estimated using ordinary least squares?
(3) If you were told to estimate the supply equation using instrumental variables, what would you do? Be explicit.
(4) If you were told to estimate the supply equation using two-stage least squares, what would you do? How does this relate to (3)?
(5) Could you use indirect least squares to estimate the demand equation? Why or why not?
(6) Would your results be different if you knew that ε was autocorrelated?

5.6 Consider the following two-equation model system:

$$Y_1 = a_1 Y_2 + a_2 Z_1 + u_1$$

$$Y_2 = b_1 Y_1 + b_2 Z_2 + u_2$$

(1) Under what conditions will ordinary least-squares estimation of the first equation lead to consistent parameter estimates? (*Hint*: There are two conditions, one relating to parameter values and the other to error variances and covariances.)
(2) Under what assumptions is the first equation identified? (*Hint*: There are two conditions once again, the first relating to parameter values and the second to error covariances.)

5.7 Consider the following two-equation model system:

$$Y_1 = a_1 + a_2 Y_2 + u_1$$

$$Y_2 = b_1 + b_2 Y_1 + b_3 Z_1 + b_4 Z_2 + u_2$$

Assess the following approaches to the estimation of the first equation in terms of possible bias, inconsistency, and efficiency. Which of the estimators are instrumental variables estimators? How does the last estimation process relate to the previous three?

a. Ordinary least-squares estimation of the first equation.
b. Indirect least-squares estimation of the first equation.
c. Instrumental variables estimation using Z_1 as an instrument in the first equation.
d. Two-stage least-squares estimation of the first equation.
e. Estimating the first equation as follows: $Y_1 = c_1 + c_2 Z_1 + c_3 Z_2$.

APPENDIX 5 / INSTRUMENTAL VARIABLES ESTIMATION IN MATRIX FORM

The technique of instrumental variables can be used to obtain consistent estimates of β when the right-hand variables are known to be correlated with the error term as a result of errors in variables or simultaneous equations bias. If our original model is

$$Y = X\beta + \varepsilon \tag{A5.1}$$

the correlation of one or more X's and the error term ε is summarized as follows:

$$\text{plim}\left(\frac{1}{N}X'\varepsilon\right) \neq 0 \tag{A5.2}$$

The expression "plim" refers to the probability limit as defined in Appendix 2.1. To see the difficulty which arises when (A5.2) holds, premultiply Eq. (A5.1) by the matrix X' to obtain

$$X'Y = X'X\beta + X'\varepsilon$$

If plim $((1/N)X'\varepsilon) = 0$, then the last term goes to 0 in the probability limit and

$$\hat{\beta} = (X'X)^{-1}X'Y \tag{A5.3}$$

is a consistent estimate of β. However, when the probability limit is nonzero, ordinary least-squares estimation becomes inconsistent.

Consistent estimates of β can be obtained through the use of an $N \times k$ matrix of instruments $\mathbf{Z} = (\mathbf{Z}_1, \mathbf{Z}_2, \ldots, \mathbf{Z}_k)$, where each instrument $\mathbf{Z}_i$ has N observations. $\mathbf{Z}$ satisfies the conditions necessary to be labeled a matrix of instruments if the following conditions hold:

i $\operatorname{plim}\left(\dfrac{1}{N} \mathbf{Z}'\varepsilon\right) = \mathbf{0}.$ $\hspace{4cm}$ (A5.4)

ii $\operatorname{plim}\left(\dfrac{1}{N} \mathbf{Z}'\mathbf{X}\right) = \Sigma$ exists and is nonsingular (has an inverse). $\hspace{1cm}$ (A5.5)

iii $\operatorname{plim}\left(\dfrac{1}{N} \mathbf{Z}'\mathbf{Z}\right) = \Sigma^*$ exists and is nonsingular. $\hspace{2.5cm}$ (A5.6)

The first condition guarantees that each instrument is uncorrelated with the error term, while the second guarantees a nonzero correlation among the Z's and the X's as well as the fact that all the Z's must be linearly independent. There is no reason that some of the original X's cannot be used as instruments in the instrumental variables estimation process. In our notation, for example, the first X variable will be appropriate as an instrument, since it is a vector of constants and is uncorrelated with the error term.

Given the appropriate instruments, we premultiply Eq. (A5.1) by $\mathbf{Z}'$ to get

$$\mathbf{Z}'\mathbf{Y} = \mathbf{Z}'\mathbf{X}\beta + \mathbf{Z}'\varepsilon$$

from which it follows that

$$\hat{\beta}^* = (\mathbf{Z}'\mathbf{X})^{-1}\mathbf{Z}'\mathbf{Y} \qquad\qquad (A5.7)$$

will be a consistent estimator of β. $\hat{\beta}^*$ will be consistent because

$$\hat{\beta}^* = (\mathbf{Z}'\mathbf{Z})^{-1}(\mathbf{Z}'\mathbf{X})\beta + (\mathbf{Z}'\mathbf{X})^{-1}(\mathbf{Z}'\varepsilon)$$

$$= \beta + (\mathbf{Z}'\mathbf{X})^{-1}(\mathbf{Z}'\varepsilon)$$

and $\operatorname{plim} \hat{\beta}^* = \beta + \operatorname{plim}\left[(\mathbf{Z}'\mathbf{X})^{-1}(\mathbf{Z}'\varepsilon)\right]$

$$= \beta + \operatorname{plim}\left[\left(\frac{1}{N}\mathbf{Z}'\mathbf{X}\right)^{-1}\left(\frac{1}{N}\mathbf{Z}'\varepsilon\right)\right] \qquad \text{from (A5.4) and (A5.5)}$$

$$= \beta + \Sigma^{-1}\mathbf{0} = \beta$$

To find the appropriate distribution of $\hat{\beta}^*$, we need to derive $\mathbf{V}$, the asymptotic variance-covariance matrix for $\hat{\beta}^*$. To accomplish this, we utilize the fact that

$$\hat{\beta}^* - \beta = (\mathbf{Z'X})^{-1}(\mathbf{Z'\varepsilon})$$

and

$$(\hat{\beta}^* - \beta)(\hat{\beta}^* - \beta)' = (\mathbf{Z'X})^{-1}\mathbf{Z'\varepsilon\varepsilon'Z}(\mathbf{X'Z})^{-1}$$

$$\mathbf{V} = \frac{1}{N}\text{plim}\left(\frac{1}{N}\mathbf{Z'X}\right)^{-1} \cdot \text{plim}\left(\frac{1}{N}\mathbf{Z'\varepsilon\varepsilon'Z}\right) \cdot \text{plim}\left(\frac{1}{N}\mathbf{X'Z}\right)^{-1}$$

from which it follows, using (A5.5) and (A5.6),[17] that

$$\mathbf{V} = \frac{1}{N}\sigma^2\mathbf{\Sigma}^{-1}\mathbf{\Sigma}^*\mathbf{\Sigma}^{-1} \tag{A5.8}$$

In practice, the true variance-covariance matrix can be consistently estimated by

$$s^2(\mathbf{Z'X})^{-1}(\mathbf{Z'Z})(\mathbf{X'Z})^{-1} \tag{A5.9}$$

where s^2 is a consistent estimate of σ^2:

$$s^2 = \frac{1}{N-k}(\mathbf{Y} - \mathbf{X}\hat{\beta}^*)'(\mathbf{Y} - \mathbf{X}\hat{\beta}^*)$$

Notice that s^2 is calculated from the residuals of the original equation, not the equation in which the instruments replace the original right-hand variables.

---

[17] See A. Goldberger, *Econometric Theory* (New York: Wiley, 1964), pp. 270–274.

6

FORECASTING WITH A SINGLE-EQUATION REGRESSION MODEL

A principal purpose for constructing the single-equation regression models that were described in the last five chapters is *forecasting*. A forecast is a quantitative estimate (or set of estimates) about the *likelihood* of future events based on past and current information. This "past and current information" is embodied in the form of a model—a single-equation structural model, or, as we will discuss in Parts Two and Three of this book, a multi-equation model or a time-series model. By extrapolating our models out beyond the period over which they were estimated, we can use the information contained in them to make forecasts about future events. In this chapter we discuss in some detail how the single-equation regression model can be used as a forecasting tool.

The term *forecasting* is often thought to apply solely to time-series problems in which we predict the future, given information about the past and the present. We shall remain consistent with this notion by orienting our notation and discussion toward time-series forecasting. We should stress, however, that our use of notation is for convenience only. Most of the analysis applies equally well to cross-section models and time-series models. In fact, our concern in this chapter is with *prediction*, the object of which is to obtain estimates or guesses as to the movement of certain variables, given additional information about the movement of other variables.

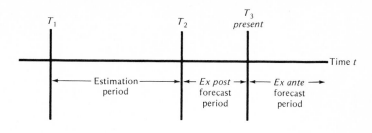

FIGURE 6.1

As we will see, two types of forecasts are found to be useful. *Point forecasts* predict a single number in each forecast period, while *interval forecasts* indicate in each forecast period an interval in which the actual realized value will hopefully lie. We begin by discussing point forecasts, after which we consider how confidence intervals (interval forecasts) can be used to provide a "margin of error" around a point forecast.

The additional information provided by the forecasting process can be used in several different ways. Frequently forecasts are used as guides for public and private policy. A forecast of a high rate of inflation based on the assumption of a large budget deficit may lead policy makers to alter their budget plans, or a forecast of an increased world demand for crude oil may lead shipbuilders to invest in new supertankers. Forecasts are also useful as "guidelines" for model building. A forecast which is found to be way off target when actual data are available provides information which may lead to the revision of the model which provided the forecast.

It is useful to distinguish between two types of forecasting, *ex post* and *ex ante*. In terms of time-series models, both forecasts predict values of a dependent variable beyond the time period in which the model is estimated. However, in an *ex post* forecast the forecast period is such that observations on both endogenous variables and the exogenous explanatory variables are known with certainty. Thus, *ex post* forecasts can be checked against existing data, and provide a means of evaluating a forecasting model. An *ex ante* forecast predicts values of the dependent variable beyond the estimation period, using explanatory variables which may or may not be known with certainty, depending on the nature of the data and the length of the lags associated with the explanatory variables. The distinction between *ex post* and *ex ante* forecasting can be seen in Fig. 6.1.

A distinction may also be made between *conditional* and *unconditional* forecasts. In an unconditional forecast, values for all the explanatory variables in the forecasting equation are known with certainty. Any *ex post* forecast is, of course, an unconditional forecast, but *ex ante* forecasts may also be unconditional. Suppose, for example, that for some industry, monthly sales, $S(t)$, are linearly related to two variables X_1 and X_2, but with lags of 3 months and 4 months, respectively:

$$S(t) = a_0 + a_1 X_1(t - 3) + a_2 X_2(t - 4) \tag{6.1}$$

If this equation were estimated, it could be used to produce unconditional forecasts of $S(t)$ 1 month, 2 months, and 3 months in the future. For example, to produce a 3-month forecast of $S(t)$, we would use the current value of X_1 and last month's value of X_2, both of which are known.

In a conditional forecast, values for one or more explanatory variables are not known with certainty, so that guesses (or forecasts) for them must be used to produce the forecast of the dependent variable. If we wanted to use Eq. (6.1) to forecast $S(t)$ 4 months into the future, we would have to also forecast $X_1(t)$ 1 month into the future, making our forecast of $S(t)$ *conditional* upon our forecast of $X_1(t)$. Of course, if the right-hand side of the forecasting equation contained no lags, e.g., if it was of the form

$$S(t) = a_0 + a_1 X_1(t) + a_2 X_2(t) \tag{6.2}$$

then every *ex ante* forecast generated by the equation would be a conditional forecast.[1]

Our primary concerns in this chapter are, first, the problem of obtaining good forecasts using a single-equation regression model, and, second, the problem of evaluating the nature of the resulting *forecast error* using appropriate statistical tests. By a good forecast we really mean the *best* forecast possible, but the problem of selecting the "best" forecast is a difficult one as a general rule. For our purposes we define the "best" forecast as the one which yields a forecast error having the *minimum variance*. In the single-equation regression model, ordinary least-squares estimation yields the best forecast among all unbiased estimators which are based on linear equations. Other definitions of the best forecast are possible and indeed plausible. We shall extend our notion of the best forecast in later chapters when we consider minimum mean-square-error forecasts based on nonlinear equations and on estimation procedures which do not guarantee unbiased parameter estimates.

We shall see that the error associated with a forecasting procedure can come from a combination of four distinct sources. First, the random nature of the additive error process in a linear regression model guarantees that forecasts will deviate from true values, even if the model is specified correctly and its parameter values are known with certainty. Second, the process of estimating the regression parameters introduces error because estimated parameter values are random variables which may deviate from the true parameter values. For any given sample, the estimated parameters are unlikely to equal the true values of the underlying parameters, even though they will (if they are unbiased) equal those parameters on the average. Third, in the case of a conditional forecast, errors are introduced when calculated guesses or forecasts are made for the values

---

[1] Even if the exogenous variables appeared with long lags in the equation, it may be the case that current values of the exogenous data are not known with certainty but contain errors and are subject to frequent and extreme revisions. The forecast would then be conditional on the exogenous data.

of the explanatory variables in the period in which the forecast is made. Finally, errors may be introduced because the model specification may not be an accurate representation of the "true" underlying model. This last source of error can be quite important and is worthy of separate treatment outside the context of the forecasting problem. We will deal with specification error in Chapter 7.

We proceed by discussing the best forecast and the properties of the resulting forecast error in three different cases. We deal first with unconditional forecasts generated by a linear regression model in which the error process obeys the classical assumptions of the linear model. Next, we treat the problem of unconditional forecasting when the error process is known to be serially correlated. Finally, we consider the added dimension of difficulty which arises when conditional forecasting is attempted.

6.1 UNCONDITIONAL FORECASTING

In order to produce an unconditional forecast from a regression model, it is necessary that the explanatory variables be known with certainty for the entire forecast period. As we saw before, one way this can occur is by having the explanatory variables appear with time lags. Even if explanatory variables do not appear with lags, we might be able to forecast them perfectly (or near perfectly)—and thus generate unconditional forecasts for the dependent variable— if they happen to be seasonal variables, or else demographic or economic variables which change slowly and predictably. For example, monthly forecasts over a 1-year horizon which use population and the month of the year as two explanatory variables will be unconditional, since population growth over this short period can be predicted rather precisely, and the month of the year is known with certainty.

In applied work it is desirable to construct models which can be used to generate unconditional forecasts, since this removes a large source of forecasting error. As a result, analysts will, when constructing a forecasting equation, attempt to use explanatory variables that have long time lags or that can themselves be forecasted easily and precisely.

We begin our discussion of unconditional forecasting by considering the simple two-variable regression model:

$$Y_t = \alpha + \beta X_t + \varepsilon_t \qquad t = 1, 2, \ldots, T \tag{6.3}$$

$$\varepsilon_t \sim N(0, \sigma^2)$$

We pose the forecasting problem as follows: Given a *known* value X_{T+1}, what is the best single forecast that can be made for Y in period $T + 1$? In solving the problem, we begin by making the assumption that *the parameters α and β are known exactly.* If this is the case, then the appropriate forecast for Y_{T+1} is given by

$$\hat{Y}_{T+1} = E(Y_{T+1}) = \alpha + \beta X_{T+1} \tag{6.4}$$

To see why this is so, consider the *forecast error*

$$\hat{e}_{T+1} = \hat{Y}_{T+1} - Y_{T+1} \tag{6.5}$$

The forecast error has two desirable properties:

1 $E(\hat{e}_{T+1}) = E(\hat{Y}_{T+1} - Y_{T+1}) = E(\varepsilon_{T+1}) = 0$. Thus, our forecast of Y_{T+1} will be *unbiased*, i.e., it will be correct on the average.
2 The forecast error variance

$$\sigma_f^2 = E[(\hat{e}_{T+1})^2] = E[(\varepsilon_{T+1})^2] = \sigma^2$$

is the minimum variance possible among all possible forecasts based on linear equations.[2]

We should note that knowledge of the slope and intercept parameters α and β does not guarantee an accurate forecast every time. We are able to say only that the forecast error will have mean 0 and variance σ^2. The existence of forecast error is brought about because the value Y_{T+1} cannot be guaranteed to lie on the true regression line due to the presence of the disturbance term ε.

Since the error of forecast is normally distributed with mean 0 and variance σ^2, it is natural to consider the problem of statistical testing. We can perform significance tests on the forecasted value of Y by calculating the normalized error

$$\lambda = \frac{\hat{Y}_{T+1} - Y_{T+1}}{\sigma} \tag{6.6}$$

Since λ is normally distributed with mean 0 and standard deviation 1, we may determine a 95 percent (or any other) confidence interval by utilizing the fact that

$$\text{Prob}\left(-\lambda_{.05} \leq \frac{\hat{Y}_{T+1} - Y_{T+1}}{\sigma} \leq \lambda_{.05}\right) = .95 \tag{6.7}$$

where $\lambda_{.05}$ is obtained from a table of the normal distribution. We write the 95 percent confidence interval as

$$\hat{Y}_{T+1} - \lambda_{.05}\sigma \leq Y_{T+1} \leq \hat{Y}_{T+1} + \lambda_{.05}\sigma \tag{6.8}$$

---

[2] σ, the square root of the forecast error variance, is called the *standard error of the forecast*.

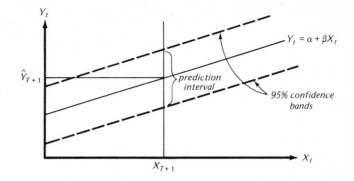

FIGURE 6.2
Forecast when equation parameters are known.

Notice that this interval is independent of values of the exogenous variable X. The 95 percent confidence interval for a typical two-variable regression model is shown in Fig. 6.2.

The confidence intervals determined above provide us with a simple means of testing the reliability of the regression model. When the actual value of Y_{T+1} is obtained, we can compare it with the previously forecasted value. If the actual observed value of Y_{T+1} lies within the 95 percent confidence interval, then we could presume that the model is performing satisfactorily, but if the value lies outside the confidence interval, we might conclude that the model is not performing well. If this poor performance is known to be due to an extraordinary event, not accounted for by the model, then we are likely to wait for a second forecast before concluding that the model is unreliable, but as a general rule we would take the poor forecast as evidence of the need to revise the basic model structure. Of course economists do not often use a single forecast alone as a basis for accepting or rejecting a model; repeated observations and statistical tests are usually needed before a more definite conclusion can be reached.

The reader should be aware that the use of forecasting as a means of evaluating model reliability is quite distinct from the classical t, F, and R^2 statistics described earlier in the book. A single-equation regression model can have significant t statistics and a high R^2 and still forecast very badly period after period. This might result from a structural change (in the economy) occurring during the forecast period and not explained by the model. Good forecasts, on the other hand, may come from regression models which have relatively low R^2's and one or more insignificant regression coefficients. This may happen because there is very little variation in the dependent variable, so that although it is not being explained well by the model, it is easy to forecast. We shall return to this model-building issue again in Parts Two and Three of the book.

Normally, of course, the parameters of our regression model are not known with certainty but instead are random variables that have been estimated. We also do not usually know the error variance σ^2, and this too is an estimated random variable. Let us therefore reconsider the problem of forecasting under the more realistic assumption that both the regression parameters and the error variance must be estimated. The best forecast for Y_{T+1} is then determined from a simple two-stage procedure:[3]

1 Estimate Eq. (6.3) using ordinary least squares.
2 Choose $\hat{Y}_{T+1} = E(Y_{T+1}) = \hat{\alpha} + \hat{\beta}X_{T+1}$.

The forecast error is then

$$\hat{e}_{T+1} = \hat{Y}_{T+1} - Y_{T+1} = (\hat{\alpha} - \alpha) + (\hat{\beta} - \beta)X_{T+1} + \varepsilon_{T+1} \tag{6.9}$$

There are two sources of error involved in Eq. (6.9), the first due to the presence of the additive error term ε_{T+1}, and the second due to the random nature of the estimated regression parameters. Recall that the estimated parameters are unbiased, but are not *identical* to the true population parameters. While the former error source is due to the basic variance in the variable Y, the latter error source is sensitive to the estimation process and, therefore, to the number of degrees of freedom involved. We will see this as we examine the distribution of the error of forecast.

To begin with, the error of forecast is normally distributed, since it is a linear function of $\hat{\alpha}$, $\hat{\beta}$, and ε_{T+1}, all of which are normally distributed. Second, it has 0 mean, since

$$E(\hat{e}_{T+1}) = E(\hat{\alpha} - \alpha) + E(\hat{\beta} - \beta)X_{T+1} + E(\varepsilon_{T+1}) = 0 \tag{6.10}$$

(Remember that $\hat{\alpha}$ and $\hat{\beta}$ are unbiased estimators, and X_{T+1} is known.) Finally, we may determine the variance of $\hat{e}_{T+1}$:

$$\sigma_f{}^2 = E[(\hat{e}_{T+1})^2] = E[(\hat{\alpha} - \alpha)^2] + E[(\hat{\beta} - \beta)^2]X_{T+1}^2 + E[(\varepsilon_{T+1})^2]$$

$$+ E[(\hat{\alpha} - \alpha)(\hat{\beta} - \beta)]2X_{T+1} \tag{6.11}$$

or $\qquad \sigma_f{}^2 = \text{Var}\,(\hat{\alpha}) + 2X_{T+1}\,\text{Cov}\,(\hat{\alpha}, \hat{\beta}) + X_{T+1}^2\,\text{Var}\,(\hat{\beta}) + \sigma^2 \qquad (6.12)$

Notice that all the cross-product terms involving estimated parameters and ε_{T+1} become 0 when expected values are taken, since $(\hat{\alpha} - \alpha)$ and $(\hat{\beta} - \beta)$ depend on

---

[3] For a proof that this forecast is the best linear unbiased forecast, see J. Johnston, *Econometric Methods*, 2d ed. (New York: McGraw-Hill, 1972), pp. 38–40.

$\varepsilon_1, \ldots, \varepsilon_T$, all of which are independent of ε_{T+1}. Recall that we have previously (Chapter 2) derived the variances of $\hat{\alpha}$ and $\hat{\beta}$ as well as their covariance:

$$\text{Var}(\hat{\alpha}) = \sigma^2 \frac{\sum X_t^2}{T \sum (X_t - \overline{X})^2} \tag{6.13}$$

$$\text{Var}(\hat{\beta}) = \frac{\sigma^2}{\sum (X_t - \overline{X})^2} \tag{6.14}$$

$$\text{Cov}(\hat{\alpha}, \hat{\beta}) = \frac{-\overline{X}\sigma^2}{\sum (X_t - \overline{X})^2} \tag{6.15}$$

where the summation runs from 1 to T and $\overline{X}$ is the sample mean of X for the first T observations. Substituting Eqs. (6.13), (6.14), and (6.15) into (6.12) and manipulating terms, we get

$$\sigma_f^2 = \sigma^2 \left[\frac{\sum X_t^2}{T \sum (X_t - \overline{X})^2} - \frac{2\overline{X}X_{T+1}}{\sum (X_t - \overline{X})^2} + \frac{X_{T+1}^2}{\sum (X_t - \overline{X})^2} + 1 \right] \tag{6.16}$$

But $$\frac{\sum X_t^2}{T \sum (X_t - \overline{X})^2} = \frac{\sum (X_t - \overline{X})^2 + T\overline{X}^2}{T \sum (X_t - \overline{X})^2} = \frac{1}{T} + \frac{\overline{X}^2}{\sum (X_t - \overline{X})^2} \tag{6.17}$$

Therefore, $$\sigma_f^2 = \sigma^2 \left[1 + \frac{1}{T} + \frac{\overline{X}^2 - 2\overline{X}X_{T+1} + X_{T+1}^2}{\sum (X_t - \overline{X})^2} \right] \tag{6.18}$$

or $$\sigma_f^2 = \sigma^2 \left[1 + \frac{1}{T} + \frac{(X_{T+1} - \overline{X})^2}{\sum (X_t - \overline{X})^2} \right] \tag{6.19}$$

Equation (6.19) is of immediate interest because it tells us that the forecast error is sensitive to the size of the sample used in the estimation process, as well as to the variance in X and to the distance between X_{T+1} and $\overline{X}$.[4] Other things being equal then, the larger the sample size and the greater the variance in X, the smaller will be the error of forecast. In addition, the error of forecast is smallest when X_{T+1} happens to be equal to the sample mean of X, since the last term in brackets in Eq. (6.19) then becomes 0. This suggests that the best forecasts about Y can be made for values of X around which the most

---

[4] Equation (6.19) shows the error for a point forecast. If we forecast the expected value of the outcome, the equation is modified by omitting the "1" in the bracketed expression. That term adds to the expected value of the forecast the error variance associated with selecting a single forecast from the distribution of possible forecasts. Thus, a point forecast will have a higher variance than a forecast of the mean or expected outcome.

sample information is available. This is not surprising; as the new value of X gets further from the mean, it moves out of the "range of experience" used to estimate the model, and generates less reliable forecasts. In general it is dangerous to extend a model much beyond its range of estimation. When time-series forecasts involve values of X_{T+1} substantially different from X, the resulting forecast error may be large.

If σ^2 were known, we could calculate σ_f^2 and then proceed to construct confidence intervals as before, relying on the knowledge that

$$\lambda = \frac{\hat{Y}_{T+1} - Y_{T+1}}{\sigma_f} \sim N(0, 1) \tag{6.20}$$

However, σ^2 is usually not known, so that as a practical matter we must use an unbiased and consistent estimate of σ^2. Such an estimate would be

$$s^2 = \frac{1}{T - 2} \sum (Y_t - \hat{Y}_t)^2 \tag{6.21}$$

As we saw in Chapter 2, this allows us to calculate confidence intervals using the t distribution. Writing the *estimated* forecast error variance,

$$s_f^2 = s^2 \left[1 + \frac{1}{T} + \frac{(X_{T+1} - \overline{X})^2}{\sum (X_t - \overline{X})^2} \right] \tag{6.22}$$

we know that the normalized error

$$\frac{\hat{Y}_{T+1} - Y_{T+1}}{s_f}$$

will be t-distributed with $T - 2$ degrees of freedom. The 95 percent confidence interval for $\hat{Y}_{T+1}$ is thus given by

$$\hat{Y}_{T+1} - t_{.05} s_f \leq Y_{T+1} \leq \hat{Y}_{T+1} + t_{.05} s_f \tag{6.23}$$

An example of the 95 percent confidence interval is shown in Fig. 6.3. It shows rather clearly the relationship between the forecast error and values of the explanatory variable X. At every value of X the distance between the regression line and one of the confidence bands is twice the estimated standard error of the forecast.

The shape of the confidence bands shown in the diagram is a natural outcome of the fact that both the slope and the intercept estimates are random variables. To see this relationship, consider the formula for the variance of the forecast error (1) when the intercept α is known exactly and the slope β is estimated,

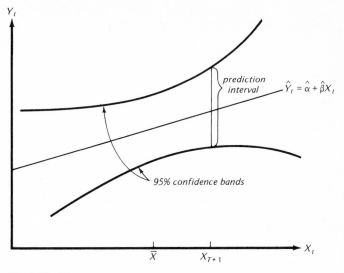

FIGURE 6.3
Forecast confidence intervals.

and (2) when the intercept is estimated and the slope is known exactly. The two variances are easily derived as special cases of the formulation leading to Eq. (6.19). They are as follows:

1 Slope estimated:
$$\sigma_f{}^2 = \sigma^2 \left[1 + \frac{X_{T+1}^2}{\sum (X_t - \overline{X})^2} \right] \tag{6.24}$$

2 Intercept estimated:
$$\sigma_f{}^2 = \sigma^2 \left[1 + \frac{1}{T} + \frac{\overline{X}^2}{\sum (X_t - \overline{X})^2} \right] \tag{6.25}$$

Notice that in case 1 the variance of the error of forecast increases with the square of X_{T+1}, while in case 2 the variance is independent of X_{T+1}. The confidence interval for case 2 is shown in Fig. 6.4; note that the confidence bands are parallel straight lines.

These results suggest that the further into the future that one forecasts, the lower the reliability of the forecast is likely to be. Note that this diminished reliability occurs simply because the values of X associated with distant forecasts are outside the range of our normal experience and, thus, far from the mean value $\overline{X}$. The unreliability is not associated with an increased possibility of specification error in the model, since we have presumed a correct specification at all times. Finally, we stress that the variance associated with the error of forecast does not imply that for a given estimated equation we get a series of distinct forecasts for every given value of X_{T+1}. Rather, it suggests that we get

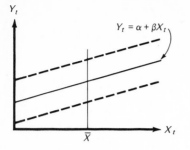

FIGURE 6.4
Confidence interval for known slope and estimated intercept.

a distribution of forecasts for each X_{T+1} only when each individual forecast is associated with a distinct sample of observations and a corresponding set of parameter estimates.

Our discussion so far has been in the context of the simple two-variable regression model, but the principles are the same and apply equally well to the multiple regression model. Confidence intervals for forecasts generated by a multiple regression model will have the same shape as those in Fig. 6.3. When two or more explanatory variables are present, however, the algebraic derivations of the forecast error distribution and forecast confidence interval become somewhat messy unless matrix notation is used. As a result, we will relegate the formal discussion of forecast error from a multiple regression model to the appendix to this chapter. For now, let us examine some simple forecasting examples.

Example 6.1   Forecasting Grade-Point Averages

Reconsider the grade-point average example discussed in Chapters 1 and 2. In that example we estimated a linear relationship between grade-point average and family income for a cross section of eight individuals. With the development of the forecasting techniques in this chapter, we are in a position to forecast the grade-point average of individuals not in the original sample, given only information about their family incomes. In terms of the notation used in Chapter 1, the relevant information about the grade-point sample is summarized as follows:

Estimated regression line:	$\hat{Y}_i = 1.375 + .120X_i \qquad i = 1, \ldots, N$
Estimated error variance:	$s^2 = .111$
Number of observations:	$N = 8$
Mean of X:	$\overline{X} = 13.5$
Variation of X:	$\sum (X_i - \overline{X})^2 = 162$

TABLE 6.1
GRADE-POINT AVERAGE FORECAST CALCULATIONS

X_{N+1}	$\hat{Y}_{N+1}$	s_f^2	$\hat{Y}_{N+1} - 1.96s_f$	$\hat{Y}_{N+1} + 1.96s_f$
6.5	2.155	.158	1.375	2.935
10.0	2.575	.133	1.860	3.415
13.5	2.995	.125	2.303	3.687
17.0	3.315	.133	2.600	4.030
20.5	3.835	.158	3.055	4.615
24.0	4.155	.201	3.277	5.033
27.5	4.675	.259	3.677	5.673

Assume for illustrative purposes that several individuals (not in the original sample) report their family income. We wish to predict grade-point average and to calculate a 95 percent confidence or prediction interval. The relevant calculations are summarized in Table 6.1, and 95 percent prediction intervals are shown graphically in Fig. 6.5.

As can be seen in Table 6.1, the smallest error of forecast is associated with the family income of $13,500, the mean family income of the original sample. For that individual we can be reasonably confident that the final grade-point average obtained will lie in the 2.3 to 3.7 range. The fact that the 95 percent prediction interval is so large, even at the point of minimum forecast error, suggests the limiting nature of the grade-point average model. A more sophisticated model (with additional explanatory variables) and more sample observations would most likely lead to a smaller forecast interval. We should note, also, that the error of forecast grows nonlinearly when family income increases beyond its mean value. In fact, the forecast interval for the last individual (with family income of $27,500) is not only large, but also

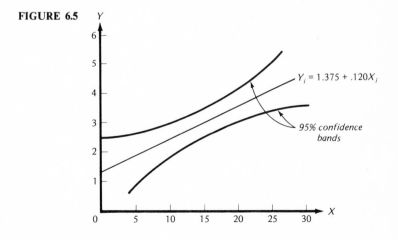

FIGURE 6.5

$Y_i = 1.375 + .120X_i$

95% confidence bands

unrealistic, since a grade-point average greater than 4.0 is not within the experience of the original sample. Forecasting in this particular cross-section example is clearly not worthwhile for family incomes outside the original range of experience.

Example 6.2 Forecasting Interest Rates

In this example we reconsider the regression model that explains the short-term interest rate (the rate on 3-month Treasury bills).[5] The linear regression model is estimated using monthly time-series data over the period January 1958 to January 1970. The interest rate R is seen to depend on total disposable income YD, a moving sum of changes in the money supply M, and a moving sum of percent changes in the price level P (i.e., the inflation rate):

$$R_t = c_0 + c_1 YD_t + c_2(\Delta M_t + \Delta M_{t-1} + \Delta M_{t-2}) + c_3\left(\frac{\Delta P_t}{P_t} + \frac{\Delta P_{t-1}}{P_{t-1}} + \frac{\Delta P_{t-2}}{P_{t-2}}\right)$$

(6.26)

The results of the estimation are shown below:

$R^2 = .853$ Corrected $R^2 = .850$

$F(3/141) = 271.9$ Standard error $= .552$

Sum of squared residuals $= 43.0$ Durbin-Watson $= .24$

Mean of $R = 3.778$

Coefficient	Estimated value	Standard error	t statistic	Mean of variable
c_0	-3.662	.388	-9.45	1.00
c_1	.053	.004	14.76	135.90
c_2	$-.280$	.046	-6.13	1.51
c_3	104.376	19.954	5.23	.006

The estimated equation is then used to generate an *ex post* forecast over a 12-month period, from February 1970 to January 1971. The forecasted path for the interest rate, together with the 95 percent confidence interval and the path that the interest rate actually followed, is shown in Fig. 6.6 and again enlarged

---

[5] See Examples 3.2 and 4.6.

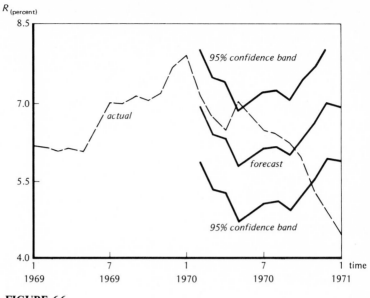

FIGURE 6.6
Interest rate forecast.

FIGURE 6.7
Interest rate forecast (enlarged).

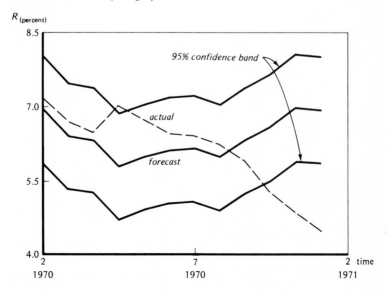

in Fig. 6.7. Note that the forecasted path is reasonably close to the actual path for the first 8 or 9 months of the forecast, but during the last 3 months the actual path is outside the boundaries of the 95 percent confidence interval. This would lead one to conclude that the model cannot be trusted for any intermediate or long-term forecasts. In fact, the main weakness of the model is revealed by the low Durbin-Watson statistic (.24), indicating that the error terms are serially correlated. We will deal with this problem of forecasting with serially correlated errors in the next section.

6.2 FORECASTING WITH SERIALLY CORRELATED ERRORS

Frequently we find that the error process is serially correlated in time-series models. When this is the case, the problem of determining the best forecast and its appropriate distribution becomes somewhat more difficult. Let us consider the two-variable model in which the errors are first-order serially correlated:

$$Y_t = \alpha + \beta X_t + \varepsilon_t \tag{6.27}$$

$$\varepsilon_t = \rho\varepsilon_{t-1} + v_t \qquad v_t \sim N(0, \sigma_v^2) \qquad |\rho| < 1$$

The difficulty arises because we now have some additional information, namely that the error term is serially correlated, and we should take advantage of this information in producing our best forecast. In the previous section our best forecast for Y_{T+1} was determined by assigning ε_{T+1} the value 0 for the forecast period. This was reasonable, given that the error had 0 mean and that error terms were assumed independent over time. In the serially correlated case, however, the time-independence assumption no longer holds. It is now reasonable to expect that knowledge of the errors (or their estimates) in periods previous to the forecast period will allow us to modify our prediction of the error in period $T + 1$.

To pursue this matter further, let us assume that all the regression parameters (α, β, and ρ) are known *a priori*. We proceed by choosing the forecasted value of Y_{T+1} as follows:

$$\hat{Y}_{T+1} = \alpha + \beta X_{T+1} + \hat{\varepsilon}_{T+1} \tag{6.28}$$

Rather than setting $\hat{\varepsilon}_{T+1} = 0$, we calculate ε_{T+1} from the previous error term. Since $\varepsilon_{T+1} = \rho\varepsilon_T + v_T$, we choose $\hat{\varepsilon}_{T+1} = \rho\varepsilon_T$ (since v_t has 0 mean and is uncorrelated over time). Therefore,

$$\hat{Y}_{T+1} = \alpha + \beta X_{T+1} + \rho\varepsilon_T \tag{6.29}$$

If we wish to forecast further into the future, the information provided by serial correlation becomes less and less useful, since

$$\hat{\varepsilon}_{T+2} = \rho\hat{\varepsilon}_{T+1} = \rho^2\varepsilon_T$$

$$\hat{\varepsilon}_{T+3} = \rho\hat{\varepsilon}_{T+2} = \rho^3\varepsilon_T$$

$$\vdots$$

$$\hat{\varepsilon}_{T+s} = \rho^s\varepsilon_T$$

and ρ^s approaches zero as s gets arbitrarily large.

The reader should note that the identical prediction of Y_{T+1} would be obtained if we wrote the model in generalized difference form:

$$Y_t^* = \alpha(1 - \rho) + \beta X_t^* + v_t \tag{6.30}$$

where $\qquad Y_t^* = Y_t - \rho Y_{t-1} \qquad$ and $\qquad X_t^* = X_t - \rho X_{t-1}$

The appropriate forecast is then

$$\hat{Y}_{T+1}^* = \alpha(1 - \rho) + \beta X_{T+1}^* \tag{6.31}$$

where $\qquad \hat{Y}_{T+1}^* = \hat{Y}_{T+1} - \rho Y_T \qquad$ and $\qquad X_{T+1}^* = X_{T+1} - \rho X_T$

The equivalence of (6.31) and (6.29) becomes apparent by writing

$$\hat{Y}_{T+1} = \hat{Y}_{T+1}^* + \rho Y_T = \alpha(1 - \rho) + \beta X_{T+1}^* + \rho Y_T$$

$$= \alpha(1 - \rho) + \beta X_{T+1} + \rho Y_T - \beta\rho X_T$$

$$= \alpha(1 - \rho) + \beta X_{T+1} + \rho(Y_T - \beta X_T) \tag{6.32}$$

But $Y_T = \alpha + \beta X_T + \varepsilon_T$. Therefore,

$$\hat{Y}_{T+1} = \alpha(1 - \rho) + \beta X_{T+1} + \rho(\alpha + \varepsilon_T)$$

$$= \alpha + \beta X_{T+1} + \rho\varepsilon_T \tag{6.33}$$

which is identical to Eq. (6.29).

If the parameters α, β, and ρ are all known, then the error of forecast is given simply by

$$\hat{e}_{T+1} = \hat{Y}_{T+1} - Y_{T+1}$$

$$= \rho\varepsilon_T - \varepsilon_{T+1} = -v_{T+1} \tag{6.34}$$

Thus the error of forecast is normally distributed with 0 mean, and has a variance

$$\sigma_f^2 = E[(\rho\varepsilon_T - \varepsilon_{T+1})^2]$$

$$= \rho^2 E(\varepsilon_T^2) + E(\varepsilon_{T+1}^2) - 2\rho E(\varepsilon_T \varepsilon_{T+1})$$

$$= \rho^2 E(\varepsilon_T^2) + E(\varepsilon_{T+1}^2) - 2\rho^2 E(\varepsilon_T^2)$$

$$= (1 - \rho^2)\sigma^2 = \sigma_v^2 \tag{6.35}$$

Note that this forecast error is *smaller*—by a factor of $(1 - \rho^2)$—than would be the case if we did not take serial correlation into account. Using the information about the serially correlated nature of the error terms makes it possible to reduce the forecast error.

Of course in practice all three parameters α, β, and ρ are usually not known, but they can be estimated using any one of the estimation techniques described in Chapter 4. To produce a best forecast, one simply uses the estimated equation in generalized difference form.[6] In other words, we calculate $\hat{Y}_{T+1}$ from

$$\hat{Y}_{T+1} = \hat{\rho}Y_T + \hat{\alpha}(1 - \hat{\rho}) + \hat{\beta}(X_{T+1} - \hat{\rho}X_T) \tag{6.36}$$

It can be proven (although we will not do so here) that the mean of the error of forecast will approach zero as the sample size gets large. It is somewhat difficult to determine an explicit expression for the variance of the error of forecast when all three parameters α, β, and ρ have been estimated, since the estimation process guarantees that the estimated slope and intercept parameters will be correlated with the residuals of the regression. In practice, to calculate the variance of the error of forecast (and thus calculate a confidence interval on the forecast itself), we assume that ρ has been estimated exactly, i.e., that $\hat{\rho} = \rho$. In this case the forecast variance of Eq. (6.19) applies to our estimated equation in *generalized difference form* (and thus with an error term v_t instead of ε_t). Once again the error of forecast for $\hat{Y}_{T+1}$ will have a smaller variance (and thus the 95 percent confidence bands will be narrower) than would be the case if serial

---

[6] For a proof that this is the best linear unbiased forecast, see A. S. Goldberger, "Best Linear Unbiased Prediction in the Linear Regression Model," *Journal of the American Statistical Association*, vol. 57, pp. 369–375.

correlation were not taken into account. We will examine this in more detail, and in the context of the multiple regression model, in the appendix to this chapter. Let us now turn to an example of forecasting in the presence of serially correlated errors.

Example 6.3 Forecasting Coal Demand[7]

In this example we construct and use a forecasting model to predict, on a monthly basis, the demand for bituminous coal. We begin by specifying a linear equation that relates coal demand (COAL) to the Federal Reserve Board index of iron and steel production (FIS), the Federal Reserve Board index of electrical utility production (FEU), the wholesale price index for coal (PCOAL), and the wholesale price index for natural gas (PGAS). We use monthly data over the period January 1965 to December 1972, and we use a seasonally adjusted series for coal demand. We begin by estimating the equation using ordinary least squares. The regression results are shown below, with t statistics in parentheses:

$$COAL = 12{,}262 + 92.34FIS + 118.57FEU - 48.90PCOAL + 118.91PGAS$$
$$(3.51) \quad (6.46) \quad\quad (7.14) \quad\quad\quad (-3.82) \quad\quad\quad (3.18)$$

$$(6.37)$$

$$R^2 = .692 \quad \bar{R}^2 = .675 \quad F(4/91) = 51.0 \quad SER = 1{,}200 \quad DW = .95$$

The fit of this equation is quite good, as can be seen both from the statistics and from Figs. 6.8 and 6.9, which compare actual and fitted coal demand over 3-year and 1-year periods, respectively. One problem with the model, however, is the low Durbin-Watson statistic, indicating a significant amount of serial correlation in the error terms.

We have seen that we can improve our forecasts by taking serial correlation into account. Therefore we will reestimate our equation using the Hildreth-Lu regression procedure, which was discussed in Chapter 4. Recall that in this procedure the equation is transformed using generalized differences:

$$(COAL - \rho COAL_{-1}) = c_0(1 - \rho) + c_1(FIS - \rho FIS_{-1}) + \cdots \quad (6.38)$$

Since ρ is not known, the Hildreth-Lu procedure performs OLS regressions on Eq. (6.38) using several different values of ρ. Each time a regression is performed, the sum of squared residuals (ESS) is calculated, and the value of ρ

---

[7] This example was generated as part of a study by Dynamics Associates, Inc., Cambridge, Mass. The model was first discussed in Example 4.5.

FIGURE 6.8
Coal demand, fitted versus actual. Time bounds: January 1970 to December 1972.

that gives the smallest ESS is used in the final result. The Hildreth-Lu regression results for our coal demand equation are as follows:

$$COAL = 16,245 + 75.29FIS + 100.26FEU - 38.98PCOAL + 105.99PGAS$$
$$(3.29) \quad (4.38) \quad (3.73) \quad (-2.02) \quad (1.96)$$

$$(6.39)$$

$$R^2 = .774 \quad \bar{R}^2 = .762 \quad F(4/90) = 77.1 \quad SER = 998 \quad DW = 2.07 \quad \hat{\rho} = .60$$

FIGURE 6.9
Coal demand, fitted versus actual. Time bounds: January 1972 to December 1972.

FIGURE 6.10
Coal demand, fitted versus actual with serial-correlation correction. Time
bounds: January 1970 to December 1972.

Note that the DW statistic is closer to 2.0, the central value in the range of
the statistic, indicative of no serial correlation, and that the standard error of
the equation is smaller (998 versus 1,200 before). All the explanatory variables
continue to be significant. The fit of the equation can be seen graphically in
Figs. 6.10 and 6.11, which compare the actual and fitted series over 3-year and
1-year periods, respectively. A comparison of Figs. 6.10 and 6.11 with Figs. 6.8
and 6.9 shows the better fit afforded by the Hildreth-Lu procedure.

FIGURE 6.11
Coal demand, fitted versus actual with serial-correlation correction. Time
bounds: January 1972 to December 1972.

FIGURE 6.12
Forecast of coal demand using OLS regression. Time bounds: January 1973
to December 1973.

We now generate *ex post* forecasts over the 12-month period January 1973
to December 1973, and compare these forecasts with actual coal demand over
that period. First we use Eq. (6.37), which does not account for serial correlation.
These forecast results, together with the 95 percent confidence band and the
actual series for coal demand, are shown in Fig. 6.12. The results are quite
good; the actual series always remains within the 95 percent confidence band,
and in fact is usually quite close to the predicted series.

We can generate better forecasts, however, by using Eq. (6.39) in its generalized
difference form, i.e., by applying Eq. (6.31). These results, again together with the
95 percent confidence band and the actual series, are shown in Fig. 6.13.

FIGURE 6.13
Forecast of coal demand using serial-correlation correction. Time bounds:
January 1973 to December 1973.

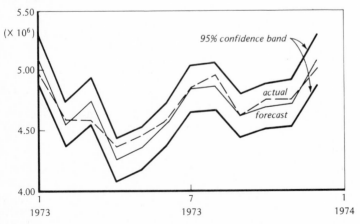

Compare Figs. 6.13 and 6.12 and notice that the 95 percent confidence band is *narrower* when the serial correlation has been taken into account. No matter whether our forecasts are *ex ante* or *ex post*, we will have greater confidence in them (i.e., expect smaller forecast errors) if we have correctly used the information provided by the serial correlation in the error terms. Finally, as we would expect, a comparison of the two figures shows that the forecasted series is closer to the actual series (i.e., the resulting forecast errors are indeed smaller) when serial correlation has been accounted for.[8]

6.3 CONDITIONAL FORECASTING

Our previous discussion about forecasting involved the assumption that all the explanatory variables are known without error, even in the forecast period. This may at times be an unrealistic assumption during *ex ante* forecasting, since some explanatory variables may have to be predicted into the future before the single-equation regression model can be used to forecast. One may intuitively expect that the stochastic nature of the predicted value of the X's will lead to forecasts of Y which are less reliable than in the fixed-X case. We shall see, in fact, that the 95 percent confidence intervals for the error of forecast are indeed increased in size when the X's must themselves be predicted. However, it is quite difficult to derive analytic results for the error of forecast in a general setting. We deal, therefore, with a special case, which, though somewhat restrictive, should be instructive.[9]

Consider the following model:

$$Y_t = \alpha + \beta X_t + \varepsilon_t \qquad t = 1, 2, \ldots, T \qquad (6.40)$$

where $\hat{X}_{T+1} = X_{T+1} + u_{T+1}$
   $\varepsilon_t \sim N(0, \sigma^2)$, $u_t \sim N(0, \sigma_u^2)$, ε_t and u_t are uncorrelated
   $E[(\hat{X}_{T+1} - X_{T+1})(\hat{\beta} - \beta)] = E[(\hat{X}_{T+1} - X_{T+1})(\hat{\alpha} - \alpha)] = 0$
   $\hat{\alpha}$ and $\hat{\beta}$ are the OLS estimates of α and β

The model presumes that X_{T+1} is forecasted in such a way that its error of forecast has 0 mean and constant variance. In addition, the error process associated with the forecast of X_{T+1} is assumed to be independent of the error process associated with each of the Y's in the model. Even though they are stochastic in nature, the X's are still presumed to be exogenous in the sense that they are uncorrelated with the equation error term. The restrictiveness of

---

[8] In Chapter 10 we present error measures that can be used to evaluate or compare forecasts. One measure that might be used is the sum of the squared errors over the forecast period. This measure is clearly smaller when the serial-correlation correction is used.

[9] This case is described in M. Feldstein, "The Error of Forecast in Econometric Models When the Forecast-Period Exogenous Variables Are Stochastic," *Econometrica*, vol. 39, pp. 55–60, Jan. 1971.

this model becomes clear when we consider the means by which forecasted values of X_{T+1} might be obtained. One frequently used procedure is to extrapolate from the sample values of X. While numerous extrapolation routines are available, the likelihood that the X variable is autocorrelated in a time-series model suggests that the error of forecast associated with the extrapolation procedure is itself likely to be serially correlated.

The forecasted value of Y in the time period $T + 1$ is defined by

$$\hat{Y}_{T+1} = \hat{\alpha} + \hat{\beta}\hat{X}_{T+1} \tag{6.41}$$

The error of forecast is then

$$\hat{e}_{T+1} = \hat{Y}_{T+1} - Y_{T+1} = (\hat{\alpha} - \alpha) + (\hat{\beta}\hat{X}_{T+1} - \beta X_{T+1}) - \varepsilon_{T+1} \tag{6.42}$$

It is easy to see that this error has 0 mean:

$$E(\hat{e}_{T+1}) = E(\hat{\alpha} - \alpha) + E(\hat{\beta}\hat{X}_{T+1}) - \beta X_{T+1} - E(\varepsilon_{T+1})$$

$$= E[\hat{\beta}(X_{T+1} + u_{T+1})] - \beta X_{T+1} = \beta X_{T+1} - \beta X_{T+1} = 0 \tag{6.43}$$

since $\hat{\beta}$ and u_{T+1} are uncorrelated.

The variance of the error of forecast is somewhat more difficult to derive:

$$\sigma_f^2 = E[(\hat{e}_{T+1})^2] = E[(\hat{\alpha} - \alpha)^2] + E[(\hat{\beta}\hat{X}_{T+1} - \beta X_{T+1})^2] + E[(\varepsilon_{T+1})^2]$$

$$+ 2E[(\hat{\alpha} - \alpha)(\hat{\beta}\hat{X}_{T+1} - \beta X_{T+1})] \tag{6.44}$$

But $\qquad \hat{\beta}\hat{X}_{T+1} - \beta X_{T+1} = \hat{\beta}(\hat{X}_{T+1} - X_{T+1}) + X_{T+1}(\hat{\beta} - \beta) \tag{6.45}$

Therefore,

$$E[(\hat{\beta}\hat{X}_{T+1} - \beta X_{T+1})^2] = E[\hat{\beta}(\hat{X}_{T+1} - X_{T+1}) + X_{T+1}(\hat{\beta} - \beta)]^2$$

$$= E[\hat{\beta}^2(\hat{X}_{T+1} - X_{T+1})^2] + X_{T+1}^2 E[(\hat{\beta} - \beta)^2]$$

$$= [\beta^2 + \text{Var}(\hat{\beta})]\sigma_u^2 + X_{T+1}^2 \text{Var}(\hat{\beta}) \tag{6.46}$$

Note that in arriving at Eq. (6.46), we took advantage of the fact that $u_{T+1} = \hat{X}_{T+1} - X_{T+1}$, that u_{T+1} and $\hat{\beta}$ are uncorrelated, and, finally, that

$\hat{\beta}^2 = \beta^2 + \text{Var}(\hat{\beta})$. Next, we can use Eq. (6.45) to simplify the last term in Eq. (6.44):

$$E[(\hat{\alpha} - \alpha)(\hat{\beta}\hat{X}_{T+1} - \beta X_{T+1})] = E[(\hat{\alpha} - \alpha)\hat{\beta}(\hat{X}_{T+1} - X_{T+1})]$$

$$+ X_{T+1}E[(\hat{\alpha} - \alpha)(\hat{\beta} - \beta)]$$

$$= X_{T+1}\,\text{Cov}(\hat{\alpha}, \hat{\beta}) \qquad (6.47)$$

Now, by combining terms, we find that

$$\sigma_f^2 = \text{Var}(\hat{\alpha}) + [\beta^2 + \text{Var}(\hat{\beta})]\sigma_u^2 + X_{T+1}^2\,\text{Var}(\hat{\beta}) + 2X_{T+1}\,\text{Cov}(\hat{\alpha}, \hat{\beta}) + \sigma^2$$

$$= \text{Var}(\hat{\alpha}) + \text{Var}(\hat{\beta})[X_{T+1}^2 + \sigma_u^2] + 2X_{T+1}\,\text{Cov}(\hat{\alpha}, \hat{\beta}) + \sigma^2 + \beta^2\sigma_u^2$$

$$(6.48)$$

Putting this in terms of our least-squares estimators, the formula for the variance of the error of forecast becomes

$$\sigma_f^2 = \sigma^2\left[1 + \frac{1}{T} + \frac{(X_{T+1} - \overline{X})^2 + X_{T+1}^2\sigma_u^2}{\sum(X_t - \overline{X})^2}\right] + \beta^2\sigma_u^2 \qquad (6.49)$$

A comparison of Eq. (6.49) with Eq. (6.19) from section 6.1 makes it clear that the stochastic nature of the forecasted value of X increases the error of forecast. There are two additional nonnegative terms involved, both of which are minimized only when the forecast of X_{T+1} is made with 0 error variance. This result makes it quite clear that the 95 percent confidence intervals associated with the forecasted value of Y_{T+1} will be larger than the intervals described in the unconditional forecasting derivation. Unfortunately, it is quite difficult to describe the confidence intervals for the conditional error of forecast. The difficulty arises because the forecast variable $\hat{Y}_{T+1}$ is not normally distributed, since it involves the sum of *products* of normally distributed variables. While confidence intervals cannot be derived analytically, they can be approximated using computer simulation techniques. A rather crude estimate of the confidence interval might be obtained as follows:

1 Calculate the 95 percent confidence intervals associated with the forecast that would be obtained were we to select $\hat{X}_{T+1}$ to be two standard deviations higher or lower, i.e., the confidence intervals associated with $Y_{T+1}^* = \hat{\alpha} + \hat{\beta}(\hat{X}_{T+1} + 2\sigma_u)$ and $Y_{T+1}^{**} = \hat{\alpha} + \hat{\beta}(\hat{X}_{T+1} - 2\sigma_u)$.
2 The final interval prediction is taken to be the union of the two confidence intervals; i.e., it contains all the values of $\hat{Y}_{T+1}$ common to both confidence intervals.

This process is depicted in Fig. 6.14.

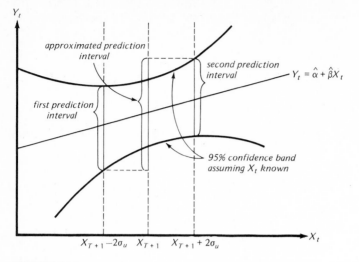

FIGURE 6.14
Approximating the predication interval for a conditional forecast.

The results of this section help to accentuate some of the difficulties involved in the forecasting process. Even if the regression model has a good fit with statistically significant parameters, unconditional forecasts may not be very accurate. In addition, the process of forecasting or extrapolating the explanatory variables into the prediction period introduces additional forecast error which diminishes the reliability of the regression model. A good regression model in terms of unconditional forecasting may perform quite badly when conditional forecasting is attempted. One should not be too quick to reject a model with a high forecast error if the primary component of that error is due to a serious error in judgment or prediction involved with the determination of the value of the explanatory variables in the forecast period. In macroeconomic forecasting, the problem is even more difficult because an accurate initial conditional forecast may lead to a shift in policy and thus to an inaccurate forecast!

Exercises

6.1 For the regression equation

$$Y_t = \alpha + \beta X_t + \varepsilon_t$$

prove that $\hat{Y}_{T+1} = \hat{\alpha} + \hat{\beta} X_{T+1}$ has the minimum variance possible among all forecasts based on linear equations.

6.2 For the regression equation

$$Y_t = \alpha + \beta X_t + \varepsilon_t$$

show that if the intercept α is known but the slope β is estimated, then a forecast generated by the equation will have an error variance given by Eq. (6.24), that is, by

$$\sigma_f^2 = \sigma^2 \left[1 + \frac{X_{T+1}^2}{\sum (X_t - \overline{X})^2} \right]$$

Show that if β is known but α is estimated, the forecast error variance will be given by Eq. (6.25), that is, by

$$\sigma_f^2 = \sigma^2 \left[1 + \frac{1}{T} + \frac{\overline{X}^2}{\sum (X_t - \overline{X})^2} \right]$$

6.3 In Example 6.2, Fig. 6.6, the actual series for the interest rate diverges considerably from the forecasted series after November 1970. Suggest why the regression model failed to predict the downturn in interest rates that occurred at the end of 1970.

APPENDIX 6 / FORECASTING WITH THE MULTIVARIATE REGRESSION MODEL

In this appendix we use matrix notation to generalize our discussion of the forecasting problem to the multivariate case. As we will see, the basic concepts that apply to the two-variable regression model also apply when additional independent variables are added to the right-hand side of the equation.

We begin by writing the general linear model in matrix form. The model contains a dependent variable and k independent variables (including the constant term) and is estimated over a total of T observations ($t = 1, 2, \ldots, T$):

$$\mathbf{Y} = \mathbf{X}\boldsymbol{\beta} + \boldsymbol{\varepsilon} \tag{A6.1}$$

Recall that $\mathbf{Y}$ is a $T \times 1$ column vector of dependent variable observations, $\mathbf{X}$ is a $T \times k$ matrix of independent variable observations, $\boldsymbol{\beta}$ is a $k \times 1$ column vector of unknown parameters, and $\boldsymbol{\varepsilon}$ is a $T \times 1$ column vector of error terms. Then the ordinary least-squares estimate of $\boldsymbol{\beta}$ will be given by

$$\hat{\boldsymbol{\beta}} = (\mathbf{X}'\mathbf{X})^{-1}\mathbf{X}'\mathbf{Y} \tag{A6.2}$$

Now let us examine the characteristics of a forecast made using this estimated equation. Suppose we have a new set of observations (or even forecasts or guesses) for the independent variables for period $T + 1$. Then the forecast for the dependent variable in period $T + 1$ will be given by

$$\hat{Y}_{T+1} = \mathbf{X}_{T+1}\hat{\boldsymbol{\beta}} \tag{A6.3}$$

Note that $\mathbf{X}_{T+1}$ is a $1 \times k$ row vector, so that $\hat{Y}_{T+1}$ is a *scalar*. Similarly, if we wanted a forecast for period $T + 2$, that would be given by

$$\hat{Y}_{T+2} = \mathbf{X}_{T+2}\,\hat{\boldsymbol{\beta}} \tag{A6.4}$$

Of course, if all the independent variables appeared with lags greater than or equal to two periods, then we could simply *observe* $\mathbf{X}_{T+2}$, but if some or all of the independent variables are not lagged, then $\mathbf{X}_{T+2}$ will itself have to be forecasted, and the forecast of Y_{T+2} will be conditional on the forecast of $\mathbf{X}_{T+2}$.

Since Eqs. (A6.3) and (A6.4) apply for any time period, let us (in the interest of notational simplicity) drop the time subscript and rewrite our forecasting equation as[10]

$$\hat{Y} = \tilde{\mathbf{X}}\hat{\boldsymbol{\beta}} \tag{A6.5}$$

where $\hat{Y}$ is a forecast of Y_t for some period, and $\tilde{\mathbf{X}}$ is a set of observations on the independent variables for that same period. Finally, let us denote the *actual* value of Y (which we must wait to observe) by $\tilde{Y}$. Then the *forecast error* is given by

$$\hat{e} = \tilde{Y} - \hat{Y} \tag{A6.6}$$

Since the actual value of Y, $\tilde{Y}$, can be written as

$$\tilde{Y} = \tilde{\mathbf{X}}\boldsymbol{\beta} + \tilde{\varepsilon} \tag{A6.7}$$

where $\tilde{\varepsilon}$ is the actual value of the additive error term in the forecast period, we can write the forecast error as

$$\hat{e} = \tilde{\mathbf{X}}\boldsymbol{\beta} + \tilde{\varepsilon} - \tilde{\mathbf{X}}\hat{\boldsymbol{\beta}}$$

$$= \tilde{\varepsilon} + \tilde{\mathbf{X}}\boldsymbol{\beta} - \tilde{\mathbf{X}}(\mathbf{X}'\mathbf{X})^{-1}\mathbf{X}'\mathbf{Y} \tag{A6.8}$$

Note that $\mathbf{Y}$ in Eq. (A6.8) is the $T \times 1$ vector of dependent variable observations as given by Eq. (A6.1). Substituting (A6.1) into (A6.8), we have

$$\hat{e} = \tilde{\varepsilon} + \tilde{\mathbf{X}}\boldsymbol{\beta} - \tilde{\mathbf{X}}(\mathbf{X}'\mathbf{X})^{-1}\mathbf{X}'(\mathbf{X}\boldsymbol{\beta} + \varepsilon)$$

$$= \tilde{\varepsilon} + \tilde{\mathbf{X}}\boldsymbol{\beta} - \tilde{\mathbf{X}}\boldsymbol{\beta} - \tilde{\mathbf{X}}(\mathbf{X}'\mathbf{X})^{-1}\mathbf{X}'\varepsilon$$

$$= \tilde{\varepsilon} - \tilde{\mathbf{X}}(\mathbf{X}'\mathbf{X})^{-1}\mathbf{X}'\varepsilon \tag{A6.9}$$

---

[10] For a proof that Eq. (A6.5) is the best predictor of Y, see H. Theil, *Principles of Econometrics* (New York: Wiley, 1971), p. 123.

We are interested in the variance of the forecast error, i.e., in

$$\sigma_f{}^2 = E[\hat{e}^2]$$

$$= E[\tilde{\varepsilon}^2] - 2\tilde{\mathbf{X}}(\mathbf{X}'\mathbf{X})^{-1}\mathbf{X}'E[\varepsilon\tilde{\varepsilon}] + \tilde{\mathbf{X}}(\mathbf{X}'\mathbf{X})^{-1}\mathbf{X}'E[\varepsilon\varepsilon']\mathbf{X}(\mathbf{X}'\mathbf{X})^{-1}\tilde{\mathbf{X}}' \quad \text{(A6.10)}$$

We are assuming here that the additive error terms are not autocorrelated, and therefore $E[\varepsilon\tilde{\varepsilon}] = 0$. We are also assuming that the error terms are homoscedastic, so that

$$E[\varepsilon\varepsilon'] = \sigma^2\mathbf{I} \quad\quad\quad\quad \text{(A6.11)}$$

We can thus write the variance of the forecast error as

$$\sigma_f{}^2 = \sigma^2 + \sigma^2\tilde{\mathbf{X}}(\mathbf{X}'\mathbf{X})^{-1}\mathbf{X}'\mathbf{I}\mathbf{X}(\mathbf{X}'\mathbf{X})^{-1}\tilde{\mathbf{X}}'$$

$$= \sigma^2(1 + \tilde{\mathbf{X}}(\mathbf{X}'\mathbf{X})^{-1}\tilde{\mathbf{X}}') \quad\quad\quad \text{(A6.12)}$$

As was the case in the two-variable regression model, this variance (and therefore the 95 percent confidence interval implied by it) depends on what the particular values of the independent variables are in the forecast period; i.e., it depends on $\tilde{\mathbf{X}}$.

We might now ask what the *smallest possible* forecast error variance could be, i.e., what value of $\tilde{\mathbf{X}}$ would minimize $\sigma_f{}^2$. We can answer this question by solving a *constrained minimization* problem in which we make use of the method of Lagrange multipliers.[11] In order to minimize $\sigma_f{}^2$ we must minimize the matrix product on the right-hand side of Eq. (A6.12); that is, we want to solve the following:

Minimize $\quad \tilde{\mathbf{X}}(\mathbf{X}'\mathbf{X})^{-1}\tilde{\mathbf{X}}'$

Subject to $\quad \tilde{X}_1 = 1$

The constraint that $\tilde{X}_1 = 1$ refers to the fact that the first element of $\tilde{\mathbf{X}}$ is the constant term, i.e., the intercept of the regression equation. Now we can write the *Lagrangian* for this problem as

$$\mathscr{L} = \tilde{\mathbf{X}}(\mathbf{X}'\mathbf{X})^{-1}\tilde{\mathbf{X}}' - \lambda(\tilde{X}_1 - 1) \quad\quad\quad \text{(A6.13)}$$

---

[11] Readers unfamiliar with the method of Lagrange multipliers can refer to M. Intriligator, *Mathematical Optimization and Economic Theory* (Englewood Cliffs, N.J.: Prentice-Hall, 1972), chap. 3; or K. Lancaster, *Mathematical Economics* (New York: Macmillan, 1968), chap. 4.

where λ is the Lagrange multiplier. Now differentiating the Lagrangian with respect to $\tilde{\mathbf{X}}$ and setting the derivative equal to 0,

$$\frac{\partial \mathcal{L}}{\partial \tilde{\mathbf{X}}} = 2(\mathbf{X}'\mathbf{X})^{-1}\tilde{\mathbf{X}}' - \lambda \begin{bmatrix} 1 \\ 0 \\ \vdots \\ 0 \end{bmatrix} = 0 \qquad (A6.14)$$

or

$$\tilde{\mathbf{X}}' = \frac{\lambda}{2}(\mathbf{X}'\mathbf{X}) \begin{bmatrix} 1 \\ 0 \\ \vdots \\ 0 \end{bmatrix} \qquad (A6.15)$$

Thus $\tilde{\mathbf{X}}'$ is proportional to the first column of $\mathbf{X}'\mathbf{X}$:

$$\tilde{\mathbf{X}}' = \frac{\lambda}{2} \begin{bmatrix} T \\ \sum X_2 \\ \sum X_3 \\ \vdots \\ \sum X_k \end{bmatrix} \qquad (A6.16)$$

The summations in Eq. (A6.16) are over the T observations. From the first row of Eq. (A6.16) we have, since $\tilde{X}_1 = 1$,

$$\frac{\lambda}{2} T = 1 \qquad \text{or} \qquad \lambda = \frac{2}{T}$$

We can thus write Eq. (A6.16) as

$$\tilde{\mathbf{X}}' = \begin{bmatrix} 1 \\ \dfrac{\sum X_2}{T} \\ \dfrac{\sum X_3}{T} \\ \vdots \\ \dfrac{\sum X_k}{T} \end{bmatrix} \qquad (A6.17)$$

But note that the right-hand side of (A6.17) is just the *point of means*. Thus, as was the case in the two-variable model, the forecast error variance is minimized when all the new observations on the independent variables are equal to their mean values. What is the value of this minimum forecast error variance? Writing (A6.17) as

$$\tilde{\mathbf{X}}' = \frac{1}{T} (\mathbf{X}'\mathbf{X}) \begin{bmatrix} 1 \\ 0 \\ \vdots \\ 0 \end{bmatrix} \tag{A6.18}$$

and substituting this into (A6.12), we have

$$\min (\sigma_f{}^2) = \sigma^2 \left\{ 1 + \frac{1}{T} [1 \quad 0 \quad \cdots \quad 0](\mathbf{X}'\mathbf{X})(\mathbf{X}'\mathbf{X})^{-1}(\mathbf{X}'\mathbf{X}) \begin{bmatrix} 1 \\ 0 \\ \vdots \\ 0 \end{bmatrix} \frac{1}{T} \right\}$$

$$= \sigma^2 \left\{ 1 + \frac{1}{T^2} [1 \quad 0 \quad \cdots \quad 0](\mathbf{X}'\mathbf{X}) \begin{bmatrix} 1 \\ 0 \\ \vdots \\ 0 \end{bmatrix} \right\}$$

$$= \sigma^2 \left(1 + \frac{T}{T^2} \right) = \sigma^2 \left(1 + \frac{1}{T} \right) \tag{A6.19}$$

Note that as the number of observations T becomes infinitely large, this minimum forecast error variance approaches the variance of the additive error term σ^2. We would expect this to be the case, since as T becomes infinitely large the estimated parameter values approach the true parameter values exactly, so that the only source of forecast error is the additive error term.

Now what will our 95 percent confidence regions look like? They will essentially be a multidimensional version of Fig. 6.3. In the case of two independent variables (in addition to the constant term), the 95 percent confidence region will be bounded by two "hyperboloids." The confidence interval will be smallest at the mean values of X_1 and X_2.

7

SINGLE EQUATION ESTIMATION— ADVANCED TOPICS

In the last six chapters we completed the development of the core of econometrics—the general linear model. We began with a discussion of ordinary least-squares estimation and continued with an analysis of adjustments which must be made to ordinary least squares to guarantee unbiased, consistent, and efficient estimation. These adjustments included corrections for serial correlation, heteroscedasticity, and correlation between the regressors and the disturbance term. Finally, we showed how the linear model can be used for forecasting. In this chapter we continue our discussion of single-equation estimation by discussing problems associated with the econometric model.[1] First, we deal with the problem of specification error, focusing on the difficulties which arise when irrelevant variables are added to a regression model and when relevant variables are omitted. The costs associated with both kinds of specification error have direct bearing on the strategy of model building. Second, we consider several means of resolving the dilemma which arises when there are missing observations. The loss of efficiency which results when observations are dropped from the sample is compared with the risks of replacing missing observations with suitable substitutes. Third, we provide a brief introduction to the estimation

---

[1] The five topics presented in this chapter may be read independently of each other, and can be treated as optional for an introductory econometrics course.

of regression models using cross-section and time-series data. Several alternative schemes for pooling data are contemplated, and whenever possible the corresponding estimation techniques are described. The fourth topic in this chapter is a description of distributed lag models and their estimation. We focus on two of the most frequently used lag structures, the geometric lag and the polynomial distributed lag. Finally, the chapter concludes with an introduction to nonlinear estimation. We focus on some alternative techniques for estimating equations that are nonlinear in the parameters, and see how these equations can be used for forecasting.

7.1 SPECIFICATION ERROR

Much of our discussion of econometrics has relied heavily upon the assumption that the model to be estimated is correctly specified, i.e., that it represents the underlying physical process. Once the correct specification of the model is assumed, model estimation and model testing become relatively straightforward. In reality, however, we can never be sure that a given model is correctly specified. In fact, applied researchers usually examine more than one possible model specification, attempting to find the specification which best describes the physical process under study. We attempt to give the reader a feeling for the hazards involved in searching for a model by discussing the costs associated with model misspecification. We concern ourselves with two types of misspecification, the first occurring when relevant variables are omitted from the linear regression, and the second occurring when irrelevant variables are added to the equation. We do not consider misspecification errors associated with the disturbance term, since much of this material was discussed in Chapters 4 and 5. Finally, we pause only briefly to discuss misspecifications associated with the incorrect choice of functional form, since much of that material will be implicitly covered in section 7.5 on nonlinear estimation. Once again, we use special cases to illustrate our major arguments, although most results can be generalized using the tools of matrix algebra.[2]

7.1.1 Omitted Variables

Consider first the case in which a variable is unknowingly omitted from a "true" or correct model specification.[3] Assume that the true model is given by Eq. (7.1),

---

[2] The material used in this section is discussed in more detail in two excellent discussions of model misspecification, P. Rao and R. L. Miller, *Applied Econometrics* (Belmont, Calif.: Wadsworth, 1971); and J. Kmenta, *Elements of Econometrics* (New York: Macmillan, 1971), pp. 391–406. The original source material is H. Theil, "Specification Errors and the Estimation of Economic Relationships," *Review of the International Statistical Institute,* vol. 25, pp. 41–51, 1957.

[3] Such a variable might be omitted by choice, if sufficiently accurate data are not available to the researcher.

while the regression model is given by Eq. (7.2):[4]

$$y_i = \beta_2 x_{2i} + \beta_3 x_{3i} + \varepsilon_i \tag{7.1}$$

$$y_i = \beta_2^* x_{2i} + \varepsilon_i^* \tag{7.2}$$

All the assumptions of the classical linear model hold for Eq. (7.1).
As was derived in Chapter 1, the estimated slope parameter is

$$\hat{\beta}_2^* = \frac{\sum x_{2i} y_i}{\sum x_{2i}^2} \tag{7.3}$$

Substituting y_i, defined as in Eq. (7.2), into Eq. (7.1) and solving, we get

$$\hat{\beta}_2^* = \frac{\sum x_{2i} \beta_2 x_{2i} + \sum x_{2i} \beta_3 x_{3i} + \sum x_{2i} \varepsilon_i}{\sum x_{2i}^2}$$

$$= \frac{\beta_2 \sum x_{2i}^2 + \beta_3 \sum x_{2i} x_{3i} + \sum x_{2i} \varepsilon_i}{\sum x_{2i}^2}$$

$$= \beta_2 + \beta_3 \frac{\sum x_{2i} x_{3i}}{\sum x_{2i}^2} + \frac{\sum x_{2i} \varepsilon_i}{\sum x_{2i}^2}$$

$$= \beta_2 + \beta_3 \frac{\sum x_{2i} x_{3i}}{\sum x_{2i}^2}$$

$$= \beta_2 + \beta_3 \frac{\text{Cov}(x_2, x_3)}{\text{Var}(x_2)} \tag{7.4}$$

Since there is no guarantee that the second term will be 0, the least-squares slope estimate of Eq. (7.2) will yield a biased estimate of the true slope parameter β_2. This bias will not disappear as the sample size grows large, so that the omission of a variable from the true model yields inconsistent parameter estimates as well. The only case in which the bias (and inconsistency) will completely disappear occurs when $\text{Cov}(x_2, x_3) = 0$, that is, when x_2 and x_3 are uncorrelated in the sample.[5] This result generalizes if there are numerous independent

---

[4] We shall work with data in deviations form to simplify the derivations. Most, but not all, of the results hold for the intercept of the equation. Since the effect of model misspecification on the intercept is not usually of paramount importance, we leave the details to the reader (see Exercise 7.1).

[5] A high variance for x_2 will lower the amount of bias, but the bias will never reach zero, since we have assumed a finite variance for all sample x's.

variables. Only when the omitted variable is uncorrelated with all the included independent variables does the bias disappear, and this is extremely unlikely with business and economic data.

The formula in Eq. (7.4) is useful because it tells that the direction of any bias which might occur depends upon the correlation between the omitted variable and all included variables, as well as on the sign of the true slope coefficient β_3. To the extent that x_2 and x_3 are highly correlated, the coefficient of x_2 will include the effect of the x_3 variable and will be biased.[6] When x_2 and x_3 are uncorrelated, x_2 picks up none of the effect of x_3 and no bias occurs. As a practical matter, it is the *extent* of the specification bias which is important. This suggests that a careful researcher will consider not only the question of missing variables, but their possible correlation with included model variables as well.

To be complete, we should pause to consider the effect of variable omission on the error variance and its estimate. First consider the case in which x_2 and x_3 are uncorrelated. Then $\hat{\beta}_2^*$ will be an unbiased estimator of β_2 and will have an identical variance with $\hat{\beta}_2$. The only difficulty with model misspecification arises because the usual *estimate* of the variance of $\hat{\beta}_2^*$ will be biased.[7] However, in the more general case when x_2 and x_3 are correlated, the two estimators will not have identical variances. In the two-variable model, the actual variance of $\hat{\beta}_2^*$ will be less than the actual variance of $\hat{\beta}_2$, even though the model is misspecified.[8] If one is willing to give up lack of bias as an important objective, then the omitted variable specification has some merit. This is particularly the case when omitted variables are thought to be uncorrelated with included variables.

7.1.2 Presence of an Irrelevant Variable

Now consider the case in which an irrelevant variable is added to the equation. Assume that the true model is given by Eq. (7.5), while the regression model is given by Eq. (7.6):

$$y_i = \beta_2 x_{2i} + \varepsilon_i \tag{7.5}$$

$$y_i = \beta_2^* x_{2i} + \beta_3^* x_{3i} + \varepsilon_i^* \tag{7.6}$$

The effects of adding an irrelevant variable are quite different from the effects of omitting a variable. The addition of the irrelevant variable x_3 implies that we are not taking into account the true parameter restriction $\beta_3^* = 0$. We would expect

---

[6] It is interesting (and useful when generalizations are made) to note that the correlation in question is simply the regression coefficient associated with the "auxiliary regression" of x_3 on x_2.

[7] It is cumbersome but not difficult to show that the estimated variance of $\hat{\beta}_2^*$ will be biased upward. See Exercise 7.3 for details.

[8] This is shown in Rao and Miller, *op. cit.*

that not taking into account all the information available about the model (the zero restriction) would lead to a loss of efficiency, but no loss of consistency and no bias. To see that this is the case, we calculate the estimated coefficient of the variable x_2 in Eq. (7.6). Using the derivation described in Chapter 3 [Eq. (3.7)], we find that

$$\hat{\beta}_2^* = \frac{(\sum x_{3i}^2 \sum x_{2i} y_i) - (\sum x_{2i} x_{3i} \sum x_{3i} y_i)}{(\sum x_{2i}^2 \sum x_{3i}^2) - (\sum x_{2i} x_{3i})^2} \tag{7.7}$$

Substituting for y_i in Eq. (7.5) and solving, we get

$$\hat{\beta}_2^* = \beta_2 + \frac{(\sum x_{3i}^2 \sum x_{2i} \varepsilon_i) - (\sum x_{2i} x_{3i} \sum x_{3i} \varepsilon_i)}{(\sum x_{2i}^2 \sum x_{3i}^2) - (\sum x_{2i} x_{3i})^2}$$

from which it follows that (taking expected values with x_2 and x_3 fixed)

$$E(\hat{\beta}_2^*) = \beta_2$$

Thus, the inclusion of an irrelevant variable does not bias the slope parameter estimates of any of the slope variables which appear in the "true" model. It is not difficult to show that the intercept of the equation is unbiased as well and that the estimate of the coefficient of x_3 will have an expected value of 0. We shall leave both of these proofs to the reader (see Exercises 7.4 and 7.5).

The inclusion of irrelevant variables does affect the efficiency of the least-squares estimator, since the variance of the estimated slope coefficient $\hat{\beta}_2^*$ will,[9] in general, be larger than the variance of the coefficient $\hat{\beta}_2$. (The only case in which a loss of efficiency will not occur is the special case when x_2 and x_3 are uncorrelated, again an unlikely possibility.) This loss of efficiency makes it more difficult to reject the null hypothesis of a zero slope parameter. However, the estimated variance of $\hat{\beta}_2^*$ will be an unbiased estimator of the true variance of $\hat{\beta}_2^*$. This suggests that the loss of efficiency will be accounted for when the standard error of the regression is calculated. Thus, we may be quite confident in rejecting the zero-slope null hypothesis when some irrelevant variables are included in the model.

7.1.3 Nonlinearities

Another specification error can occur when the researcher chooses to estimate a linear regression model that is linear in the explanatory variables when the true regression model is nonlinear in the explanatory variables. A simple example of

---

[9] For further details, see J. Kmenta, *op. cit.*, pp. 396–399.

such a specification error occurs when the true model is of the polynomial form described in Eq. (7.8), while the estimated model is that of Eq. (7.9):[10]

$$y_i = \beta_2 x_{2i} + \beta_3 x_{2i}^2 + \beta_4 x_{2i}^3 + \varepsilon_i \tag{7.8}$$

$$y_i = \beta_2^* x_{2i} + \varepsilon_i^* \tag{7.9}$$

The choice of the model in Eq. (7.9) is a special case of omitted variables as described earlier. This suggests that specification of a linear model when the true model is nonlinear can lead to biased and inconsistent parameter estimates. The same conclusion holds when a polynomial approximation to an inherently nonlinear equation is used (see section 7.5).

7.1.4 Costs of Model Building

The previous analysis of specification error suggests some of the serious difficulties involved with the model-building process. If we are unsure of which explanatory variables ought to appear in a model, we face several trade-offs. The analysis suggests that the cost of excluding a variable which should appear in the model is bias and inconsistency. The cost of adding one or more irrelevant variables, on the other hand, is loss of efficiency. If the number of observations available is rather large, it seems reasonable to opt for the risk of adding irrelevant variables because the loss of degrees of freedom associated with the addition of several independent variables to the model is unlikely to be serious. If the number of observations is not large, however, loss of efficiency becomes a serious matter. If all potential model variables are known, the choice of model form must be made in terms of the bias-efficiency trade-off, with the result dependent upon our objectives. If accurate forecasting is the goal, minimizing mean square error appears to be one reasonable objective, since it accounts for both bias and efficiency.[11] Thus, we might estimate each of several alternative models over a given time period and compare the mean square errors associated with each model.[12] This notion of validating models, or of choosing among model forms by means of simulation, is described in detail in Part Two of the book.

In terms of classical statistics, it is not difficult to test whether irrelevant variables are present. Since the coefficients of irrelevant variables have expected values of 0, we need simply apply standard t tests if we wish to evaluate the relevancy of individual variables, and an F test if we wish to test the relevancy of a group of variables. Such testing is feasible if we know the set of variables which might conceivably appear in the model, but it fails completely when we

---

[10] We often estimate polynomial equations such as that given in Eq. (7.8) as a test for nonlinearity in the independent variables.

[11] Recall from Chapter 2 that mean square error = variance + bias².

[12] One of the difficulties with such a procedure is that knowledge of mean square error does not give us independent knowledge of bias (and variance).

are unsure as to which variables ought to appear in the model. As a rule, standard statistical testing is inappropriate when two essentially unrelated models are to be compared. Once again, we must rely upon the use of simulation techniques to make such comparisons.[13] In the case of omitted variables, simple statistical tests are also unlikely to be available, since we usually cannot measure or do not have any knowledge of the omitted variable. t tests and F tests are appropriate only when the omitted variables are known.

Example 7.1 Demand for Money

In a study of the long-run and short-run demand for money, Chow estimated the following demand equation (standard errors are in parentheses and all data are quarterly):[14]

$$M_t = .1365 + 1.069 Y_{pt} - .01321 Y_t - .7476 R_t \qquad R^2 = .9965$$
$$\phantom{M_t = .1365 + 1.069 Y_{pt}} (.148) \qquad (.13897) \quad (.0540)$$

where M = natural logarithm of total money stock
$\quad Y_p$ = natural logarithm of permanent income
$\quad Y$ = natural logarithm of current income
$\quad R$ = natural logarithm of rate of interest

Since Chow views the estimated equation as a long-run equation for the demand for money, he concludes that permanent income is more important than current income as the long-run constraint on individual assets. (The Y variable is insignificant, while the Y_p variable is highly significant.) However, it is possible to argue that the estimated equation is in fact a misspecification of the correct long-run demand-for-money equation. Taylor and Newhouse argue that the correct specification is as follows:[15]

$$M_t = \beta_1 + \beta_2 Y_{pt} + \beta_3 Y_t + \beta_4 R_t + \beta_5 M_{t-1} + \varepsilon_t$$

If this specification is correct, then we would expect the coefficients of the estimated equation to be biased. We can approximate the extent of this bias by utilizing our results on the effects of omitted-variable specification error.

[13] Bayesian econometrics provides a suitable framework in which the limitations of the classical methods of model construction and model testing can be seen. See, for example, A. Zellner, *An Introduction to Bayesian Inference in Econometrics* (New York: Wiley, 1971).

[14] G. C. Chow, "On the Long-Run and Short-Run Demand for Money," *Journal of Political Economy*, vol. 74, pp. 111–131, Apr. 1966.

[15] L. D. Taylor and J. P. Newhouse, "On the Long-Run and Short-Run Demand for Money: A Comment," *Journal of Political Economy*, vol. 77, pp. 851–856, 1969.

Consider the estimated permanent income coefficient, since it is crucial to the policy conclusion which was reached. If the correct model had been

$$M_t = \alpha_1 + \alpha_2 Y_{pt} + \alpha_3 M_{t-1} + u_t$$

then from Eq. (7.4) we could conclude that the bias in the estimated coefficient $\hat{\alpha}_2$ of the equation $M_t = \alpha_1 + \alpha_2 Y_{pt}$ would be

$$E(\hat{\alpha}_2) - \alpha_2 = \alpha_3 \frac{\text{Cov}(Y_{pt}, M_{t-1})}{\text{Var}(Y_{pt})}$$

While we have not done so in the text, it is possible to extend the formula for specification bias to apply to equations with numerous explanatory variables. In our case the bias in the permanent income term is estimated by

$$E(\hat{\beta}_2) - \beta_2 = \beta_5 d_2 + v_t$$

where d_2 is the coefficient of Y_{pt} in the "auxiliary" regression of M_{t-1} on Y_{pt}, Y_t, and R_t, that is,

$$M_{t-1} = d_1 + d_2 Y_{pt} + d_3 Y_t + d_4 R_t + v_t$$

If the variable M_{t-1} is unavailable, we would have to speculate about the extent of any specification bias present. However, in this particular example M_{t-1} is available, since it involves a one-period lag of a variable present in the misspecified equation. Since M_{t-1} and Y_{pt} are known to be highly correlated and we expect the sign of M_{t-1} to be positive when the correctly specified equation is run, we would predict that the bias is positive and substantial. In other words, the extent of the importance of permanent income is overstated because of the specification error. This guess is borne out when the correctly specified model is estimated. The results are as follows:

$$M_t = .3067 + .06158 Y_{pt} + .3274 Y_t - .3325 R_t + .5878 M_{t-1} \qquad R^2 = .9988$$
$$ (.14284) \quad (.0940) \quad (.0597) \quad (.0669)$$

The M_{t-1} coefficient is positive and significant, while the Y_{pt} coefficient is positive but is insignificant at the 5 percent level. Thus, the original conclusion ought to be revised to state that current income is more important than permanent income in explaining the demand for money.

7.2 MISSING OBSERVATIONS

Our empirical work is often complicated by the fact that observations for one or more variables may be missing. Since there is no best approach for dealing with the problem of missing observations, we proceed by discussing some of the relevant issues and suggesting some possible solutions. The choice of method for dealing with missing observations depends upon the nature of each particular regression model and the related data. For this reason, it is very difficult to state rules of thumb for dealing with missing observations. There is no substitute for careful thought on the part of the analyst.

Assume that the regression model is given by

$$Y_i = \beta_1 + \beta_2 X_i + \varepsilon_i \tag{7.10}$$

We shall deal solely with the situation in which the right-hand variable (or variables when we generalize) has some missing observations.[16] If N observations on both X and Y are available, then the least-squares estimator of the slope is

$$\hat{\beta}_2 = \frac{\sum\limits_{i=1}^{N}(X_i - \overline{X}_N)(Y_i - \overline{Y}_N)}{\sum\limits_{i=1}^{N}(X_i - \overline{X}_N)^2} \tag{7.11}$$

where $\overline{X}_N$ and $\overline{Y}_N$ represent the sample means calculated for the first N observations. Assume that M additional observations are available for the dependent variable, but that there are M missing observations for the independent variable (there are a total of $M + N$ observations). A straightforward solution to the missing observations problem is simply to drop the last M observations of Y from consideration. The resulting slope estimate is $\hat{\beta}_2$. If we are dealing with a cross-section problem and the missing observations appear to be missing at random (e.g., not available because of data reporting problems), then eliminating the observations is a reasonable procedure. Because the observations dropped are random, the least-squares slope estimator $\hat{\beta}_2$ will be an unbiased and consistent estimator of β_2, and the only effect of dropping the observations is a loss of efficiency. The loss of efficiency can be seen by comparing the variance

---

[16] In most cross-section studies the unavailability of observations on the dependent variable makes any information about the explanatory variables useless. For example, if we are predicting individual auto purchases on the basis of annual income, data on income for which there are no corresponding automobile expenditures data are likely to be of no value. The income observations (without expenditures) are best dropped from the model. In time-series analysis, however, missing dependent variable observations present a serious problem and necessitate a solution procedure.

of the slope estimator $(\hat{\beta}_2)$ when missing observations are dropped to the variance of the slope estimator $(\hat{\beta}_2^*)$ if all observations are available:

$$\text{Var}(\hat{\beta}_2) = \frac{\sigma^2}{\sum_{i=1}^{N}(X_i - \overline{X}_N)^2} \tag{7.12}$$

$$\text{Var}(\hat{\beta}_2^*) = \frac{\sigma^2}{\sum_{i=1}^{N+M}(X_i - \overline{X}_{N+M})^2} \tag{7.13}$$

where $\overline{X}_{N+M}$ is the overall mean of X. Then

$$\frac{\text{Var}(\hat{\beta}_2)}{\text{Var}(\hat{\beta}_2^*)} = \frac{\sum_{i=N+1}^{N+M}(X_i - \overline{X}_{N+M})^2}{\sum_{i=1}^{N}(X_i - \overline{X}_N)^2}$$

But

$$\sum_{i=1}^{N+M}(X_i - \overline{X}_{N+M})^2 = \sum_{i=1}^{N}[(X_i - \overline{X}_N) + (\overline{X}_N - \overline{X}_{N+M})]^2 + \sum_{i=N+1}^{N+M}(X_i - \overline{X}_{N+M})^2$$

$$= \sum_{i=1}^{N}(X_i - \overline{X}_N)^2 + N(\overline{X}_N - \overline{X}_{N+M})^2$$

$$+ \sum_{i=N+1}^{N+M}(X_i - \overline{X}_{N+M})^2$$

Therefore,

$$\frac{\text{Var}(\hat{\beta}_2)}{\text{Var}(\hat{\beta}_2^*)} = 1 + \frac{N(\overline{X}_N - \overline{X}_{N+M})^2 + \sum_{i=N+1}^{N+M}(X_i - \overline{X}_{N+M})^2}{\sum_{i=1}^{N}(X_i - \overline{X}_N)^2} \tag{7.14}$$

It should be apparent from Eq. (7.14) that dropping the observations with only partial information available will increase the variance of the estimated slope parameter (note that all terms are nonnegative). Only when all missing observations are identical in value to the sample mean of the available X's will there be no loss of efficiency. In general, the closer the missing X's to the sample mean and the smaller the sample variance of the missing X's, the lower the efficiency loss caused by dropping the observations.

If many observations are missing, the potential loss of efficiency necessitates an alternative to simply dropping incomplete observations. If some *a priori* knowledge is available, the best alternative may very well be to assign values for the missing observations.[17] If the missing observations are random, with no *a priori* information available, another solution must be found. The most natural solution is to replace the missing observations by the sample mean of the available X observations. This is equivalent to regressing X on a constant and assigning to each missing observation the estimated coefficient. To see the effect of this substitution, compare the least-squares estimator $\hat{\beta}_2$ with the least-squares estimator $\tilde{\beta}_2$ computed with the sample mean of X substituted for all missing observations:

$$
\tilde{\beta}_2 = \frac{\sum_{i=1}^{N}(X_i - \overline{X}_{N+M})(Y_i - \overline{Y}_{N+M}) + \sum_{i=N+1}^{N+M}(\overline{X}_N - \overline{X}_{N+M})(Y_i - \overline{Y}_{N+M})}{\sum_{i=1}^{N}(X_i - \overline{X}_{N+M})^2 + \sum_{i=N+1}^{N+M}(\overline{X}_N - \overline{X}_{N+M})^2}
$$

By construction, $\overline{X}_N = \overline{X}_{N+M}$. Therefore,

$$
\tilde{\beta}_2 = \frac{\sum_{i=1}^{N}(X_i - \overline{X}_N)(Y_i - \overline{Y}_{N+M})}{\sum_{i=1}^{N}(X_i - \overline{X}_N)^2} \tag{7.15}
$$

But $\tilde{\beta}_2$ is identically equal to the least-squares estimator $\hat{\beta}_2$. To show this, we need simply to prove that the numerators of both estimators are equal [from (7.11) and (7.15)]. This result holds since

$$
\sum_{i=1}^{N}(X_i - \overline{X}_N)(Y_i - \overline{Y}_N) = \sum_{i=1}^{N}(X_i - \overline{X}_N)Y_i - \overline{Y}_N\sum_{i=1}^{N}(X_i - \overline{X}_N) = \sum_{i=1}^{N}(X_i - \overline{X}_N)Y_i
$$

and

$$
\sum_{i=1}^{N}(X_i - \overline{X}_N)(Y_i - \overline{Y}_{N+M}) = \sum_{i=1}^{N}(X_i - \overline{X}_N)Y_i - \overline{Y}_{N+M}\sum_{i=1}^{N}(X_i - \overline{X}_N)
$$

$$
= \sum_{i=1}^{N}(X_i - \overline{X}_N)Y_i
$$

---

[17] One must keep in mind, however, that the degrees of freedom in the model may be different from the degrees of freedom printed by the computer, so that statistical tests may be misleading.

In addition, the variance of the estimator with the observations replaced will be identical to the estimator with observations dropped; that is,

$$\text{Var}\ (\tilde{\beta}_2) = \frac{\sigma^2}{\displaystyle\sum_{i=1}^{N} (X_i - \overline{X}_{N+M})^2 + \sum_{i=N+1}^{N+M} (\overline{X}_N - \overline{X}_{N+M})^2} = \frac{\sigma^2}{\displaystyle\sum_{i=1}^{N} (X_i - \overline{X}_N)^2}$$

$$= \text{Var}\ (\hat{\beta}_2) \tag{7.16}$$

Thus, the substitution of variable means for missing observations does not change the least-squares slope estimator or its variance. This result is discouraging, but should not be taken out of context. If we were to generalize the model to one containing several independent variables, only one of which had missing observations, then the substitution procedure described here *might* well yield different slope estimators and an improvement in efficiency. The proof of this is too complex to describe here,[18] but some examples in which the substitution of variable means is helpful appear later in the chapter.

In practice, the assumption that missing observations are random is unlikely to be realistic. More often than not, the pattern of missing observations is systematic. For example, in a study relating automobile expenditures to income, there may systematically be missing observations for low-income individuals, who tend to spend little on automobiles. Dropping observations, or using the sample mean of X to replace missing observations, is not the correct procedure, because no account is taken of the known correlation between income and expenditures. Equivalently, in doing time-series analysis, we can improve our analysis by accounting for the fact that most time-series variables tend to undergo relatively predictable rates of growth. To do so, we search for proxy variables which are highly correlated with the variables whose observations are missing, and which involve little measurement error.

An elementary solution to the time-series problem would involve replacing missing observations with proxy observations obtained by regressing the known values of the independent variable X on time and by replacing the missing observations by the fitted values of the regression. In other words, the regression $X_t = \alpha_1 + \alpha_2 t + u_t$ would be run for all available X observations and $\hat{X}_t = \hat{\alpha}_1 + \hat{\alpha}_2 t$ would be calculated, where values of t are chosen to correspond to the time period of the missing observations. This procedure is only one of several ways in which missing observations can be replaced through the interpolation of the X variable.[19] It yields consistent parameter estimates *if the time variable t*

---

[18] See Y. Haitovsky, "Estimation of Regression Equations When a Block of Observations Is Missing," *Proceedings of the American Statistical Association,* Business and Economics Statistics Section, 1968; A. A. Afifi and R. M. Elashoff, "Missing Observations in Multivariate Statistics II. Point Estimates in Simple Linear Regression," *Journal of the American Statistical Association,* vol. 62, pp. 10–29, 1967; and M. G. Dagenais, "The Use of Incomplete Observations in Multiple Regression Analysis," *Journal of Econometrics,* vol. 1, pp. 317–328, 1973.

[19] There are numerous methods of linear and geometric interpolation from which to choose.

is uncorrelated with the error term in the original equation. The procedure is perhaps most useful because it suggests a more general approach to the systematic missing observations problem which also yields consistent parameter estimates.

Let us presume that a set of "instruments," $Z_2, \ldots, Z_k$, is available with respect to the variable with the missing observations. The nature of the instruments would vary, depending upon the particular problem and whether the data are cross-sectional or time-series. The instruments are presumed to be highly correlated with the variable X and uncorrelated with error term ε; that is, Cov $(Z_i, \varepsilon) = 0$, $i = 2, 3, \ldots, k$. It is necessary, of course, that all the observations be available for the instruments, which might be chosen (see Chapter 9) because they appear as predetermined variables in a simultaneous equation system. We can increase the efficiency of the original parameter estimates while maintaining the consistency of the parameter estimates by proceeding in a manner which resembles the two-stage least-squares procedure described in Chapter 5.[20]

First regress X on the set of instruments for all observations with complete information:

$$X_i = \alpha_1 + \alpha_2 Z_{2i} + \cdots + \alpha_k Z_{ki} + u_i \qquad i = 1, 2, \ldots, N \qquad (7.17)$$

Then calculate fitted values for the missing observations:[21]

$$\hat{X}_i = \hat{\alpha}_1 + \hat{\alpha}_2 Z_{2i} + \cdots + \hat{\alpha}_k Z_{ki} \qquad i = N + 1, \ldots, N + M \qquad (7.18)$$

We may then reestimate the original equation as follows:

$$Y_i = \beta_1 + \beta_2 \hat{X}_i + v_i \qquad (7.19)$$

where $\hat{X}_i = X_i$ for $i = 1, 2, \ldots, N$

$$v_i = \begin{cases} \varepsilon_i & \text{for } i = 1, 2, \ldots, N \\ \varepsilon_i - \beta_2 u_i & \text{for } i = N + 1, \ldots, N + M \end{cases} \qquad (7.20)$$

As long as the instruments are correctly chosen, the estimation of Eq. (7.19) will yield a consistent slope estimate.[22]

There are several problems associated with the instrumental variables approach

---

[20] If X is an endogenous variable, then 2SLS can be used without any difficulty (as far as that particular equation is concerned), and the missing observations problem disappears!

[21] In time-series analysis, it is unlikely that the last set of observations will be missing. The analysis is quite general, however, because we need simply rearrange the numbering of the observations appropriately and all results will follow.

[22] The proof is too difficult to describe here, but is similar in nature to the proof that two-stage least-squares parameter estimates are consistent.

just described. First, the error variances associated with missing observations will be larger than the remaining error variances [from Eq. (7.20)]:

$$\text{Var }(v_i) = \begin{cases} \sigma^2 & \text{for } i = 1, 2, \ldots, N \\ \sigma^2 + \beta_2{}^2 \text{ Var }(u_i) & \text{for } i = N + 1, \ldots, N + M \end{cases}$$

A more refined technique would utilize weighted least squares to adjust for the efficiency loss associated with heteroscedasticity. Such an approach is likely to be important only when many observations are missing. Second, it is possible that observations will be missing for more than one right-hand variable. Then, a series of instrumental variable regressions must be run to fill in the missing observations. Unfortunately, the order in which these procedures occur can affect the estimated parameters. Finally, the choice of proper instruments is often difficult. If the instruments are not uncorrelated with the error term, then measurement error (a form of errors in variables) will be introduced when the missing observations are replaced by observations from the constructed proxy variable. For further details the reader should review Chapter 5, in which errors in variables and instrumental variables are discussed.[23]

Example 7.2   Dividend Policy

The dividend behavior of firms is a subject of frequent study by business analysts. The following model was developed in an attempt to study the dividend policies of firms in the electrical industry (all data pertain to the year 1965):

$$\frac{\text{DPS}}{P} = \beta_1 + \beta_2 \frac{\text{EPS}}{P} + \beta_3 \frac{\text{DL} + \text{DS}}{A} + \beta_4 \frac{\text{DEPR}}{A} + \beta_5 \text{OI} + \varepsilon$$

where DEPR = depreciation
DPS = dividends per share
EPS = earnings per share
P = end of year security price
DL = long-term debt
DS = short-term debt
A = asset value of the firm
OI = operating income

It is believed that earnings per share will be positively correlated with dividends per share, since companies with a high rate of earnings are more likely to pay out larger dividends. On the other hand, the debt-asset ratio should

---

[23] For a distinctive and useful procedure for dealing with missing observations, see M. Glasser, "Linear Regression Analysis with Missing Observations among the Independent Variables," *Journal of the American Statistical Association*, 59 (1964), pp. 834–844.

be negatively correlated with dividends. Other things equal, one would expect that firms with large debt-asset ratios would be concerned with long-term growth and would choose to increase retained earnings rather than dividends. The depreciation-asset ratio was included to account for the fact that firms with high depreciation levels are likely to have a large cash flow and greater dividend potential. Finally, the operating income term was added with the thought that operating income might be positively related to dividends. The relationship is a questionable one, because dividend policy usually involves a long-run planning decision, while operating income is a function primarily of short-run factors.

The estimation of the linear regression was complicated by the fact that five observations were missing from variable A, six from P, four from DS, six from DEPR, five from DPS, six from EPS, five from DL, and five from OI: The original sample consisted of 77 firms, but only 68 of the observations were complete. As a first attempted solution to the missing observations problem, the 68 complete observations were used to estimate the regression equation. The results are as follows (t statistics are in parentheses):

$$\frac{\text{DPS}}{P} = \underset{(3.31)}{.015} + \underset{(1.43)}{.082}\frac{\text{EPS}}{P} - \underset{(-1.92)}{.016}\frac{\text{DL}+\text{DS}}{A} + \underset{(.77)}{.039}\frac{\text{DEPR}}{A} + \underset{(.18)}{3.1\times10^{-6}\text{OI}}$$

$$R^2 = .159 \qquad \text{SER} = .0151 \qquad \text{DW} = 1.92 \qquad F(4/63) = 2.990$$

Only two of the coefficients are significant at the 5 percent level and the general predictive power of the equation appears to be quite low. When each of the missing observations is replaced by the appropriate sample means, the results are somewhat more promising:

$$\frac{\text{DPS}}{P} = \underset{(4.68)}{.017} + \underset{(1.28)}{.048}\frac{\text{EPS}}{P} - \underset{(-3.27)}{.017}\frac{\text{DL}+\text{DS}}{A} + \underset{(1.75)}{.028}\frac{\text{DEPR}}{A} + \underset{(.23)}{3.7\times10^{-6}\text{OI}}$$

$$R^2 = .182 \qquad \text{SER} = .0144 \qquad \text{DW} = 2.01 \qquad F(4/72) = 3.997$$

The t statistics suggest that some efficiency has been gained by the replacement procedure, while the relative stability of the coefficients is to be expected, since the replacement process does not cause any bias in the coefficient estimates.

The results of the regression lend support to the original hypotheses. The coefficient of the EPS/P term is positive, but not significant at the 5 percent level. The debt-asset term is negative and highly significant, while the depreciation term is positive and significant at the 10 percent level. The OI term is positive, but is not significant.

Example 7.3   Security Prices

The same sample of electrical firms as described in Example 7.2 was used to study the determinants of security prices. One would expect that EPS and DPS would be positively correlated with price, since, other things equal, firms with high earnings per share and high dividends are valued higher than firms with low earnings per share and lower dividends. The model was completed by adding a third term to account for the effects of leverage on price. It was thought, on the one hand, that a high degree of leverage would be associated with a slow and sometimes interrupted period of earnings for the investor, and therefore a lower stock valuation. On the other hand, a highly leveraged firm has certain tax advantages and usually a greater potential for growth. For this reason, the correlation between price and leverage is hard to predict. The complete model is

$$P = \beta_1 + \beta_2 \text{EPS} + \beta_3 \text{DPS} + \beta_4 \frac{\text{DL}}{\text{DL} + \text{EQTY}} + \varepsilon$$

where EQTY = equity value of the firm
and the remaining terms are defined in Example 7.2.

Two sets of regression results were obtained, the first based on the reduced but complete set of 68 observations, and the second obtained when missing observations on each variable were replaced by the sample means of those variables.

Missing Observations Dropped

$$P = -1.42 + 17.10\text{EPS} + 4.78\text{DPS} + 14.54 \frac{\text{DL}}{\text{DL} + \text{EQTY}}$$
$$\quad (-.39) \quad (5.08) \qquad (.72) \qquad (1.53)$$

$$R^2 = .64 \qquad \text{SER} = 14.1 \qquad \text{DW} = 2.31 \qquad F(3/64) = 38.5$$

Missing Observations Replaced

$$P = -1.59 + 15.52\text{EPS} + 8.35\text{DPS} + 15.66 \frac{\text{DL}}{\text{DL} + \text{EQTY}}$$
$$\quad (-.46) \quad (5.11) \qquad (1.40) \qquad (1.76)$$

$$R^2 = .63 \qquad \text{SER} = 13.6 \qquad \text{DW} = 2.31 \qquad F(3/73) = 41.9$$

Both regression results are quite similar. The smaller reduced sample results in a slightly higher R^2 than the larger sample, but the t statistics in the latter are generally higher than those of the reduced sample. Both results suggest that earnings per share are an important determinant of stock price and that leverage bears a direct relationship with price. Dividends per share are statistically insignificant in both regressions, although the sign is as expected. In this case, the gain from replacing the missing observations is small. The choice to drop all missing observations would be a reasonable one.

7.3 POOLING OF CROSS-SECTION AND TIME-SERIES DATA

A practical problem of some importance occurs when observations are available for several individual units (households, firms, cities, etc.) over a period of time (usually years). Occasionally sufficient observations will not be available to estimate either a time-series or a cross-section equation, suggesting that some method of combining the data be used. As an example, assume that we are modeling the determination of profits of firms in an industry. A single-year cross-section model might include such cross-section explanatory variables as attributes of the firms' management, type of physical capital, and financial leverage.[24] If data were available for each firm over a series of years, then we might question whether cross-section parameters remain constant over time. If they do, we can consider the possibility of combining the data to obtain more efficient parameter estimates. The process of combining cross-section and time-series data is called *pooling*. Cross-section parameters may shift over time, in which case pooling is not the appropriate procedure. On the other hand, there may be time-series-related explanatory variables such as expectations, prices, and interest rates which could be included in a pooled model. Pooling data in a model with both time-series and cross-section explanatory variables then becomes an acceptable procedure. However, the necessity of combining time-series and cross-section variables in the model adds a new dimension of difficulty to the problem of model specification. The model specification problem in turn suggests that the structure of the disturbance term may be a complex one, since the disturbance term is assumed to result in part from the effects of omitted explanatory variables. The difficulty arises because the disturbance term is likely to consist of time-series-related disturbances, cross-section disturbances, and a combination of both.

We proceed by considering a simple regression model for which time-series and cross-section data are available. We discuss several alternative schemes

---

[24] This example was used by E. Kuh to discuss the stability of cross-section models and the specification of variables in *Capital Stock Growth: A Micro-Econometric Approach* (Amsterdam: North-Holland, 1963), pp. 116–117. Cross-section explanatory variables differ over individuals, but remain constant over time. Time-series variables remain constant over individuals, but vary over time. Some variables can both differ over individuals and vary over time.

by which the data might be pooled. The first technique is to combine all cross-section and time-series data and perform ordinary least-squares regression on the entire data set. A second procedure involves the recognition that omitted variables may lead to changing cross-section and time-series intercepts. *Covariance analysis* involves the addition of dummy variables to the model to allow for these changing intercepts. A third pooling technique improves the efficiency of the first least-squares estimation process by accounting for the existence of cross-section and time-series disturbances. The *error components* pooling procedure is a variation of the generalized least-squares estimation process described in the appendix to Chapter 4. Finally, we consider a set of techniques which accounts for the fact that the error term may be correlated over time and over cross-section units. Once again a variation of generalized least-squares estimation provides a useful solution to the problem.

Consider the two-variable model:[25]

$$Y_{it} = \alpha + \beta X_{it} + \varepsilon_{it} \tag{7.21}$$

where $i = 1, 2, ..., N$ $N =$ number of cross-section units (individuals)
       $t = 1, 2, ..., T$ $T =$ number of time periods

If all the classical error term assumptions hold (no correlation with X, no autocorrelation, no heteroscedasticity, etc.), then, in principle, we could estimate separate cross-section regressions, each regression involving N observations. For time period $t = 1$, the cross-section regression would be

$$Y_{i1} = \alpha + \beta X_{i1} + \varepsilon_{i1} \qquad i = 1, 2, ..., N$$

There would be a total of T such equations. Similarly, we could estimate N time-series regressions with T observations in each. However, if both α and β are constant over time and over cross-section units, more efficient parameter estimates can be obtained if all the data are combined so that one large pooled regression is run with NT observations. In this most elementary pooling technique, there will be $NT - 2$ degrees of freedom (since estimation of the two parameters uses up 2 degrees of freedom).

7.3.1 Covariance Model

The difficulty with the least-squares procedure just described is that the assumption of constant intercept and slope may be unreasonable in a pooled model. The obvious generalization of the ordinary least-squares model is to introduce dummy variables which allow for the intercept term to vary over time and to vary over cross-section units. If the slopes were to vary as well, then each separate cross-section regression would involve a distinct model and pooling would be

---

[25] The use of a single explanatory variable does not limit the results of this section.

inappropriate.[26] We can introduce the dummy variables by writing the *covariance model* as follows:

$$Y_{it} = \alpha + \beta X_{it} + \gamma_2 W_{2t} + \gamma_3 W_{3t} + \cdots + \gamma_N W_{Nt}$$

$$+ \delta_2 Z_{i2} + \delta_3 Z_{i3} + \cdots + \delta_T Z_{iT} + \varepsilon_{it} \tag{7.22}$$

where $W_{it} = \begin{cases} 1 & \text{for the } i\text{th individual} \quad i = 2, \ldots, N \\ 0 & \text{otherwise} \end{cases}$

$Z_{it} = \begin{cases} 1 & \text{for the } t\text{th time period} \quad t = 2, \ldots, T \\ 0 & \text{otherwise} \end{cases}$

We have added $(N - 1) + (T - 1)$ dummy variables to the model and have omitted the remaining two, since their addition would result in perfect collinearity among the explanatory variables. If this model were estimated using ordinary least squares, unbiased and consistent estimates of all parameters (including the slope β) would be obtained. A total of $NT - 2 - (N - 1) - (T - 1)$, or $NT - N - T$, degrees of freedom would be involved. The dummy variable coefficients would measure the change in the cross-section and time-series intercepts (with respect to the first individual in the first period of time). To see this, we can eliminate the dummy variables and rewrite the model associated with each of the NT observations:

$$Y_{11} = \alpha + \beta X_{11} + \varepsilon_{11}$$

$$Y_{12} = (\alpha + \delta_2) + \beta X_{12} + \varepsilon_{12}$$

$$\vdots$$

$$Y_{1T} = (\alpha + \delta_T) + \beta X_{1T} + \varepsilon_{1T}$$

$$Y_{21} = (\alpha + \gamma_2) + \beta X_{21} + \varepsilon_{21}$$

$$Y_{22} = (\alpha + \gamma_2 + \delta_2) + \beta X_{22} + \varepsilon_{22}$$

$$\vdots \tag{7.23}$$

$$Y_{2T} = (\alpha + \gamma_2 + \delta_T) + \beta X_{2T} + \varepsilon_{2T}$$

$$\vdots$$

$$Y_{N1} = (\alpha + \gamma_N) + \beta X_{N1} + \varepsilon_{N1}$$

$$Y_{N2} = (\alpha + \gamma_N + \delta_2) + \beta X_{N2} + \varepsilon_{N2}$$

$$\vdots$$

$$Y_{NT} = (\alpha + \gamma_N + \delta_T) + \beta X_{NT} + \varepsilon_{NT}$$

---

[26] Allowance for random variation in slope parameters is made in the random coefficients model literature. See, for example, H. Theil, *Principles of Econometrics* (New York: Wiley, 1971), pp. 622–627; and P. A. V. B. Swamy, "Efficient Inference in a Random Coefficient Regression Model," *Econometrica*, vol. 38, pp. 311–323, 1970.

The effect of the missing δ_1 and γ_1 coefficients is accounted for in the parameter α, the intercept of the first equation. Each of the δ's is then measured in terms of deviations from δ_1 (and the γ's in terms of deviations from γ_1) and thus from the "true" intercept α.

The choice of whether to pool data using ordinary least squares or to sacrifice degrees of freedom by using ordinary least squares with dummy variables is one which can be made on the basis of statistical testing. The test involves a comparison of the residual sum of squares associated with the two estimation techniques. Since the ordinary least-squares model includes more parameter restrictions than the covariance model (the intercepts are restricted to be equal over time and over individuals), we would expect the residual sum of squares to be higher for the ordinary least-squares model. If the increase in the residual sum of squares is not significant when the restrictions are added, then we conclude that the restrictions are proper and ordinary least squares can be applied. If the residual sum of squares changes substantially, we opt for the covariance model. In our model the appropriate test statistic would be[27]

$$F_{N+T-2,\ NT-N-T} = \frac{(\text{ESS}_1 - \text{ESS}_2)/(N+T-2)}{(\text{ESS}_2)/(NT-N-T)} \qquad (7.24)$$

where ESS_1 = residual sum of squares using ordinary least squares
ESS_2 = residual sum of squares using covariance model

The numerator represents the increase in the residual sum of squares divided by the number of additional degrees of freedom when moving from the covariance model to the ordinary least-squares model, while the denominator represents the residual sum of squares for the covariance model divided by the number of degrees of freedom in the covariance model. On the null hypothesis that the equal-intercept restrictions are correct, the statistic F follows the F distribution with $N + T - 2$ and $NT - N - T$ degrees of freedom.

There are several important problems associated with the use of the covariance model for purposes of pooling. First, the use of dummies does not directly identify the variables which might cause the regression line to shift over time and over individuals. The use of dummy variables is an attempt to adjust for important missing information in the model. In doing so, a substantial portion of the error variation may be "explained" without the analyst's obtaining any useful knowledge about the model. Because of this fact, dummy variable coefficients are difficult to interpret. Second, the dummy variable technique uses up a substantial number of degrees of freedom ($N + T - 2$ in our model). The loss of degrees of freedom may substantially decrease the statistical power of the model.

---

[27] For details concerning testing of the covariance model see J. Johnston, *Econometric Methods*, 2d ed. (New York: McGraw-Hill, 1972), pp. 192–207, as well as G. C. Chow, "Tests of Equality between Sets of Coefficients in Two Linear Regressions," *Econometrica*, vol. 28, pp. 591–605, 1960; and F. M. Fisher, "Tests of Equality between Sets of Coefficients in Two Linear Regressions: An Expository Note," *Econometrica*, vol. 38, pp. 361–366, 1970. As the titles of the latter two items imply, the authors deal with a more general set of statistical tests than the one described above.

For example, the use of dummy variables for a study of 15 firms over a 4 year period would involve a reduction of degrees of freedom from 58 to 41, not an inconsequential number.[28]

7.3.2   Error Components Model

Since the inclusion of dummy variables represents a lack of knowledge about the model, it is natural to describe this lack of knowledge through the disturbance term of the equation. We might thus wish to choose a pooled cross-section and time-series model in which error terms may be correlated across time and correlated across individual units. Because of the limited number of available degrees of freedom, further restrictions on the error correlations must be made before a useful estimation procedure can be devised. The *error components model* is a natural solution to this problem.[29]

The model is as follows:

$$Y_{it} = \alpha + \beta X_{it} + \varepsilon_{it} \tag{7.25}$$

$$\varepsilon_{it} = u_i + v_t + w_{it} \tag{7.26}$$

where $u_i \sim N(0, \sigma_u^2)$ is the cross-section error component
$v_i \sim N(0, \sigma_v^2)$ is the time-series error component
$w_{it} \sim N(0, \sigma_w^2)$ is the combined error component

We assume also that individual error components are uncorrelated with each other and are not autocorrelated (across both cross-section and time-series units), that is,

$$\text{Cov}\,(u_i, v_t) = \text{Cov}\,(u_i, w_{it}) = \text{Cov}\,(v_t, w_{it}) = 0$$

$$\text{Cov}\,(u_i, u_j) = 0 \qquad i \neq j$$

$$\text{Cov}\,(v_t, v_{t'}) = 0 \qquad t \neq t'$$

$$\text{Cov}\,(w_{it}, w_{jt}) = 0 \qquad i \neq j$$

$$\text{Cov}\,(w_{it}, w_{it'}) = 0 \qquad t \neq t'$$

$$\text{Cov}\,(w_{it}, w_{jt'}) = 0 \qquad i \neq j, t \neq t'$$

---

[28] Despite the loss of degrees of freedom associated with the use of dummy variables, it is incorrect to drop those dummy variables whose coefficients are insignificant. This would bias the statistical tests when the new regression is run.

[29] The model is discussed in P. Balestra and M. Nerlove, "Pooling Cross-Section and Time Series Data in the Estimation of a Dynamic Model: The Demand for Natural Gas," *Econometrica*, vol. 34, no. 4, pp. 585–612, 1966; T. D. Wallace and A. Hussain, "The Use of Error Components Models in Combining Cross Section with Time Series Data," *Econometrica*, vol. 37, no. 1, pp. 55–72, 1969; G. S. Maddala, "The Use of Variance Components Models in Pooling Cross Section and Time Series Data," *Econometrica*, vol. 39, no. 2, pp. 341–358, 1971; and M. Nerlove, "Further Evidence on the Estimation of Dynamic Economic Relations from a Time Series of Cross Sections," *Econometrica*, vol. 39, no. 2, pp. 359–381, 1971.

The relationship between the error components model and the covariance model can be seen by treating the intercept terms in the covariance model not as a set of distinct parameters, but as two random variables, one a time-series variable and the other a cross-section variable. If both random variables are assumed to be normally distributed, degrees of freedom are saved because we need to be concerned only with the mean and variance of each of the error components.

The error components formulation is obtained from the covariance model by assuming that the mean effect of the random time-series and cross-section variables is included in the intercept term, and the random deviations about the mean are equated to the error components, u_i and v_i, respectively.[30] To see this more clearly, consider the case in which no time-series error component exists. The use of dummy variables would force no restrictions on the pattern of shifting regression intercepts, while the error components model would presume that the pattern follows a normal distribution. Specifically, we would assume that the cross-section intercepts have mean α_u and variance σ_u^2. The combined error component (which is analogous to the error term in the least-squares regression equation) is assumed to have mean 0 and variance σ_w^2. These two assumptions are equivalent to the assumption that the error component has variance $\sigma_u^2 + \sigma_w^2$, since

$$\text{Var}\,(\varepsilon_{it}) = \text{Var}\,(u_i) + \text{Var}\,(w_{it}) = \sigma_u^2 + \sigma_w^2 \tag{7.27}$$

The effect of the mean of the normally distributed intercepts (α_u) will be accounted for by the inclusion of a constant term in the pooled regression equation. If time-series intercepts had also been random, normally distributed with mean α_v and variance σ_v^2, we could allow the mean effect of the random intercepts (α_v) to be picked up by the constant term. At the same time the error term would consist of three components and would have variance

$$\text{Var}\,(\varepsilon_{it}) = \sigma_u^2 + \sigma_v^2 + \sigma_w^2 \tag{7.28}$$

The relationship between the error components model and the pooled model using ordinary least squares can be seen directly from Eq. (7.28). If both σ_u^2 and σ_v^2 are identically equal to 0, then the error term consists of a single combined disturbance and the correct procedure is to apply ordinary least-squares regression to the pooled data. In this case, we are assuming that intercept terms do not vary, either systematically as in the covariance model, or randomly as in the error components model.

Since all the estimation techniques described will give unbiased and consistent parameter estimates, the central issue associated with pooling is one of efficiency.

---

[30] The relationship between the covariance model and the error components model is described in greater detail in Maddala, *op. cit.*

Error components models are useful in this respect because they are estimated using a form of generalized least-squares regression (see Appendix 4) and can be shown under reasonable conditions to be more efficient than the covariance model estimation process.[31] The estimation of the error components model is a generalization of the weighted least-squares technique because it weights observations in inverse relationship to their variances. To accomplish the weighting, a two-stage estimation process must be used, since error component variances are generally not known. In the first stage, ordinary least squares is run on the entire pooled sample. The ordinary least-squares regression residuals are then used to calculate sample estimates of the variance components. The estimated variances are used in the second stage, in which the generalized least-squares parameter estimates are obtained.[32]

7.3.3 Time-Series Autocorrelation Model

There are several difficulties associated with the error components model. First, its estimation can be computationally quite expensive, since the application of the generalized least-squares estimation procedure involves the inversion of an $NT \times NT$ matrix. Second, the technique is not directly applicable if there are lagged dependent variables in the equation or if the equation is part of a simultaneous equations model.[33] Finally, the error components specification is not the only error specification possible. It has the property that the correlation of disturbances over time is independent of the time gap between the disturbance terms.[34] An alternative specification would predict a decline in the error correlation over time. This suggests that one ought to consider pooling cross-section and time-series data under error assumptions involving time-series (or cross-section) autocorrelation as well as cross-section (or time-series) heteroscedasticity. As one example of how this might be accomplished consider the following model:

$$Y_{it} = \alpha + \beta X_{it} + \varepsilon_{it}$$

$$\varepsilon_{it} = \rho_i \varepsilon_{i, t-1} + u_{it}$$

(7.29)

where
$$E(\varepsilon_{it}^2) = \sigma^2$$
$$E(\varepsilon_{it} \varepsilon_{jt}) = 0 \qquad i \neq j$$
$$E(\varepsilon_{i, t-1} u_{jt}) = 0 \qquad i \neq j$$
$$u_{it} \sim N(0, \sigma_u^2)$$

The assumptions imply that cross-section disturbances are uncorrelated and have constant variance, but time-series disturbances are autocorrelated. We allow

---

[31] See Wallace and Hussain, *op. cit.*

[32] More of the details are available in Wallace and Hussain, *op. cit.*, and J. Kmenta, *op. cit.*, pp. 515–516.

[33] For a discussion of some of these issues, see Maddala, *op. cit.*

[34] Recall that the time-series error components are assumed to be *independent*, identically distributed random variables.

ρ to vary from individual observation to individual observation, but fix each error structure to involve first-order serial correlation. Efficient parameter estimates can be obtained by using a variant of generalized least squares, analogous to that described in Chapter 4. We estimate each ρ_i and then use the estimated $\hat{\rho}_i$ as a basis for the generalized least-squares regression. To estimate ρ_i, $i = 1, 2, \ldots, N$, we estimate the entire pooled sample using ordinary least squares. Since the parameter estimates are consistent (as well as unbiased), we may use them to calculate the regression residuals $\hat{\varepsilon}_{it}$. We then estimate each ρ_i consistently as follows:

$$\hat{\rho}_i = \frac{\sum\limits_{t=2}^{T} \hat{\varepsilon}_{it}\, \hat{\varepsilon}_{i,\,t-1}}{\sum\limits_{t=2}^{T} \hat{\varepsilon}_{i,\,t-1}^2} \qquad \text{for } i = 1, 2, \ldots, N \qquad (7.30)$$

We proceed by forming the generalized difference form of the original model:

$$Y_{it}^* = \beta X_{it}^* + u_{it}^* \qquad (7.31)$$

where $Y_{ii}^* = Y_{it} - \hat{\rho}_i\, Y_{i,\,t-1}$
$X_{it}^* = X_{it} - \hat{\rho}_i\, X_{i,\,t-1}$
$u_{it}^* = \varepsilon_{it} - \hat{\rho}_i\, \varepsilon_{i,\,t-1}$

The generalized difference form may now be estimated by applying ordinary least squares to the pooled model. $NT - N$ observations are used in the estimation, since one observation from each individual unit is dropped in the generalized differencing process. Corrections for heteroscedasticity or cross-section correlation among individual units would proceed in a similar fashion to that just described. If heteroscedasticity had been present in the model of Eq. (7.29), for example, we would use the residuals of the generalized difference model (pooled) to estimate the individual error variances and then apply weighted least squares in the third stage of the estimation process.

Example 7.4[35] Foreign Aid

An important empirical question facing development economists concerns the effect of foreign aid on the investment expenditures of less-developed countries

[35] This example is adapted from Peter S. Heller, "An Econometric Analysis of the Fiscal Behavior of the Public Sector in Developing Countries: Aid, Investment and Taxation," *Univ. of Michigan Center for Research on Economic Development, Discussion Paper* 30, Oct. 1973. An updated version appears as "A Model of Public Fiscal Behavior in Developing Countries: Aid, Investment, and Taxation," *American Economic Review*, pp. 368–379, June 1975.

(LDCs). Some economists have argued that inflows of foreign capital to less-developed countries do not lead to increased investment, but rather to increased public and private consumption. In order to deal with this issue, an economic model was developed which accounts for the interrelationship between taxing, spending, and borrowing decisions. The model makes a clear distinction between alternative types of foreign aid, such as grants and loans. The model used in the study of the fiscal behavior of LDCs presumes that local officials seek to maximize an objective function which is influenced by allocative choices between private consumption, public "civil" consumption, public "socioeconomic" consumption, public investment for development purposes, and public borrowing from domestic sources. Maximization of this objective function subject to a budget constraint yields a series of five simultaneous equations which must hold if maximization is to be achieved. In order to simplify matters we shall examine two of these five equations:

1 $T_t = \alpha_1 + \alpha_2 A_{1t} + \alpha_3 A_{2t} + \alpha_4 Y_t + \alpha_5 M_{t-1} + \alpha_6 I_t + \alpha_7 G_{s,t} + \alpha_8 G_{c,t-1} + \varepsilon_{1t}$

2 $I_t = \beta_1 + \beta_2 T_t + \beta_3 A_{1t} + \beta_4 A_{2t} + \beta_5 Y_{t-1} + \varepsilon_{2t}$

where T_t = level of tax and nontax revenues at time t
  I_t = public investment expenditure for development purposes at time t
  B_t = level of domestic borrowing at time t
  $G_{c,t}$ = public "civil" consumption (government administration, debt service, police, military) at time t
  $G_{s,t}$ = public "socioeconomic" consumption (schools, hospitals, roads, agricultural projects) at time t
  A_{1t} = grants to the public sector at time t
  A_{2t} = loans to the public sector at time t
  Y_t = gross domestic product at time t
  M_t = imports at time t
  P_t = primary school enrollments at time t

The sample of LDCs included 11 African countries: Nigeria, Ghana, Zambia, Kenya, Uganda, Tanzania, Malawi, Liberia, Ethiopia, Tunisia, and Morocco. Time-series data on all variables were available for periods of approximately 6 years. The limited quantity of individual time-series and cross-section data necessitated that the data be pooled to obtain parameter estimates in each of the structural equations. Because the system of equations is simultaneous in nature, the two-stage least-squares technique was chosen to estimate each equation. In addition, a decision was made to use an error components model with two error components, a cross-section error term, and a combined error term, that is, $\varepsilon_{it} = u_{it} + w_{it}$. It was implicitly assumed that time-series intercepts remained constant during the period of study. However, the cross-section error component does account for the random nature of the cross-section intercepts.

The error components technique is likely to be more efficient than the direct inclusion of cross-section dummy variables in the model.

The estimation process proceeded in two steps. First, the reduced-form equations were estimated using ordinary least squares. The fitted values of the right-hand endogenous variables were calculated and substituted in the structural equations. The second stage of this 2SLS procedure was then estimated using a variant of the two-step generalized least-squares procedure described in the text. For each equation, the ratio of cross section to total variance θ was calculated: $\theta = \sigma_u^2 / \sigma_w^2$. The estimated equations (with t statistics in parentheses and constant terms dropped) are as follows:

1 $\quad T_t = -.32A_{1t} - .84A_{2t} + .23Y_t - .39M_{t-1} + 1.03I_t - .71G_{s,t} + 1.51G_{c,t-1}$
$\qquad (-.58) \quad (-1.98) \quad (4.54) \quad (-3.40) \qquad (3.37) \quad (-2.24) \qquad (6.25)$

$\qquad \theta = .45 \qquad N = \text{number of observations} = 57 \qquad R^2 = .89$

2 $\qquad\qquad\qquad\qquad I_t = .70A_{1t} + .24A_{2t} + .49T_t - .02Y_{t-1}$
$\qquad\qquad\qquad\qquad\quad (3.21) \quad (1.64) \quad (11.10) \quad (-1.23)$

$\qquad\qquad\qquad\qquad \theta = .65 \qquad N = 61 \qquad R^2 = .89$

The first equation verifies the expected result that higher grants and loans lead to lower domestically raised revenues (although the grants term is insignificant). Government investment and government "civil" consumption have a strong positive effect on tax revenues, but this is offset to some extent by the negative coefficient on the public "socioeconomic" consumption term. The results of the second equation indicate that foreign aid does have a positive effect on investment, but the value being less than 1 indicates that some of the foreign aid "leaks" into other expenditure areas. We may conclude that the estimated equations do verify the fiscal interdependence associated with current and capital budgets. Foreign loans can and do affect public consumption as well as investment.

7.4 DISTRIBUTED LAGS

When constructing models, it is important to recognize that some amount of time usually lapses between the movement of the independent variables and the response of the dependent variable. In time-series models in particular, a substantial period of time may pass between the economic decision-making period and the final impact of a change in a given policy variable. If the decision-and-response period associated with a given model is sufficiently long, then lagged explanatory variables should be included explicitly in the model specification. As an example, consider the specification of an aggregate consumption function which is to be estimated using quarterly macroeconomic data. One might specify aggregate consumption C_t to be a function of aggregate disposable income lagged one quarter Y_{t-1}. The one-period lag allows for the time involved in the consumption response to a change in disposable income. The specification of a model's lag structure is very much dependent on the time units of the data. If the same consumption function were specified using annual data, it might be reasonable to drop the lag in the income variable, since the period of measurement is substantially larger than the hypothesized reaction period.

This simple example assumes that the entire effect of the explanatory variable occurs in one time period $(t - 1)$. More generally, one would account for the fact that economic changes take place gradually over time. For example, aggregate consumption may be a function of disposable income lagged one, two, three, or more periods. The fact that the impact of a variable can be distributed over a number of time periods is the basis of the *distributed lag model*, in which a series of lagged explanatory variables accounts for the time adjustment process. In its most general form, the distributed lag model can be written as follows:

$$Y_t = \alpha + \beta_0 X_t + \beta_1 X_{t-1} + \beta_2 X_{t-2} + \cdots = \alpha + \sum_{s=0}^{\infty} \beta_s X_{t-s} + \varepsilon_t \quad (7.32)$$

Unless we state otherwise, we shall assume that the error term is normally distributed, independent of X, and neither serially correlated nor heteroscedastic. We allow the number of lags to be infinite in our specification, although many practical examples involve a finite lag structure. If the lag structure is infinite, however, the sequence of lag weights which describe the pattern of the lag response must have a finite sum. If this were not the case, the model would not have a finite solution.

If the number of terms in the distributed lag is very small, then the equation can be estimated using ordinary least-squares regression. However, when there are many terms and little is known about the form of the lag, direct estimation becomes difficult for several reasons. First, the estimation of a lengthy lag structure uses up a large number of degrees of freedom, which are often in short supply in time-series models. Second, the estimation of an equation with a substantial number of lagged explanatory variables is likely to lead to imprecise parameter estimates because of the presence of multicollinearity. Multicollinearity arises when the X variable is highly autocorrelated; i.e., the variable observed at time t bears a close relationship to the variable measured at times $t - 1$, $t - 2$, etc. Both these difficulties can be resolved if one can specify a priori some conditions about the form of the distributed lag. We shall pursue this matter further by describing two of the most frequently posited lag structures. Our purpose is to introduce the reader to some of the problems involved in the specification of distributed lag models.[36]

---

[36] For a more advanced discussion of distributed lag models, the reader is referred to P. Dhrymes, *Distributed Lags: Problem of Estimation and Formulation* (San Francisco: Holden-Day, 1971); Z. Griliches, "Distributed Lags: A Survey," *Econometrica*, vol. 35, pp. 16–49, 1967; L. M. Koyck, *Distributed Lags and Investment Analysis* (Amsterdam: North-Holland 1954); and M. Nerlove, "Lags in Economic Behavior," *Econometrica*, vol. 40, pp. 221–251, 1972.

7.4.1 Geometric Lag

The geometric lag assumes that the weights of the lagged explanatory variables are all positive and decline geometrically with time. The model is as follows:

$$Y_t = \alpha + \beta(X_t + wX_{t-1} + w^2X_{t-2} + \cdots) + \varepsilon_t$$

$$= \alpha + \beta \sum_{s=0}^{\infty} w^s X_{t-s} + \varepsilon_t \qquad 0 < w < 1 \qquad (7.33)$$

The pattern of parameters associated with the model is depicted in Fig. 7.1 (for $w = 1/2$). While the weights of the geometric lag model never become zero, they diminish so that beyond a reasonable time period the effect of the explanatory variable becomes negligible.

It is often useful to describe the lag structure of a distributed lag model in terms of its mean or average lag, and in terms of the long-run response of the dependent variable to a permanent change in one of the explanatory variables. The *long-run response m* in the geometric lag model is simply the parameter β times the sum of the lag weights $\sum w^s$ or $\beta/(1-w)$. m measures the change in Y associated with a one-unit increase in X which stays in effect for all time. The *mean lag*, on the other hand, is defined as a time-weighted average of the individual lag weights, that is,

$$\text{Mean lag} = \frac{\sum\limits_{s=0}^{\infty} s\beta_s}{\sum\limits_{s=0}^{\infty} \beta_s} \qquad \text{where } \beta_s = \beta w^s$$

In the geometric lag model, the mean lag is $w/(1-w)$, since

$$\frac{\sum\limits_{s=0}^{\infty} s\beta_s}{\sum\limits_{s=0}^{\infty} \beta_s} = \frac{\beta \sum sw^s}{\beta \sum w^s} = \frac{w/(1-w)^2}{1/(1-w)} = \frac{w}{(1-w)}$$

If $w = 1/2$, for example, the mean lag of 1 suggests that half the impact of a change in Y will be felt during the first time period.

FIGURE 7.1
Geometric lag parameters.

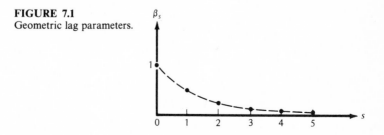

In its present form, the Koyck geometric lag model appears quite difficult to estimate, since it involves an infinite number of regressors. However, the parametric form of the lag weights allows for a substantial simplification of the model. To see this, we rewrite the original model [Eq. (7.33)] with all observations lagged one period:

$$Y_{t-1} = \alpha + \beta(X_{t-1} + wX_{t-2} + \cdots) + \varepsilon_{t-1} \tag{7.34}$$

Then we calculate the expression $Y_t - wY_{t-1}$ to obtain the following:

$$Y_t - wY_{t-1} = \alpha(1 - w) + \beta X_t + u_t \tag{7.35}$$

where $u_t = \varepsilon_t - w\varepsilon_{t-1}$

Rewriting, we find that

$$Y_t = \alpha(1 - w) + wY_{t-1} + \beta X_t + u_t \tag{7.36}$$

Equation (7.36) can be estimated more easily, since only three parameters remain unknown. However, before considering the estimation of the equation, we shall pause to consider when such a model specification is appropriate. This is a relevant concern, because the autoregressive model [Eq. (7.36)], containing a single lagged endogenous variable, is frequently specified outside the distributed lag context.

Adaptive Expectations Model

The *adaptive expectations model* postulates that changes in Y are related to changes in the "expected" level of the explanatory variable X. We would write this model as

$$Y_t = \alpha^* + \beta^* X_t^* + \varepsilon_t \tag{7.37}$$

where X^* represents the desired or expected level of X. X^* might represent a notion of permanent income in the aggregate consumption example described previously, or it might represent an expected price in a microeconometric model. The expected level of X is defined by a second relationship, in which expectations are assumed to be altered every time period as an adjustment between the current observed value of X and the previous expected value of X. The relationship is

$$X_t^* - X_{t-1}^* = \theta(X_t - X_{t-1}^*) \tag{7.38}$$

where $0 < \theta \leq 1$

It is sometimes more useful to rewrite Eq. (7.38) as

$$X_t^* = \theta X_t + (1 - \theta)X_{t-1}^* \tag{7.39}$$

This suggests that the expected level of X (permanent income or expected price) is a weighted average of the present level of X and the previous expected level of X. Expected levels of X are adjusted period-by-period by taking into account present levels of X. To posit the adaptive expectations model in a form which allows econometric estimation, rewrite Eq. (7.39) by lagging the model period-by-period, while at the same time multiplying by $(1 - \theta)^s$, where s is the number of periods involved in the lag process:

$$(1 - \theta)X^*_{t-1} = \theta(1 - \theta)X_{t-1} + (1 - \theta)^2 X^*_{t-2}$$

$$(1 - \theta)^2 X^*_{t-2} = \theta(1 - \theta)^2 X_{t-2} + (1 - \theta)^3 X^*_{t-3} \tag{7.40}$$

$$\vdots$$

Now, substitute (7.40) into (7.39) and combine terms:

$$X^*_t = \theta[X_t + (1 - \theta)X_{t-1} + (1 - \theta)^2 X_{t-2} + \cdots] = \theta \sum_{s=0}^{\infty} (1 - \theta)^s X_{t-s} \tag{7.41}$$

Notice that the desired level of X is a weighted average of all present and previous values of X, since the weights sum to unity $[\theta\Sigma(1 - \theta)^s = 1]$. Substituting (7.41) into (7.37), we get

$$Y_t = \alpha^* + \beta^*\theta \sum_{s=0}^{\infty} (1 - \theta)^s X_{t-s} + \varepsilon^*_t \tag{7.42}$$

The equivalence of this model to the original geometric lag model [Eq. (7.33)] can be seen by letting

$$\alpha = \alpha^* \qquad \beta = \beta^*\theta \qquad w = (1 - \theta) \qquad \text{and} \qquad \varepsilon_t = \varepsilon^*_t$$

Thus, estimation of the economic specification associated with the adaptive expectations model is identical to the problem of estimating the Koyck geometric lag, with Eq. (7.36) now becoming

$$Y_t = \alpha^*\theta + \beta^*\theta X_t + (1 - \theta)Y_{t-1} + u^*_t \tag{7.43}$$

where $u^*_t = \varepsilon^*_t - (1 - \theta)\varepsilon^*_{t-1}$

Stock Adjustment Model

The *stock adjustment model* assumes that the desired level of Y is dependent upon the current level of X, that is,

$$Y^*_t = \alpha' + \beta'X_t + \varepsilon'_t \tag{7.44}$$

In the consumption example Y_t^* might represent a desired or optimal expenditure level, while in the demand example it might represent the desired quantity to be supplied or the desired acreage to be farmed. In any given period, the actual value of Y may not adjust completely to obtain the desired level. Lack of knowledge, technical constraints, and other items might be responsible for this partial adjustment. We may represent the adjustment process as follows:

$$Y_t - Y_{t-1} = \gamma(Y_t^* - Y_{t-1}) \qquad 0 < \gamma < 1 \qquad (7.45)$$

The equation specifies that the change in Y will respond only partially to the difference between the desired stock of Y and the past value of Y, the rate of response being a function of the adjustment coefficient γ. Substituting for Y_t^* in Eq. (7.45) and solving for Y_t yields

$$Y_t = \alpha'\gamma + \gamma\beta'X_t + (1 - \gamma)Y_{t-1} + \gamma\varepsilon_t' \qquad (7.46)$$

Once again the stock adjustment model bears a close relationship to the geometric lag model. The two are equivalent in form [see Eq. (7.36)], if we let

$$\alpha = \alpha' \qquad \beta = \gamma\beta' \qquad w = 1 - \gamma \qquad \text{and} \qquad u_t = \gamma\varepsilon_t'$$

However, the equivalence of the models is not complete, because they involve a different set of assumptions about the error structure. To see this, rewrite Eq. (7.46), lagging the model one period and then substituting for Y_{t-1}. Iterating this procedure and collecting terms, we obtain

$$Y_t = \alpha' + \beta'\gamma[X_t + (1 - \gamma)X_{t-1} + (1 - \gamma)^2 X_{t-2} + \cdots] + v_t$$
$$v_t = \gamma\varepsilon_t' + \gamma(1 - \gamma)\varepsilon_{t-1}' + \gamma(1 - \gamma)^2\varepsilon_{t-2}' + \cdots \qquad (7.47)$$

or

$$Y_t = \alpha' + \beta'\gamma \sum_{s=0}^{\infty} (1 - \gamma)^s X_{t-s} + \gamma \sum_{s=0}^{\infty} (1 - \gamma)^s \varepsilon_{t-s}' \qquad (7.48)$$

Unlike the original error specification, the error process associated with the stock adjustment model is a moving-average error process (moving-average error processes are discussed in another context in Chapter 14).

7.4.2 Geometric Lag Estimation

In this section we briefly outline some of the issues involved in the estimation of the geometric lag model.[37] Recall that such a model can be transformed into a single-equation autoregressive model with a single lagged dependent variable:

$$Y_t = \alpha(1 - w) + wY_{t-1} + \beta X_t + u_t \qquad (7.49)$$

---

[37] These estimation techniques also apply when we extend the two models just described by combining stock adjustment and adaptive expectations models, or by allowing more than one explanatory variable to involve a distributed lag.

Depending on the model chosen, the error process may follow several alternative assumptions. Not surprisingly, the choice of estimation process depends heavily on the nature of the assumption that one is willing to make about the error process. Consider first the case in which the error term is normally distributed with constant variance and is not serially correlated. As a general rule, the Koyck specification will introduce serial correlation if the original error specified is not autocorrelated. However, the transformation procedure might conceivably eliminate any serial correlation that was originally present.[38] In such a case, the presence of a lagged dependent variable in the model causes ordinary least-squares parameter estimates to be biased, although they remain consistent.[39] While it is possible to devise estimation procedures which remain consistent and are adjusted to remove bias, such procedures are not very popular, because the variance of the adjusted unbiased estimator tends to be large relative to the variance of the biased ordinary least-squares estimator.

Now consider the estimation problem when the error term follows the pattern suggested by the Koyck and adaptive expectations models, that is, $u_t = \varepsilon_t - w\varepsilon_{t-1}$. In this case we are less fortunate, because ordinary least-squares estimates become inconsistent as well as biased. The difficulty arises because u_t and Y_{t-1} are correlated and the correlation does not disappear as the sample size gets larger (in the probability limit). A number of estimation procedures are available which involve the use of either an instrumental variables technique or a maximum-likelihood technique, but they are too complex to present in detail here.[40] Perhaps the simplest procedure would be to use instrumental variables estimation with X_{t-1} serving as an instrument for Y_{t-1}. This procedure will yield consistent estimates, but is not likely to be very efficient in practice.

Finally, consider a third error specification involving first-order serial correlation, that is,

$$u_t = \rho u_{t-1} + \varepsilon_t$$

While this specification does not follow directly from any of the Koyck-related models, it should receive serious consideration, because autocorrelated disturbances often occur in models with lagged dependent variables. Once again, ordinary least-squares parameter estimates will be inconsistent and biased, with the direction of the large sample bias relating directly to the sign of ρ.[41] Both instrumental variables and maximum-likelihood estimation procedures are available to deal with the autoregressive model in the presence of serially correlated

---

[38] If $\varepsilon_t = w\varepsilon_{t-1} + u_t$, then the transformation process will yield the error process u_t, which is not autocorrelated.

[39] For further details, see J. Johnston, *op. cit.*, pp. 305–306.

[40] For further details, see P. J. Dhrymes, "Efficient Estimation of Distributed Lags with Autocorrelated Error Terms," *International Economic Review*, vol. 10, pp. 47–67, Feb. 1969; or A. Zellner and M. S. Geisel, "Analysis of Distributed Lag Models with Applications to Consumption Function Estimation," *Econometrica* (forthcoming). Two excellent discussions of distributed lag estimation appear in J. Johnston, *op. cit.*, pp. 304–321, and J. Kmenta, *op. cit.*, pp. 473–498.

[41] See Z. Griliches, "A Note on the Serial Correlation Bias in Estimates of Distributed Lags," *Econometrica*, vol. 29, pp. 65–73, 1971.

errors. The instrumental variables estimation process yields consistent estimates, but tends to be inefficient, given the known presence of serial correlation.[42] The instrument to replace Y_{t-1} can be obtained by a first-stage regression in which Y_t is the dependent variable and a series of lagged values of X make up the explanatory variables. The efficiency of this estimator can be improved if the estimated intercept and slope parameters are used to obtain an estimate of the serial correlation coefficient ρ.[43] We do this by calculating the residuals associated with the estimated intercept and slope parameters. A regression of u_t on u_{t-1} yields an estimate of the serial correlation coefficient. Once ρ is estimated, the generalized differencing process can be used to reestimate the parameters of the original equation (see Chapter 4).

7.4.3 Polynomial Distributed Lag

While the geometric lag formulation is quite useful, it is limited in its range of potential uses because it hypothesizes a declining set of lag weights.[44] A much more general formulation is the *polynomial distributed lag* model. The polynomial lag model assumes that the lag weights can be specified by a continuous function, which in turn can be approximated by evaluating a polynomial function at the appropriate discrete points in time. We might assume, for example, that $w_i = c_0 + c_1 i + c_2 i^2$ for $i = 0, 1, 2, 3, \ldots, 6$ and $w_i = 0$ for i less than 0 and greater than 6. This specifies lag weights that are to follow a second-degree polynomial for the first six lagged values and are 0 otherwise. The lag weights might appear as shown in Fig. 7.2.

We have considerable flexibility involved in specifying a polynomial distributed lag model. We should be careful, however, to be sure the degree of the polynomial is less than the number of terms in the distributed lag, or there will be no reduction in the number of lag parameters to be estimated.[45] The choice of endpoint restrictions is an optional one, however. If we do not wish to restrict the lag weights to be 0 outside the lag interval, one or both of the endpoint restrictions may be eliminated.

Usually a third- or fourth-degree polynomial will provide a sufficiently accurate approximation to the lag structure, although higher-degree polynomials are occasionally specified when sufficient data are available. The choice of length of lag depends more on the nature of the problem being specified, so that useful rules of thumb are not available. In practice it is common for researchers to vary

---

[42] See N. Liviatan, "Consistent Estimation of Distributed Lags," *International Economic Review*, vol. 4, pp. 44–52, 1963.

[43] See K. F. Wallis, "Lagged Dependent Variables and Serially Correlated Errors: A Reappraisal of Three-Pass Least Squares," *Review of Economics and Statistics*, vol. 49, pp. 555–567, 1967.

[44] It is quite possible, of course, to allow the first several lag terms to be estimated freely and to impose the geometric lag assumption on lagged values of the explanatory variable beyond the first several terms. This allows for greater flexibility in the form of the distributed lag, while maintaining the advantages associated with the simple geometric lag form.

[45] In addition, the number of observations available must be greater than or equal to the degree of the polynomial plus two. The two extra observations are needed if the endpoints of the lag are fixed by assumption.

FIGURE 7.2
Polynomial distributed lag
weights.

the degree of the polynomial, the length of the lag, and the endpoint restrictions. Such a procedure is dangerous, however, because (see Chapters 6 and 10) a good-fitting equation as measured by a high R^2 may turn out to be a poor-predicting equation.

To understand how the polynomial distributed lag model is estimated, consider the case of a third-degree polynomial with a five-period lag (no endpoint restrictions). The original lag specification is

$$Y_t = \alpha + \beta(w_0 X_t + w_1 X_{t-1} + \cdots) + \varepsilon_t \tag{7.50}$$

Assume that

$$w_i = c_0 + c_1 i + c_2 i^2 + c_3 i^3 \qquad i = 0, 1, 2, 3, 4 \tag{7.51}$$

Substituting and rewriting the original specification, we get

$$Y_t = \alpha + \beta c_0 X_t + \beta(c_0 + c_1 + c_2 + c_3)X_{t-1}$$

$$+ \beta(c_0 + 2c_1 + 4c_2 + 8c_3)X_{t-2}$$

$$+ \beta(c_0 + 3c_1 + 9c_2 + 27c_3)X_{t-3}$$

$$+ \beta(c_0 + 4c_1 + 16c_2 + 64c_3)X_{t-4} + \varepsilon_t \tag{7.52}$$

Combining terms, we have

$$Y_t = \alpha + \beta c_0(X_t + X_{t-1} + X_{t-2} + X_{t-3} + X_{t-4})$$

$$+ \beta c_1(X_{t-1} + 2X_{t-2} + 3X_{t-3} + 4X_{t-4})$$

$$+ \beta c_2(X_{t-1} + 4X_{t-2} + 9X_{t-3} + 16X_{t-4})$$

$$+ \beta c_3(X_{t-1} + 8X_{t-2} + 27X_{t-3} + 64X_{t-4}) + \varepsilon_t \tag{7.53}$$

Equation (7.53) can be estimated using ordinary least squares. If the error term obeys the classical assumptions of econometrics, the estimated c's will be best linear unbiased estimates[46] (once the c's are known, it is a simple procedure to calculate the original lag weights, that is, the w's). Standard errors for each of the lag weights can be obtained from the variance-covariance matrix of the c's, but the calculations are too involved to display here.[47] In general, statistical tests that are performed must be done through the estimated equation (7.53) and not directly through the specified equation (7.52).

Example 7.5 Capital Expenditures

In her 1965 article,[48] Almon used the polynomial distributed lag model to examine the relationship between capital expenditures of manufacturing industries and capital appropriations. The model specified that capital expenditures E were determined by a series of seasonal dummy variables, S_1, S_2, and S_3, and by present and past values of appropriations A. The model was estimated using a seven-period lag structure and a third-degree polynomial, with both endpoints restricted to be equal to 0. The manufacturing industry results are as follows:

$$E_t = -283 + 13S_{1t} - 50S_{2t} + 320S_{3t} + .048A_t + .900A_{t-1} + .141A_{t-2}$$

$$+ .165A_{t-3} + .167A_{t-4} + .146A_{t-5} + .105A_{t-6} + .053A_{t-7}$$

$$\bar{R}^2 = .92$$

A quick glance at the lag-weight coefficients shows that the lag structure follows an inverted U shape, lag weights first increasing and then decreasing. While not guaranteed by the specification of the model, this result is quite common when working with polynomial distributed lags.

Example 7.6 Consumption Function

In modeling the aggregate consumption function, it is plausible to assume that consumption in the present period C_t is a direct function of personal disposable

---

[46] As written, it is impossible to estimate β directly. One simply assumes that β equals 1, allowing the estimated lag weights to incorporate the effect of the true parameter β.

[47] See J. L. Murphy, *Introductory Econometrics* (Homewood, Ill.: Irwin, 1973), p. 277, for details.

[48] See S. Almon, "The Distributed Lag between Capital Appropriations and Expenditures," *Econometrica*, vol. 33, pp. 178–196, 1965.

income Y_t in the present and past periods and the interest rate r_t. We expect that a higher interest rate, other things equal, will be associated with more savings and less consumption. If we were to regress C_t on Y_t and r, a low Durbin-Watson statistic would result, signaling the presence of positive first-order serial correlation. For this reason, a decision was made to estimate an elementary form of the aggregate consumption function, using first differences and a polynomial distributed lag formulation. The model is as follows:

$$\Delta C_t = \alpha + \beta_0 \Delta Y_t + \beta_1 \Delta Y_{t-1} + \cdots + \beta_4 \Delta Y_{t-4} + \gamma r_t + \varepsilon_t$$

where C_t = quarterly personal consumption expenditures
   $\Delta C_t = C_t - C_{t-1}$
   Y_t = quarterly disposable personal income
   $\Delta Y_t = Y_t - Y_{t-1}$
   r_t = 3-month average of open market new issue rates of 3-month Treasury bills

A first attempt at model estimation using a five-period third-degree polynomial with no endpoint restrictions yielded the following regression results (t statistics in parentheses):

$$\Delta C_t = .299 + .445\Delta Y_t + .219\Delta Y_{t-1} + .086\Delta Y_{t-2} + .045\Delta Y_{t-3} + .098\Delta Y_{t-4}$$
$$(.43) \quad (4.68) \quad\quad (4.18) \quad\quad\quad (1.28) \quad\quad\quad (.82) \quad\quad\quad (.93)$$

$$-.037 r_t$$
$$(-.09)$$

T (number of observations) = 68 (1953-1 to 1969-4) $R^2 = .62$ $F = 25.6$

DW = 2.56   Mean lag = 1.03   Sum of lag coefficients = .895

The coefficients of the lags may be interpreted as follows: An increase of $1 billion in the quarterly change in disposable income in the present time will result in an increase in the change in consumption of $445 million in the first quarter, $219 million in the second quarter, $86 million in the third quarter, etc. The interest rate is inversely related to changes in consumption, but the coefficient is not statistically significant. If one has reason to believe that the effect of changes in personal disposable income on changes in consumption will not be felt after four periods, then it is reasonable to set the tail of the lag distribution equal to 0 in period $t - 5$. For illustrative purposes, we have reestimated the model using the zero tail restriction. The results exhibited in the following regression output show that the zero tail restriction forces neighboring lag weights

FIGURE 7.3
Consumption function lag structures.

to become close to zero. This is a natural consequence of the fact that polynomial functions are continuous.

$$\Delta C_t = .258 + .394\Delta Y_t + .241\Delta Y_{t-1} + .125\Delta Y_{t-2} + .125\Delta Y_{t-3} + .046\Delta Y_{t-4}$$
$$\quad\quad (.37) \quad (4.99) \quad\quad (5.09) \quad\quad\quad (2.33) \quad\quad\quad (.82) \quad\quad\quad (.11)$$

$$+ .004r_t$$
$$\quad (.30)$$

$$T = 68 \quad\quad R^2 = .61 \quad\quad F = 33.8 \quad\quad DW = 2.57$$

$$\text{Mean lag} = .80 \quad\quad \text{Sum of lag coefficients} = .81$$

Finally, consider the regression output in which both the tail and the head of the lag distribution are assumed equal to 0:

$$\Delta C_t = .186 + .166\Delta Y_t + .241\Delta Y_{t-1} + .224\Delta Y_{t-2} + .115\Delta Y_{t-3} - .086\Delta Y_{t-4}$$
$$\quad\quad (.25) \quad (4.27) \quad\quad (4.24) \quad\quad\quad (4.11) \quad\quad\quad (2.09) \quad\quad (-.91)$$

$$+ .416r_t$$
$$\quad (.96)$$

$$T = 68 \quad\quad R^2 = .56 \quad\quad F = 26.9 \quad\quad DW = 2.31$$

$$\text{Mean lag} = 1.05 \quad\quad \text{Sum of lag coefficients} = .66$$

The zero restriction on the head of the distribution substantially alters the pattern of the lag weights. The weights now approximate an inverted U structure. Once again the zero restriction and the continuity of the polynomial are crucial determinants of the lag pattern. The lag structures resulting from each of the three regressions are graphed in Fig. 7.3.

Example 7.7   Inventory Investment

In this example we construct a single-equation regression model which contains polynomial distributed lags, and then use that equation for forecasting.[49] The example estimates the monthly change in manufacturers' inventories in the durable goods industries IND (end-of-period book value) as a function of shipments SHD, unfilled orders UNOD, and the wholesale price index WHMD. (All the independent variables relate to the category manufacturers' durable goods industries.) Monthly data from January 1965 to December 1972 have been used, and a polynomial distributed lag regression has been performed. The estimation results are shown below, with t statistics in parentheses, and a plot of estimated and actual values of the change in manufacturing durable inventories is presented in Fig. 7.4:

$$\Delta IND_t = \underset{(-3.15)}{-876.5} + \sum_{i=0}^{19} a_i SHD_{t-i} - \underset{(-3.50)}{.0809} IND_{t-i}$$

$$+ \underset{(2.44)}{45.82} \frac{WHMD_t - WHMD_{t-3}}{3} + \underset{(2.50)}{.177} \frac{UNOD_{t-3} - UNOD_{t-9}}{6}$$

$$R^2 = .573 \qquad \bar{R}^2 = .539 \qquad F(7/100) = 19.2 \qquad SER = 168.14 \qquad DW = 1.81$$

Third-degree polynomial lag coefficients:

$a_0 = -.0394$	$a_7 = .0295$	$a_{14} = .0103$
(-2.91)	(5.53)	(1.46)
$a_1 = -.0196$	$a_8 = .0294$	$a_{15} = .0073$
(-2.69)	(6.77)	(1.03)
$a_2 = -.0038$	$a_9 = .0278$	$a_{16} = .0053$
$(-.94)$	(7.77)	$(.75)$
$a_3 = .0086$	$a_{10} = .0251$	$a_{17} = .0046$
(1.97)	(6.89)	$(.58)$
$a_4 = .0177$	$a_{11} = .0217$	$a_{18} = .0056$
(3.17)	(4.79)	$(.51)$
$a_5 = .0241$	$a_{12} = .0178$	$a_{19} = .0086$
(3.88)	(3.15)	$(.51)$
$a_6 = .0279$	$a_{13} = .0139$	$\sum a_i = .222$
(4.60)	(2.11)	(3.64)

[49] This example came from a study done by Dynamics Associates, Inc., Cambridge, Mass. The reader may wish to refer to Chapter 6, in which the use of the single-equation model for forecasting is discussed.

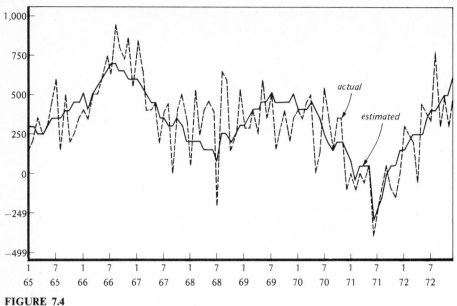

FIGURE 7.4
Change in manufacturer inventories in durable goods industries (in millions of dollars).

Note that the final form of the equation expresses the relationship of inventories to shipments as a third-degree polynomial—the polynomial then defining 20 coefficients of current and lagged shipments. The lagged level of inventories is included; the wholesale price index is introduced as the monthly

FIGURE 7.5
Ex post forecast of the change in manufacturers' durable goods inventories.

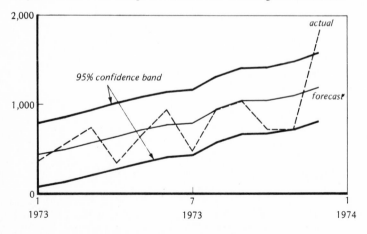

change (averaged over 3 months); and unfilled orders are added using the monthly change (averaged over 6 months), lagged one quarter.

The regression equation can now be used to generate a set of *ex post* monthly forecasts (thus allowing us to compare the results with actual data) for the period January 1973 to December 1973. The resulting forecasted series, together with 95 percent confidence interval and the actual series, is shown in Fig. 7.5.

One can observe that the forecasted series turned out to be a "smoothed" version of the actual series. Although the forecast did not successfully predict the short month-to-month "turning points" in the actual series, it did predict the overall trend. In fact the forecasted series is quite close to the actual series, at least for the first 9 or 10 months. Only in the last month of the forecast period is the actual value of the dependent variable outside the 95 percent confidence interval, and this may be due to an occurrence not properly modeled by the regression equation. On the whole we would probably be satisfied with the predictive performance of the regression equation.

7.5 NONLINEAR ESTIMATION

All the single-equation regression models that we have studied to this point have been linear in their coefficients, and thus ordinary least squares, or variations on ordinary least squares, could be used to estimate them. In this section we examine the problem of estimating equations that are nonlinear in their coefficients. Although procedures for *nonlinear estimation* can be computationally expensive, they greatly increase the scope of model structures that can be fitted to data.

Recall that there is no problem in applying ordinary least squares to an equation that is nonlinear in the *independent variables*. Equations such as

$$Y = \alpha_0 + \alpha_1 X_1^2 + \alpha_2 \log X_2 + \varepsilon \tag{7.54}$$

or

$$Y = \alpha_0 + \alpha_1 X_1^2 + \alpha_2 X_1 X_2 + \varepsilon \tag{7.55}$$

can be estimated using the methods discussed earlier in the book. In addition, some equations that are nonlinear in the coefficients can be transformed into linear equations. For example, the equation

$$Y = \alpha_0 X_1^{\alpha_1} X_2^{\alpha_2} \varepsilon \tag{7.56}$$

can be written equivalently as

$$\log Y = \log \alpha_0 + \alpha_1 \log X_1 + \alpha_2 \log X_2 + \log \varepsilon \tag{7.57}$$

and estimated by ordinary least squares. Our concern will be directed toward equations that are *inherently* nonlinear. For example, the equations

$$Y = \alpha_0 + \alpha_1 X_1^{\beta_1} + \alpha_2 X_2^{\beta_2} + \varepsilon \tag{7.58}$$

$$Y = \alpha_1 e^{\beta_1 X_1} + \alpha_2 e^{\beta_2 X_2} + \varepsilon \tag{7.59}$$

cannot be transformed into linear equations, and thus do not lend themselves to linear regression.

Specifically, we consider equations of the form

$$Y = f(X_1, X_2, \ldots, X_k, \beta_1, \beta_2, \ldots, \beta_p) + \varepsilon \tag{7.60}$$

where f is a nonlinear function of the k independent variables $X_1, \ldots, X_k$ and the p coefficients $\beta_1, \ldots, \beta_p$. The criterion used for determining the estimated values for the coefficients is the same as that used in a linear regression—minimization of the *sum of squared errors*. If we have T observations on $Y, X_1, \ldots, X_k$, then we can write the sum of squared errors as

$$S = \sum_{t=1}^{T} [Y_t - f(X_{1t}, \ldots, X_{kt}, \beta_1, \ldots, \beta_p)]^2 \tag{7.61}$$

We call $\hat{\beta}_1, \ldots, \hat{\beta}_p$ the nonlinear least-squares estimates of $\beta_1, \ldots, \beta_p$, i.e., the values of $\beta_1, \ldots, \beta_p$ that minimize the sum of squared errors S. If the error term ε is normally distributed, then these estimates are equivalent to the maximum-likelihood estimates of $\beta_1, \ldots, \beta_p$.[50]

In the case of a linear regression, obtaining least-squares estimates is computationally straightforward. For a nonlinear equation, however, there are alternative computational approaches to finding coefficient estimates that minimize the sum of squared errors in Eq. (7.61).

7.5.1 Computational Methods for Nonlinear Estimation

There are three general approaches to the solution of the nonlinear estimation problem. Most numerical estimation methods involve one of the approaches, or a combination of two of them. As we will see, the choice of approach will depend on the type of equation being estimated.

First, a *direct search* may be used; in this case the sum-of-squared-errors function is evaluated for alternative sets of coefficient values. Those values which

---

[50] The technique of maximum-likelihood estimation is discussed in Appendix 2.2. Since the likelihood function is

$$L = (2\pi\sigma_\varepsilon^2)^{-T/2} e^{-S/2\sigma_\varepsilon^2}$$

maximizing L with respect to $\beta_1, \ldots, \beta_p$ is equivalent to minimizing S with respect to $\beta_1, \ldots, \beta_p$.

result in a minimum are chosen as the estimates. This method may be effective if only one or two coefficients must be estimated. However, if more than two coefficients are involved (which is usually the case), an extremely large number of calculations must be made, so that the method becomes computationally very expensive. For example, if 4 coefficients must be estimated, and 20 alternative values for each coefficient are to be considered, then the sum of squared errors must be calculated $(20)^4 = 160,000$ times! As a result, this method is almost never used, and we will not discuss it any further.

A second approach involves *direct optimization*. Parameter estimates are obtained by differentiating the sum-of-squared-errors function with respect to each coefficient, setting the derivatives equal to zero (thus defining a minimum), and solving the resulting set of nonlinear equations (which are called the *normal equations*). Taking the derivatives of Eq. (7.61) with respect to $\beta_1, \ldots, \beta_p$ and setting them equal to zero, we find that the normal equations are

$$\sum_{t=1}^{T} 2[Y_t - f(X_{1t}, \ldots, X_{kt}, \beta_1, \ldots, \beta_p)]\frac{\partial f}{\partial \beta_i} = 0 \qquad \text{for } i = 1, \ldots, p \quad (7.62)$$

These nonlinear equations must be solved simultaneously for $\beta_1, \ldots, \beta_p$, since each equation may contain all p coefficients. As one might expect, this approach can present computational difficulties, and is therefore seldomly applied directly. One variation of this approach that is computationally feasible is the *steepest-descent* method, which involves an iterative process to find the minimum of S. The method works by moving from one trial set of coefficient values for $\beta_1, \ldots, \beta_p$ to a new set in such a way that the derivatives $-\partial S/\partial \beta_1, \ldots, -\partial S/\partial \beta_p$ are as large as possible, resulting in rapid progress to those values of $\beta_1, \ldots, \beta_p$ that minimize S (and for which the derivatives are zero).[51]

The third approach is an iterative linearization method in which the nonlinear equation is linearized (using a Taylor series expansion) around some initial set of coefficient values. Then ordinary least squares is performed on this linear equation, generating a new set of coefficient values. The nonlinear equation is relinearized around these new coefficient values, ordinary least squares is again performed to generate new coefficient values, and the equation is relinearized around these values. This iterative process is repeated until *convergence* is attained, i.e., until the coefficient values do not change substantially after each new ordinary least-squares regression.

This approach has certain advantages, the first of which is computational efficiency. If the equation to be estimated is closely approximated by a linear equation, very few iterations may be necessary. A second advantage of the approach is that it provides a clear guideline for applying statistical tests that

---

[51] This technique is described in more detail in N. Draper and H. Smith, *Applied Regression Analysis* (New York: Wiley, 1966), pp. 270–272; and in H. A. Spang, "A Review of Minimization Techniques for Nonlinear Functions," *SIAM Review*, vol. 4, pp. 343–365, 1962.

are usually applied only to linear regression. Since a linear regression is performed at each iteration, one may use standard statistics (R^2, t statistics, etc.) to evaluate the fit of the linearized equation. Because this approach has found application to computer systems for econometric modeling, we examine it in more detail.[52]

We utilize the fact that any nonlinear function can be expressed as a *Taylor series expansion*. Specifically, we may write Eq. (7.60) in an expansion around a set of initial values $\beta_{1,0}, \ldots, \beta_{p,0}$ for the coefficients $\beta_1, \ldots, \beta_p$. (How these initial values were obtained is not important at this point; let us assume that they represent "guesses" of the true values.) The expanded equation would be

$$
Y = f(X_1, \ldots, X_k, \beta_{1,0}, \ldots, \beta_{p,0}) + \sum_{i=1}^{p} \left[\frac{\partial f}{\partial \beta_i} \right]_0 (\beta_i - \beta_{i,0})
$$

$$
+ \tfrac{1}{2} \sum_{i=1}^{p} \left[\frac{\partial^2 f}{\partial \beta_i^2} \right]_0 (\beta_i - \beta_{i,0})^2 + \cdots + \varepsilon \tag{7.63}
$$

Here the subscript 0 on the partial derivatives denotes that the derivatives are evaluated at $\beta_1 = \beta_{1,0}, \ldots, \beta_p = \beta_{p,0}$. A linear approximation to our nonlinear function is provided by the first two terms in the Taylor series expansion. Dropping the second- and higher-order terms, and rewriting the equation, we get

$$
Y - f(X_1, \ldots, X_k, \beta_{1,0}, \ldots, \beta_{p,0}) + \sum_{i=1}^{p} \beta_{i,0} \left[\frac{\partial f}{\partial \beta_i} \right]_0 = \sum_{i=1}^{p} \beta_i \left[\frac{\partial f}{\partial \beta_i} \right]_0 + \varepsilon \tag{7.64}
$$

Observe that Eq. (7.64) has the form of a linear regression equation. The left-hand side is a constructed dependent variable. The right-hand side consists of (in addition to the additive error term) a set of unknown coefficients $(\beta_1, \ldots, \beta_p)$ multiplying a set of constructed independent variables. Thus, the coefficients can be estimated by performing an ordinary least-squares regression on Eq. (7.64).

The estimated coefficient values for $\beta_1, \ldots, \beta_p$ from Eq. (7.64), which are labeled $\beta_{1,1}, \ldots, \beta_{p,1}$, are used as a new set of "initial estimates," and the nonlinear equation is *relinearized* around these values. The result is a new linear regression equation:

$$
Y - f(X_1, \ldots, X_k, \beta_{1,1}, \ldots, \beta_{p,1}) + \sum_{i=1}^{p} \beta_{i,1} \left[\frac{\partial f}{\partial \beta_i} \right]_1 = \sum_{i=1}^{p} \beta_i \left[\frac{\partial f}{\partial \beta_i} \right]_1 + \varepsilon \tag{7.65}
$$

---

[52] The approach, and its application to an econometric software system, is described in detail in M. Eisner and R. S. Pindyck, "A Generalized Approach to Estimation as Implemented in the TROLL/1 System," *Annals of Economic and Social Measurement*, vol. 2, no. 1, pp. 29–51, 1973.

Ordinary least squares is applied to this equation, and a new set of coefficient estimates $\beta_{1,2}, \ldots, \beta_{p,2}$ is obtained. The process of relinearization is repeated until convergence occurs, i.e., until

$$\left| \frac{\beta_{i,j+1} - \beta_{i,j}}{\beta_{i,j}} \right| < \delta \qquad i = 1, 2, \ldots, p \qquad (7.66)$$

where δ is a small number whose choice depends in part on how much computational expense one is willing to entail in making repeated iterations.

There is no guarantee that this iterative process will converge to the maximum-likelihood estimate of the coefficients. The process may, for example, converge to a local, as opposed to global, minimum of the sum-of-squared-errors function. One way to check if this has occurred is to repeat the estimation starting with a different set of initial guesses for the coefficients. Usually the initial guesses $\beta_{1,0}, \ldots, \beta_{p,0}$ are based on values that would seem reasonable from a theoretical point of view. However, the set of guesses chosen for the second estimation should differ substantially from the first set of guesses.

Of crucial importance is the fact that the iterative process may not converge *at all*. Succeeding estimates of the coefficients may differ, and the left-hand side of Eq. (7.66) may grow larger with each new iteration (i.e., the process may *diverge*). Should divergence occur, one might begin the process over again using a new set of initial guesses for the coefficients. (Occasionally convergence is dependent on the particular initial guesses chosen.) If the process still does not converge, then it becomes necessary to try a different estimation method (e.g., the direct optimization approach—through the solution of a set of normal equations—mentioned earlier).

An alternative method involves a variation on the iterative linearizatio.1 method. Instead of using the successive estimates resulting from each linearization, estimates are computed from

$$\beta_{i,j+1} = \beta_{i,j} + \alpha(\hat{\beta}_{i,j+1} - \beta_{i,j}) \qquad (7.67)$$

where $\hat{\beta}_{i,j+1}$ is the least-squares estimate from the $(j + 1)$st iteration, and α is a damping factor $(0 < \alpha < 1)$. The damping factor α can be chosen to keep from "overshooting" the minimum of the sum-of-squared-errors function.[53]

---

[53] The damping factor can also be used to change the step $\beta_{i,j+1} - \beta_{i,j}$ so that it is somewhere between that which would be indicated by the linearization method and that which would be indicated by the steepest-descent method. This is the basis for Marquardt's method. See D. W. Marquardt, "An Algorithm for Least Squares Estimation of Nonlinear Parameters," *Journal of the Society of Industrial and Applied Mathematics*, vol. 2, 1963, p. 431.

Other methods for nonlinear estimation are available and may provide convergent estimates when the methods described above fail.[54] There is really no "best" method, since one method might converge more easily while another might involve less computational expense. Often alternative methods will be used as a way of checking that the global minimum of the sum-of-squared-errors function has been reached.

7.5.2   Evaluation of Nonlinear Regression Equations

The statistical tests used to evaluate the fit of a linear regression equation are not directly applicable to a nonlinear regression. An F statistic, for example, cannot be used to perform a significance test on the overall fit of a nonlinear regression, nor can t statistics be used in the usual manner. One reason for this is that we cannot obtain an unbiased estimate of σ^2, the true variance of the error term ε, from the regression residuals. Even if ε is normally distributed with 0 mean, the residuals u_t given by

$$u_t = Y_t - f(X_{1t}, \ldots, X_{kt}, \hat{\beta}_1, \ldots, \hat{\beta}_p) \tag{7.68}$$

will not be normally distributed (nor will they have 0 mean). Thus the sum of squared residuals will not follow a chi-square distribution, the estimated coefficients themselves will not be normally distributed, and standard t tests and F tests cannot be applied.

What we can do, however, is perform t tests and F tests on the *linear* regression that applies to the *final linearization of the iterative process* (if indeed we have estimated the equation using a linearization approach). These tests will provide some information about the fit of the regression for this last linearization. We would hope that this linearization provides a reasonable approximation to the nonlinear equation, and that it fits the data. If this is not the case (as indicated by the statistics), then doubt would be cast on the fit of the nonlinear equation as a whole. As a result, computer programs that perform nonlinear estimation via the linearization approach usually calculate t statistics (and associated standard errors) for the last linearization.[55]

The R^2, however, can be applied in its conventional sense to a nonlinear regression. Recall that the R^2 is calculated from

$$R^2 = 1 - \frac{\sum u_t^2}{\sum y_t^2} \tag{7.69}$$

---

[54] For other methods that seem computationally quite efficient, see S. M. Goldfeld, R. E. Quandt, and H. F. Trotter, "Maximization by Quadratic Hill-Climbing," *Econometrica*, vol. 34, pp. 541–551, 1966; and V. Corbo, "A Non-Linear Estimation Procedure for a CES Production Function" (unpublished, 1974). For a discussion of several alternative estimation methods and their statistical properties, see S. M. Goldfeld and R. E. Quandt, *Nonlinear Methods in Econometrics* (Amsterdam: North-Holland, 1972).

[55] See M. Eisner and R. S. Pindyck, *op. cit.*

(where y_t is measured in deviation form) and represents the fraction of the variation in y_t that is "explained" by the regression. The R^2 will retain this meaning if the equation is nonlinear and the residuals are calculated from Eq. (7.69). Recall, though, that the R^2 is solely a descriptive statistic that can be associated with overall fit. It cannot be used for significance or hypothesis testing.[56]

7.5.3   Forecasting with a Nonlinear Regression Equation

Once a nonlinear regression equation has been estimated, it can be used to obtain forecasts. A forecast of Y_t is given by

$$Y_{T+1} = f(X_{1,\,T+1}, \ldots, X_{k,\,T+1}, \hat{\beta}_1, \ldots, \hat{\beta}_p) \qquad (7.70)$$

We saw in Chapter 6 that for a linear regression this forecast is unbiased and has the minimum mean square error. This claim cannot be made, however, for a forecast generated from a nonlinear regression as in equation (7.69). The reason is that the forecast errors will not be normally distributed with 0 mean as was the case for a linear equation. In such a case we cannot determine whether the forecast error is smaller than the error generated by a different set of coefficient estimates.

Furthermore, the formulas for the standard error of forecast (i.e., the standard deviation of the forecast error) and corresponding confidence intervals that were derived in Chapter 6 for the linear case do not apply to Eq. (7.70). There is, in fact, no analytical formula that can be used to compute directly forecast confidence intervals for the general nonlinear equation. One solution might involve the generation of confidence intervals through the use of Monte Carlo forecasting, as described in Chapter 11. This, however, requires that the coefficients be normally distributed (which is not the case) and that estimates be available for the coefficient standard errors and the standard error of the equation itself (which is also not the case). Thus, Monte Carlo techniques are not directly applicable here.

We suggest the following "compromise" approach. A Monte Carlo forecast is performed using normally distributed errors for the coefficients and the additive error term, and using the linear regression results from the last iteration to provide estimates for the standard errors. As an illustration, consider the following nonlinear regression equation:

$$Y_t = \beta_0 + \beta_1 X_t^{\beta_2} + \varepsilon_t \qquad (7.71)$$

After the equation has been estimated and a forecast $\hat{Y}_{T+1}$ has been computed, the standard error of forecast would be computed as follows:

---

[56] When the linearization approach is used for estimation, a second R^2 is usually calculated for the linear regression at the last iteration.

1 Rewrite the equation as

$$Y_t = (\beta_0 + \eta_0) + (\beta_1 + \eta_1)X_t^{\beta_2 + \eta_2} + \varepsilon_t \qquad (7.72)$$

where η_0, η_1, η_2, and ε_t are assumed to be normally distributed random variables with 0 mean and standard deviations equal to the *computed standard errors from the linear regression corresponding to the last iteration* of the estimation process.

2 Generate random numbers (from the appropriate normal distributions) for η_0, η_1, η_2, and ε_{T+1} to use for the forecast $\hat{Y}_{T+1}$. Compute this forecast accordingly.

3 Repeat step 2 approximately 50 times. Use the sample standard derivation of the resulting distribution of values for $\hat{Y}_{T+1}$ as the standard error of forecast. This "approximate" standard error of forecast can then be used to calculate confidence intervals.

There is no guarantee that this method provides even a close approximation to the true standard error of forecast. It does, however, at least provide some measure of forecast confidence.

Example 7.8 Consumption Function

In this example we estimate a *consumption function* that is nonlinear in the coefficients. The objective is to relate aggregate real (constant-dollar) consumption C to aggregate real disposable income YD in the United States, using quarterly time-series data. We would also like to test the hypothesis that the *marginal propensity to consume* MPC, defined as

$$\text{MPC} = \frac{dC}{d\text{YD}} \qquad (7.73)$$

declines as disposable income increases. This hypothesis is easy to support using cross-section data (regressing consumption against income for groups at different income levels), but not using time-series data.

Typically, the following consumption function, which is linear in the coefficients, is estimated:

$$C = \alpha_0 + \alpha_1 \text{YD} + \alpha_2 \text{YD}^2 + \varepsilon \qquad (7.74)$$

One would expect α_1 to be positive and α_2 to be negative, so that MPC decreases as YD increases. If Eq. (7.74) is estimated using cross-section data, a significant and negative value of α_2 will usually result, while if time-series data are used, the estimate of α_2 will invariably be insignificant, implying a constant MPC (α_1 is always significant and positive).[57]

As an alternative to Eq. (7.74), we estimate the following nonlinear consumption function:

$$C = \alpha_0 + \alpha_1 YD^{\alpha_2} + \varepsilon \qquad (7.75)$$

The quarterly time-series data used cover the period 1946-1 to 1974-3. The estimation is performed using the iterative linearization process. We use the value 1.0 as an initial guess for all three coefficients (we would expect α_1 and α_2 to be close to this value, but we have no expectation regarding the value of α_0).

The estimation results are shown below for each iteration:

Iteration	α_0	α_1	α_2
Initial guess	1.0000	1.0000	1.0000
1	−9.4974	1.1856	.9589
2	−10.3366	1.2400	.9539
3	−10.3517	1.2409	.9539
4	−10.3507	1.2409	.9539

Convergence occurs quickly, requiring only four iterations. Standard errors are also calculated for the linear regression at the last iteration. The standard error for the equation as a whole is 4.732, and the standard errors for α_0, α_1, and α_2 are 4.192, .0876, and .0098, respectively. Thus, the regression estimates at the last iteration are all significant. Finally, the R^2 for the fitted nonlinear equation is .9994. The estimated nonlinear equation is as follows:

$$C = -10.3507 + 1.2409YD^{.9539} \qquad (7.76)$$

For comparison, the following linear regression equation was also estimated (coefficient standard errors are in parentheses):

$$C = 7.9852 + .8905YD \qquad (7.77)$$
$$(1.0349) \quad (.0022)$$

$$R^2 = .9993 \qquad SER = 5.154$$

---

[57] See, for example, R. D. Husby, "A Nonlinear Consumption Function Estimated from Time-Series and Cross-Section Data," *Review of Economics and Statistics*, vol. 53, Feb. 1971. Husby's consumption functions are nonlinear only in the independent variables, and not in the coefficients.

Note that the MPC for this linear equation is a constant, .8905. For our nonlinear equation, the MPC is

$$\text{MPC} = \frac{dC}{d\text{YD}} = \alpha_1 \alpha_2 \text{YD}^{\alpha_2 - 1} \tag{7.78}$$

The mean value of YD (in billions of 1958 dollars) is 417, and at this value MPC is .876. Note that MPC indeed declines as YD increases; for YD equal to 600, MPC is .860.

It is important to stress that our estimation results are dependent upon the particular nonlinear estimation method used. As an illustration of this, Eq. (7.75) was reestimated using a steepest-descent method of direct optimization. Convergence occurred after 17 iterations, and the resulting equation is

$$C = .005 + 1.0424 \text{YD}^{.9779} \tag{7.79}$$

The result is a lower marginal propensity to consume. For YD equal to 417, the MPC is .850, and for YD equal to 600, the MPC is .841. While the results in Eqs. (7.76) and (7.79) differ, it is impossible to determine which is more "correct" on statistical grounds, since we lack statistical tests for nonlinear regression estimates. Therefore, the evaluation of the two equations would require comparing their performance in a series of *ex post* forecasts.

Exercises

7.1 Prove that the omission of a variable from a "true" regression model will lead in general to a biased estimate of the regression intercept. Under what special conditions will the bias become zero? [*Hint:* Recall that $\overline{Y} = \beta_1^* + \beta_2^* \overline{X}_2$ in Eq. (7.2) and that $\overline{Y} = \beta_1 + \beta_2 \overline{X}_2 + \beta_3 \overline{X}_3$ in Eq. (7.1).]

7.2 Assume that the true regression model is of the form

$$y_i = \beta_2 x_{2i} + \beta_3 x_{2i}^2 + \varepsilon_i$$

If the regression $y_i = \beta_2^* x_{2i} + \varepsilon_i^*$ is run, what can you say about the direction of the bias of the slope coefficient?

7.3 Prove that in the case of omitted-variable specification error, the estimated variance of the slope parameter when the omitted variable is correlated with the included variable will be greater than the estimated variance when the omitted variable is uncorrelated with the included variable. [*Hint:* When the omitted variable is uncorrelated with the included variable, one can show that $\text{Var}(\hat{\beta}_2^*) = \text{Var}(\varepsilon_i)/\sum x_{2i}^2 = \sigma^2/\sum x_{2i}^2$. To find the estimated variance, substitute the estimated error variances and then take expected values.]

7.4 Prove that the inclusion of an irrelevant variable does not bias the estimated intercept parameter.

7.5 Prove that the coefficient of an irrelevant variable will have expected value of 0. [*Hint:* Using the analog of Eq. (7.7), solve for the estimated parameter $\hat{\beta}_3^*$ and then take expected values.]

7.6 A given explanatory variable for a regression model is unavailable. The researcher is forced to omit the relevant variable, but replaces it with a "proxy" variable, which is believed to be highly correlated with the missing variable. Discuss the properties of the estimated coefficient of the proxy variable. Why is the high correlation between the original variable and the proxy so important?

7.7 Consider the following model:

$$Y_t = \alpha + \beta X_t + \varepsilon_t \qquad t = 1, 2, \ldots, T$$

Discuss the appropriate method or methods for dealing with missing observations when:

(1) The last (Tth) observation on X is missing.
(2) The last (Tth) observation on Y is missing.
(3) The last observation on both X and Y is missing.

Suggestion: Relate answers to (2) and (3) to the material on single-equation forecasting in Chapter 6.

7.8 Prove that replacing the missing X observation in the model described in Exercise 7.7 [case (1)] by using time t as an instrument will yield a consistent slope estimate. What will happen if the error term is serially correlated?

7.9 Consider the following model:

$$Y_{it} = \alpha + \beta X_{it} + \varepsilon_{it} \qquad i = 1, 2, \ldots, N \qquad t = 1, 2, \ldots, T$$

Assume that it is known that the time-series intercepts are constant. How would you test to see whether the covariance model ought to be used to account for varying cross-section intercepts?

7.10 How would you go about estimating a pooled time-series cross-section econometric model when the time-series error component is known to be heteroscedastic? How would this differ from the case when the cross-section error component is heteroscedastic?

7.11 Prove that the mean geometric lag is $w/(1 - w)$. [*Hint:* Apply the formula for the sum of a geometric series: $a(1 + r + r^2 + r^3 + \cdots) = a/(1 - r)$ for $0 \leq r < 1$.]

7.12 Assume that you are estimating a model with two explanatory variables, each of which has a Koyck geometric lag. Derive an equation to be estimated when both lags have identical weights.

7.13 Consider the following model:

$$Y_t = \alpha + \beta(w_0 X_t + w_1 X_{t-1} + w_2 X_{t-2} + w_3 X_{t-3}) + \varepsilon_t$$

Show how to estimate the model using the polynomial distributed lag model and a second-degree polynomial if:

(1) There are no endpoint restrictions.
(2) The tail and head of the distribution are assumed equal to 0 ($w_{-1} = w_4 = 0$).

7.14 Expand the consumption function

$$C = a_0 + a_1 YD^{a_2}$$

in a Taylor series expansion around some initial "guess" for a_0, a_1, and a_2. Set up the linear regression equation. Explain how the equation would be relinearized around the OLS estimates from the first regression.

7.15 Write the sum-of-squared-errors function S for the nonlinear consumption function

$$C = a_0 + a_1 YD^{a_2}$$

Take the derivatives of S with respect to a_0, a_1, and a_2 to obtain the *normal equations* that correspond to Eq. (7.62). Describe how these normal equations could be solved to yield estimates of a_0, a_1, and a_2.

8

MODELS OF QUALITATIVE CHOICE

Our objective in this chapter is to extend the tools of linear regression to construct models in which the dependent variable is not continuous. Specifically, we concern ourselves with models in which the dependent variable is associated with two or more qualitative choices. Such models are finding wider application to economics (and business) in part because of the recent emphasis on the analysis of survey data. In most surveys the behavioral responses are qualitative in nature—one either votes yes or votes no in an election; one uses either the subway, the bus, or the automobile; one is either in the labor force or out of the labor force; etc.

Our approach will be to focus primarily on the analysis of models in which binary choices are made. In particular, we will discuss the specification and estimation of three models—the linear probability model, the probit model, and the logit model. The linear probability model provides a suitable starting point because it can be viewed as a direct extension of our earlier discussion (Chapter 3) of the use of dummy variables. Some of the difficulties associated with the interpretation of the probabilistic nature of this model suggest the usefulness of the probit and logit models. Throughout the chapter we attempt only to introduce the important modeling concepts involved and to outline some of the estimation problems which arise. To extend their understanding of this subject, some readers may wish to read some of the relevant source materials cited within the chapter. These studies include further details about the estimation processes described in the chapter as well as proofs of some of the results.

8.1 BINARY CHOICE MODELS

When one or more of the *explanatory* variables in a regression model are dichotomous in nature, we may represent them as dummy variables and proceed as in Chapter 3. However the application of the linear regression model when the *dependent variable* is dichotomous is more complex. *Binary choice models* assume that individuals[1] are faced with a choice between two alternatives, and that the choice they make depends on the characteristics of the alternatives. Assuming that we have information about the attributes of each of the individuals and the choices that they make, it is natural to ask whether we can estimate an equation which will predict the choices of individuals not in the original sample.[2] Suppose, for example, that we wish to build a model which will allow us to make predictions about how individuals will vote on a local bond issue. We might expect that individual income is a primary determinant of voting choice, and that (other things equal) high-income individuals are more likely to vote yes on a bond issue than are low-income individuals. Although it is reasonable to expect a direct relationship between income and voting behavior, our information is not sufficient to predict how each and every individual will vote with perfect accuracy. A more plausible objective is to predict the *likelihood* that an individual with a given income will vote yes.

As in the regression model, one purpose of qualitative choice models is to determine the probability that an individual with a given set of attributes will make one choice rather than the alternative. A suitable model is one which (when properly estimated) will allow us to make statements of the following type: "The probability that an individual with an income of $15,000 will vote yes on the upcoming bond issue is .6." More generally, we wish to find a relationship between a set of attributes describing an individual and the probability that the individual will make a given choice. The choice model, like most models that we have studied, must be written in a form which is both useful for predictive purposes and easily estimated.

We will describe several possible model specifications and some of the

---

[1] We use the expression *individual* to refer to any choice-making entity. Thus, households, cities, and firms are all considered to be "individuals" in the discussion which follows.

[2] The problem of model estimation and its relationship to the theory of choice is described thoroughly in D. McFadden, "Conditional Logit Analysis of Qualitative Choice Behavior," in P. Zarembka (ed.), *Frontiers in Econometrics* (New York: Academic Press, 1973), and T. Domencich and D. McFadden, *Urban Travel Demand: A Behavioral Analysis* (Amsterdam: North-Holland, 1975). We shall implicitly restrict our analysis to cases in which prediction is to occur over the same set of choices available during the period of model estimation.

trade-offs involved in selecting the appropriate one. In order to simplify our discussion, we will always assume that the probability of an individual making a given choice is a *linear* function of the individual attributes. Alternative model specifications arise because it is possible to make several assumptions about the probabilistic nature of the decision process. We will have more to say about the importance of the assumptions relating to probability after we study the most elementary specification of a binary choice model—the linear probability model.

8.1.1 Linear Probability Model

We begin by examining the *linear probability model*. The regression form of the model is[3]

$$Y_i = \alpha + \beta X_i + \varepsilon_i \qquad (8.1)$$

where X_i = the value of an attribute (e.g., income) for the ith individual

$$Y_i = \begin{cases} 1 \text{ if the first option is chosen (buy a car, vote yes)} \\ 0 \text{ if the second option is chosen (not buy, vote no)} \end{cases}$$

ε_i = an independently distributed random variable with 0 mean[4]

The interpretation of Eq. (8.1) as a linear probability model comes about when we take the expected value of each dependent variable observation Y_i:

$$E(Y_i) = \alpha + \beta X_i \qquad (8.2)$$

Since Y_i can take on only two values, 1 and 0, we can describe the probability distribution of Y by letting $P_i = \text{Prob}\,(Y_i = 1)$ and $1 - P_i = \text{Prob}\,(Y_i = 0)$. Then,

$$E(Y_i) = 1(P_i) + 0(1 - P_i)$$

$$= P_i$$

Thus, the regression equation may be interpreted as describing the probability that an individual will vote yes, given information about the person's income. The slope of the regression line measures the effect on the probability of voting yes of a unit change in the individual's income. Formally, the linear probability model is often written in the following form, which allows the dependent variable to be interpreted as a probability:

$$P_i = \begin{cases} \alpha + \beta X_i & \text{when } 0 < \alpha + \beta X_i < 1 \\ 1 & \text{when } \alpha + \beta X_i \geq 1 \\ 0 & \text{when } \alpha + \beta X_i \leq 0 \end{cases}$$

---

[3] We shall work with a single explanatory variable purely for purposes of simplicity.

[4] As in the classical linear regression model, we are assuming that X_i is either fixed (or, if random, is independent of ε_i).

TABLE 8.1
PROBABILITY DISTRIBUTION OF ε_i

	ε_i	**Probability**
$Y_i = 1$	$1 - \alpha - \beta X_i$	P_i
$Y_i = 0$	$-\alpha - \beta X_i$	$1 - P_i$

We have not yet described the probability distribution of the error term in the model. The actual distribution is determined by substituting the values of Y_i (1 and 0) in Eq. (8.1), and is exhibited in Table 8.1.[5] When X_i is fixed, the probability distribution of ε_i must be equivalent to the probability distribution of Y_i. (When X_i is stochastic, the probability distribution will be more complicated.) We can determine the relationship between the probability P_i and X_i by utilizing our assumption that the error has 0 mean. It follows that

$$E(\varepsilon_i) = (1 - \alpha - \beta X_i)P_i + (-\alpha - \beta X_i)(1 - P_i) = 0$$

Solving for P_i, we find that

$$P_i = \alpha + \beta X_i$$

$$1 - P_i = 1 - \alpha - \beta X_i$$

The variance of the error term can now be calculated:

$$E(\varepsilon_i^2) = (1 - \alpha - \beta X_i)^2 P_i + (-\alpha - \beta X_i)^2 (1 - P_i)$$

$$= (1 - \alpha - \beta X_i)^2 (\alpha + \beta X_i) + (\alpha + \beta X_i)^2 (1 - \alpha - \beta X_i)$$

$$= (1 - \alpha - \beta X_i)(\alpha + \beta X_i) = P_i(1 - P_i)$$

or

$$\sigma_i^2 = E(\varepsilon_i^2) = E(Y_i)[1 - E(Y_i)]$$

This suggests quite properly that the error term is heteroscedastic; i.e., the variance of the error term is not constant for all observations. Observations for which P_i is close to 0 or close to 1 will have relatively low variances, while observations with P_i closer to 1/2 will have higher variances. The presence of heteroscedasticity results in a loss of efficiency, but does not in itself result in either biased or inconsistent parameter estimates.

---

[5] P_i measures the probability that $\varepsilon_i = 1 - \alpha - \beta X_i$, etc.

An obvious means of correcting for heteroscedasticity is to estimate the variances of *each* of the Y_i and then to apply weighted least-squares estimation. To do this, we perform ordinary least squares on the original (0, 1) dichotomous dependent variable model, and estimate each of the error variances as follows:[6]

$$\hat{\sigma}_i^2 = \hat{Y}_i(1 - \hat{Y}_i) \qquad \text{where } \hat{Y}_i = \hat{\alpha} + \hat{\beta}X_i \qquad (8.3)$$

The difficulty with weighted least squares is that there is no guarantee that the predicted value $\hat{Y}_i$ will lie in the (0, 1) interval.[7] If some values of $\hat{Y}_i$ do lie outside the (0, 1) range, the observations must either be dropped from the model or arbitrarily be set equal to numbers such as .01 and .99. In either case, the weighted least-squares procedure may not be efficient. It can be shown that as the sample size becomes arbitrarily large, weighted least squares is efficient, but it is not efficient for small samples. Since the weighted least-squares procedure is also quite sensitive to errors of specification, we advise against the indiscriminate use of the technique. Ordinary least-squares estimation is most likely a better alternative. An additional problem arises from the fact that the error distribution is not normal. We cannot apply the classical statistical tests to the estimated parameters, since the tests depend on the normality of the errors. (It is possible to develop statistical tests which are appropriate when the sample size gets large. However, the issues involved are too complex to be discussed here.[8])

When we attempt to use the linear probability model for prediction, a serious weakness of the model becomes apparent. Since the linear probability model involves the interpretation of predicted values of Y as probabilities, we are faced with a problem when the predicted value lies outside the (0, 1) range. This possibility is depicted in Fig. 8.1. Even if the true linear probability model is correct, it is certainly possible that a given sample value of X will lie outside the $(-2, 2)$ interval. The fitted value of Y associated with this observation on X will be greater than 1 or less than 0 as the occasion arises. The obvious correction for this problem is to set extreme predictions equal to either 1 or 0, thereby constraining predicted probabilities to be within the (0, 1) interval. This solution is not very satisfying, because it suggests that we might predict an occurrence with a probability of 1 when it is entirely possible that it may not occur, or we might predict an occurrence with probability 0 when it may actually occur. While the estimation procedure might yield unbiased estimates, the predictions obtained from the estimation process are clearly biased.

An alternative approach is to reestimate the parameters α and β subject to the

---

[6] $\hat{\sigma}_i^2$ will be a consistent estimate of σ_i^2.

[7] This, of course, presents a serious problem when the linear probability model is used for purposes of forecasting. See the discussion which follows.

[8] For a discussion of some of the relevant issues, see S. Warner, "Asymptotic Variances for Dummy Variable Regression under Normality Assumptions," *Journal of the American Statistical Association*, vol. 62, pp. 1305–1314, 1967; and S. Warner, "Multivariate Regression of Dummy Variates under Normality Assumptions," *Journal of the American Statistical Association*, vol. 58, pp. 1054–1063, 1963.

FIGURE 8.1
Prediction with the linear probability model.

constraint that $0 \le \hat{Y}_i \le 1$. The determination of least-squares parameter estimates subject to inequality constraints is a nonlinear estimation problem, which in this particular case can be solved using a mathematical programming routine. The available evidence suggests that the addition of the inequality constraint leads to parameter estimates with lower variances, as expected, but there is no guarantee that the estimates will be unbiased.[9] Given this fact, and given the sensitivity of the constrained estimation procedure, it seems more appropriate to use the ordinary least-squares version of the linear probability model.

The problem of predicting outside the unit interval with the linear probability model suggests an additional problem associated with the model specification. The problem arises because observations in a given sample may be drawn excessively from attributes whose values are associated with extreme values of

FIGURE 8.2
Underestimated slope.

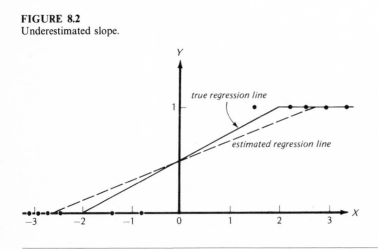

---

[9] See Domencich and McFadden, *op. cit.*, chap. 5.

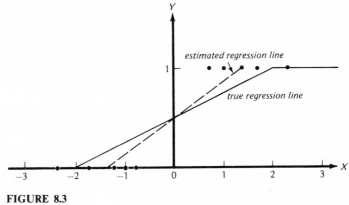

FIGURE 8.3
Overestimated slope.

choice probabilities (0 and 1). Suppose, for example, that the independent attribute values are drawn randomly from a known population and that several observations lie outside the $(-2, 2)$ interval shown in Fig. 8.1. This possibility is depicted graphically in Fig. 8.2. In this case, the true regression model associates a probability of 1 with values of X greater than 2 and a probability of 0 with values of X less than 0. The sample contains several X values greater than 2 for which the first option was chosen, and several values of X less than -2 for which the second option was chosen. The resulting ordinary least-squares slope estimate will be biased, since it will underestimate the true regression slope. This bias is in reality a form of specification bias and cannot be eliminated by the use of nonlinear estimation procedures which account for loss of efficiency. It suggests the particular sensitivity to specification error which is associated with the linear probability model. We should note that the underestimated slope as shown in Fig. 8.2 is not a general result. If the attribute data are bunched somewhat differently, the slope might be over-estimated. An example of this case is shown in Fig. 8.3.[10]

Example 8.1 Predicting Bond Defaults

A useful means of predicting bond failures is to analyze the factors that correlate highly with actual bond defaults.[11] If we view the decision to default and the decision not to default as two options for local governments, then we may estimate the probability of default using the linear probability model.

---

[10] This bunching example is described in M. Nerlove and S. J. Press, "Univariate and Multivariate Log-Linear and Logistic Models," *Rand Corporation, R-1306-EDA/NIH,* Dec. 1973, Santa Monica, Calif.

[11] A bond default occurs when there is a delayed payment of either principal or interest on a bond. Some bondholders are repaid for partial or total loss of interest and payment, but only after some length of time.

A sample of 35 Massachusetts communities, several of which actually defaulted, was used in a cross-section study using 1930 data.[12] The goal of the estimation was to find a subset of characteristics of communities which best allows one to predict the probability of default. The model is as follows:

$$P_i = \beta_1 + \beta_2\,\text{TAX}_i + \beta_3\,\text{INT}_i + \beta_4\,\text{AV}_i + \beta_5\,\text{DAV}_i + \beta_6\,\text{WELF}_i + \varepsilon_i$$

where $P = 0$ if the municipality defaulted and 1 otherwise
   TAX = average of 1929, 1930, and 1931 tax rates
   INT = percentage of current budget allocated to interest payments in 1930
    AV = percentage growth in assessed property valuation from 1925 to 1930
   DAV = ratio of total direct net debt to total assessed valuation in 1930
  WELF = percentage of 1930 budget allocated to charities, pensions, and
         soldiers' benefits

The regression results were as follows (standard errors are in parentheses):

$$P = 1.96 - .029\text{TAX} - 4.86\text{INT} + .063\text{AV} + .007\text{DAV} - .48\text{WELF}$$
$$\quad\ (.29)\quad (.009)\qquad (2.13)\qquad (.028)\qquad (.003)\qquad (.88)$$

$$R^2 = .36$$

The R^2 of .36 suggests that a good deal of variance in the model is still unexplained. Nonetheless one can still use the results of the model to study several economic factors which do correlate highly with defaults. The coefficient of the tax rate variable is negative and significant, implying that, *ceteris paribus*, an increase in the tax rate of $1 per thousand will raise the probability of default by .029. The percentage of the budget allocated to interest payments also appears to be a good predictor of defaults, with higher-interest budget shares being positively correlated with the probability of default. This result is to be expected, given the near-guarantee of the claim of interest payments on the current budget. The percentage of current budget allocated to welfare bears the same relationship to probability of default as the interest budget share, but is not significant. The rate of growth of actual assessed valuation is significant and inversely related to default probability. A growing tax base implies a low probability of default, at least in the short run. Finally, the debt-to-assessed-valuation ratio is also inversely related to default probability.

---

[12] See D. Rubinfeld, "An Econometric Analysis of the Market for General Obligation Municipal Bonds," unpublished doctoral dissertation, M.I.T., June 1972.

8.1.2   Probit Model

All the difficulties associated with the linear probability model point to the need for alternative model specifications. Since the most serious set of difficulties arises from the fact that predictions may lie outside the (0, 1) interval, it is natural to search for alternative distributional assumptions for which all predictions must lie within the appropriate interval. The obvious solution to the problem is to transform the original model in such a way that for all X, predictions will lie in the (0, 1) interval. The constrained form of the linear probability model achieves this goal, but at some cost. Since our primary concern is to interpret the "dependent" variable in our model as the probability of making a choice (given information about the individual's attributes), it is reasonable to utilize some notion of probability as the basis of the transformation. The requirement of such a process is that it translate the values of the attribute X, which may range in value over the entire real line, to a probability which ranges in value from 0 to 1. We would also like the transformation to maintain the property that increases in X are associated with increases (or decreases) in the dependent variable for all values of X.[13] These requirements suggest that use of the *cumulative probability function* will provide a suitable transformation.[14] The resulting probability distribution might be represented as follows:

$$P_i = F(\alpha + \beta X_i) = F(Z_i) \tag{8.4}$$

where F = a cumulative probability function

Under the assumption that we transform the model using a cumulative *uniform* probability function, we get the constrained version of the linear probability model, $P_i = \alpha + \beta X_i$. (See Exercise 8.4.) While numerous alternative cumulative probability functions are possible, we shall consider only two, the *normal* and the *logistic*.

The *probit probability model* is associated with the cumulative normal probability function.[15] To understand this model, assume that there exists an index Z_i which measures an individual's feeling toward voting in an election. If properly chosen, Z_i will be defined so that the higher its value, the greater the likelihood that the individual will vote yes. In our special case, we hypothesize that Z_i is a linear function of the individual's attribute X_i (income):

$$Z_i = \alpha + \beta X_i \tag{8.5}$$

---

[13] Such a transformation is called a *monotonic* transformation.

[14] The reader should recall that a *cumulative probability function* is defined as having as its value the probability that an observed value of a variable X (for every X) will be less than or equal to a particular X. The range of the cumulative probability function is the (0, 1) interval, since all probabilities lie between 0 and 1.

[15] For further details see D. J. Finney, *Probit Analysis*, 2d ed. (Cambridge, England: Cambridge University Press, 1964), and J. Tobin, "The Application of Multivariate Probit Analysis to Economic Survey Data," *Cowles Foundation Discussion Paper* 1, 1955.

TABLE 8.2

Z	$F(Z)$	Z	$F(Z)$
-3.0	.001	.5	.691
-2.5	.006	1.0	.841
-2.0	.023	1.5	.933
-1.5	.067	2.0	.977
-1.0	.159	2.5	.994
$-.5$	.309	3.0	.999
0	.500	3.5	.999

In addition, we assume that associated with *each individual* is a critical value Z_i^* of the index Z_i. The critical value allows us to describe an explicit criterion for predicting voting behavior:

$$\text{If } Z_i > Z_i^*, \text{ vote yes}$$

$$\text{If } Z_i \leq Z_i^*, \text{ vote no}$$

(8.6)

The probit model assumes that Z_i^* is a normally distributed random variable, so that the probability that Z_i^* is less than (or equal to) Z_i can be computed from the cumulative normal probability function. (The cumulative normal function assigns to a number Z the probability that any arbitrary Z^* will be less than or equal to Z.) The cumulative normal function is written as follows:

$$P_i = F(Z_i) = \frac{1}{\sqrt{2\pi}} \int_{-\infty}^{Z_i} e^{-s^2/2} \, ds$$

(8.7)

By construction, the variable P_i will lie in the $(0, 1)$ interval. The reader unfamiliar with the cumulative normal function may find it helpful to examine Table 8.2, in which the relationship in Eq. (8.7) is described for particular values of Z. (The normal distribution has mean 0 and variance 1.) The cumulative normal function is shown graphically in Fig. 8.4, which compares the probit and linear probability models.

To obtain the variable Z_i, which is assumed to be linear in the unknown parameters, we apply the inverse of the cumulative normal function to Eq. (8.7):[16]

$$Z_i = F^{-1}(P_i) = \alpha + \beta X_i$$

We may interpret the probability P_i resulting from the probit model as an estimate

---

[16] The variable Z_i can take on any real value.

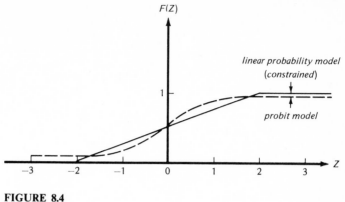

FIGURE 8.4
Probit model.

of the conditional probability that an individual will vote yes (or an individual will go to college), given that his/her income is X_i. This is equivalent to the probability that a standard normal variable will be less than or equal to $\alpha + \beta X_i$.

Note that the slope of the probit function as shown in Fig. 8.4 is larger than that of the linear probability function in the middle range, but smaller at the extremes of the interval $(-2, 2)$. Outside the $(-2, 2)$ interval the linear probability model has a slope of 0. The graph is suggestive of some of the difficulties which might be associated with a misspecified probability model. Assume, for example, that the probit specification is correct. Then estimation of the incorrect linear probability model will lead to the false inference that the slope of the function is constant, when in fact the change in probability associated with a change in X is dependent upon the particular value of X selected.

While the probit model is more appealing than the linear probability model, it generally involves nonlinear estimation and thus added computational costs.[17] In addition, the theoretical justification for employing the probit model is often rather limited. We shall now consider a somewhat more appealing model specification—the *logit model*.

8.1.3 *Logit Model*

The *logit model* is based on the cumulative logistic probability function:[18]

$$P_i = F(Z_i) = \frac{1}{1 + e^{-Z_i}} = \frac{1}{1 + e^{-(\alpha + \beta X_i)}} \tag{8.8}$$

---

[17] Because the cumulative normal transformation is nonlinear, ordinary least squares cannot generally be applied to estimate the probit model. However, we can obtain values for α and β using maximum-likelihood estimation. The use of maximum-likelihood estimation ensures that the parameter estimates will be consistent and the appropriate statistical tests can be performed. For further details, see Domencich and McFadden, *op. cit.*

[18] e is the base of natural logarithms ($e \approx 2.718$).

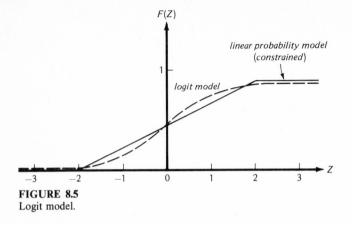

FIGURE 8.5
Logit model.

where P_i represents the probability that an individual will make a certain choice, given knowledge of X_i. In our voting example, P_i would represent the probability that an individual will vote yes, given that his/her income is equal to X_i. The cumulative logistic function is graphed in Fig. 8.5. Because it is quite similar in form to the cumulative normal function, but computationally more tractable, the logistic function is often used as a replacement for the cumulative normal function. We obtain an equation to be estimated by rewriting Eq. (8.8) as follows:

$$(1 + e^{-Z_i})P_i = 1$$

Then,
$$e^{-Z_i} = \frac{1 - P_i}{P_i}$$

and
$$e^{Z_i} = \frac{P_i}{1 - P_i}$$

and taking logarithms of both sides,

$$Z_i = \log\left(\frac{P_i}{1 - P_i}\right)$$

Thus,
$$\log\left(\frac{P_i}{1 - P_i}\right) = \alpha + \beta X_i \tag{8.9}$$

The dependent variable in this regression equation is simply the logarithm of the odds that a particular choice will be made. One important appeal of the logit model is that it transforms the problem of predicting probabilities within a $(0, 1)$ interval to the problem of predicting the odds of an event occurring within the range of the entire real line. The slope of the cumulative logistic distribution is greatest at $P = 1/2$. In terms of the regression model, this implies that changes in independent variables will have their greatest impact on the probability of choosing a given option at the midpoint of the distribution. The rather low slopes near the endpoints of the distribution imply that large changes in X are necessary to bring about a small change in probability.[19] In our voting example, the logit model presumes that an increase in income will increase the probability of a yes vote only slightly for very-low-income individuals, who are unlikely to alter their vote under any conditions, and for high-income individuals, who are very likely to have voted yes before the increase in income. Only in the middle-income ranges, where individuals are more or less indifferent to voting yes or voting no, is the change in income likely to have a substantial impact on the probability of a yes vote.

If we were to attempt to estimate Eq. (8.9) directly, a serious difficulty would arise. If P_i happens to equal either 0 or 1, then the odds, $P_i/(1 - P_i)$, will equal 0 or infinity and the logarithm of the odds will be undefined. Thus, the application of ordinary least-squares estimation to Eq. (8.9), where P_i is set equal to 1 if a given choice is made and 0 otherwise, is clearly inappropriate. The correct estimation of the logit model can best be understood by distinguishing between studies depending upon whether or not the sample includes repeated observations for each value of the explanatory variable.[20] Consider first the case in which the independent variable, e.g., income, is represented in the sample by k different values, with n_1 individuals having income X_1, n_2 individuals having income X_2, and so forth. Also, let r_1 represent the number of times the first alternative is chosen by individuals with income X_1 (voting yes), r_2 the number of times the first alternative is chosen by individuals with income X_2, etc. Then it seems reasonable to estimate the logit model by utilizing an estimate of the probability of a given choice *for each group* of identical individuals. Specifically, we approximate P_i as[21]

$$\hat{P}_i = \frac{r_i}{n_i}$$

We may then estimate the logit probability model in the following form:

$$\log\left(\frac{r_i/n_i}{1 - r_i/n_i}\right) = \log\left(\frac{r_i}{n_i - r_i}\right) = \alpha^* + \beta^* X_i \tag{8.10}$$

---

[19] The properties described hold in the probit model as well.

[20] For details see J. Berkson, "Application of the Logistic Function to Bio-Assay," *Journal of the American Statistical Association*, vol. 39, pp. 357–365, 1944; and D. R. Cox, *Analysis of Binary Data* (London: Methuen, 1970).

[21] This approximation is sensible if we take into account the fact that r_i obeys the binomial probability distribution for which the mean frequency of occurrence is r_i/n_i.

Equation (8.10) is linear in the parameters and ordinary least-squares estimation can be applied. The procedure will yield parameter estimates which are consistent only when the number of repetitions for each of the k levels of X grows arbitrarily large. The necessity for a large number of observations arises because the dependent variable is not normally distributed for small samples, but does approximate the normal distribution when the sample size is large. In addition, the efficiency of the estimation technique can be improved if modifications are made to the form of Eq. (8.10). One suggestion is to correct for heteroscedasticity resulting from the fact that $\log[r_i/(n_i - r_i)]$ is approximately normally distributed with mean 0 and variance

$$V_i = \frac{n_i}{r_i(n_i - r_i)} \tag{8.11}$$

An additional adjustment suggested by Cox and by Domencich and McFadden helps to improve the approximation involved in the specification given by Eq. (8.10).[22] They suggest that the following equation be run in its place:

$$\log\left(\frac{r_i + \frac{1}{2}}{n_i - r_i + \frac{1}{2}}\right) = \alpha + \beta X_i \tag{8.12}$$

An improved adjustment for heteroscedasticity is obtained if we use as weights the following estimates of the error variance:

$$V_i^* = \frac{(n_i + 1)(n_i + 2)}{n_i(r_i + 1)(n_i - r_i + 1)}$$

Both corrections help with the small-sample properties of the estimation process, but have no effect on the large-sample properties.

The approximation leading to the specification of Eq. (8.10) is reasonable *only when sufficient repetitions occur*. In fact, when only one choice is associated with each set of explanatory variables, the left-hand side of Eq. (8.10) is undefined, so that the approximation to Eq. (8.9) is of no use. A useful rule of thumb for the application of the least-squares approximation is that for each value of X, n_i be at least equal to 5, but a more accurate rule would account for the fact that the least-squares approximation is poorest for levels of X in which the frequency of a given choice is close to either 0 or 1. This can be seen in Eq. (8.11). When r_i/n_i approaches either 0 or 1, the expression for V_i gets arbitrarily large. (This is not true in the adjustment which yields a variance of V_i^*.) The large variance in the frequency estimates guarantees inaccurate parameter estimates,

---

[22] Cox, *op. cit.*, and Domencich and McFadden, *op. cit.*

making additional observations desirable. We should note that the approximation implicit in Eq. (8.10) is not strictly appropriate when the explanatory variable is continuous, since the continuous variable must be partitioned before the technique can be applied. Unfortunately, this partitioning process can introduce bias because of the potentially serious errors-in-variables problem.

All these qualifications are rather discouraging, since most economic data are likely to be continuous, necessitating the use of a partitioning process. In addition, economic models are likely to contain several independent variables. With limited sample sizes, it is unlikely that sufficient repetitions will be available for groups of individuals defined over all possible combinations of attribute values, even if the attributes are qualitative rather than quantitative variables. To see this, assume that income and number of children are the two attributes which are used to predict voting behavior. If there are four income categories ($0–$10,000; $10,000–$20,000; $20,000–$30,000; $30,000+) and three categories representing the number of children (0, 1–2, 3+), then there will be *twelve* groups of individuals (individuals with less than $10,000 in income and no children; $10,000–$20,000 and no children; etc.).

The existence of continuous variables in models with several attributes as explanatory variables suggests that in the context of economic and business models it may be necessary to estimate a logit model in which only *one* choice is associated with each set of independent variables. Fortunately a maximum-likelihood estimation procedure which can be applied to the model in Eq. (8.9) does exist. Because it is possible to prove that a unique maximum always exists for the logit model, maximum-likelihood estimation is particularly appealing. Almost any nonlinear estimation routine will find the estimated parameters—the only question is one of computing costs. It is possible to prove that the maximum-likelihood estimation technique yields consistent parameter estimates, and the calculation of the appropriate large-sample statistics is not difficult. Thus, the only disadvantage of nonlinear logit estimation is its cost. Small-sample studies suggest that the signs (and frequently the magnitudes) of the estimated parameters obtained from the linear probability models and the maximum-likelihood logit estimators are usually the same. This provides an additional rationalization for the use of the linear probability model.

Example 8.2   Predicting College-going Behavior

In a recent study of college choice,[23] a model was constructed to predict whether students attending college would choose to live on campus or to commute. This is a binary choice problem for which the logit probability model was utilized. The goal was to predict the "odds" of a student attending college

---

[23] M. G. Kohn, C. F. Manski, and D. S. Mundel, "An Empirical Investigation of Factors Which Influence College Going Behavior," *Rand Corporation Report, R1470–NSF*, September 1974.

on campus, conditional upon information about *individual* attributes and attributes of the particular college. The model is as follows:

$$\log\left(\frac{P_i}{1 - P_i}\right) = \beta_1 I_1 + \beta_2 I_2 + \beta_3 I_3 + \beta_4 I_4 + \beta_5 D + \beta_6 S + \beta_7 R$$

where P_i = probability that a student will choose to live on campus
Y = logarithm (base 10) of family income
X = distance from home to campus
$I_1 = (100 - X)(5 - Y)/500$
$I_2 = X(5 - Y)/500$
$I_3 = (100 - X)Y/500$
$I_4 = XY/500$
D = percentage of students at college who live on campus
S = dummy variable representing sex of student; $S = 1$ if female and 0 otherwise
R = dummy variable representing residency preference; $R = 1$ if students said they preferred to live on campus even if money were no problem and 0 otherwise

The logit model was estimated using the maximum-likelihood nonlinear estimation routine and a sample of students who actually attended college.[24] The sample was part of the 1966 SCOPE survey, and consisted of a total of 10,600 college respondents. The estimation results are as follows (with standard errors in parentheses):

$$\log\left(\frac{P_i}{1 - P_i}\right) = \underset{(1.73)}{-16.59 I_1} \ \underset{(.90)}{-8.680 I_2} \ \underset{(.40)}{-.6277 I_3} \ \underset{(.70)}{+10.81 I_4} \ \underset{(.0023)}{+.01929 D}$$

$$\underset{(.11)}{-.04789 S} \ \underset{(.16)}{+1.470 R}$$

The distance-income interaction variables are somewhat difficult to interpret on their own, but their import can be seen in the graph of Fig. 8.6. The graph shows that the probability of living on campus increases with distance from campus and is higher at all distances for the students with higher family incomes. The probability of campus residency increases with the percentage of students living on campus in the absence of monetary constraints. Finally, there is a slightly higher, but insignificant, probability of living on campus for males rather than females.

---

[24] The ordinary least-squares approximation was not used here most likely because of the difficulty of grouping or categorizing individuals according to the set of attributes given. Despite the large sample size, the seven explanatory variables would have necessitated a substantial number of groups and would have involved arbitrary partitioning of the indices I_i and the D variable.

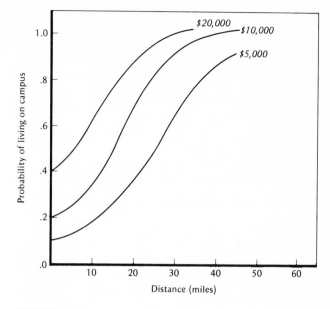

FIGURE 8.6
Probability of living on campus (for males attending a college with 50 percent dormitory capacity who prefer to live on campus).

The interpretation of the individual estimated parameters must be done with care, since the left-hand side of the equation is the logarithm of the odds of choice, not the actual probability. For example, a 1 percent increase in the percentage of students living on campus at a given college will lead to an increase of .019 in the logarithm of the odds that the individual will choose to reside on that campus. To interpret the effect of a change in D on the probability of campus residence, we need to solve for the change in probability ΔP_i as follows:

$$\Delta \log \left(\frac{P_i}{1 - P_i}\right) = .019\Delta D$$

To simplify, we utilize the fact that for any variable x, $\Delta \log x \approx \Delta x/x$, and the fact that $\log (x/y) = \log x - \log y$. Then,

$$\Delta \log \left(\frac{P_i}{1 - P_i}\right) \approx \left(\frac{1}{P_i} + \frac{1}{1 - P_i}\right)\Delta P_i = \left[\frac{1}{P_i(1 - P_i)}\right]\Delta P_i$$

Since we have chosen $\Delta D = 1$, it follows that

$$\Delta P_i \approx .019[P_i(1 - P_i)]$$

We find that the change in probability is a function of the probability itself.

If P_i were equal to .5, for example, then ΔP_i would equal .076. Perhaps the most useful single value of P_i to choose for this interpretation is the mean, but examination of the response in campus choice for numerous points of the probability distribution can be illuminating.

The campus choice model can easily be used to make predictions. Assume for example that we wish to predict the probability that a male student, whose family income is $6,000 and who has stated a preference for living on campus rather than at home, will indeed live on campus. We will assume that he attends a university located very near his home at which 50 percent of the students live on campus. To predict the odds of living on campus, we simply evaluate the right-hand side of the estimated equation:

$$I_1 = .2(5 - \log_{10} 6000) = .2444 \qquad D = 50$$

$$I_3 = .2(\log_{10} 6000) = .7556 \qquad S = 0$$

$$I_2 = I_4 = 0 \qquad R = 1$$

The calculated logarithm (base e) of the odds is -2.10. Taking antilogarithms and solving, we find that $P_i = .108$. Thus we predict that the student will live on campus with a probability of .108. We might wish to see how the probability of the student's living on campus would change as the distance between the university and home increased. Calculating P_i for different values of distance X, we would obtain the following:

Distance	Probability of living on campus
0	.108
10	.258
20	.500
30	.742
40	.892
50	.960
60	.986
70	.995

Notice that once the student's home is more than 50 miles from the campus, he will almost certainly choose to live on campus.

8.1.4 Forecasting

Forecasting with models that have a dichotomous dependent variable is somewhat more difficult than the continuous dependent variable case. As a general rule, the models developed in this chapter can be applied directly toward forecasting the probability (or the odds) that a given choice will be made. In the voting case, for example, assume that whatever the choice of specification, the predicted probability associated with one new individual observation is .8. We may interpret .8 as measuring our best forecast of the probability that an individual with a given income will vote yes in an election.[25] Of course, if we are forecasting the *explicit* behavior of a single individual, then a forecast of .8 can never be strictly correct.[26] If we wish to forecast individual choices, we are likely to predict an outcome of 1 (vote yes) if the predicted probability is greater than .5 and 0 if the predicted probability is less than .5.

This discussion suggests a problem with the use of R^2 as a measure of the goodness of fit of a linear equation. In the classical regression model R^2 can range in value between 0 and 1, with a value close to 1 indicating a good fit. We have seen, however, that the dichotomous dependent variable model is not likely to yield an R^2 close to 1. Only in the extreme case that all predicted probabilities are either 0 or 1 can such a result possibly occur. Thus, if we are to use R^2 as a measure of goodness of fit, we must realize[27] that its upper limit is likely to be substantially less than 1. If we were to assume, for example, that the true probabilities of an event occurring were uniformly distributed across a given interval,[28] then it is possible to show [29] an upper bound for R^2 of

---

[25] Assume, for example, that our objective is to forecast so as to minimize the variance of the error of forecast. As before, let P equal the probability that an event occurs ($Y = 1$); and $1 - P$ equal the probability that the event does not occur ($Y = 0$). Let $\hat{P}$ be the forecast value of the probability that a given choice will be made. (Assume, for the moment, that our model is known so that the estimated probability is the true probability of the event occurring.) Then the error of forecast will be $(1 - \hat{P})$ if the event occurs, and $(0 - \hat{P})$ otherwise. The variance of the error of forecast is as follows:

$$\sigma_\varepsilon^2 = P(1 - \hat{P})^2 + (1 - P)(-\hat{P})^2 = P(1 - \hat{P})^2 + (1 - P)\hat{P}^2$$

Minimizing σ_ε^2 with respect to $\hat{P}$ yields $\hat{P} = P$. Thus, to minimize the error of forecast, or equivalently to maximize the correlation between Y and the predicted probabilities, we choose our forecast to be the true probability of occurrence each time, rather than alternating between values of 0 and 1. The same general result would hold when we expand our derivation to include the effect of errors associated with the estimation and prediction processes.

[26] It will be accurate only in the sense that it reflects the individual's uncertainty about a choice to be made.

[27] This issue is discussed in D. G. Morrison, "Upper Bounds for Correlations between Binary Outcomes and Probabilistic Predictions," *Journal of the American Statistical Association*, vol. 67, 1972; and J. Neter and E. S. Maynes, "Correlation Coefficient with a 0, 1 Dependent Variable," *Journal of the American Statistical Association*, vol. 65, pp. 501–509, 1970.

[28] In the example given in the text the distribution of probabilities would result from an underlying distribution of the independent explanatory variable X.

[29] These results are described in D. G. Morrison, *op. cit.*

1/3. Thus, it is not surprising that one who estimates a linear probability model is likely to obtain[30] a low R^2.

8.2 MULTIPLE CHOICE MODELS

We now consider generalizing the results of the previous section to cases in which individuals make choices among three or more alternatives. (For example, an individual might choose to vote yes, vote no, or abstain.) In each case, we assume that all choices are mutually exclusive. There are several ways in which to analyze this problem, each dependent upon the statistical assumptions made, and upon whether or not a natural ranking can be associated with each of the possible choices. We focus here on the case in which alternatives are unranked.[31]

First, consider the extension of the linear probability model to the multiple choice case. If there are three choices $j = 1, 2, 3$, we would write

$$P_{1i} = \alpha_1 + \beta_1 X_i$$

$$P_{2i} = \alpha_2 + \beta_2 X_i \qquad (8.13)$$

$$P_{3i} = \alpha_3 + \beta_3 X_i$$

P_{ji} is the probability that individual i will choose the jth option, while X_i is the value of X for the ith individual. It appears reasonable to estimate each of the three equations in the model by ordinary least squares. In each case the dependent variable utilized will equal 1 if the choice is actually made and 0 otherwise. In practice it is not necessary to run all three of the linear probability regressions. Since the estimated probabilities are constrained to sum to 1, the estimated intercepts sum to 1 and the slope parameters sum to 0. To prove this, we utilize the fact that every observation is assigned to one and only one group. Then,

$$P_{1i} + P_{2i} + P_{3i} = 1 \qquad \text{for each } i$$

Averaging over all observations in the group, it follows that

$$\bar{P}_1 + \bar{P}_2 + \bar{P}_3 = 1$$

where $\bar{P}_j$ is the mean probability of choice j.

---

[30] There are, of course, alternative measures of goodness of fit for such models, but they are too involved to discuss at this point. One useful measure is the average conditional entropy as described by H. Theil in *Economics and Information Theory* (Chicago: Rand McNally, 1967, and Amsterdam: North-Holland, 1967).

[31] In the case of ranked alternatives, it is possible to estimate a scale or set of scores associated with the available choices.

First examine the sum of the least-squares slope estimates:

$$\hat{\beta}_1 + \hat{\beta}_2 + \hat{\beta}_3 = \frac{\sum (P_{1i} - \bar{P}_1)(X_i - \bar{X})}{\sum (X_i - \bar{X})^2} + \frac{\sum (P_{2i} - \bar{P}_2)(X_i - \bar{X})}{\sum (X_i - \bar{X})^2}$$

$$+ \frac{\sum (P_{3i} - \bar{P}_3)(X_i - \bar{X})}{\sum (X_i - \bar{X})^2}$$

$$= \frac{\sum (P_{1i} + P_{2i} + P_{3i})(X_i - \bar{X}) - (\bar{P}_1 + \bar{P}_2 + \bar{P}_3) \sum (X_i - \bar{X})}{\sum (X_i - \bar{X})^2}$$

$$= \frac{\sum (X_i - \bar{X}) - \sum (X_i - \bar{X})}{\sum (X_i - \bar{X})^2} = 0$$

On the other hand, the intercepts sum to 1, since

$$\hat{\alpha}_1 + \hat{\alpha}_2 + \hat{\alpha}_3 = (\bar{P}_1 - \hat{\beta}_1 \bar{X}) + (\bar{P}_2 - \hat{\beta}_2 \bar{X}) + (\bar{P}_3 - \hat{\beta}_3 \bar{X})$$

$$= (\bar{P}_1 + \bar{P}_2 + \bar{P}_3) - \bar{X}(\hat{\beta}_1 + \hat{\beta}_2 + \hat{\beta}_3)$$

$$= 1$$

Therefore,

$$\hat{P}_{1i} + \hat{P}_{2i} + \hat{P}_{3i} = (\hat{\alpha}_1 + \hat{\beta}_1 X_i) + (\hat{\alpha}_2 + \hat{\beta}_2 X_i) + (\hat{\alpha}_3 + \hat{\beta}_3 X_i)$$

$$= (\hat{\alpha}_1 + \hat{\alpha}_2 + \hat{\alpha}_3) + (\hat{\beta}_1 + \hat{\beta}_2 + \hat{\beta}_3) X_i$$

$$= 1$$

Thus, we need to run only two of the three least-squares regressions. A solution for the parameters of the third equation follows immediately.

If the X variables in each equation are not identical, then the analysis becomes more difficult. The estimation process will not guarantee that the probabilities sum to 1, and ordinary least squares is no longer the most appropriate technique. A useful approach to this problem is provided by Zellner and Lee, who propose that a generalized least-squares estimation procedure be used to account for the correlation among the error terms associated with each equation in the multiple choice model.[32]

---

[32] See A. Zellner and T. H. Lee, "Joint Estimation of Relationships Involving Discrete Random Variables," *Econometrica*, vol. 33, Apr. 1965.

The extension of the logit model in a manner analogous to that of the linear probability model is quite promising.[33] To extend the binary choice logit model to the three-choice case, for example, we write the following equations:

$$\log\left(\frac{P_2}{P_1}\right) = \alpha_{21} + \beta_{21}X$$

$$\log\left(\frac{P_3}{P_1}\right) = \alpha_{31} + \beta_{31}X \tag{8.14}$$

$$\log\left(\frac{P_3}{P_2}\right) = \alpha_{32} + \beta_{32}X$$

The subscript i, designating individual observations, has been dropped for notational simplicity. In this case, $P_j, j = 1, 2, 3$, indicates the probability that the jth choice will be made. Each equation presumes that the logarithm of the odds of one choice relative to a second choice is a linear function of the attribute X. These odds are dependent on the odds associated with the remaining two equations only in the sense that the system must be constrained so that the sum of the individual probabilities equals 1. As in the case of the linear probability model, it is unnecessary to estimate each of the three equations separately. We may simplify matters by accounting for the fact that the choice of logit form forces constraints on the model which reduces the number of parameters to be estimated from six to four. To see why this is true, notice that

$$\log\left(\frac{P_3}{P_2}\right) = \log\left(\frac{P_3}{P_1}\right) + \log\left(\frac{P_1}{P_2}\right) = \log\left(\frac{P_3}{P_1}\right) - \log\left(\frac{P_2}{P_1}\right)$$

$$= (\alpha_{31} + \beta_{31}X) - (\alpha_{21} + \beta_{21}X)$$

$$= (\alpha_{31} - \alpha_{21}) + (\beta_{31} - \beta_{21})X$$

This creates two additional parameter constraints:

$$\alpha_{32} = \alpha_{31} - \alpha_{21} \qquad \beta_{32} = \beta_{31} - \beta_{21}$$

[33] See D. McFadden, *op. cit.*; H. Theil, "A Multinomial Extension of the Linear Logit Model," *International Economic Review*, vol. 10, pp. 251–259, 1969; H. Theil, "On the Estimation of Relationships Involving Qualitative Variables," *American Journal of Sociology*, vol. 76, pp. 103–154, 1970; and M. Nerlove and S. J. Press, *op. cit.* The probit extension is also possible. See, for example, J. Aitchison and S. Silvey, "The Generalization of Probit Analysis to the Case of Multiple Responses," *Biometrika*, pp. 131–140, 1957.

It is somewhat easier to view the logit model's form if we redefine all the unknown parameters as follows:

$$\alpha_{21} = \alpha_2 - \alpha_1 \qquad \beta_{21} = \beta_2 - \beta_1$$

$$\alpha_{31} = \alpha_3 - \alpha_1 \qquad \beta_{31} = \beta_3 - \beta_1 \qquad (8.15)$$

$$\alpha_{32} = \alpha_3 - \alpha_2 \qquad \beta_{32} = \beta_3 - \beta_2$$

Then the model system of Eq. (8.14) can be rewritten

$$\log\left(\frac{P_2}{P_1}\right) = (\alpha_2 - \alpha_1) + (\beta_2 - \beta_1)X$$

$$\log\left(\frac{P_3}{P_1}\right) = (\alpha_3 - \alpha_1) + (\beta_3 - \beta_1)X \qquad (8.16)$$

$$\log\left(\frac{P_3}{P_2}\right) = (\alpha_3 - \alpha_2) + (\beta_3 - \beta_2)X$$

Since the parameters of the third equation can be calculated once we know the parameters of the first two equations, the third equation need not be estimated. Assume first that sufficient repetitions are available so that we may use the ordinary least-squares approximation to the correct estimation procedure. Then we proceed by using ordinary least squares to estimate the following two equations (i refers to each one of the k levels of X for which repetitions are available, not to the individual observations):

$$\log\left(\frac{r_{2i}/n_i}{r_{1i}/n_i}\right) = \log\left(\frac{r_{2i}}{r_{1i}}\right) = (\alpha_2 - \alpha_1) + (\beta_2 - \beta_1)X_i$$

$$(8.17)$$

$$\log\left(\frac{r_{3i}/n_i}{r_{1i}/n_i}\right) = \log\left(\frac{r_{3i}}{r_{1i}}\right) = (\alpha_3 - \alpha_1) + (\beta_3 - \beta_1)X_i$$

The estimated parameters will determine the effect of changes in X on the logarithm of the ratios of the probabilities, which is sufficient for some uses of the model. If actual magnitudes are needed, one must take into account the constraint that the estimated probabilities must sum to 1. This can be done by renormalizing the estimated parameter values after the initial least-squares regression has been run. There are two difficulties associated with such a procedure.

First, the errors are likely to be heteroscedastic, just as in the binary choice model. A correction analogous to the one described previously can be applied to deal with this problem. Second, the cross-equation error correlation ought to be accounted for directly in the estimation process. As described before, this can be accomplished by the application of a form of generalized least-squares regression. [34]

If sufficient repetitions are not available, then a generalized version of the nonlinear maximum-likelihood procedure must be used. Once again the derivation of the estimator is not difficult, nor is the process of finding the maximum, but there is a large computing cost associated with the procedure. If computational costs are not a problem, the maximum-likelihood procedure should be considered desirable because it guarantees consistent parameter estimates and correct large-sample statistics.

Example 8.3 Occupational Attainment

In a recent study a multiple logit model was constructed to analyze occupational attainment of individuals.[35] The object was to predict the relative probability that an individual is in each of five occupational categories—"professional," "white collar," "craft," "blue collar," or "menial"—on the basis of individual's race, sex, education, and labor-market experience. One thousand observations were used from years 1960 and 1970, each pertaining to a full-time working member of the labor force. The following model was estimated:

$$\log_e \left(\frac{P_2}{P_1}\right) = \alpha_{21} + \beta_{21}E_i + \gamma_{21}X_i + \delta_{21}R_i + \theta_{21}S_i$$

$$\log_e \left(\frac{P_3}{P_1}\right) = \alpha_{31} + \beta_{31}E_i + \gamma_{31}X_i + \delta_{31}R_i + \theta_{31}S_i$$

$$\log_e \left(\frac{P_4}{P_1}\right) = \alpha_{41} + \beta_{41}E_i + \gamma_{41}X_i + \delta_{41}R_i + \theta_{41}S_i$$

$$\log_e \left(\frac{P_5}{P_1}\right) = \alpha_{51} + \beta_{51}E_i + \gamma_{51}X_i + \delta_{51}R_i + \theta_{51}S_i$$

where subscript 1 = "menial" occupation
subscript 2 = "blue-collar" occupation
subscript 3 = "craft" occupation
subscript 4 = "white-collar" occupation

---

[34] See Zellner and Lee, *op. cit.*, and H. Theil, *op. cit.*

[35] P. Schmidt and R. P. Strauss, "The Prediction of Occupation Using Multiple Logit Models," *International Economic Review* (forthcoming, 1975).

subscript 5 = "professional" occupation

E_i = years of schooling of individual i

X_i = years of work experience of individual i (age minus E minus five)

R_i = race of individual i (1 if white, 0 if black)

S_i = sex of individual i (1 if male, 0 if female)

Statements for $\log_e P_3/P_2$, etc., may be derived from the above equations; for example,

$$\alpha_{32} = \alpha_{31} - \alpha_{21} \qquad \beta_{32} = \beta_{31} - \beta_{21}$$

The estimated coefficients are as follows (with the ratios of the coefficient to the asymptotic error, i.e., "t ratio," given in parentheses):

Coefficients and "t ratios," 1960†

Dependent variable	Constant	Education	Experience	Race	Sex
$\log_e (P_2/P_1)$	1.293	−.1238	−.02432	1.244	.7988
	(2.18)	(−2.71)	(−2.74)	(4.46)	(3.23)
$\log_e (P_3/P_1)$	−4.086	.0490	−.00957	2.747	2.138
	(−4.56)	(.92)	(−.94)	(5.02)	(5.34)
$\log_e (P_4/P_1)$	−3.358	.2163	−.01682	2.8517	−.8087
	(−4.05)	(4.17)	(−1.70)	(5.11)	(−3.14)
$\log_e (P_5/P_1)$	−6.025	.4128	−.00126	1.879	.2263
	(−7.11)	(7.59)	(−.12)	(3.83)	(.80)
$\log_e (P_3/P_2)$	−5.379	.1728	.01475	1.5030	1.3395
	(−6.78)	(4.11)	(1.85)	(2.85)	(3.61)
$\log_e (P_4/P_2)$	−4.651	.3401	.00750	1.6074	−1.6075
	(−6.26)	(7.94)	(.95)	(2.93)	(−7.62)
$\log_e (P_5/P_2)$	−7.318	.5366	.02306	.6347	−.5725
	(−9.09)	(11.66)	(2.72)	(1.32)	(−2.33)
$\log_e (P_4/P_3)$	.7280	.1673	−.00725	.1044	−2.947
	(.76)	(3.58)	(−.80)	(.14)	(−8.00)
$\log_e (P_5/P_3)$	−1.939	.3638	.00831	−.8683	−1.912
	(−2.05)	(7.58)	(.89)	(−1.31)	(−4.93)
$\log_e (P_5/P_4)$	−2.667	.1965	.01556	−.9727	1.035
	(−3.11)	(4.69)	(1.86)	(−1.45)	(4.66)

Coefficients and "t ratios," 1970†

Dependent variable	Constant	Education	Experience	Race	Sex
$\log_e (P_2/P_1)$	1.056	−.1239	−.01491	.7000	1.2519
	(1.56)	(−2.53)	(−1.75)	(2.32)	(5.15)
$\log_e (P_3/P_1)$	−3.769	−.0014	.00776	1.4575	3.1117
	(−4.18)	(−.03)	(.80)	(3.35)	(6.56)

(continued)

Coefficients and "t ratios," 1970† *(continued)*

Dependent variable	Constant	Education	Experience	Race	Sex
$\log_e (P_4/P_1)$	−3.305	.2254	.00300	1.7624	−.5233
	(−4.22)	(4.27)	(.35)	(4.27)	(−2.22)
$\log_e (P_5/P_1)$	−5.959	.4292	.00779	.9758	.6557
	(−7.51)	(7.96)	(.88)	(2.62)	(2.65)
$\log_e (P_3/P_2)$	−4.825	.1225	.02268	.7575	1.8598
	(−6.14)	(2.86)	(2.85)	(1.90)	(4.02)
$\log_e (P_4/P_2)$	−4.361	.3493	.01792	1.0624	−1.775
	(−6.25)	(7.69)	(2.43)	(2.60)	(−8.35)
$\log_e (P_5/P_2)$	−7.015	.5531	.02270	.2758	−.5962
	(−10.03)	(11.89)	(3.02)	(.77)	(−2.62)
$\log_e (P_4/P_3)$	.4640	.2268	−.00476	.3049	−3.635
	(.52)	(4.57)	(−.56)	(.59)	(−7.97)
$\log_e (P_5/P_3)$	−2.190	.4306	.00002	−.4817	−2.456
	(−2.49)	(8.71)	(.00)	(−1.03)	(−5.30)
$\log_e (P_5/P_4)$	−2.654	.2038	.00478	−.7866	1.179
	(−3.77)	(4.95)	(.67)	(−1.77)	(5.96)

† Group 5 = professional, 4 = white collar, 3 = craft, 2 = blue collar, 1 = menial.

The estimation results demonstrate that more education makes it more likely for one to be in a higher-numbered occupation. Presumably, this is what one expects—education enables one to move "up" the job scale. The only exception is that more education makes it less likely to be in a blue-collar position than a menial position. The effects of labor-market experience are much less strong across occupations and indicate that blue-collar workers tend to have little experience while professionals tend to have much more experience.

The results for sex are fairly apparent. If we order the occupations as follows:

white collar
menial
professional
blue collar
craft

then, other things held constant, being female (male) makes one more likely to be in any occupational group relative to any other occupational group *lower* (higher) on the list.

Finally, if we order the occupations as follows:

menial
blue collar
craft, professional
white collar

then being *black* (white) makes it more likely to be in any group relative to any other group *lower* (higher) on the list. Essentially what these results show is that being black makes it more likely to be in one of the less desirable groups—menial and blue collar. Furthermore, the worst discrimination is encountered in white-collar positions, not, as some might have expected, in the craft positions.

A final point worth noting is the intertemporal change of the race and sex variables. Movements toward zero represent decreases in discrimination. With this in mind, it is interesting to note that the race coefficient decreased in 9 out of 10 equations, while the sex coefficient increased in 9 out of 10 equations. While this suggests a decrease in occupational differences due to race and an increase in occupational differences due to sex, the reader is warned that none of the changes is significant at the 5 percent level.

Exercises

8.1 In correcting the linear probability model for heteroscedasticity, why can't the least-squares residuals be used directly to calculate an estimate of the error variance σ_i^2 rather than using the formula in Eq. (8.3)?

8.2 What would happen to the coefficients of the linear probability model if the binary dependent variable were represented by a (0, 2) variable rather than by a (0, 1) variable? What does this suggest to you about the interpretation of the estimated least-squares parameters?

8.3 Assume that the true binary choice model is represented by the logit model, but a linear probability model is estimated. What can you conclude about the likely effects of this specification error?

8.4 Prove that the transformation of the probability model described in Eq. (8.4) using a cumulative uniform probability function yields the constrained version of the linear probability model.

8.5 Consider the municipal bond default example (Example 8.1). Explain how you might reinterpret the bond default issue in terms of the probit model. What are some of the advantages and disadvantages of using the probit specification rather than the linear probability specification?

8.6 The logit model of Eq. (8.9) is linear in the parameters and yet must (usually) be estimated using a nonlinear estimation package. Explain this seeming inconsistency.

8.7 Using the following six data points, estimate a linear probability model using ordinary least squares:

X	-1	-2	0	1	1	1
Y	0	0	0	1	1	1

Calculate R^2 for the model. Then utilize the estimated model to classify individuals into the two categories. Calculate the number of correct classifications using the following classification rule:

$$\text{Classify in first group } (Y = 1) \text{ if } \hat{Y} > \tfrac{1}{2}$$

$$\text{Classify in second group } (Y = 0) \text{ if } \hat{Y} \leq \tfrac{1}{2}$$

Discuss the advantages and disadvantages of using R^2 and the percentage of correct classifications as measures of goodness of fit in the linear probability model.

TWO

MULTI-EQUATION SIMULATION MODELS

In the next four chapters we concern ourselves with models that consist of more than one equation. In a single-equation regression model a dependent variable is related to a set of explanatory variables; for example, an interest rate might be related to GNP, the rate of inflation, and the money supply. However, the single-equation model does not explain the interdependencies that may exist among the explanatory variables themselves, or how these explanatory variables are related to other variables. In addition, the single-equation model explains causality in one direction; i.e., explanatory variables determine a dependent variable, but there is no "feedback" relationship between the dependent variable and the explanatory variables.

Multi-equation simulation models allow us to account simultaneously for all the interrelationships between a set of variables. Often these models consist of a set of regression equations which, after having been estimated, are solved simultaneously on a computer. However, simulation models can also consist of equations which are not estimated, such as accounting identities, or behavioral "rules of thumb."

In Chapter 9 we describe some of the estimation problems involved in multi-equation models as well as the problem of model identification that was introduced in Chapter 5. We also examine some estimation techniques developed especially for multi-equation models, including two-stage and three-stage least squares.

In Chapters 10 and 11 we discuss some general issues involved in the construction, evaluation, and use of simulation models. In Chapter 10 we describe how the simulation of a model is actually carried out, how a simulation model can be evaluated, and how the particular estimation method used for the model affects its simulation performance. In Chapter 11 we examine the dynamic behavior of simulation models, methods of adjusting simulation models, and the use of stochastic simulation to determine confidence intervals for model forecasts.

Finally, in Chapter 12 we present three examples of simulation models. These include a model of the United States macroeconomy, a model of a particular industry, and a financial planning model for a corporation.

9

SIMULTANEOUS EQUATION ESTIMATION

In the first part of this book we concerned ourselves primarily with single-equation models. We found that in many cases, ordinary least-squares estimation was the most appropriate estimation procedure. We showed in Chapter 5, however, that the presence of simultaneity in a two-equation model causes ordinary least-squares parameter estimates to be inconsistent, so that an alternative method must be used to estimate each equation. In this chapter we change our emphasis by dealing explicitly with models consisting of several equations, in which the behavior of the variables is jointly determined.

Perhaps the simplest example of a simultaneous equation model is a two-equation model of market demand and supply, where price and quantity are both endogenous variables. More complex examples include industry, regional, and national economic models. All these examples are similar in that each model includes several endogenous variables which are simultaneously determined by an interrelated series of equations. The presence of two or more endogenous variables necessitates some additional model-building and estimation tools. We shall develop these tools by working with examples of two- or three-equation models. Our objective is to develop the important modeling and estimation techniques in as comprehensible a fashion as possible. The examples and derivations in the text have been chosen with an eye toward clarity and intuition, at the risk of loss of generality. However, Appendixes 9.1 to 9.4 do contain a more complete mathematical development of many of the techniques described in the text.

This chapter begins with a description of several types of *equation systems*. The discussion focuses on the distinction between alternative model systems, with emphasis given to the question of whether or not ordinary least squares is an appropriate estimation method. In the second section we return to the *identification problem* first discussed in Chapter 5. Model identification is analyzed in detail, with emphasis placed on rules of thumb which might be of use in the model-building process. The remaining sections of the chapter deal briefly with some of the estimation techniques available for multi-equation models. Section 9.3 completes the discussion of single-equation estimation techniques which can be applied to multi-equation models. In section 9.4 we first introduce estimation techniques in which all the equations in the model are estimated simultaneously, thus providing greater estimation efficiency. These techniques include three-stage least squares, Zellner and full-information maximum likelihood estimation.

9.1 TYPES OF EQUATION SYSTEMS

We assume that in our econometric model there are as many equations as there are endogenous variables. If this were not the case, it would be impossible to solve the model to determine values for these endogenous variables (associated with values for the predetermined variables). A model with more equations than endogenous variables could have an infinite number of solutions, while one with fewer equations than endogenous variables would have no solution.

For purposes of model estimation it is important to distinguish between models which are truly simultaneous in nature and models which are not. We are referring, of course, to the structural form of the model which must be specified on the basis of known information. We shall proceed by describing several types of model systems, limiting ourselves on behalf of clarity to a three-equation system with two predetermined (exogenous and lagged endogenous) variables. We shall not concern ourselves with the identification of the structural parameters in the model until the following section.

9.1.1 *Simultaneous Equation Systems*

The most general form of a three-equation simultaneous system is as follows:

$$Y_1 = \alpha_0 \qquad\qquad + \alpha_2 Y_2 + \alpha_3 Y_3 + \alpha_4 Z_1 + \alpha_5 Z_2 + u_1 \qquad (9.1)$$

$$Y_2 = \beta_0 + \beta_1 Y_1 \qquad\quad + \beta_3 Y_3 + \beta_4 Z_1 + \beta_5 Z_2 + u_2 \qquad (9.2)$$

$$Y_3 = \gamma_0 + \gamma_1 Y_1 + \gamma_2 Y_2 \qquad\quad + \gamma_4 Z_1 + \gamma_5 Z_2 + u_3 \qquad (9.3)$$

Here each of the three endogenous variables, Y_1, Y_2, and Y_3, appears on the left-hand side of one and only one equation. The two predetermined variables,

Z_1 and Z_2, appear on the right-hand side of the equations, along with the error terms, u_1, u_2, and u_3. We assume for now that the error term in each equation obeys the classical assumptions of least squares, that is, $u_i \sim N(0, \sigma_{u_i}^2)$ for $i = 1, 2, 3$. We also assume that there is no direct relationship between the three error processes, i.e., that $E(u_{it} u_{jt}) = 0$ for all t and for all $i \neq j$. (We shall drop this assumption in section 9.4.)

If none of the coefficients in Eqs. (9.1), (9.2), and (9.3) are 0, the model is a completely interdependent system, since it is impossible to solve for any single endogenous variable, say Y_1, without simultaneously solving all three equations. As a rule, ordinary least-squares estimation of this model will yield biased and inconsistent parameter estimates; we have seen why this is true in the two-equation model described in Chapter 5, and the logic extends to a model of three (or more) equations. Assume, for example, that we are trying to estimate Eq. (9.1). Ordinary least-squares estimates will be consistent only if both Y_2 and Y_3 are uncorrelated with the disturbance term u_1. Notice, however, what happens if there is a small movement in u_1. The movement in u_1 will cause an equivalent movement in Y_1 as depicted in Eq. (9.1). But Y_2 [in Eq. (9.2)] and Y_3 [in Eq. (9.3)] are both determined in part by Y_1, so that the movement in Y_1 will lead to a movement in Y_2 and Y_3. The result is that both Y_2 and Y_3 will be correlated with u_1, making ordinary least squares an inappropriate method of estimating Eq. (9.1).

Example 9.1

Consider the following three-equation macroeconomic model:

$$C_t = \alpha_0 + \alpha_2 I_t + \alpha_3 Y_t + \alpha_4 C_{t-1} + \alpha_5 R_t + u_{1t}$$

$$I_t = \beta_0 \qquad\quad + \beta_3 Y_t \qquad\qquad + \beta_5 R_t + u_{2t}$$

$$Y_t = C_t + I_t + G_t$$

where C = aggregate consumption
I = gross investment
Y = gross national product
G = government spending
M = money supply
R = short-term interest rate

The three endogenous variables are C, I, and Y, while the predetermined variables are C_{t-1}, G_t, and R_t. The model is simultaneous, despite the fact that aggregate consumption is not a direct determinant of gross investment. Simultaneity occurs because the estimation of C and I in the first two equations cannot be accomplished unless values for Y are available, but Y is a function of C and I (as well as of G) in the third equation. Only when all three equations are solved simultaneously can a solution be found. (The fact that the third equation is an identity should not be a cause for concern. The identity differs from the previous behavioral equations only in that all its coefficients are known to be equal to 1.)

9.1.2 Recursive Equation Systems

A system of equations is *recursive* (rather than simultaneous) if each of the endogenous variables can be determined sequentially. Consider the following model:

$$Y_1 = \alpha_0 \qquad\qquad\qquad + \alpha_4 Z_1 + \alpha_5 Z_2 + u_1 \qquad\qquad (9.4)$$

$$Y_2 = \beta_0 + \beta_1 Y_1 \qquad\qquad + \beta_4 Z_1 + \beta_5 Z_2 + u_2 \qquad\qquad (9.5)$$

$$Y_3 = \gamma_0 + \gamma_1 Y_1 + \gamma_2 Y_2 + \gamma_4 Z_1 + \gamma_5 Z_2 + u_3 \qquad\qquad (9.6)$$

$$\text{Cov}\,(u_1, u_2) = \text{Cov}\,(u_1, u_3) = \text{Cov}\,(u_2, u_3) = 0$$

Although this system of equations seems simultaneous, it is actually recursive. To see this, assume that the true structural parameters are known. Given values for Z_1 and Z_2, we can solve directly for Y_1 in Eq. (9.4). Then, knowing Y_1 allows us to solve for Y_2 in Eq. (9.5). Finally, values for Y_1, Y_2, Z_1, and Z_2 allow us to solve for Y_3 in Eq. (9.6).

In a more general recursive model we see that (if the model is written appropriately) the solution for the nth endogenous variable involves only the first n equations of the model; thus the right-hand endogenous variables need not be correlated with the error terms. This property of recursive models makes ordinary least squares (OLS) an appropriate estimation procedure. OLS is obviously appropriate for the first equation, since Z_1 and Z_2 are predetermined and therefore uncorrelated with u_1. OLS is also appropriate for the second equation because the endogenous variable Y_1 is uncorrelated with u_2 (since the only error term affecting Y_1 is u_1 in the first equation). Finally, OLS can be applied to the third equation because (by similar reasoning) Y_1 and Y_2 are uncorrelated with u_3.

Remember that we have assumed that the errors across equations are themselves not correlated. We should note that the application of ordinary least squares would be inappropriate if this were not the case. We shall return to this problem in section 9.4.

Example 9.2

Consider the following three-equation model:

$$P = \alpha_0 \qquad\qquad\qquad + \alpha_3 W \qquad\qquad + u_1$$

$$P' = \beta_0 + \beta_1 P \qquad\qquad\qquad + \beta_4 T + u_2$$

$$Q = \gamma_0 + \gamma_1 P + \gamma_2 P' + \gamma_3 W \qquad\qquad + u_3$$

where P = price of cotton
  P' = price of cotton goods
  Q = quantity of cotton goods sold
  W = index of weather conditions
  T = effective tax rate on cotton goods

The model specification is based on the presumption that the price of cotton is determined solely by weather conditions (there is no simultaneous interaction of demand and supply). The price of cotton goods is determined by the price of cotton and by the tax rate on cotton goods. Finally, the quantity of cotton goods sold is determined by the two previously determined prices and by weather conditions. The model is clearly a recursive model and can be estimated using ordinary least squares.

9.1.3 Block-Recursive Equation Systems

A block-recursive equation system is a group of equations which can be broken up into groups or blocks of equations in such a way that equations *within* each block are simultaneous, but groups of equations *across* blocks are recursive; i.e., knowledge of the endogenous variables in the first block permits the determination of the endogenous variables in the second block, etc. Consider the following model:

$$Y_1 = \alpha_0 \qquad + \alpha_2 Y_2 + \alpha_4 Z_1 + \alpha_5 Z_2 + u_1 \qquad (9.7)$$

$$Y_2 = \beta_0 + \beta_1 Y_1 + \qquad + \beta_4 Z_1 + \beta_5 Z_2 + u_2 \qquad (9.8)$$

$$Y_3 = \gamma_0 + \gamma_1 Y_1 + \gamma_2 Y_2 + \gamma_4 Z_1 + \gamma_5 Z_2 + u_3 \qquad (9.9)$$

Equations (9.7) and (9.8) make up a block, i.e., a system of two equations which must be solved simultaneously to obtain values for Y_1 and Y_2. Once solutions are obtained, values for Y_1 and Y_2 may be substituted into Eq. (9.9) to obtain a value for Y_3. This particular model consists of two blocks, the first containing two equations and the second containing only one. To estimate this block-recursive system, we proceed by estimating the block of equations in which Y_1 and Y_2 are simultaneously determined. If identified, these equations can be estimated using either the instrumental variables or the two-stage least-squares technique. The third equation, however, can be estimated using ordinary least squares, since the recursive nature of the model guarantees that Y_1 and Y_2 will both be uncorrelated with u_3.

9.1.4 Systems of Seemingly Unrelated Equations

The seemingly unrelated model is a specific type of recursive model which occurs occasionally in business and economic modeling. It consists of a series of endogenous variables which are considered as a group because they bear a close conceptual relationship to each other. An example of such a model is as follows:

$$Y_1 = \alpha_0 + \alpha_4 Z_1 + \alpha_5 Z_2 + u_1 \tag{9.10}$$

$$Y_2 = \beta_0 + \beta_4 Z_3 + \beta_5 Z_4 + u_2 \tag{9.11}$$

$$Y_3 = \gamma_0 + \gamma_4 Z_5 + \gamma_5 Z_6 + u_3 \tag{9.12}$$

A set of demand equations for related products might be specified in this form. If, in fact, the *disturbances* of each equation are unrelated (uncorrelated), then there is indeed no relationship between the equations. (Notice that no pre-determined variable appears in more than one equation.) In such a case, ordinary least-squares estimation is quite proper. If the error terms are correlated between equations, efficient estimates can be obtained using a more sophisticated estimation technique.[1] Further details and examples appear in section 9.4.

9.1.5 Modeling of Equation Systems

After having categorized equation systems, we might ask whether it is preferable to build models of one category (e.g., recursive) or another (e.g., simultaneous). The answer depends upon how one views the economic (and related) processes in the real world. One might argue that the world is best represented by a recursive model because very few markets are actually perfectly competitive; usually either price or quantity (or both) is influenced by a firm or firms with market power. Under monopoly, for example, one firm is a price setter, so that the notion of the simultaneous determination of price and quantity is irrelevant. In addition, the existence of lags in the reactions of buyers and sellers leads one to believe that with a proper time frame all variables to be explained could be seen as a function of predetermined variables (consisting of many lagged endogenous variables, of course). On the other hand, the nature of the data available for econometric analysis makes analysis of reaction time very difficult, if not impossible, in most cases. The fact that quarterly macroeconomic data are available but weekly and daily are often not means that we may not be able to model weekly and daily lag adjustments. As a result, the majority of econometric models are appropriately simultaneous equation models. However, the choice of the type of equation system to be used depends in the end upon the judgment of the model builder.

9.2 THE IDENTIFICATION PROBLEM

We have seen in Chapter 5 that the study of a model's structure for purposes of identification is a prior step to model estimation. Within the context of a two-equation model, we discussed the relationship among structural forms,

---

[1] Ordinary least-squares estimation will remain consistent and may be appropriate when the added computational costs are weighed against the gain in efficiency.

reduced forms, and the problem of identification. We found in certain cases that, given the reduced-form representation of the model, it was impossible to find the values of the parameters of the structural model. This corresponds, of course, to the case in which an equation is *unidentified* (or *underidentified*). When structural equation parameters can be uniquely determined, the equation in question is said to be *exactly identified*, and when more than one set of parameter estimates is available for one or more parameters, the equation is *overidentified*. Over-identification and underidentification are not symmetric concepts. Under-identification implies that structural model estimation is impossible. Over-identification implies only that a surfeit of information is available, forcing us to choose carefully among a set of possible estimation processes. Unless we specify otherwise, we shall apply the concept of identification to individual equations in a model system. It is quite possible, of course, for one equation to be identified while another is unidentified.

In order to delve further into the nature of the identification problem, we consider a rather simple three-equation model:

$$y_1 = \qquad \alpha_3 y_3 + \alpha_4 z_1 + \alpha_5 z_2 + u_1 \qquad (9.13)$$

$$y_2 = \beta_1 y_1 \qquad\qquad\qquad + u_2 \qquad (9.14)$$

$$y_3 = \qquad \gamma_2 y_2 \qquad\qquad\quad + u_3 \qquad (9.15)$$

We have written the model using data in deviations form to eliminate unnecessary use of algebra. No loss of generality is involved in this simplification. If we were to solve the structural model for its reduced form, we would obtain the following:

$$y_1 = \pi_{11} z_1 + \pi_{12} z_2 + v_1 \qquad (9.16)$$

$$y_2 = \pi_{21} z_1 + \pi_{22} z_2 + v_2 \qquad (9.17)$$

$$y_3 = \pi_{31} z_1 + \pi_{32} z_2 + v_3 \qquad (9.18)$$

where $\pi_{11} = \alpha_4/\delta \qquad \pi_{12} = \alpha_5/\delta \qquad\qquad (9.19)$
$\qquad \pi_{21} = \beta_1 \alpha_4/\delta \qquad \pi_{22} = \alpha_5 \beta_1/\delta \qquad (9.20)$
$\qquad \pi_{31} = \beta_1 \gamma_2 \alpha_4/\delta \qquad \pi_{32} = \beta_1 \gamma_2 \alpha_5/\delta \qquad (9.21)$
$\qquad \delta = 1 - \alpha_3 \beta_1 \gamma_2$
$\qquad v_1 = u_1 + \alpha_3 \gamma_2 u_2 + \alpha_3 u_3$
$\qquad v_2 = \beta_1 u_1 + (1 + \beta_1 \alpha_3 \gamma_2) u_2 + \beta_1 \alpha_3 u_3$
$\qquad v_3 = \beta_1 \gamma_2 u_1 + (1 + \beta_1 \alpha_3 \gamma_2) \gamma_2 u_2 + (1 + \beta_1 \alpha_3 \gamma_2) u_3$

Since the right-hand variables are all predetermined, it is quite simple to estimate the reduced-form parameters using ordinary least squares. The identification problem poses the issue of whether structural-form parameter estimates can be deduced from the reduced-form estimates. From the reduced-form system we can see that the parameters β_1 and γ_2 can be obtained in two ways:

$$\hat{\beta}_1 = \frac{\hat{\pi}_{21}}{\hat{\pi}_{11}} \quad \text{or} \quad \hat{\beta}_1' = \frac{\hat{\pi}_{22}}{\hat{\pi}_{12}}$$

and

$$\hat{\gamma}_2 = \frac{\hat{\pi}_{31}}{\hat{\pi}_{11}} \quad \text{or} \quad \hat{\gamma}_2' = \frac{\hat{\pi}_{32}}{\hat{\pi}_{11}}$$

We conclude that Eqs. (9.14) and (9.15) are both identified (in fact, overidentified), since each of the parameters in the equation can be determined directly from the reduced-form parameter estimates in two different ways. A more careful examination of the reduced form should convince the reader that the first equation, (9.13), is unidentified, since there is no way to obtain estimates of the structural parameters α_3, α_4, and α_5.

As long as our concern lies solely with Eqs. (9.14) and (9.15), we may proceed with model estimation and use the resulting parameter estimates for prediction or other purposes. However, our analysis tells us that estimation of the first structural equation is not viable. While we could make calculated guesses as to the parameter estimates, we would not be able to place much reliance, if any, on those guesses, since correct statistical estimation procedures are not applicable.

Although we will always check for identification before estimating a model, there may be cases in which prediction is our primary objective. In such cases models with unidentified equations may be valuable. If parameter estimates can be made for the unidentified equation, satisfactory predictions can be obtained. The gain in knowledge about the interaction of variables in the model may outweigh the costs associated with the potential unreliability of parameter estimates in unidentified equations. In fact, prediction can be accomplished directly with the use of the reduced-form parameters, so that knowledge of the structural form parameters is not necessary for forecasting.

We have seen in Chapter 5 that identification necessitates *prior* information which allows us to distinguish the parameters of each equation from those of any other equation of the same form. While many kinds of prior information can help to resolve the identification problem, we limit ourselves to dealing with restrictions in the form of 0 coefficients on the endogenous and predetermined variables in the model.[2] Such a 0 coefficient occurs every time a variable which is present in at least one equation in the model is excluded from another equation. In our cotton example (Example 9.2), the first equation contains three zero restrictions, since only weather is expected to have a direct effect on the

---

[2] Much of what we say about zero restrictions can be extended to all linear restrictions on the parameters. For details of this and related matters, see F. M. Fisher, *The Identification Problem in Econometrics* (New York: McGraw-Hill, 1966).

price of cotton. The second equation has two zero restrictions, given that neither weather nor the quantity of cotton goods affects the price of cotton goods directly. Finally, the third equation contains the single zero restriction that the tax rate will not directly affect the quantity of cotton goods sold.

Given that the test of whether an equation is identified involves a test of whether one can solve for the structural form from the reduced form, the most general conditions for identification in the case of zero restrictions involve some matrix-related conditions associated with the solution of a system of equations. These general conditions are described in Appendix 9.1. For our purposes it is useful only to describe in somewhat greater detail than in Chapter 5 what is necessary for identification to be possible.

The most useful rule for the purposes of identification is called the *order condition*. The order condition states that if an equation is to be identified, *the number of predetermined variables excluded from the equation must be greater than or equal to the number of included endogenous variables minus one*. The list of included endogenous variables should contain variables on the left-hand side and the right-hand side of the equation. For some purposes it is useful to express the order condition in a somewhat different, but equivalent, form. A necessary condition for an equation to be identified is that the number of all variables excluded from the equation be greater than or equal to the number of endogenous variables in the model system minus one.[3]

Perhaps the best way to gain some intuition into why the order condition is necessary for identification is to consider the problem of estimating Eq. (9.13). Since the model is simultaneous, the variable y_3 will be correlated with the error term u_1. Consistent parameter estimates can be obtained if two-stage least squares or instrumental variables estimation is used. If we were to proceed thoughtlessly to use 2SLS, we would estimate y_3 in the reduced form as a weighted average of the two predetermined variables z_1 and z_2. We would then replace y_3 by $\hat{y}_3$ in the original equation and attempt to utilize an ordinary least-squares estimation procedure. Such a procedure would fail, however, because of the perfect collinearity between $\hat{y}_3$ and the variables z_1 and z_2 guaranteed by the first stage of the estimation process. In order for 2SLS to be used, at least one of the predetermined variables in the model must be excluded from the first equation. If y_2 were included in Eq. (9.13), then the number of excluded predetermined variables would need to be at least two to guarantee identification. The presence of two right-hand endogenous variables necessitates the use of two potential instruments, both not already present in the equation.

The difficulty with the order condition is that it is not a sufficient condition; i.e., it is possible for the condition to be satisfied and for the equation to be unidentified. While the order condition is likely to be a satisfactory rule of thumb for identification, there is a possibility that it will fail on occasion. The

---

[3] The order condition is described in full generality in Appendix 9.1.

extension of the order condition to include sufficient as well as necessary conditions for identification is somewhat difficult. Since it involves an understanding of the rank of a matrix, we leave that discussion to Appendix 9.1.[4]

Example 9.3

Reconsider the three-equation macroeconomic model described in Example 9.1. The first equation is clearly unidentified, since there are three endogenous variables and only one excluded predetermined variable (G_t). Estimation of the first equation using 2SLS is impossible, and prediction using any parameter estimates must be suspect. A more realistic consumption equation, not containing I_t (gross investment) as an explanatory variable, would be identified. The second equation is overidentified according to the order condition, since there are two excluded predetermined variables and only two included endogenous variables. Finally, the third equation is identified, without regard to the order condition, since it is an identity with all parameters known by definition. In this particular example the order condition is sufficient to guarantee identification of the investment equation, since the rank condition also holds.

Example 9.4

Let us return to one of the rather simple supply-demand models examined in Chapter 5. The model is as follows:

Supply: $$Q_t = \alpha_1 + \alpha_2 P_t \qquad + u_{1t}$$

Demand: $$Q_t = \beta_1 + \beta_2 P_t + \beta_3 Y_t + u_{2t}$$

where P = price
Q = quantity
Y = income

The demand equation is not identified by the order condition, since no predetermined variables are excluded. The necessary condition for the supply curve to be identified is satisfied, since there are two endogenous variables and one excluded predetermined variable. The sufficient condition will also hold when $\beta_3 \neq 0$. This makes intuitive sense, since $\beta_3 = 0$ implies that the original zero exclusion restriction has no force in the model. With $\beta_3 = 0$ there is no way to distinguish between the supply and demand equations.

This simple example is useful because it suggests that the problem of

---

[4] The sufficient condition for identifiability is called the *rank condition.*

identification should not be approached in a rigid manner. Assume, for example, that there is very little variability in the income variable Y, and that the associated coefficient is close to 0. While the strict rules for identification will be satisfied, it will still be difficult to distinguish the supply equation from the demand equation. This suggests that attempts to guarantee identifiability in each model equation by adding and deleting variables randomly will most likely lead to problems. While the strict order and rank conditions might be satisfied by such a process, the model is unlikely to have much predictive power, since some or all of the added variables may have little effect on the corresponding endogenous variables.

9.3 SINGLE-EQUATION ESTIMATION

Before discussing methods by which systems of equations can be estimated, let us once again consider the subject of single-equation estimation. We concern ourselves with the estimation of an overidentified equation, since the choice of estimation technique becomes uninteresting if the equation is exactly identified.[5] Our objective is to put the estimation techniques of instrumental variables and two-stage least squares in proper perspective by pointing out some practical difficulties. Each of the single-equation estimation techniques discussed here is a limited-information estimator in the sense that it does not utilize all the information available in the model. In particular, no account is taken of information associated with overidentifying restrictions in equations not being estimated.

Consider the following simple two-equation model:[6]

$$y_1 = \alpha_2 y_2 + u_1 \tag{9.22}$$

$$y_2 = \beta_1 y_1 + \beta_3 z_1 + \beta_4 z_2 + u_2 \tag{9.23}$$

The first equation is overidentified (as long as $\beta_3 \neq 0$ and $\beta_4 \neq 0$), while the second is unidentified. The reader should recall that the order condition is satisfied for Eq. (9.22) because there are two excluded predetermined variables and only two included endogenous variables. In Eq. (9.23), on the other hand, there are no excluded predetermined variables, so that the order condition is not satisfied.

For our purposes it will be sufficient to consider the problem of estimating the first equation. Ordinary least squares is clearly an inappropriate estimation procedure, since the simultaneous nature of the model guarantees that y_2 and u_1 will be correlated, regardless of sample size. One plausible estimation process

---

[5] All the estimation techniques described here yield equivalent sample estimators if the equation is exactly identified.

[6] Portions of this section rely upon an excellent discussion in Malinvaud, *Principles of Econometrics* (Paris: North-Holland, 1966), pp. 534–540.

is instrumental variables, since the proper choice of instruments guarantees that consistent parameter estimators will be utilized. If we were to choose the instrumental variables technique as an estimation procedure, we would have a choice between at least two estimators of the parameter α_2, each choice associated with the use of a different predetermined variable as instrument $(\hat{\alpha}_2 = \sum z_1 y_1 / \sum z_1 y_2$ and $\hat{\hat{\alpha}}_2 = \sum z_2 y_1 / \sum z_2 y_2)$. The two estimators will not coincide in the sample, so that we are faced with the necessity of finding a decision rule which allows us to choose between the two. Since both parameter estimators are consistent (i.e., in a large enough sample they will converge to the same estimate), some criterion must be used to choose between the two. One useful criterion[7] is to choose as an instrument the predetermined variable which is most highly correlated with y_2. This criterion guarantees that the *single* instrument chosen will lead to parameter estimators with the smallest variance among the set of parameter estimators associated with all predetermined variables taken individually. It makes sense intuitively,[8] because an instrument which is very highly correlated with y_2 would be expected to lead to more accurate results than an instrument having a substantially lower correlation with y_2.

The choice of instruments just made is rather limiting, however, since we have restricted ourselves to choosing as our instrument one element from a set of predetermined variables. A more reasonable (and more efficient) procedure would be one which chooses as an instrument a weighted average of the two available predetermined variables, with the weights being selected so as to maximize the correlation between the single instrument and y_2. To get such an instrument, we simply regress y_2 on both z_1 and z_2, and calculate the fitted values $\hat{y}_2$. This procedure should be familiar to the reader, since it is the first stage of two-stage least squares. The 2SLS estimator is $\alpha_2^* = \sum \hat{y}_2 y_1 / \sum \hat{y}_2 y_2$. Thus, the 2SLS estimator is an instrumental variables estimator, where the instrument is chosen to maximize its correlation with y_2 and indirectly to minimize the variance of the estimated parameter.[9]

The 2SLS technique is frequently used in the estimation of business and economic models. As long as the number of predetermined variables in the reduced form of the model is relatively small (less than 20), 2SLS presents no computational problems. However, when the number of predetermined variables is quite large, the computational cost of 2SLS necessitates an alternative means of determining instruments. One solution is to reduce the number of predetermined variables through the technique of *principal components*. Principal components is a computational process in which a group of variables is reduced in number to a more fundamental set of variables. The reduced set of variables is used

---

[7] This method of choosing instruments suggests one potential pitfall. If lagged endogenous variables are added to a model artificially to make each of the equations identified, the lagged variables may not be suitable choices as instruments. A variable such as y_{2t-1} is likely to be highly correlated with y_{2t}, but the high correlation makes it likely that it will also be correlated with u_{1t}, the error term. If such is the case, inconsistent parameter estimates will be obtained.

[8] This result is quite difficult to prove. For details see Malinvaud, *op. cit.*, p. 536.

[9] *Ibid.*

(sometimes in a modified form) as the reduced form for the first-stage estimation.[10] A second procedure selects a subset of predetermined variables from the original set according to a well-defined selection rule.[11] Both techniques are used frequently in the estimation (and later simulation) of large econometric models.

Another complication with the use of 2SLS occurs when the error process in one or more equations of a model is autoregressive, i.e., when errors in a given equation are correlated over time. If the equations with autocorrelated errors do not contain lagged endogenous variables and if the errors are first-order serially correlated, then the estimation problem is not very difficult.[12] Consider the following simple example:

$$y_{1t} = \alpha_2 y_{2t} + u_{1t} \tag{9.24}$$

$$y_{2t} = \beta_1 y_{1t} + \beta_3 z_t + u_{2t} \tag{9.25}$$

$$u_{1t} = \rho u_{1t-1} + \varepsilon_{1t} \tag{9.26}$$

where ε_{1t} and u_{2t} are not autocorrelated. We proceed first by applying the generalized differencing process to each equation and then by solving for the reduced form. This yields

$$y_{1t} = \frac{1}{1 - \alpha_2 \beta_1} (\rho y_{1t-1} - \alpha_2 \rho y_{2t-1} + \alpha_2 \beta_3 z_t + v_{1t}) \tag{9.27}$$

$$y_{2t} = \frac{1}{1 - \alpha_2 \beta_1} (\beta_1 \rho y_{1t-1} - \beta_1 \alpha_2 \rho y_{2t-1} + \beta_3 z_t + v_{2t}) \tag{9.28}$$

In order to estimate the first equation, (9.24), we obtain fitted values for y_{2t} by applying ordinary least squares to the second reduced-form equation, (9.28). Then, rewriting the first equation in generalized difference form and substituting the fitted values for y_{2t}, we obtain

$$y_{1t} - \rho y_{1t-1} = \alpha_2(\hat{y}_{2t} - \rho \hat{y}_{2t-1}) + \hat{\varepsilon}_{1t}$$

The modified two-stage least-squares procedure is completed by estimating this equation using any one of the autoregressive estimation procedures described in Chapter 4.

---

[10] For details see T. Kloek and L. B. Mennes, "Simultaneous Equation Estimation Based on Principal Components of Predetermined Variables," *Econometrica*, vol. 28, pp. 45–61, 1960; and L. R. Klein, "Estimation of Interdependent Systems in Macroeconometrics," *Econometrica*, vol. 37, pp. 171–192, 1969.

[11] See F. M. Fisher, "Dynamic Structure and Estimation in Economy-wide Econometric Models," chap. XV in J. Duesenberry, G. Fromm, L. Klein, and E. Kuh (eds.), *The Brookings Quarterly Econometric Model of the United States*, 1965.

[12] The correct estimation technique when lagged endogenous variables appear in the equations is described by R. Fair in "The Estimation of Simultaneous Equation Models with Lagged Endogenous Variables and First Order Serially Correlated Errors," *Econometrica*, vol. 38, pp. 507–516, May 1970.

9.4 ESTIMATION OF EQUATION SYSTEMS

All the single-equation estimation procedures just described yield consistent parameter estimates. As a general rule, however, each estimation technique yields inefficient parameter estimates (for large samples) because all the information available in the description of the system of equations is not utilized in the estimation procedure. We have argued that one way to view this loss of information is through the overidentifying restrictions in the system of equations that are not taken into account when single-equation estimation is done. An alternative source of inefficiency arises because single-equation estimation does not account for the fact that error terms across equations (for corresponding observations) are likely to be correlated. In either case, the problem of loss of efficiency can be resolved with the utilization of any of several methods of estimating systems of equations, in which parameters for all equations are determined in a single procedure.

We describe in this section how techniques to estimate equation systems might be applied first to the seemingly unrelated equations model and then to the simultaneous equations model. Because of the complexity of the techniques, much of the mathematical detail is presented in the appendixes to the chapter. Our purpose is simply to provide an introduction to each of the important estimation procedures.

9.4.1 Seemingly Unrelated Equations Model

The seemingly unrelated equations model consists of a series of equations linked because the error terms across equations are correlated. As an example, assume that we are attempting to predict the percentage shares of a local government budget to be allocated to fire and police FP, to schools S, and to all other purposes O. The explanatory variables might include population density D, number of school-age children C, and median family income Y. Formally, the model is as follows (T = total budget):

$$\frac{FP_i}{T_i} = \alpha_0 + \alpha_1 D_i + \alpha_2 Y_i \qquad\qquad + u_{1i} \tag{9.29}$$

$$\frac{S_i}{T_i} = \beta_0 \qquad\qquad + \beta_2 Y_i + \beta_3 C_i + u_{2i} \tag{9.30}$$

$$\frac{O_i}{T_i} = \gamma_0 + \gamma_1 D_i + \gamma_2 Y_i + \gamma_3 C_i + u_{3i} \tag{9.31}$$

where the subscript i refers to individual cities. When none of the dependent budget-share variables appears on the right-hand side of any equation, the seemingly unrelated equations model is appropriate. Each equation could be estimated independently using ordinary least-squares, and consistent and unbiased parameter estimates would be obtained. However, the efficiency of the parameter estimates could be improved if explicit account were taken of the correlation between error terms across equations. The correlation arises because of the restriction (by definition) that the sum of the individual budget shares is 100 percent, or 1. If in a given year a higher-than-average prediction is made for percentage expenditures on fire and police and on schools, the arithmetic of the model guarantees that a lower-than-average prediction should be made for the residual budget item. This correlation may be seen more formally by summing each of the three equations for each individual observation (city):

$$1 = (\alpha_0 + \beta_0 + \gamma_0) + (\alpha_1 + \gamma_1)D_i + (\alpha_2 + \beta_2 + \gamma_2)Y_i + (\beta_3 + \gamma_3)C_i$$

$$+ (u_{1i} + u_{2i} + u_{3i}) \tag{9.32}$$

Since Eq. (9.32) must hold identically for each observation, we conclude that $u_{1i} + u_{2i} + u_{3i} = 0$ for every observation.[13]

For efficient estimation one must take into account the correlation between equations by using a systems method of estimation. This can be done using a method devised by Zellner (called *Zellner estimation*).[14] Zellner suggests that efficiency in estimation can be gained if one views the system of seemingly unrelated equations as a single large equation to be estimated. Estimation of this single (system) equation is accomplished efficiently through the use of generalized least-squares estimation (see Appendix 4). Zellner estimation achieves an improvement in efficiency by taking into explicit account the fact that cross-equation error correlations may not be zero.

While the details of the method are left to Appendix 9.3, it is instructive to examine a simple application of seemingly unrelated equations estimation. Consider the following two-equation model:[15]

$$y_1 = \alpha x + u_1 \tag{9.33}$$

$$y_2 = \beta z + u_2 \tag{9.34}$$

We assume that the model is a cross-section model and that N observations are available for each of the variables in the model. Were the error terms in the two equations to be uncorrelated, then we would obtain efficient estimates of α and β by performing ordinary least-squares estimation on each separate equation, using N observations for each regression. However, under the assumption that u_1

---

[13] There are additional parameter restrictions, of course, but they are not of immediate concern to us. The parameter restrictions are relevant, however, when the actual estimation process is undertaken. The restrictions that the sum of the intercept coefficients be 1 and that the sum of all slope coefficients be 0 necessitates the estimation of only two of the three equations listed. The coefficients of the third can be solved directly from the estimated coefficients of the first two equations.

[14] See A. Zellner, "An Efficient Method of Estimating Seemingly Unrelated Regressions and Tests for Aggregation Bias," *Journal of the American Statistical Association*, vol. 57, pp. 348–368, 1962.

[15] The observational subscripts have been dropped to simplify the exposition.

and u_2 are correlated for identical cross-section units, we can improve upon the efficiency of ordinary least squares by writing the equation system as one combined equation, estimating that equation using generalized least-squares estimation.

In order to write the system as one large equation rather than two smaller equations, it is necessary to distinguish between observations associated with the first equation, (9.33), and observations associated with the second equation, (9.34). To do so, we shall relabel the observations, arbitrarily assigning observations 1 to N to the first-equation variables and observations $N + 1$ to $2N$ to the second-equation variables. We now define four new variables as follows:

$$y^* \begin{cases} = y_{1i} & \text{if } i = 1, \ldots, N \\ = y_{2i} & \text{if } i = N + 1, \ldots, 2N \end{cases} \qquad x^* \begin{cases} = x_i & \text{if } i = 1, \ldots, N \\ = 0 & \text{otherwise} \end{cases}$$

$$z^* \begin{cases} = 0 & \text{if } i = 1, \ldots, N \\ = z_i & \text{if } i = N + 1, \ldots, 2N \end{cases} \qquad u^* \begin{cases} = u_{1i} & \text{if } i = 1, \ldots, N \\ = u_{2i} & \text{if } i = N + 1, \ldots, 2N \end{cases}$$

Also, $\qquad \sigma_1 = \text{Var}\,(u_1) \qquad \sigma_2 = \text{Var}\,(u_2) \qquad \sigma_{12} = \text{Cov}\,(u_1, u_2)$

With this new notation the combined equation may be written

$$y^* = \alpha x^* + \beta z^* + u^* \tag{9.35}$$

Applying the generalized least-squares procedure to Eq. (9.35) allows us to obtain parameter estimates for α and β. Since the algebra involved is substantial (despite the fact that we are working with data in deviations form), we shall simply present the results here:

$$\hat{\alpha} = \frac{1}{C} \left(A\sigma_1{}^2 \sum z^2 + B\sigma_{12} \sum xz \right) \tag{9.36}$$

$$\hat{\beta} = \frac{1}{C} \left(A\sigma_{12} \sum xz + B\sigma_2{}^2 \sum z^2 \right) \tag{9.37}$$

where $A = \sigma_2{}^2 \sum xy_1 - \sigma_{12} \sum xy_2$
$B = \sigma_1{}^2 \sum xy_2 - \sigma_{12} \sum zy_1$
$C = \sigma_1{}^2\sigma_2{}^2 \sum x^2 \sum z^2 - \sigma_{12}^2(\sum xz)^2$

This example is instructive because it allows us to illustrate the two important cases in which Zellner estimation and ordinary least-squares estimation are identical. The first, and most obvious, situation occurs when the cross-equation covariance is identically 0 ($\sigma_{12} = 0$). The second, less obvious, situation occurs when the two explanatory variables (x and z) are identical. The details of these derivations are left to the reader (Exercise 9.8).

The application of generalized least squares necessitates obtaining estimates of the error covariances between equations. These estimates are obtained by first estimating each single equation using ordinary least squares. The variances and covariances of the estimated residuals then provide consistent estimators of the error variances and covariances. In our two-equation example, we would estimate $\sigma_1{}^2$, $\sigma_2{}^2$, and σ_{12} as follows:

$$\hat{\sigma}_1{}^2 = \frac{1}{N-2} \sum_{i=1}^{N} \hat{u}_{1i}^2 \qquad \hat{\sigma}_2{}^2 = \frac{1}{N-2} \sum_{i=N+1}^{2N} \hat{u}_{2i}^2 \qquad \hat{\sigma}_{12} = \frac{1}{N-2} \sum_{i=1}^{N} \hat{u}_{1i}\hat{u}_{2i+N}$$

$$(9.38)$$

As a practical matter, Zellner estimation is a two-stage estimation procedure. It can be shown to be consistent as well as (asymptotically) efficient, but its small-sample properties are not well known.[16]

9.4.2 Simultaneous Equation Model

The notion that the efficiency of parameter estimates can be improved using system estimation methods can be extended to simultaneous equation models. The natural extension of Zellner estimation is the technique of three-stage least squares (3SLS).[17] 3SLS involves the application of generalized least-squares estimation to the system of equations, each of which has first been estimated using 2SLS. In the first stage of the process, the reduced form of the model system is estimated. The fitted values of the endogenous variables are then used to get 2SLS estimates of all the equations in the system. Once the 2SLS parameters are calculated, the residuals of each equation are utilized to estimate the cross-equation variances and covariances, just as in the Zellner estimation process described previously. In the third and final stage of the estimation process, generalized least-squares parameter estimates are obtained. The 3SLS procedure can be shown to yield more efficient parameter estimates than 2SLS because it takes into account cross-equation correlation.[18]

If one considers applying 3SLS, several items of information will prove valuable. First, all identities must be removed from the equation system before the estimation process is used.[19] Second, the application of the third stage of the procedure will not alter the 2SLS estimates in the special case in which all the cross-equation covariances are 0. Finally, any equation which is unidentified

---

[16] For some information about the properties of Zellner estimation, see A. Zellner, "Estimators of Seemingly Unrelated Regressions: Some Exact Finite Sample Results," *Journal of the American Statistical Association*, vol. 58, pp. 977–992, 1963; and J. Kmenta and R. F. Gilbert, "Small Sample Properties of Alternative Estimators of Seemingly Unrelated Regressions," *Journal of the American Statistical Association*, vol. 63, pp. 1180–1200, 1968.

[17] See A. Zellner and H. Theil, "Three-Stage Least Squares: Simultaneous Estimation of Simultaneous Relations," *Econometrica*, vol. 30, pp. 54–78, 1962.

[18] See A. Madansky, "On the Efficiency of Three-Stage Least Squares Estimation," *Econometrica*, vol. 32, p. 55, 1964.

[19] This can be seen by substituting variables to eliminate the identities from the model, but such a procedure is unnecessary.

must be dropped from the equation system before 3SLS is applied. (Recall that 2SLS parameter estimates cannot be obtained for unidentified equations.)

Example 9.5 Public Assistance

The growth of public relief payments has long been a concern of professional economists. In an attempt to further knowledge of the public relief problem, Brehm and Saving used statewide data to study the demand for public assistance.[20] Data were collected on the number of general assistance recipients on an average per-month basis, annually by state for the period 1951–1959. The model developed by the authors focuses on the effects of interstate migration on levels of participation in the general assistance program. This suggests the use of a cross-section estimation with individual observations associated with states of the United States. However, because time-series data were available for a period of 9 years, the authors decided that pooling their data might allow them to obtain more efficient parameter estimates. One equation which was estimated is of the following form:

$$N_{ij} = \beta_0 + \beta_1 \frac{P_{ij}}{W_{ij}} + \beta_2 U_{ij} + \beta_3 A_{ij} + \varepsilon_{ij}$$

where $i = 1, 2, \ldots, 48$ refers to observations across states

$j = 1, 2, \ldots, 9$ refers to observations over time

N_{ij} = percentage of ith state's population receiving general assistance payments (GAP) in the jth year

P_{ij} = average monthly GAP in the ith state for the jth year

W_{ij} = average monthly manufacturing wage in the ith state for the jth year

U_{ij} = unemployment rate in the ith state for the jth year

A_{ij} = nonagricultural employment as a percentage of population in the ith state for the jth year

On the basis of an extensive theoretical development the authors were able to predict that the percentage of the population receiving assistance will be directly related to average monthly assistance payments and inversely related to the on-going wage rate. The latter result is expected because higher wages imply a higher opportunity cost of choosing to receive public assistance rather than to work. The unemployment rate appears in the model because it measures the number of individuals whose alternative to general assistance is a zero (or very low) wage. We would expect unemployment rates and public assistance recipient rates to be positively related. Finally, the nonagricultural employment rate that is included is used as a proxy variable for the ease of getting on general

---

[20] C. T. Brehm and T. R. Saving, "The Demand for General Assistance Payments," *American Economic Review*, vol. LIX, pp. 1002–1018, 1964.

assistance rolls. The coefficient is expected to be positive since previous studies have shown a direct relationship between the degree of urbanization in a state and the assistance recipient rate.

In attempting to pool the data, the authors were concerned with the potential links that might exist between the nine individual cross-section relationships—one for each year in which data are available. The primary link is caused by the fact that the effect of migration of individuals from low to high general-assistance-level states takes place over a period of years. Since no lags are included explicitly in the model, it is reasonable to expect that disturbance terms for one state in a given year will be positively related to disturbance terms for that state in preceding as well as future years. The authors decided to improve the efficiency of the estimation process by using Zellner's seemingly unrelated regression technique rather than ordinary least squares. Zellner's generalized least-squares estimation process improves on efficiency by taking explicit account of the expected correlation between disturbance terms associated with separate cross-section equations. The results of their estimations are listed in Table 9.1 (with standard errors in parentheses):

TABLE 9.1
RESULTS OF SEEMINGLY UNRELATED
ESTIMATION

Year	Constant	P/W	U	A
1951	−.7300 (.4817)	.0684 (.0245)	.1418 (.0671)	.0649 (.0167)
1952	−.8122 (.4237)	.0317 (.0198)	.1952 (.0516)	.0666 (.0147)
1953	.0673 (.5558)	.0808 (.0257)	.0938 (.0760)	.0177 (.0198)
1954	−.1399 (.4992)	.1006 (.0189)	.0443 (.0388)	.0251 (.0174)
1955	−.2245 (.5043)	.0967 (.0185)	−.0422 (.0510)	.0435 (.0161)
1956	.2102 (.4985)	.0729 (.0175)	.0402 (.0469)	.0254 (.0148)
1957	.2868 (.5371)	.0732 (.0177)	.0583 (.0391)	.0198 (.0169)
1958	−.8801 (.8324)	.0825 (.0250)	.1799 (.0550)	.0544 (.0298)
1959	−1.0300 (.9018)	.0952 (.0274)	.2180 (.0898)	.0515 (.0339)
Mean	−.3614	.0780	.1033	.0400

The P/W term is generally the most significant of all the variables (significantly different from 0 at the 5 percent level in all cases but one). In all cases, the coefficient has the expected sign. The unemployment variable coefficient is significant in only 3 of the 9 years, although it had an unexpected sign only once. Finally, the proxy variable for the ease of becoming a general assistance recipient has the expected sign in every case and is significantly different from 0 in four of the nine cases. The results of the study give additional support to the view that income-related variables such as the ratio of assistance payments to the wage rate are important determinants of recipient levels. The remaining variables have a somewhat lesser effect. The authors conclude that general assistance recipients are not unlike most consumers in that they react in expected ways to the economic incentives which exist.

Example 9.6 Macroeconomic Model

In their original article dealing with three-stage least-squares estimation, Zellner and Theil provide an insightful illustrative example.[21] In the example, 2SLS and 3SLS estimates of a simple macroeconomic model are compared. The model, known as "Klein's Model I," includes three behavioral equations and three identities.[22] The behavioral equations are as follows:
Consumption:

$$C = \alpha_0 + \alpha_1 \Pi + \alpha_2 (W_1 + W_2) + \alpha_3 \Pi_{-1} + u_1$$

Investment:

$$I = \beta_0 + \beta_1 \Pi + \beta_2 \Pi_{-1} + \beta_3 K_{-1} + u_2$$

Demand for labor:

$$W_1 = \gamma_0 + \gamma_1 (Y + T - W_2) + \gamma_2 (Y + T - W_2)_{-1} + \gamma_3 t + u_3$$

where C = consumption
Π = profits
W_1 = private wage bill
W_2 = government wage bill
I = investment
K = capital stock
Y = national income
T = indirect taxes
t = time (in years)

---

[21] Zellner and Theil, *op. cit.*

[22] From L. R. Klein, *Economic Fluctuations in the U.S., 1921-1941* (New York: Wiley, 1950).

TABLE 9.2
THREE-STAGE AND TWO-STAGE LEAST-SQUARES ESTIMATES OF PARAMETERS

Equation	Coefficient of	3SLS		2SLS	
		Coefficient estimate	Variance of coefficient estimator	Coefficient estimate	Variance of coefficient estimator
Consumption	Π	.0479	.013119	.0173	.013936
	$W_1 + W_2$	.8170	.001490	.8102	.001620
	Π_{-1}	.1897	.010946	.2162	.011506
	1	16.1923	1.690	16.5548	1.745
Investment	Π	.2111	.028505	.1502	.030084
	Π_{-1}	.5667	.025220	.6159	.026499
	K_{-1}	−.1472	.001202	−.1578	.001305
	1	17.9210	52.516	20.2782	56.892
Demand for labor	$Y + T - W_2$	.4282	.001203	.4389	.001270
	$(Y + T - W_2)_{-1}$	.1543	.001422	.1467	.001508
	t	.1356	.000821	.1304	.000849
	1	1.6935	1.302	1.5003	1.317

The three behavioral equations are linked by three identities:

$$Y + T = C + I + G$$

$$Y = W_1 + W_2 + \Pi$$

$$K = K_{-1} + I$$

In total, the model includes six endogenous variables and eight predetermined variables. All three behavioral equations are overidentified. The results of the 2SLS and 3SLS estimations are provided in Table 9.2. The reader should pay particular attention to the variances of the coefficient estimators associated with both estimation processes. In all cases (as guaranteed by the estimation process), 3SLS parameter estimates have smaller variances than their 2SLS counterparts. The gain in efficiency associated with 3SLS is usually in the neighborhood of 5 percent. The example illustrates the benefits of using 3SLS but does not prove its necessity, since computational costs may be high enough to outweigh the efficiency gain.

9.5 COMPARISON OF ALTERNATIVE ESTIMATORS

We have now completed a survey of several single-equation and system estimation procedures. It is useful to pause for a moment and ask how one selects between alternative estimation techniques. The answer is a difficult one, for two reasons. First, the choice of estimation procedure may depend in part upon the purpose for which the estimated system of equations is to be used. We shall see in the next chapter, for example, that the choice of estimation technique can have substantial effects on the dynamic properties of the estimated model. Second, most of our knowledge about the properties of estimators relates to large samples; i.e., we know that estimators will be consistent and (sometimes) asymptotically efficient. We know little, however, about the small-sample properties of these estimators. Some small-sample studies examine the sensitivity of estimated parameters to different estimation techniques using real world data and previously developed models, while others apply *Monte Carlo* experimentation techniques to known artificial model structures.[23] While the results of the studies are varied and difficult to summarize, it would be worthwhile to mention a few of the important issues which arise from them.

Given a truly simultaneous system of equations, we know that ordinary least-squares estimation is inconsistent as well as biased. Two-stage least squares and instrumental variables provide consistent single-equation parameter estimates, but they are biased as well. On the other hand, studies suggest that 2SLS estimates have larger variance than OLS. Thus, if one's criterion is to minimize mean square error (which combines bias and variance), it is conceivable that OLS estimation will be more suitable than 2SLS and other consistent single-equation techniques. On the other hand, studies suggest that systems methods of estimation yield lower variance estimates than do single-equation methods. Since most modern computer packages allow for the use of generalized least-squares estimation, it is not unusual for one to bear the added expense of performing Zellner and 3SLS estimation. The difficulty with all systems estimation techniques, however, is that individual parameter estimates (by construction) are sensitive to the specification of the entire model system. A serious specification error in one equation can affect the parameter estimates in all equations of the model. Thus, the decision to use systems estimation involves a trade-off between the gain in efficiency and the potential costs of specification error.

Example 9.7 Monte Carlo Study

In an attempt to study some of the small sample properties of alternative estimators, Robert Summers[24] performed a series of Monte Carlo experiments in which a hypothetical two-equation simultaneous equation model was estimated using (among others) ordinary least squares (OLS), two-stage least squares

---

[23] See, for example, R. Summers, "A Capital Intensive Approach to the Small Sample Properties of Various Simultaneous Equation Estimators," *Econometrica*, vol. 33, pp. 1–41, 1965; J. Johnston, *Econometric Methods*, 2d ed. (New York: McGraw-Hill, 1972), pp. 408–420; G. Chow, "A Comparison of Alternative Estimators for Simultaneous Equations," *Econometrica*, vol. 32, pp. 532–553, Oct. 1964.

[24] Summers, *op. cit.*

(2SLS), limited-information maximum likelihood (LIML), and full-information maximum likelihood (FIML).[25] The model is as follows:

$$Y_1 + \beta_{12} Y_2 + \gamma_{11} Z_1 + \gamma_{12} Z_2 + \gamma_{10} = u_1 \tag{9.39}$$

$$Y_2 + \beta_{22} Y_2 + \gamma_{23} Z_3 + \gamma_{24} Z_4 + \gamma_{20} = u_2 \tag{9.40}$$

It should be readily apparent to the reader that both equations are overidentified.

The experiment proceeded in the following manner. First, specific values were chosen for all the parameters in the structural form of the model as well as for the individual error variances and the cross-equation error covariance. Second, the values of all the predetermined variables were given. As specified in one of the experiments, the model looks as follows:

$$Y_1 - .7Y_2 + .8Z_1 + .7Z_2 - 149.5 = u_1 \tag{9.41}$$

$$Y_1 + .4Y_2 + .6Z_3 - .4Z_4 - 149.6 = u_2 \tag{9.42}$$

$$\text{Var}(u_1) = 400 \qquad \text{Var}(u_2) = 400 \qquad \text{Cov}(u_1, u_2) = 200$$

where Z_1 = labor income originating in government
$\quad Z_2$ = nonfarm residential construction
$\quad Z_3$ = stock of nonfarm housing
$\quad Z_4$ = excise taxes

Data sets were generated by assuming that the error process in each equation was normally distributed. Each observation on the endogenous variables was calculated (conditional on the values of the predetermined variables) by randomly sampling values for u_1 and u_2 and solving in Eqs. (9.41) and (9.42). Once a sample of endogenous (as well as predetermined) variables was available, structural parameters were estimated using each of the estimation techniques listed. Because of the complexities involved in an attempt to compare alternative estimators, numerous models were estimated and compared, each involving slightly different assumptions about specification and correlation among variables. In addition, the comparison of the alternative estimators was accomplished using several distinct approaches. For our purposes, the most interesting comparison was made by randomly determining 50 individual data samples in the manner just described. This allows for the determination of a distribution of estimated parameters associated with each of the alternative estimation processes. A comparison of these alternative distributions is best made by listing the bias, standard deviation, and root-mean-square error associated with each estimation process.

---

[25] Limited-information maximum-likelihood and full-information maximum-likelihood estimation are discussed in Appendix 9.4.

TABLE 9.3†

SMALL-SAMPLE PROPERTIES OF ESTIMATION

Bias appears on the top line, standard deviation in the lower left, and root mean square on the lower right.

Parameters	β_{12}	γ_{11}	γ_{12}	γ_{10}	β_{22}	γ_{23}	γ_{24}	γ_{20}
True values	−.7	.8	.7	−149.5	.4	.6	−.4	−149.6
LIML	.013	−.035	−.017	4.141	−.020	−.259	.015	28.819
	.089 .089	.177 .180	.104 .105	22.1 22.5	.106 .107	.582 .638	.052 .054	68.6 74.4
2SLS	.017	−.041	−.019	4.375	−.025	−.260	.017	29.415
	.089 .091	.177 .181	.103 .105	22.0 22.4	.106 .109	.582 .638	.052 .053	68.6 74.6
OLS	.073	−.120	−.049	7.398	−.085	−.270	.042	36.602
	.085 .112	.175 .212	.101 .112	21.8 23.0	.098 .130	.579 .639	.049 .064	66.3 75.7
FIML	.011	−.028	−.019	3.769	−.021	−.157	.002	17.571
	.090 .091	.150 .161	.103 .105	20.8 21.2	.106 .108	.477 .502	.051 .051	55.7 58.4

† Adapted from Table 1A, p. 34, of Summers.

For review purposes the three terms are redefined here (for an arbitrary coefficient α):

$$\text{Bias} = \frac{1}{N} \sum_i \hat{\alpha}_i - \alpha = \bar{\hat{\alpha}} - \alpha$$

$$\text{Standard deviation (SD)} = \sqrt{\frac{1}{N} \sum_i (\hat{\alpha}_i - \bar{\hat{\alpha}})^2}$$

$$\text{Root-mean-square error (RMSE)} = \sqrt{\frac{1}{N} \sum_i (\hat{\alpha}_i - \alpha)^2}$$

The reader should check that

$$\text{RMSE}^2 = \text{SD}^2 + \text{Bias}^2$$

The results of the Monte Carlo experiment are summarized in Table 9.3. From a careful examination of Table 9.3 several tentative conclusions can be reached. First, OLS is clearly inferior to the three other estimation processes. Not surprisingly (since OLS is an inconsistent estimator), OLS exhibits the greatest bias of all the estimators. While OLS frequently has a smaller standard deviation than some other estimators, this gain is swamped by the cost in terms of the extent of bias present. This result is most clearly illustrated by the fact that OLS parameter estimates have the largest root-mean-square error of all the estimates. Second, the remaining three estimation processes are difficult to rank order. All do substantially better than OLS in terms of bias and root-mean-square error. FIML has the smallest root-mean-square error for several of the coefficients, but the result is not true in every case.

While the conclusion is not readily apparent from this single example, Summers is able to conclude from the entirety of his results that FIML does marginally better than the alternative consistent estimators when model misspecification is not a serious problem. 2SLS is better than the alternative estimators when the predetermined variables are highly interrelated, but it is inferior when the correlation becomes small. It appears, therefore, that the added computational costs associated with LIML and FIML make 2SLS an appropriate estimation process for most econometric models. The future availability of low-cost maximum-likelihood estimation packages (full-information, in particular) may necessitate a modification of this conclusion.

Exercises

9.1 Explain intuitively (using a three-equation model) why the omission of one variable from each equation of a system of equations is insufficient to guarantee that each equation in the system is identified.

9.2 Prove that the two forms of the order condition for identifiability which are described in the text are equivalent.

9.3 Consider the following three-equation model system:

$$Y_1 = \alpha_1 + \alpha_2 Y_2 \qquad + \alpha_4 X_1 + \alpha_5 Z_2 + u_1$$

$$Y_2 = \beta_1 \qquad + \beta_3 Y_3 \qquad + \beta_5 X_2 + u_2$$

$$Y_3 = \gamma_1 + \gamma_2 Y_2 \qquad + u_3$$

Which of the above equations (if any) are unidentified? Exactly identified? Overidentified?

9.4 Consider the following simple macroeconomic model of an economy:

$$C_t = \alpha_1 + \alpha_2 Y_t + \alpha_3 r_t + u_{1t}$$

$$I_t = \beta_1 + \beta_2 r_t + \beta_3 (Y_t - Y_{t-1}) + u_{2t}$$

$$r_t = \gamma_1 + \gamma_2 I_t + \gamma_3 M_t + u_{3t}$$

$$Y_t = C_t + I_t + G_t$$

Which of the equations are identified? Unidentified? How might you estimate the identified equations?

9.5 Consider the following two-equation recursive model:

$$Y_1 = \alpha_1 \qquad + \alpha_3 X + u_1$$

$$Y_2 = \beta_1 + \beta_2 Y_1 \qquad + u_2$$

(1) Explain why ordinary least squares is the appropriate estimation technique (assuming u_1 and u_2 are uncorrelated).
(2) Suppose that a naive researcher, seeing Y_1 on the right-hand side of the second equation, attempts to estimate it using two-stage least squares, i.e., regressing Y_2 on the fitted values of Y_1 determined by using ordinary least squares on the first equation. What will be the outcome of such an attempt? How might one obtain a value for $\hat{\beta}_2$ if such a procedure is used?
(3) How would the answers to (2) differ if the second equation contained X explicitly as an independent variable?

9.6 Using the example in the text [Eqs. (9.33) and (9.34)], prove that Zellner estimation reduces to ordinary least-squares estimation when the cross-equation error covariance is 0 and when the independent variables in each equation are identical.

9.7 Consider the following two-equation supply-demand model:

Demand: $\qquad\qquad P_t = \alpha_1 + \alpha_2 Q_t + u_{1t}$

Supply: $\qquad\qquad Q_t = \beta_1 + \beta_2 P_{t-1} + \beta_3 W_t + u_{2t}$

(1) Discuss the identifiability of each equation.
(2) Under what condition is the model recursive?
(3) If the model is recursive, how would you estimate the demand equation?
(4) If the model is not recursive, how would you estimate the demand equation?

9.8 Explain why the simple process of lagging all right-hand variables in a simultaneous equation system does not necessarily make the model recursive.

9.9 Consider the following model:

$$y_1 = \qquad \alpha_2 y_2 + \alpha_3 x + u_1$$

$$y_2 = \beta_1 y_1 + \beta_4 z + \beta_5 w + u_2$$

Assume that you have estimated the reduced form of this model, first using ordinary least squares, and then using two-stage least-squares estimates of the structural parameters to solve for the reduced form. Explain why these estimates will differ.

APPENDIX 9.1 / THE IDENTIFICATION PROBLEM IN MATRIX FORM

Representation of the Simultaneous Equations Model

In order to consider the identification problem in its most general form, we need to develop some additional notation which will allow us to distinguish between endogenous and exogenous variables as well as structural and reduced forms. We assume that the model under investigation consists of G equations. Each equation contains G endogenous variables (some may have coefficients which are known to be equal to 0), K predetermined variables, and a randomly distributed error term. Written equation by equation, the structural form of the model is as follows:[26]

---

[26] We have chosen a notation which is most nearly consistent with the notation used in other econometrics textbooks. In this notation, lowercase letters do not imply that variables are measured as deviations about their means.

$$\beta_{11}y_{1i} + \beta_{12}y_{2i} + \cdots + \beta_{1G}y_{Gi} + \gamma_{11}x_{1i} + \gamma_{12}x_{2i} + \cdots + \gamma_{1K}x_{Ki} = u_{1i}$$

$$\beta_{21}y_{1i} + \beta_{22}y_{2i} + \cdots + \beta_{2G}y_{Gi} + \gamma_{21}x_{1i} + \gamma_{22}x_{2i} + \cdots + \gamma_{2K}x_{Ki} = u_{2i}$$

$$\cdots\cdots\cdots\cdots\cdots\cdots\cdots\cdots\cdots\cdots\cdots\cdots\cdots\cdots\cdots\cdots\cdots\cdots\cdots\cdots$$

$$\beta_{G1}y_{1i} + \beta_{G2}y_{2i} + \cdots + \beta_{GG}y_{Gi} + \gamma_{G1}x_{1i} + \gamma_{G2}x_{2i} + \cdots + \gamma_{GK}x_{Ki} = u_{Gi}$$

for $i = 1, 2, \ldots, N$. As in the text, the y's are the endogenous variables and the x's the predetermined variables. In each equation some of the coefficients are equal to 0, and one of the endogenous variables is chosen to have a coefficient of 1. The variable with the coefficient 1 is viewed as the dependent variable (equations in the text are written in this form). The set of equations given previously may be written in matrix form as follows:

$$\mathbf{B}\mathbf{y}_i + \mathbf{\Gamma}\mathbf{x}_i = \mathbf{u}_i \tag{A9.1}$$

where

$$\mathbf{y}_i = \begin{bmatrix} y_{1i} \\ y_{2i} \\ \vdots \\ y_{Gi} \end{bmatrix} \quad \mathbf{x}_i = \begin{bmatrix} x_{1i} \\ x_{2i} \\ \vdots \\ x_{Ki} \end{bmatrix} \quad \mathbf{u}_i = \begin{bmatrix} u_{1i} \\ u_{2i} \\ \vdots \\ u_{Gi} \end{bmatrix}$$

$$\mathbf{B} = \begin{bmatrix} \beta_{11} & \beta_{12} & \cdots & \beta_{1G} \\ \beta_{21} & \beta_{22} & \cdots & \beta_{2G} \\ \cdots\cdots\cdots\cdots\cdots \\ \beta_{G1} & \beta_{G2} & \cdots & \beta_{GG} \end{bmatrix} \quad \mathbf{\Gamma} = \begin{bmatrix} \gamma_{11} & \gamma_{12} & \cdots & \gamma_{1K} \\ \gamma_{21} & \gamma_{22} & \cdots & \gamma_{2K} \\ \cdots\cdots\cdots\cdots\cdots \\ \gamma_{G1} & \gamma_{G2} & \cdots & \gamma_{GK} \end{bmatrix}$$

where $\mathbf{y}_i$ = a $G \times 1$ vector of endogenous variables
$\mathbf{x}_i$ = a $K \times 1$ vector of predetermined variables
$\mathbf{u}_i$ = a $G \times 1$ vector of disturbance terms
$\mathbf{B}$ = a $G \times G$ matrix of endogenous variable coefficients
$\mathbf{\Gamma}$ = a $G \times K$ matrix of predetermined variable coefficients

If we wish to include all N observations available for each y and each x and utilize the matrix notation, we can rewrite the model as follows:

$$\mathbf{B}\mathbf{Y} + \mathbf{\Gamma}\mathbf{X} = \mathbf{U} \tag{A9.2}$$

where $\mathbf{Y}$ = a $G \times N$ matrix
$\mathbf{X}$ = a $K \times N$ matrix
$\mathbf{U}$ = a $G \times N$ matrix

$$\mathbf{Y} = \begin{bmatrix} y_{11} & y_{12} & \cdots & y_{1N} \\ y_{21} & y_{22} & \cdots & y_{2N} \\ \cdots\cdots\cdots\cdots\cdots \\ y_{G1} & y_{G2} & \cdots & y_{GN} \end{bmatrix} \qquad \mathbf{X} = \begin{bmatrix} x_{11} & x_{12} & \cdots & x_{1N} \\ x_{21} & x_{22} & \cdots & x_{2N} \\ \cdots\cdots\cdots\cdots\cdots \\ x_{K1} & x_{K1} & \cdots & x_{KN} \end{bmatrix}$$

$$\mathbf{U} = \begin{bmatrix} u_{11} & u_{12} & \cdots & u_{1N} \\ u_{21} & u_{22} & \cdots & u_{2N} \\ \cdots\cdots\cdots\cdots\cdots \\ u_{G1} & u_{G2} & \cdots & u_{GN} \end{bmatrix}$$

The structural equation contains G equations and G unknowns. If all β's and γ's are known, we can in principle solve for the values of each of the y's, given values of the predetermined x's. To do so, we assume that $\mathbf{B}$ is nonsingular and solve to get the reduced-form representation of the model. Premultiplying both sides of Eq. (A9.1) by the matrix $\mathbf{B}^{-1}$, we get

$$\mathbf{y}_i + \mathbf{B}^{-1}\mathbf{\Gamma}\mathbf{x}_i = \mathbf{B}^{-1}\mathbf{u}_i$$

or

$$\mathbf{y}_i = \pi\mathbf{x}_i + \mathbf{v}_i$$

where $\pi = -\mathbf{B}^{-1}\mathbf{\Gamma}$
$\mathbf{v}_i = \mathbf{B}^{-1}\mathbf{u}_i$

π is a $G \times K$ matrix of reduced-form coefficients:

$$\pi = \begin{bmatrix} \pi_{11} & \pi_{12} & \cdots & \pi_{1K} \\ \pi_{21} & \pi_{22} & \cdots & \pi_{2K} \\ \cdots\cdots\cdots\cdots\cdots \\ \pi_{G1} & \pi_{G2} & \cdots & \pi_{GK} \end{bmatrix}$$

$\mathbf{v}_i$ is a $G \times 1$ vector of reduced-form disturbances. The reduced form of the model is as follows:

$$y_{1i} = \pi_{11}x_{1i} + \pi_{12}x_{2i} + \cdots + \pi_{1K}x_{Ki} + v_{1i}$$

$$y_{2i} = \pi_{21}x_{1i} + \pi_{22}x_{2i} + \cdots + \pi_{2K}x_{Ki} + v_{2i}$$

$$\cdots\cdots\cdots\cdots\cdots\cdots\cdots\cdots\cdots\cdots\cdots$$

$$y_{Gi} = \pi_{G1}x_{1i} + \pi_{G2}x_{2i} + \cdots + \pi_{GK}x_{Ki} + v_{Gi}$$

In terms of all N equations, we would rewrite the system of equations as

$$\mathbf{Y} = \pi\mathbf{X} + \mathbf{V} \qquad\qquad\qquad (A9.3)$$

where $\mathbf{Y}$ = a $G \times N$ matrix
π = a $G \times K$ matrix
$\mathbf{X}$ = a $K \times N$ matrix
$\mathbf{V}$ = a $G \times N$ matrix

In order to complete our description of the simultaneous equations model, we need to specify the assumptions which involve the error term $\mathbf{u}_i$. We shall assume the following:

1
$$E(\mathbf{u}_i) = \mathbf{0} \tag{A9.4}$$

2
$$E(\mathbf{u}_i \mathbf{u}_i') = \sum \tag{A9.5}$$

where $\sum$ is a $G \times G$ matrix of variances and covariances between error terms of identical observations across equations. $\sum$ need not be a multiple of the identity matrix, since covariances of identical observations across different equations may be nonzero. We also assume:

3
$$E(\mathbf{u}_i \mathbf{u}_j') = \mathbf{0} \qquad i, j = 1, 2, \ldots, N \qquad i \neq j \tag{A9.6}$$

This assumption eliminates all correlations between errors associated with different observations, both within equations and across different equations.

It is also useful to relate the reduced-form error term to the structural error term. Reduced-form errors have 0 mean since

$$E(\mathbf{v}_i) = E(\mathbf{B}^{-1}\mathbf{u}_i) = \mathbf{B}^{-1}E(\mathbf{u}_i) = \mathbf{0} \qquad i = 1, 2, \ldots, N \tag{A9.7}$$

The variance-covariance matrix of the reduced-form errors $\mathbf{\Omega}$ is as follows:

$$\mathbf{\Omega} = E(\mathbf{v}_i \mathbf{v}_i') = E[\mathbf{B}^{-1}\mathbf{u}_i \mathbf{u}_i'(\mathbf{B}')^{-1}] = \mathbf{B}^{-1}E(\mathbf{u}_i \mathbf{u}_i')(\mathbf{B}')^{-1}$$

$$= \mathbf{B}^{-1} \sum (\mathbf{B}')^{-1} \tag{A9.8}$$

Conditions for Identification

The presence of right-hand endogenous variables in the simultaneous equations model guarantees that ordinary least-squares estimates of the structural form of the model will be inconsistent. However, ordinary least-squares estimates of the reduced form will be consistent, since only predetermined variables appear on the right-hand side of the reduced-form equations. Thus, it is natural to ask whether it is possible to obtain information about structural parameters, given that consistent estimates of reduced-form parameters can be obtained. The problem of expressing the β's and γ's in terms of the reduced-form coefficients (the π's) is the identification problem. We shall say that a structural parameter is identified if and only if it can be uniquely determined from the set of reduced-form parameters. In our notation, the link between the structural and reduced forms is provided by two equations:

$$\pi = -\mathbf{B}^{-1}\Gamma \tag{A9.9}$$

$$\Omega = \mathbf{B}^{-1} \sum (\mathbf{B}')^{-1} \tag{A9.10}$$

Knowledge of the reduced form is provided by the $G \times K$ elements of π. Unfortunately, our goal is to determine the $G \times G$ elements of $\mathbf{B}$ and the $G \times K$ elements of Γ. Unless further information is known *a priori*, the goal will be impossible to obtain. What is required is information about restrictions on the structural-form parameters. As we have suggested in the text, *a priori* restrictions can be of several types. Restrictions may involve linear relationships between structural parameters as well as restrictions on elements of the variance-covariance matrix of the structural disturbances. We shall focus our attention on the most prevalent form of identifying restriction—the zero restriction on structural-form parameters.

We concentrate, without loss of generality, on the identification of the first equation. In addition, we presume that the variables with 0 coefficient restrictions are grouped after the variables with nonzero coefficients. We assume that of the G endogenous variables in the first equation, the first G_* have nonzero coefficients, while the remaining G_{**} are assumed to have 0 coefficients $(G = G_* + G_{**})$. In addition, K_0 of the predetermined variables have nonzero coefficients, while K_{00} are equal to 0 $(K = K_0 + K_{00})$. In other words, the first equation has G_{**} excluded endogenous variables and K_{00} excluded predetermined variables. The first equation may then be written as follows:

$$[\beta_{11} \quad \beta_{12} \quad \cdots \quad \beta_{1G_*} \quad 0 \quad 0 \quad \cdots \quad 0]\begin{bmatrix} y_{1i} \\ y_{2i} \\ \vdots \\ y_{Gi} \end{bmatrix}$$

$$+ [\gamma_{11} \quad \gamma_{12} \quad \cdots \quad \gamma_{1K_0} \quad 0 \quad 0 \quad \cdots \quad 0]\begin{bmatrix} x_{1i} \\ x_{2i} \\ \vdots \\ x_{Ki} \end{bmatrix} = \begin{bmatrix} u_{1i} \\ u_{2i} \\ \vdots \\ u_{Gi} \end{bmatrix}$$

We shall find it valuable to represent the equation as follows:

$$[\beta_* \quad \beta_{**}]\begin{bmatrix} \mathbf{y}_* \\ \mathbf{y}_{**} \end{bmatrix} + [\gamma_0 \quad \gamma_{00}]\begin{bmatrix} \mathbf{x}_0 \\ \mathbf{x}_{00} \end{bmatrix} = \mathbf{u}_i \tag{A9.11}$$

where $\mathbf{y}_* = $ a $G_* \times 1$ vector of observations on included endogenous variables

$\mathbf{y}_{**} = $ a $G_{**} \times 1$ vector of observations on excluded endogenous variables

$\boldsymbol{\beta}_* = $ a $1 \times G_*$ vector of nonzero coefficients

$\boldsymbol{\beta}_{**} = $ a $1 \times G_{**}$ vector of 0's

$\boldsymbol{\gamma}_0 = $ a $1 \times K_0$ vector of nonzero coefficients

$\boldsymbol{\gamma}_{00} = $ a $1 \times K_{00}$ vector of 0's

We have dropped the i subscript in order to simplify the notation. We may rewrite the first equation as

$$\boldsymbol{\beta}_*\mathbf{y}_* + \boldsymbol{\gamma}_0\mathbf{x}_0 = \mathbf{u} \qquad (A9.12)$$

by eliminating the terms with 0 coefficients. Using a similar notation, we may rewrite the reduced-form equation as follows:

$$[\mathbf{y}_* \quad \mathbf{y}_{**}] = \begin{bmatrix} \pi_{*,0} & \pi_{*,00} \\ \pi_{**,0} & \pi_{**,00} \end{bmatrix}[\mathbf{x}_0 \quad \mathbf{x}_{00}] + [\mathbf{v}_* \quad \mathbf{v}_{**}]$$

In the partitioned matrix of reduced-form coefficients the first subscript refers to the endogenous variables and the second to the predetermined variables:

$\pi_{*,0} = $ a $G_* \times K_0$ matrix

$\pi_{*,00} = $ a $G_* \times K_{00}$ matrix

$\pi_{**,0} = $ a $G_{**} \times K_0$ matrix

$\pi_{**,00} = $ a $G_{**} \times K_{00}$ matrix

$\mathbf{v}_* = $ a $G_* \times 1$ vector of the first G_* reduced-form disturbances

$\mathbf{v}_{**} = $ a $G_{**} \times 1$ vector of the remaining reduced-form disturbances

Now we are in a position to examine the conditions which are necessary and sufficient to identify the structural parameters. To do so, we rewrite Eq. (A9.9) as follows:

$$\mathbf{B}\pi = -\boldsymbol{\Gamma} \qquad (A9.13)$$

and then rewrite (A9.13) only in terms of the first equation of the simultaneous equation system:

$$[\boldsymbol{\beta}_* \quad \mathbf{0}]\begin{bmatrix} \pi_{*,0} & \pi_{*,00} \\ \pi_{**,0} & \pi_{**,00} \end{bmatrix} = -[\boldsymbol{\gamma}_0 \quad \mathbf{0}]$$

It is useful to divide the previous matrix equation into two separate sub-equations:

$$\boldsymbol{\beta}_* \pi_{*,0} = -\boldsymbol{\gamma}_0 \qquad (A9.14)$$

$$\boldsymbol{\beta}_* \pi_{*,00} = \mathbf{0} \qquad (A9.15)$$

We have previously normalized one of the β's in the first equation to be equal to 1. Then Eq. (A9.14) has $G_* - 1$ unknown β's and K_0 unknown γ's. Equation (A9.15) involves only the $G_* - 1$ unknown β's. We shall focus for the moment on the second equation, which consists of K_{00} individual equations. We know that a necessary condition for the existence of a solution to (A9.15) is that there are at least $G_* - 1$ equations. This leads directly to the *order condition* for identification:

$$K_{00} \geq G_* - 1 \qquad (A9.16)$$

where K_{00} = the number of excluded predetermined variables
G_* = the number of included endogenous variables

The order condition is not a sufficient condition for identification, because not all the K_{00} equations need be independent of each other. This suggests that a necessary and sufficient condition for identification will be one which guarantees that $G_* - 1$ of the K_{00} equations are in fact independent. This condition is often called the *rank condition* and may be stated as follows:[27]

$$\text{rank}\,[\pi_{*,\,00}] = G_* - 1 \qquad (A9.17)$$

Once the $G_* - 1$ unknown β's are determined from Eq. (A9.15), there is no difficulty in solving Eq. (A9.14) for the coefficients of the predetermined variables.

APPENDIX 9.2 / TWO-STAGE LEAST SQUARES IN MATRIX FORM

Recall from Appendix 9.1 that the determination of the unknown structural coefficients depends upon a solution to the equation

$$\boldsymbol{\beta}_* \, \pi_{*,\,00} = \mathbf{0} \qquad (A9.18)$$

Given that one β has been set equal to 1, we seek (directly) to obtain values for the remaining $G_* - 1$ unknown β's. Such a solution will exist if rank $[\pi_{*,\,00}] = G_* - 1$. If the rank condition is satisfied and $K_{00} = G_* - 1$, then the first equation is exactly identified. If $K_{00} > G_* - 1$, however, then the equation is overidentified. Overidentification occurs because there are more than $G_* - 1$ equations in (A9.18) from which we desire to find estimates of the $G_* - 1$ unknown β's. There are several ways to combine the set of equations to obtain the value of $\boldsymbol{\beta}_*$. In the overidentified case, two-stage least squares becomes an

---

[27] Since a detailed explanation of the rank condition necessitates a lengthy discussion of certain aspects of matrix algebra, we shall not pursue the matter further here.

appropriate estimation procedure. Two-stage least squares uses all the information available in the equation system (A9.18) to obtain unique structural parameter estimates.

We shall describe the application of 2SLS to the estimation of the first structural equation, which we presume to be overidentified. To do so, it is useful to alter the notation of Appendix 9.1, expressing the first equation as follows:

$$\mathbf{y}_1 = \mathbf{Y}_1\boldsymbol{\beta}_1 + \mathbf{X}_1\boldsymbol{\gamma}_1 + \mathbf{u}_1 \tag{A9.19}$$

where $\mathbf{y}_1$ = an $N \times 1$ vector of observations on the endogenous variable with a coefficient of 1 in the first equation

$\mathbf{Y}_1$ = an $N \times (G_* - 1)$ matrix of observations on the endogenous variables included in the first equation (on the right-hand side)

$\boldsymbol{\beta}_1$ = a $(G_* - 1) \times 1$ vector of coefficients for the included endogenous variables

$\mathbf{X}_1$ = an $N \times K_0$ matrix of observations on the included predetermined variables

$\boldsymbol{\gamma}_1$ = a $K_0 \times 1$ vector of predetermined variable coefficients

$\mathbf{u}_1$ = an $N \times 1$ vector of disturbances associated with the first equation

As we have described in the text, the application of ordinary least squares to Eq. (A9.19) will yield inconsistent parameter estimates due to the fact that $\mathbf{Y}_1$ and $\mathbf{u}_1$ are (asymptotically) correlated. 2SLS yields consistent estimates by purging $\mathbf{Y}_1$ of the component which is correlated with $\mathbf{u}_1$ and then rerunning the new regression using OLS.

In the first stage, each of the right-hand endogenous variables is regressed on the *entire* set of predetermined variables in the model. This is equivalent to estimating the reduced-form equations associated with the $G_* - 1$ right-hand endogenous variables. We might represent this as follows:

$$\mathbf{Y}_1 = \mathbf{X}_1\boldsymbol{\pi}_1 + \mathbf{X}_2\boldsymbol{\pi}_2 + \mathbf{V} \tag{A9.20}$$

or
$$\mathbf{Y}_1 = \mathbf{X}\boldsymbol{\pi} + \mathbf{V} \tag{A9.21}$$

where $\mathbf{X}_2$ = an $N \times K_{00}$ matrix of observations on the predetermined variables excluded from the first equation

$\boldsymbol{\pi}_1$ = a $K_0 \times (G_* - 1)$ matrix of reduced-form coefficients

$\boldsymbol{\pi}_2$ = a $K_{00} \times (G_* - 1)$ matrix of reduced-form coefficients

$\mathbf{V}$ = an $N \times (G_* - 1)$ matrix of reduced-form disturbances

The resulting first-stage estimator is

$$\hat{\boldsymbol{\pi}} = (\mathbf{X}'\mathbf{X})^{-1}\mathbf{X}'\mathbf{Y}_1 \tag{A9.22}$$

from which we calculate the fitted values for $\mathbf{Y}_1$:

$$\hat{\mathbf{Y}}_1 = \mathbf{X}\hat{\pi} \tag{A9.23}$$

In the second stage we perform an ordinary least-squares procedure of $\mathbf{Y}$ on $\hat{\mathbf{Y}}_1$ and $\mathbf{X}_1$. The estimated coefficients are the 2SLS parameter estimates of $\boldsymbol{\beta}_1$ and $\boldsymbol{\gamma}_1$. In terms of our matrix formulation, the second-stage estimators are as follows:

$$\begin{bmatrix} \hat{\boldsymbol{\beta}}_1 \\ \hat{\boldsymbol{\gamma}}_1 \end{bmatrix} = [(\hat{\mathbf{Y}}_1 \quad \mathbf{X}_1)'(\hat{\mathbf{Y}}_1 \quad \mathbf{X}_1)]^{-1}(\hat{\mathbf{Y}}_1 \quad \mathbf{X}_1)'\mathbf{y}_1 \tag{A9.24}$$

or

$$\begin{bmatrix} \hat{\boldsymbol{\beta}}_1 \\ \hat{\boldsymbol{\gamma}}_1 \end{bmatrix} = \begin{bmatrix} \hat{\mathbf{Y}}_1'\hat{\mathbf{Y}}_1 & \hat{\mathbf{Y}}_1'\mathbf{X}_1 \\ \mathbf{X}_1'\hat{\mathbf{Y}}_1 & \mathbf{X}_1'\mathbf{X}_1 \end{bmatrix}^{-1} \begin{bmatrix} \hat{\mathbf{Y}}_1'\mathbf{y}_1 \\ \mathbf{X}_1'\mathbf{y}_1 \end{bmatrix} \tag{A9.25}$$

We can rewrite the 2SLS estimators in a more useful form by taking into account the fact that the residuals of the first-stage regression are uncorrelated with all the predetermined variables, that is,

$$\hat{\mathbf{V}}'\mathbf{X} = \mathbf{0} = \mathbf{X}'\hat{\mathbf{V}} \tag{A9.26}$$

where $\mathbf{Y}_1 = \hat{\mathbf{Y}}_1 + \hat{\mathbf{V}}$

Also,

$$\hat{\mathbf{Y}}_1'\hat{\mathbf{V}} = \mathbf{0} \tag{A9.27}$$

since $\hat{\mathbf{Y}}_1$ is a linear combination of predetermined variables. Thus,

$$\mathbf{Y}_1'\mathbf{Y}_1 = (\hat{\mathbf{Y}}_1 + \hat{\mathbf{V}})'(\hat{\mathbf{Y}}_1 + \hat{\mathbf{V}})$$

$$= \hat{\mathbf{Y}}_1'\hat{\mathbf{Y}}_1 + \hat{\mathbf{V}}'\hat{\mathbf{V}}$$

Also

$$\mathbf{X}_1'\hat{\mathbf{Y}}_1 = \mathbf{X}_1'(\mathbf{Y}_1 - \hat{\mathbf{V}}) = \mathbf{X}_1'\mathbf{Y}_1$$

Therefore, we may rewrite Eq. (A9.25) in the following manner:

$$\begin{bmatrix} \hat{\boldsymbol{\beta}}_1 \\ \hat{\boldsymbol{\gamma}}_1 \end{bmatrix} = \begin{bmatrix} \mathbf{Y}_1'\mathbf{Y}_1 - \hat{\mathbf{V}}'\hat{\mathbf{V}} & \mathbf{Y}_1'\mathbf{X}_1 \\ \mathbf{X}_1'\mathbf{Y}_1 & \mathbf{X}_1'\mathbf{X}_1 \end{bmatrix}^{-1} \begin{bmatrix} (\mathbf{Y}_1 - \hat{\mathbf{V}})'\mathbf{y}_1 \\ \mathbf{X}_1'\mathbf{y}_1 \end{bmatrix} \tag{A9.28}$$

As a comparison to the 2SLS estimator, the reader might find it useful to examine the inconsistent estimators which would be obtained if ordinary least squares were applied to the structural equation directly. The estimators are

$$\begin{bmatrix} \hat{\boldsymbol{\beta}}_1{}^0 \\ \hat{\boldsymbol{\gamma}}_1{}^0 \end{bmatrix} = \begin{bmatrix} \mathbf{Y}_1'\mathbf{Y}_1 & \mathbf{Y}_1'\mathbf{X}_1 \\ \mathbf{X}_1'\mathbf{Y}_1 & \mathbf{X}_1'\mathbf{X}_1 \end{bmatrix}^{-1} \begin{bmatrix} \mathbf{Y}_1'\mathbf{y}_1 \\ \mathbf{X}_1'\mathbf{y}_1 \end{bmatrix} \tag{A9.29}$$

Incidentally, it is not difficult to show that 2SLS is an instrumental variables estimator, where the fitted values of the first stage and the included predetermined variables of the first stage are the appropriate instruments. To see this, we write the instrumental variables estimator as follows:

$$\begin{bmatrix} \hat{\beta}_1^* \\ \hat{\gamma}_1^* \end{bmatrix} = [(\hat{Y}_1 \quad X_1)'(Y_1 \quad X_1)]^{-1}(\hat{Y}_1 \quad X_1)'y_1$$

Expanding terms and simplifying, we find that

$$\begin{bmatrix} \hat{\beta}_1^* \\ \hat{\gamma}_1^* \end{bmatrix} = \begin{bmatrix} \hat{Y}_1'Y_1 & \hat{Y}_1'X_1 \\ X_1'\hat{Y}_1 & X_1'X_1 \end{bmatrix}^{-1} \begin{bmatrix} \hat{Y}_1'y_1 \\ X_1'y_1 \end{bmatrix}$$

$$= \begin{bmatrix} Y_1'Y_1 - \hat{V}'\hat{V} & Y_1'X_1 \\ X_1'Y_1 & X_1'X_1 \end{bmatrix}^{-1} \begin{bmatrix} \hat{Y}_1'y_1 \\ X_1'y_1 \end{bmatrix} = \begin{bmatrix} \hat{\beta}_1 \\ \hat{\gamma}_1 \end{bmatrix}$$

The consistency of 2SLS is too difficult to prove here, but it is important for statistical purposes to outline a derivation of the asymptotic variance-covariance matrix of the estimated parameters. To do so, we can utilize the formula for the asymptotic variance-covariance matrix of the instrumental variables estimator as described in the appendix to Chapter 5. In our notation the variance-covariance matrix is

$$\text{Var} \begin{bmatrix} \hat{\beta}_1 \\ \hat{\gamma}_1 \end{bmatrix} = \sigma^2[(\hat{Y}_1 \quad X_1)'(Y_1 \quad X_1)]^{-1}$$

$$\times [(\hat{Y}_1 \quad X_1)'(\hat{Y}_1 \quad X_1)][(Y_1 \quad X_1)'(\hat{Y}_1 \quad X_1)]^{-1}$$

But

$$Y_1'X_1 = (\hat{Y}_1 + \hat{V})'X_1 = \hat{Y}_1'X_1$$

Expanding the expression for $\text{Var} \begin{bmatrix} \hat{\beta}_1 \\ \hat{\gamma}_1 \end{bmatrix}$ using the previous result, we get the following:

$$\text{Var} \begin{bmatrix} \hat{\beta}_1 \\ \hat{\gamma}_1 \end{bmatrix} = \sigma^2[(\hat{Y}_1 \quad X_1)'(Y_1 \quad X_1)]^{-1}$$

$$= \sigma^2 \begin{bmatrix} Y_1'Y_1 - \hat{V}'\hat{V} & Y_1'X_1 \\ X_1'Y_1 & X_1'X_1 \end{bmatrix}^{-1} \tag{A9.30}$$

In practice, σ^2 is estimated by

$$s^2 = \frac{\hat{u}_1'\hat{u}_1}{N - [(G_* - 1) + K_0]}$$

where $\hat{u}_1 = y_1 - Y_1\hat{\beta}_1 - X_1\hat{\gamma}_1$

Notice that the residuals utilized to calculate s^2 do not come from the second-stage regression alone. Rather, they are calculated from the *original* structural equation with the estimated parameters replacing the true parameters. The variance-covariance matrix, on the other hand, does account for the second-stage use of fitted values for $\mathbf{Y}_1$, as seen by the fact that $\mathbf{Y}_1'\mathbf{Y}_1 - \hat{\mathbf{V}}'\hat{\mathbf{V}}(= \hat{\mathbf{Y}}_1'\hat{\mathbf{Y}}_1)$ appears in the matrix to be inverted (rather than $\mathbf{Y}_1'\mathbf{Y}_1$ alone).

APPENDIX 9.3 / ZELLNER ESTIMATION IN MATRIX FORM

As we described in the text, Zellner estimation is simply the application of generalized least-squares estimation to a group of seemingly unrelated equations. The equations are related through the nonzero covariances associated with error terms across different equations at a given point in time. We can generalize the seemingly unrelated model by writing the system of G equations as follows:

$$\mathbf{Y}_i = \mathbf{X}_i\boldsymbol{\beta}_i + \mathbf{u}_i \qquad i = 1, 2, \ldots, G \qquad \text{(A9.31)}$$

where $\mathbf{Y}_i =$ an $N \times 1$ vector
$\mathbf{X}_i =$ an $N \times K_i$ matrix
$\boldsymbol{\beta}_i =$ a $K_i \times 1$ vector
$\mathbf{u}_i =$ an $N \times 1$ vector

It will be useful to write the model in shorthand form as $\mathbf{Y} = \mathbf{X}\boldsymbol{\beta} + \mathbf{u}$, or

$$\begin{bmatrix} \mathbf{Y}_1 \\ \mathbf{Y}_2 \\ \vdots \\ \mathbf{Y}_G \end{bmatrix} = \begin{bmatrix} \mathbf{X}_1 & 0 & \cdots & 0 \\ 0 & \mathbf{X}_2 & \cdots & 0 \\ \multicolumn{4}{c}{\dotfill} \\ 0 & 0 & \cdots & \mathbf{X}_G \end{bmatrix} \begin{bmatrix} \boldsymbol{\beta}_1 \\ \boldsymbol{\beta}_2 \\ \vdots \\ \boldsymbol{\beta}_G \end{bmatrix} + \begin{bmatrix} \mathbf{u}_1 \\ \mathbf{u}_2 \\ \vdots \\ \mathbf{u}_G \end{bmatrix} \qquad \text{(A9.32)}$$

where $\mathbf{Y} =$ a $GN \times 1$ matrix

$\mathbf{X} =$ a $GN \times \left(\sum\limits_{i=1}^{G} K_i\right)$ matrix

$\boldsymbol{\beta} =$ a $\left(\sum\limits_{i=1}^{G} K_i\right) \times 1$ matrix

$\mathbf{u} =$ a $GN \times 1$ matrix

According to the assumptions of the seemingly unrelated model, there is no autocorrelation within equations, but there does exist cross-equation correlation, that is,

$$E(\mathbf{u}_i\mathbf{u}_j') = \begin{bmatrix} \sigma_{ij} & 0 & \cdots & 0 \\ 0 & \sigma_{ij} & \cdots & 0 \\ \multicolumn{4}{c}{\dotfill} \\ 0 & 0 & \cdots & \sigma_{ij} \end{bmatrix} = \sigma_{ij}\mathbf{I} \qquad \text{(A9.33)}$$

where $\mathbf{I} =$ a $G \times G$ identity matrix

This relationship applies to the covariances between two arbitrary equations in the system of G equations. To generalize this result in matrix form, we write

$$\Omega = E(\mathbf{uu'}) = \begin{bmatrix} E(\mathbf{u}_1\mathbf{u}_1') & E(\mathbf{u}_1\mathbf{u}_2') & \cdots & E(\mathbf{u}_1\mathbf{u}_G') \\ E(\mathbf{u}_2\mathbf{u}_1') & E(\mathbf{u}_2\mathbf{u}_2') & \cdots & E(\mathbf{u}_2\mathbf{u}_G') \\ \cdots\cdots\cdots\cdots\cdots\cdots\cdots\cdots\cdots \\ E(\mathbf{u}_G\mathbf{u}_1') & E(\mathbf{u}_G\mathbf{u}_2') & \cdots & E(\mathbf{u}_G\mathbf{u}_G') \end{bmatrix}$$

Substituting from (A9.33),

$$\Omega = \begin{bmatrix} \sigma_{11}\mathbf{I} & \sigma_{12}\mathbf{I} & \cdots & \sigma_{1G}\mathbf{I} \\ \sigma_{21}\mathbf{I} & \sigma_{22}\mathbf{I} & \cdots & \sigma_{2G}\mathbf{I} \\ \cdots\cdots\cdots\cdots\cdots\cdots\cdots \\ \sigma_{G1}\mathbf{I} & \sigma_{G2}\mathbf{I} & \cdots & \sigma_{GG}\mathbf{I} \end{bmatrix}$$

All information about error covariances is contained in the matrix Ω. The most efficient estimation of Eq. (A9.32) is obtained by applying generalized least-squares estimation to get

$$\hat{\boldsymbol{\beta}} = (\mathbf{X'\Omega^{-1}X})^{-1}(\mathbf{X'\Omega^{-1}Y}) \tag{A9.34}$$

with

$$E[(\hat{\boldsymbol{\beta}} - \boldsymbol{\beta})(\hat{\boldsymbol{\beta}} - \boldsymbol{\beta})'] = (\mathbf{X'\Omega^{-1}X})^{-1} \tag{A9.35}$$

In practice the elements of Ω must be estimated. This is accomplished with the use of the residuals which are obtained when ordinary least-squares estimation is applied to each of the G equations:

$$\hat{\sigma}_{ii} = \frac{\hat{\mathbf{u}}_i\hat{\mathbf{u}}_i'}{N - K_i}$$

$$\hat{\sigma}_{ij} = \frac{\hat{\mathbf{u}}_i\hat{\mathbf{u}}_j'}{\sqrt{(N - K_i)(N - K_j)}}$$

$$\hat{\mathbf{u}}_i = \mathbf{Y}_i - \mathbf{X}_i\hat{\boldsymbol{\beta}}_i$$

There are two important cases in which Zellner estimation is equivalent to the equation-by-equation application of ordinary least squares. The first case occurs when $\sigma_{ij} = 0$ for every i and j, $i \neq j$. Then Ω simplifies to

$$\Omega = \begin{bmatrix} \sigma_{11}\mathbf{I} & 0 & \cdots & 0 \\ 0 & \sigma_{22}\mathbf{I} & \cdots & 0 \\ \cdots\cdots\cdots\cdots\cdots\cdots\cdots \\ 0 & 0 & \cdots & \sigma_{GG}\mathbf{I} \end{bmatrix} \tag{A9.36}$$

The use of simple matrix algebra [substituting (A9.36) into (A9.35)] is sufficient to prove the stated result. A second, less obvious case occurs when $\mathbf{X}_i = \mathbf{X}$ for every $i = 1, 2, \ldots, G$ ($K_i = K$ is implicit). This occurs when the identical set of independent variables appears in each equation. Once again the proof involves a straightforward application of the techniques of matrix algebra.

APPENDIX 9.4 / MAXIMUM-LIKELIHOOD ESTIMATION OF EQUATION SYSTEMS

Limited-Information Maximum-Likelihood Estimation

Recall briefly that the material on errors in variables discussed in Chapter 5 mentioned a disturbing property of the 2SLS estimation process. Before describing problems of simultaneity, we found that it was important to distinguish between errors in the dependent variable (no problem) and errors in the right-hand variables (a serious problem). In fact, the choice of left- and right-hand variables was related to our basic assumptions about both variable and equation error. Now reconsider Eqs. (9.22) and (9.23). Despite the fact that the endogenous variables are correlated with u_1, they are treated in the same way as predetermined variables when the 2SLS procedure is used. Both variables are replaced using the first-stage process, of course, but the residual sum of squares to be minimized in the second stage is based on deviations from the left-hand variable. The arbitrariness of this procedure is brought about because of the implicit normalization associated with the choice of dependent variable (with a coefficient of 1) for each equation. To see the arbitrariness of this normalization, rewrite each of the two equations, by solving the first for y_2 and the second for y_1. The revised equations are as follows:

$$y_2 = \frac{1}{\alpha_2} y_1 - \frac{u_1}{\alpha_2} \tag{A9.37}$$

$$y_1 = \frac{1}{\beta_1} y_2 - \frac{\beta_3}{\beta_1} z_1 - \frac{\beta_4}{\beta_1} z_2 - \frac{u_2}{\beta_1} \tag{A9.38}$$

Once again the first equation (A9.37) is overidentified, so that we might attempt to estimate α_2 by using 2SLS. In the first stage we would regress y_1 on the predetermined reduced-form variables z_1 and z_2 and obtain fitted values $\hat{y}_1$. A regression of y_2 on $\hat{y}_1$ would allow us to estimate the unknown parameter α_2:

$$\tilde{\alpha}_2 = \frac{1}{\sum \hat{y}_1 y_2 / \sum \hat{y}_1 \hat{y}_1} \tag{A9.39}$$

A careful check shows that $\tilde{\alpha}_2$ and α_2^* will not yield the same parameter estimate. The difficulty is equivalent to that discussed in Chapter 1 when minimization using vertical deviations was seen to be different from minimization using horizontal deviations.

As a solution to this troubling problem it is natural to look for an estimation process which is invariant to the type of normalization made, i.e., to the choice of left-hand variables in each equation. While the derivation of this new limited-information estimator[28] is beyond the scope of this book, we shall attempt to motivate it to some extent by using our original example. Our desire to find a "neutral" estimation process involves the search for a technique which yields parameter estimates somewhere between the two versions of 2SLS just described.

To motivate best the derivation of the new limited-information estimator, consider the following two-equation model:

$$y_1 = \alpha_2 y_2 + \alpha_4 z_1 + u_1 \tag{A9.40}$$

$$y_2 = \beta_1 y_1 + \beta_5 z_2 + \beta_6 z_3 + u_2 \tag{A9.41}$$

Assume that we wish to estimate the first equation without making the normalization that the coefficient of y_1 is equal to 1. To do so, we rewrite the first (overidentified) equation, replacing y_1 as the endogenous variable with a weighted average of the two endogenous variables y_1 and y_2. The artificially constructed variable is

$$y^* = \gamma_1 y_1 + \gamma_2 y_2 \tag{A9.42}$$

and the first equation may now be written

$$y^* = \gamma_4 z_1 + u_1 \tag{A9.43}$$

If our estimation procedure is properly chosen, then y^* should be constructed so that Eq. (A9.43) fits the data as closely as possible. This objective is achieved by selecting γ_1 and γ_2 so that the coefficient γ_4 is significantly different from 0, while at the same time the deleted variables z_2 and z_3 add little or no explanatory power to the model. The only additional explanatory power which might exist will arise because the zero restrictions are only approximately satisfied in the particular sample being used.

If substantial explanatory power were added by the addition of z_2 and z_3 to Eq. (A9.43), then the restriction that allowed for the equation to be identified

---

[28] For an extensive discussion of this estimator see T. C. Koopmans and W. C. Hood, "The Estimation of Simultaneous Linear Economic Relationships," in Hood and Koopmans, *Studies in Econometric Method* (New York: Wiley, 1953), pp. 166–177. The authors prove that this estimation process is a limited-information maximum-likelihood estimator. It involves the use of a likelihood function relating to the observations on all endogenous variables included in the equation to be estimated.

would be incorrect. This suggests that we ought to choose y_1 and y_2 jointly to minimize the following ratio:[29]

$$\lambda = \frac{\text{residual variance after regressing } y^* \text{ on } z_1}{\text{residual variance after regressing } y^* \text{ on } z_1, z_2, \text{ and } z_3} \qquad \text{(A9.44)}$$

This ratio can never be less than unity, since the addition of any variable to a regression equation cannot increase the unexplained variance. If our model was correctly specified, we would expect λ to be close to 1 (but always greater than 1). This least-variance ratio technique (LVR) can be extended to apply to single-equation estimation in larger equation systems. The numerator becomes the residual variance associated with regressing the weighted endogenous variable y^* on all predetermined variables appearing in the equation, while the denominator becomes the residual variance associated with the regression of the weighted endogenous variable on all predetermined variables in the equation system. The solution values for the parameters will be good only up to scalar multiples,[30] so that a final normalization must be made. We usually achieve this by arbitrarily setting one of the parameters equal to 1. Note, however, that the normalization comes after the estimation procedure, not before, and is, therefore, quite distinct from the 2SLS normalization. Unlike 2SLS, least-variance ratio estimation has the property that parameter estimates are insensitive or invariant (up to scalar multiples) with respect to the choice of endogenous variable whose coefficient is to be set equal to 1.

The least-variance ratio estimator can be shown to be a maximum-likelihood estimator. As such, it is frequently referred to as the *limited-information maximum-likelihood* estimation process.[31] Least-variance ratio estimation can be applied to each identified equation in a model. It requires knowledge of the parametric form of the individual equation and knowledge of the list of all predetermined variables in the model system. It is a limited-information estimator, however, because it does not take into account any restrictions on the model which arise because equations other than the one to be estimated might be overidentified. As a practical matter, least-variance ratio estimation (or limited-information maximum-likelihood estimation) is not often utilized. The major reason is that LVR estimation is computationally much more difficult than 2SLS or IV estimation. In addition, researchers have found (using small-sample studies of limited-information estimators) that LVR is more sensitive to problems of multicollinearity than is 2SLS.

While the least-variance ratio estimator appears to be quite distinct from the

---

[29] Because the solution to this problem involves the use of eigenvalues and matrix algebra, we do not include it here. For a brief summary of this material see J. Johnston, *Econometric Methods*, 2d ed. (New York: McGraw-Hill, 1972), pp. 384–387.

[30] If a given set of parameter values is a solution to the estimation problem, then multiplying each parameter by an identical constant will yield another solution.

[31] See T. C. Koopmans and W. C. Hood, *op. cit.*, for a proof of this equivalence.

least-squares estimators described previously, there is, in reality, a close relationship. Recalling that in our earlier discussion of instrumental variables estimation, we found that 2SLS is an instrumental variables estimator with $\hat{y}_2$ the appropriately chosen instrument. (Ordinary least squares, on the other hand, involves the use of y_2 as an instrument.) It seems reasonable, therefore, to ask what would happen if we took a weighted average of the 2SLS and OLS instruments. This is achieved by defining a new variable y_2^* as follows:

$$y_2^* = (1 - k)y_2 + k\hat{y}_2$$

As a general rule, all instruments of this type will not yield consistent parameter estimators (recall that OLS is inconsistent). However, if k is chosen appropriately, consistent estimation is possible.[32] What is surprising about this new class of instruments is that the least-variance ratio estimator is a *k-class estimator*, for k chosen equal to λ.[33] When the equation to be estimated is exactly identified, then $\lambda = 1$ and LVR and 2SLS become equivalent. However, if the equation is overidentified, λ can be substantially greater than 1. Unfortunately, the larger the value of λ, the more unstable the parameter estimates are likely to be.

Full-Information Maximum-Likelihood Estimation

One of the difficulties with 3SLS arises because of the arbitrary nature of the normalization involved when 2SLS is used. This difficulty can be eliminated by an estimation procedure which is a generalization of the least-variance ratio, limited-information maximum-likelihood estimator described in the previous section. The new estimation process is alternately called a *full-information maximum-likelihood* (FIML) or a *least generalized residual variance* (LGRV) estimator. The former name applies because the estimation procedure arises as the solution to the application of the maximum-likelihood concept to the entire simultaneous equation system. The latter arises because the estimators can also be obtained by minimizing the determinant of the covariance matrix associated with the residuals of the reduced form of the equation system.[34] Because it is not frequently utilized and is quite complex both theoretically and computationally, we shall not pursue the full-information maximum-likelihood estimator further.[35]

---

[32] k must approach 1 in the probability limit.

[33] For a more thorough discussion of k-class estimators see A. Goldberger, *Econometric Theory* (New York: Wiley, 1964), pp. 341–344; or J. Kmenta, *Elements of Econometrics* (New York: Macmillan, 1972), pp. 565–571.

[34] See Goldberger, *op. cit.*, pp. 353–356, and Kmenta, *op. cit.*, pp. 578–581, for details.

[35] For further details see the references of the preceding footnote.

10

INTRODUCTION TO SIMULATION MODELS

In this and the next two chapters we discuss the construction of simultaneous equation simulation models and their use in analysis and forecasting. Our coverage is somewhat limited, as most of our examples will be *econometric* simulation models. These models have an economic orientation and are made up of equations which (except for accounting identities) are estimated using the standard econometric techniques described in Part One of this book. It is important to point out now, however, that the model-building techniques discussed in these chapters can also be applied to other types of models, including models of corporations[1] and models of social or political behavior.[2] Economists do not have a monopoly on simulation models; corporate planners, sociologists, political scientists, and others have been making increasing use of models as a framework for analysis and prediction.

---

[1] See, for example, J. W. Elliott, *Econometric Analysis for Management Decisions* (Homewood, Ill.: Irwin, 1973), Chap. 13, or B. E. Davis, G. J. Cacappolo, and M. A. Chaudry, "An Econometric Planning Model for American Telephone and Telegraph Company," *Bell Journal of Economics and Management Science*, vol. 4, no. 1, 1973. In Chapter 12 of this book we will present an example of a corporate financial planning model.

[2] See, for example, N. Choucri, M. Laird, and D. L. Meadows, "Resource Scarcity and Foreign Policy: A Simulation Model of International Conflict," *M.I.T. Center for International Studies Tech. Report* C/72-9, Mar. 1972, and R. D. Brunner and G. D. Brewer, *Organized Complexity* (New York: Free Press, 1971).

One of our goals is to give the reader some idea of how a simulation model is constructed, since (unfortunately) much more is involved than simply putting together several individually estimated single equations. We will see that when individual regression equations, which may fit the historical data very well, are combined to form a simultaneous equation model, simulation results may bear little resemblance to reality. The difficulty arises because the construction of a simulation model often involves understanding the dynamic structure of the system that results when individual equations are combined, and thus may not be a straightforward process.

In order to construct and use simulation models, one must be able to evaluate them and to compare alternative models of the same physical process. Thus, we will be concerned at an early stage with the question of evaluating and validating simultaneous equation simulation models. Model validation presents a less serious problem in the case of the single-equation regression, since one can look at a set of statistics such as the R^2 and t statistics to make a judgment about the goodness of fit of the equation. In a multiple-equation model each individual equation may have a very good statistical fit, but the model as a whole may do a very bad job in reproducing the historical data. The converse may also be true; the individual equations of a simulation model may have a very poor statistical fit, but the model when taken as a whole may reproduce the historical time series very closely. An important problem, then, is how to evaluate a simulation model properly.

Another objective is to compare the benefits of a simultaneous equation model with the costs of building one. If our goal, for example, is to forecast a short-term interest rate, we know that it will be easier to produce a forecast using a single-equation regression model than using a multiple-equation simulation model of the money market. The question is whether the added benefit (measured in terms of an improved forecast) of the simultaneous equation model outweighs the added cost involved in building it.

In this chapter we begin with a very elementary introduction to the simulation process. We then introduce the problem of evaluating simulation models and discuss some particular evaluation criteria. This discussion will be important for later developments, where we use these criteria routinely to evaluate alternative methods (and examples) of model construction. In the next section we discuss the problem of estimating a simultaneous equation model (a problem which was discussed in great detail in the last chapter) and we relate the estimation method used to the simulation performance of the resulting model. Finally, we close the chapter with a brief discussion of alternative (noneconometric) approaches to the construction of simulation models. For example, we discuss the problem of building models of processes for which little or no data are available. In such a case, hypothetical relationships which cannot be statistically fitted or tested must be utilized.

10.1 THE SIMULATION PROCESS

Simulation, as we will use the word, is simply the mathematical solution of a simultaneous set of difference equations.[3] A *simulation model* refers to that set of equations. As an example, consider the extremely simple macroeconomic model represented by Eqs. (10.1), (10.2), and (10.3) below (the error terms are suppressed):

$$C_t = a_1 + a_2 Y_{t-1} \tag{10.1}$$

$$I_t = b_1 + b_2(Y_{t-1} - Y_{t-2}) \tag{10.2}$$

$$Y_t = C_t + I_t + G_t \tag{10.3}$$

where C = consumption
$\quad I$ = investment
$\quad Y$ = gross national product
$\quad G$ = government spending

C, I, and Y are the *endogenous* variables, while G is an *exogenous* variable, i.e., determined from outside the model. This is the standard multiplier-accelerator model introduced in most elementary macroeconomics textbooks. Consumption is proportional to GNP (the multiplier), but investment is proportional to changes in GNP (the accelerator).

If values are given for the parameters a_1, a_2, b_1, and b_2, initial values are specified for the variables C and I, and a time path is given for the exogenous variable G, then the simultaneous solution of these three equations will give us time paths for each of the endogenous variables C, I, and Y. This is what is meant by the "simulation process." Given a model whose parameters have been estimated (or numerical values have been otherwise supplied), given initial values for the endogenous variables (i.e., "base year" values), and given time series for the exogenous variables (these may be historical series, or they may represent hypotheses about the future behavior of the series), the model is "solved" over some range of time to yield solutions for each of the endogenous variables.

The model above is rather simple, and can be solved analytically by substituting Eqs. (10.1) and (10.2) into Eq. (10.3) and rearranging:

$$Y_t - (a_2 + b_2)Y_{t-1} + b_2 Y_{t-2} = (a_1 + b_1) + G_t \tag{10.4}$$

The result is a second-order difference equation whose solution will depend on two initial conditions, as well as all future values of the exogenous variable G_t.[4] We will see in the next chapter that the solution may not be stable; i.e., it may

---

[3] A difference equation relates the current value of one variable to current and past values of other variables. Good examples of difference equations are given by the distributed lag models discussed in Chapter 7.

[4] For an introduction to difference equations and their solution, see W. J. Baumol, *Economic Dynamics* (New York: Macmillan, 1970).

GNP

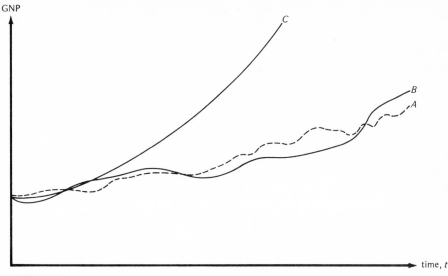

time, t

FIGURE 10.1
Stable and unstable solutions.

become increasingly large, or it may oscillate. In the case of a simple model, it is easy to determine the conditions that must hold for the parameters of the model for it to be stable, while in the case of a more complex model (which may be nonlinear), the conditions for stability may be difficult to ascertain.

Model stability is important because we believe the real world (or at least most of it) to be stable. If, for example, the GNP moved over the past 20 years according to dotted line A in Fig. 10.1, then we would expect a model which explained GNP to yield a solution which moved in the same characteristic way, perhaps as represented by solid line B. Solid line C would represent an unstable solution, since it diverges more and more rapidly from the range of actual values of GNP.[5] Other "nonrepresentative" modes of behavior are possible, such as the damped oscillations of solid line D in Fig. 10.2, and the explosive oscillations of line E in the same figure. Of course in some cases nonexplosive oscillations might be a desirable solution—if, for example, the model in question was being used to explain (or predict) business cycles for some commodity, and the frequency of the oscillations closely matched the frequency of the actual cycles.

Solution characteristics such as these are important and will be discussed in some detail in the next chapter. For now, however, we will limit ourselves to the problem of obtaining a solution (i.e., performing a simulation). If the parameters are known for the small model of Eqs. (10.1), (10.2), and (10.3), then the solution is simple and can be obtained analytically. For a larger and

---

[5] A more precise definition of stability will be given in the next chapter.

GNP

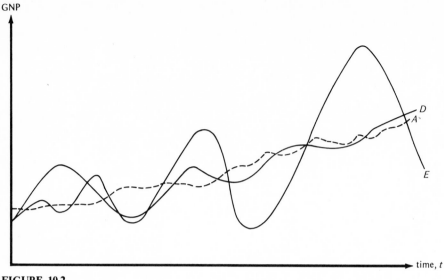

time, t

FIGURE 10.2
Oscillatory solutions.

perhaps nonlinear model, the simultaneous equations must be solved numerically (i.e., simulated) on a computer. Several computer programs exist that make the simulation of even a very large model quite easy, so that it is usually not necessary for an analyst to write a program of his/her own.[6] Most of these programs obtain solutions using an iterative procedure in which the nonlinear model is repeatedly linearized, perhaps renormalized, and then solved.[7]

Simulations of a model might be performed for a variety of reasons, including model testing and evaluation, historical policy analysis, and forecasting. Usually the *time horizon* over which the simulation is performed will depend on the objective of the simulation. To see this, we examine some of the different types of simulations that might be performed over different time horizons.

In Fig. 10.3, T_1 and T_2 represent the time bounds over which the equations of a hypothetical model are estimated (the estimation period). T_3 represents the time today. The first mode of simulation is called an *ex post*, or "historical," simulation. The simulation begins in year T_1 and runs forward until year T_2.

---

[6] Examples of more sophisticated simulation systems include the TROLL system, developed initially at M.I.T. and then at the National Bureau of Economic Research, and now used in many universities (see "TROLL—A User's Manual," NBER Computer Research Center, Cambridge, Mass.). Designed more for a commercial or applied environment is the XSIM system, developed by Dynamics Associates, Inc., Cambridge, Mass. (see "XSIM Manual," Dynamics Associates, Inc.).

[7] We will not attempt to describe or explain these numerical solution methods; rather, it is assumed that readers who want to construct and simulate their own models will have access to the appropriate computer programs. Those readers interested in mathematical solution techniques and algorithms are referred to T. H. Naylor (ed.), *The Design of Computer Simulation Experiments* (Durham, N.C.: Duke University Press, 1969).

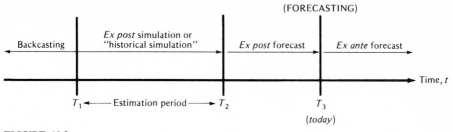

FIGURE 10.3
Simulation time horizons.

Historical values in year T_1 are supplied as initial conditions for the endogenous variables, and historical series beginning in T_1 and ending in T_2 are used for the exogenous variables. There is no "reinitialization" of the endogenous variables; after year T_1 values for the endogenous variables are determined by the simulation solution. By simulating the model during the period for which historical data for all variables are available, a comparison of the original data series with the simulated series for each endogenous variables can provide a useful test of the validity of the model. *Ex post* simulations can also be useful in policy analysis. By changing parameter values or letting exogenous policy variables follow different time paths, one can examine and compare what might have taken place as a result of alternative policies. One can use a macroeconometric model to examine, for example, the economic consequences that would have resulted from changes in the level of government spending, tax rates, or the money supply.[8] Similarly, industry-wide models can be used to study the effects of alternative government regulatory policies, or the impact of macroeconomic growth and fluctuations on the industry.[9]

Forecasting involves a simulation of the model forward in time beyond the estimation period. Of course, before a forecast can be made, one must have time series covering the entire forecast period for all the exogenous variables. In the simple macroeconomic model of Eqs. (10.1), (10.2), and (10.3), for example, one must first predict (or at least make some assumption about) future values of government spending G_t. Typically, an analyst will generate a set of alternative forecasts, each of which is conditional on one particular set of assumptions about the exogenous variables. In the case of the small macroeconomic model, for example, one might produce three sets of forecasts, the

---

[8] We will examine how a macroeconometric model can be used for policy analysis in Chapter 12. The reader is also referred to G. Fromm and P. Taubman, *Policy Simulations with an Econometric Model* (Washington: Brookings, 1968).

[9] We will provide an example of an industry-wide model in Chapter 12. Other examples can be found in T. Naylor, *Computer Simulation Experiments with Economic Systems* (New York: Wiley, 1971). For a detailed example of an application of an industry-wide econometric model to the analysis of government price regulatory policy, see P. W. MacAvoy and R. S. Pindyck, "Alternative Regulatory Policies for Dealing with the Natural Gas Shortage," *Bell Journal of Economics and Management Science,* Autumn 1973; and P. W. MacAvoy and R. S. Pindyck, *The Economics of the Natural Gas Shortage* (Amsterdam, North-Holland, 1975).

first based on the assumption that G_t grows at 3 percent per year, the second based on a 5 percent growth rate, and the third based on a 7 percent growth rate.

As we saw in Chapter 6, we can distinguish between two types of forecasts. If the estimation period did not extend to the current year (that is, T_2 is less than T_3), then one might want to begin the forecast at the end of the estimation period and extend it to the present, perhaps comparing the results with available data. This type of simulation is called an *ex post* forecast, and is often performed to test the forecasting accuracy of a model. On the other hand, a forecast made by beginning the simulation in the current year and extending it into the future is called an *ex ante* forecast.

It should be clear that forecasting is useful not only for predictive purposes, but also for policy analysis. Forecasts can be used to compare the effects of alternative policies, where policies are stated as movements in exogenous variables that are controllable (such as G_t in our examples), or as changes in the values of policy parameters (such as tax rates). We will examine in more detail in Chapter 12 how policy analyses of this sort can be performed.[10]

One last type of simulation, the "backcast" simulation, should also be mentioned. It is occasionally of interest to simulate a model *backward* in time beginning at the start of the estimation period. One reason for doing this would be to test a model's dynamic stability as it evolved backward in time instead of forward. Another reason might be to analyze hypotheses about events that took place just prior to the estimation period. Note that in a backcast one begins with initial conditions for all variables in period T_1 (see Fig. 10.3 again) and then, using specified values for the exogenous variables prior to period T_1, solves the model backward one period at a time. Since time runs forward in the real world, there is little reason to expect the model to reproduce the real world when it is simulated backward; for this reason backcasting is usually done only over a short time period. The word *backcasting* is often misused and confused with *ex post*, or historical, simulation. Occasionally books or articles describing simulation models will refer to an historical simulation as a "backcast." However, for purposes of clarity we will use the definition of backcasting given above.

10.2 EVALUATING SIMULATION MODELS

In constructing a simulation model, we are faced with the same difficulty that exists in constructing a single-equation regression model (or, as we will see in Part Three of this book, that exists in constructing a time-series model). The problem is how to evaluate or test the "goodness" of the model. We have seen that in the case of the single-equation regression model there exists a set of statistical tests (R^2, F test, t tests, etc.) that can be used to judge the significance

---

[10] The reader is also referred to the examples cited in footnotes 8 and 9.

(in a statistical sense) of the model and its individual estimated coefficients. Other statistics exist (e.g., the Durbin-Watson statistic) to test the underlying assumptions of the model. Even with these tests, however, the choice of whether to accept or reject a single-equation model, particularly in comparison with other single-equation models, is not a straightforward task. One must decide whether the structural specification of the model is reasonable, and whether the estimated coefficients make sense. The model's evaluation must also depend on the *purpose* for which the model was built. A model designed for forecasting purposes should have as small a standard error of forecast as possible, while a model designed to test a specific hypothesis or measure some elasticity should have high *t* statistics.

The same considerations apply to a multi-equation simulation model, except that the evaluation criteria become more complicated. The fact that there are several equations means that high statistical significance for some equations may have to be balanced against low statistical significance for other equations. Even more important, however, is the fact that the model as a whole will have a dynamic structure which is much richer than that of any one of the individual equations of which it is composed. Thus even if all the individual equations fit the data well and are statistically significant, we have no guarantee that the model as a whole, when simulated, will reproduce those same data series closely. Finally, it is possible that in an *ex post* (or historical) simulation some of the endogenous variables will "track" the original data series closely while others will not. Just as in the case of a single-equation model, the evaluation of the multi-equation model must depend on the purpose for which the model was built. Some models are built primarily for forecasting, while others are built primarily for descriptive purposes and hypothesis testing. As in the single-equation case, different criteria will apply depending on the model's purpose.

We shall examine criteria that can be used to evaluate multi-equation models, beginning with the individual equations of the model. Do the equations, on a one-by-one basis, fit the data well; i.e., are they statistically significant? This question can be answered by using the same criteria (statistical and otherwise) that were used in the construction and evaluation of single-equation regression models. As we saw in Part One of this book, judgments can be made regarding the theoretical "reasonableness" of each equation, as well as the statistical significance of the equation's coefficients and overall fit.

Even if a multi-equation estimation procedure was used to estimate all the model's coefficients, the statistical fit of each of the model's individual equations can be judged. Recall from Chapter 9 that Zellner and three-stage least-squares estimates increase the estimation efficiency by accounting for cross-equation error covariances. Each individual equation, however, will still have an associated set of standard errors and *t* statistics which can be used to evaluate statistical fit just as in the case of ordinary least squares or other single-equation estimation methods.

In examining the equation of a model, one typically finds that some of the equations fit the data very well while others do not. Thus a judgment must be made regarding the overall statistical "fit" of the multi-equation model. The model builder makes this judgment as the model is constructed. One might find, for example, that some of the model's equations are easy to fit, in the sense that there is little difficulty in specifying equation forms which fit the data well. Construction of other parts of the model might prove more difficult. In fact the estimated forms of some equations may not fit the data well even when several alternative specifications are tried. In practice, it may be necessary to use specifications for some of the equations in the model that are less desirable from a statistical point of view, but that improve the ability of the model to simulate "well" (according to criteria that we will discuss below). The model builder is thus forced to make some compromises, accepting some equations which do not have a particularly good statistical fit in order to build a complete structural model.

Another criterion that is used to evaluate a simulation model is the "fit" of the individual variables in a *simulation context*. One would expect the results of a historical simulation (i.e., a simulation through the estimation period) to match the behavior of the real world rather closely. One way to "test" the performance of the model is to perform an historical simulation and examine how closely each endogenous variable tracks its corresponding historical data series. It is therefore desirable to have some quantitative measure of how closely individual variables track their corresponding data series. The measure that is most often used is called the *RMS* (root-mean-square) *simulation error*. The RMS simulation error for the variable Y_t is defined as follows:

$$\text{RMS error} = \sqrt{\frac{1}{T} \sum_{t=1}^{T} (Y_t^s - Y_t^a)^2} \tag{10.5}$$

where Y_t^s = the simulated value of Y_t
$\qquad Y_t^a$ = the actual value
$\qquad T$ = the number of periods in the simulation

The RMS error is thus a measure of the deviation of the simulated variable from its actual time path. Of course, the magnitude of this error can be evaluated only by comparing it with the average size of the variable in question.

Other measures of simulation fit exist and are often used. One is the *RMS* (root-mean-square) *percent error*, which is defined as

$$\text{RMS percent error} = \sqrt{\frac{1}{T} \sum_{t=1}^{T} \left(\frac{Y_t^s - Y_t^a}{Y_t^a} \right)^2} \tag{10.6}$$

This is also a measure of the deviation of the simulated variable from its actual time path, but in percentage terms. Other measures are the *mean simulation error*, defined as

$$\text{Mean error} = \frac{1}{T} \sum_{t=1}^{T} (Y_t^s - Y_t^a) \tag{10.7}$$

FIGURE 10.4

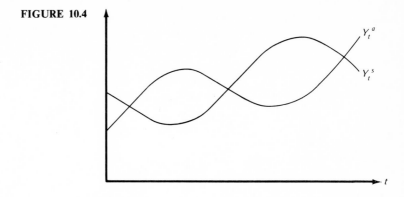

and the *mean percent error*, defined as

$$\text{Mean percent error} = \frac{1}{T} \sum_{t=1}^{T} \left(\frac{Y_t^s - Y_t^a}{Y_t^a} \right) \tag{10.8}$$

The problem with mean errors is that they may be close to 0 if large positive errors cancel out large negative errors. In Fig. 10.4, for example, the mean simulation error would probably be close to 0, while the RMS simulation error would be large. The RMS simulation error would be a better measure of the simulation performance.[11]

Note that it is entirely possible for an equation that has a very good statistical fit to have a very poor simulation fit. In an industry market model, for example, an equation which explains the market price of the good being sold (i.e., price is the dependent variable) may have a very good statistical fit (large R^2, small standard errors, etc.). At the same time, however, when the model as a whole is simulated, that same price variable might have a very poor simulation fit—i.e., it might have a very large RMS simulation error. Such an occurrence is not only possible, but likely, since the behavior of the model as a dynamic system may bear little relation to the way individual equations fit the historical data. It is for this reason that RMS simulation errors are an important criterion for evaluating a multi-equation model, while statistical considerations alone are insufficient.

It is also possible that the results of an historical simulation will show some endogenous variables to have a small RMS simulation error while others will have large errors. In this case model evaluation will involve a consideration of which variables are most critical as well as the *reasons* that large errors have occurred. Usually one can trace through the structure of the model in order to

---

[11] Mean *absolute* errors (and mean absolute percent errors) can also be calculated to avoid the problem of positive and negative errors canceling, but RMS errors are used more often in practice, since they penalize large individual errors more heavily. See Exercise 10.1.

FIGURE 10.5

find out why certain variables seem to diverge from their historical paths during the simulation. The simulation performance of the model can often be improved by substituting new equation forms, which may have poorer statistical fits but improve the dynamic structure of the model.

Low RMS simulation errors are only one desirable measure of simulation fit. Another important criterion is how well the model simulates *turning points* in the historical data. Consider Fig. 10.5, where dotted line *A* represents the historical time series for some endogenous variable *X*, and solid lines *B* and *C* represent the simulated values of that same variable using two different models. Based on that figure alone, one would probably pick the model that produced line *C* as the "better" model, since despite its larger RMS simulation error it duplicates the marked change in variable *X* that occurred historically. The model that produced line *B* failed to predict the *turning point*, i.e., the sudden change in the historical data. It did track the historical data closely during the rest of the simulation period, but any simple trend model could have done this without really explaining the underlying physical processes. Thus the ability of a simulation model to duplicate turning points or rapid changes in the actual data is an important criterion for model evaluation.

If the model has been designed for forecasting purposes, then the *ex post RMS forecast error* is another very important criterion for model performance. In an *ex post* forecast, the forecast results can be compared to recent data. The RMS forecast error, i.e., the RMS simulation error computed over the forecast range, provides a measure of the ability of the model to forecast well. Again it is possible in a multi-equation model for some endogenous variables to have large RMS forecast errors while others have very small errors. Unless the forecasting objective is centered on only one or two variables, all the RMS forecast errors must be evaluated together to judge the model as a whole.

It would be useful to have a measure of performance associated with an *ex ante* forecast for a multi-equation model. We saw in Chapter 6, for example, that for a single-equation regression model a standard error of forecast and a corresponding confidence interval could be computed. Unfortunately there is no simple way to calculate analytically confidence intervals for the forecast from a multi-equation model. This is due to the fact that forecast errors can be compounded in a complex way by the feedback structure of the model. One can, however, *experimentally* compute confidence intervals for the *ex ante* forecast through the process of *stochastic*, or *Monte Carlo*, simulation, as will be discussed in Chapter 11. Often *ex post* RMS forecast errors are used as criteria for forecast performance. However, one must remember that the *ex ante* errors are likely to be larger than the *ex post* errors.

Even if a model "tracked" well, i.e., had small RMS simulation and forecast errors for most or all of the endogenous variables, one would also want to investigate whether or not it responds to stimuli (e.g., large changes in exogenous variables or policy parameters) in a manner consistent with economic theory and with empirical observation. In the case of a macroeconometric model, for example, the simulation of a $1 billion increase in government expenditures should result in increases in GNP (over time) that at least roughly match both our theoretical expectations and recent observations of the relationship of these two variables. Thus the *dynamic response* of the model (which will be discussed in some detail on the next chapter) is another evaluation criterion.[12]

An additional criterion of model performance is the overall *sensitivity* of the model to such factors as the initial period in which the simulation is begun, minor changes in estimated coefficients, and small changes in the time paths of exogenous variables. If, for example, a model was estimated using data from 1955 to 1970, then one would expect the historical simulation to "fit" well whether it was begun in 1955 or in 1960. If the model truly represents the real world, then it should not matter very much in what year the simulation is begun. Thus alteration of the initial simulation period provides one test for model sensitivity. We would also expect that small changes in the model's coefficients (at least within one-half of the estimated standard error for the coefficient) should not affect the model's simulation performance very drastically. Another sensitivity test, then, is to simulate the model after making small changes in individual coefficients. A third sensitivity test is to alter the time paths for exogenous variables over the simulation period. Again, *small* changes in these time paths for exogenous variables should not affect the simulation performance drastically.

We have seen that there is a wide variety of criteria which can be (and are) used to evaluate the performance of a simulation model—but problems may

---

[12] This and other evaluation criteria are discussed in H. T. Shapiro, "Is Verification Possible? The Evaluation of Large Econometric Models," *American Journal of Agricultural Economics*, vol. 55, May 1973; and in L. R. Klein, *An Essay on the Theory of Economic Prediction* (Chicago: Markham, 1971).

arise in the use of these criteria.[13] What can one say if the RMS simulation errors are all very small but the model is very sensitive to the initial starting date in the simulation? What if the *ex post* RMS forecast errors are all small, but the model fails to reproduce turning points? Unfortunately, we can offer no formulas for what should be done in cases like these. Model building is very much an art, and part of that art is learning to trade off alternate criteria in different ways.

10.3   A SIMULATION EXAMPLE

As a simple example of a multi-equation simulation model we look at a small linear macroeconomic model, which is given by Eqs. (10.9), (10.10), (10.11), and (10.12). (The reader can check that all the equations are identified.)

$$C_t = 2.537 + .185Y_t + .714C_{t-1} \tag{10.9}$$
$$(1.90)\quad(5.95)\quad(13.8)$$

$$R^2 = .999 \qquad SER = 2.40 \qquad DW = 2.08$$

$$I_t = 5.020 + .392(Y_t - Y_{t-1}) + .1634Y_{t-1} - 3.856R_{t-4} \tag{10.10}$$
$$(2.69)\quad(4.25)\qquad\qquad(23.80)\qquad(-5.23)$$

$$R^2 = .980 \qquad SER = 4.22 \qquad DW = .62$$

$$R_t = -.072 + .0024Y_t + .011(Y_t - Y_{t-1}) - .189(M_t - M_{t-1})$$
$$(-.25)\quad(2.14)\quad\;\;(.74)\qquad\qquad(-2.30)$$

$$+ .347(R_{t-1} + R_{t-2}) \tag{10.11}$$
$$(6.24)$$

$$R^2 = .867 \qquad SER = .59 \qquad DW = .92$$

$$Y_t = C_t + I_t + G_t \tag{10.12}$$

---

[13] For examples of recent research in the development of other evaluation criteria for econometric models, see M. K. Evans, Y. Haitkovsky, and G. Treyz, "An Analysis of the Forecasting Properties of U.S. Econometric Models," and V. Zarnowitz, C. Boschan, and G. H. Moore, "Business Cycle Analysis of Econometric Model Simulations," both articles in B. Hickman (ed.), *Econometric Models of Cyclical Behavior* (New York: National Bureau of Economic Research, 1972). For a summary of the state of the art of model evaluation, see P. J. Dhrymes *et al.*, "Criteria for Evaluation of Econometric Models," *Annals of Economic and Social Measurement*, vol. 1, 1972, pp. 291–324.

where C = aggregate personal consumption
$\quad$ I = gross domestic investment
$\quad$ Y = GNP (net of exports and imports)
$\quad$ G = government spending
$\quad$ M = money stock
$\quad$ R = a short-term interest rate

C, Y, I, and G are all measured in billions of 1958 dollars, while R is in percent per year. The equations are estimated using quarterly time-series data from 1955 through the end of 1971. The t statistics (in parentheses below each estimated coefficient), the R^2, the standard error, and the Durbin-Watson statistic are shown for each equation.[14] The equations [with the exception of (10.12), which is an identity] were all estimated using ordinary least squares, a method which could be improved upon, as will be demonstrated in the next section.

Equation (10.9) for aggregate consumption consists of a multiplier with a Koyck lag distribution.[15] The investment equation contains both a multiplier and an accelerator, with investment also depending on the short-term interest rate R, with a long time delay. An equation is also estimated for this interest rate, which is positively related to the GNP and changes in the GNP, and negatively related to changes in the money stock. Finally, the model is completed with the addition of the GNP accounting identity in Eq. (10.12). The model thus consists of four endogenous variables and four equations, as well as two exogenous variables—the money stock and government expenditures.

Despite the simplicity of this model, its simulation performance is surprisingly good. To see this, we can examine an *ex post* (historical) simulation over the estimation period 1955-1 to 1971-4. In performing this simulation, the historical values are used for the two exogenous variables—government spending and the money supply. The results are shown graphically in Figs. 10.6 to 10.9, in which

---

[14] The reader should be aware of the fact that because Eqs. (10.9) and (10.11) contain lagged dependent variables, their Durbin-Watson statistics are biased toward 2, and thus provide no guarantee that there is no serial correlation. This point is discussed in Chapter 4.

[15] The use of the lagged dependent variable C_{t-1} in Eq. (10.9) is equivalent to a lag distribution of Y_t with geometrically declining weights. Consider the equation

$$C_t = a_0 + a_1 Y_t + a_1 \lambda Y_{t-1} + a_1 \lambda^2 Y_{t-2} + a_1 \lambda^3 Y_{t-3} + \cdots$$

where λ is a coefficient greater than 0 but less than 1. Now subtract from the left- and right-hand sides of this equation the equation

$$\lambda C_{t-1} = \lambda a_0 + a_1 \lambda Y_{t-1} + a_1 \lambda^2 Y_{t-2} + a_1 \lambda^3 Y_{t-3} + \cdots$$

The result is the equation

$$C_t = a_0(1 - \lambda) + a_1 Y_t + \lambda C_{t-1}$$

as in Eq. (10.9). This geometrically declining lag distribution is called a Koyck distribution, and is described in some detail in Chapter 7.

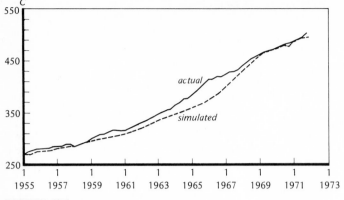

FIGURE 10.6
Historical simulation—consumption. Time bounds: 1955 first quarter to
1971 fourth quarter.

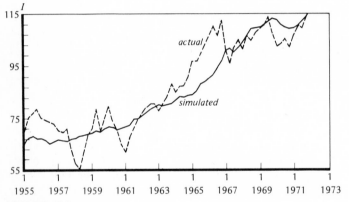

FIGURE 10.7
Historical simulation—investment. Time bounds: 1955 first quarter to
1971 fourth quarter.

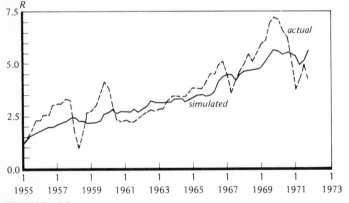

FIGURE 10.8
Historical simulation—interest rate. Time bounds: 1955 first quarter to
1971 fourth quarter.

FIGURE 10.9
Historical simulation—GNP. Time bounds: 1955 first quarter to 1971
fourth quarter.

the actual and simulated series for each endogenous variable are plotted on the
same set of axes.

Presumably one would use the results of this historical simulation to help
in evaluating the model. Looking at Figs. 10.6 to 10.9, we observe that the
simulated series do seem to reproduce the general long-run behavior of the actual
series, although short-run fluctuations in the actual series are not reproduced
well, and some turning points are missed altogether. We could also examine the
RMS and mean simulation errors and percent simulation errors for each variable,
which are shown in Table 10.1 along with the mean value of each variable.

The results are reasonable, given the simplistic nature of the model. Recall
also that the model was estimated using ordinary least squares. We will see in
the next section that the use of alternative estimation methods can result in an
improved simulation performance. In the meanwhile, however, we will illustrate
the use of this model for forecasting.

We begin with an *ex post* forecast, in which the model is simulated forward
starting at the end of the estimation period (1971–4) and continuing as long as
historical data are available (in this case 1973–2). The results of this simulation are
shown in Figs. 10.10 to 10.13. The results are also shown numerically for each
endogenous variable in Table 10.2.

TABLE 10.1
RESULTS OF HISTORICAL SIMULATION

	C	I	R	Y
Mean	369.8	87.3	3.72	574.0
RMS error	15.3	7.04	.776	24.0
RMS percent error	3.97%	8.26%	26.2%	4.12%
Mean error	− 11.3	− 1.95	− .284	− 16.9
Mean percent error	− 3.10%	− 1.92%	− 3.90%	− 3.04%

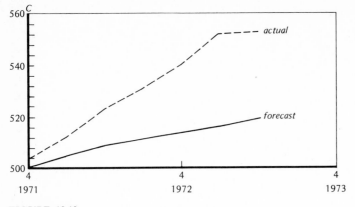

FIGURE 10.10
Ex post forecast—consumption. Time bounds: 1971 fourth quarter to
1973 second quarter.

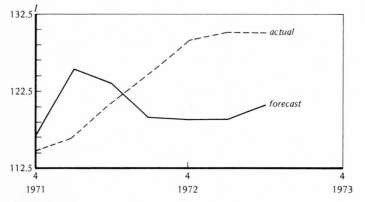

FIGURE 10.11
Ex post forecast—investment. Time bounds: 1971 fourth quarter to 1973
second quarter.

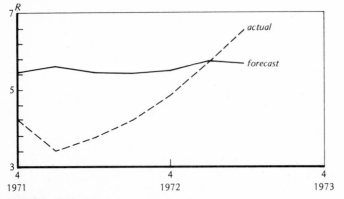

FIGURE 10.12
Ex post forecast—interest rate. Time bounds: 1971 fourth quarter to
1973 second quarter.

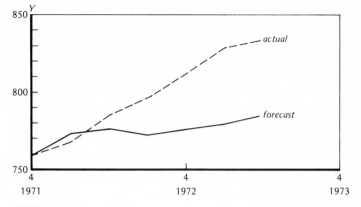

FIGURE 10.13
Ex post forecast—GNP. Time bounds: 1971 fourth quarter to 1973
second quarter.

TABLE 10.2
EX POST FORECAST RESULTS

		C—Consumption			
		Actual	**Forecast**	**Error**	**Percent error**
1971	4	504.1	500.81	−3.28	−.651
1972	1	512.5	505.28	−7.21	−1.408
1972	2	523.4	509.27	−14.12	−2.697
1972	3	531.	511.71	−19.28	−3.632
1972	4	540.5	514.21	−26.28	−4.863
1973	1	552.7	516.66	−36.03	−6.520
1973	2	553.3	519.40	−33.89	−6.126
Mean		531.1	511.1	−20.02	−3.7
RMS		531.4†	511.1†	23.22	4.25

		I—Investment			
		Actual	**Forecast**	**Error**	**Percent error**
1971	4	114.8	116.54	1.74	1.516
1972	1	116.5	125.44	8.94	7.674
1972	2	121.	123.63	2.63	2.176
1972	3	124.8	119.24	−5.55	−4.448
1972	4	129.1	118.97	−10.12	−7.844
1973	1	130.2	118.92	−11.27	−8.657
1973	2	130.2	120.72	−9.47	−7.278
Mean		123.8	120.5	−3.30	−2.41
RMS		123.9	120.5	7.93	6.27

TABLE 10.2
CONTINUED

		R—Interest rate			
		Actual	**Forecast**	**Error**	**Percent error**
1971	4	4.23	5.44	1.21	28.66
1972	1	3.43	5.60	2.16	63.11
1972	2	3.77	5.45	1.68	44.62
1972	3	4.22	5.43	1.21	28.68
1972	4	4.86	5.49	.63	13.00
1973	1	5.7	5.75	.05	1.03
1973	2	6.60	5.67	−.92	−14.04
Mean		4.69	5.55	.86	23.58
RMS		4.80	5.55	1.29	33.78

		Y—GNP			
		Actual	**Forecast**	**Error**	**Percent error**
1971	4	759.	758.9	−.04	−.00
1972	1	768.	773.4	5.42	.70
1972	2	785.6	776.9	−8.68	−1.10
1972	3	796.7	772.7	−23.94	−3.00
1972	4	812.3	776.6	−35.61	−4.38
1973	1	829.3	779.9	−49.30	−5.94
1973	2	834.3	785.3	−48.97	−5.87
Mean		797.9	774.9	−23.02	−2.80
RMS		798.3	774.9	31.11	3.78

† These are the root-mean-square values of the actual and forecasted series, for example,

$$\text{RMS (actual)} = \sqrt{\frac{1}{T} \sum_{t=1}^{T} C_t^2}$$

Note that the RMS errors and RMS percent errors for the *ex post* forecast are for the most part larger than those for the historical simulation. This is not surprising, since in the *ex post* forecast the model is being extrapolated outside the period over which its coefficients were estimated. In Fig. 10.10, for example, the forecasted series for consumption fails to predict the upturn in consumer spending that actually occurred in 1972 and the first quarter of 1973. One reason for this might have been an increase in the actual propensity to consume, which the model, with its constant coefficients, could not have accounted for.[16]

---

[16] The forecasts for the interest rate and gross investment also contain sizable errors, with the interest rate failing to reproduce the sharp upturn that actually occurred in 1972 and early 1973, and forecasted investment decreasing while actual investment increased. The reader can investigate the reasons for this (see Exercise 10.3). One would not expect to be able to predict macroeconomic behavior in any detail with a four-equation model; we present it only as an example of how a simulation is performed and how the results can be analyzed.

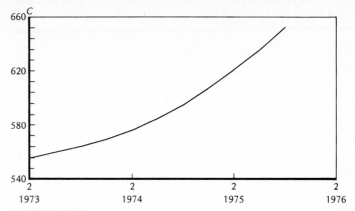

FIGURE 10.14
Ex ante forecast—consumption. Time bounds: 1973 second quarter to 1975 fourth quarter.

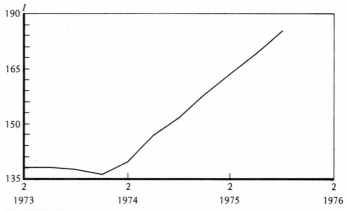

FIGURE 10.15
Ex ante forecast—investment. Time bounds: 1973 second quarter to 1975 fourth quarter.

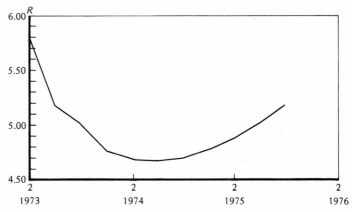

FIGURE 10.16
Ex ante forecast—interest rate. Time bounds: 1973 second quarter to 1975 fourth quarter.

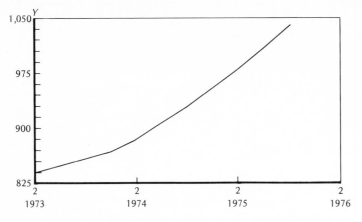

FIGURE 10.17
Ex ante forecast—GNP. Time bounds: 1973 second quarter to 1975
fourth quarter.

We will take the example one step further and use the model to produce an *ex ante* forecast. We begin the simulation in the second quarter of 1973 (using the actual data as initial values for the endogenous variables), and continue the simulation through the fourth quarter of 1975. Before this simulation can be performed, however, some forecast or assumption must be made regarding the exogenous variables G_t and M_t. We will assume that G_t and M_t will grow at an annual rate of 4 percent from their actual values in the second quarter of 1973 (this is close to their average historical growth rates). The simulation can now be performed, with the results dependent on this assumption about G_t and M_t.

The results of this *ex ante* forecast are shown in Figs. 10.14 to 10.17. Even though the *ex ante* forecast is not compared with actual data, some judgment can be made regarding "reasonableness." The *ex ante* forecasts for consumption and GNP predict a growth rate after the second quarter of 1974 of about 10 percent, which is probably too high to be reasonable. Rapid forecasted investment growth during this period (in response to falling forecasted interest rates earlier) may be part of the reason for this, but in any case these forecasts invite skepticism.

10.4   MODEL ESTIMATION

In this section we demonstrate how alternative estimation methods can affect the simulation performance of a model. The model given by Eqs. (10.9) to (10.12) was estimated using ordinary least squares, which can result in inconsistent and biased estimates of the coefficients. It is interesting to see how the choice of estimation method affects the performance of the model when simulated as a whole. To see this we estimate the model using two-stage least squares (2SLS).

The 2SLS estimates are shown in Eqs. (10.13) to (10.15) below:

$$C_t = .940 + .125Y_t + .814C_{t-1} \tag{10.13}$$
$$ (.54) \quad (2.86) \quad (11.15)$$

$$R^2 = .999 \qquad SER = 2.82 \qquad DW = 2.23$$

$$I_t = 4.964 + .341(Y_t - Y_{t-1}) + .164Y_{t-1} - 3.948R_{t-4} \tag{10.14}$$
$$ (2.44) \quad (3.86) (22.13) (-4.83)$$

$$R^2 = .976 \qquad SER = 4.62 \qquad DW = .94$$

$$R_t = -.057 + .016Y_t + .041(Y_t - Y_{t-1}) - .265(M_t - M_{t-1}) + .384(R_{t-1} + R_{t-2})$$
$$ (-.22) \quad (1.71) \quad (3.39) (-3.34) (4.48)$$
$$\tag{10.15}$$

$$R^2 = .886 \qquad SER = .55 \qquad DW = .93$$

Presumably the use of 2SLS will reduce the possibility of inconsistency introduced by the model's simultaneity. The equations look reasonable, except that two of them, (10.14) and (10.15), have rather low Durbin-Watson statistics, indicating likely serial correlation in the error terms. If these equations could be reestimated using an autoregressive transformation to correct for this serial correlation, more efficient estimates would be obtained. Using the Hildreth-Lu method[17] to reestimate the equations gives the results shown in Eqs. (10.16) to (10.18) below.[18] The value of ρ used in the autoregressive correction is shown with each equation.

$$C_t = .940 + .125Y_t + .814C_{t-1} \tag{10.16}$$
$$ (.54) \quad (2.86) \quad (11.15)$$

$$R^2 = .999 \qquad SER = 2.82 \qquad DW = 2.23 \qquad \rho = 0$$

$$I_t = 5.239 + .207(Y_t - Y_{t-1}) + .161Y_{t-1} - 3.247R_{t-4} \tag{10.17}$$
$$ (1.33) \quad (3.19) (17.07) (-3.15)$$

$$R^2 = .984 \qquad SER = 3.81 \qquad DW = 2.01 \qquad \rho = .6$$

---

[17] The Hildreth-Lu technique is described in Chapter 4.

[18] Combining 2SLS with an autoregressive correction as we have done actually may yield inconsistent estimates. A method for obtaining consistent estimates using these two methods together has been derived by Fair (R. Fair, "The Estimation of Simultaneous Equation Models with Lagged Endogenous Variables and First Order Serially Correlated Errors," *Econometrica*, May 1970), but was not computationally available. In any case, it was felt here that the benefit from more efficient estimates outweighed the probably small error introduced by combining the techniques. An alternative estimation method is used to construct a larger macroeconomic model in Chapter 12.

$$R_t = .433 + .004Y_t + .020(Y_t - Y_{t-1}) - .194(M_t - M_{t-1})$$
$$(.49) \quad (2.77) \quad (2.52) \quad\quad\quad (-2.96)$$

$$+ .144(R_{t-1} + R_{t-2}) \tag{10.18}$$
$$(2.06)$$

$$R^2 = .926 \quad\quad \text{SER} = .43 \quad\quad \text{DW} = 1.50 \quad\quad \rho = .8$$

We now have three versions of this model, the first estimated by ordinary least squares, the second by two-stage least squares, and the third combining two-stage least squares with an autoregressive correction. Each of these models was simulated from the first quarter of 1961 to the last quarter of 1971, and the RMS simulation error and RMS percent error were computed for each endogenous variable. The results are shown in Table 10.3.

Note that the simulation of the two-stage least-squares version of the model yields smaller RMS simulation errors than the ordinary least-squares version for every variable except the interest rate. Version 3, which contains the autoregressive correction for serial correlation in the error terms, does even better, with the RMS errors for investment and the interest rate less than one-third of what they were before.[19] The reason that the autoregressive corrections improve the performance of the model is that they add information to it. Even though we

TABLE 10.3
SUMMARY SIMULATION STATISTICS

	Root-mean-square errors		
	Version 1 OLS	Version 2 2SLS	Version 3 autoregressive
Gross national product Y	16.44	12.43	8.15
Consumption C	10.03	6.86	6.22
Investment I	7.22	6.62	2.29
Interest rate R	.86	.88	.27
	Root-mean-square percent errors		
Gross national product	2.16	1.70	1.12
Consumption	2.06	1.50	1.35
Investment	6.49	6.00	1.96
Interest rate	17.67	19.03	5.43

[19] The reason that the RMS error for consumption does not decrease as dramatically is that the estimated value for ρ in that equation was 0, so that in effect there was no autoregressive correction in the consumption equation.

may not know why the additive error terms behave the way they do, we can observe that they are serially correlated, and include that information in the model.

In Part Three of this book we will discuss time-series models, i.e., models which describe and predict the behavior of random processes. The autoregressive correction that we employed to estimate the third version of our small model makes the implicit assumption that the additive error terms are of the form

$$\varepsilon_t = \rho \varepsilon_{t-1} + \varepsilon_t^* \tag{10.19}$$

where ε_t^* is the uncorrelated part of ε_t. Equation (10.19) is actually a simple time-series model for ε_t (a first-order autoregressive model, to be exact). By combining this model with the structural relationships of each equation, the predictive performance of the model as a whole can be improved. In fact a more complicated time-series model than that of Eq. (10.19) can be used to "explain" the behavior of the additive error term, and we will see in Chapter 17 of this book that the result can be an even greater improvement in model performance.

The important point for the time being, however, is that the ability of a model to simulate and forecast well can depend on the particular method used to estimate the model's coefficients. We have examined only two alternatives to ordinary least squares, but a variety of other estimation methods are available. R. Fair recently made a comparison of 10 alternative estimation methods.[20] Each method was used to estimate the seven behavioral equations of a macro-economic forecasting model that had been previously developed.[21] Historical simulations were then performed for each of the 10 resulting versions of the model, and the RMS simulation errors for each endogenous variable compared. Nine of the estimation methods used were[22]

1 Ordinary least squares (OLS)
2 Two-stage least squares (2SLS)
3 OLS plus first-order autoregressive correction (OLSAUTO1)
4 2SLS plus first-order autoregressive correction (2SLSAUTO1)
5 OLS plus second-order autoregressive correction (OLSAUTO2)
6 2SLS plus second-order autoregressive correction (2SLSAUTO2)
7 Full-information maximum likelihood (FIML)
8 FIML plus first-order autoregressive correction (FIMLAUTO1)
9 FIML plus second-order autoregressive correction (FIMLAUTO2)

---

[20] See R. Fair, "A Comparison of Alternative Estimators of Macroeconomic Models," *International Economic Review*, vol. 14, no. 2, pp. 261–277, June 1973.

[21] The model is described in detail in R. Fair, *A Short-Run Forecasting Model of the United States Economy* (Lexington, Mass.: Heath, 1971).

[22] The tenth method was an experimental procedure that accounts for the dynamic structure of the equations on a one-by-one basis. This method has rarely been used in practice, and so we will not describe it here.

The RMS simulation errors are shown below for one variable, GNP, for the entire sample period (42 observations) and for a four-quarter forecast:

	Entire period	Four quarters
1 OLS	8.45	7.51
2 2SLS	8.07	7.21
3 OLSAUTO1	8.61	6.44
4 2SLSAUTO1	8.27	6.42
5 OLSAUTO2	8.40	6.14
6 2SLSAUTO2	7.78	5.90
7 FIML	7.38	5.34
8 FIMLAUTO1	6.55	4.79
9 FIMLAUTO2	6.99	4.95

Note that it is with the four-quarter forecast that the estimation method used is most critical, with the range of RMS errors extending from 7.51 (OLS) to 4.79 (FIMLAUTO1). Since most forecasting is done over the short term, the results for the first four quarters are presented separately from those for the entire sample period. In both cases, however, the use of FIMLAUTO1 seems to yield the best result. This method accounts for correlations between error terms across equations as well as first-order serial correlation in the individual error terms, and the gain that results in its use seems quite large. The results, however, do not prove one method to be better than any other; they simply demonstrate the use of the alternative methods on one particular model. In general, the model builder must experiment with alternative estimation methods on each and every model being developed.

10.5 OTHER KINDS OF MULTI-EQUATION SIMULATION MODELS

Our discussion of multi-equation simulation models has focused largely on econometric models, i.e., models constructed from sets of equations that were estimated using standard econometric techniques. One of the criteria that we used to judge or evaluate a simulation model, for example, was the degree of statistical fit of the model's individual equations. We said that if the model contained several equations that did not fit the data well or were otherwise statistically insignificant, then we might question the validity of the model as a whole. Thus, the reader may have been led to believe that econometric estimation is essential to the construction of a simulation model. In fact there exist other approaches to modeling, and there are other applications of multi-equation simulation models besides micro- and macroeconomic forecasting and policy analysis.[23]

A simulation model need not contain equations that are estimated by fitting them to data. One of the newest and most important applications of multi-equation simulation is in corporate financial planning. A financial simulation model can be thought of as an econometric model in which the equations describe the financial accounting structure of a particular corporation. Since all the equations are accounting relationships (as opposed to behavioral relationships), the model consists of a set of identities, and there is no estimation involved in its construction. Financial simulation models can be extremely useful for forecasting and analyzing the impact of alternative financial strategies on a company's development. By simulating such a model into the future using different assumptions about capitalization, debt, future revenue streams, etc., one can generate *pro forma* balance sheets and income statements that can provide a useful input to corporate planning. We will present an example of a financial simulation model and demonstrate its use in Chapter 12.[24]

There may be other situations in which a simulation model is constructed without the use of econometric estimation. Suppose that one wanted to construct a model to be simulated over a very long time horizon, perhaps 100 years. Such a model might be used to explain long-run economic growth; changes in population and fertility rates; or some other economic, social, or political process which evolves slowly over a long period of time. It is very possible that data would not exist for many of the variables in such a model. One reason for this might be that some of the variables are unobservable and thus unmeasurable; an example would be some "attitudinal" parameters in a sociological model. On the other hand, the variable may be observable, but perhaps data have never been collected for it. This is often the case in less-developed countries and presents a problem to the economist constructing a planning model for economic development policy. Finally, even if data were available, they might span only a short time period, say 10 or 20 years. Even if the data were used to estimate the coefficients of the model, the resulting estimates might have limited meaning when the model was simulated over a 100-year period.

In this situation the model builder could begin by specifying a set of hypothetical relationships. In the case of an econometric model, those relationships would be estimated and tested by fitting them to available data. If data were not available (or the model builder chose not to use available data), then it would be necessary to "specify" values for the coefficients based either on "intuition" or else on estimates produced by examining averages, sporadic data points, or perhaps just the opinion of "experts." As far as the testing of the individual relationships is concerned, all one can really do in this case is to simulate the

---

[23] For an overview of simulation techniques as they apply to economic problems, see T. Naylor, *Computer Simulation Experiments with Economic Systems* (New York: Wiley, 1971).

[24] For another example of a financial simulation model, see J. M. Warren and J. P. Shelton, "A Simultaneous Equation Approach to Financial Planning," *Journal of Finance*, Dec. 1971.

model as a whole and assess its performance over some limited time period for which data are available.

One of the problems with this modeling technique is that it provides no safety check on the reasonableness of the individual relationships that make up the model. Anyone who has constructed an econometric model knows that many hypothetical relationships must be tested against data before one is found that is statistically acceptable. This provides an important check on the model builder, forcing him/her to test statistically each of the relationships originally specified. This check is missing in the "data-less" approach to modeling, and it is thus important that that approach be used only with great caution.[25]

Simulation models have over the past few years found acceptance and application in a wide variety of social science disciplines. Sociologists and political scientists, finding them a natural vehicle for the representation, analysis, and forecasting of complex social phenomena, have been applying them to a variety of problems. Sociological and political simulation models have been constructed by combining econometric estimation methods with the "data-less" techniques described above. In fact, some of these modeling efforts have resulted in methodological advances for dealing with situations when data are limited or unreliable. Although the perspective of this book is largely limited to econometric models of the economy, individual markets, and individual firms, the reader should be aware that the applicability of the techniques that we are presenting is quite broad.[26]

Exercises

10.1 The RMS simulation error penalizes heavily for large individual errors. In what cases is it a more, or less, desirable performance criterion than the mean absolute error (MAE), defined as

$$\text{MAE} = \frac{1}{T} \sum_{t=1}^{T} \frac{|Y_t^s - Y_t^a|}{Y_t^a}$$

---

[25] One of the more prominent proponents of the "data-less" approach to modeling has been J. W. Forrester, who has constructed models of, among other things, the dynamics of urban growth and world resource use. While Forrester's work has been criticized because many of the relationships used in his models have not been substantiated or validated, he has at least shown that certain problems could be approached from a simulation context. See J. W. Forrester, *Urban Dynamics* (Cambridge, Mass.: M.I.T., 1969); J. W. Forrester, *World Dynamics* (Wright-Allen, 1971); D. Meadows *et al.*, *The Limits to Growth* (Wright-Allen, 1972); and W. D. Nordhaus, "World Dynamics: Measurement without Data," *Economic Journal*, December 1974.

[26] For examples of some of the more interesting applications of multi-equation simulation models to sociology and political science, see R. D. Brunner and G. D. Brewer, *Organized Complexity* (New York: Free Press, 1971); G. D. Brewer, *Politicians, Bureaucrats, and the Consultant: a Critique of Urban Problem Solving* (New York: Basic Books, 1973); J. M. Dutton and W. H. Starbuck, *Computer Simulation of Human Behavior* (New York: Wiley, 1971); and J. P. Crecine, "A Computer Simulation Model of Municipal Budgeting," *Management Science*, vol. 13, pp. 786–815, July 1967. This last model, which describes the process by which mayors make their budgeting decisions, consists of a set of logical "rules of thumb," and is not unlike the financial simulation models described above.

10.2 The mean error may be small even though the RMS error is large, if positive and negative errors cancel. In what situation does the mean error provide useful information for evaluating a model not provided by the RMS error?

10.3 Reexamine the historical simulation of the four-equation macroeconometric model in Figs. 10.6 to 10.9. Based on this historical simulation (and the model itself), explain why the *ex post* forecast (Figs. 10.10 to 10.13) underpredicts GNP.

10.4* Specify, estimate, and simulate your own macroeconometric model. [Equations (10.9) to (10.12) could be used as a starting point.] Produce *ex post* and *ex ante* forecasts, and evaluate these forecasts. If possible, experiment with alternative estimation techniques. Attempt to improve upon the performance of the four-equation model in the text. (The experience gained in this kind of exercise is invaluable for learning the art of model building.)

---

* This exercise applies to students who have access to an econometric computer facility.

11

DYNAMIC BEHAVIOR OF SIMULATION MODELS

We saw in the last chapter that a multi-equation simulation model provides a representation of the real world that is considerably richer than that of a single-equation regression model. Because variables can interact with each other across equations and through time, a multi-equation model can describe and explain the dynamic behavior of the world in a much more complete way than can a single-equation model. Because the multi-equation model is constructed to represent the dynamic behavior of the real world, its own time-dynamic behavior is of central concern in both its construction and its use. It is the time-dynamic behavior of multi-equation simulation models that is the focus of this chapter.

Since a simulation model is a set of difference equations that can be solved simultaneously through time, we are interested in the properties of difference equation solutions. We want to know, for example, what makes the solution to a difference equation (or set of difference equations) oscillate, since oscillatory behavior would be important in a model designed to explain (or forecast) cyclical market phenomena. We begin, then, by reviewing difference equations and their solutions.

Simulation models are often used to study and compare the short-run and the long-run responses of one variable (or set of variables) to another variable. The second section of this chapter deals with the notion of *dynamic multipliers* and dynamic response. We may know, for example, that a change in price may result in a change in demand for some good—but how long does it take for that change in demand to occur? We know that an increase in government spending results in an increase in GNP with a "multiplier" effect—but the size of that multiplier depends on how much time elapses after the level of government spending is increased. By discussing dynamic multipliers, we will see how simulation models can be used as a tool for analyzing the dynamic response of one set of economic variables to changes in other variables.

In the third section of the chapter we describe how a simulation model can be modified or adjusted to improve its performance, i.e., to improve its forecasting ability or its ability to provide information regarding policy alternatives. As we will see, misspecification or biased estimation in one part of a model may cause the whole model to perform poorly in a simulation context. These problems can sometimes be reduced or eliminated by modifying the structure of the model slightly.

The chapter closes with an introductory discussion of *stochastic simulation*. Since the equations of an econometric model are estimated by fitting them to data, the resulting parameter estimates are themselves random variables. Furthermore, each equation has an implicit additive error term associated with it. Stochastic simulation allows us to recognize explicitly this random character of the model—as well as the simulation and forecast errors that it implies. When a model is used for policy analysis, the results are subject to some margin of error. Stochastic simulation allows one to get a better quantitative grasp of what this margin of error is, and to estimate its magnitude. Stochastic simulation is similarly useful when a model is used for forecasting, as it allows one to obtain confidence intervals for the forecast.

11.1 MODEL BEHAVIOR—STABILITY AND OSCILLATIONS

The structural richness of a multi-equation simulation model makes it somewhat more difficult to build, analyze, evaluate, and use. Life is relatively simple in a single-equation world—a regression equation can easily be evaluated based on its statistical fit, and directly used to produce a forecast. As we saw in the last chapter, however, things may not be so simple in the case of a simulation model. Each of the regression equations that make up the model may have an excellent statistical fit, but when they are put together and simulated, the results may be meaningless. The reason for this may be that a *structural instability* was built into the model that is unrepresentative of the real world. Such an instability may not appear in any single equation, but could result when the equations of the model are combined and solved simultaneously. Of course a single-equation model can be simulated by itself, and it too may (or may not) be structurally unstable. A single-equation model can in fact have a rather complicated dynamic structure (e.g., long and complicated distributed lags), but it is more crucial that one be concerned about questions of stability when dealing with multi-equation models.

In this section we present the conditions for determining stability (and oscillations) in simple linear simulation models. In particular, we show how these conditions depend not only on the structure of the model (i.e., the particular causal relationships that have been specified), but also on the estimated values of the coefficients of the individual equations. We discuss nonlinear models only briefly, since there is little in the way of analytical tools available for analyzing their dynamic properties. Some discussion is necessary, however, since many econometric models are nonlinear.

11.1.1   Linear Models[1]

We say that a model is *linear* if all the difference equations that constitute it are linear. Sets of linear difference equations can usually be solved rather easily, and the determination of whether or not the system is stable is relatively straightforward. We will begin by demonstrating how one can analyze a linear model to determine whether or not it is stable and/or oscillatory. We will illustrate the method using as an example the simple three-equation multiplier-accelerator model presented at the beginning of the last chapter:

$$C_t = a_1 + a_2\, Y_{t-1} \tag{11.1}$$

$$I_t = b_1 + b_2(Y_{t-1} - Y_{t-2}) \tag{11.2}$$

$$Y_t = C_t + I_t + G_t \tag{11.3}$$

where C = consumption
  I = investment
  G = government spending (exogenous)
  Y = GNP

The analysis of this linear model begins by combining the three equations into a *single* difference equation, which we call the *fundamental dynamic equation*. Substituting (11.1) and (11.2) into (11.3), we have as our fundamental dynamic equation the following second-order difference equation for Y_t:

$$Y_t - (a_2 + b_2)Y_{t-1} + b_2\, Y_{t-2} = (a_1 + b_1) + G_t \tag{11.4}$$

We are interested in determining if and how the endogenous variable Y_t reaches a new equilibrium value in response to a change in the exogenous variable G_t. In other words, if at time $t = 0$, G_t increases by 1 and then *remains fixed at that higher level*, what will happen to Y_t over all future time? We are thus

---

[1] Readers who are not familiar with the solution of linear difference equations and the analysis of their properties may have some difficulty with this section. These readers may wish to read W. J. Baumol, *Economic Dynamics* (New York: Macmillan, 1951), or R. G. D. Allen, *Mathematical Economics* (New York: Macmillan, 1956), for a detailed but introductory presentation of difference equations.

interested in the pattern by which Y_t reaches a new equilibrium value (if indeed it does reach a new equilibrium value). This pattern, called the *transient solution* for Y_t, is found by setting the right-hand side of the fundamental dynamic equation equal to 0:

$$Y_t - (a_2 + b_2)Y_{t-1} + b_2 Y_{t-2} = 0 \qquad (11.5)$$

and then *assuming* the solution of this equation to be of the form[2]

$$Y_t = A\lambda^t \qquad (11.6)$$

If (11.6) above is a solution, then it should satisfy Eq. (11.5). Substituting (11.6) into (11.5) and dividing through the equation by $A\lambda^{t-2}$, we obtain the *characteristic equation* for our model:

$$\lambda^2 - (a_2 + b_2)\lambda + b_2 = 0 \qquad (11.7)$$

The solutions to the characteristic equation, called the *characteristic roots* of the model, determine the solution properties of the model. In our example the characteristic equation is quadratic, and so the characteristic roots (i.e., the solutions to the equation) are easy to find:

$$\lambda_1, \lambda_2 = \frac{(a_2 + b_2) \pm \sqrt{(a_2 + b_2)^2 - 4b_2}}{2} \qquad (11.8)$$

We now have two transient solutions to our model, $Y_t = A_1\lambda_1^t$ and $Y_t = A_2\lambda_2^t$, where A_1 and A_2 are constants that depend on the initial value that Y_t happens to take. We had assumed that the solutions were of the form $A\lambda^t$, but since λ_1 and λ_2 both satisfy the characteristic equation, we can verify that $A_1\lambda_1^t$ and $A_2\lambda_2^t$ are indeed solutions. If we substitute $A_1\lambda_1^t$ for Y_t in Eq. (11.5), we will obtain the characteristic equation in terms of λ_1, and since λ_1 is known to be a solution to the characteristic equation, we can be sure that $A_1\lambda_1^t$ is a transient solution. In fact, it is easy to see that if $A_1\lambda_1^t$ and $A_2\lambda_2^t$ are both solutions to (11.5), then the *sum* $Y_t = A_1\lambda_1^t + A_2\lambda_2^t$ is also a solution. The reader can verify this by substituting $A_1\lambda_1^t + A_2\lambda_2^t$ for Y_t in (11.5).

Depending on the values of a_2 and b_2, the behavior of the solution can be characterized in four possible ways: (1) The solution may be stable, converging without oscillation. This requires that both λ_1 and λ_2 be less than 1 in magnitude and have no imaginary component. (2) The solution may be stable,

---

[2] Again we are assuming that the reader has some familiarity with difference equation solutions. If our discussion seems somewhat confusing, the reader should turn to one of the references mentioned in the last footnote.

converging with damped oscillations. This occurs if the solutions to the characteristic equation are both less than 1 in magnitude, but have imaginary components. (3) The solution may be unstable and nonoscillatory. This results if either solution to the characteristic equation is greater than 1 in magnitude, but there is no imaginary component. (4) The solution may be unstable and oscillatory (i.e., it exhibits ever-diverging oscillations). This occurs if one or both of the characteristic roots are greater than 1 in magnitude and there is an imaginary component.

It is easy to see how these conditions on the characteristic roots λ_1 and λ_2 determine the behavior of the model if one remembers that the transient solution to the fundamental dynamic equation is given by

$$Y_t = A_1\lambda_1{}^t + A_2\lambda_2{}^t$$

Clearly if either λ_1 or λ_2 is greater than 1 in magnitude, the solution will grow explosively, and if λ_1 and λ_2 are complex (i.e., have imaginary components), then the solution will be sinusoidal (i.e., will oscillate).[3]

The type of solution which results will depend on the values of the two parameters a_2 and b_2. For example, if a_2 and b_2 take on the values .6 and .1, respectively, then the characteristic roots are given by

$$\lambda_1, \lambda_2 = \frac{.7 \pm \sqrt{.49 - .4}}{2} = .35 \pm .15$$

Since the largest root has a value of .5 and neither root has an imaginary component, the solution will be stable and nonoscillatory. If a_2 and b_2 have the values .6 and .8, respectively, then the characteristic roots would be

$$\lambda_1, \lambda_2 = \frac{1.4 \pm \sqrt{1.96 - 3.2}}{2} \simeq .7 \pm .56i$$

Now the characteristic roots are both less than 1 in magnitude, but they have an imaginary component, so that the solution will be stable but will oscillate. The reader can see that values of a_2 and b_2 equal to .6 and 1.5, respectively, would result in a solution that is unstable (explosive) and oscillatory, while values of .6 and 3.0 would result in a solution that is unstable and nonoscillatory. In fact (and the reader can verify this), as long as a_2 and b_2 are both less than 1.0, the solution will be stable, while if either is larger than 1.0,

---

[3] If the characteristic roots are complex, then they will occur as complex conjugates; i.e., they will be of the form

$$\lambda_1, \lambda_2 = \alpha \pm \beta i$$

These complex roots, when substituted into $Y_t = A_1\lambda_1{}^t + A_2\lambda_2{}^t$, will result in a solution for Y_t that will be a sinusoidal function of time. For a proof and further discussion of this, see Baumol, *op. cit.*

the solution will be unstable. We can also find an algebraic relationship between a_2 and b_2 that will determine if the solution is oscillatory. The characteristic roots [see Eq. (11.8)] will have an imaginary component if

$$4b_2 > (a_2 + b_2)^2 \tag{11.9}$$

or

$$a_2 < 2\sqrt{b_2} - b_2 \tag{11.10}$$

In Fig. 11.1 the plane is divided up into regions that indicate the range of parameter values that would result in each of the four types of solutions. The region that indicates those values of a_2 and b_2 that would result in a stable and nonoscillatory solution has been shaded.

In Fig. 11.2 and Table 11.1 we show as an illustration four solutions for Y_t corresponding to the four pairs of values for a_2 and b_2 from above, that is, $(a_2, b_2) = (.6, .1), (.6, .8), (.6, 1.5),$ and $(.6, 3.0)$. These solutions begin with the initial conditions $C_t = 90, I_t = 0, G_t = 10,$ and $Y_t = 100$. After three periods G_t is increased to 12, and a solution is obtained for the next 30 periods. In each case, the values 30 and 0 are used for the parameters a_1 and b_1 respectively.

In order to obtain the fundamental dynamic equation for our three-equation model (and thus the characteristic equation and characteristic roots), we could have begun by combining the equations of the model for any one endogenous variable. If, for example, we had substituted Eqs. (11.2) and (11.3) into Eq. (11.1) for C_t, we would have the following fundamental dynamic equation in terms of C_t:

$$C_t = a_1 + a_2 C_{t-1} + a_2 b_1 + a_2 b_2 \left(\frac{C_{t-1}}{a_2} - \frac{a_1}{a_2} \right) - a_2 b_2 \left(\frac{C_{t-2}}{a_2} - \frac{a_1}{a_2} \right) + G_t \tag{11.11}$$

or

$$C_t - (a_2 + b_2)C_{t-1} + b_2 C_{t-2} = (a_1 + a_2 b_1 - a_1 b_2 + a_1 a_2) + G_t \tag{11.12}$$

FIGURE 11.1
Solution behavior for simple multiplier-accelerator model.

FIGURE 11.2
Simulations of multiplier-accelerator model. Case I: $b_2 = .1$; case II: $b_2 = .8$; case III: $b_2 = 1.5$; case IV: $b_2 = 3.0$.

It is easy to see that this yields the same characteristic equation as (11.7) and thus the same characteristic roots. The reader can verify that the same characteristic equation would also result if Eqs. (11.1) and (11.3) were substituted into Eq. (11.2) to yield a single fundamental dynamic equation in terms of investment I_t.

Suppose that we *estimate* the coefficients of our model and obtain values for a_2 and b_2 that result in an oscillatory (but stable) solution. How should the model then be interpreted? If the oscillations in GNP predicted by the model in a historic simulation bear no resemblance to the actual past behavior of GNP, then we should doubt the validity of the model (even if the *individual* equations have good statistical fit). On the other hand, if the periodicity and magnitude of the oscillations predicted by the model bear a reasonable resemblance to the

TABLE 11.1

SIMULATIONS OF MULTIPLIER-ACCELERATOR MODEL

t	Case I $(b_2 = .1)$	Case II $(b_2 = .8)$	Case III $(b_2 = 1.5)$	Case IV $(b_2 = 3.0)$
0	100	100	100	100
1	100	100	100	100
2	102.	102.	102.	102.
3	103.4	104.8	106.2	109.2
4	104.18	107.12	112.02	129.12
5	104.586	108.128	117.942	179.232
6	104.792	107.683	121.648	299.875
7	104.896	106.254	120.548	583.854
8	104.948	104.609	112.679	1244.25
9	104.974	103.45	97.8034	2769.74
10	104.987	103.142	78.3680	6280.3
11	104.993	103.639	59.8696	14341.9
12	104.997	104.581	50.1727	32831.8
13	104.998	105.502	57.5584	75210.9
14	104.999	106.038	87.6135	172306.
15	105.	106.052	139.651	394710.
16	105.	105.642	203.846	904080.
17	105.	105.057	260.601	2.071×10^6
18	105.	104.566	283.493	4.742×10^6
19	105.	104.347	246.433	1.086×10^7
20	105.	104.433	134.27	2.487×10^7
21	105.	104.728	-45.6819	5.695×10^7
22	105.	105.073	-255.337	1.304×10^8
23	105.	105.32	-425.685	2.986×10^8
24	105.	105.389	-468.933	6.838×10^8
25	105.	105.289	-304.231	1.566×10^9
26	105.	105.093	106.513	3.586×10^9
27	105.	104.899	722.025	8.210×10^9
28	105.	104.784	1398.48	1.880×10^{10}
29	105.	104.779	1895.77	4.305×10^{10}
30	105.	104.863	1925.4	9.859×10^{10}

actual behavior of the economy, we might conclude that the dynamic structure of the model is representative of that of the actual economy. One might, for example, try to explain the presence of business cycles in the American economy using a multiplier-accelerator interaction. From Eq. (11.8) a range of values for a_2 and b_2 could be found that would result in oscillations with periodicity close to that observed in business cycles. Statistical tests could then be performed to determine whether data could support values of a_2 and b_2 in that range.[4]

---

[4] See, for example, P. A. Samuelson, "Interactions between the Multiplier Analysis and the Principle of Acceleration," *Review of Economics and Statistics*, May 1939; and G. C. Chow, "Multiplier, Accelerator, and Liquidity Preference in the Determination of National Income in the United States," *Review of Economics and Statistics*, February 1967.

A simple multiplier-accelerator model would probably not suffice to explain the cycles and other fluctuations in the economy. However, the larger and more complicated models which have been constructed recently have to some extent been able to explain and predict economic fluctuations. The principle holds that the dynamic structure implicit in a set of simultaneous time-dependent equations can provide a model of real world structure. It is for this reason that a multi-equation model can often describe more about the actual physical system being modeled than can single-equation models.

11.1.2   Analyzing Larger Models

As models become larger, an analysis of their dynamic behavior becomes more difficult and less straightforward. As long as the model remains linear, a character-istic equation can be derived, although a solution to that equation may offer computational problems. Consider, for example, the four-equation macro-economic model that was constructed in the last chapter [Eqs. (10.7), (10.8), (10.9), and (10.10)].

This is a very simple model, but if the equations are combined into a single fundamental dynamic equation for Y, the difference equation will be of fifth order, i.e., of the form

$$Y_t + \alpha_1 Y_{t-1} + \alpha_2 Y_{t-2} + \alpha_3 Y_{t-3} + \alpha_4 Y_{t-4} + \alpha_5 Y_{t-5} = \alpha_6 Z_t \qquad (11.13)$$

The characteristic equation will also be fifth order, and will have five solutions (i.e., five characteristic roots). A fifth-order equation is harder to solve analytically than the simple characteristic equation of (11.7). Thus if the size of the econometric model is substantial, an analysis of the properties of the solution becomes difficult.

Computer programs exist that can be used to solve a characteristic equation of high order. In fact some of the computer packages that have been written to solve simulation models also provide a solution of the characteristic equation. If an appropriate program is available, then one can examine the characteristic roots of a model, assuming, of course, that it is linear (there might be 100 or 200 such characteristic roots if the model is large). Those characteristic roots which are greater than 1 in magnitude will yield instabilities in the model, and those characteristic roots which are complex (i.e., have imaginary components) will contribute to the oscillatory behavior of the model.

When actually simulating a linear econometric model, it might be useful to look at the values of the characteristic roots. It is possible that the model may exhibit oscillatory or unstable behavior, but that the period of the oscillation may be much larger than the simulation period being used, or that the rate of divergence might be very slow. For example, if an econometric model is built to be simulated over 40 time periods, it might be that the period of oscillation is more than 100 or 200 time periods and will not become apparent in a 40-period simulation. By examining the values of the characteristic roots, the model builder can immediately determine whether or not the model will have long-term oscillatory or unstable characteristics.

It is quite possible that a large model will have some characteristic roots that are greater than 1 (and some that are complex) but that the model will be quite useful as a forecasting tool. If a few roots exist that are only slightly larger than 1, their destabilizing effects may be minimal, becoming evident only if the model is simulated over a long time horizon. The importance of stability for a model's forecasting performance thus depends very much on the length of the forecast. In particular, a technical instability may be of little consequence for a short-term forecasting model.

In the simple model of Eqs. (11.1), (11.2), and (11.3), it was easy to determine whether or not the solution was stable, and to determine whether or not a small change in one of the coefficients (that is, a_2 or b_2) would change the solution characteristic from stable to unstable. Suppose, for example, that the estimated values of a_2 and b_2 yield a stable and nonoscillatory solution, and we would like to know if a small change in a_2 would result in unstable behavior. It is very easy to determine analytically whether or not this would be the case, since one need look only at how the solution to the characteristic equation changes as a result of the change in a_2. Such an analysis is difficult or impossible, however, if the model is large. Even if we can determine the characteristic roots for the model, we would probably not be able to determine how those characteristic roots are related to all the individual coefficients in the model. Thus, it becomes difficult to determine analytically how sensitive the solution is to small changes in any of the coefficients. We usually cannot say (without actually performing a simulation) whether or not a small change in one of the coefficients will move the solution from stable to unstable or from nonoscillatory to oscillatory.

If the model is nonlinear, the situation becomes even more difficult, because we cannot use the solution to a characteristic equation to tell us about the stability or instability of the model solution. Most computer solution algorithms for nonlinear models involve iterative solutions in which a linearization is made in each iteration. Thus, as far as characteristic roots are concerned, the best that one can do is to derive a set of characteristic roots based on a linearization about some nominal solution path. (The model might, for example, be simulated and then linearized around the resulting solution.) If these characteristic roots are all less than 1 in magnitude, then the *linearization* of the nonlinear model (i.e., about the particular nominal path) is stable. We still have no guarantee, however, that the full nonlinear model will exhibit stability. Unfortunately, the current state of the art of mathematical stability theory is of limited use when it comes to nonlinear models. Methods do exist for determining the stability of nonlinear models, but these methods are largely analytical and do not readily yield computational algorithms that can be applied to models of any reasonable size. As a result we have no simple and direct way of determining the stability of a nonlinear model.[5]

Is there any way to determine the solution properties for a medium-to-large-size simultaneous equation model that contains nonlinearities (as many models do)? Usually one must resort to performing a series of simulations, over different periods of time, and using different time paths for the exogenous variables in the model. If the model is nonlinear and complex, then the best that one can do to determine whether or not it is stable in the long term is to simulate it over a long period of time. Similarly, in analyzing the sensitivity of the model to parameter changes, often the simplest thing to do (and the most revealing) is to make trial-and-error experiments with parameter values. After experimenting with models over a period of time, one usually obtains a "sense" of a model's characteristics and how they are determined. Experimentation with parameter changes, etc., then becomes more intuitive and less a matter of trial and error. Clearly, this aspect of model building is more of an art than a science.

11.2 MODEL BEHAVIOR—MULTIPLIERS AND DYNAMIC RESPONSE

We often build models to predict how a change in one variable is likely to affect other variables over time. We might construct a macroeconometric model, for example, to determine how changes in government expenditures, the money supply, or some other exogenous policy variable will affect future values of the GNP and its components, prices, employment, etc. We might construct a microeconometric model of some industry to forecast the future impact on market equilibrium of changes in personal income (or other demand-determining exogenous variables), changes in export demand, or (if the industry is a regulated one) changes in the government's regulatory policy. In any case, we will want to use our models to make statements about the *dynamic response*, i.e., the response over time, of the macroeconomy, an industry, or a firm to changes in particular variables. One way to quantify these statements is to calculate and examine the *multipliers* associated with the model's exogenous variables.

In the case of our simple three-equation multiplier-accelerator model—Eqs. (11.1), (11.2), and (11.3)—we can determine what change in Y_t would result from a \$1 increase in G_t (or we could determine the corresponding change in C_t or I_t). Assuming that the model's parameters are such that the simulation solution is

---

[5] Most of the analytical methods that do exist have come out of the field of control theory. An approach that has recently received some attention by economists and econometricians (called "Lyapunov's direct method") provides a sufficient condition for stability in the form of an existence theorem. If a certain function (called a "Lyapunov function") can be shown to exist for a given model, then the model is guaranteed to be stable. Unfortunately there is no simple computational algorithm for determining whether or not such a function exists for a particular model. For an introduction to the applications of Lyapunov's method to economic models the reader is referred to K. Fox, J. Sengupta, and E. Thorbecke, *The Theory of Quantitative Economic Policy* (Amsterdam: North-Holland, 1966). For a detailed treatment of the dynamic analysis of both linear and nonlinear models, see G. C. Chow, *Analysis and Control of Dynamic Economic Systems* (New York: Wiley, 1975).

stable, we would expect that the initial increase in G_t would result in ever-diminishing increases in Y_t. These changes in Y_t are called *dynamic multipliers*. The initial (first-period) change in Y_t is called the *impact multiplier*, while the *total long-run multiplier* is just the sum of all the dynamic multipliers over time. Thus, the long-run multiplier indicates the total long-run change in Y_t that results from a unit change in G_t. In this section we examine dynamic multipliers in some detail, and see how they can be used to provide information about a model's behavior.[6]

11.2.1 Dynamic Multipliers

Let us return to our simple model of Eqs. (11.1), (11.2), and (11.3), with parameter values $a_1 = 30, a_2 = .6, b_1 = 0$, and $b_2 = .1$. We can obtain the dynamic multipliers directly from our simulation of the model in which we increased G_t by 2. Taking the *changes* in Y_t, and dividing these changes by 2 (to correspond to an increase in G_t of 1), we obtain the dynamic multipliers, tabulated in Table 11.2. We also show in Table 11.2 the dynamic multipliers that result for $a_2 = .6$ and $b_2 = .8$, which, as expected, are oscillatory. The impact multiplier is the initial first-period change in Y_t (1.0), and the total long-run multiplier is the sum of all the dynamic multipliers. Note that in both cases the total long-run multiplier is 2.50. The two transient solutions are quite different, but they both bring Y_t to the same equilibrium value.

The impact multiplier can also be determined algebraically. First, rewrite Eq. (11.4) as

$$Y_t = (a_2 + b_2)Y_{t-1} - b_2 Y_{t-2} + (a_1 + b_1) + G_t \qquad (11.14)$$

Now taking first differences across this equation,

$$\Delta Y_t = (a_2 + b_2)\Delta Y_{t-1} - b_2 \Delta Y_{t-2} + \Delta G_t \qquad (11.15)$$

we see that for $\Delta G_t = 1$ the first-period change in Y_t will also be 1. In general, one can obtain the impact multipliers directly from the reduced-form version of a model—the reduced-form coefficient of each unlagged exogenous variable is that variable's impact multiplier. The remaining dynamic multipliers, however, cannot be determined from inspection of the model. Instead, one must perform a simulation in which each exogenous variable is increased appropriately, and the resulting changes in the endogenous variables are obtained by examining the simulation solution.

---

[6] For a detailed discussion of dynamic multipliers and their application to the analysis of a larger econometric model, see A. S. Goldberger, *Impact Multipliers and the Dynamic Properties of the Klein-Goldberger Model* (Amsterdam: North-Holland, 1959).

TABLE 11.2
DYNAMIC MULTIPLIERS FOR
MULTIPLIER-ACCELERATOR
MODEL

t	Case I $(b_2 = .1)$	Case II $(b_2 = .8)$
2	1.0	1.0
3	.699997	1.39999
4	.389999	1.16
5	.202995	.503998
6	.103096	−.222397
7	.051872	−.714554
8	.025993	−.822464
9	.013008	−.579803
10	.006508	−.153755
11	.003258	.248581
12	.001625	.471016
13	.000816	.460564
14	.000404	.267975
15	.000206	.006714
16	.000099	−.204979
17	.000053	−.292343
18	.000023	−.2453
19	.000015	−.109543
20	.000007	.042877
21	.000004	.147667
22	0	.172432
23	0	.123268
24	0	.03463
25	0	−.050133
26	0	−.097885
27	0	−.096931
28	0	−.057396
29	0	−.002815
30	0	.041977
⋮		
Sum	2.5000	2.5000

Example 11.1   St. Louis Model

An application of dynamic multipliers is provided by the "St. Louis model"
of Andersen and Carlson of the St. Louis Federal Reserve Bank.[7] They set out

---

[7] L. C. Andersen and K. M. Carlson, "A Monetarist Model for Economic Stabilization," *Federal Reserve Bank of St. Louis, Monthly Review*, April 1970. For a general reference on the monetarist view, see K. Brunner, "The Role of Money and Monetary Policy," *Federal Reserve Bank of St. Louis, Monthly Review*, July 1968.

to test the "monetarist" position regarding macroeconomic policy. This viewpoint holds that only the money supply (and therefore monetary policy) has any long-run impact on the GNP, and that government expenditures, while perhaps having some immediate impact on GNP, have almost no long-run impact. The model constructed by Andersen and Carlson included as exogenous variables both government expenditures and the money supply. Simulations of the model were used to determine the dynamic and total long-run multipliers corresponding to each of these exogenous variables. The result was that the total long-run multiplier for government expenditures was close to zero, while that for the money supply was large.

We will not describe the St. Louis model in detail, since that would require a lengthy discussion. The results described above, however, are largely the outcome of only one of the model's eight equations, one which relates changes in total spending (in current dollars) ΔY to changes in the money supply ΔM and changes in government expenditures ΔG. The estimated form of that equation uses polynomial distributed lags (see Chapter 7), and constrains each of the independent variables to lie on a fourth-degree polynomial with the head and tail set at 0. The estimated equation is shown below, with t statistics in parentheses:

$$\Delta Y_t = 2.67 + \sum_{i=0}^{4} m_i \Delta M_{t-1} + \sum_{i=0}^{4} g_i \Delta G_{t-1} \qquad (11.16)$$
$$(3.46)$$

$$m_0 = 1.22 \quad (2.73) \qquad g_0 = .56 \quad (2.57)$$

$$m_1 = 1.80 \quad (7.34) \qquad g_1 = .45 \quad (3.43)$$

$$m_2 = 1.62 \quad (4.25) \qquad g_2 = .01 \quad (.08)$$

$$m_3 = .87 \quad (3.65) \qquad g_3 = -.43 \quad (-3.18)$$

$$m_4 = .06 \quad (.12) \qquad g_4 = -.54 \quad (-2.47)$$

$$\sum m_i = 5.57 \quad (8.06) \qquad \sum g_i = .05 \quad (.17)$$

As can be seen from this equation, an increase in G will initially have a positive impact on Y, but after two or three quarters it will have a negative impact, with a total (long-run) impact that is close to zero. The money supply, on the other hand, has a rather large long-run impact ($\sum m_i = 5.57$).[8]

---

[8] One criticism of the model has been that this equation is not easily justified. It is not our purpose to enter into this debate, but rather to use it as an example of how impact multipliers alone (describing a static or short-run response) are not sufficient as a mode of analysis. It is the dynamic response of the St. Louis model that makes it interesting.

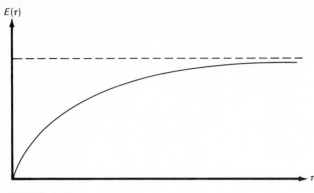

FIGURE 11.3
Dynamic elasticity.

11.2.2 Dynamic Elasticities

When constructing a microeconometric model, we are usually interested in describing (and predicting) the dynamic response of a particular industry or market. Corresponding to the dynamic multipliers described above, we would calculate dynamic *elasticities*. A dynamic elasticity would tell how the demand for a good would change *over time* in response to a change in price or in consumers' incomes. We often make statements about the price or income elasticity of some good without explicitly recognizing that the value of the elasticity depends on how much time is allowed to elapse after price or income has changed.[9] In fact it is much more meaningful to look at a dynamic elasticity, such as

$$E_p(\tau) = -\frac{P_t}{Q_t}\frac{(Q_{t+\tau} - Q_t)}{\Delta P_t} \qquad (11.17)$$

Here ΔP_t is a change in price (occurring at time t), and $Q_{t+\tau} - Q_t$ is the change in quantity demanded after a time interval τ has elapsed. Other dynamic elasticities (e.g., income, cross-price, etc.) would be defined in the same way.

By simulating the model (with a change in price), we can calculate and

---

[9] The price elasticity of demand is defined as

$$E_p = -\frac{P}{Q}\frac{\Delta Q}{\Delta P}$$

and the income elasticity as

$$E_I = \frac{I}{Q}\frac{\Delta Q}{\Delta I}$$

The problem, of course, is that given some ΔP (or ΔI), how much time should be allowed to elapse before we measure ΔQ?

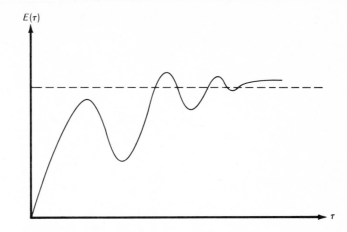

FIGURE 11.4
Oscillating dynamic elasticity.

plot the elasticity as a function of the time interval τ. We would normally expect the elasticity to grow monotonically with increasing τ, and approach some asymptotic value, as in Fig. 11.3. It is quite possible, however, that as a result of the model's structure (which hopefully reflects the true market structure) the elasticity would oscillate (still approaching some asymptotic long-run value as long as the model is stable), as in Fig. 11.4.

The behavior of dynamic elasticities is clearly important if a model is being used to forecast or analyze the impact of a price increase, or a change in the price of some competing good, on an industry's (or a company's) sales. That impact must be described in dynamic terms. It is possible that a price increase would result in a drop in demand, but only after a long period of time has elapsed. On the other hand, it might result in an initially large drop in demand, but later (after consumers' perceptions of relative prices have changed) an increase in demand, so that the net decrease is small. The time required for these changes to occur is likely to vary considerably from industry to industry. Because of this, a company, trying to plan its production and marketing in anticipation of a planned change in prices, must have some idea of how much time will pass before it experiences a resulting change in sales.

Example 11.2 Another Macroeconometric Model

The St. Louis model discussed above represents just one example of an attempt to study fiscal and monetary policy. As a second example, let us look at a quarterly model constructed recently by Kmenta and Smith.[10] Their model is

---

[10] J. Kmenta and P. E. Smith, "Autonomous Expenditures versus Money Supply: An Application of Dynamic Multipliers," *Review of Economics and Statistics*, Aug. 1973.

also rather simple, and should help to make clear the notion of dynamic multipliers and their application.

The equations of the model, which were estimated with quarterly data over the period 1954 to 1963, using three-stage least squares, are shown below with standard errors in parentheses below each coefficient:

$$C_t = -1.7951 + .1731Y_t + .0421(L_t - .7275L_{t-1}) + .7275C_{t-1} \quad (11.18)$$
$$\quad (.7803) \quad (.0131) \quad (.0277) \quad (.0665) \quad (.0665)$$

$$R^2 = .9968$$

$$I_t^d = 2.5624 - .4411r_t + .1381(S_{t-1} - S_{t-2}) + .0237t + .8917I_{t-1}^d \quad (11.19)$$
$$\quad (1.0759) \quad (.1891) \quad (.0501) \quad (.0110) \quad (.0700)$$

$$R^2 = .8961$$

$$I_t^r = 3.6083 - .5127r_t + .1267(S_{t-1} - S_{t-2}) + .0218t + .6483I_{t-1}^r \quad (11.20)$$
$$\quad (.5779) \quad (.1133) \quad (.0335) \quad (.0059) \quad (.0668)$$

$$R^2 = .8394$$

$$I_t^i = 3.0782 - .8934r_t + .3713(S_{t-1} - S_{t-2}) + .0450t + .3178I_{t-1}^i \quad (11.21)$$
$$\quad (1.3610) \quad (.4089) \quad (.1301) \quad (.0208) \quad (.1181)$$

$$R^2 = .5341$$

$$r_t = 13.8928 + .0261Y_t - .1501M_t + .0588M_{t-1} \quad (11.22)$$
$$\quad (1.8706) \quad (.0042) \quad (.0335) \quad (.0338)$$

$$R^2 = .8538$$

$$Y_t = C_t + I_t^d + I_t^r + I_t^i + G_t \quad (11.23)$$

$$S_t = Y_t - I_t^i \quad (11.24)$$

$$L_t = M_t + TD_t \quad (11.25)$$

where Y = gross national product

  C = consumption expenditures

  I^d = producer's outlays on durable plant and equipment

  I^r = residential construction

  I^i = increase in inventories

  G = government purchases of goods and services plus net foreign investment

  S = final sales of goods and services

  t = time in quarters (first quarter of 1954 = 0)

  r = yield on all corporate bonds, percent per annum

  M = money supply, i.e., demand deposits plus currency outside banks

  TD = time deposits in commercial banks

  L = money supply plus time deposits in commercial banks (representing liquid wealth)

All the variables except for t and r are measured in billions of 1958 dollars, and the variables G, M, TD, and t are taken to be exogenous (there are thus eight equations and eight endogenous variables). No prices or wages are included in the model, since during the time period which it describes, prices were relatively stable.

To examine the dynamic characteristics of this model, we can begin by writing the reduced-form equation for GNP. This is found by expressing the current endogenous variables in Eq. (11.23) in terms of the exogenous and lagged endogenous variables. Making those substitutions gives us the following reduced-form equation:

$$Y_t = -20.8070 + .3168M_t - .1242M_{t-1} + .0481L_t - .0350L_{t-1}$$
$$(.1024) (.0755)\phantom{M_{t-1}} (.0308) (.0224)$$

$$+ 1.1427G_t + .1035t + .8313C_{t-1} + .7270(S_{t-1} - S_{t-2})$$
$$(.0286) (.0489) (.0356)\phantom{C_{t-1}} (.1796)$$

$$+ 1.0190I^d_{t-1} + .7409I^r_{t-1} + .3631I^i_{t-1} \tag{11.26}$$
$$(.0853)\phantom{I^d_{t-1}} (.0802)\phantom{I^r_{t-1}} (.1350)$$

According to this equation the impact effect of a $1 billion increase in government expenditures G_t is to increase GNP by $1.1427 billion, while the impact effect of a $1 billion increase in money supply M_t is to increase GNP by $.3649 billion (.3168 plus .0481, since M_t is a component of L_t).

Before examining the dynamic multipliers, let us determine what type of solution the model will have by finding the characteristic roots. First, by substituting for C_{t-1}, S_{t-1}, S_{t-2}, I^d_{t-1}, I^r_{t-1}, and I^i_{t-1} in Eq. (11.26), we obtain the fundamental dynamic equation, which expresses current GNP in terms of its own lagged values and in terms of current and lagged values of the exogenous variables:

$$
\begin{aligned}
Y_t = \quad & 3.0716\,Y_{t-1} \quad - 3.6561\,Y_{t-2} \quad + 2.0850\,Y_{t-3} \\
& - .5585\,Y_{t-4} \quad + .0535\,Y_{t-5} \quad + 1.1427G_t \\
& - 2.5300G_{t-1} \quad + 1.3779G_{t-2} \quad + .5853G_{t-3} \\
& - .7463G_{t-4} \quad + .1784G_{t-5} \quad + .3168M_t \\
& - .7499M_{t-1} \quad + .6253M_{t-2} \quad - .2000M_{t-3} \\
& + .0082M_{t-4} \quad + .0046M_{t-5} \quad + .0481L_t \\
& - .1065L_{t-1} \quad + .0580L_{t-2} \quad + .0246L_{t-3} \\
& - .0314L_{t-4} \quad + .0075L_{t-5} \quad + .1034t \\
& - .2050(t-1) + .1267(t-2) \\
& - .0192(t-3) - .0032(t-4) - .5113
\end{aligned}
\tag{11.27}
$$

From Eq. (11.27) we can determine the characteristic equation of the model:

$$
\lambda^5 - 3.0716\lambda^4 + 3.6561\lambda^3 - 2.0850\lambda^2 + .5585\lambda - .0535 = 0 \tag{11.28}
$$

The characteristic roots (i.e., the solutions to this equation) are

$$
\lambda_1 = .2081
$$

$$
\lambda_{2,3} = .8475 \pm .0809i
$$

$$
\lambda_{4,5} = .5843 \pm .1156i
$$

Since all the roots are less than 1 in magnitude (λ_2 and λ_3 have a magnitude of .8513), and four of them are complex, the solution will be stable, and we will observe damped oscillations. The dynamic multipliers, then, should also exhibit damped oscillations and should converge toward 0 as the length of the time lag increases. This is indeed the case, as can be seen in Table 11.3.

By summing the multipliers listed in the table, we see that the total long-run multiplier for government expenditures is 1.8406, that for the money supply (the combined effect of M_t and L_t) is 1.2270, and that for the time trend is .6363.

TABLE 11.3
DYNAMIC GNP MULTIPLIERS

	Multipliers of			
Lag k	G_{t-k}	M_{t-k}	L_{t-k}	$t-k$
0	1.14271	.31683	.04811	.10341
1	.98001	.22330	.04126	.11262
2	.21029	.15287	.00885	.09459
3	.03086	.11372	.00130	.07525
4	−.01519	.08722	−.00064	.05920
5	−.02878	.06775	−.00121	.04660
6	−.03352	.05291	−.00141	.03679
7	−.03539	.04135	−.00149	.02908
8	−.03604	.03210	−.11052	.02298
9	−.03592	.02487	−.00151	.01808
10	−.03520	.08196	−.00148	.01412
11	−.00396	.01410	−.00143	.01091
12	−.03227	.01036	−.00136	.00820
13	−.03024	.00729	−.00127	.00619
14	−.02795	.00486	−.00188	.00448
15	−.02552	.00295	−.00107	.00312
16	−.02303	.00148	−.00097	.00204
17	−.02056	.00037	−.00086	.00120
18	−.01816	−.00044	−.00076	.00055
19	−.01589	−.00102	−.00067	.00006
⋮	⋮	⋮	⋮	⋮

These results are quite different from those of the St. Louis model, and support the view that both government expenditures and money supply are effective as policy instruments.[11]

11.3 TUNING AND ADJUSTING SIMULATION MODELS

It often may be the case that by making changes or adjustments in a simulation model, its forecasting performance can be improved. The structure of a model might be such that its dynamic behavior verges on being unstable, and minor changes in the structure might be sufficient to stabilize the behavior. On the other hand, a bias in an individual estimated coefficient might result in consistent under or over prediction by the model as a whole which could be corrected by an adjustment in the coefficient value. In this section we discuss how one

---

[11] The reader might wish to examine this model, the St. Louis model, and the macroeconometric model developed in the next chapter in more detail and make a personal evaluation of their rather different implications for fiscal and monetary policy.

can "tune," or make changes in, a simulation model so as to improve its forecasting performance. We begin with a brief review of how we might change a regression equation so as to improve its fit and explanatory power.

Suppose we estimated a regression equation to forecast an interest rate into the future. The result might have been Eq. (10.11) in Chapter 10. Presumably, this equation has been compared with other regression equations that used different explanatory variables, different lag structures, and even different functional forms. The reason for having selected this particular equation might have been based solely on statistical grounds; i.e., it might have a higher R^2, better t statistics, etc. Suppose we take the equation and use it to produce a "predicted" series for the interest rate over the historical time period, by using historical values for the independent variables. It may turn out to be the case that the predicted series is very close to the actual series for the interest rate during those periods when the interest rate does not change very much, i.e., during periods of relative interest rate stability. On the other hand, during periods when the interest rate is changing rapidly, the predicted series may miss the turns in the actual series. Thus, although the overall fit of the equation is good, the equation may fail to pick up turns in the variable that is being explained. If this is the case, we might want to change the equation, perhaps by introducing additional explanatory variables, or by changing the functional form or the lag structure. The result might have an overall statistical fit that is not as good, but might be more useful for purposes of prediction or analysis. The point is that in selecting an individual regression equation one must usually experiment with different equations and keep in mind the ultimate purpose of building the single-equation model.

Once a single-equation regression model has been built, one would probably not want to manipulate the coefficient values that have been estimated (although alternative estimation techniques might be used). This may not be the case with a simulation model. Let us consider as an example the four-equation model from Chapter 10, the equations of which (ordinary least-squares version) are shown again below:

$$C_t = 2.537 + .185Y_t + .714C_{t-1} \tag{10.9}$$
$$\quad\;\; (1.90) \quad (5.95) \quad (13.8)$$

$$R^2 = .999 \qquad \text{SER} = 2.40 \qquad \text{DW} = 2.08$$

$$I_t = 5.020 + .392(Y_t - Y_{t-1}) + .1634Y_{t-1} - 3.856R_{t-4} \tag{10.10}$$
$$\quad\;\; (2.69) \quad (4.25) \qquad\qquad (23.80) \qquad (-5.23)$$

$$R^2 = .980 \qquad \text{SER} = 4.22 \qquad \text{DW} = .62$$

$$R_t = -.072 + .0024Y_t + .011(Y_t - Y_{t-1}) - .189(M_t - M_{t-1})$$
$$(-.25) \quad (2.14) \quad (.74) \quad (-2.30)$$

$$+ .347(R_{t-1} + R_{t-2})$$
$$(6.24) \tag{10.11}$$

$$R^2 = .867 \qquad SER = .59 \qquad DW = .92$$

$$Y_t = C_t + I_t + G_t \tag{10.12}$$

Suppose we wanted to use this model to forecast the interest rate. We might be satisfied with each of the above equations taken by themselves, but we might not be happy with the simulation performance of the model as a whole. The model might be overly sensitive to changes in an exogenous variable, or it simply may be unstable or oscillate. One approach to improve its performance (as discussed in Chapter 10) is to use alternative methods for estimating the model's coefficients. Aside from the use of two-stage least squares to ensure consistency (which was discussed in some detail in Chapter 9), we saw in section 10.4 that the use of simple single-equation estimation techniques such as an autoregressive correction (for serially correlated error terms) can greatly improve a model's forecasting performance, and the use of full-information techniques can result in still further improvement. Let us assume, then, that the model builder has used the estimation "tool kit" as extensively as possible to obtain coefficient estimates, and see what else can be done to improve the performance of the model.[12]

Other techniques are available for making major or minor changes in the model, and are often used interdependently. The first of these is to analyze all the feedback and feedforward loops in the model. To do this, one begins with a *block diagram* of the model. A block diagram, an example of which is shown for our simple four-equation model in Fig. 11.5, illustrates all the causal flows between variables, and blocks of variables. Feedback loops are essentially circular causal flows; an example in Fig. 11.5 is the "loop" between consumption and GNP—consumption is at least in part determined by GNP, but it is also a component of (and therefore helps determine) GNP.

The model builder can use a block diagram to identify mechanisms in the model that could result in an unstable performance. In our four-equation model, for example, consumption and investment both depend on total GNP, while at

---

[12] It should be noted that some estimation methods, such as three-stage least squares and full-information maximum likelihood, can require a large amount of numerical computation, and thus may not be feasible for a model builder whose computational facilities are limited. The estimation "tool kit," then, should be used as extensively as possible, given such constraints.

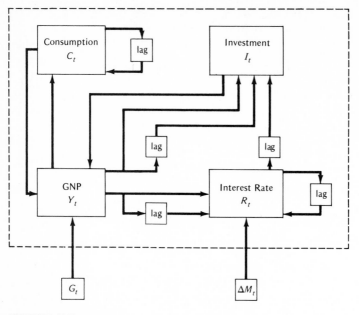

FIGURE 11.5
Block diagram for simple four-equation model.

the same time contribute to total GNP. Thus, if the multiplier coefficients in these equations are too large, a feedback loop could result that would continually magnify small changes in consumption or investment demand into very large changes in the GNP. If this is the case, one might want to restructure one of the demand equations, e.g., the consumption equation, so as to reduce the dependence on total GNP. One could, for example, introduce another explanatory variable that would eliminate some of the dependence of consumption on GNP. Thus a restructuring of the model can be used to eliminate feedback loops or at least reduce their impact. Note that the restructuring of individual equations will be done for very different reasons than would be the case in a single-equation model. In a single-equation model, one is usually concerned only with the statistical fit, either overall or at particular turning points. In a simulation model, however, one is also concerned with the dynamic interaction of the equations which compose the model. Thus, we might want to restructure an equation even though it has a very satisfactory statistical fit.

There is a second method that is often used to make minor adjustments in large econometric models, particularly those that are used for forecasting purposes. This method is called "tuning," and consists of making small changes in some of the model's coefficients, as well as introducing adjustable parameters at key points in the model so as to improve the ability of the model to forecast.[13] Suppose, for example, that one of the variables in a model is consistently simulated above its actual values. There might be several reasons for this; one or more of the coefficients in the consumption equation might be biased, some of the coefficients in other equations that feed into the consumption equation might be biased, or the structure of the model may simply build an upward trend into that particular variable. One way of dealing with this problem is to adjust some of the coefficients in the equation for the variable that is simulating badly.

Some equations may have autoregressive terms, i.e., lagged dependent variables. An adjustment of the coefficient of the autoregressive term provides a simple means of changing the overall dynamic response of the particular dependent variable, and is thus another means by which trend effects and built-in dynamic adjustments can be modified.

"Tuning" a model can be a somewhat tricky business. By adjusting some of the coefficients, the analyst might make the model track the historical data very well, even though it is really a very poor representation of the real world, with little predictive value. Coefficients should be adjusted only with great caution and to a very limited extent, and only if they are not statistically significant. A statistically significant coefficient indicates that the data have information to convey, and this information should be accounted for when making a forecast.

There are other techniques for the construction and adjustment of simulation models that are still in the forefront of econometric research. One technique that has received recent attention involves constructing a separate model for the random error term of each equation. In effect, the use of an autoregressive correction is an example of this technique, since one is constructing (and estimating) a simple serial correlation model of the error term. In the case of first-order serial correlation, one constructs the following model:

$$\varepsilon_t = \rho\varepsilon_{t-1} + \varepsilon_t^* \tag{11.29}$$

Note that Eq. (11.29) does not *explain* the behavior of the error term; it simply replicates (to some extent) its past behavior, and conveys some information about its future behavior. If Eq. (11.29) is a correct representation of the error term, then its inclusion in the model will improve the model's forecasting performance.

Much more complicated and sophisticated models can be constructed for the random error term than that of Eq. (11.29). These models, called *time-series models*, are the subject of Part Three of this book. After discussing how to

---

[13] These parameters are often called "add factors" and "mul factors," depending on whether they are introduced additively or multiplicatively in the equation. Add and mul factors have come to be used in large macroeconometric forecasting models, particularly those constructed for commercial or business application (often they are adjusted to keep the forecast "in line" with intuitive forecasts—thus to some extent negating the predictions of the model). Needless to say, they can easily be misused (and often are).

build time-series models in Chapters 13 to 16, we will see in Chapter 17 how they can be used to improve the forecasting performance of a structural econometric model (and how they can be used for other forecasting purposes).

11.4 STOCHASTIC SIMULATION

In Chapter 6 we saw how the forecasts produced by a single-equation regression model are subject to four sources of error:

1 The regression equation contains an implicit additive error term.
2 The estimated values of the coefficients of the equation are themselves random variables and will therefore differ from the true values.
3 The exogenous variables may have to be forecasted themselves, and these forecasts may contain errors.
4 The equation itself may be misspecified; i.e., the functional form may not be representative of the real world.

We showed in Chapter 6 how we could calculate a confidence interval on a forecast that would account for the first three sources of error. (We cannot account for the fourth source of error, so that all our confidence intervals are calculated under the assumption that the model is correctly specified.)

In the case of a multi-equation simulation model, the four sources of error listed above still apply, although now misspecification can occur not only for individual equations but also for the dynamic structure contained in the model as a whole. Furthermore, even if the model is totally specified correctly, errors in each equation of the first three types may become multiplied across equations and thus magnified.

As an example, consider the four-equation model of Eqs. (10.9) to (10.12) which appears on pages 356 and 357, along with the corresponding block diagram in Fig. 11.5. When the model is simulated, the consumption equation will generate a prediction of consumption which will be in error as a result of both the implicit additive error term in that equation, and as a result of the fact that the equation's coefficients are not known with certainty. Since consumption is a component of GNP, the error in consumption will contribute to an error in GNP, and this error in GNP will contribute to the error in the prediction of investment (together with the additive error term and coefficient errors in the investment equation). Investment is also a component of GNP, so that the error in investment will also contribute to an error in GNP. Likewise, consumption is a function of GNP, so that the error in consumption will become still larger as a result of the accumulated error in GNP.

If the model is linear, the final forecasting error variances associated with each endogenous variable can be calculated exactly, although to do so is not computationally trivial.[14] Generally a more fruitful approach (particularly for nonlinear models) is to perform a *stochastic simulation*. This is done by specifying, for each equation of the model, a probability distribution for the additive error term and for each estimated coefficient. Next, a large number (say 50 or 100) of simulations are performed, and in each simulation values for the additive error terms and estimated coefficients are chosen at random from the corresponding probability distributions. For any particular endogenous variable, the results of the simulation (i.e., the resulting set of forecasts) yield points that trace out a probability distribution of that variable's forecasted value. Thus the dispersion of the forecasts about their mean value can be used to define a forecast confidence interval.

If unbiased and consistent estimates have been obtained for all the model's coefficients, then the determination of the appropriate probability distributions for the additive error terms and the estimated coefficients is straightforward. For each equation, the additive error can be assumed to be normally distributed with 0 mean and standard deviation equal to the standard error of the regression. The coefficients of each equation can be assumed to follow a *joint* normal distribution, where the mean of each coefficient is given by its estimated value, the standard deviation of each coefficient is given by its estimated standard error, and the covariances between coefficients are given by the estimated covariance matrix.

In order to illustrate the technique, let us take the four-equation model as an example. To perform a stochastic simulation, the equations of the model would be written as follows:

$$C_t = (2.537 + v_{11}) + (.185 + v_{12})Y_t + (.714 + v_{13})C_{t-1} + \varepsilon_{1t} \tag{11.30}$$

$$I_t = (5.020 + v_{21}) + (.392 + v_{22})(Y_t - Y_{t-1}) + (.1634 + v_{23})Y_{t-1}$$
$$- (3.856 + v_{24})R_{t-4} + \varepsilon_{2t} \tag{11.31}$$

$$R_t = -(.072 + v_{31}) + (.0024 + v_{32})Y_t + (.011 + v_{33})(Y_t - Y_{t-1})$$
$$- (1.89 + v_{34})(M_t - M_{t-1}) + (.347 + v_{35})(R_{t-1} + R_{t-2}) + \varepsilon_{3t} \tag{11.32}$$

$$Y_t = C_t + I_t + G_t \tag{11.33}$$

In the first equation the "error terms" v_{11}, v_{12}, and v_{13} should be assumed to follow a joint normal distribution, but in practice it may be computationally

---

[14] The techniques for doing this are the result of recent advances in modern control and system theory, and are beyond the scope of this book. The interested reader is referred to K. Anstrom, *Introduction to Stochastic Control Theory* (New York: Academic, 1970).

difficult to generate random numbers from joint distributions. It is often reasonable, however, to perform the stochastic simulation under the approximating assumption that the covariances between coefficients are 0. In this case, the error term v_{11} is assumed to be a normally distributed random variable with 0 mean and a standard deviation of 1.33 (which is the estimated standard error of the coefficient 2.537 in the consumption equation). Similarly, v_{12} is normally distributed with 0 mean and a standard deviation of .031, and v_{13} is normally distributed with 0 mean and a standard deviation of .051.[15] The additive error term ε_{1t} is, *for each period t*, a normally distributed random variable with 0 mean and a standard deviation of 2.40 (the standard error of the equation). The remaining error terms in Eqs. (11.31) and (11.32) are similarly defined.

Now suppose that we would like to obtain a stochastic one-period-ahead forecast of the interest rate R_t (under the assumption that the exogenous variables M_t and G_t are known with certainty). We do this by performing 50 or 100 simulations of the model one period ahead.[16] In each simulation we select a value for v_{11} at random from a normal distribution with mean 0 and standard deviation 1.33, we select a value for v_{12} at random from a normal distribution with mean 0 and standard deviation .031, etc. The result of these 50 or 100 simulations will be a range of forecasted values of R_t. This range will have some sample mean, and the 50 or 100 simulated values themselves will determine a probability distribution about this mean (if the model is nonlinear, this probability distribution will not be normal). Next, we can calculate the standard deviation of this sample distribution, which will give us an estimated value for the standard error of the forecast. We can then use this standard error of forecast just as we did in Chapter 6 to determine forecast confidence intervals.

It should be pointed out that if the model is linear, then as the number of simulations included in the sample becomes large, the sample mean will approach the deterministic forecast (i.e., the forecast corresponding to all the random parameters set at 0). If the model is nonlinear, however, there is no guarantee that the sample mean will approach the deterministic forecast as the sample size increases, and in fact it usually will not. In addition, it may be necessary for an unacceptably large number of simulations to be performed before the sample means for each variable converge at all. We therefore center our confidence intervals on the *deterministic forecast*, rather than on the sample mean of the stochastic simulations.

The process would be exactly the same if we wanted to forecast over a time

---

[15] Ignoring the covariances between coefficients, as we have done here, will usually tend to *overestimate* the size of the model's forecast errors. The majority of the estimated covariances are usually negative, and cancel part of the variance in each coefficient. Ignoring the covariances thus tends to overemphasize the degree of fluctuation in the coefficients. Forecast confidence intervals obtained in this way will thus be somewhat overly conservative.

[16] The choice of how many simulations to perform may depend somewhat on one's research budget. Obviously, performing a large number of simulations can entail a considerable computational expense.

horizon longer than one period. For each simulation we simply select a *different* random value for ε_{1t}, ε_{2t}, and ε_{3t} for *each period*, but we use the *same* random value for v_{11}, v_{12}, etc., during the entire simulation (since the equations of the model were specified and estimated under the assumption that the coefficients are constant over time). Furthermore, if the future values of the exogenous variables G_t and M_t were not known with certainty but had to be forecasted themselves, standard errors could be associated with their forecasts. The exogenous variables could then be treated as normally distributed random variables (with means equal to their forecasted values and standard deviations equal to their standard errors of forecast) in our stochastic simulation. For example, Eq. (11.33) could be rewritten to include an error term associated with G_t (which now must itself be forecasted):

$$Y_t = C_t + I_t + (\hat{G}_t + \eta_t) \tag{11.34}$$

Here $\hat{G}_t$ is a forecast of G_t, and η_t is a normally distributed random variable (defined for each period t) with mean 0 and standard deviation equal to the standard error of the forecast $\hat{G}_t$. Note that our forecast is now a *conditional* forecast; i.e., it is conditional on $\hat{G}_t$.

Example 11.3

Let us examine the results of an actual stochastic simulation based on Eqs. (11.30) to (11.33). We forecast the model over four periods, beginning with the first quarter of 1972 and ending with the last quarter of that year. Actual values for G_t are used, so that the forecast is unconditional.

The results of a sample of 25 simulations are shown in Figs. 11.6 to 11.9 for each of the four endogenous variables. Each figure shows the 25 different forecast paths for a particular variable that resulted from different random errors. Note that there is a good deal of dispersion in the forecasts.

A sample standard deviation can be calculated for each variable for each of the four periods in the forecast. These sample standard deviations can be interpreted as estimated standard errors of forecast, and thus can be used to determine confidence intervals for the forecast. In Figs. 11.10 to 11.13 we show forecasts for each variable from a simulation in which no random errors are introduced, and these forecasts can be compared with the actual values of the variables. Also shown in each figure are 95 percent confidence intervals for the forecasts. These are based on the sample standard deviations calculated from the stochastic simulation (the 95 percent confidence interval is approximately two standard deviations above and below the forecast). These confidence intervals are rather large, and would have been somewhat smaller had we accounted for the covariances between the coefficients of each equation. However they provide a conservative measure of the model's forecasting accuracy.

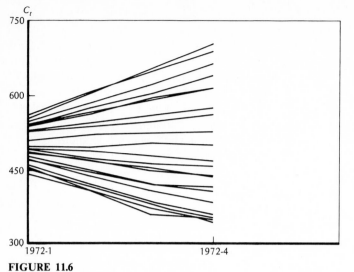

FIGURE 11.6
Stochastic simulation—consumption.

FIGURE 11.7
Stochastic simulation—investment.

FIGURE 11.8
Stochastic simulation—interest rate.

FIGURE 11.9
Stochastic simulation—GNP.

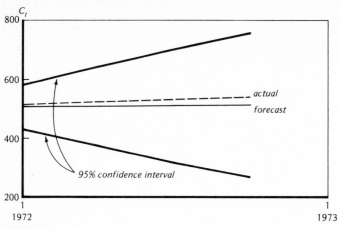

FIGURE 11.10
Forecast of consumption.

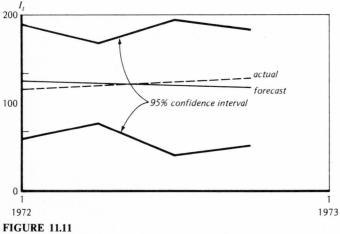

FIGURE 11.11
Forecast of investment.

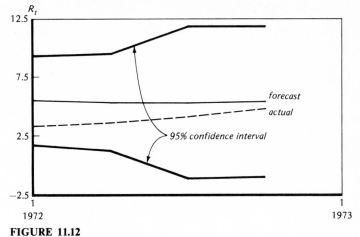

FIGURE 11.12
Forecast of interest rate.

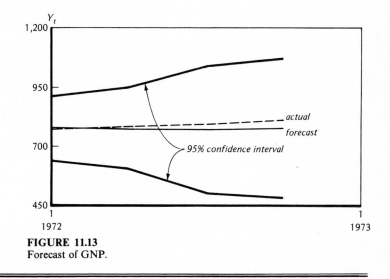

FIGURE 11.13
Forecast of GNP.

Exercises

11.1 Show that if $A_1 \lambda_1{}^t$ and $A_2 \lambda_2{}^t$ are both transient solutions to a model, i.e., both satisfy an equation such as (11.5), then the sum $A_1 \lambda_1{}^t + A_2 \lambda_2{}^t$ must also be a solution.

11.2 Consider the following simple multiplier-accelerator macroeconomic model:

$$C_t = a_1 + a_2 Y_{t-1}$$

$$I_t = b_1 + b_2(C_t - C_{t-1})$$

$$Y_t = C_t + I_t + G_t$$

Note that investment is now a function of changes in consumption, rather than changes in total GNP.

(1) Determine the characteristic equation for this model, and find the associated characteristic roots.
(2) Find the relationships between values of a_2 and b_2 that determine what kind of solution the model will have. Draw a diagram that corresponds to that of Fig. 11.1.
(3) What is the impact multiplier corresponding to a change in G_t? What is the *total* long-run multiplier corresponding to a change in G_t?

11.3 The following equations describe a simple "cobweb" model of a competitive market:

Demand: $\qquad Q_t{}^D = a_1 + a_2 P_t \qquad a_2 < 0$

Supply: $\qquad Q_t{}^S = b_1 + b_2 P_{t-1} \qquad b_2 > 0$

When the market is in equilibrium, $Q_t{}^D = Q_t{}^S$. Now suppose that the market is temporarily out of equilibrium, i.e., that $Q_t{}^D \neq Q_t{}^S$ temporarily.

(1) Show that the price will converge stably to an equilibrium value if

$$\frac{b_2}{a_2} < 1$$

(2) Show that the path to equilibrium will be oscillatory if

$$b_2 > 0$$

and will not be oscillatory if $b_2 < 0$.

11.4 Examine the 95 percent confidence intervals in Figs. 11.10 to 11.13 from the stochastic simulation of Example 11.3. What can you say about the forecasting accuracy of the four-equation model used in the simulation? Examine the model again [Eqs. (10.9) to (10.12)] and the corresponding block diagram in Fig. 11.5, and indicate potential sources of forecasting error. Which coefficients of the model seem to be most critical in terms of introducing forecast error? How might you restructure and/or reestimate the model to improve its forecasting performance?

12

EXAMPLES OF SIMULATION MODELS

In this chapter we present three examples of multi-equation simulation models. We begin with a small model of the United States economy. This model is designed to demonstrate how one might construct a macroeconometric model and use it to forecast over a 2-year period. Because the model is illustrative, it is therefore simple and highly aggregated, representing the economy in a way that is consistent with most introductory Keynesian macroeconomics textbooks. As a result, it does not represent the state of the art of macroeconometric modeling and forecasting; other models exist (most of them much larger) that are likely to be more reliable as tools for forecasting and policy analysis.[1] It is, however,

---

[1] One of the well-known large models is the Wharton econometric model, which is described in M. D. McCarthy, *The Wharton Quarterly Econometric Forecasting Model, Mark III*, Wharton School of Finance and Commerce, University of Pennsylvania, and in V. G. Duggal, L. R. Klein, and M. D. McCarthy, "The Wharton Model Mark III: A Modern IS-LM Construct," *International Economic Review*, October 1974. Two other good examples of large econometric models are the "MPS Model," developed jointly at M.I.T., the University of Pennsylvania, and the Federal Reserve, and described in A. Ando and F. Modigliani, *The MPS Econometric Model: Its Theoretical Foundation and Empirical Findings* (forthcoming), and the University of Michigan Model, described in S. H. Hymans and H. T. Shapiro, "The Structure and Properties of the Michigan Quarterly Econometric Model of the U.S. Economy," *International Economic Review*, October 1974. For examples of smaller quarterly models see R. Fair, *A Short-Run Forecasting Model of the United States Economy* (Lexington, Mass.: Heath, 1971); and E. Kuh and R. Schmalensee, *An Introduction to Applied Macroeconomics* (Amsterdam: North-Holland, 1973). Finally, for an example of a *monthly* macroeconometric model, see T. C. Liu and E. C. Hwa, "Structure and Applications of a Monthly Econometric Model of the U.S.," *International Economic Review*, June 1974.

a very good starting point for students who are interested in macroeconomic modeling.

The second example is a model of a particular industry. It is also small and relatively simple, but serves to show how a *microeconometric* model can be constructed and used for forecasting and analysis. As we shall see, an industry-wide econometric model can provide a consistent framework which accounts for the interactions of producers and consumers that determine market behavior.

Finally, the last example is a "noneconometric" simulation model of a corporation's financial structure. Since all the equations in the model represent financial accounting identities or decision rules, no statistical estimation was required for the model's construction. The example shows, however, how a set of simultaneous time-dependent equations can provide a useful tool for corporate analysis and planning.

12.1 A SMALL MACROECONOMETRIC MODEL

Our first example is designed to take the reader through the steps involved in the construction of a small, quarterly model of the United States economy, and to demonstrate how that model can be used to perform some simple policy experiments. As we discussed in Chapter 10, the design or construction of any model, as well as the criteria used to validate the model, depends very much on the purpose for which the model is built. Since the major objective of our model is short-term macroeconomic forecasting, to be useful the model must contain several basic macroeconomic variables—consumption, investment, GNP, an interest rate, a price level, wages, and unemployment. Because we are also concerned with the means by which the government might control the economy, we will include in the model some basic "policy" variables—the money supply, government spending, and a crude tax mechanism. Since the model is intended to be illustrative, it is convenient to design its structure to be consistent with conventional macroeconomic theory. Therefore, validation of the model will involve a check to see whether the estimated coefficients are statistically significant with the proper sign, as well as whether the simulated time series correlate well with the historical time series.

We begin by specifying the overall structure of the model, including the rough functional form for each equation. Since our purpose in this book is not to teach macroeconomic theory, the theoretical motivation for each equation is presented in a compressed summary form.[2] We then discuss the estimation of the model's equations, and the evaluation of the model's simulation performance. Finally, we use the model to perform some simple forecasting and policy experiments.

---

[2] The reader interested in the application of macroeconomic theory to macroeconometric modelling is referred to E. Kuh and R. Schmalensee, *An Introduction to Applied Macroeconomics* (Amsterdam: North-Holland, 1973), or M. K. Evans, *Macroeconomic Activity* (New York: Harper & Row, 1969).

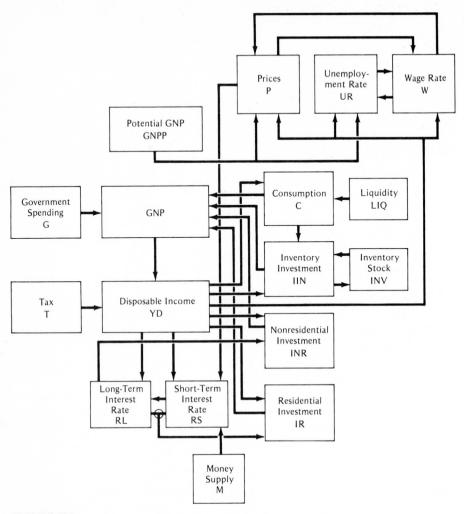

FIGURE 12.1
Block diagram of macroeconometric model.

12.1.1 Structure of the Model

The model consists of 13 equations, of which ten are behavioral and three are identities. The specification of the model involves a considerable degree of inter-relationship between the endogenous variables. This interrelationship is easiest to see from a block diagram, and one is presented in Fig. 12.1. The endogenous and exogenous variables of the model (with equation references) are listed in Table 12.1. The reader may find it useful to refer to Fig. 12.1 and Table 12.1 during the discussion of the model's structure.

The model assumes that exports and imports are always equal and therefore

TABLE 12.1
VARIABLES IN THE MODEL

Endogenous variables		Equation number
C	Consumption	(12.6)
GNP	Gross national product	(12.1) (identity)
IIN	Inventory investment	(12.16)
INR	Nonresidential investment	(12.11)
INV	Stock of inventories	(12.13) (identity)
IR	Residential investment	(12.12)
P	Price level	(12.19)
RL	Long-term interest rate	(12.18)
RS	Short-term interest rate	(12.17)
T	Taxes	(12.2)
UR	Unemployment rate	(12.21)
W	Wage rate	(12.20)
YD	Disposable income	(12.3) (identity)

Exogenous variables	
G	Government spending
GNPP	Potential GNP
LIQ	Liquidity
M	Money supply
T_0	Surtax

can be dropped from the GNP accounting relationship. GNP and its components—consumption C, total investment I, and government expenditures G—are all in real (constant dollar) terms. Total investment is disaggregated and separate equations are estimated to explain nonresidential investment (plant and equipment) INR, residential investment IR, and investment in inventories IIN. The GNP identity, then, can be written as

$$GNP = C + INR + IR + IIN + G \qquad (12.1)$$

The tax mechanism in the model is extremely simple. The total tax flow T (net of transfer payments) is given by

$$T = t \cdot GNP + T_0 \qquad (12.2)$$

where t is an average tax rate and T_0 is a surtax.[3] Thus, disposable income

---

[3] Thus personal income taxes, corporate profits taxes, and indirect business taxes are averaged together. If GNP is roughly constant at some nominal level $(GNP)_0$, then we could think of T_0 in terms of a tax surcharge of S percent, where $S = T_0/t \cdot (GNP)_0$.

YD is given by the identity

$$YD = (1 - t)GNP - T_0 \tag{12.3}$$

Let us now turn to the specification of the consumption function. As one might expect, consumption can be largely explained by disposable income. A consumption function of the form

$$C_t = \sum_{i=0}^{n} \beta_i YD_{t-i} \tag{12.4}$$

or, using a Koyck lag distribution,

$$C_t = a_0 + a_1 YD_t + a_2 C_{t-1} \tag{12.5}$$

should provide a reasonable fit to the data.[4] However, we have chosen to restructure the consumption function to include some measure of wealth, which would have an impact on consumption independent from that of income.[5] Since wealth can be defined in a variety of ways and is difficult to measure, we use as a proxy total liquidity in real (constant dollar) terms, LIQ, which is equal to the sum of demand deposits plus time (savings) deposits. This variable can be controlled (at least roughly) by the Federal Reserve, and therefore can be treated as a government policy variable. Our consumption function, then, is of the form

$$C = f_1(YD, LIQ, C_{-1}) \tag{12.6}$$

Nonresidential investment is also taken to depend on disposable income.[6] Because there is usually a significant lead time between an investment decision and an investment expenditure, income should enter the investment function as a distributed lag. Nonresidential investment should also depend on long-term interest rates RL (probably with a long lag) and on the capital stock K.[7] Our equation is of the form

$$INR = f_2(YD, RL, K) \tag{12.7}$$

---

[4] The reader might wish to review the discussion of distributed lags in Chapter 7.

[5] The problem with Eqs. (12.4) and (12.5) is that the heavy dependence of consumption on income (together with the fact that consumption is itself a large proportion of income) may result in a structural instability in this simultaneous equation model. If the coefficients in (12.4) or (12.5) were large enough, some of the characteristic roots of the (linearized) model would be greater than 1 in magnitude (see Chapter 11). Then, an overprediction of C_t would result in an overprediction of YD_t, which would result in *still larger* overprediction of C_t, etc. This instability is inconsistent with our expectations concerning the behavior of the entire system of equations, rather than the consumption equation alone.

[6] It could be argued that GNP should be used instead, but this would eliminate the influence of direct and indirect business taxes. Thus in order to keep the tax mechanism simple and consistent, we use YD instead of GNP both here and throughout the rest of the model.

[7] If the capital stock is large relative to the *desired* capital stock (which in turn would be roughly proportional to planned output), then the level of investment will be lower. Thus investment should depend *negatively* on the capital stock.

However, since there is no published capital stock data, we treat the investment equation in *differenced* form. To do this, we use the identity that the level of investment in plant and equipment is equal to the change in the stock of plant and equipment, ΔK, plus the rate of depreciation, D:

$$INR = \Delta K + D \tag{12.8}$$

Now by assuming that the capital stock variable is separable from the disposable income and interest rate variables, we may write the investment function as

$$INR = f_2(YD, RL) + \beta_1 K \qquad \beta_1 < 0 \tag{12.9}$$

and by first-differencing we get

$$\Delta INR = \Delta f_2(YD, RL) + \beta_1 \Delta K \tag{12.10}$$

or $\qquad\qquad\qquad \Delta INR = f_2^*(\Delta YD, \Delta RL, INR, D) \tag{12.11}$

In our model D is assumed to be relatively constant, so that its effect is measured by the constant in the estimated nonresidential investment equation.

Residential (housing) investment is difficult to explain accurately in a small macroeconomic model. It depends on mortgage interest rates, mortgage availabilities, and construction costs, none of which are included in our model. We explain residential investment by relating it to income, the short-term interest rate RS, and the difference between the long-term and short-term interest rates:

$$IR = f_3(YD, RS, RL - RS) \tag{12.12}$$

The interest rates are used both as a proxy for mortgage rates and as a crude measure of credit availability (credit becomes tighter as the short-term rate approaches the long-term rate). The dependence on interest rates is expected to be greater than is the case with nonresidential investment, in terms of both magnitude and speed of response.

Inventory investment IIN is related to the stock of inventories INV by the identity

$$INV_t = INV_{t-1} + IIN_t \tag{12.13}$$

To describe inventory investment, we assume that the present stock of inventories is a linear function of present GNP, present consumption, and the stock of inventories last quarter:

$$INV_t = d_1 GNP_t + d_2 C_t + d_3 INV_{t-1} \tag{12.14}$$

The coefficient d_1 should be positive, and the coefficient d_2 should be negative, since consumption spending is expected to deplete the stock of inventories. First-differencing this equation, recognizing from (12.13) that $IIN = \Delta INV$, and replacing GNP with our income variable YD, we have

$$IIN_t = d_1 \Delta YD_t + d_2 \Delta C_t + d_3 IIN_{t-1} \tag{12.15}$$

We would also expect inventory investment to depend negatively on the *stock* of inventories, since if the stock is large (relative to the desired stock), downward adjustments are made by decreasing inventory investment. This means that we must add to our model the identity in Eq. (12.13). Thus inventory investment can be specified as

$$IIN = f_4(\Delta YD, \Delta C, INV, IIN_{-1}) \tag{12.16}$$

Our model contains both a short-term and a long-term interest rate, with the long-term rate assumed to adjust with lags to the expected value of the short-term rate. The short-term interest rate RS is a function of the level of income YD, the rate of change in the real money supply $\Delta M/M$, and current and past values of the rate of inflation $\Delta P/P$. The interest rate does not depend explicitly on the level of the money supply, but there is an indirect dependence through the income variable YD.[8] Our equation, then, has the form

$$RS = f_5\left(YD, \frac{\Delta M}{M}, \frac{\Delta P}{P}\right) \tag{12.17}$$

The long-term interest rate RL responds (with a Koyck lag) to both the level of the short-term rate and changes in the short-term rate. In addition, the long-term rate depends on changes in the income variable. Hence monetary policy (i.e., changes in the money supply) can affect RL only indirectly (through RS), but changes in GNP can affect RL both indirectly through RS and directly through YD. The equation for the long-term interest rate, then, is of the form

$$RL = f_6(RS, \Delta RS, \Delta YD, RL_{-1}) \tag{12.18}$$

An important variable in the model is the price level P, which we would expect to depend on the wage rate W and the level of income. Our equation

---

[8] We are viewing the demand for money as proportional to YD, so that if YD increases, the demand for money increases, and if M is held fixed, the interest rate must rise. We could have included the level of the money supply in the interest rate equation, but collinearity with YD would make a good estimate of its coefficient impossible.

explains the rate of change in the price level, i.e., the inflation rate, which is linked to the rate of change in the wage rate and the rate of change in income. The rate of inflation should also be a function of the excess demand for goods and services that exists in the economy. To describe excess demand, we introduce an exogenous variable into the model—"potential GNP" (GNPP). Excess demand is measured by the difference GNP − GNPP.[9] This difference can, of course, be negative, as it is for most of the period over which the model is estimated. Finally, today's rate of inflation should also depend on rates of inflation that existed in the recent past. When the rate of inflation is high for a year or more, people develop inflationary expectations, which in turn has an inflationary impact on current and future prices. Thus we include a moving average of past inflation rates in our price equation. That equation is thus of the form

$$\frac{\Delta P}{P} = f_7\left(\frac{\Delta W}{W}, \frac{\Delta \text{YD}}{\text{YD}}, \text{GNP} - \text{GNPP}, \frac{\Delta P_{-1}}{P_{-1}}\right) \tag{12.19}$$

What remains now is to explain the wage rate W and the unemployment rate UR. The wage rate depends on past values of the price level, changes in income, the unemployment rate, and past levels of the wage rate:[10]

$$W = f_8(P, \Delta \text{YD}, \text{UR}, W_{-1}) \tag{12.20}$$

Finally, the unemployment rate depends on past and current changes in income (the unemployment rate is lowest when GNP is growing rapidly), the level of excess demand (again, the unemployment rate is low when actual GNP is close to potential GNP), and the wage rate (when wages rise, firms hire fewer workers and the unemployment rate rises). Our equation is

$$\text{UR} = f_9(\Delta \text{YD}, \text{GNP} - \text{GNPP}, W) \tag{12.21}$$

12.1.2 Estimation of the Model

All the equations of the model were estimated using quarterly data over the period 1956–1 to 1973–4.[11] The average tax rate t was found by regressing T (taxes net of transfer payments) on GNP and forcing the regression line through

---

[9] Potential GNP is that GNP which would result if the economy were operating at full capacity. It is measured in real terms, and is essentially a 4 percent trend line. For a discussion of the concept of potential GNP, see A. M. Okun, "Potential GNP: Its Measurement and Significance," *Papers and Proceedings of the Business and Economic Statistics Section of the American Statistical Association*, pp. 98–104, 1962.

[10] The derivation of the wage and unemployment rate equations is too lengthy to be presented here. For a more detailed explanation of why these equations are specified as they are, see R. S. Pindyck, *Optimal Planning for Economic Stabilization* (Amsterdam: North-Holland, 1973), chap. 4.

[11] The data were obtained from the National Bureau of Economic Research Data Bank.

the origin. The estimated value of t was .1538. The tax "surcharge" variable T_0 was set at 0 when estimating all the behavioral equations.

All the other behavioral equations were estimated using two-stage least squares, but for those equations which do not contain a lagged dependent variable a correction for first-order serial correlation was also used. In order to obtain consistent estimates of both the equation coefficients and the serial correlation coefficient, a procedure was devised to combine these estimation techniques. This procedure involves an iterative process in which a first estimate of the serial correlation coefficient ρ is obtained, two-stage least squares is performed on the equation in its generalized difference form, a new estimate of ρ is obtained, two-stage least squares is again performed, etc. This procedure is described in more detail in the appendix to this chapter.

This estimation technique cannot be applied to all the equations of the model, even if serial correlation is present. The estimate of ρ would be inconsistent for those equations which contain a lagged dependent variable; these equations are estimated using two-stage least squares without a serial-correlation correction.[12] In presenting the behavioral equations, we simply show the final estimates obtained in the last step of the procedure. Equations are presented in their original form, even if they have been estimated in generalized difference form, but the estimated value for ρ is included.

Most of the explanation for consumption is provided by a Koyck lag in disposable income, so that disposable income and lagged consumption appear in the equation. The lagged dependent variable also imposes a Koyck lag on liquidity. Because of this, and also because we expect increases (and decreases) in liquidity to affect consumption, we use the change in liquidity rather than the level of liquidity in our equation. The final estimated consumption function, then, is (t statistics are in parentheses):

$$C = 11.11 + .0831\text{YD} + .5047\Delta\text{LIQ} + .8624C_{-1} \qquad (12.22)$$
$$\quad\ (1.98)\quad (1.81)\qquad (4.11)\qquad\quad (11.15)$$

$$R^2 = .998 \qquad \text{SER} = 3.27 \qquad F(3/68) = 1.6 \times 10^4 \qquad \text{DW} = 1.72$$

As we explained earlier, our equation for nonresidential investment is estimated in differenced form so that we may capture the capital stock effect. A polynomial lag distribution is used for the income term; five lag coefficients are fitted to a second-degree polynomial.[13] The long-term interest rate appears in the equation with a four-quarter lag. Finally, a two-quarter moving sum of

---

[12] If the error terms are serially correlated, then the estimate of the coefficient of the lagged dependent variable will also be inconsistent. It could be argued that for this reason it is not desirable to include lagged dependent variables in equations. The lagged dependent variable, however, sometimes provides the best means of imposing a lag distribution on the equation, and this benefit may outweigh the associated statistical problems.

[13] See Chapter 7 for a review of polynomial distributed lags.

the level of nonresidential investment is used as the capital stock proxy. The estimated equation is

$$\Delta INR = .569 + .1198\Delta YD + .0564\Delta YD_{-1} + .0287\Delta YD_{-2} + .0368\Delta YD_{-3}$$
$$(.98) \quad (4.86) \qquad\quad (4.35) \qquad\qquad (1.72) \qquad\qquad (2.76)$$

$$+ .0806\Delta YD_{-4} - .5012\Delta RL_{-4} - .0153(INR_{-1} + INR_{-2}) \qquad (12.23)$$
$$(3.27) \qquad\quad (-1.26) \qquad\quad (-2.74)$$

$$R^2 = .548 \qquad SER = 1.14 \qquad F(5/66) = 16.02 \qquad DW = 1.92$$

$$\hat{\rho} = .037$$

Despite the fact that the estimated coefficient of the long-term interest rate is not significant at the 5 percent level, we do not drop the variable from the equation. Because we believe *a priori* that the interest rate variable provides the link between monetary policy and investment, it is necessary that we include an interest rate as one of the determinants of investment.

Residential investment is related to income, the difference between the long- and short-term interest rates, and the short-term interest rate (with lags). These variables are not sufficient to explain the steep drop in housing starts (and thus in residential investment) that occurred between the second quarter of 1966 and the end of 1967. Since we are restricted to the use of a simple macroeconomic model, we account for this phenomenon by including a dummy variable (DUM1) in the equation. This dummy variable has the value 1 during the period 1966–2 to 1967–4, and has the value 0 at all other times. We would expect the coefficient of this dummy variable to be negative. The estimated equation is shown below:

$$IR = 12.79 + .0351YD + .8354(RL_{-2} - RS_{-2}) - 1.016RS_{-2} - 1.090RS_{-4}$$
$$(10.03) \quad (10.73) \qquad (1.65) \qquad\qquad\qquad (-3.63) \qquad\quad (-5.36)$$

$$- 1.694DUM1 \qquad\qquad\qquad\qquad\qquad\qquad\qquad\qquad (12.24)$$
$$(-2.68)$$

$$R^2 = .729 \qquad SER = .887 \qquad F(5/66) = 35.52 \qquad DW = 1.22$$

$$\hat{\rho} = .674$$

Note that all the explanatory variables are significant at the 5 percent level with the exception of the difference between the long- and short-term interest rates. We include this last variable in the equation, however, since it does provide some measure of credit availability.

Inventory investment is regressed against the income level YD, two-quarter differences in income and consumption, the stock of inventories INV, and a lagged dependent variable:[14]

$$\text{IIN} = 9.174 + .0737\text{YD}_{-1} + .2791(\text{YD} - \text{YD}_{-2}) - .4530(C - C_{-2})$$
$$\quad\;\; (2.80) \quad (3.18) \qquad\qquad (4.40) \qquad\qquad\qquad (-3.97)$$

$$\quad - .3014\text{INV}_{-1} + .5190\text{IIN}_{-1} \tag{12.25}$$
$$\quad\;\; (-3.04) \qquad\quad (5.62)$$

$$R^2 = .621 \qquad \text{SER} = 2.75 \qquad F(5/66) = 21.60 \qquad \text{DW} = 2.11$$

Note that all the explanatory variables are statistically significant and have the correct signs.

The short-term interest rate is related to income, changes in income, the rate of growth of the money supply, and a two-period moving sum of past inflation rates:

$$\text{RS} = -.499 + .0069\text{YD} + .0140\,\Delta\text{YD}_{-1} - 30.51\,\frac{\Delta M}{M}$$
$$\quad\;\; (-.53) \quad\;\; (3.86) \qquad\;\; (1.26) \qquad\quad (-2.80)$$

$$\quad + 57.21 \left(\frac{\Delta P_{-1}}{P_{-1}} + \frac{\Delta P_{-2}}{P_{-2}} \right) \tag{12.26}$$
$$\quad\;\; (3.15)$$

$$R^2 = .431 \qquad \text{SER} = .500 \qquad F(4/67) = 12.70 \qquad \text{DW} = 1.54 \qquad \hat{\rho} = .755$$

The long-term interest rate responds, with a Koyck lag, to the short-term rate and to changes in the short-term rate. We also include a two-quarter difference in income in the equation to allow for a direct impact between changes in output (and thus changes in the demand for money) and the long-term rate. The estimated equation is

$$\text{RL} = .317 + .1597\text{RS} + .1750\,\Delta\text{RS} + .0113(\text{YD} - \text{YD}_{-2}) + .7771\text{RL}_{-1} \tag{12.27}$$
$$\quad\;\; (2.03) \;\; (1.86) \qquad\; (1.91) \qquad\quad (2.73) \qquad\qquad\quad (8.55)$$

$$R^2 = .940 \qquad \text{SER} = .348 \qquad F(4/67) = 261.8 \qquad \text{DW} = 1.92$$

The price equation is estimated in terms of the rate of inflation, $\Delta P/P$. The explanatory variables include a two-period moving sum of the rate of growth

---

[14] Single-quarter differences in income and consumption could have been used instead of two-quarter differences, and would result in a good fit. The resulting equation, however, would be somewhat unstable in a simulation framework. This would be an example of statistical fit that is somewhat artificial—we are in effect regressing a noisy variable against its own noise. For this reason two-quarter differences are used.

in the wage rate, excess demand (as measured by the difference between GNP and potential GNP), the rate of change in lagged income, and a three-quarter moving sum of past inflation rates (which is used to represent the expected rate of inflation). In addition, a dummy variable (DUM2) is included to account for the drop in the rate of inflation that occurred as a result of price and wage controls during the period 1971–3 through 1972–4. The dummy takes on the value 1 during that period and is 0 otherwise. The estimated equation is shown below:

$$
\frac{\Delta P}{P} = -.00055 + .1637\left(\frac{\Delta W}{W} + \frac{\Delta W_{-1}}{W_{-1}}\right) + 4.35 \times 10^{-5}(GNP_{-1} - GNPP_{-1})
$$
$$
\quad (-.44) \qquad (4.51) \qquad\qquad\qquad\qquad\qquad (2.21)
$$

$$
+ .0470\frac{\Delta YD_{-3}}{YD_{-3}} - .0034DUM2 + .2375\left(\frac{\Delta P_{-2}}{P_{-2}} + \frac{\Delta P_{-3}}{P_{-3}} + \frac{\Delta P_{-4}}{P_{-4}}\right) \quad (12.28)
$$
$$
\quad (1.47) \qquad\quad (-2.54) \qquad\quad (6.87)
$$

$$
R^2 = .684 \qquad SER = .0026 \qquad F(5/66) = 28.53 \qquad DW = 1.47
$$

The wage equation explains the average money wage rate expressed in dollars per hour. Explanatory variables include the price level (lagged), changes in income, the unemployment rate (lagged), and the same dummy variable to account for price and wage controls. In addition, a lagged dependent variable is included. The estimated equation is

$$
W = -.275 + .6870P_{-3} + .0016\,\Delta YD - .0084UR_{-2} + .8376W_{-1} - .0142DUM2
$$
$$
\quad (-3.19) \;\; (3.05) \qquad\quad (4.52) \qquad\quad (-3.32) \qquad\quad (13.94) \qquad (-1.56)
$$
$$
\qquad\qquad\qquad\qquad\qquad\qquad\qquad\qquad\qquad\qquad\qquad\qquad (12.29)
$$

$$
R^2 = .999 \qquad SER = .015 \qquad F(5/66) = 2.35 \times 10^4 \qquad DW = 1.84
$$

Finally, the unemployment rate (measured in percent) is related to current and past changes in income (and thus output), the difference between actual and potential GNP, and the wage rate (lagged). The estimated equation includes a lagged dependent variable:

$$
UR = 1.266 - .0205\,\Delta YD - .0152\,\Delta YD_{-1} - .0066\,\Delta YD_{-2}
$$
$$
\quad (3.11) \quad (-3.49) \qquad (-2.33) \qquad\quad (-1.09)
$$

$$
- .0187(GNP_{-1} - GNPP_{-1}) + .0972W_{-2} + .6773UR_{-1} \qquad (12.30)
$$
$$
\quad (-4.00) \qquad\qquad\qquad\qquad (1.42) \qquad\quad (8.40)
$$

$$
R^2 = .949 \qquad SER = .243 \qquad F(6/65) = 201.0 \qquad DW = .96
$$

TABLE 12.2
RESULTS OF HISTORICAL SIMULATIONS

Variable	1956–1 to 1974–2		1970–1 to 1974–2	
	RMS error	RMS percent error	RMS error	RMS percent error
C	15.35	3.66	8.013	1.51
INR	6.177	9.55	2.89	3.28
IR	2.301	9.259	4.165	12.74
IIN	6.514	102.22	7.589	85.82
RS	.887	28.49	1.38	32.54
RL	.717	14.34	.761	12.77
P	.038	3.14	.017	1.07
W	.093	3.34	.03	.8
UR	1.355	31.34	.638	12.85
GNP	23.81	3.56	13.606	1.43

Note that most of the explanation in the equation comes from income. If GNP and income are rising rapidly, the equation will predict a low unemployment rate.

12.1.3 Simulation of the Model

The model can now be simulated as a complete system. Two historical simulations were performed in order to evaluate the model's ability to replicate the actual data.[15] The first simulation was begun at the beginning of the estimation period (1956–1) and ended in 1974–2 (two-quarters beyond the end of the estimation period), while the second runs from the first quarter of 1970 to the second quarter of 1974. The results of these simulations are summarized in Table 12.2. For each simulation, RMS errors and RMS percent errors are shown for 10 endogenous variables in the model. In addition, actual and simulated values for all the endogenous variables are plotted in Figs. 12.2 to 12.11 for the simulation that begins in 1970.

Note that although the model reproduces the time path for GNP rather closely (the RMS percent error is about 1.5 percent for the shorter simulation), the simulated values for most of the other endogenous variables deviate considerably from the actual series. Because residential investment fails to pick up the sharp upturn and then downturn in that variable that occurred between 1971 and 1974, GNP and its components are underpredicted from 1972 onward.

---

[15] All simulations are *dynamic*, in the sense that *simulated* (rather than actual) values for endogenous variables in a given period are used as inputs when the model is solved in future periods. See Chapter 10 for details on the simulation process.

FIGURE 12.2
Historical simulation—GNP.

FIGURE 12.3
Historical simulation—consumption.

FIGURE 12.4
Historical simulation—nonresidential investment.

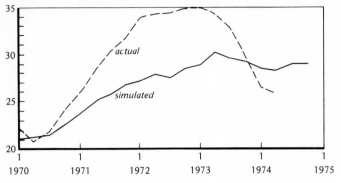

FIGURE 12.5
Historical simulation—residential investment.

FIGURE 12.6
Historical simulation—inventory investment.

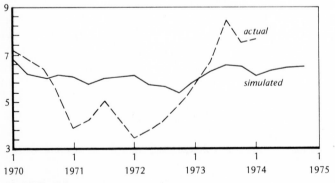

FIGURE 12.7
Historical simulation—short-term interest rate.

FIGURE 12.8
Historical simulation—long-term interest rate.

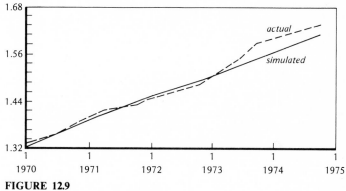

FIGURE 12.9
Historical simulation—price level.

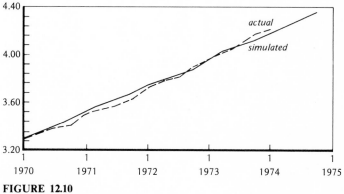

FIGURE 12.10
Historical simulation—wage rate.

FIGURE 12.11
Historical simulation—unemployment rate.

The result is that the simulated unemployment rate is also considerably higher than the actual unemployment rate after 1972. It is difficult to say whether the major source of error in the model lies in the equation for residential investment or in the equation for the short-term interest rate. The simulated values for the short-term interest rate failed to reproduce the downturn and then upturn in that variable between 1970 and 1974. Overpredicting interest rates in 1971 contributed to the underprediction of residential investment in 1972 and 1973. Since the simulation errors are in some cases large, and turning points in several variables are not reproduced, we might not want to rely on this model as a serious tool for macroeconomic forecasting. Nonetheless, the model still provides a good example for macroeconometric policy analysis, as we will see below.

Dynamic Multipliers

Before using the model to perform some simple policy experiments, it would be interesting to calculate the dynamic GNP multipliers that correspond to changes in government spending and the money supply. These total multipliers, representing the net change in GNP after the specified number of periods has elapsed, are shown in Table 12.3. The government spending multipliers were obtained by increasing that variable by \$1 billion above its historical path beginning in the first quarter of 1967. The simulated series for GNP corresponding to the historical series

TABLE 12.3
GOVERNMENT SPENDING AND MONEY SUPPLY MULTIPLIERS

Period	0	1	2	3	4	5	6	7	8	9	10	11	12	13	14
ΔGNP from ΔG	1.68	2.21	1.81	1.26	1.35	1.80	2.21	2.34	2.27	2.17	2.17	2.26	2.36	2.41	2.41
ΔGNP from ΔM	.517	.132	.261	$-.044$	$-.068$	$-.002$	.13	.127	.068	$-.002$	-0.14	.003	.023	.025	.015

for government spending was then subtracted from the simulated series for GNP resulting from this higher value of government spending. Next, the money supply was increased by \$1 billion in the first quarter of 1967 and all quarters thereafter, and corresponding changes in GNP were similarly calculated. Note that the government spending multiplier oscillates. The impact multiplier is 1.68 and the long-run multiplier is 2.41, but the multiplier increases and decreases before reaching this equilibrium value. The money supply multiplier approaches 0 after several periods, as expected, since it is only *changes* in the money supply that enter the interest rate equation. Thus, a change in the money supply has an impact on the GNP only in the first few quarters. Monetary policy experiments in this model must therefore involve changes in the *percentage growth rates* in the money supply, and not in a change in the level of the money supply.

12.1.4 Use of the Model for Forecasting and Policy Analysis

We now use the model to perform some simple forecasting and policy experiments. In each experiment we simulate the model 2 years into the future, beginning in the second quarter of 1974. Our objective is to forecast the effects of alternative economic policies by formulating those policies in terms of trajectories for the exogenous policy variables. In particular, we perform the following five simulation experiments:

1 *Base Forecast* In this first experiment, we generate a forecast out to the middle of 1976 under the assumption that all the exogenous variables, including the policy variables, grow at their historical rates of growth. This means that liquidity (in real terms) grows at a rate of 2 percent per year, the money supply (in real terms) grows at 2 percent per year, and government spending (also in real terms) grows at 4 percent per year. In addition, the tax surcharge variable (T_0) is set at 0.

2 *Tax Surcharge Experiment* In this experiment, liquidity, the money supply, and government spending all grow at the same rates as in experiment 1, but a 5 percent tax surcharge is imposed over the period 1974-3 to 1976-2. The objective is to determine how large an impact this tax surcharge will have on GNP, interest rates, unemployment, and the rate of inflation.

3 *Money Growth Experiment* Now liquidity and the money supply both grow at an annual rate of 6 percent per year; government spending again grows at 4 percent per year; and the tax surcharge is set at 0. This more rapid expansion of the money supply should result in a more rapid growth of GNP (through lower interest rates and more investment), but may also result in more inflation.

4 *Wage and Price Controls* In this experiment, we manipulate the dummy variable DUM2 that is used in the price and wage equations to account for the phase I and phase II wage and price controls. That dummy variable is now assigned the value of 1 over the period 1974-3 to 1976-2. This is intended to replicate roughly the effects of wage and price controls that were in existence over the period 1971-3 to 1972-4. All other exogenous variables follow the same paths as in experiment 1.

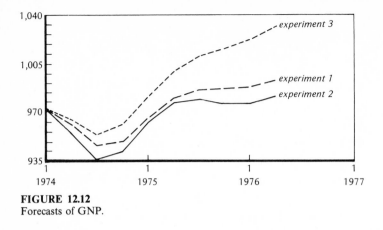

FIGURE 12.12
Forecasts of GNP.

5 *Expansion of Government Spending*   In this last experiment, the rate of growth of government spending is set at 6 percent. The objective is to examine how an increase in government spending will affect GNP, prices, and other variables. The wage-price dummy variable is again set at 0, and the other exogenous variables follow the same paths as in experiment 1.

The results of all these experiments are presented graphically. Forecasts for several endogenous variables corresponding to experiments 1, 2, and 3 are shown in Figs. 12.12 to 12.20, while the results for experiments 1, 4, and 5 are compared in Figs. 12.21 to 12.27.

The results are not at all surprising. The 5 percent tax surcharge (experiment 2) results in lower levels of GNP, consumption, nonresidential investment, and residential investment through the multiplier effect. Note that residential investment, however, is only slightly below its level for the base case. This is because the drop in GNP results in lower interest rates, which in turn stimulates residential investment (and, to some extent, nonresidential investment). The tax

FIGURE 12.13
Consumption.

FIGURE 12.14
Nonresidential investment.

FIGURE 12.15
Residential investment.

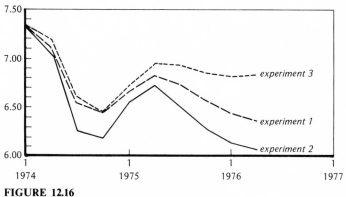

FIGURE 12.16
Short-term interest rate.

FIGURE 12.17
Long-term interest rate.

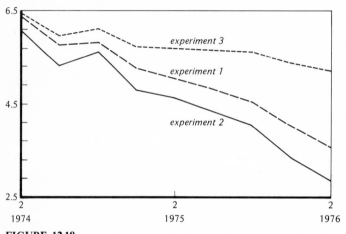

FIGURE 12.18
Annual rate of inflation.

FIGURE 12.19
Wage rate.

FIGURE 12.20
Unemployment rate.

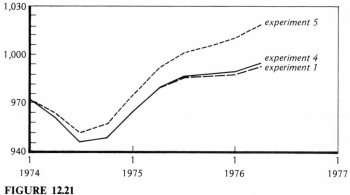

FIGURE 12.21
Forecasts of GNP.

FIGURE 12.22
Residential investment.

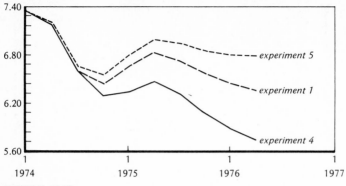

FIGURE 12.23
Short-term interest rate.

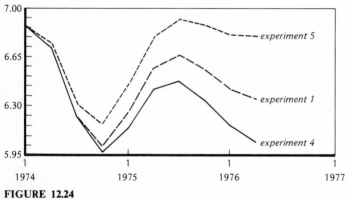

FIGURE 12.24
Long-term interest rate.

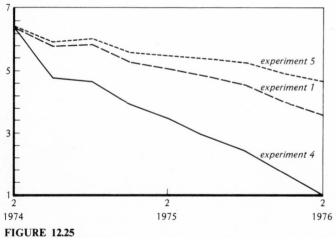

FIGURE 12.25
Annual rate of inflation.

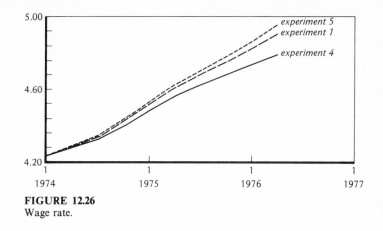

FIGURE 12.26
Wage rate.

surcharge also results in lower rates of inflation, lower wage rates, and a higher unemployment rate, all as a result of the more slowly growing GNP.

The more rapid growth of the money supply and liquidity (experiment 3) results in an increase in GNP and its components. The growth in liquidity stimulates consumption directly, and this results in more rapid growth in GNP, and in a higher rate of inflation. More rapid growth in the money supply tends to depress interest rates, but this is more than compensated for by the increase in GNP growth and the higher rate of inflation, so that the net effect is a *rise* in interest rates. Of course the rapid growth in GNP results in less unemployment, but this is at the expense of a higher rate of inflation.

The use of wage-price controls (experiment 4) has little effect on GNP, consumption, and the unemployment rate, but it does result in a lower annual rate of inflation, lower interest rates, and a slight increase in residential investment. The interpretation of these results, as well as the results of experiment 5, are left to the reader (see Exercises 12.1 and 12.2).

FIGURE 12.27
Unemployment rate.

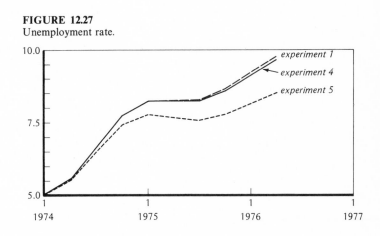

The model could, of course, be used to perform other forecasting experiments. For example, the effects of a change in the propensity to consume could be measured by changing the coefficient multiplying disposable income in the consumption equation, and then simulating the model into the future. The reader who has access to the appropriate computer simulation package may wish to utilize this model and perform his/her own simulation experiments (see Exercise 12.3).

12.2 AN INDUSTRY-WIDE ECONOMETRIC MODEL

As our microeconometric example we examine a model of the United States tobacco industry constructed by Vernon, Rives, and Naylor.[16] The model attempts to explain the behavior of the tobacco industry over the 18-year period 1949–1966, and was constructed using annual data for that time period. The model determines the annual production (supply) of flue-cured tobacco leaf, the annual production of cigarettes (and thus the demand for tobacco leaf), and by equating demand and supply, the price of tobacco leaf. All these variables are at least partly dependent on certain government controls. An important use of the model, then, would be as a tool to forecast tobacco prices and measure the impact on prices of government controls.

The model is completely recursive; i.e., endogenous variables affect other endogenous variables only with a time lag, so that there is no simultaneity, and ordinary least squares (rather than two-stage least squares) is used to estimate the model's behavioral equations. The model, which contains a total of seven behavioral equations and eleven identities, can best be understood by breaking it up into three blocks, as is shown in Fig. 12.28. The first block contains six equations which explain the production of tobacco leaf and the effect of government restrictions on leaf output. The second block describes the determination of leaf price and the effects of government support prices. Finally, the third block describes cigarette manufacturing, which in turn determines the demand for tobacco leaf. The leaf price is determined in the second block of equations by equilibrating leaf supply (from the first block) with this demand for tobacco leaf.

Since 1933, the United States government has placed certain controls on the operation of the tobacco leaf market which are accounted for in the model. In particular, output restrictions have been placed on leaf production, and

---

[16] J. M. Vernon, N. W. Rives, Jr., and T. H. Naylor, "An Econometric Model of the Tobacco Industry," *Review of Economics and Statistics*, May 1969. For other examples of microeconometric simulation models, see W. H. Wallace, T. H. Naylor, and W. E. Sasser, "An Econometric Model of the Textile Industry in the United States," *Review of Economics and Statistics*, Feb. 1968; F. M. Fisher, P. H. Cootner, and M. N. Baily, "An Econometric Model of the World Copper Industry," *Bell Journal of Economics and Management Science*, vol. 3, no. 2, 1972; J. M. Griffin, "The Effects of Higher Prices on Electricity Consumption," *Bell Journal of Economics and Management Science*, vol. 5, no. 2, 1974; and P. W. MacAvoy and R. S. Pindyck, *The Economics of the Natural Gas Shortage* (Amsterdam: North-Holland, 1975).

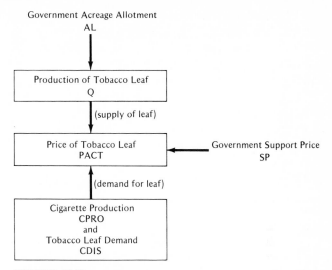

FIGURE 12.28
Simplified block diagram of tobacco leaf model.

support prices for tobacco leaf were maintained by the government.[17] These controls are embodied in the model via two policy variables, acreage allotment AL and the support price SP.

Let us now turn to the econometric model, and examine it on a block-by-block basis.

12.2.1   Production of Tobacco Leaf

In this model, leaf production is treated separately from the determination of leaf price. This is based on the assumption that price and production are not determined simultaneously. Rather, it is assumed that production depends on the lagged price, while price depends on current production. Thus production and price are determined recursively.[18]

Leaf production Q is determined in the model as being proportional to the amount of acreage planted A. This first equation, then, can be written as

$$Q = A \times \overline{\text{YPA}} \tag{12.31}$$

---

[17] The maintenance of high leaf prices by the government was justified on the grounds that leaf producers formed a competitive industry whereas the buyers of tobacco leaf, namely the cigarette manufacturing companies, were highly concentrated and thus represented an oligopsony. Government policies were intended to offset the oligopsony power of the cigarette manufacturers.

[18] This assumption is reasonable, since tobacco growers decide on leaf production in the spring of each year, based upon the price received for the crop in the preceding fall. The tobacco is then harvested during the summer and taken to market.

$\overline{\text{YPA}}$ is the yield per acre, which should depend on such factors as weather and technical change. This variable is made exogenous to the model, however, so that once the amount of producing acreage is determined, production is also determined.[19] The remaining equations, then, serve to determine A, the amount of acreage planted.

The dollar value of producing acreage AVAL is determined by the following identity:

$$\text{AVAL} = \frac{\overline{\text{YPA}} \times \text{PACT}}{\overline{\text{WPX}}} \qquad (12.32)$$

where PACT = the tobacco leaf price

$\overline{\text{WPX}}$ = the wholesale price index

Thus, acre value is just the yield per acre times the price per unit of that yield, deflated by the wholesale price index so that the value is in real terms.

Under free-market conditions, one would expect a supply relationship to exist between producing acreage and the value of acreage, i.e., $A = f(\text{AVAL}_{-1})$. Because of government intervention, however, it is impossible to estimate such a supply relationship. Instead of explaining acreage directly, an equation is estimated to explain the difference between the acreage allotment of the government $\overline{\text{AL}}$ and the acreage planted A. This difference is called the underage (UND = $\overline{\text{AL}} - A$), and is the number of acres not planted even though permitted by the government allotment. We would expect that UND will be lower the greater is the economic incentive to growers.

The authors of the model take the approach of estimating an acreage equation using 1910–1930 data, and then extrapolating this equation forward to create a hypothetical free-market acreage (AFR) over the 1949–1966 time period. The estimated equation for free-market acreage is shown below, with standard errors in parentheses:

$$\text{AFR} = 197.60 + .9089A_{-1} + 3.1058\text{AVAL}_{-1} \qquad (12.33)$$
$$\quad\;\; (89.07) \quad (.0738) \qquad (.8684)$$

$$\overline{R}^2 = .9025 \qquad \text{DW} = 2.14 \qquad \text{SER} = 84.54$$

Using the estimate of free-market acreage obtained from Eq. (12.33), free-market acreage less the government allotment (AFRMAL) is determined by the identity

$$\text{AFRMAL} = \widehat{\text{AFR}} - \overline{\text{AL}} \qquad (12.34)$$

Underage can now be estimated econometrically by relating it to the free-market acreage less allotment. The underage equation contains two dummy variables in

---

[19] Exogenous variables have a bar over them.

addition to AFRMAL. The first (SBDMY) is equal to 1 during the years 1957 and 1958 and is 0 otherwise, and accounts for the effects of the government soil bank program at that time. The second dummy variable (LBDMY) represents the year 1965, and accounts for a change in allotments that occurred after planting was over in that year.[20]

The estimated equation for underage is as follows:

$$UND = 26.964 - .0160AFRMAL + 46.397SBDMY + 33.642LBDMY \qquad (12.35)$$
$$(6.672) \quad (.0085) \qquad\qquad (5.227) \qquad\qquad (7.537)$$

$$\bar{R}^2 = .8296 \qquad DW = 1.56 \qquad SER = 6.90$$

Finally, actual acreage is determined as the difference between the acreage allotment and estimated underage:

$$\hat{A} = \overline{AL} - \widehat{UND} \qquad (12.36)$$

12.2.2 The Price of Tobacco Leaf

This part of the model determines the actual leaf price (PACT) by explaining the mutual dependence between that variable and the amount of leaf pledged by growers (T) at the support price $(\overline{SP})$. Since T depends upon the support price, the model thus explains the impact of the support price on the actual price.

One would expect that T, the amount of leaf pledged at the support price, would depend upon the difference between $\overline{SP}$ and a hypothetical free-market price, PFR, which represents what the price would have been if the government control program were not in effect. As we shall see, this hypothetical free-market price can be estimated from an equation for the actual price by setting the amount of leaf pledged under the support program to 0.

The actual leaf price is a function of two variables, disposable income and the ratio of the net leaf supply to domestic leaf consumption (or "disappearance"). This second variable (SQNET) is given by the identity

$$SQNET = \frac{STK_{-1} + Q - T - \overline{X}}{DDISP} \qquad (12.37)$$

where STK_{-1} = stock of tobacco leaf remaining from the previous year
$\overline{X}$ = exports of tobacco leaf
Q = leaf production
$DDISP$ = leaf disappearance, determined from cigarette consumption in the third block of the model

---

[20] The original allotment was set at 515,425 acres in December 1964, but was increased in May 1965 to 607,335 acres as a result of a new government control program.

Q was determined in the first block of equations, and the determination of T will be discussed shortly. The leaf stock is also given by an identity:

$$STK = STK_{-1} + Q - DDISP - \overline{X} \tag{12.38}$$

The variable SQNET thus represents a ratio of inventory stock to sales. Since cigarette manufacturers attempt to maintain a constant ratio of leaf supply to leaf usage, this variable should have a negative effect on the leaf price.

The other explanatory variable in the leaf price equation is per capita disposable income ($\overline{PCAPY}$). This variable accounts for shifts in demand, and thus should have a positive impact on the price. The estimated equation for the leaf price is

$$\log PACT = -.2833 \log SQNET + .5858 \log \overline{PCAPY} \tag{12.39}$$
$$(.1108) \qquad\qquad (.0189)$$

$$\overline{R}^2 = .7873 \qquad DW = 1.66 \qquad SER = .043$$

It is still necessary to determine the amount of leaf pledged, which is related to the support price less the free-market price. The hypothetical free-market price is determined from the actual leaf price equation under the assumption that $T = 0$, that is, from

$$\log PFR = -.2833 \log SQ + .5858 \log \overline{PCAPY} \tag{12.40}$$

where
$$SQ = \frac{STK_{-1} + Q - \overline{X}}{DDISP} \tag{12.41}$$

The support price less the free-market price (SPMFP) is thus determined by the identity

$$SPMFP = \overline{SP} - PFR \tag{12.42}$$

Finally, the amount of leaf pledged under the support program is given by the following estimated equation:

$$\log T = 5.4038 + .1472 SPMFP \tag{12.43}$$
$$(.1609) \quad (.0352)$$

$$\overline{R}^2 = .4922 \qquad DW = 1.27 \qquad SER = .439$$

12.2.3   Cigarette Production and the Demand for Tobacco Leaf

One of the variables that determines leaf price is DDISP, the domestic disappearance of tobacco leaf, and this of course is related to cigarette production.

Domestic leaf disappearance is given by

$$DDISP = CDIS + \overline{OTHDIS} \qquad (12.44)$$

where CDIS = leaf disappearance into cigarette production
$\overline{OTHDIS}$ = disappearance into other tobacco products

The variable CDIS is in turn determined by the identity

$$CDIS = 1000(LFPCIG \times CPRO) \qquad (12.45)$$

where LFPCIG = quantity of leaf per cigarette
CPRO = cigarette production

The quantity of leaf per cigarette has been declining slightly over time, and is predicted using the following exponential trend equation:

$$\log LFPCIG = .6161 - .0289\overline{TIME} \qquad (12.46)$$
$$(.0156) \quad (.0017)$$

$$\overline{R}^2 = .9531 \qquad DW = 1.38 \qquad SER = .028$$

Cigarette production is equal to domestic cigarette consumption (CCON, measured in packs) plus tax-free withdrawals and exports of cigarettes ($\overline{TXFWD}$):

$$CPRO = 20(CCON) + \overline{TXFWD} \qquad (12.47)$$

One remaining equation is needed to explain domestic cigarette consumption. A log-log demand function is estimated that relates cigarette consumption to the real retail price of cigarettes ($\overline{RPCIG}$) and real disposable income ($\overline{RDISY}$):

$$\log CCON = -.4250 \log \overline{RPCIG} + .7721 \log \overline{RDISY} \qquad (12.48)$$
$$(.1349) \qquad\qquad (.0765)$$

$$\overline{R}^2 = .9094 \qquad DW = .5900 \qquad SER = 0.467 \qquad (1949-1966)$$

The estimated price elasticity of $-.425$ and income elasticity of $.772$ are comparable to estimates obtained from other studies.

12.2.4 Simulation of the Model

The authors of this model performed an historical simulation to test the model's validity. The simulated and actual values for the more important endogenous variables in the model are shown graphically in Figs. 12.29 to 12.32.

Note that flue-cured underage tracks the historical series quite closely, while the stock of flue-cured tobacco leaf veers away from the actual series after several

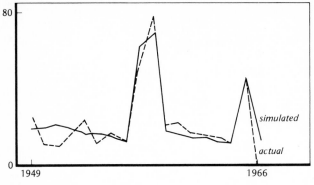

FIGURE 12.29
Flue-cured underage (1,000 acres).

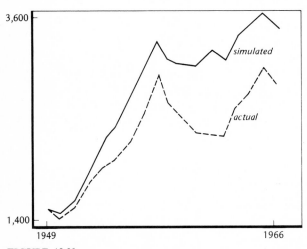

FIGURE 12.30
Stocks of flue-cured tobacco leaf (1,000 lb).

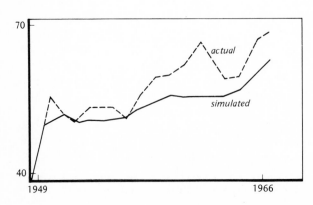

FIGURE 12.31
Actual price of flue-cured
tobacco leaf (cents).

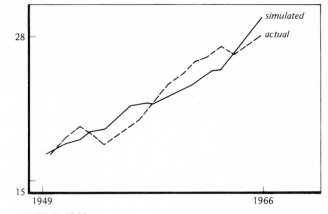

FIGURE 12.32
Domestic cigarette consumption, United States (billions of cigarettes).

years. Since the stock of tobacco leaf in the current year depends in part on the stock of the previous year, there is a tendency for errors in the estimation of this variable to accumulate over time.

The actual price of tobacco leaf tracks only the broad trend of the historical series, missing the sharp upturn that occurs around 1960, and the usefulness of the model as a tool for forecasting tobacco leaf prices is thus rather limited. One reason for this is that the equations that determine cigarette production—and thus leaf demand—fail to pick up the turning points in these variables. Note, for example, that the simulated values for domestic cigarette consumption also track only the broad trend in the actual series.

These results indicate that the model, while providing an overall description of the tobacco industry, would be of only limited use for forecasting. This is not surprising. The model is rather simple, so that one would not expect it to provide a full representation for what is a rather complex industry.[21] The model does, however, provide a good starting point for what could be a more detailed econometric analysis of the tobacco industry.

12.3 A SIMULATION MODEL FOR CORPORATE FINANCIAL PLANNING

As we explained in Chapter 10, a simulation model need not consist only of equations that are statistically estimated. A *financial simulation model*, containing equations all of which are accounting identities that describe the financial structure of a particular corporation, is an example of a "noneconometric"

---

[21] In addition, the difficulty of obtaining information about some of the exogenous variables (such as acreage allotment and tobacco leaf exports) may substantially complicate the forecasting process.

model. Although the equations of a financial simulation model are not behavioral, many of them will be *time-dependent*, enabling the model to describe the dynamic characteristics of the firm's financial structure. By simulating the model into the future, one can forecast and analyze the effects of economic conditions, changing revenue streams, or alternative financial strategies on the firm's financial position. Typically, these models are used to generate *pro forma* balance sheets and *pro forma* income statements, i.e., balance sheets and income statements that would apply in the future under specific assumptions about capitalization, debt, future costs and revenues, etc.

Financial simulation models have become a recent addition to the quantitative tool kit of corporate planners and business analysts. They are particularly valuable for planning because they provide a consistent framework that simultaneously accounts for all the interrelationships in a firm's financial structure. Thus, although they are new, their usefulness is becoming increasingly accepted.

In this section a simple example of a financial simulation model[22] is presented. The firm described by the example is imaginary, and its financial structure is intentionally a simple one. It was designed only to illustrate how such a model is constructed and applied to corporate financial planning. The example embodies many of the principles of financial decision making encountered in actual situations, but it abstracts from the detail associated with operational firms.

The objective of this model is to generate *pro forma* financial statements that describe the financial condition of the firm for any assumed pattern of sales in the future. Particular attention is paid to the determination of retained earnings, dividends paid, and the securing of additional funds through the flotation of long-term debt or the sale of common and preferred stock. A given sales pattern implies a set of asset requirements; these, in turn, are combined with a number of decision rules supplied by management to calculate the distribution of retained earnings and the levels and types of new financing.

The equations of the model include both descriptive relationships among financial variables and basic decision rules specified in a very general form. The descriptive relationships are accounting relationships and definitions. The decision rules, on the other hand, are not written in the form of conventional algebraic equations. They are described algebraically using *conditional operators*, consisting of statements of the type: "IF ... THEN ... ELSE." A decision rule describes what to do given a binary choice (or series of binary choices). For example, suppose we wanted to express the following decision rule algebraically: "If X is greater than 0, then Y is set equal to X divided by 2. Otherwise, Y is set equal to 0." Using the symbol "GT" to represent "greater than," we use the conditional operator "IF ... THEN ... ELSE" to write the decision rule algebraically as:

$$Y = \text{IF } X \text{ GT } 0 \text{ THEN } X/2 \text{ ELSE } 0 \tag{12.49}$$

---

[22] This example was constructed by Robert B. Anthonyson and J. Phillip Cooper for Dynamics Associates, Inc., Cambridge, Mass., and is used here by permission.

Suppose that we wanted the decision rule instead to read: "If X is greater than 0, then Y is set equal to X divided by 2. Otherwise, Y depends on Z. If Z is less than 3 times X, then Y is set equal to 0, but otherwise Y is set equal to Z." The equation for this rule would be

$$Y = \text{IF } X \text{ GT } 0 \text{ THEN } X/2 \text{ ELSE IF } Z \text{ LT } 3X \text{ THEN } 0 \text{ ELSE } Z \quad (12.50)$$

Equations (12.49) and (12.50) are highly nonlinear relationships, and models that include relationships of this kind can be solved using appropriate computer simulation packages.

Data for our corporate model include a set of financial variables calculated by the equations of the model and various types of parameters which are supplied by management. Examples of input data are: historical values such as stock outstanding in a previous period, "environmental" data such as the expected interest rate on new debt or tax rates, observed or assumed characteristics of the business operation such as the ratio between accounts receivable and sales, and financial decision variables such as the maximum desired debt-equity ratio. In the present example, the focus is on the pattern of sales, and the financing decision problem is solved for alternative sales scenarios. The technique is perfectly general, however, since any one or any combination of the input variables or parameters could be chosen for a sensitivity analysis.

Table 12.4 presents a list of the variables used in the model; there are 37

TABLE 12.4

UNKNOWNS AND PARAMETERS SUPPLIED BY MANAGEMENT

Unknowns

1.	A	Total assets
2.	AP	Accounts payable
3.	AR	Accounts receivable
4.	CA	Current assets
5.	CASH	Cash
6.	CGS	Cost of goods sold
7.	CL	Current liabilities
8.	CMDIV	Common dividends
9.	DEP	Depreciation
10.	DPS	Dividends per share
11.	EAFCD	Earnings available for common dividends
12.	EAT	Earnings after taxes
13.	EBT	Earnings before taxes
14.	EPS	Earnings per share
15.	EQTY	Total equity
16.	FA	Net plant and equipment
17.	INT	Interest
18.	INV	Inventories
19.	L	Long-term debt
20.	LIAB	Total liabilities and equity

TABLE 12.4 (*continued*)

21. NF	Needed funds	
22. NFA	New fixed assets	
23. NL	New long-term debt	
24. NPFDSK	New preferred stock	
25. NS	New common stock	
26. NUMCS	Number of common shares outstanding	
27. OC	Operating costs	
28. OCL	Other current liabilities	
29. OI	Operating income	
30. P	Price per common share	
31. PFDIV	Preferred dividends	
32. PFDSK	Preferred stock	
33. R	Retained earnings	
34. RCASH	Minimum cash requirement	
35. RETMIN	Desired addition to retained earnings	
36. S	Common stock	
37. TAX	Income taxes	

Parameters supplied by management

1. B	Retention rate as percentage of earnings
2. DPSMAX	Maximum desired common dividend per share
3. DPSMIN	Minimum desired common dividend per share
4. FINV	Fixed (buffer) inventory
5. FRETMIN	Minimum desired addition to retained earnings
6. I	Interest rate in percent
7. K	Maximum desired debt as fraction of debt + equity
8. M	Multiplier (*P/E* ratio)
9. NFAS	Minimum increment size for plant and equipment
10. PROD	Turnover rate for plant and equipment
11. RAP	Accounts payable as percentage of inventory
12. RAR	Accounts receivable as percentage of sales
13. RCGS	Cost of goods sold as percentage of sales
14. RDEP	Depreciation as percentage of fixed assets
15. RINV	Variable inventory as percentage of sales
16. RL	Current portion of long-term debt as percentage of long-term debt
17. ROCA	Operating costs dependent on fixed assets as percentage
18. ROCS	Operating costs dependent on sales as percentage
19. RPFDIV	Preferred stock dividend rate as percent
20. RRCASH	Minimum cash requirement as percentage of sales
21. SALES	Sales
22. T	Tax rate in percent

unknown variables that are solved for by the model and 22 parameters to be supplied by management. There are a total of 37 equations in the model, and they are listed in Table 12.5, broken down into three functional blocks.[23] The basic logic of the model is described below.

---

[23] The equations are written in the format of the XSIM simulation language. The model itself was simulated using XSIM, a system that is particularly applicable to the construction and solution of financial simulation models.

TABLE 12.5

EQUATIONS OF THE FINANCIAL SIMULATION MODEL†

Block I: Generation of sales and earnings
CGS = RCGS / 100 * SALES
OC = ROCS / 100 * SALES + ROCA / 100 * (FA + FA(−1)) / 2
OI = SALES − CGS − OC
INT = I / 100 * (L + L(−1)) / 2
DEP = RDEP / 100 * (FA(−1) + NFA / 2)
PFDIV = RPFDIV / 100 * PFDSK
EBT = OI − INT − DEP
TAX = EBT * T / 100
EAT = EBT − TAX
EAFCD = EAT − PFDIV
EPS = EAFCD / NUMCS
P = EPS * M

Block II: Generation of required assets
AR = RAR / 100 * SALES
INV = RINV / 100 * SALES + FINV
RCASH = RRCASH / 100 * SALES
CA = CASH + AR + INV
NFA = IF SALES(−1)/PROD GT FA(−1) − DEP THEN (SALES(−1)/PROD − (FA(−1)
    − DEP)) ELSE 0
FA = FA(−1) − DEP + NFA
A = CA + FA

Block III: Financing the required asset level
AP = RAP / 100 * INV
OCL = RL / 100 * L(−1)
CL = AP + OCL
RETMIN = IF B / 100 * EAFCD GT EAFCD − DPSMIN * NUMCS AND EAFCD −
    DPSMIN * NUMCS GT FRETMIN THEN EAFCD − DPSMIN * NUMCS ELSE IF
    B / 100 * EAFCD GT FRETMIN THEN B / 100 * EAFCD ELSE FRETMIN
CMDIV = IF EAFCD − RETMIN GT DPSMAX * NUMCS THEN DPSMAX * NUMCS
    ELSE IF EAFCD − RETMIN LT 0 THEN 0 ELSE EAFCD − RETMIN
R = R(−1) + EAFCD − CMDIV
EQTY = PFDSK + S + R
NF = NFA + DEL(AR) + DEL(INV) − DEL(AP) + OCL(−1) + CMDIV − EAFCD −
    DEP + RCASH − CASH(−1)
NL = IF NF GT 0 THEN IF NF LT K * (EQTY + L(−1) − OCL + NF) − L(−1) +
    OCL THEN NF ELSE K * (EQTY + L) − L(−1) + OCL ELSE IF − NF GT L(−1)
    − OCL THEN − L(−1) + OCL ELSE NF
L = L(−1) − OCL + NL
NS = IF NF − NL GT 0 THEN IF EAFCD − RETMIN GT NUMCS(−1) * DPSMIN
    THEN IF NF − NL GT P * (EAFCD − RETMIN − NUMCS(−1) * DPSMIN) /
    DPSMIN THEN P * (EAFCD − RETMIN − NUMCS(−1) * DPSMIN) / DPSMIN
    ELSE NF − NL ELSE 0 ELSE 0
NUMCS = NUMCS(−1) + NS / P
S = S(−1) + NS
NPFDSK = IF NF − NL − NS GT 0 THEN NF − NL − NS ELSE IF − (NF − NL − NS)
    GT PFDSK(−1) THEN − PFDSK(−1) ELSE NF − NL − NS
DPS = CMDIV / NUMCS
PFDSK = PFDSK(−1) + NPFDSK
CASH = RCASH − NF + NL + NS + NPFDSK
LIAB = CL + L + EQTY

† The symbols GT and LT refer to "greater than" and "less than," respectively. The symbol "DEL" refers to a first difference, for example, DEL(AR) = AR − AR(−1). An asterisk (*) refers to multiplication.

In each time period, the assumed level of sales is used to generate the earnings of the firm in the first block of equations. Input parameters (supplied by management) relate the cost of goods sold to sales, operating costs to both sales and fixed assets, depreciation to fixed assets, and so on, leading to values for earnings before and after taxes. Earnings per share are converted to an implied stock price using a supplied price-earnings ratio.

The asset side of the balance sheet is also highly aggregated. Assets required to support the sales level are generated as simple functions of sales in the second block of equations. (The net book value is assumed to be an appropriate measure of assets for this purpose.) The asset equations determine expected values for accounts receivable and "required" values for inventories, cash, and fixed assets.

The liability side of the balance sheet includes relationships similar to those used above; for example, accounts payable is related proportionally to inventories, and other current liabilities is a simple function of last year's long-term debt. There are, in addition, more complicated equations which embody the decision rules used by the hypothetical financial officer. Some examples of these decision rules follow:

1 A minimum desired dollar addition to retained earnings (FRETMIN) and a normal retention rate for earnings (B) are specified as parameters by management. The targeted addition to retained earnings (RETMIN) is chosen (in the fourth equation of block III) according to the relationship between the two constraints imposed by management and the simulated (i.e., calculated) value for earnings available for common stock less a minimum dividend payout.

2 The determination of actual dividends paid (CMDIV) takes into account the targeted addition to retained earnings and also a maximum dividend payout ratio (DPSMAX).

3 After calculating the funds needed (NF) to meet asset changes, dividends, and maturing debt, the amount of long-term debt to be floated (NL) is chosen in light of a prespecified leverage ratio; if no new debt is needed, the amount of existing debt that should be retired is chosen.

4 The amount of common stock to be issued (NS) is chosen on the basis of funds needed which are not financed by new long-term debt, but is constrained by the responsibility to meet minimum dividend payments. Preferred stock (NPFDSK) is issued to make up any remaining deficiency. Excess funds can be used to retire preferred stock.

It would be difficult to diagram the decision tree reflecting the set of rules referred to above for two reasons. First, these rules have been stated succinctly using conditional statements (IF...THEN...ELSE). If the options involved were to be written in detail, a very large number of possibilities would have to be evaluated. Second, and far more important, these calculations could not progress in a straightforward manner from start to end. Because the branches of the decision tree are tied together in a number of places, there are many feedback loops in the model, so that the determination of additions to retained

TABLE 12.6
SIMULATION RESULTS

	1974	1975	1976	1977
Pro forma income statement for 1974–1977				
Sales	$1,000,000	$900,000	$1,100,000	$1,400,000
Cost of goods sold	600,000	540,000	660,000	840,000
Operating costs	125,000	115,600	140,400	176,200
Operating income	$ 275,000	$244,400	$ 299,600	$ 383,800
Depreciation	25,000	26,200	31,200	37,100
Interest	2,000	1,400	4,300	12,900
Earnings before taxes	$ 247,200	$216,700	$ 264,100	$ 333,800
Income taxes	118,600	104,000	126,800	160,200
Earnings after taxes	$ 128,500	$112,700	$ 137,400	$ 173,600
Preferred dividends	0	0	0	0
Earnings available for common	$128,500	$112,700	$137,400	$173,600
Earnings per share	1.29	1.13	1.37	1.74
Common dividends	$ 75,000	$ 56,400	$ 75,000	$ 86,800
Dividends per share	.75	.56	.75	.87
Pro forma balance sheet for 1974–1977				
Assets				
Cash	$ 126,000	$ 90,200	$ 110,000	$ 140,000
Accounts receivable	70,000	63,000	77,000	98,000
Inventories	430,000	397,000	463,000	562,000
Current assets	$ 626,000	$ 550,200	$ 650,000	$ 800,000
Net plant and equipment	475,000	548,800	667,600	780,400
Total assets	$1,101,000	$1,098,900	$1,317,600	$1,580,400
Liabilities				
Accounts payable	$107,500	$ 99,200	$115,700	$140,500
Other current liabilities	5,000	2,400	0	7,100
Current liabilities	$112,500	$101,600	$115,700	$147,600
Long-term debt	47,500	0	142,100	286,400
Equity				
Preferred stock	0	0	0	0
Common stock	500,000	500,000	500,000	500,000
Retained earnings	441,000	497,400	559,700	646,500
Total equity	$ 941,000	$ 997,400	$1,059,700	$1,146,500
Total liabilities and equity	$1,101,000	$1,099,000	$1,317,600	$1,580,500

earnings, dividends paid, debt floated, and stock issued must be a simultaneous one.

The concept of simultaneity, as it enters our example, can be illustrated as follows. A sales figure was used to generate earnings and this in turn led to, among other items, the level of long-term debt required. Yet the level of debt affects the interest expense incurred within the current year and therefore earnings. Furthermore, as earnings are affected, so is the price at which new shares are issued, the number of shares to be sold, and thus earnings per share. Earnings per share then "feeds back" into the stock price calculation.

Let us now examine how this model can be used. The model was simulated into the future to generate a *pro forma* income statement and balance sheet. "Actual" data were used for 1974, and the simulation was run through 1977. The variable SALES was set at its "actual" value of $1 million in 1974, and was assumed to drop to $900,000 in 1975, and then increase to $1.1 million in 1976 and $1.4 million in 1977.[24] The results of this simulation are shown in Table 12.6.

Observe from the income statement that the decrease and then increase in sales result in a decrease and then increase in both earnings and dividends. We see in the balance sheet that no new stock (preferred or common) is issued, however, and long-term debt drops to zero in 1975 and then increases in the following two years. An additional sale of stock is unnecessary, because retained earnings increase steadily over the 4 years. The 1-year drop in sales, then, has no adverse long-term effect on the company's financial position. This may not be the case, however, if sales drop more dramatically and remain low over a longer period of time. The model can easily be simulated to determine the impact of alternative sales flows on the company's future income statements and balance sheets.

Note that in this simulation, we chose sales to be an external input variable and we solved the model for various financial measures contingent upon the given values for sales. We might also have asked the following question: What would the value of sales have to be for earnings to be zero; i.e., what is the *breakeven* point for sales? This question could be answered easily by re-solving the model, making sales an internal unknown variable and earnings an external input parameter. (See Exercise 12.7.)

Exercises

12.1 Note in Figs. 12.21 to 12.27 that the use of wage-price controls in the macroeconomic model (experiment 4 in which the wage-price dummy variable is used) has little effect on the GNP and the unemployment rate, although it

---

[24] Note that an econometric forecasting model could have been used to generate these sales forecasts. Typically, a financial simulation model is "linked" in this way to an econometric model.

results in a considerably lower rate of inflation. Explain this impact of wage-price controls in terms of the structure of the model. Also explain why interest rates are lower (and residential investment is slightly higher) in experiment 4.

12.2 Explain the results of experiment 5, in which the rate of growth of government spending is increased. Again, refer to Figs. 12.21 to 12.27. Why are interest rates and the rate of inflation higher in this experiment?

12.3 (Possible term project.) The data that were used in the estimation of the macroeconomic model are listed in the appendix to this chapter, and should be used to reconstruct the model. Begin by reestimating all the equations as they are specified in the text. Next experiment with alternative equation specifications. For example, alternative lag structures might be used in the consumption or investment equations. After the student has estimated a new version of the model, he/she should test it by performing a historical simulation and calculating RMS simulation errors. Finally, the student should use the model to conduct a set of forecasting experiments. For example, the model might be used to predict the effects of a change in the propensity to consume or a change in the average tax rate.

12.4 Construct a complete block diagram for the tobacco model discussed in section 12.2. The diagram should show the interrelationships between all the variables in the model. Use arrows in your diagram to indicate directions of causality.

12.5 (1) Suppose the government increases the tobacco support price SP. Using the tobacco model, explain how this will affect the actual price of tobacco leaf PACT and the production of tobacco leaf Q. Indicate all the causal links and time lags (if any) between a change in the support price and changes in leaf price and leaf production. You may refer to the block diagram from Exercise 12.4.

(2) Repeat the above analysis for a change in the government acreage allotment AL. Again, indicate all causal links and time lags between a change in acreage allotment and changes in leaf price and leaf production.

12.6 In using the financial simulation model to generate *pro forma* income statements and balance sheets, it was hypothesized that sales would drop to $900,000 in 1975 and then increase to $1.1 million in 1976 and $1.4 million in 1977. Suppose instead that sales drop to $800,000 in 1976 and $700,000 in 1977. Trace through the equations of the model to explain (qualitatively) how this would affect the company's financial position in 1976 and 1977. Indicate where preferred or common stock might be issued, and how long-term debt would change. (Students with access to a computer simulation package should actually perform the simulation.)

12.7 Rewrite the equations of the financial simulation model (Table 12.5) so that the model can be used to determine the breakeven point for sales, i.e., the value of sales that produces zero earnings. Note that this can be done by making sales an endogenous variable and earnings an input parameter.

APPENDIX 12 / ESTIMATION METHOD AND DATA SERIES FOR THE MACROECONOMETRIC MODEL

Estimation

Three of the behavioral equations in the macroeconomic model [Eqs. (12.23), (12.24), and (12.26)] were estimated using a procedure that combines two-stage least squares with a first-order serial-correlation correction. To explain this procedure, let us go through the steps involved in estimating Eq. (12.26) for the short-term interest rate.

The short-term interest rate is taken to be related linearly to income, changes in income, the rate of growth in the money supply, and a moving sum of recent inflation rates. This equation was first estimated using a simple Hildreth-Lu procedure for first-order serial-correlation correction.[25] The estimation results are shown below, with t statistics in parentheses. The R^2, F statistic, standard error (SER), Durbin-Watson (DW) statistic, and the estimated value of ρ used in the serial correlation correction are also shown.

$$RS = \underset{(-.792)}{-.747} + \underset{(4.02)}{.0072YD} + \underset{(1.26)}{.0138\Delta YD_{-1}} - \underset{(-2.75)}{29.66} \frac{\Delta M}{M}$$

$$+ \underset{(3.23)}{58.33} \left(\frac{\Delta P_{-1}}{P_{-1}} + \frac{\Delta P_{-2}}{P_{-2}} \right) \tag{A12.1}$$

$$R^2 = .404 \qquad SER = .498 \qquad F(4/67) = 11.35 \qquad DW = 1.59 \qquad \hat{\rho} = .783$$

Note that this equation contains an unlagged endogenous variable, namely, YD. Two-stage least squares must therefore be applied, with YD being regressed against the set of exogenous variables in the model as well as lagged endogenous variables. This results in a "fitted" series for YD, which we call YDFIT. We now reestimate our equation using *ordinary least squares*, but with YDFIT instead of YD:

$$RS = \underset{(-1.78)}{-.701} + \underset{(6.91)}{.0076YDFIT} + \underset{(.21)}{.0042\Delta YD_{-1}} - \underset{(-3.10)}{49.03} \frac{\Delta M}{M}$$

$$+ \underset{(2.72)}{50.49} \left(\frac{\Delta P_{-1}}{P_{-1}} + \frac{\Delta P_{-2}}{P_{-2}} \right) \tag{A12.2}$$

$$R^2 = .757 \qquad SER = .784 \qquad F(4/67) = 52.28 \qquad DW = .48$$

---

[25] For a review of the Hildreth-Lu procedure, see Chapter 4.

The residuals u_t from Eq. (A12.2) are then regressed against their own lagged values u_{t-1} to obtain a new estimate for the coefficient of serial correlation:

$$u_t = .755u_{t-1} + .0056 \qquad \text{(A12.3)}$$
$$\quad (9.65) \qquad (.09)$$

Our original equation is now transformed autoregressively using .755 as an estimated value for ρ. Note that this value for ρ is slightly different from that obtained when the Hildreth-Lu procedure was applied to the original equation. Our equation is now of the form

$$(RS - .755RS_{-1}) = \beta_0(1 - .755) + \beta_1(YD - .755YD_{-1})$$

$$+ \beta_2(\Delta YD_{-1} - .755\Delta YD_{-2}) + \cdots \qquad \text{(A12.4)}$$

This equation is now estimated using two-stage least squares. This is done by regressing the generalized difference $YD - .755YD_{-1}$ against a set of exogenous and lagged endogenous variables that are in the same generalized difference form; i.e., we perform the regression

$$(YD - .755YD_{-1}) = \alpha_0 + \alpha_1(Z_1 - .755Z_{1,-1})$$

$$+ \alpha_2(Z_2 - .755Z_{2,-1}) + \cdots \qquad \text{(A12.5)}$$

where Z_1, Z_2, etc., are exogenous and lagged endogenous variables. A "fitted" series thus results for the generalized difference $YD - .755YD_{-1}$, which we call YDDIF. This fitted series is now substituted for $YD - .755YD_{-1}$ in Eq. (A12.4):

$$(RS - .755RS_{-1}) = \beta_0(1 - .775) + \beta_1 YDDIF + \beta_2(\Delta YD_{-1} - .755YD_{-2}) + \cdots$$
$$\text{(A12.6)}$$

Equation (A12.6) can now be estimated using ordinary least squares. The results, which are shown below, provide the final coefficient estimates for our interest rate equation:

$$(RS - .755RS_{-1}) = -.499(1 - .755) + .0069 YDDIF$$
$$\qquad\qquad (-.53) \qquad\qquad (3.86)$$

$$+ .0140(\Delta YD_{-1} - .755\Delta YD_{-2})$$
$$\quad (1.26)$$

$$-30.51 \left(\frac{\Delta M}{M} - .755\frac{\Delta M_{-1}}{M_{-1}}\right) + 57.21 \left[\left(\frac{\Delta P_{-1}}{P_{-1}} - .755\frac{\Delta P_{-2}}{P_{-2}}\right)\right.$$
$$(-2.80) \qquad\qquad\qquad\qquad (3.15)$$

$$\left. + \left(\frac{\Delta P_{-2}}{P_{-2}} - .755\frac{\Delta P_{-3}}{P_{-3}}\right)\right] \qquad \text{(A12.7)}$$

$$R^2 = .431 \qquad SER = .500 \qquad F(4/67) = 12.70 \qquad DW = 1.54$$

Note that this procedure could be continued iteratively; i.e., Eq. (A12.7) could be written in undifferenced form and estimated using the Hildreth-Lu technique, resulting in a new value for ρ. If the value for ρ differed significantly from the value obtained in the regression equation (A12.3), two-stage least squares would be repeated (beginning with a new computation of the fitted series YDDIF). This was not the case for our model, however, and in fact for most applications of this procedure further iterations are not necessary.

Data Series

Some readers may wish to repeat the estimation of the model themselves, or estimate alternative versions of one or more equations (see Exercise 12.3). The data series used in the construction of the model are therefore presented here.

C—Consumption
(In billions of dollars deflated)

Quarter	1	2	3	4
1953	250.1	251.5	251.1	250.4
1954	250.8	253.3	256.9	261.9
1955	267.6	273.	276.3	279.9
1956	279.8	280.3	280.8	284.7
1957	286.6	287.	289.3	289.7
1958	285.6	287.5	291.9	295.2
1959	302.3	307.	309.9	310.
1960	313.8	317.7	316.4	316.4
1961	316.2	320.4	323.9	329.5
1962	333.3	335.7	340.1	344.6
1963	348.5	350.9	356.1	357.7
1964	366.3	370.7	378.6	379.3
1965	387.9	393.4	400.3	409.2
1966	415.3	415.1	421.3	420.7
1967	424.2	430.3	431.6	434.3
1968	444.6	448.4	457.7	460.2
1969	465.5	469.3	469.5	472.2
1970	474.3	477.5	480.9	477.5
1971	490.1	493.8	497.7	504.1
1972	512.8	523.2	531.2	542.2
1973	552.9	553.7	555.4	546.3
1974	539.7	542.3		

G—Government spending
(In billions of dollars deflated)

	1	2	3	4
1954	77.5	72.6	71.8	69.7
1955	70.6	71.6	72.6	73.9
1956	74.1	74.7	74.6	75.1
1957	78.	79.5	81.1	83.
1958	87.6	90.4	93.	96.6
1959	97.5	98.3	96.2	95.7
1960	94.6	95.3	96.1	95.9
1961	97.7	101.1	103.5	106.
1962	109.8	111.3	112.1	114.4
1963	117.3	114.7	117.3	117.2
1964	117.5	121.4	120.7	121.3
1965	125.3	126.3	131.6	137.3
1966	141.8	147.8	156.3	160.3
1967	168.7	172.6	175.7	182.5
1968	191.	194.6	198.2	204.4
1969	205.	207.	209.	211.3
1970	213.6	213.4	216.1	220.5
1971	224.1	231.	234.4	244.4
1972	255.8	259.9	258.5	264.2
1973	268.6	272.5	271.4	272.8
1974	278.8	281.6		

GNP—Gross national product
(*In billions of dollars deflated*)

1953	394.	397.4	393.6	387.7
1954	384.6	382.9	388.5	395.9
1955	409.	420.1	425.8	432.4
1956	429.5	429.5	429.4	433.1
1957	435.1	436.4	441.3	436.6
1958	430.7	433.9	446.5	460.3
1959	470.6	483.9	476.4	480.7
1960	488.3	486.4	483.5	477.4
1961	476.3	489.3	498.5	510.2
1962	520.3	526.	532.8	539.7
1963	544.5	546.2	556.5	562.7
1964	569.1	579.5	586.9	591.4
1965	610.1	616.5	631.6	649.9
1966	663.9	673.6	684.6	693.5
1967	693.6	699.7	709.8	721.9
1968	737.2	749.9	760.8	772.3
1969	780.2	787.	792.5	790.9
1970	790.5	794.4	802.3	800.1
1971	822.1	836.5	842.	863.3
1972	887.9	906.3	916.3	937.2
1973	956.	962.4	962.5	964.9
1974	976.5	988.3		

GNPP—Potential GNP
(*In billions of dollars deflated*)

1953	386.5	389.1	391.2	394.6
1954	400.3	403.1	407.	409.9
1955	414.3	421.8	424.4	430.8
1958	434.6	436.4	441.1	443.2
1957	446.1	451.5	458.	464.5
1958	473.2	478.6	484.	491.4
1959	498.8	505.5	507.	510.3
1960	512.4	515.5	519.4	520.9
1961	525.5	533.2	538.2	544.4
1962	551.8	553.8	559.6	566.7
1963	573.7	575.7	582.6	586.8
1964	589.5	597.6	603.6	610.7
1965	622.3	625.2	633.9	643.9
1966	651.7	661.9	674.1	681.4
1967	689.3	696.9	706.3	720.5
1968	733.9	740.4	751.2	765.8
1969	774.7	785.3	794.1	803.8
1970	814.3	824.6	834.6	848.2
1971	862.6	880.1	886.9	905.1
1972	930.	938.4	944.6	958.7
1973	966.5	976.7	975.1	983.2
1974	994.5	1006.		

IIN—Inventory investment (*change in inventories*)
(*In billions of dollars deflated, annual rate*)

1953	3.1	3.8	1.2	−4.3
1954	−2.9	−3.6	−2.5	0.9
1955	5.	6.7	6.4	7.6
1956	6.2	4.6	4.1	4.4
1957	2.1	2.4	3.	−2.5
1958	−5.6	−5.	0.3	4.3
1959	3.8	8.9	0.5	6.2
1960	9.6	3.8	3.	−2.6
1961	−3.4	2.1	3.8	5.5
1962	6.5	5.9	5.3	6.2
1963	4.6	4.8	5.9	8.1
1964	4.8	6.1	4.8	7.6
1965	10.	8.3	8.6	9.3
1966	10.7	15.3	11.1	18.5
1967	9.1	4.3	8.3	9.2
1968	2.6	8.8	7.	7.4
1969	6.	6.8	9.4	4.6
1970	1.9	4.4	4.9	4.5
1971	6.5	6.8	3.4	4.6
1972	4.2	6.6	8.5	8.8
1973	7.3	7.8	8.	20.
1974	10.6	9.1		

INV—Level of inventories
(*In billions of dollars deflated*)

1953	105.1	106.	106.	105.3
1954	104.5	103.6	103.05	102.8
1955	104.	105.7	107.35	109.2
1956	110.8	111.9	112.9	114.
1957	114.6	115.2	115.9	115.3
1958	113.9	112.6	112.7	113.8
1959	114.7	117.	117.1	118.6
1960	121.	122.	122.7	122.1
1961	121.2	121.8	122.7	124.1
1962	125.7	127.2	128.5	130.1
1963	131.2	132.4	133.9	135.9
1964	137.1	138.6	139.8	141.7
1965	144.2	146.3	148.5	150.8
1966	153.5	157.3	160.1	164.7
1967	167.	168.	170.1	172.4
1968	173.1	175.3	177.3	181.1
1969	180.4	182.1	184.4	185.6
1970	186.4	187.5	188.7	189.8
1971	191.5	193.2	194.	195.2
1972	196.2	197.9	200.	202.2
1973	204.	206.	208.	213.
1974	215.6	217.9		

INR—Nonresidential investment
(*In billions of dollars deflated*)

1953	40.4	40.4	41.1	40.7
1954	39.5	39.5	39.9	39.6
1955	40.2	43.	45.4	47.1
1956	46.5	47.3	48.	47.5
1957	47.7	47.3	48.	46.4
1958	43.3	41.3	40.5	41.4
1959	42.2	44.3	45.1	44.9
1960	46.6	47.6	47.	47.
1961	44.9	44.6	45.7	46.6
1962	47.6	49.3	51.1	50.7
1963	49.8	51.1	52.5	54.3
1964	55.5	57.	58.9	59.7
1965	62.8	64.8	67.3	70.3
1966	72.5	73.2	75.	75.4
1967	73.6	73.3	72.9	72.9
1968	76.2	74.4	75.3	76.6
1969	79.2	79.3	80.9	80.9
1970	78.5	78.3	78.6	73.5
1971	75.5	76.6	76.2	78.6
1972	81.3	82.4	83.8	87.2
1973	92.2	94.3	95.1	96.
1974	96.3	96.4		

IR—Residential investment
(*In billions of dollars deflated*)

1953	19.9	19.9	19.3	19.2
1954	19.7	21.1	22.4	23.8
1955	25.6	25.8	25.1	33.9
1956	22.9	22.6	21.9	21.4
1957	20.7	20.2	19.9	20.
1958	19.8	19.7	20.8	22.8
1959	24.8	25.4	24.7	23.9
1960	23.7	22.	21.	20.7
1961	20.9	21.1	21.6	22.6
1962	23.1	23.8	24.2	23.8
1963	24.3	24.7	24.7	25.4
1964	25.	24.3	23.9	23.5
1965	24.1	23.7	23.8	23.8
1966	23.6	22.2	20.9	18.6
1967	18.	19.2	21.3	23.
1968	22.8	23.7	22.6	23.7
1969	24.5	24.6	23.7	21.9
1970	22.2	20.8	21.8	24.1
1971	25.9	28.3	30.3	31.6
1972	33.8	34.2	34.3	34.8
1973	35.	34.1	32.6	29.8
1974	26.4	25.8		

LIQ—Liquidity
(*In billions of dollars deflated*)

1953	191.4	193.4	194.4	195.6
1954	194.7	196.3	199.2	200.6
1955	202.	202.4	202.5	201.9
1956	200.4	199.6	197.9	197.4
1957	197.1	197.1	196.6	196.2
1958	196.5	200.6	203.3	204.6
1959	206.5	207.4	207.7	206.7
1960	204.7	204.	206.2	208.1
1961	210.4	213.6	217.	219.3
1962	222.7	226.9	228.9	232.1
1963	236.3	240.2	244.3	248.1
1964	251.2	254.6	258.7	263.1
1965	267.8	271.6	276.9	283.1
1966	286.6	289.5	289.7	288.2
1967	293.4	299.8	305.7	308.4
1968	311.	313.1	317.6	323.5
1969	323.9	320.8	312.6	307.8
1970	304.3	308.4	317.2	323.2
1971	331.9	340.4	345.5	351.5
1972	356.4	365.	373.3	381.1
1973	388.2	396.4	399.9	397.3
1974	399.9	401.9		

M—Money supply
(*In billions of dollars deflated*)

1953	144.3	145.5	145.5	145.6
1954	144.2	144.4	146.	147.
1955	148.	148.2	148.2	147.5
1956	146.4	145.5	143.7	143.2
1957	142.	141.	139.8	138.3
1958	137.	138.	138.9	139.9
1959	141.	141.7	141.8	140.7
1960	139.4	138.5	139.	138.7
1961	138.9	139.7	140.5	141.1
1962	141.4	141.9	141.3	141.5
1963	142.3	143.3	144.4	145.1
1964	145.4	146.4	148.	149.1
1965	149.3	149.8	151.1	152.9
1966	154.1	154.5	152.8	151.8
1967	152.3	153.7	155.6	156.
1963	156.6	158.1	159.7	161.
1969	162.3	162.1	160.6	159.3
1970	158.5	159.4	160.1	159.9
1971	160.3	162.7	164.2	164.5
1972	164.4	167.1	169.4	171.5
1973	171.9	172.1	171.5	169.6
1974	169.8	170.6		

P—Price level
(1958 = 100)

1953	88.4	88.3	88.4	88.4
1954	89.5	89.6	89.5	89.8
1955	90.2	90.6	91.	95.4
1956	92.6	93.4	94.6	98.5
1957	96.4	97.1	98.	100.6
1958	99.3	99.7	100.1	102.1
1959	101.1	101.5	101.9	104.
1960	102.6	103.1	103.5	105.1
1961	104.3	104.5	104.5	106.3
1962	105.5	105.6	105.8	107.8
1963	106.7	107.	107.2	109.6
1964	108.2	108.5	109.1	111.5
1965	110.2	110.7	111.	115.4
1966	112.4	113.5	114.5	119.3
1967	116.2	116.8	118.	124.3
1968	120.4	121.6	122.9	130.9
1969	125.5	127.2	129.1	137.9
1970	132.9	134.4	135.8	142.7
1971	139.5	141.1	142.	148.
1972	144.6	145.3	146.5	158.9
1973	149.9	152.6	155.7	
1974	163.6	167.3	172.	

RL—Long-term interest rate
(In percent per annum)

1953	2.423	2.797	2.727	2.307
1954	1.893	1.76	1.743	1.897
1955	2.197	2.403	2.663	2.703
1956	2.74	3.007	3.253	3.477
1957	3.37	3.617	3.91	3.553
1958	2.647	2.277	3.073	3.627
1959	3.863	4.173	4.543	4.793
1960	4.59	4.237	3.57	3.6
1961	3.5	3.457	3.753	3.713
1962	3.72	3.507	3.613	3.453
1963	3.483	3.6	3.823	3.973
1964	4.077	4.093	4.003	4.05
1965	4.087	4.107	4.177	4.52
1966	4.95	4.937	5.473	5.293
1967	4.653	4.7	5.283	5.657
1968	5.63	5.783	5.353	5.627
1969	6.177	6.373	7.227	7.673
1970	7.713	7.773	7.46	6.43
1971	5.257	5.933	6.373	5.533
1972	5.527	5.823	5.98	6.07
1973	6.583	6.76	7.467	6.857
1974	7.013			

RS—Short-term interest rate
(In percent per annum)

1953	2.047	2.203	2.022	1.486
1954	1.084	0.814	0.87	1.036
1955	1.256	1.514	1.861	2.349
1956	2.379	2.597	2.597	3.064
1957	3.172	3.157	3.382	3.343
1958	1.838	1.018	1.711	2.788
1959	2.8	3.019	3.533	4.299
1960	3.943	3.092	2.39	2.361
1961	2.377	2.325	2.325	2.475
1962	2.739	2.716	2.858	2.803
1963	2.909	2.941	3.281	3.499
1964	3.538	3.481	3.504	3.685
1965	3.9	3.879	3.86	4.159
1966	4.631	4.597	5.048	5.246
1967	4.534	3.657	4.345	4.787
1968	5.065	5.51	5.226	5.581
1969	6.138	6.24	7.047	7.318
1970	7.263	6.752	6.375	5.358
1971	3.863	4.206	5.05	4.234
1972	3.435	3.748	4.241	4.851
1973	5.64	6.608	8.388	7.462
1974	7.6			

UR—Unemployment rate
(In percentage rates)

1953	2.7	2.567	2.733	3.7
1954	5.267	5.8	5.967	5.333
1955	4.733	4.4	4.1	4.233
1956	4.033	4.2	4.133	4.133
1957	3.933	4.1	4.233	4.933
1958	6.3	7.367	7.333	6.367
1959	5.833	5.1	5.267	5.6
1960	5.133	5.233	5.533	6.267
1961	6.8	7.	6.767	6.2
1962	5.633	5.533	5.567	5.533
1963	5.767	5.733	5.5	5.567
1964	5.467	5.2	5.	4.967
1965	4.9	4.667	4.367	4.1
1966	3.867	3.833	3.767	3.7
1967	3.833	3.833	3.8	3.9
1968	3.733	3.567	3.533	3.4
1969	3.4	3.433	3.567	3.567
1970	4.167	4.733	5.167	5.8
1971	5.967	5.9	5.933	5.933
1972	5.867	5.7	5.567	5.3
1973	5.033	4.9	4.7	4.7
1974	5.167			

W—Wage rate
(In dollars per hour)

1953	1.72	1.733	1.75	1.763
1954	1.773	1.777	1.77	1.797
1955	1.82	1.843	1.863	1.893
1956	1.91	1.943	1.957	2.003
1957	2.023	2.033	2.05	2.073
1958	2.08	2.093	2.107	2.143
1959	2.177	2.203	2.187	2.207
1960	2.26	2.257	2.26	2.277
1961	2.287	2.31	2.317	2.357
1962	2.377	2.39	2.38	2.413
1963	2.433	2.45	2.453	2.49
1964	2.507	2.527	2.537	2.55
1965	2.587	2.607	2.61	2.65
1966	2.677	2.707	2.72	2.76
1967	2.787	2.81	2.83	2.88
1968	2.947	2.987	3.013	3.083
1969	3.123	3.163	3.21	3.267
1970	3.297	3.34	3.383	3.407
1971	3.507	3.547	3.577	3.623
1972	3.72	3.777	3.813	3.9
1973	3.977	4.023	4.083	4.17
1974	4.217			

YD—Disposable income
(In billions of dollars deflated)

1953	333.4	336.3	333.1	328.1
1954	325.5	324.	328.8	335.
1955	346.1	355.5	360.3	365.9
1956	363.5	363.5	363.4	366.5
1957	368.2	369.3	373.4	369.5
1958	364.5	367.2	377.8	389.5
1959	398.2	409.5	403.1	406.8
1960	413.2	411.6	409.2	404.
1961	403.1	414.1	421.8	431.7
1962	440.3	445.1	450.9	456.7
1963	460.8	462.2	470.9	476.2
1964	481.6	490.4	496.7	500.5
1965	516.3	521.7	534.5	550.
1966	561.8	570.	579.3	586.9
1967	586.9	592.1	600.7	610.9
1968	623.8	634.6	643.8	653.5
1969	660.2	666.	670.6	669.3
1970	668.9	672.2	678.9	677.1
1971	695.7	707.9	712.5	730.5
1972	751.4	766.9	775.4	793.1
1973	809.	814.4	814.5	816.5

THREE

TIME-SERIES MODELS

In the first two parts of this book we saw how econometric models—both single-equation regression models and multi-equation simulation models—can be constructed and used to explain and forecast the future movements of one or more variables. In Part Three of the book we are again interested in constructing models and using them for forecasting, but these models are quite different in nature from those that we worked with earlier. We no longer predict future movements in a variable by relating it to a set of other variables in a causal framework; instead we base our prediction solely on the past behavior of the variable and that variable alone.

As an example, consider the time function $y(t)$ drawn in the figure below, which might represent the historical performance of some economic or business variable—a stock market index, an interest rate, a production index, or perhaps the daily sales volume for some commodity. We may or may not be able to explain (based on economic theory, intuitive reasoning, etc.) why $y(t)$ behaved the way it did. If $y(t)$ represents the sales volume of some good, for example, it may have moved up or down partly in response to changes in prices, personal income, and interest rates (or so we might believe). However, much of its movement may have been due to factors that we may simply not be able to explain, such as the weather, changes in consumer taste, or simply seasonal (or aseasonal) cycles in consumer spending.

It may be difficult or impossible to explain the movement of $y(t)$ through the use of a structural model, i.e., by relating it explicitly to other economic variables. This might happen if, for example, data are not available for those explanatory variables which are believed to affect $y(t)$. Or if data were available, the estimation of a regression model for $y(t)$ might result in standard errors that are so large as to make most of the estimated coefficients insignificant and the standard error of forecast unacceptably large.

Even if we could estimate a statistically significant regression equation for $y(t)$, the result may not be useful for forecasting purposes. To obtain a forecast for $y(t)$ from a regression equation, those explanatory variables that are not lagged must themselves be forecasted, and this may be more difficult than forecasting $y(t)$ itself. The standard error of forecast for $y(t)$ with future values of the explanatory variables known may be small (if the regression equation fits well), but the forecast errors for the explanatory variables themselves may be so large as to make the total forecast error for $y(t)$ too large to be acceptable.

Clearly, then, situations may exist where it is impossible or undesirable to "explain" $y(t)$ using a structural model, and we might ask whether there is an alternative means of obtaining a forecast of $y(t)$. Are there ways in which we can observe the time series in the figure and draw some conclusions about its *past* behavior that would allow us to infer something about its probable *future* behavior? For example, is there some kind of overall upward trend in $y(t)$ which, because it has dominated the past behavior of the series, might dominate its future behavior? Or does the series exhibit some kind of cyclical behavior which we could extrapolate into the future? If some kind of systematic behavior of this type is present, we can attempt to construct a *model* for the time series which does not offer a structural explanation for its behavior in terms of other variables, but does replicate its past behavior in a way that might help us forecast its future behavior. On this basis the *time-series model* accounts for patterns in the past movements of a particular variable, and uses that information to predict future movements of the variable. In a sense a time-series model is just a sophisticated method of extrapolation. Yet, as we will see in this part of the book, it may often provide a very effective tool for forecasting.

In this book we have divided economic and business forecasting models into three general classes, each of which involves a different level of comprehension about the real world processes that one is trying to model. In Part One of the book we discussed single-equation regression models, where the variable of interest is explained by a single function (linear or nonlinear) of explanatory variables. Next, in Part Two of the book we examined multi-equation simulation models where two or more endogenous variables are related to each other (and perhaps to one or more exogenous variables) through a set of equations, which can be solved simultaneously (i.e., simulated) to produce forecasts over time. In this third part of the book we concern ourselves with time-series models, in which we have no structural knowledge about the real world causal relationships that affect the variable we are trying to forecast.

Clearly a choice will often have to be made as to which type of model should be developed in order to best make a forecast. This choice may be difficult and will depend not only on how much we know about the workings of the real world process, but also on how much time and energy we can afford to spend on the modeling process. The development of a single-equation regression model may not be too difficult, but the construction of a multi-equation simulation model might require large expenditures of time and effort. The gains that result from this effort might include a better understanding of the relationships and structure involved as well as the ability to make a better forecast. However, in some cases, these gains may be so small that they are outweighed by the heavy cost involved.

The choice of a time-series model will usually result in those cases where little information is known about the determinants of the variable of primary concern, and a sufficiently large amount of data is available to construct a time series of reasonable length. An example might be to forecast on a weekly or monthly basis a cyclical series for the production of a commodity (we will present as an example a time-series model to forecast monthly hog production). In some cases we will have information about the physical processes involved, and it will not be obvious as to whether a time-series model or a single-equation regression model is preferable as a means of forecasting. One choice would be to build a regression model; a second choice would be to build a time-series model; and as we will see in Chapter 17, a third choice is to *combine* time-series analysis with regression analysis. We will see that a powerful method of forecasting involves constructing a regression model in which, say, an interest rate is related to several economic variables, after which a time-series model is constructed to "explain" the behavior of the residual term from the regression.

The following chapters will present an introduction, on a rather elementary level, to the science and art of developing time-series models for purposes of forecasting. The models that we deal with are actually only a subset of a broader class of models and techniques for data analysis that falls under the general rubric of "time-series analysis." We do not discuss, for example, recent developments in the theory of *spectral analysis* and its application to economic modeling and forecasting. Rather, we concentrate on a class of linear time-series models introduced by G. E. P. Box and G. M. Jenkins that have recently found wide application to economic and business forecasting.[1]

Since time-series analysis builds on the development of the single-equation regression model, we treat time-series models in the last part of the book, even though they are the "simplest" class of models in terms of their explanation of the real world. To forecast a short-term interest rate, we might use a regression model to relate that variable to GNP, prices, and the money supply. A time series for interest rates would relate that variable to its past values, and to variables that describe the "random" nature of its past behavior. The model, like most regression models, is an equation that contains a set of coefficients that

---

[1] G. E. P. Box and G. M. Jenkins, *Time Series Analysis* (San Francisco: Holden-Day, 1970).

must be estimated. Unlike the majority of regression models, however, the equation is nonlinear in the coefficients, so that a nonlinear version of ordinary least squares is necessary for estimation purposes.

Part Three begins with a brief introduction to the nature of stochastic (i.e., random) time series. We discuss how stochastic processes are generated, what they look like, and, most important, how they are described. We discuss some of the characteristics of stochastic processes, and in particular develop the concept of stationarity. Then we describe autocorrelation functions, and show how they can be used as a means of describing time series and as a tool for testing their properties.

Chapter 14 develops linear models for time series, including moving average models, autoregressive models, and mixed autoregressive-moving average models for stationary time series. We show how certain types of nonstationary time series can be differenced one or more times so as to produce a stationary series. This enables us to develop a general integrated autoregressive-moving average model (ARIMA model) for time series. Finally, we show how autocorrelation functions can be used to specify and characterize a time-series model for any particular time series.

Chapters 15 and 16 deal with use of time-series models to make forecasts. Chapter 15 explains how the parameters of a time-series model are estimated and how a specification of the model can be verified. Chapter 16 discusses how the model can then be used to produce a forecast. We also show how time series are "adaptive" in nature, i.e., how they produce forecasts in a way that adapts to new information. The last part of Chapter 16 deals with forecast errors, and shows how confidence intervals can be determined for forecasts.

The last chapter of Part Three develops some examples of applications of time-series models to economic and business forecasting. While Chapters 13 to 16 concentrate on the "science" of time-series model building, Chapter 17 is concerned largely with the "art" of time-series models. In that chapter we lead the reader step-by-step through the construction of several time-series models and their application to forecasting problems.

13

PROPERTIES
OF
STOCHASTIC
TIME SERIES

As explained in the introduction to Part Three, time-series models provide a sophisticated method of extrapolating time series. We see in this chapter, however, that extrapolations using time-series models differ from simple extrapolations. The difference arises because time-series analysis presumes that the series to be forecasted has been generated by a *stochastic* (or *random*) *process*, with a structure that can be characterized and described. In other words, a time-series model provides a description of the random nature of the (stochastic) process that generated the sample of observations under study. The description is given not in terms of a cause-and-effect relationship (as would be the case in a regression model), but rather in terms of the way that randomness is embodied in the process. Time-series analysis is, therefore, more "sophisticated" than simple extrapolation, since extrapolation does not account for the fact that the time series is stochastic. This point will become clearer as we proceed through the chapter.

We begin by discussing some simple (and not so simple) methods of extrapolation, recognizing the fact that these extrapolation techniques represent *deterministic models* of time series. We see that a stochastic model of a time series, which provides more information than a deterministic model, allows for improved forecasting. We introduce stochastic time-series models in the second section of this chapter, after which we discuss the properties of stochastic processes. This provides the groundwork for Chapters 14 to 16, in which the methodology for constructing and using time-series models is developed.

13.1 DETERMINISTIC MODELS OF TIME SERIES

We begin by explaining how to construct simple models that can be used to forecast the future behavior of a time series on the basis of its past behavior. These models are deterministic in that no reference is made to the sources or nature of the underlying randomness in the series. Essentially the models involve extrapolation techniques that have been standard "tools of the trade" in economic and business forecasting for years. It is therefore important that they be reviewed, even though they often do not provide as much forecasting accuracy as the more modern stochastic time-series models.

Most of the time series that we encounter are not continuous in time; instead they consist of discrete observations made at regular intervals of time. A typical time series might be given by Fig. 13.1. We denote the values of that series by y_t, so that y_1 represents the first observation, y_2 the second, and y_T the *last* observation that we have for the series.[1] Our objective is to build a model describing the series y_t and to use that model to make a forecast of y_t beyond the last observation y_T. We denote the forecast one period ahead by $\hat{y}_{T+1}$, two periods ahead by $\hat{y}_{T+2}$, and l periods ahead by $\hat{y}_{T+l}$.

If the number of observations is not too large, then the simplest and most complete representation of y_t would be given by a polynomial whose degree is one less than the number of observations; i.e., we could describe y_t by a continuous function of time $f(t)$, where

$$f(t) = a_0 + a_1 t + a_2 t^2 + \cdots + a_n t^n \tag{13.1}$$

and $n = T - 1$. Such a polynomial will (if the a's are chosen correctly) pass through *every point* in the time series y_t. Thus, we can be sure that $f(t)$ will equal y_t at every time t from 1 to T. Can we, however, have any confidence that the *forecast* of y_t one or more periods ahead generated by $f(t)$ will be at all close to the actual future values taken on by y_t? Will, for example, the forecast

$$f(T + 1) = a_0 + a_1(T + 1) + a_2(T + 1)^2 + \cdots + a_{T-1}(T + 1)^{T-1} = \hat{y}_{T+1}$$

be close to the actual future value y_{T+1}? Unfortunately, we have no way of knowing the answer to this question, unless additional prior information is

---

[1] In Part Three of the book we use small letters, for example, y_t, to denote time series. The reader should not confuse this with the notation in Part One of the book, where a small letter denotes deviations from the mean.

FIGURE 13.1
Discrete time series.

available. The difficulty with the model given by Eq. (13.1) is that it does not describe y_t; it merely *reproduces* y_t. It does not capture any characteristics of y_t that might repeat themselves in the future. Thus, although $f(t)$ correlates perfectly with y_t, it is of little use for forecasting y_t.

13.1.1 Simple Extrapolation Models

One of the basic characteristics of y_t that can be described is its long-run growth pattern. Despite the short-run up-and-down movement, it is possible that y_t might exhibit a clear-cut upward trend. If we believe that this upward trend exists and will continue (and there may not be any reason why we should), we can construct a simple model that describes that trend and can be used to forecast, i.e., extrapolate, y_t.

The simplest extrapolation model is the *linear trend model*. If one believes that a series y_t will increase in constant absolute amounts each time period, then one can predict y_t in the future by fitting the "trend line"

$$y_t = c_1 + c_2 t \tag{13.2}$$

where t = time
$\quad y_t$ = the value of y at time t

t is usually chosen to equal 0 in the base period (first observation) and to increase by 1 during each successive period. For example, if we determine by regression that

$$y_t = 27.5 + 3.2t \tag{13.3}$$

we can predict that the value of y in period $t + 1$ will be 3.2 units higher than the previous value.

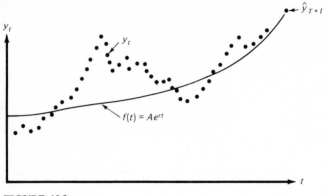

FIGURE 13.2
Exponential growth curve.

It may be more realistic to assume that the series y_t grows with constant percentage increases, rather than constant absolute increases. This assumption is the basis for the second simple example of a trend model which is the *exponential growth curve*:

$$y_t = f(t) = Ae^{rt} \tag{13.4}$$

Here A and r would be chosen to maximize the correlation between $f(t)$ and y_t. A forecast one period ahead would then be given by

$$\hat{y}_{T+1} = Ae^{r(T+1)} \tag{13.5}$$

and l periods ahead by

$$\hat{y}_{T+l} = Ae^{r(T+1)} \tag{13.6}$$

This is illustrated in Fig. 13.2. The parameters A and r can be estimated by taking the logarithms of both sides of (13.4), and fitting the log-linear regression equation[2]

$$\log y_t = c_1 + c_2 t \tag{13.7}$$

where $c_1 = \log A$
$\quad\quad c_2 = r$

---

[2] Note that in the exponential growth model the logarithm of y_t is assumed to grow at a constant rate. If $y_{t+1} = Ae^{rt}$, then $y_{t+1}/y_t = e^r$, and $\log(y_{t+1}) - \log(y_t) = r$.

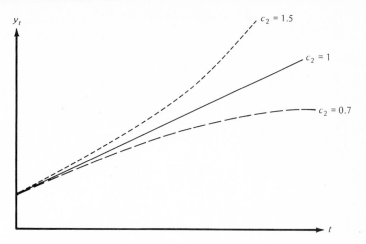

FIGURE 13.3
Autoregressive trend model.

A third extrapolation method is based on the *autoregressive trend model*:

$$y_t = c_1 + c_2 y_{t-1} \tag{13.8}$$

In using such an extrapolation procedure, one has the option of fixing $c_1 = 0$, in which case c_2 represents the rate of change of the series y. If, on the other hand, c_2 is set equal to 1, with c_1 not equal to 0, the extrapolated series will increase by the same absolute amount each time period. The autoregressive trend model is illustrated in Fig. 13.3 for three different values of c_2 (in all cases $c_1 = 1$).

A variation of the previous model is the *logarithmic autoregressive trend model*:

$$\log y_t = c_1 + c_2 \log y_{t-1} \tag{13.9}$$

If c_1 is fixed to be 0, then the value of c_2 is the compounded rate of growth of the series y. Both linear and compound extrapolation based on the autoregressive model are commonly used as a simple means of forecasting.

Example 13.1 Forecasting Department Store Sales

In this example simple extrapolation models are used to forecast monthly retail sales of department stores. The time series is listed below, where monthly observations are seasonally adjusted and cover the period from January 1968 to March 1974, the units of measurement are millions of dollars, and the source of the data is the U.S. Department of Commerce.

	1968	1969	1970	1971	1972	1973	1974
January	2,582	2,839	3,034	3,287	3,578	4,121	4,456
February	2,621	2,876	3,029	3,342	3,650	4,233	4,436
March	2,690	2,881	3,045	3,336	3,664	4,439	4,699
April	2,635	2,967	3,066	3,427	3,643	4,167	
May	2,676	2,944	3,077	3,413	3,838	4,326	
June	2,714	2,939	3,046	3,503	3,792	4,329	
July	2,834	3,014	3,094	3,472	3,899	4,423	
August	2,789	3,031	3,053	3,511	3,845	4,351	
September	2,768	2,995	3,071	3,618	4,007	4,406	
October	2,785	2,998	3,186	3,554	4,092	4,357	
November	2,886	3,012	3,167	3,641	3,937	4,485	
December	2,842	3,031	3,230	3,607	4,008	4,445	

One might desire to forecast monthly sales for April, May, and the months following in 1974. For instructional purposes, we extrapolate sales for April 1974. The results of four regressions associated with the four alternative trend models are listed below. Standard regression statistics are shown (see Chapters 1 to 3 for a review of their meaning), with t statistics in parentheses:

Linear trend model:

$$\text{SALES}_t = 2463.1 + 26.70t \tag{13.10}$$
$$(84.9) \quad (39.5)$$

$$R^2 = .955 \qquad F(1/73) = 2,000 \qquad \text{SER} = 126.9 \qquad \text{DW} = .38$$

Log-linear trend model (exponential growth):

$$\log \text{SALES}_t = 7.849 + .0077t \tag{13.11}$$
$$(1,000) \quad (52.6)$$

$$R^2 = .974 \qquad F(1/73) = 3,000 \qquad \text{SER} = .027 \qquad \text{DW} = .56$$

Autoregressive trend model:

$$\text{SALES}_t = 4.918 + 1.007\text{SALES}_{t-1} \tag{13.12}$$
$$(.09) \quad (65.05)$$

$$R^2 = .983 \qquad F(1/73) = 4,000 \qquad \text{SER} = 78.07 \qquad \text{DW} = 2.82$$

Logarithmic autoregressive trend model:

$$\log SALES_t = .0188 + .9987 \log SALES_{t-1} \qquad (13.13)$$
$$(.16) \qquad (70.37)$$

$$R^2 = .985 \qquad F(1/73) = 5,000 \qquad SER = .021 \qquad DW = 2.80$$

In the first regression, a time variable running from 0 to 74 was constructed and then used as the independent variable. When $t = 75$ is placed in the right-hand side of the equation

$$SALES = 2463.1 + 26.70t$$

the resulting forecast is 4,465.8. The use of the second log-linear equation yields

FIGURE 13.4
Simulated and actual sales.

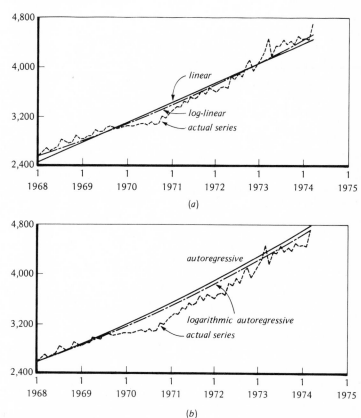

(a)

(b)

a forecast of 4,551.5. The third regression, based on an autoregressive process, yields an extrapolated value for April 1974 of 4,736.8:

$$4{,}736.8 \simeq 4.92 + 1.007 \times 4{,}699$$

If the constant term were dropped from Eq. (13.12), the extrapolated value would be 4,738.24. The fourth regression result is based on the logarithmic autoregressive model. The extrapolated value in this case is 4,735.6. If one were to calculate a compounded growth rate for the series and to extrapolate on the basis that the growth rate remains unchanged, the extrapolated value would be 4,739.3.

The simulated and actual series are plotted for each of the four extrapolation models in Fig. 13.4a and b. Note that the two autoregressive models are closer to the actual series at the end of the time period.

Simple extrapolation methods such as those used in the preceding example are frequently the basis for making "casual" long-range forecasts of variables ranging from GNP to population to pollution indices. Although they can be useful as a way of quickly formulating initial forecasts, they usually provide little forecasting accuracy. The analyst who estimates an extrapolation model is at least advised to calculate a standard error of forecast and forecast confidence interval following the methods presented in Chapter 6.[3] More important, the analyst should realize that there are alternative models that can be used to obtain forecasts with smaller standard errors.

13.1.2 Moving Average Models

Another class of deterministic models that are often used for forecasting consists of *moving average models*. As a simple example, assume that we are forecasting a monthly time series. We might use the following model:

$$f(t) = \tfrac{1}{12}(y_{t-1} + y_{t-2} + \cdots + y_{t-12}) \tag{13.14}$$

Then, a forecast one period ahead would be given by

$$\hat{y}_{T+1} = \tfrac{1}{12}(y_T + y_{T-1} + \cdots + y_{T-11}) \tag{13.15}$$

The moving average model is useful if we believe that a likely value for our series next month is a simple average of its values over the past 12 months. It may be unrealistic, however, to assume that a good forecast of y_t would be given by a simple average of its past values. It is often more reasonable to

---

[3] One should keep in mind that the autoregressive models of Eqs. (13.8) and (13.9) involve regression with a lagged dependent variable. If the additive error process is serially correlated, then the coefficient estimates will be biased, as will the estimate of the standard error of forecast.

have more recent values of y_t play a greater role than earlier values. In such a case recent values should be weighted more heavily in the moving average. In other words, if y_{T+1} is to be an average of all the past values of y_t, we might, in taking the average, want to weight y_T most heavily, y_{T-1} somewhat less heavily, etc. A deterministic forecasting model that accomplishes this is the *exponentially weighted moving average* (EWMA) model:

$$\hat{y}_{T+1} = \alpha y_T + \alpha(1 - \alpha)y_{T-1} + \alpha(1 - \alpha)^2 y_{T-2} + \cdots$$

$$= \alpha \sum_{\tau=0}^{\infty} (1 - \alpha)^{\tau} y_{T-\tau} \tag{13.16}$$

Here α is a number between 0 and 1 that indicates how heavily we weight recent values relative to older ones.[4] With $\alpha = 1$, for example, our forecast becomes

$$\hat{y}_{T+1} = y_T \tag{13.17}$$

and we ignore any values of y that occurred before y_T. As α becomes smaller, we place greater emphasis on more distant values of y.[5] Note that Eq. (13.16) represents a true average, since

$$\alpha \sum_{\tau=0}^{\infty} (1 - \alpha)^{\tau} = \frac{\alpha}{1 - (1 - \alpha)} = 1 \tag{13.18}$$

so that the weights indeed sum to unity.

If we want to make a forecast $\hat{y}_{T+l}$ more than one period ahead using an exponentially weighted moving average model, we can modify Eq. (13.16) to include a weighted average of the more recent short-run forecasts $\hat{y}_{T+l-1}$, $\hat{y}_{T+l-2}, \ldots, \hat{y}_{T+1}$. This logical extension of the EWMA model is given by

$$\hat{y}_{T+l} = \alpha \hat{y}_{T+l-1} + \alpha(1 - \alpha)\hat{y}_{T+l-2} + \cdots + \alpha(1 - \alpha)^{l-2}\hat{y}_{T+1}$$

$$+ \alpha(1 - \alpha)^{l-1} y_T + \alpha(1 - \alpha)^{l} y_{T-1} + \alpha(1 - \alpha)^{l+1} y_{T-2}$$

$$+ \alpha(1 - \alpha)^{l+2} y_{T-3} + \cdots \tag{13.19}$$

---

[4] The reader might note that this model is similar to the Koyck distributed lag model discussed in Chapter 7. In fact Eq. (13.16) says that y_t is related to a Koyck lag distribution of past values of y_t—rather than past values of some explanatory variable x_t, as in Chapter 7.

[5] The reader might suspect that if the series has an upward (downward) trend, the EWMA model will underpredict (overpredict) future values of y_t. This will indeed be the case, since the model averages past values of y_t to produce a forecast. If y_t has been growing steadily in the past, the EWMA forecast $\hat{y}_{T+1}$ will thus be *smaller* than the most recent value y_T, and if the series continues to grow steadily in the future, $\hat{y}_{T+1}$ will be an underprediction of the true value y_{T+1}. This suggests that one ought to remove any trend from the data before using the EWMA technique. Once an untrended initial forecast has been made, the trend term can be added in order to obtain a final forecast for the time series.

As an example, consider a forecast two periods ahead ($l = 2$), which would be given by

$$\hat{y}_{T+2} = \alpha\hat{y}_{T+1} + \alpha(1 - \alpha)y_T + \alpha(1 - \alpha)^2 y_{T-1} + \cdots$$

$$= \alpha[\alpha y_T + \alpha(1 - \alpha)y_{T-1} + \cdots] + \alpha(1 - \alpha)y_T + \alpha(1 - \alpha)^2 y_{T-1} + \cdots$$

$$= \alpha^2 \sum_{\tau=0}^{\infty} (1 - \alpha)^\tau y_{T-\tau} + \alpha(1 - \alpha) \sum_{\tau=0}^{\infty} (1 - \alpha)^\tau y_{T-\tau}$$

$$= \alpha \sum_{\tau=0}^{\infty} (1 - \alpha)^\tau y_{T-\tau} \qquad (13.20)$$

Note that the two-period forecast is the same as the one-period forecast. The weightings on y_T, y_{T-1}, ..., in the EWMA model are the same as they were before, but we are now extrapolating the average ahead an extra period. In fact, it is not difficult to show (see Exercise 13.3) that the l-period forecast $\hat{y}_{T+l}$ is also given by Eq. (13.20).

The moving average forecasts represented by Eqs. (13.15), (13.16), and (13.19) are all *adaptive forecasts*. By "adaptive" we mean that they automatically adjust themselves to the most recently available data. Consider, for example, a simple four-period moving average. Suppose y_{20} in Fig. 13.5 represents the most recent data point. Then our forecast will be given by

$$\hat{y}_{21} = \tfrac{1}{4}(y_{20} + y_{19} + y_{18} + y_{17}) \qquad (13.21)$$

and a forecast two periods ahead will be given by

$$\hat{y}_{22} = \tfrac{1}{4}(\hat{y}_{21} + y_{20} + y_{19} + y_{18})$$

$$= \tfrac{5}{16}y_{20} + \tfrac{5}{16}y_{19} + \tfrac{5}{16}y_{18} + \tfrac{1}{16}y_{17} \qquad (13.22)$$

These forecasts are represented by $\times$'s in Fig. 13.5. If y_{21} were known, then we would forecast y_{22} one period ahead as follows:

$$\hat{\hat{y}}_{22} = \tfrac{1}{4}(y_{21} + y_{20} + y_{19} + y_{18})$$

This forecast is represented by an $\otimes$ in Fig. 13.5. Now suppose that the *actual* value of y_{21} turns out to be larger than the predicted value, that is,

$$y_{21} > \hat{y}_{21}$$

The actual value of y_{22} is, of course, not known, but we would expect that $\hat{\hat{y}}_{22}$ would provide a better forecast than $\hat{y}_{22}$ because of the extra information used

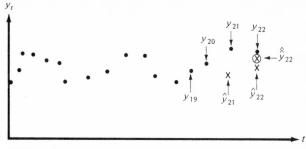

FIGURE 13.5
Adaptive forecasts.

in the adaptive process. The EWMA forecast would exhibit the same adaptive behavior. Note, however, that the simple exponential trend model of Eq. (13.4) is not adaptive, i.e., does not change in response to a new data point.

Although the moving average models described above are certainly useful, they do not provide us with information about *forecast confidence*. The reason is that no regression is used to estimate the model, so that we cannot calculate standard errors, nor can we describe or explain the stochastic (or "unexplained") component of the time series. It is this stochastic component that creates the error in our forecast. Unless the stochastic component is explained through the modeling process, little can be said about the kinds of forecast errors that might be expected. For this reason, we turn to stochastic models of time series, i.e., models that attempt to describe the stochastic properties of a given time series.

13.2 STOCHASTIC MODELS OF TIME SERIES

The models that are introduced in this section all make the assumption that the time series to be forecasted has been generated by a *stochastic process*, that is, that each value $y_1, y_2, \ldots, y_T$ in the series is drawn randomly from a probability distribution. In modeling such a process, we attempt to describe the characteristics of its randomness. This should help us to infer something about the probabilities associated with alternative future values of the series. To be completely general, we assume that the series $y_1, \ldots, y_T$ is a set of *jointly distributed random variables*, i.e., that there exists some probability distribution function $p(y_1, \ldots, y_T)$ that assigns probabilities to all possible combinations of values of $y_1, \ldots, y_T$. If we could somehow numerically specify the probability distribution function for our series, then we could actually determine the probability of one or another future outcome.

Unfortunately, the complete specification of the probability distribution function for a time series is almost always impossible. However, it usually is possible to construct a simplified model of the time series which explains its randomness in a manner that is useful for forecasting purposes. For example, we might believe that the values of $y_1, \ldots, y_T$ are normally distributed, and are correlated with each other according to a simple first-order Markov process (recall the serially correlated error process described in Chapter 4). The actual distribution of $y_1, \ldots, y_T$ may in fact be much more complicated, but this simple model may be a reasonable approximation. Of course, the usefulness of such a model depends on how closely it captures the true probability distribution and thus the true random behavior of the series. Note that it *need not* (and usually will not) match the actual past behavior of the series *since the series and the model are stochastic*. It should simply capture the characteristics of the series' randomness.

We take as our first (and most simple) example of a stochastic time series the *random walk* process.[6] Of course, there are few series that are actually random walk processes, but there are several for which a random walk model is not a bad approximation. In the simplest random walk process, each successive *change* in y_t is drawn *independently* from a probability distribution with 0 mean. Thus, y_t is determined by

$$y_t = y_{t-1} + \varepsilon_t \tag{13.23}$$

with $E[\varepsilon_t] = 0$ and $E[\varepsilon_t \varepsilon_s] = 0$ for $t \neq s$. Such a process could be generated by successive flips of a coin, where a head receives a value of $+1$ and a tail receives a value of -1.

Suppose we wanted to make a forecast for such a random walk process; i.e., we knew the past history $y_1, y_2, \ldots, y_T$ and we wanted to obtain a forecast $\hat{y}_{T+1}$. The forecast is given by

$$\hat{y}_{T+1} = E[y_{T+1} | y_T, \ldots, y_1] \tag{13.24}$$

But $y_{T+1} = y_T + \varepsilon_{T+1}$, and ε_{T+1} is independent of $y_T, y_{T-1}, \ldots, y_1$. Thus, the forecast one period ahead is simply

$$\hat{y}_{T+1} = y_T + E[\varepsilon_{T+1}] = y_T \tag{13.25}$$

The forecast two periods ahead is

$$\hat{y}_{T+2} = E[y_{T+2} | y_T, \ldots, y_1]$$

$$= E[y_{T+1} + \varepsilon_{T+2}]$$

$$= E[y_T + \varepsilon_{T+1} + \varepsilon_{T+2}] = y_T \tag{13.26}$$

Similarly, the forecast l periods ahead is also y_T.

---

[6] The random walk process has often been used as a model for the movement of stock market prices. See, for example, E. F. Fama, "Random Walks in Stock Market Prices," *Financial Analysts Journal*, Sept.–Oct. 1965; or P. H. Cootner (ed.), *The Random Character of Stock Market Prices* (Cambridge, Mass.: M.I.T., 1964).

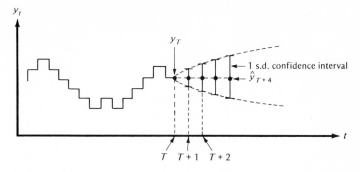

FIGURE 13.6
Forecasting a random walk.

Although the forecast $\hat{y}_{T+l}$ will be the same no matter how large l is, the variance of the forecast error will grow as l becomes larger. For the one-period forecast, the forecast error is given by

$$e_1 = y_{T+1} - \hat{y}_{T+1}$$

$$= y_T + \varepsilon_{T+1} - y_T = \varepsilon_{T+1} \qquad (13.27)$$

and its variance is just $E[\varepsilon_{T+1}^2] = \sigma_\varepsilon^2$. For the two-period forecast,

$$e_2 = y_{T+2} - \hat{y}_{T+2}$$

$$= y_T + \varepsilon_{T+1} + \varepsilon_{T+2} - y_T = \varepsilon_{T+1} + \varepsilon_{T+2} \qquad (13.28)$$

and its variance is

$$E[(\varepsilon_{T+1} + \varepsilon_{T+2})^2] = E[\varepsilon_{T+1}^2] + E[\varepsilon_{T+2}^2] + 2E[\varepsilon_{T+1}\varepsilon_{T+2}] \qquad (13.29)$$

Since ε_{T+1} and ε_{T+2} are independent, the third term in (13.29) is 0, and the error variance is $2\sigma_\varepsilon^2$. Similarly, for the l-period forecast, the error variance is $l\sigma_\varepsilon^2$. Thus, the *standard error of forecast* (i.e., the standard deviation of the forecast error) increases with the square root of l. We can thus obtain *confidence intervals* for our forecasts, and these intervals will become wider as the forecast horizon increases. This is illustrated in Fig. 13.6. Note that the forecasts $\hat{y}_{T+1}, \hat{y}_{T+2}$, etc., are all equal to the last observation y_T, but the confidence intervals represented by one standard deviation in the forecast error increase as the square root of l.

A simple variation on this theme is the random walk with "drift," which accounts for a trend (upward or downward) in the series y_t, and allows us to embody that trend in our forecast. In this process, y_t is determined by

$$y_t = y_{t-1} + d + \varepsilon_t \qquad (13.30)$$

FIGURE 13.7
Forecasting a random walk with drift.

so that on the average the process will tend to move upward (for $d > 0$). Now the one-period forecast is

$$\hat{y}_{T+1} = E[y_{T+1} | y_T, \dots, y_1] = y_T + d \tag{13.31}$$

and the l-period forecast is

$$\hat{y}_{T+l} = y_T + ld \tag{13.32}$$

The standard error of forecast will be the same as before. For one period,

$$e_1 = y_{T+1} - \hat{y}_{T+1}$$

$$= y_T + d + \varepsilon_{T+1} - y_T - d = \varepsilon_{T+1} \tag{13.33}$$

as before. The process, together with forecasts and forecast confidence intervals, is illustrated in Fig. 13.7. As can be seen in that figure, the forecasts increase linearly with l, and the standard error of forecast increases with the square root of l.

In the next chapter of this book we examine a general class of stochastic time-series models. Later, we will see how that class of models can be used to make forecasts for a wide variety of time series. First, however, it is necessary to review some basic concepts about stochastic processes and their properties.

13.3 STATIONARY AND NONSTATIONARY TIME SERIES

As we begin to develop models for time series, we want to know whether or not the underlying stochastic process that generated the series can be assumed to be *invariant with respect to time*. If the characteristics of the stochastic process change over time, i.e., if the process is *nonstationary*, then it will often be difficult to represent the time series over past and future intervals of time by a simple algebraic model.[7] On the other hand, if the stochastic process is fixed in time, i.e., if it is *stationary*, then, as we will see, it is possible to model the process via an equation with fixed coefficients that can be estimated from past data. This is analogous to the single-equation regression model in which one economic variable is related to other economic variables, with coefficients that are estimated under the assumption that the structural relationship described by the equation is invariant over time (i.e., is stationary). If the structural relationship changed over time (i.e., was nonstationary), then we could hardly expect to follow the techniques of Chapter 6 in using a regression model estimated from past data to forecast future data. Time-series models do not utilize economic relationships. However, our task of describing a stochastic process will be much easier if the characteristics of that process do not change over time. Thus, stationarity is an important characteristic of the stochastic processes that we will model.

The stochastic time-series models which are developed in detail in the next chapter of the book are stationary models. Specifically, the stochastic processes are assumed to be in equilibrium over time about a constant mean level. The probability of a given fluctuation in the process from that mean level is assumed to be the same *at any point in time*. In other words, the stochastic properties of the stationary process are assumed to be *invariant with respect to time*.

One would suspect that many of the time series that one encounters in business and economics are not generated by stationary processes. The gross national product, for example, has for the most part been growing steadily, and for this reason alone its stochastic properties in 1973 are different from those in 1933. Although it is quite difficult to build models of nonstationary processes, we will see that certain classes of nonstationary processes can easily be transformed into stationary or approximately stationary processes. Many time series that arise in economic and business applications belong to one of these classes of non-stationary processes.

13.3.1 *Properties of Stationary Processes*

We have said that any stochastic time series $y_1, \ldots, y_T$ can be thought of as having been generated by a set of jointly distributed random variables; i.e., the set of data points $y_1, \ldots, y_T$ represents a particular outcome of the joint

---

[7] The random walk with drift is one example of a nonstationary process for which a simple forecasting model can be constructed.

probability distribution function $p(y_1, \ldots, y_T)$.[8] Similarly, a *future* observation y_{T+1} can be thought of as being generated by a *conditional probability distribution function* $p(y_{T+1} | y_1, \ldots, y_T)$, that is, a probability distribution for y_{T+1} given the past observations $y_1, \ldots, y_T$. We define a *stationary* process, then, as one whose joint distribution and conditional distribution both are *invariant with respect to displacement in time*. In other words, if the series y_t is stationary, then

$$p(y_t, \ldots, y_{t+k}) = p(y_{t+m}, \ldots, y_{t+k+m}) \tag{13.34}$$

and
$$p(y_t) = p(y_{t+m}) \tag{13.35}$$

for any t, k, and m.

Note that if the series y_t is stationary, then the *mean* of the series, defined as

$$\mu_y = E[y_t] \tag{13.36}$$

must also be stationary, so that $E[y_t] = E[y_{t+m}]$, for any t and m. Furthermore, the *variance* of the series,

$$\sigma_y^2 = E[(y_t - \mu_y)^2] \tag{13.37}$$

must be stationary, so that $E[(y_t - \mu_y)^2] = E[(y_{t+m} - \mu_y)^2]$, and finally, for any lag k, the *covariance* of the series,

$$\gamma_k = \text{Cov}\,(y_t, y_{t+k}) = E[(y_t - \mu_y)(y_{t+k} - \mu_y)] \tag{13.38}$$

must be stationary, so that $\text{Cov}\,(y_t, y_{t+k}) = \text{Cov}\,(y_{t+m}, y_{t+m+k})$.[9]

If a stochastic process is stationary, then the probability distribution $p(y_t)$ is the same for all time t, and its shape (or at least some of its properties) can be inferred by looking at a histogram[10] of the observations $y_1, \ldots, y_T$ that make up the observed series. Also, an estimate of the mean μ_y of the process can be obtained from the *sample mean* of the series

$$\bar{y} = \frac{1}{T} \sum_{t=1}^{T} y_t \tag{13.39}$$

---

[8] This outcome is called a *realization*. Thus $y_1, \ldots, y_T$ represent one particular realization of the stochastic process represented by the probability distribution $p(y_1, \ldots, y_T)$.

[9] It is possible for the mean, variance, and covariances of the series to be stationary but not the joint probability distribution. If the probability distributions are stationary, then we term the series *strict-sense stationary*. If the mean, variance, and covariances are stationary, then we term the series *wide-sense stationary*. Note that strict-sense stationarity implies wide-sense stationarity but that the converse is not true.

[10] A histogram is a plot of the frequency distribution of a set of observations.

and an estimate of the variance σ_y^2 can be obtained from the *sample variance*

$$\hat{\sigma}_y^2 = \frac{1}{T} \sum_{t=1}^{T} (y_t - \bar{y})^2 \qquad (13.40)$$

13.3.2 The Autocorrelation Function

While it is usually impossible to obtain a complete description of a stochastic process (i.e., actually specify the underlying probability distributions), the autocorrelation function is extremely useful in helping us to obtain a partial description of the process for modeling purposes. The autocorrelation function provides us with a measure of how much correlation there is (and by implication how much interdependency there is) between neighboring data points in the series y_t. We define the *autocorrelation with lag k* as

$$\rho_k = \frac{E[(y_t - \mu_y)(y_{t+k} - \mu_y)]}{\sqrt{E[(y_t - \mu_y)^2]E[(y_{t+k} - \mu_y)^2]}} = \frac{\text{Cov}(y_t, y_{t+k})}{\sigma_{y_t}\sigma_{y_{t+k}}} \qquad (13.41)$$

For a stationary process the variance at time t in the denominator of (13.41) is the same as the variance at time $t + k$; thus the denominator is just the variance of the stochastic process, and

$$\rho_k = \frac{E[(y_t - \mu_y)(y_{t+k} - \mu_y)]}{\sigma_y^2} \qquad (13.42)$$

Note that the numerator of (13.42) is the covariance between y_t and y_{t+k}, γ_k, so that

$$\rho_k = \frac{\gamma_k}{\gamma_0} \qquad (13.43)$$

and thus $\rho_0 = 1$.

The autocorrelation function in (13.42) is purely theoretical, in that it describes a stochastic process for which we have only a limited number of observations. In practice, then, we must calculate an *estimate* of the autocorrelation function, called the *sample autocorrelation function:*[11]

$$\hat{\rho}_k = \frac{\sum_{t=1}^{T-k} (y_t - \bar{y})(y_{t+k} - \bar{y})}{\sum_{t=1}^{T} (y_t - \bar{y})^2} \qquad (13.44)$$

---

[11] Other estimates of the autocorrelation function have been suggested. For a discussion of their properties, see G. M. Jenkins and D. G. Watts, *Spectral Analysis and Its Applications* (San Francisco: Holden-Day, 1968). Equation (13.44), however, seems to provide the most robust estimate.

FIGURE 13.8
Nonfarm inventory investment.

If the number of observations in the time series is large, then the estimated autocorrelation function will closely approximate the true population autocorrelation function.

It is easy to see from their definitions that both the theoretical and estimated autocorrelation functions are symmetrical, i.e., that the correlation for a positive displacement is the same as that for a negative displacement, so that

$$\rho_k = \rho_{-k} \tag{13.45}$$

Then, when plotting an autocorrelation function (i.e., plotting ρ_k for different values of k), one need consider only positive values of k.

As an example of an estimated autocorrelation function for a stationary economic time series, we have calculated $\hat{\rho}_k$ for quarterly data on nonfarm inventory investment. The time series itself (covering the years 1946 to 1972) is shown in Fig. 13.8, and the sample autocorrelation function is shown in Fig. 13.9. Note that the autocorrelation function falls off rather quickly as the lag k increases. This is typical of a stationary time series, such as inventory investment. In fact, as we will see, the autocorrelation function can be used to test whether or not a series is stationary. If ρ_k does not fall off quickly as k increases, this is an indication of nonstationarity.[12]

---

[12] One can statistically test the null hypothesis that a particular value of the autocorrelation function ρ_k is equal to 0. Bartlett has derived an approximate formula for the variance of the sample autocorrelation. Using his formula, one can estimate how many standard deviations away from 0 the sample autocorrelation is. For details see M. S. Bartlett, "On the Theoretical Specification of Sampling Properties of Autocorrelated Time Series," *Journal of the Royal Statistical Society*, ser. B8, vol. 27, 1946. Also see G. E. P. Box and G. M. Jenkins, *Time Series Analysis* (San Francisco: Holden-Day, 1970).

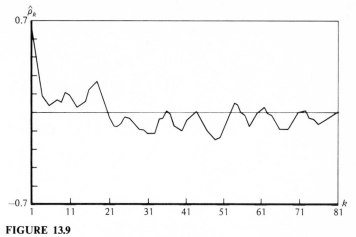

FIGURE 13.9
Nonfarm inventory investment—sample autocorrelation function.

If a time series is stationary, then there exist certain analytical conditions which place bounds on the values that can be taken by the individual points of the autocorrelation function. However, the derivation of these conditions is somewhat complicated and will not be presented at this point. Furthermore, the conditions themselves are rather cumbersome and of limited usefulness in applied time-series modeling. Therefore, we have chosen to include the mathematical details in a short appendix to this chapter. We turn our attention now to the properties of those time series which are nonstationary, but which can be transformed into stationary series through a simple mathematical operation.

13.3.3 Homogeneous Nonstationary Processes

Probably very few of the time series that one encounters in practice are stationary. Fortunately, however, many of the nonstationary time series encountered (and this includes most of those that arise in economics and business) have the desirable property that if they are *differenced one or more times, the resulting series will be stationary.* Such a nonstationary series is termed *homogeneous.* The number of times that the original series must be differenced before a stationary series results is called the *order* of homogeneity. Thus, if y_t is first-order homogeneous nonstationary, the series

$$w_t = y_t - y_{t-1} = \Delta y_t \tag{13.46}$$

is stationary. If y_t happened to be second-order homogeneous, then the series

$$w_t = \Delta^2 y_t = \Delta y_t - \Delta y_{t-1} \tag{13.47}$$

would be stationary.

As an example of a first-order homogeneous nonstationary process, consider the simple random walk process that we introduced earlier:

$$y_t = y_{t-1} + \varepsilon_t \tag{13.48}$$

Let us examine the variance of this process:

$$\gamma_0 = E[y_t^2] = E[(y_{t-1} + \varepsilon_t)^2]$$

$$= E[y_{t-1}^2] + \sigma_\varepsilon^2$$

$$= E[y_{t-2}^2] + 2\sigma_\varepsilon^2 \tag{13.49}$$

or
$$\gamma_0 = E[y_{t-n}^2] + n\sigma_\varepsilon^2 \tag{13.50}$$

Observe that the variance grows over time. In fact the variance becomes infinite and is undefined. In addition, the covariances grow over time, since, for example

$$\gamma_1 = E[y_t y_{t-1}] = E[y_{t-1}(y_{t-1} + \varepsilon_t)]$$

$$= E[y_{t-1}^2] \tag{13.51}$$

Now let us look at the series that results from differencing the random walk process, i.e., the series

$$w_t = \Delta y_t$$

$$= y_t - y_{t-1} = \varepsilon_t \tag{13.52}$$

Since the ε_t are assumed independent over time, w_t clearly is a stationary process. Thus, we see that the random walk process is first-order homogeneous. If we calculate the covariances and autocorrelation function for w_t, it is trivial to see that $\rho_0 = 1$, but $\rho_k = 0$ for $k > 0$. This is not surprising, since the ε_t's are independent over time.

13.3.4   Stationarity and the Autocorrelation Function

The GNP or a series of sales figures for a firm are both likely to be non-stationary. Each has been growing (on average) over time, so that the mean of each series is time dependent. It is quite likely, however, that if the GNP or company sales figures are first-differenced one or more times, the resulting series will be stationary. Thus, if we want to build a time-series model to forecast the GNP, we can difference the series one or two times, construct a model for this new series, make our forecasts, and then *integrate* (i.e., remove the

FIGURE 13.10
Stationary series.

effect of the differencing) the model and its forecasts to arrive back at the GNP.

How can we decide if a series is stationary, or determine the appropriate number of times a homogeneous nonstationary series should be differenced to arrive at a stationary series? Usually these questions can be answered by looking at a plot of the autocorrelation function (called a *correlogram*). Figures 13.10 and 13.11 show autocorrelation functions for stationary and nonstationary series. The autocorrelation function for a stationary series drops off as k, the number of lags, becomes large, but this is usually not the case for a nonstationary series. If we are differencing a nonstationary series, we can test each succeeding difference by looking at the autocorrelation function. If, for example, the second round of differencing results in a series whose autocorrelation function drops off rapidly, then we can determine that the original series is second-order homogeneous. If the resulting series is still nonstationary, the autocorrelation function will remain large even for long lags.

FIGURE 13.11
Nonstationary series.

Example 13.2   Interest Rate

Often in applied work it will not be clear how many times a nonstationary series should be differenced. Then one must make a judgment based on experience and intuition. As an example, take the time series for the interest rate on 4–6 month commercial paper. This series (consisting of quarterly data from 1947 to 1973) is shown in Fig. 13.12, and its sample autocorrelation function is shown in Fig. 13.13. The autocorrelation function does seem to

FIGURE 13.12
Interest rate on commercial paper.

FIGURE 13.13
Interest rate on commercial paper—sample autocorrelation function.

FIGURE 13.14
Interest rate on commercial paper: Δy_t.

decline as the number of lags becomes large, so that one might at first suspect that the series is stationary. The series, however, exhibits an upward trend (so that the mean is not constant over time), and the autocorrelation function declines only slowly. This series is thus a candidate for a homogeneous non-stationary process. To check, we difference the series and recalculate the sample autocorrelation function.

The differenced series is shown in Fig. 13.14. Its sample autocorrelation function, shown in Fig. 13.15, appears more stationary (as does the series

FIGURE 13.15
Interest rate on commercial paper: autocorrelation function of Δy_t.

FIGURE 13.16
Interest rate on commercial paper: $\Delta^2 y_t$.

itself). The series is then differenced a second time (see Fig. 13.16) and the resulting autocorrelation function (Fig. 13.17) appears stationary. In fact, it declines more rapidly than does the autocorrelation function associated with differencing only once.[13] To conclude our example, we can attempt to obtain a "more stationary" series by differencing a third time. The thrice-differenced

FIGURE 13.17
Interest rate on commercial paper: autocorrelation function of $\Delta^2 y_t$.

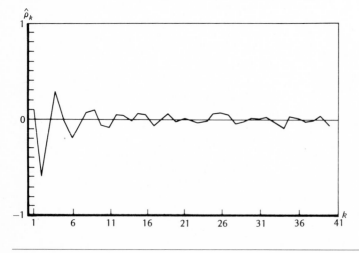

---

[13] For our purposes what is important for stationarity is the sharp decline in ρ_k for the first four time periods. The remaining portion of the graph appears to be random with 0 mean.

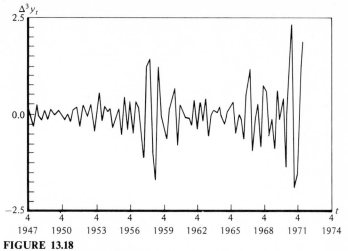

FIGURE 13.18
Interest rate on commercial paper: $\Delta^3 y_t$.

FIGURE 13.19
Interest rate on commercial paper: autocorrelation function of $\Delta^3 y_t$.

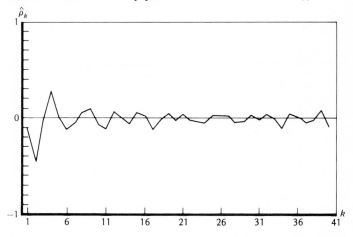

series is shown in Fig. 13.18 and the corresponding sample autocorrelation function in Fig. 13.19. The results do not seem qualitatively different than the previous case. Our conclusion, then, would be that differencing once, or at most twice, should be sufficient to ensure stationarity.

13.3.5 Seasonality and the Autocorrelation Function

We have just seen that the autocorrelation function can reveal information about the stationarity of a time series. In the remaining chapters of this book we will see that a good deal of other information about a time series can also be obtained from its autocorrelation function. This information will be useful in helping us to construct stochastic models of time series. However, we continue here by examining the relationship between the autocorrelation function and the *seasonality* of a time series.

Seasonality is defined as cyclical behavior that occurs on a regular calendar basis, i.e., in cycles with periodicity that is annual, semiannual, quarterly, monthly, or any other unit of calendar time. An example of a highly seasonal time series would be toy sales, which exhibit a strong peak every Christmas. Sales of ice cream and iced-tea mix show seasonal peaks each summer in response to increased demand brought about by warmer weather; Peruvian anchovy production shows seasonal troughs once every 7 years in response to decreased supply brought about by cyclical changes in the ocean currents.

Often seasonal peaks and troughs are easy to spot simply by direct observation of the time series. On many occasions, however, if the time series fluctuates considerably, seasonal peaks and troughs will not be distinguishable from the other fluctuations. Recognition of seasonality is important, since it provides information about "regularity" in the series that can aid us in making a forecast. Fortunately, that recognition can be made easier with the help of the autocorrelation function.

If a monthly time series y_t exhibits annual seasonality, then the data points in the series should show some degree of correlation with the corresponding data points which lead or lag by 12 months. In other words, we would expect to see some degree of correlation between y_t and y_{t-12}. Since y_t and y_{t-12} will be correlated, as will y_{t-12} and y_{t-24}, we should also see correlation between y_t and y_{t-24}. Similarly there will be correlation between y_t and y_{t-36}, y_t and y_{t-48}, etc. These correlations should manifest themselves in the autocorrelation function ρ_k, which will exhibit peaks at $k = 12, 24, 36, 48$, etc. Thus we can identify seasonality by observing regular peaks in the autocorrelation function, even if seasonal peaks cannot be discerned in the time series itself.

Example 13.3   Hog Production

As an example, look at the time series for the monthly production of hogs in the United States, shown in Fig. 13.20. It would take a somewhat experienced eye to discern easily seasonality in that series. The seasonality of the series, however, is readily apparent in its sample autocorrelation function, which is shown in Fig. 13.21. Note the peaks that occur at $k = 12, 24$, and 36, indicating annual cycles in the series.

A crude method of removing the annual cycles ("deseasonalizing" the data) would be to take a 12-month difference, obtaining a new series $z_t = y_t - y_{t-12}$. As can be seen in Fig. 13.22, the autocorrelation function for this 12-month differenced series does not exhibit strong seasonality. We will see in later chapters that z_t represents an extremely simple time-series model for hog production,

FIGURE 13.20
Hog production (in thousands of hogs per month). Time bounds: January
1962 to December 1971. (*Source: Survey of Current Business.*)

FIGURE 13.21
Autocorrelation function for hog production series.

FIGURE 13.22
Hog production: autocorrelation function of $(y_t - y_{t-12})$.

FIGURE 13.23
Hog production: autocorrelation function of $\Delta(y_t - y_{t-12})$.

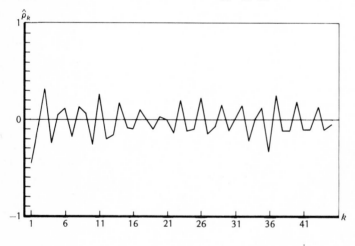

since it accounts only for the annual cycle. We can complete this example by observing that the autocorrelation function in Fig. 13.22 declines only slowly, so that there is some doubt as to whether z_t is a stationary series. We therefore first-differenced this series, to obtain $w_t = \Delta z_t = \Delta(y_t - y_{t-12})$. The autocorrelation function of this series, shown in Fig. 13.23, declines rapidly and remains small, so that we may be confident that w_t is a stationary, nonseasonal time series.

Exercises

13.1 Which (if any) of the simple extrapolation models presented in section 13.1.1 do you think might be suitable for forecasting the GNP? The Consumer Price Index? A short-term interest rate? Annual production of wheat? Explain.

13.2 Show that the exponentially weighted moving average (EWMA) model will generate forecasts that are adaptive in nature.

13.3 Show that the EMWA forecast l periods ahead is the same as the forecast one period ahead, i.e.,

$$\hat{y}_{T+l} = \alpha \sum_{\tau=0}^{\infty} (1 - \alpha)^\tau y_{T-\tau}$$

13.4 Show that the random walk process with drift is first-order homogeneous nonstationary.

13.5 Consider the time series 1, 2, 3, 4, 5, 6, ..., 20. Is this series stationary? Calculate the sample autocorrelation function $\hat{\rho}_k$ for $k = 1, 2, ..., 5$. Can you explain the shape of this function?

APPENDIX 13 / THE AUTOCORRELATION FUNCTION FOR A STATIONARY PROCESS

In this appendix we derive a set of conditions that must hold for an auto-correlation function of a stationary process. Let y_t be a stationary process and let L_t be any linear function of y_t and lags in y_t, for example,

$$L_t = \alpha_1 y_t + \alpha_2 y_{t-1} + \cdots + \alpha_k y_{t-k+1} \qquad (A13.1)$$

Now since y_t is stationary, the covariances of y_t are stationary, and

$$\text{Cov}\,(y_{t+i}, y_{t+j}) = \gamma_{|i-j|} \qquad (A13.2)$$

independent of t. Then, by squaring both sides of Eq. (A13.1), we see that the variance of L_t is given by

$$\text{Var}\,(L_t) = \sum_{i=1}^{n} \sum_{j=1}^{n} \alpha_i \alpha_j \gamma_{|i-j|} \qquad (A13.3)$$

If the α's are not all 0, then the variance of L_t must be greater than 0, and therefore we must have, for all i and j,

$$\gamma_{|i-j|} > 0 \qquad \text{for } i = j \tag{A13.4}$$

Now, for n observations, write the covariances of y_t as a matrix:

$$\mathbf{\Gamma}_n = \begin{bmatrix} \gamma_0 & \gamma_1 & \gamma_2 & \cdots & \gamma_{n-1} \\ \gamma_1 & \gamma_0 & \gamma_1 & \cdots & \gamma_{n-2} \\ \cdots\cdots\cdots\cdots\cdots\cdots\cdots\cdots\cdots\cdots \\ \gamma_{n-1} & \gamma_{n-2} & \gamma_{n-3} & \cdots & \gamma_0 \end{bmatrix} \tag{A13.5}$$

This matrix must be positive definite because the variance of L_t is always greater than zero. Note that

$$\mathbf{\Gamma}_n = \sigma_y^2 \begin{bmatrix} 1 & \rho_1 & \rho_2 & \cdots & \rho_{n-1} \\ \rho_1 & 1 & \rho_1 & \cdots & \rho_{n-2} \\ \cdots\cdots\cdots\cdots\cdots\cdots\cdots\cdots\cdots\cdots \\ \rho_{n-1} & \rho_{n-2} & \rho_{n-3} & \cdots & 1 \end{bmatrix} = \sigma_y^2 \mathbf{P}_n \tag{A13.6}$$

where $\mathbf{P}_n$ is the matrix of autocorrelations, and is itself positive definite. Thus the determinant of $\mathbf{P}_n$ and its principal minors must be greater than 0.

As an example, let us consider the case of $n = 2$. The condition on the determinant of $\mathbf{P}_n$ becomes

$$\det \begin{bmatrix} 1 & \rho_1 \\ \rho_1 & 1 \end{bmatrix} > 0$$

which implies that

$$1 - \rho_1^2 > 0$$

or

$$-1 < \rho_1 < 1 \tag{A13.7}$$

Similarly, for $n = 3$, it is easy to see that the following three conditions must all hold:

$$-1 < \rho_1 < 1 \tag{A13.8}$$

$$-1 < \rho_2 < 1 \tag{A13.9}$$

$$-1 < \frac{\rho_2 - \rho_1^2}{1 - \rho_1^2} < 1 \tag{A13.10}$$

Sets of conditions can also be derived for $n = 4$, $n = 5$, etc., but it should become clear that as the number of observations n becomes large, the number of conditions that must hold also becomes quite large. Although these conditions can provide an analytical check on the stationarity of a time series, in applied work it is more typical to judge stationarity from a visual examination of both the series itself and the sample autocorrelation function. For our purposes it will be sufficient to remember that for $k > 0$, $-1 < \rho_k < 1$ for a stationary process.

14

LINEAR TIME-SERIES MODELS

In the last chapter we introduced stochastic processes and discussed some of their properties. Now we turn to the main focus of the remainder of this book—the construction of models of stochastic processes and their use in forecasting. Our objective is to develop models that "explain" the movement of a time series y_t. Unlike the regression model, however, a set of explanatory variables will not be utilized. Instead we explain y_t by relating it to its own past values and to a weighted sum of current and lagged random disturbances.

While there are many functional forms that can be used to relate y_t to its past values and lagged random disturbances, we use here a linear specification. The assumption of linearity allows us to make quantitative statements about the stochastic properties of the models and the forecasts generated by the models (e.g., to calculate confidence intervals around our forecasts). In addition, our models apply to stationary processes and to homogeneous non-stationary processes (which can be differenced one or more times to yield stationary processes). Finally, the models are written as equations with fixed estimated coefficients, representing a stochastic structure that does not change over time. Although models with time-varying coefficients of nonstationary processes have been developed recently, they are well beyond the scope of this book.

In the first two sections of the chapter we examine simple moving average and autoregressive models for stationary processes. In a moving average model, the process y_t is described completely by a weighted sum of current and lagged random disturbances. In the autoregressive model, y_t depends on a weighted sum of its past values and a random disturbance term. In the third section we introduce mixed autoregressive-moving average models. In these models the process y_t is a function of both lagged random disturbances and its past values, as well as a current disturbance term. Even if the original process is nonstationary, it often can be differenced one or more times to produce a new series that is stationary and for which a mixed autoregressive-moving average model can be constructed. This model can be used to produce a forecast one or more periods into the future, after which the forecasted stationary series can be integrated one or more times to yield a forecast for the original time series. The integrated autoregressive-moving average model is the most complex model that we discuss in this chapter. It provides a general framework for the modeling of homogeneous nonstationary time series.

When building an integrated autoregressive-moving average model for a non-stationary time series, we must first specify how many times the series is to be differenced before a stationary series results. We must also specify the number of autoregressive terms and lagged disturbance terms to be included in the model of the stationary series. We have seen in Chapter 13 that the autocorrelation function can be used to tell us how many times we must difference a homogeneous nonstationary process in order to produce a stationary process. In this chapter, we see how the autocorrelation function can also be used to help determine the number of disturbance terms in the moving average portion and the number of lags in the autoregressive portion of our model.

14.1 MOVING AVERAGE MODELS

In the *moving average process of order* q each observation y_t is generated by a weighted average of random disturbances going back q periods. We denote this process as MA(q), and write its equation as

$$y_t = \mu + \varepsilon_t - \theta_1 \varepsilon_{t-1} - \theta_2 \varepsilon_{t-2} - \cdots - \theta_q \varepsilon_{t-q} \tag{14.1}$$

where the parameters $\theta_1, \ldots, \theta_q$ may be positive or negative.

In the moving average model (and also in the autoregressive model which will follow) the random disturbances are assumed to be generated by a *white noise* process. In other words, each disturbance term ε_t is assumed to be a normal random variable with mean 0, variance σ_ε^2, and covariance $\gamma_k = 0$ for $k \neq 0$.[1]

---

[1] Thus the autocorrelation function for a white noise process is simply

$$\rho_k = \begin{cases} 1 & \text{for } k = 0 \\ 0 & \text{for } k \neq 0 \end{cases}$$

White noise processes may not occur very commonly in nature, but, as we will see, weighted sums of a white noise process provide a good representation of processes that are nonwhite.

The reader should observe that the *mean* of the moving average process is independent of time, since $E[y_t] = \mu$. Each ε_t is assumed to be generated by the same white noise process, so that $E[\varepsilon_t] = 0$, $E[\varepsilon_t^2] = \sigma_\varepsilon^2$, and $E[\varepsilon_t \varepsilon_{t-k}] = 0$ for $k \neq 0$. The process MA(q) is thus described by exactly $q + 2$ parameters, the mean μ, the disturbance variance σ_ε^2, and the parameters $\theta_1, \theta_2, \ldots, \theta_q$ that determine the weights in the moving average.

Let us now look at the *variance*, denoted by γ_0, of the moving average process of order q:

$$\text{Var } (y_t) = \gamma_0 = E[(y_t - \mu)^2]$$

$$= E[\varepsilon_t^2 + \theta_1^2 \varepsilon_{t-1}^2 + \cdots + \theta_q^2 \varepsilon_{t-q}^2 - 2\theta_1 \varepsilon_t \varepsilon_{t-1} - \cdots]$$

$$= \sigma_\varepsilon^2 + \theta_1^2 \sigma_\varepsilon^2 + \cdots + \theta_q^2 \sigma_\varepsilon^2$$

$$= \sigma_\varepsilon^2 (1 + \theta_1^2 + \theta_2^2 + \cdots + \theta_q^2) \tag{14.2}$$

Note that the expected values of the cross terms are all 0, since we have assumed that the ε_t's are generated by a white noise process for which $\gamma_k = E[\varepsilon_t \varepsilon_{t-k}] = 0$ for $k \neq 0$.

Equation (14.2) imposes a restriction on the values that are permitted for $\theta_1, \ldots, \theta_q$. We would expect the variance of y_t to be finite, since otherwise a realization of the random process (i.e., a time series generated by it) would involve larger and larger deviations from a fixed reference point as time increased. This, in turn, would violate our assumption of stationarity, since stationarity requires that the probability of being some arbitrary distance from a reference point be invariant with respect to time. Thus, if y_t is the realization of a stationary random process, we must have

$$\sum_{i=1}^{q} \theta_i^2 < \infty \tag{14.3}$$

In a sense this result is trivial, since we have only a finite number of θ_i's, and thus their sum is finite. However, the assumption of a fixed number of θ_i's can be considered to be an approximation to a more general model. A complete model of most random processes would require an infinite number of lagged disturbance terms (and their corresponding weights). Then, as q, the order of the moving average process, becomes infinitely large, we must require that the sum $\sum_{i=0}^{\infty} \theta_i^2$ converge. Convergence will usually occur if the θ's become smaller as i becomes larger. Thus, if we are representing a process, believed to be stationary, by a moving average model of order q, we expect the θ_i's to become smaller as i becomes larger. We will see later that this implies that if the process is stationary, its correlation function ρ_k will become smaller as k becomes larger. This is consistent with our result of the last chapter that one indicator of stationarity is an autocorrelation function that approaches zero.

Now we examine some simple moving average processes, calculating the mean, variance, covariances, and autocorrelation function for each. These statistics are important, first because they provide information that helps characterize the process, and second because they will help us to identify the process when we actually construct models in the next chapter.

We begin with the simplest moving average process, the moving average process of order 1. The process is denoted by MA(1), and its equation is

$$y_t = \mu + \varepsilon_t - \theta_1 \varepsilon_{t-1} \tag{14.4}$$

This process has mean μ and variance $\gamma_0 = \sigma_\varepsilon^2(1 + \theta_1^2)$. Now let us derive the *covariance* for a one-lag displacement, γ_1:

$$\gamma_1 = E[(y_t - \mu)(y_{t-1} - \mu)]$$

$$= E[(\varepsilon_t - \theta_1 \varepsilon_{t-1})(\varepsilon_{t-1} - \theta_1 \varepsilon_{t-2})]$$

$$= -\theta_1 \sigma_\varepsilon^2 \tag{14.5}$$

In general we can determine the covariance for a k-lag displacement to be

$$\gamma_k = E[(\varepsilon_t - \theta_1 \varepsilon_{t-1})(\varepsilon_{t-k} - \theta_1 \varepsilon_{t-k-1})]$$

$$= 0 \qquad \text{for } k > 1 \tag{14.6}$$

Thus the MA(1) process has a covariance of 0 when the displacement is more than one period. We say, then, that the process has a *memory* of only one period—any value y_t is correlated with y_{t-1} and with y_{t+1}, but with no other time-series values. In effect, the process "forgets" what happened more than one period in the past; i.e., events occurring more than one period in the past (and that are independent of y_{t-1}) have no effect on where the process is now. In general the "limited memory" of a moving average process is important. It suggests (and we will see this to be the case in Chapter 16) that a moving average model provides forecasting information only a limited number of periods into the future [one period into the future for an MA(1) model].

We can now determine the autocorrelation function for the process MA(1):

$$\rho_k = \frac{\gamma_k}{\gamma_0} = \begin{cases} \dfrac{-\theta_1}{1 + \theta_1^2} & k = 1 \\[2ex] 0 & k > 1 \end{cases} \tag{14.7}$$

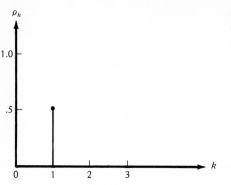

FIGURE 14.1
Autocorrelation function for
$y_t = 2 + \varepsilon_t + .8\varepsilon_{t-1}$.

An example of a first-order moving average process might be given by

$$y_t = 2 + \varepsilon_t + .8\varepsilon_{t-1} \tag{14.8}$$

The autocorrelation function for y_t is shown in Fig. 14.1, and a typical realization is shown in Fig. 14.2.

Now let us proceed by examining the moving average process of order 2. The process is denoted by MA(2), and its equation is

$$y_t = \mu + \varepsilon_t - \theta_1\varepsilon_{t-1} - \theta_2\varepsilon_{t-2} \tag{14.9}$$

This process has mean μ, variance $\sigma_\varepsilon^2(1 + \theta_1^2 + \theta_2^2)$, and covariances given by

$$\gamma_1 = E[(\varepsilon_t - \theta_1\varepsilon_{t-1} - \theta_2\varepsilon_{t-2})(\varepsilon_{t-1} - \theta_1\varepsilon_{t-2} - \theta_2\varepsilon_{t-3})]$$

$$= -\theta_1\sigma_\varepsilon^2 + \theta_2\theta_1\sigma_\varepsilon^2$$

$$= -\theta_1(1 - \theta_2)\sigma_\varepsilon^2 \tag{14.10}$$

$$\gamma_2 = E[(\varepsilon_t - \theta_1\varepsilon_{t-1} - \theta_2\varepsilon_{t-2})(\varepsilon_{t-2} - \theta_1\varepsilon_{t-3} - \theta_2\varepsilon_{t-4})]$$

$$= -\theta_2\sigma_\varepsilon^2 \tag{14.11}$$

and $\qquad \gamma_k = 0 \qquad$ for $k > 2$ $\tag{14.12}$

The autocorrelation function is given by

$$\rho_1 = \frac{-\theta_1(1 - \theta_2)}{1 + \theta_1^2 + \theta_2^2} \tag{14.13}$$

$$\rho_2 = \frac{-\theta_2}{1 + \theta_1^2 + \theta_2^2} \tag{14.14}$$

and $\qquad \rho_k = 0 \qquad$ for $k > 2$ $\tag{14.15}$

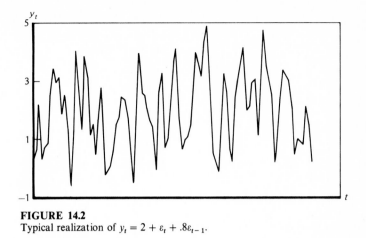

FIGURE 14.2
Typical realization of $y_t = 2 + \varepsilon_t + .8\varepsilon_{t-1}$.

The process MA(2) has a memory of exactly two periods, so that the value of y_t is influenced only by events that took place in the current period, one period back, and two periods back.

An example of a second-order moving average process might be

$$y_t = 2 + \varepsilon_t + .6\varepsilon_{t-1} - .3\varepsilon_{t-2} \tag{14.16}$$

The autocorrelation function is shown in Fig. 14.3, and a typical realization is shown in Fig. 14.4.

We leave to the reader a proof that the moving average process of order q has a memory of exactly q periods, and that its autocorrelation function ρ_k is given by the following (see Exercise 14.3):

$$\rho_k = \begin{cases} \dfrac{-\theta_k + \theta_1\theta_{k+1} + \cdots + \theta_{q-k}\theta_q}{1 + \theta_1{}^2 + \theta_2{}^2 + \cdots + \theta_q{}^2} & k = 1, \ldots, q \\[2mm] 0 & k > q \end{cases} \tag{14.17}$$

FIGURE 14.3
Autocorrelation function for
$y_t = 2 + \varepsilon_t + 6\varepsilon_{t-1} - .3\varepsilon_{t-2}$.

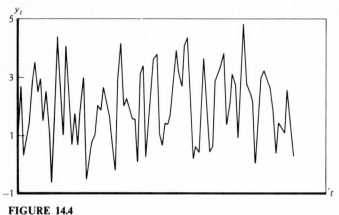

FIGURE 14.4
Typical realization of $y_t = 2 + \varepsilon_t + .6\varepsilon_{t-1} - .3\varepsilon_{t-2}$.

We can now see why the sample autocorrelation function can be useful in specifying the order of a moving average process (assuming that the time series of concern is generated by a moving average process). The autocorrelation function ρ_k for the MA(q) process has q positive and negative values, and is then 0 for $k > q$. As we proceed through this and later chapters, we will attempt to give the reader an understanding of how the sample autocorrelation function can be used to identify the stochastic process that may have generated a particular time series.

14.2   AUTOREGRESSIVE MODELS

In the *autoregressive process of order p* the current observation y_t is generated by a weighted average of past observations going back p periods, together with a random disturbance in the current period. We denote this process as AR(p), and write its equation as

$$y_t = \phi_1 y_{t-1} + \phi_2 y_{t-2} + \cdots + \phi_p y_{t-p} + \delta + \varepsilon_t \qquad (14.18)$$

Here δ is a constant term which relates (as we will see) to the mean of the stochastic process.

If the process is stationary, then its mean, which we denote by μ, must be invariant with respect to time; that is, $E[y_t] = E[y_{t-1}] = E[y_{t-2}] = \cdots = \mu$. The mean μ is thus given by

$$\mu = \phi_1 \mu + \phi_2 \mu + \cdots + \phi_p \mu + \delta \qquad (14.19)$$

or

$$\mu = \frac{\delta}{1 - \phi_1 - \phi_2 - \cdots - \phi_p} \qquad (14.20)$$

This formula for the mean of the process also gives us a condition for stationarity. If the process is stationary, then the mean μ in (14.20) must be finite. If this were not the case, the process would drift farther and farther away from any fixed reference point and could not be stationary. (Consider the example of the random walk with drift—that is, $y_t = y_{t-1} + \delta + \varepsilon_t$. Here $\phi_1 = 1$, and $\mu = \infty$, and if $\delta > 0$, the process continually drifts upward.) If μ is to be finite, it is necessary that

$$\phi_1 + \phi_2 + \cdots + \phi_p < 1 \tag{14.21}$$

This condition is not sufficient to ensure stationarity, since there are other necessary conditions that must hold if the $AR(p)$ process is to be stationary. We discuss these additional conditions in more detail in the appendix to this chapter.

Now let us examine the properties of some simple autoregressive processes. Again we will determine the mean, covariances, etc., for each. We begin with the first-order process $AR(1)$:

$$y_t = \phi_1 y_{t-1} + \delta + \varepsilon_t \tag{14.22}$$

[The reader should notice the resemblance between $AR(1)$ and the first-order autoregressive error process discussed in Chapter 4.] This process has mean

$$\mu = \frac{\delta}{1 - \phi_1} \tag{14.23}$$

and is stationary if $|\phi_1| < 1$. Again, recall that the random walk with drift is a first-order autoregressive process that is *not* stationary. In that process $\phi_1 = 1$, and, as we saw in Chapter 13, the variance of the process becomes larger and larger with time.

Let us now calculate γ_0, the variance of this process about its mean. Assuming stationarity, so that we know that the variance is constant, and setting $\delta = 0$ (to scale the process to one that is zero mean), we have[2]

$$\gamma_0 = E[(\phi_1 y_{t-1} + \varepsilon_t)^2]$$

$$= E[\phi_1^2 y_{t-1}^2 + \varepsilon_t^2 + 2\phi_1 y_{t-1}\varepsilon_t]$$

$$= \phi_1^2 \gamma_0 + \sigma_\varepsilon^2$$

so that

$$\gamma_0 = \frac{\sigma_\varepsilon^2}{1 - \phi_1^2} \tag{14.24}$$

---

[2] Setting $\delta = 0$ is equivalent to measuring y_t in terms of deviations about its mean, since if y_t follows Eq. (14.22), then the series $\tilde{y}_t = y_t - \mu$ follows the process $\tilde{y}_t = \phi_1 \tilde{y}_{t-1} + \varepsilon_t$. The reader can check to see that the result in Eq. (14.24) is also obtained (although with more algebraic manipulation) by calculating $E[(y_t - \mu)^2]$ directly.

We can also calculate the covariances of y_t about its mean:

$$\gamma_1 = E[y_{t-1}(\phi_1 y_{t-1} + \varepsilon_t)]$$

$$= \phi_1 \gamma_0 = \frac{\phi_1 \sigma_\varepsilon^2}{1 - \phi_1^2} \tag{14.25}$$

$$\gamma_2 = E[y_{t-2}(\phi_1^2 y_{t-2} + \phi_1 \varepsilon_{t-1} + \varepsilon_t)]$$

$$= \phi_1^2 \gamma_0 = \frac{\phi_1^2 \sigma_\varepsilon^2}{1 - \phi_1^2} \tag{14.26}$$

Similarly the covariance for a k-lag displacement is

$$\gamma_k = \phi_1^k \gamma_0 = \frac{\phi_1^k \sigma_\varepsilon^2}{1 - \phi_1^2} \tag{14.27}$$

The autocorrelation function for AR(1) is thus particularly simple—it begins at $\rho_0 = 1$ and then declines geometrically:

$$\rho_k = \frac{\gamma_k}{\gamma_0} = \phi_1^k \tag{14.28}$$

Note that this process has an *infinite memory*. The current value of the process depends on *all past values*, although the magnitude of this dependence declines with time.[3]

An example of a first-order autoregressive process would be the process defined by the equation

$$y_t = .9 y_{t-1} + 2 + \varepsilon_t \tag{14.29}$$

The autocorrelation function for this process is shown in Fig. 14.5, and a typical realization is shown in Fig. 14.6. The realization differs from that of a first-order moving average process in that each observation is highly correlated with those surrounding it, resulting in discernible overall up-and-down patterns.

---

[3] It can be shown that if the AR(1) process is stationary, then it is equivalent to a moving order process of *infinite order* (and thus with infinite memory). In fact, for any stationary autoregressive process of any order there exists an equivalent moving average process of infinite order (so that the autoregressive process is *invertible* into a moving average process). Similarly, if certain *invertibility conditions* are met (and these will be discussed in the appendix to this chapter) any finite-order moving average process has an equivalent autoregressive process of infinite order. For a more detailed discussion of invertibility, the reader is referred to G. E. P. Box and G. M. Jenkins, *Time Series Analysis* (San Francisco: Holden-Day, 1970), or C. Nelson, *Applied Time Series Analysis* (San Francisco: Holden-Day, 1973), chap. 3.

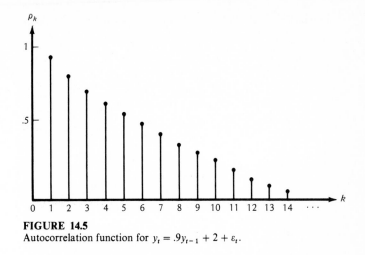

FIGURE 14.5
Autocorrelation function for $y_t = .9y_{t-1} + 2 + \varepsilon_t$.

Let us now look at the second-order autoregressive process, AR(2):

$$y_t = \phi_1 y_{t-1} + \phi_2 y_{t-2} + \delta + \varepsilon_t \tag{14.30}$$

The process has mean

$$\mu = \frac{\delta}{1 - \phi_1 - \phi_2} \tag{14.31}$$

and a necessary condition for stationarity is that $\phi_1 + \phi_2 < 1.$[4]

FIGURE 14.6
Typical realization of the process $y_t = .9y_{t-1} + 2 + \varepsilon_t$.

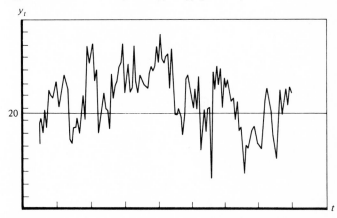

---

[4] This is not a sufficient condition for stationarity. Necessary and sufficient conditions are presented in Appendix 14.

Let us now calculate the variances and covariances of y_t:

$$\gamma_0 = E[y_t(\phi_1 y_{t-1} + \phi_2 y_{t-2} + \varepsilon_t)]$$

$$= \phi_1 \gamma_1 + \phi_2 \gamma_2 + \sigma_\varepsilon^2 \qquad (14.32)$$

$$\gamma_1 = E[y_{t-1}(\phi_1 y_{t-1} + \phi_2 y_{t-2} + \varepsilon_t)]$$

$$= \phi_1 \gamma_0 + \phi_2 \gamma_1 \qquad (14.33)$$

$$\gamma_2 = E[y_{t-2}(\phi_1 y_{t-1} + \phi_2 y_{t-2} + \varepsilon_t)]$$

$$= \phi_1 \gamma_1 + \phi_2 \gamma_0 \qquad (14.34)$$

and in general, for $k \geq 2$,

$$\gamma_k = E[y_{t-k}(\phi_1 y_{t-1} + \phi_2 y_{t-2} + \varepsilon_t)]$$

$$= \phi_1 \gamma_{k-1} + \phi_2 \gamma_{k-2} \qquad (14.35)$$

We can solve (14.32), (14.33), and (14.34) simultaneously to get γ_0 in terms of ϕ_1, ϕ_2, and σ_ε^2. Equation (14.33) can be rewritten as

$$\gamma_1 = \frac{\phi_1 \gamma_0}{1 - \phi_2} \qquad (14.36)$$

Substituting (14.34) into (14.32) yields

$$\gamma_0 = \phi_1 \gamma_1 + \phi_2 \phi_1 \gamma_1 + \phi_2^2 \gamma_0 + \sigma_\varepsilon^2 \qquad (14.37)$$

Now using (14.36) to eliminate γ_1 gives us

$$\gamma_0 = \frac{\phi_1^2 \gamma_0}{1 - \phi_2} + \frac{\phi_2 \phi_1^2 \gamma_0}{1 - \phi_2} + \phi_2^2 \gamma_0 + \sigma_\varepsilon^2$$

which, after rearranging, yields

$$\gamma_0 = \frac{(1 - \phi_2)\sigma_\varepsilon^2}{(1 + \phi_2)[(1 - \phi_2)^2 - \phi_1^2]} \qquad (14.38)$$

These equations can also be used to derive the autocorrelation function ρ_k. From (14.34) and (14.36),

$$\rho_1 = \frac{\phi_1}{1 - \phi_2} \tag{14.39}$$

$$\rho_2 = \phi_2 + \frac{\phi_1{}^2}{1 - \phi_2} \tag{14.40}$$

From (14.35) one can see that for $k \geq 2$,

$$\rho_k = \phi_1 \rho_{k-1} + \phi_2 \rho_{k-2} \tag{14.41}$$

and this can be used to calculate the autocorrelation function for $k > 2$.

A comment is in order regarding Eqs. (14.39) and (14.40), which are called the *Yule-Walker equations*. Suppose we have the sample autocorrelation function for a time series which we believe was generated by a second-order autoregressive process. We could then take a measurement of ρ_1 and ρ_2 and substitute these numbers into Eqs. (14.39) and (14.40). We would then have two algebraic equations which could be solved simultaneously for the two unknowns ϕ_1 and ϕ_2. Thus, we could use the Yule-Walker equations to obtain estimates of the autoregressive parameters ϕ_1 and ϕ_2. (We will discuss the methods by which we obtain estimates for the parameters of our time-series models in considerable detail in the next chapter.)

Let us look at an example of a second-order autoregressive process:

$$y_t = .9y_{t-1} - .7y_{t-2} + 2 + \varepsilon_t \tag{14.42}$$

The autocorrelation function for this process is shown in Fig. 14.7. Note that it is a sinusoidal function that is geometrically damped. As we will see from further examples, autocorrelation functions for autoregressive processes (of order greater than 1) are typically geometrically damped, oscillating, sinusoidal functions.

The reader should note that *realizations* of second- (and higher-) order autoregressive processes may or may not be cyclical depending on the numerical values of the parameters ϕ_1, ϕ_2, etc. Equation (14.30), for example, is a second-order difference equation in y_t (with an additive error term). We saw in Chapter 11 that the values of ϕ_1 and ϕ_2 determine whether the solution to this difference equation is oscillatory.

Let us now turn to the covariances and autocorrelation function for the autoregressive process of order p. First, notice that the covariance with displacement k is determined from the following equation:

$$\gamma_k = E[y_{t-k}(\phi_1 y_{t-1} + \phi_2 y_{t-2} + \cdots + \phi_p y_{t-p} + \varepsilon_t)] \tag{14.43}$$

FIGURE 14.7
Autocorrelation function for $y_t = .9y_{t-1} - .7y_{t-2} + 2 + \varepsilon_t$.

Now letting $k = 0, 1, \ldots, p$, we obtain the following $p + 1$ difference equations that can be solved simultaneously for $\gamma_0, \gamma_1, \ldots, \gamma_p$:

$$\gamma_0 = \phi_1 \gamma_1 + \phi_2 \gamma_2 + \cdots + \phi_p \gamma_p + \sigma_\varepsilon^2$$

$$\gamma_1 = \phi_1 \gamma_0 + \phi_2 \gamma_1 + \cdots + \phi_p \gamma_{p-1}$$

$$\vdots \qquad\qquad\qquad\qquad\qquad (14.44)$$

$$\gamma_p = \phi_1 \gamma_{p-1} + \phi_2 \gamma_{p-2} + \cdots + \phi_p \gamma_0$$

For displacements k greater than p the covariances are determined from

$$\gamma_k = \phi_1 \gamma_{k-1} + \phi_2 \gamma_{k-2} + \cdots + \phi_p \gamma_{k-p} \qquad (14.45)$$

Now by dividing the left-hand and right-hand sides of the equations in (14.44) by γ_0, we can derive a set of p equations that together determine the first p values of the autocorrelation function:

$$\rho_1 = \phi_1 + \phi_2 \rho_1 + \cdots + \phi_p \rho_{p-1}$$

$$\vdots \qquad\qquad\qquad\qquad\qquad (14.46)$$

$$\rho_p = \phi_1 \rho_{p-1} + \phi_2 \rho_{p-2} + \cdots + \phi_p$$

For displacement k greater than p we have, from Eq. (14.45),

$$\rho_k = \phi_1 \rho_{k-1} + \phi_2 \rho_{k-2} + \cdots + \phi_p \rho_{k-p} \tag{14.47}$$

The equations (14.46) are the Yule-Walker equations; if ρ_1, ρ_2, ..., ρ_p are known (i.e., measured from a sample autocorrelation function), then the equations can be solved for ϕ_1, ϕ_2, ..., ϕ_p. As in the case of the second-order autoregressive process, the Yule-Walker equations provide one means of obtaining estimates of the parameters ϕ_1, ..., ϕ_p.

14.3 MIXED AUTOREGRESSIVE-MOVING AVERAGE MODELS

Many stationary random processes cannot be modeled as purely moving average or as purely autoregressive, since they have the qualities of both types of processes. The logical extension of the models presented in the last two sections is the *mixed autoregressive-moving average process of order* (p,q). We denote this process as ARMA(p,q) and represent it by the equation

$$y_t = \phi_1 y_{t-1} + \cdots + \phi_p y_{t-p} + \delta + \varepsilon_t - \theta_1 \varepsilon_{t-1} - \cdots - \theta_q \varepsilon_{t-q} \tag{14.48}$$

We assume that the process is stationary, so that its mean is constant over time and is given by

$$\mu = \phi_1 \mu + \cdots + \phi_p \mu + \delta$$

or

$$\mu = \frac{\delta}{1 - \phi_1 - \cdots - \phi_p} \tag{14.49}$$

This gives a necessary condition for the stationarity of the process, that is,[5]

$$\phi_1 + \phi_2 + \cdots + \phi_p < 1 \tag{14.50}$$

Now let us consider the simplest mixed autoregressive-moving average process, the process ARMA$(1,1)$:

$$y_t = \phi_1 y_{t-1} + \delta + \varepsilon_t - \theta_1 \varepsilon_{t-1} \tag{14.51}$$

---

[5] Again, this is not a sufficient condition. See Appendix 14.

The variances and covariances of this process are determined jointly as follows (setting $\delta = 0$):

$$\gamma_0 = E[y_t(\phi_1 y_{t-1} + \varepsilon_t - \theta_1 \varepsilon_{t-1})]$$

$$= E[(\phi_1 y_{t-1} + \varepsilon_t - \theta_1 \varepsilon_{t-1})^2]$$

$$= \phi_1{}^2 \gamma_0 - 2\phi_1 \theta_1 E[y_{t-1}\varepsilon_{t-1}] + \sigma_\varepsilon{}^2 + \theta_1{}^2 \sigma_\varepsilon{}^2 \qquad (14.52)$$

Since $E[y_{t-1}\varepsilon_{t-1}] = \sigma_\varepsilon{}^2$, we have

$$\gamma_0(1 - \phi_1{}^2) = \sigma_\varepsilon{}^2(1 + \theta_1{}^2 - 2\phi_1\theta_1) \qquad (14.53)$$

so that the variance is given by

$$\gamma_0 = \frac{1 + \theta_1{}^2 - 2\phi_1\theta_1}{1 - \phi_1{}^2} \sigma_\varepsilon{}^2 \qquad (14.54)$$

We can now determine the covariances $\gamma_1, \gamma_2, \ldots,$ recursively:

$$\gamma_1 = E[y_{t-1}(\phi_1 y_{t-1} + \varepsilon_t - \theta_1 \varepsilon_{t-1})]$$

$$= \phi_1 \gamma_0 - \theta_1 \sigma_\varepsilon{}^2$$

$$= \frac{(1 - \phi_1\theta_1)(\phi_1 - \theta_1)}{1 - \phi_1{}^2} \sigma_\varepsilon{}^2 \qquad (14.55)$$

$$\gamma_2 = E[y_{t-2}(\phi_1 y_{t-1} + \varepsilon_t - \theta_1 \varepsilon_{t-1})]$$

$$= \phi_1 \gamma_1 \qquad (14.56)$$

and similarly,

$$\gamma_k = \phi_1 \gamma_{k-1} \qquad k \geq 2 \qquad (14.57)$$

The autocorrelation function, then, is given by

$$\rho_1 = \frac{\gamma_1}{\gamma_0} = \frac{(1 - \phi_1\theta_1)(\phi_1 - \theta_1)}{(1 + \theta_1{}^2 - 2\phi_1\theta_1)} \qquad (14.58)$$

and for displacement k greater than 1,

$$\rho_k = \phi_1 \rho_{k-1} \qquad k \geq 2 \qquad (14.59)$$

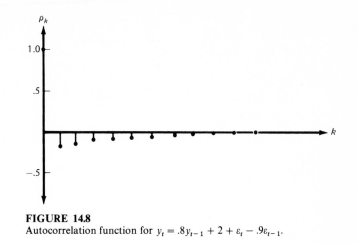

FIGURE 14.8
Autocorrelation function for $y_t = .8y_{t-1} + 2 + \varepsilon_t - .9\varepsilon_{t-1}$.

Thus, the autocorrelation function begins at its starting value ρ_1 (which is a function of both ϕ_1 and θ_1), and then decays geometrically from this starting value. This reflects the fact that the moving average part of the process has a memory of only one period.

Let us examine the autocorrelation functions of some typical ARMA(1,1) processes. The autocorrelation function for the process

$$y_t = .8y_{t-1} + 2 + \varepsilon_t - .9\varepsilon_{t-1} \tag{14.60}$$

is shown in Fig. 14.8. The starting value ρ_1 is negative, and the function decays toward 0 from this value.

The autocorrelation function for the process

$$y_t = -.8y_{t-1} + 2 + \varepsilon_t + .9\varepsilon_{t-1} \tag{14.61}$$

will exhibit oscillatory behavior, as shown in Fig. 14.9. Note that it oscillates between positive and negative values, since ϕ_1 is negative.

For higher-order processes, i.e., the general ARMA(p,q) process, the variance, covariances, and autocorrelation function are solutions to difference equations that usually cannot be solved by inspection. It can be shown easily, however, that

$$\gamma_k = \phi_1 \gamma_{k-1} + \phi_2 \gamma_{k-2} + \cdots + \phi_p \gamma_{k-p} \qquad k \geq q+1 \tag{14.62}$$

and thus, $\quad \rho_k = \phi_1 \rho_{k-1} + \phi_2 \rho_{k-2} + \cdots + \phi_p \rho_{k-p} \qquad k \geq q+1 \tag{14.63}$

Note that q is the memory of the moving average part of the process, so that for $k \geq q+1$ the autocorrelation function (and covariances) exhibit the properties of a purely autoregressive process.

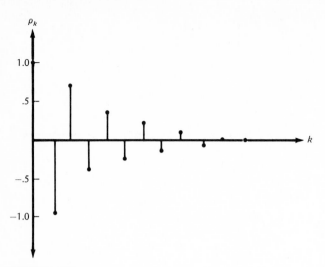

FIGURE 14.9
Autocorrelation function for $y_t = -.8y_{t-1} + 2 + \varepsilon_t + .9\varepsilon_{t-1}$.

This completes our discussion of models for stationary stochastic processes. Before we turn to models for homogeneous nonstationary processes, it will be useful to introduce a new notational device. Often it is convenient to write or describe time lags using the *backward shift operator* B. The operator B imposes a one-period time lag each time it is applied to a variable. Thus, $B\varepsilon_t = \varepsilon_{t-1}$, $B^2\varepsilon_t = \varepsilon_{t-2}, \ldots, B^n\varepsilon_t = \varepsilon_{t-n}$. Using this operator, we can now rewrite Eq. (14.1) for the MA(q) process as

$$y_t = \mu + (1 - \theta_1 B - \theta_2 B^2 - \cdots - \theta_q B^q)\varepsilon_t$$

$$= \mu + \theta(B)\varepsilon_t \tag{14.64}$$

where $\theta(B)$ denotes a polynomial function of the operator B. Similarly Eq. (14.18) for the AR(p) process can be rewritten as

$$(1 - \phi_1 B - \phi_2 B^2 - \cdots - \phi_p B^p)y_t = \delta + \varepsilon_t \tag{14.65}$$

or

$$\phi(B)y_t = \delta + \varepsilon_t \tag{14.66}$$

Finally, Eq. (14.48) for the ARMA(p,q) process can be rewritten as

$$(1 - \phi_1 B - \phi_2 B^2 - \cdots - \phi_p B^p)y_t = \delta + (1 - \theta_1 B - \theta_2 B^2 - \cdots - \theta_q B^q)\varepsilon_t \tag{14.67}$$

or

$$\phi(B)y_t = \delta + \theta(B)\varepsilon_t \tag{14.68}$$

We will use the backward-shift operator for notational ease throughout the remainder of Part Three of the book.

14.4 HOMOGENEOUS NONSTATIONARY PROCESSES— ARIMA MODELS

In practice, many of the time series that we will work with are nonstationary, so that the characteristics of the underlying stochastic process change over time. In this section we construct models for those nonstationary series which can be transformed into stationary series by differencing one or more times. We say that y_t is *homogeneous nonstationary of order d* if

$$w_t = \Delta^d y_t \tag{14.69}$$

is a stationary series. Here Δ denotes differencing, i.e.,

$$\Delta y_t = y_t - y_{t-1}$$

$$\Delta^2 y_t = \Delta y_t - \Delta y_{t-1}$$

and so forth. A discussion of the autoregressive characteristics of homogeneous nonstationary series is given in the appendix to this chapter.

Observe that if we have a series w_t, we can get back to y_t by *summing* w_t a total of d times. We write this as

$$y_t = \sum{}^d w_t \tag{14.70}$$

where $\sum$ is the summation operator:

$$\sum w_t = \sum_{i=-\infty}^{t} w_i \tag{14.71}$$

$$\sum{}^2 w_t = \sum_{j=-\infty}^{t} \sum_{i=-\infty}^{j} w_i \tag{14.72}$$

and so forth. Note that the summation operator $\sum$ is just the *inverse* of the difference operator Δ. Since $\Delta y_t = y_t - y_{t-1}$, we can write that $\Delta = 1 - B$, and thus $\sum = \Delta^{-1} = (1 - B)^{-1}$.

When computing this sum for an actual time series, we begin with the first observation on the original undifferenced series (y_0), and then add successive values of the differenced series. Thus if $w_t = \Delta y_t$, we would compute y_t from

$$y_t = \sum w_t = \sum_{i=-\infty}^{t} w_i$$

$$= \sum_{i=-\infty}^{0} w_i + \sum_{i=1}^{t} w_i$$

$$= y_0 + w_1 + w_2 + \cdots + w_t \tag{14.73}$$

FIGURE 14.10
An ARIMA process with $d = 1$.

If y_t had been differenced twice, so that $w_t = \Delta^2 y_t$, we could compute y_t from w_t by summing w_t twice.[6]

After we have differenced the series y_t to produce the stationary series w_t, we can model w_t as an ARMA process. If $w_t = \Delta^d y_t$, and w_t is an *ARMA* (p,q) *process, then we say that* y_t *is an integrated autoregressive-moving average process of order* (p,d,q), or simply ARIMA(p,d,q). We can write the equation for the process ARIMA(p,d,q), using the backward shift operator, as

$$\phi(B)\Delta^d y_t = \delta + \theta(B)\varepsilon_t \tag{14.74}$$

with
$$\phi(B) = 1 - \phi_1 B - \phi_2 B^2 - \cdots - \phi_p B^p \tag{14.75}$$

and
$$\theta(B) = 1 - \theta_1 B - \theta_2 B^2 - \cdots - \theta_q B^q \tag{14.76}$$

We call $\phi(B)$ the *autoregressive operator*, and we call $\theta(B)$ the *moving average operator*.

---

[6] Summing w_t the first time gives us Δy_t:

$$\Delta y_t = \sum w_t = \sum_{i=-\infty}^{0} w_i + \sum_{i=1}^{t} w_i$$

$$= \Delta y_0 + w_1 + w_2 + \cdots + w_t$$

Now summing Δy_t yields y_t:

$$y_t = \sum (\Delta y_t)$$

$$= \sum (\Delta y_0 + w_1 + w_2 + \cdots + w_t)$$

$$= y_0 + (\Delta y_0 + w_1) + (\Delta y_0 + w_1 + w_2) + \cdots$$

$$+ (\Delta y_0 + w_1 + w_2 + \cdots + w_t)$$

FIGURE 14.11
An ARIMA process with $d = 2$.

Note that the mean of $w_t = \Delta^d y_t$ is given by

$$\mu_w = \frac{\delta}{1 - \phi_1 - \phi_2 - \cdots - \phi_p} \tag{14.77}$$

Thus if δ is not equal to 0, the *integrated series* y_t will have a built-in *deterministic trend*. Suppose, for example, that $d = 1$ and $\delta > 0$. Then $y_t = \sum w_t$ will grow linearly over time. An example of such a series might be the one drawn in Fig. 14.10. The series has a linear time trend that is independent of the random disturbances, i.e., that is deterministic. The series drawn in Fig. 14.11, on the other hand, has an average slope that is increasing linearly in time. This series would most likely have been generated by a process that is ARIMA with $d = 2$ and $\delta > 0$. Thus $w_t = \Delta^2 y_t$ will have no time trend, $\sum w_t = \Delta y_t$ will have a linear time trend, and $\sum \sum w_t = y_t$ will have a time trend whose rate of increase is constant.

It is possible that the stationary series w_t will not be mixed, i.e., will be completely autoregressive or moving average. If w_t is just AR(p), then we call y_t an integrated autoregressive process of order (p,d), and denote it as ARI($p,d,0$). If w_t is just MA(q), then we call y_t an integrated moving average process of order (d,q), and denote it as IMA($0,d,q$).

14.5 SPECIFICATION OF ARIMA MODELS

We have seen that any homogeneous nonstationary time series can be modeled as an ARIMA process of order (p,d,q). The practical problem is to choose the most appropriate values for p, d, and q, that is, to *specify* the ARIMA model.

This problem is partly resolved by examining the autocorrelation function for the time series of concern.

Given a series y_t that one would like to model, the first problem is to determine the degree of homogeneity d, that is, the number of times that the series must be differenced to produce a stationary series. To determine the appropriate value of d, we make use of the fact that the autocorrelation function ρ_k for a stationary series must approach 0 as the displacement k becomes large. To see why this must be so, consider a stationary ARMA process of order (p,q). We know that the autocorrelation function for the *moving average part* of this process becomes 0 for $k > q$, as the process has a memory of only q periods. Thus, if y_t is MA(q), then $\rho_k = 0$ for $k > q$. We also know that the autocorrelation function for the *autoregressive part* of a stationary ARMA process is geometrically damped (see the examples in Figs. 14.5, 14.6, and 14.7). Finally, the autocorrelation function for the complete ARMA process has moving average characteristics for the first $q - p$ periods, but after that it is autoregressive in character; i.e., it has an envelope that declines geometrically.

The procedure for specifying the value of d is straightforward. Look at the autocorrelation function of the original series y_t and determine whether it is stationary. If it is not, difference the series and examine the autocorrelation function for Δy_t to determine stationarity. Repeat this process until a value for d is reached such that $\Delta^d y_t$ is stationary; i.e., the autocorrelation function goes to 0 as k becomes large.[7] One should also examine the time series itself to check for stationarity. If the series appears to have an overall trend, then it is probably not stationary.

After d is determined, one can work with the stationary series $w_t = \Delta^d y_t$ and its autocorrelation function to determine the proper specification of p and q. For low-order processes this can be rather simple, since the autocorrelation functions for processes such as AR(1), AR(2), MA(1), MA(2), and ARMA(1,1) are easy to recognize and distinguish from each other (see Figs. 14.1 to 14.9). Fortunately, many of the time series encountered in economic applications can, if they are seasonally adjusted, be modeled as low-order ARMA processes, i.e., as processes with $p \leq 2$ and $q \leq 2$. When this is not the case, the specification of p and q becomes more difficult.

If the series is not of low order, then one may only be able to make a tentative "guess" for p and q. As we will see later, however, it is possible to check that "guess" after the parameters in the ARMA(p,q) model have been estimated. As a first step in this process of *diagnostic checking* one can calculate the autocorrelation function for the estimated ARMA(p,q) model and compare it with

---

[7] Remember that in practice we have no guarantee that the time series being modeled is homogeneous nonstationary. One might be unlucky and discover that his/her time series is *nonhomogeneous* nonstationary. In this case, no matter how many times the series was differenced, the autocorrelation function would not damp down to 0. Models of nonhomogeneous nonstationary series are beyond the scope of this book; suffice it to say that they are difficult to construct and estimate.

the autocorrelation function of the original series to see how well the two match. If they do not match well, a new specification can be tried.

The process of diagnostic checking will be discussed in more detail in Chapter 15. However, it is important to realize that the specification of an ARMA model is an art, rather than a science. As one gains more experience in constructing time-series models, it becomes easier to recognize autocorrelation functions and to link them to the appropriate specification of p and q. When sound judgment is used, diagnostic checking becomes simpler.

Example 14.1 Interest Rate

As an example of model specification, reconsider the time series for the interest rate on commercial paper that we examined in Chapter 13. After repeatedly differencing the series and examining the autocorrelation functions, we established that it was probably second-order homogeneous nonstationary, so that d equals 2 in a specification of an ARIMA model. Now if we examine the autocorrelation function for $\Delta^2 y_t$ in Fig. 14.12 in more detail, we see that it exhibits moving average properties that are second order; i.e., it begins decaying after the point $k = 2$. The periodicity of the oscillations in the autocorrelation function would probably indicate that the autoregressive part of the model should be of order 4, although a second-order autoregressive specification might also be suggested by the periodic behavior. Thus two specifications might be appropriate, namely the ARIMA(2,2,2) and the ARIMA(4,2,2) models.

FIGURE 14.12
Interest rate on commercial paper: autocorrelation function of $\Delta^2 y_t$.

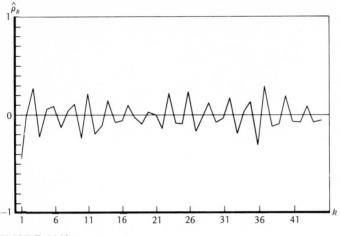

FIGURE 14.13
Monthly hog production: autocorrelation function of $(1 - B)(1 - B^{12})y_t$.

Example 14.2   Hog Production

A second example is the monthly series for hog production which was also examined in the last chapter. We took a 12-month difference of the series to eliminate seasonal cycles and then found that differencing once was sufficient to ensure stationarity. The autocorrelation function for $(1 - B)(1 - B^{12})y_t$ is shown again in Fig. 14.13.[8] Observe that the autocorrelation function begins declining immediately at $k = 1$, and has peaks roughly once every three periods. We might thus suspect that $(1 - B)(1 - B^{12})y_t$ is autoregressive of order 3, so that y_t could be specified by the model (using backward-shift operator notation):

$$(1 - \phi_1 B - \phi_2 B^2 - \phi_3 B^3)(1 - B)(1 - B^{12})y_t = \varepsilon_t \qquad (14.78)$$

The reader should not be disturbed at this point if he/she finds the "art" of model specification somewhat bewildering. We will go through several more examples of model specification in Chapter 17.

---

[8] Recall the meaning of the backward shift operator B:

$$(1 - B)(1 - B^{12})y_t = \Delta(y_t - y_{t-12})$$

Exercises

14.1 Calculate the covariances γ_k for MA(3), the moving average process of order 3. Determine the autocorrelation function for this process. Plot the autocorrelation function for the MA(3) process

$$y_t = 1 + \varepsilon_t + .8\varepsilon_{t-1} - .5\varepsilon_{t-2} + .3\varepsilon_{t-3}$$

14.2 What are the characteristics that one would expect of a realization of the following MA(1) process?

$$y_t = 1 + \varepsilon_t + .8\varepsilon_{t-1}$$

How would these characteristics differ from those of a realization of the following MA(1) process?

$$y_t = 1 + \varepsilon_t - .8\varepsilon_{t-1}$$

14.3 Show that the covariances γ_k of MA(q), the moving average process of order q, are given by

$$\gamma_k = \begin{cases} (-\theta_k + \theta_1\theta_{k+1} + \cdots + \theta_{q-k}\theta_q)\sigma_\varepsilon^2 & k = 1, \ldots, q \\ 0 & k > q \end{cases}$$

and that the autocorrelation function for MA(q) is given by

$$\rho_k = \begin{cases} \dfrac{-\theta_k + \theta_1\theta_{k+1} + \cdots + \theta_{q-k}\theta_q}{1 + \theta_1^2 + \theta_2^2 + \cdots + \theta_q^2} & k = 1, \ldots, q \\ 0 & k > q \end{cases}$$

as in Eq. (14.17) of the text.

14.4 Derive the autocorrelation function for the ARMA(2,1) process:

$$y_t = \phi_1 y_{t-1} + \phi_2 y_{t-2} + \varepsilon_t - \theta_1\varepsilon_{t-1}$$

that is, determine ρ_1, ρ_2, etc., in terms of ϕ_1, ϕ_2, and θ_1. Draw this autocorrelation function for $\phi_1 = .6$, $\phi_2 = .3$, and $\theta_1 = .9$. Repeat for $\phi_1 = .6$, $\phi_2 = .3$, and $\theta_1 = -.9$. Repeat for $\phi_1 = .6$, $\phi_2 = -.3$, and $\theta_1 = -.9$.

14.5 Show that the autocorrelation function for the general ARMA(p,q) process is given by

$$\rho_k = \phi_1\rho_{k-1} + \phi_2\rho_{k-2} + \cdots + \phi_p\rho_{k-p} \qquad k \geq q + 1$$

as in Eq. (14.63) of the text.

14.6 Suppose that y_t is first-order homogeneous nonstationary, and that $w_t = \Delta y_t$ can be represented by the ARMA(1,1) model

$$w_t = .9w_{t-1} + \varepsilon_t - .6\varepsilon_{t-1} + 1$$

If $y_t = 0$ for $t = 0$, what is $E[y_t]$ as a function of time?

14.7 Relate the summation operator to the backward-shift operator by showing that

$$\sum = (1 - B)^{-1} = 1 + B + B^2 + B^3 + \cdots$$

14.8 Refer back to the time series for nonfarm inventory investment in Fig. 13.7 of the last chapter, and its sample autocorrelation function in Fig. 13.8. Can you suggest one or more ARMA(p,q) processes that might have generated that time series? (In other words, how many autoregressive terms p and moving average terms q should the process have?)

APPENDIX 14 / STATIONARITY, INVERTIBILITY, AND HOMOGENEITY

We saw before that a necessary condition for an ARMA(p,q) process to be stationary is that

$$\phi_1 + \phi_2 + \cdots + \phi_p < 1 \tag{A14.1}$$

We now present a strict (i.e., necessary and sufficient) condition for stationarity, and use it to demonstrate a particular property of homogeneous nonstationary processes.

Note that the process ARMA(p,q) can be written in the form

$$(1 - \phi_1 B - \cdots - \phi_p B^p)\tilde{y}_t = (1 - \theta_1 B - \cdots - \theta_q B^q)\varepsilon_t \tag{A14.2}$$

or

$$\phi(B)\tilde{y}_t = \theta(B)\varepsilon_t \tag{A14.3}$$

where B is the backward-shift operator, and $\tilde{y}_t$ is the deviation of y_t from its mean, that is,

$$\tilde{y}_t = y_t - \mu \tag{A14.4}$$

Now let us rewrite Eq. (A14.3) as

$$\tilde{y}_t = \phi^{-1}(B)\theta(B)\varepsilon_t \tag{A14.5}$$

If y_t is a stationary process, then $\phi^{-1}(B)$ must converge. This requires that the roots of the *characteristic equation*

$$\phi(B) = 0 \tag{A14.6}$$

all be *outside* the unit circle.[9] Thus the solutions $B_1, \ldots, B_p$ to (A14.6) must all be greater than 1 in magnitude.

Now suppose that the process $\tilde{y}_t$ in (A14.3) is *nonstationary*, but in such a way that exactly d of the roots of $\phi(B)$ are on the unit circle and the remainder are outside the unit circle. This process can then be rewritten in the form

$$\omega(B)(1 - B)^d \tilde{y}_t = \theta(B)\varepsilon_t \tag{A14.7}$$

where $\omega(B)$ is a stationary autoregressive operator of order $p - d$, and the operator $(1 - B)^d$ has d roots all equal to unity. But $(1 - B)$ is a *first-difference* operator, that is,

$$(1 - B)\tilde{y}_t = \Delta\tilde{y}_t = \tilde{y}_t - \tilde{y}_{t-1} \tag{A14.8}$$

Thus (A14.7) can be rewritten as

$$\omega(B)\Delta^d \tilde{y}_t = \theta(B)\varepsilon_t \tag{A14.9}$$

or

$$\omega(B)w_t = \theta(B)\varepsilon_t \tag{A14.10}$$

where $w_t = \Delta^d \tilde{y}_t$ is stationary, since it resulted from differencing $\tilde{y}_t$ d times. We call $\tilde{y}_t$ *homogeneous nonstationary with order d*, and we note the conclusion that such a process has an autoregressive operator $\phi(B)$ such that

$$\phi(B) = \omega(B)(1 - B)^d \tag{A14.11}$$

where the roots of $\omega(B)$ are all outside the unit circle.

Analogous to the stationarity condition for the autoregressive operator is the *invertibility condition* for the moving average operator. We say that y_t is invertible if we can write (A14.3) as

$$\theta^{-1}(B)\phi(B)\tilde{y}_t = \varepsilon_t \tag{A14.12}$$

i.e., if the ARMA process (or more specifically the moving average part of the ARMA process) can be inverted into a purely autoregressive process. Now, if y_t

[9] See G. E. P. Box and G. M. Jenkins, *Time Series Analysis* (San Francisco: Holden-Day, 1970), for a proof of this.

is invertible, then $\theta^{-1}(B)$ must converge. This requires that the roots of the *characteristic equation*

$$\theta(B) = 1 - \theta_1 B - \theta_2 B^2 - \cdots - \theta_q B^q = 0 \tag{A14.13}$$

must all lie outside the unit circle; i.e., the solutions $B_1, B_2, \ldots, B_q$ to Eq. (A14.13) must all be greater than 1 in absolute value.[10]

As an example, consider the first-order moving average process (that is, $q = 1$), whose characteristic equation is

$$1 - \theta_1 B = 0 \tag{A14.14}$$

Then the invertibility condition becomes

$$|B| = \frac{1}{|\theta_1|} > 1 \tag{A14.15}$$

or

$$|\theta_1| < 1$$

For the second-order moving average process ($q = 2$) the characteristic equation is

$$1 - \theta_1 B - \theta_2 B^2 = 0 \tag{A14.16}$$

and

$$B = \frac{+\theta_1 \pm \sqrt{\theta_1^2 + 4\theta_2}}{2\theta_2} \tag{A14.17}$$

Both these values of B must be outside the unit circle, which implies that

$$\theta_2 + \theta_1 < 1 \tag{A14.18}$$

$$\theta_2 - \theta_1 < 1 \tag{A14.19}$$

and

$$|\theta_2| < 1 \tag{A14.20}$$

---

[10] This invertibility condition is proved in detail in U. Grenander and M. Rosenblatt, *Statistical Analyses of Stationary Time Series* (New York: Wiley, 1957). A brief discussion is also presented in G. E. P. Box and G. M. Jenkins, *op. cit.*

15

In this chapter we discuss the procedure by which the parameters of an ARIMA model are estimated. As we shall see, this involves the application of a nonlinear estimation method similar to that described in Chapter 7. Following this we describe diagnostic checking, a procedure used to test whether the model has been correctly specified (i.e., whether p, d, and q have been chosen correctly).

The material in this chapter is at a somewhat more advanced mathematical level than that in the previous two chapters. Those readers unfamiliar with vector and matrix notation should skip over some of the mathematical details involved in the estimation procedure. A basic understanding of the estimation procedure and its application can be obtained by reading through the chapter and giving special attention to the examples.

We begin by summarizing the procedures involved in the estimation and diagnostic checking of a time-series model. Once a tentative specification of the time-series model has been made, i.e., once values of p, d, and q have been chosen for the ARIMA model,[1]

$$\phi(B)\Delta^d y_t = \phi(B)w_t = \theta(B)\varepsilon_t \qquad (15.1)$$

with $\phi(B) = 1 - \phi_1 B - \phi_2 B^2 - \cdots - \phi_p B^p$ and

ESTIMATION OF TIME-SERIES MODELS

---

[1] We assume for simplicity here that $\delta = 0$, that is, that w_t is measured as a deviation from its mean value.

$\theta(B) = 1 - \theta_1 B - \theta_2 B^2 - \cdots - \theta_q B^q$, then estimates can be obtained for the p autoregressive parameters $\phi_1, \ldots, \phi_p$ and the q moving average parameters $\theta_1, \ldots, \theta_q$. As in the case of the regression model, we choose parameter values that will minimize the sum of squared differences between the actual time series and $\hat{\theta} = (\hat{\theta}_1, \ldots, \hat{\theta})$, and the residuals associated with these parameter values by $\hat{\varepsilon}_t$, so that $\hat{\varepsilon}_t = \hat{\theta}^{-1}(B)\hat{\phi}(B)w_i$. Thus,

$$\varepsilon_t = \theta^{-1}(B)\phi(B)w_t \tag{15.2}$$

The objective in estimation is to find a vector of autoregressive parameters $\phi = (\phi_1, \ldots, \phi_p)$ and a vector of moving average parameters $\theta = (\theta_1, \ldots, \theta_q)$ that *minimize the sum of squared errors*

$$S(\phi, \theta) = \sum_t \varepsilon_t^2 \tag{15.3}$$

We denote the vectors of parameters that minimize (15.3) by $\hat{\phi} = (\hat{\phi}_1, \ldots, \hat{\phi}_p)$ and $\hat{\theta} = (\hat{\theta}_1, \ldots, \hat{\theta}_q)$, and the residuals associated with these parameter values by $\hat{\varepsilon}_t$, so that $\hat{\varepsilon}_t = \hat{\theta}^{-1}(B)\hat{\phi}(B)w_t$. Thus,

$$S(\hat{\phi}, \hat{\theta}) = \sum_t \hat{\varepsilon}_t^2$$

This estimation is difficult, since Eq. (15.2) is nonlinear in the parameters. For this reason an iterative method of nonlinear estimation must be used in the minimization of (15.3). In addition, the first error term in the series, ε_1, depends on the past and unobservable values $w_0, w_{-1}, \ldots, w_{-p+1}$ and $\varepsilon_0, \varepsilon_{-1}, \ldots, \varepsilon_{-q+1}$. Thus some method must be used to "initialize" the series (i.e., choose numbers for these unobservable values) before the nonlinear estimation process is applied.

After the parameters of the model have been estimated, a procedure of *diagnostic checking* is used to test whether the initial specification of the model was correct. We would expect the *residuals* $\hat{\varepsilon}_t$, $t = 1, \ldots, T$, to resemble closely the true errors ε_t, which, by assumption, are uncorrelated. A diagnostic check is used to test whether these residuals are indeed uncorrelated. If they are not, we would want to respecify the model (i.e., choose new values for p, d, and q), estimate this new model, and perform another diagnostic check to determine if it has been correctly specified.

Once the model has been checked to satisfaction, it can be used for forecasting future movements in the time series. We will see that the optimal (minimum

---

[2] It should be more clear now why we were concerned with the invertibility of $\theta(B)$ in the appendix to the last chapter.

mean square error) forecast $\hat{y}_T(l)$ of the series y_t made at time T for the value l periods in the future is the conditional expectation of y_{T+l} taken at time T. The properties of this forecast, as well as the method of determining confidence intervals, will be discussed in Chapter 16.

15.1   THE ESTIMATION PROCEDURE

We assume that a total of $T + d$ observations are available for the homogeneous nonstationary time series of order d, y_t, and we denote these observations as $y_{-d+1}, \ldots, y_0, y_1, \ldots, y_T$. After differencing this series d times, we obtain a stationary series w_t with T observations $w_1, \ldots, w_T$. The problem is to estimate the parameter vectors ϕ and θ for the ARMA(p,q) model which has been specified for the series w_t. To do this, we utilize the fact that (by assumption) the error terms $\varepsilon_1, \ldots, \varepsilon_T$ are all *normally distributed* and independent, with mean 0 and variance σ_ε^2. Then the *conditional log likelihood function* associated with the parameter values (ϕ, θ, σ_ε) is given by

$$L(\phi, \theta, \sigma_\varepsilon) = -T \ln \sigma_\varepsilon - \frac{S(\phi, \theta)}{2\sigma_\varepsilon^2} \tag{15.4}$$

We say that $L(\phi, \theta, \sigma_\varepsilon)$ is the *conditional* log likelihood function because the sum of squared errors $S(\phi, \theta)$ depends on (i.e., is conditional on) the past and unobservable values $w_0, w_{-1}, \ldots, w_{-p+1}, \varepsilon_0, \varepsilon_{-1}, \ldots, \varepsilon_{-q+1}$. This can be seen by writing the equation for the first observable error term ε_1 in the expanded form of the ARMA model:

$$\varepsilon_1 = w_1 - \phi_1 w_0 - \phi_2 w_{-1} - \cdots - \phi_p w_{-p+1} + \theta_1 \varepsilon_0 + \cdots + \theta_q \varepsilon_{-q+1} \tag{15.5}$$

Setting aside for the moment the problem of determining the past values of w_t and ε_t, Eq. (15.4) makes it clear that the maximum-likelihood estimate of ϕ and θ is given by the *minimization* of the sum of squared residuals $S(\phi, \theta)$. Thus, under the assumption of normally distributed errors, the maximum-likelihood estimate is the same as the *least-squares* estimate.[3]

15.1.1   Initialization of the Series

Because the sum-of-squares function $S(\phi, \theta)$ and thus the likelihood function $L(\phi, \theta, \sigma_\varepsilon)$ are both conditional on the past unobservable values of w_t and ε_t ($w_0, \ldots, w_{-p+1}$ and $\varepsilon_0, \ldots, \varepsilon_{-q+1}$), the least-squares estimates that we obtain depend on the choice of values made for $w_0, w_{-1}, \ldots$, etc. For this reason

---

[3] For a review of maximum-likelihood estimation, the reader should refer back to Appendix 2.2.

we must choose initial starting values for w_0, w_{-1}, ..., to be used in the minimization of the conditional sum-of-squares function.

One solution is to set w_0, ..., w_{-p+1} and ε_0, ..., ε_{-q+1} equal to their *unconditional expected values*. The unconditional expected values of $\varepsilon_0, ..., \varepsilon_{-q+1}$ are all 0, and, if $\delta = 0$ (i.e., the process has no deterministic component), the unconditional expected values of $w_0, ..., w_{-p+1}$ are 0 as well. This solution will provide a reasonably good approximation to the correct procedure if the actual values of ϕ_1, ..., ϕ_p are not very close to 1 and if the number of observations T is large relative to p and q.

In the appendix to this chapter we discuss an alternative method of initializing the series. The procedure determines *conditional expected values* for $w_0, ..., w_{-p+1}$, that is, values that are conditional on the observed values of w_1, ..., w_T and the estimated values of ε_1, ..., ε_T. This procedure is technically difficult and computationally expensive, however, and its benefits (in terms of increased efficiency in the parameter estimates) may not be substantial. In fact, as the sample size becomes large, the influence of the initial values disappears. We therefore recommend using the unconditional expected values for w_0, ..., w_{-p+1}, that is, setting them equal to 0.

15.1.2   Nonlinear Estimation of Model Parameters

Our estimation problem is to find values of ϕ and θ that minimize the sum of squared errors

$$S(\phi, \theta) = \sum_t \varepsilon_t^2 = \sum_t [\varepsilon_t | \phi, \theta, \mathbf{w}]^2 \tag{15.6}$$

where $\mathbf{w}$ is the vector of observations of w_t, and the errors ε_t are conditional on ϕ, θ, and $\mathbf{w}$. Assuming that the initialization of the series is based, as we suggest, on the unconditional expected values (which are all 0) of $w_0, ..., w_{-p+1}$ and $\varepsilon_0, ..., \varepsilon_{-q+1}$, then the time bounds in the summation of Eq. (15.6) would be $t = 1$ to T. Thus our problem is to minimize

$$S(\phi, \theta) = \sum_{t=1}^{T} [\varepsilon_t | \phi, \theta, \mathbf{w}]^2 \tag{15.7}$$

Now suppose that the model was purely autoregressive, i.e., was of the form

$$\phi(B)w_t = \varepsilon_t \tag{15.8}$$

or
$$w_t = \phi_1 w_{t-1} + \cdots + \phi_p w_{t-p} + \varepsilon_t \tag{15.9}$$

Observe that since Eq. (15.9) is of the general form

$$y_t = \beta_0 + \beta_1 x_{1t} + \beta_2 x_{2t} + \cdots + \varepsilon_t \tag{15.10}$$

it can be estimated simply as a linear regression.[4] Although for a purely autoregressive model the estimation process is essentially a linear regression, the problem is more difficult if the model contains a moving average component as well. In that case we can represent the model as

$$\theta^{-1}(B)\phi(B)w_t = \varepsilon_t \tag{15.11}$$

Clearly, this "regression equation" is nonlinear in the parameters, and cannot be estimated by a simple application of ordinary least squares. However, it can be estimated by a general iterative nonlinear estimation routine. The process is nearly identical to that discussed in section 7.5 and used in standard nonlinear regression programs.

The nonlinear estimation process uses the first two terms in a Taylor series expansion to linearize Eq. (15.11) around an initial "guess" for ϕ and θ. A linear regression is then performed on this linearized equation, least-squares estimates of θ and ϕ are obtained, and a new linearization of (15.11) is made around these estimates. Again a linear regression is performed, a second set of estimates of θ and ϕ is obtained, and a new linearization of (15.11) is made around this second set of estimates. This process is repeated iteratively until convergence occurs, i.e., until the estimates of θ and ϕ do not change after repeated iterations.

To look at this iterative estimation process in more detail, let the vector β represent the $p + q$ parameters (θ, ϕ) that we wish to estimate. We wish to choose numerical values for β which minimize

$$S(\beta) = \sum_{t=1}^{T} [\varepsilon_t | \mathbf{w}, \beta]^2 = \sum_{t=1}^{T} [\varepsilon_t]^2 \tag{15.12}$$

Remember that the notation $[\varepsilon_t]$ means that the errors are conditional on the

---

[4] Ignoring problems of initialization (i.e., selection of values for $w_0, w_{-1}, \ldots, w_{-p+1}$), our estimate for ϕ would be given by

$$\hat{\phi} = (\mathbf{X}'\mathbf{X})^{-1}\mathbf{X}'\mathbf{Y}$$

where $\mathbf{X}$ is the $(T - p) \times p$ matrix

$$\mathbf{X} = \begin{bmatrix} w_p & w_{p-1} & \cdots & w_1 \\ w_{p+1} & w_p & \cdots & w_2 \\ \cdots\cdots\cdots\cdots\cdots\cdots\cdots \\ w_{T-1} & w_{T-2} & \cdots & w_{T-p} \end{bmatrix}$$

and $\mathbf{Y}$ is the $(T - p) \times 1$ vector

$$\mathbf{Y} = \begin{bmatrix} w_{p+1} \\ w_{p+2} \\ \vdots \\ w_T \end{bmatrix}$$

values of $\mathbf{w}$ and $\boldsymbol{\beta}$. Now let us expand $[\varepsilon_t]$ in a Taylor series around some initial guess $\boldsymbol{\beta}_0$ for the parameter values:[5]

$$[\varepsilon_t] = [\varepsilon_t | \mathbf{w}, \boldsymbol{\beta}_0] + \sum_{i=1}^{p+q} (\beta_i - \beta_{i,0}) \frac{\partial [\varepsilon_t]}{\partial \beta_i} \bigg|_{\boldsymbol{\beta}=\boldsymbol{\beta}_0} + \frac{1}{2} \sum_{i=1}^{p+q} (\beta_i - \beta_{i,0})^2 \frac{\partial^2 [\varepsilon_t]}{\partial \beta_i^2} \bigg|_{\boldsymbol{\beta}=\boldsymbol{\beta}_0} + \cdots$$

$$(15.13)$$

Here $\beta_{i,0}$ is the value of the first guess for the parameter β_i, and thus is the ith component of the vector $\boldsymbol{\beta}_0$. We will approximate $[\varepsilon_t]$ by the first two terms of this Taylor series expansion. Letting

$$x_{i,t} = -\frac{\partial [\varepsilon_t]}{\partial \beta_i} \bigg|_{\boldsymbol{\beta}=\boldsymbol{\beta}_0} \qquad (15.14)$$

and

$$[\varepsilon_{t,0}] = [\varepsilon_t | \mathbf{w}, \boldsymbol{\beta}_0] \qquad (15.15)$$

it follows that (approximately)

$$[\varepsilon_t] = [\varepsilon_{t,0}] - \sum_{i=1}^{p+q} (\beta_i - \beta_{i,0}) x_{i,t} \qquad (15.16)$$

which can be rewritten as

$$[\varepsilon_{t,0}] + \sum_{i=1}^{p+q} \beta_{i,0} x_{i,t} = \sum_{i=1}^{p+q} \beta_i x_{i,t} + [\varepsilon_t] \qquad (15.17)$$

The left-hand side of Eq. (15.17) can be thought of as a composite dependent variable, which will have different numerical values for $t = 1, 2, \ldots, T$. (Note that $[\varepsilon_{t,0}]$ is just the value of the error term at time t, given the first guess $\boldsymbol{\beta}_0$.) On the right-hand side of (15.17) are $p + q$ independent variables (multiplied by the $p + q$ unknown parameters β_i) as well as an additive error term. It should

---

[5] Recall that if $y = f(x_1, x_2)$ is a nonlinear function of two variables x_1 and x_2, it can be represented by a Taylor series around the numerical values $x_{1,0}$ and $x_{2,0}$ as follows:

$$y = f(x_{1,0}, x_{2,0}) + (x_1 - x_{1,0}) \frac{\partial f}{\partial x_1} \bigg|_{\substack{x_1=x_{1,0} \\ x_2=x_{2,0}}} + (x_2 - x_{2,0}) \frac{\partial f}{\partial x_2} \bigg|_{\substack{x_1=x_{1,0} \\ x_2=x_{2,0}}} + \tfrac{1}{2}(x_1 - x_{1,0})^2 \frac{\partial^2 f}{\partial x_1^2} \bigg|_{\substack{x_1=x_{1,0} \\ x_2=x_{2,0}}}$$

$$+ \tfrac{1}{2}(x_2 - x_{2,0})^2 \frac{\partial^2 f}{\partial x_2^2} \bigg|_{\substack{x_1=x_{1,0} \\ x_2=x_{2,0}}} + (x_1 - x_{1,0})(x_2 - x_{2,0}) \frac{\partial^2 f}{\partial x_1 \partial x_2} \bigg|_{\substack{x_1=x_{1,0} \\ x_2=x_{2,0}}} + \cdots$$

(Note that the derivatives are evaluated at $x_{1,0}$ and $x_{2,0}$.) A linear approximation of $f(x_1, x_2)$ is thus given by the first three terms on the right-hand side of the above equation.

be clear, then, that the parameters β_i can be estimated from Eq. (15.17) via a linear regression.[6] This ordinary least-squares regression is performed to produce a new estimate of $\boldsymbol{\beta}$, which we call $\hat{\boldsymbol{\beta}}_1$.

Next, using a new Taylor series expansion of $[\varepsilon_t]$ around this $\hat{\boldsymbol{\beta}}_1$, we obtain a new version of (15.17) which can also be estimated by ordinary least squares to yield a new estimate $\hat{\boldsymbol{\beta}}_2$. This process is repeated over and over again until

$$\hat{\boldsymbol{\beta}}_k - \hat{\boldsymbol{\beta}}_{k-1} \approx \mathbf{0} \tag{15.18}$$

We call k the *convergence number*, i.e., the number of iterations required until convergence occurs. $\hat{\boldsymbol{\beta}}_k$ will then be our final estimate of the parameters $\phi_1, \ldots, \phi_p$ and $\theta_1, \ldots, \theta_q$.

The standard errors and t statistics for our parameter estimates would be calculated from the *last* linearization—as is typically done in a nonlinear estimation procedure (see Chapter 7). Thus t statistics have limited meaning, indicating only the significance of the least-squares parameter estimates obtained for the final linearization of the nonlinear equation. An R^2 can be calculated in the same way, and has similar relevance. For this reason, we should not necessarily reject a time-series equation with a low R^2. Despite a low R^2 for the last iteration, it is possible that the full nonlinear model will have considerable predictive power.

It is important to point out that there can be no guarantee that the estimation process described above will converge *at all* to a final estimate of the parameters.

---

[6] Let $\mathbf{Y}$ be the $T \times 1$ vector representing the left-hand side of (15.17) for different values of t:

$$\mathbf{Y} = \begin{bmatrix} [\varepsilon_{1,0}] + \sum_{i=1}^{p+q} \beta_{i,0} x_{i,1} \\ \vdots \\ [\varepsilon_{T,0}] + \sum_{i=1}^{p+q} \beta_{i,0} x_{i,T} \end{bmatrix}$$

Let $\mathbf{X}$ be the $T \times (p+q)$ matrix of independent variables:

$$\mathbf{X} = \begin{bmatrix} x_{1,1} & x_{2,1} & \cdots & x_{p+q,1} \\ \cdots\cdots\cdots\cdots\cdots\cdots\cdots\cdots \\ x_{1,T} & x_{2,T} & \cdots & x_{p+q,T} \end{bmatrix}$$

and let $\boldsymbol{\beta}$ be the $(p+q) \times 1$ vector of unknown parameters:

$$\boldsymbol{\beta} = \begin{bmatrix} \beta_1 \\ \vdots \\ \beta_{p+q} \end{bmatrix}$$

Now letting $[\varepsilon]$ be the $T \times 1$ vector of (unobservable) error terms, we obtain the linear regression equation

$$\mathbf{Y} = \mathbf{X}\boldsymbol{\beta} + [\varepsilon]$$

It is quite possible for the process to *diverge*, i.e., for the successive estimates $\hat{\beta}_1$, $\hat{\beta}$, ..., $\hat{\beta}_k$ to be farther and farther apart. Furthermore, it is also possible for *multiple solutions* to exist—in this case convergence occurs, but different initial guesses result in different final estimates for one or more of the parameters. Whether or not divergence or multiple solutions occur would depend both on the specification of the ARIMA model and on the data to which that specification is fitted.

Should divergence occur, the model can be reestimated one or more times using different initial guesses. Hopefully a new initial guess will result in convergence, although one cannot be sure that this will be the case. If it turns out to be impossible to reach a convergent solution, then a new model specification will have to be chosen.

Even if convergence occurs on the first try, it is wise to test for multiple solutions by reestimating the model with a different initial guess. If multiple solutions do occur, then the final estimate should be that which gives the smallest value of the sum of squared errors. This estimate would correspond to the global minimum of the sum of squared errors function, as opposed to one or more local minima.

15.1.3 *Obtaining an Initial Guess for the Parameter Values*

Before a nonlinear estimation can be performed on Eq. (15.11), an initial guess $\beta_0 = (\phi_0, \theta_0)$ must be made for the parameter values. Convergence of the estimation process may be faster if the initial guess is a good one, i.e., if β_0 is close to the "true" parameter values. On the other hand, if the initial guess is very poor, it is possible that the iterative process may not converge at all.

The sample autocorrelation function can sometimes be used to help produce the initial guess. As one might expect, this may work for a simple (i.e., low-order) time-series model, but can be virtually useless if the model is at all complicated. For example, if the series w_t is modeled as first-order autoregressive, then one need only look at the sample value of ρ_1. If that is, say, .9, then a reasonable first guess for ϕ_1 is $\phi_{1,0} = .9$. If, however, our model for w_t is complex, then this inspection method is unlikely to produce much useful information.

Even if we cannot determine the initial guess by simply inspecting a correlogram, we can still use the numerical values for the sample autocorrelation function to obtain the initial guess. As we demonstrated in the last chapter, the theoretical autocorrelation function can be related to the theoretical parameter values through a series of equations. If these equations are "inverted," they can be used to solve for the parameter values *in terms of the autocorrelation function*. This is straightforward at least in the case of a purely autoregressive model. As an example, consider the autoregressive process of order p, and recall from Eq. (14.47) of the last chapter that the difference equation for its autocorrelation function is given by

$$\rho_k = \phi_1 \rho_{k-1} + \phi_2 \rho_{k-2} + \cdots + \phi_p \rho_{k-p}$$

Utilizing the fact that $\rho_k = \rho_{-k}$, we can rewrite this equation as a set of p simultaneous linear equations relating the parameters $\phi_1, \ldots, \phi_p$ to $\rho_1, \ldots, \rho_p$:

$$\rho_1 = \phi_1 \qquad + \phi_2 \rho_1 \quad + \cdots + \phi_p \rho_{p-1}$$

$$\rho_2 = \phi_1 \rho_1 \quad + \phi_2 \qquad + \cdots + \phi_p \rho_{p-2}$$

$$\vdots$$

$$\rho_p = \phi_1 \rho_{p-1} + \phi_2 \rho_{p-2} + \cdots + \phi_p$$

(15.19)

Recall from the last chapter that these are the *Yule-Walker equations.*[7] By using them to solve for the parameters $\phi_1, \ldots, \phi_p$ in terms of the *estimated* values of the autocorrelation function, we arrive at what are called the *Yule-Walker estimates* of the parameters. These estimates can be used to provide a reasonable first guess for the parameter values.[8] This first guess is, however, of limited value, since the purely autoregressive model can be estimated by ordinary least squares.

If the time-series model contains a moving average part, then the Yule-Walker equations that relate the values of the autocorrelation function to the values of the parameters will not be linear. Recall, for example, that the process MA(1) has the autocorrelation function

$$\rho_k = \begin{cases} \dfrac{-\theta_1}{1 + \theta_1{}^2} & k = 1 \\[2mm] 0 & k > 1 \end{cases}$$

Suppose in this example that $\rho_1 = .4$ in the sample autocorrelation function. Then

$$\theta_1 = \frac{-1 \pm \sqrt{1 - \rho_1{}^2}}{2\rho_1} = \frac{-1 \pm .6}{.8} \tag{15.20}$$

---

[7] G. U. Yule, "On a Method of Investigating Periodicities in Disturbed Series, with Special Reference to Wölfer's Sunspot Numbers," *Philosophical Transactions*, vol. A226, p. 267, 1927; and G. Walker, "On Periodicity in Series of Related Terms," *Proceedings of the Royal Society*, vol. A131, p. 518, 1931.

[8] Writing Eq. (15.19) in matrix notation,

$$\rho = P\phi$$

where
$$\rho = \begin{bmatrix} \rho_1 \\ \rho_2 \\ \vdots \\ \rho_p \end{bmatrix} \qquad P = \begin{bmatrix} 1 & \rho_1 & \cdots & \rho_{p-1} \\ \rho_1 & 1 & \cdots & \rho_{p-2} \\ \multicolumn{4}{c}{\dotfill} \\ \rho_{p-1} & \rho_{p-2} & \cdots & 1 \end{bmatrix} \qquad \text{and} \qquad \phi = \begin{bmatrix} \phi_1 \\ \phi_2 \\ \vdots \\ \phi_p \end{bmatrix}$$

We can solve for ϕ as simply

$$\phi = P^{-1}\rho$$

Thus the first estimate for θ_1 is -2 or $-.5$. Since invertibility necessitates that $|\theta_1| < 1$, we select the value $\theta_{1,0} = -.5$ for our first guess in the nonlinear estimation process. Unfortunately, the solution for θ in terms of ρ becomes more difficult as the moving average order q becomes larger. In fact, to get initial estimates for the model MA(q), it is necessary to solve q simultaneous nonlinear equations.

One might ask why a first guess for the parameter values based on the Yule-Walker equations is not sufficient for practical purposes. This would eliminate the use of the iterative nonlinear estimation method. One reason is that the sample autocorrelation function is only an *estimate* of the actual autocorrelation function, and thus is subject to error. In fact, for small samples (e.g., time series with less than 50 data points) the sample autocorrelation function will be biased (downward) from the true autocorrelation function. A second reason is that the sample autocorrelation function does not contain as much information as the actual time series. It contains only a part of the information that is very useful for model specification. In order to use as much information as possible in the estimation of the model's parameters, we calculate our final estimates based on the actual time series.

Example 15.1   Estimation of ARMA(1,1)

As an example of the iterative nonlinear estimation method described in section 15.1.2, let us see how the estimation of ϕ_1 and θ_1 in an ARMA(1,1) model for a stationary series w_t would be carried out. Writing the ARMA(1,1) model in terms of Eq. (15.11), we have

$$\varepsilon_t = \left(\frac{1 - \phi_1 B}{1 - \theta_1 B}\right) w_t \tag{15.21}$$

This equation is nonlinear in θ_1, but it can be approximated by a Taylor series expansion. This involves calculating the first derivatives of ε_t with respect to ϕ_1 and θ_1, and evaluating them at the initial guess $\phi_{1,0}$ and $\theta_{1,0}$:[9]

$$x_{1,t} = -\left.\frac{\partial \varepsilon_t}{\partial \phi_1}\right|_{\phi_{1,0},\theta_{1,0}} = \frac{B}{1 - \theta_{1,0} B} w_t \tag{15.22}$$

$$x_{2,t} = -\left.\frac{\partial \varepsilon_t}{\partial \theta_1}\right|_{\phi_{1,0},\theta_{1,0}} = -\frac{B - \phi_{1,0} B^2}{(1 - \theta_{1,0} B)^2} w_t \tag{15.23}$$

---

[9] Recall that the initial guesses for $\phi_{1,0}$ and $\theta_{1,0}$ could be obtained from inspection of the autocorrelation function. If one is unable to make a reasoned initial guess (e.g., for a high-order model), then initial guesses of 0 could be used.

Numerical time series can be computed for $x_{1,t}$ and $x_{2,t}$ (they will be used to perform the linear regression) over the time period $t = 1$ to T by expanding Eqs. (15.22) and (15.23). Taking Eq. (15.22) for $x_{1,t}$, for example, we get

$$x_{1,t} = \theta_{1,0} x_{1,t-1} + w_{t-1} \tag{15.24}$$

Setting $w_0 = x_{1,0} = 0$, Eq. (15.24) can be solved repeatedly to generate a series for $x_{1,t}$. The first value $x_{1,1}$ would be equal to 0, the second value $x_{1,2}$ would equal w_1, the third value $x_{1,3}$ would equal $\theta_{1,0} w_1 + w_2$, etc. The same thing is done for $x_{2,t}$ by expanding Eq. (15.23):

$$x_{2,t} = 2\theta_{1,0} x_{2,t-1} - \theta_{1,0}^2 x_{2,t-2} + w_{t-1} - \phi_{1,0} w_{t-2} \tag{15.25}$$

We would begin the computation of $x_{2,t}$ by setting

$$x_{2,1} = x_{2,0} = w_0 = w_{-1} = 0 \tag{15.26}$$

Thus, the first value $x_{2,1}$ would just be equal to 0, while $x_{2,2}$ would be equal to w_1, $x_{2,3}$ would be equal to $2\theta_{1,0} x_{2,2} + w_2 - \phi_{1,0} w_1$, etc.

Finally, a time series must also be computed for $\varepsilon_{t,0}$ for t ranging from 1 to T. This is done simply by writing

$$\varepsilon_{t,0} = \left(\frac{1 - \phi_{1,0} B}{1 - \theta_{1,0} B} \right) w_t \tag{15.27}$$

and using the series for w_t to obtain the series for $\varepsilon_{t,0}$. Note that this is just a series of residuals based on the first-guess estimates $\phi_{1,0}$ and $\theta_{1,0}$.

We are now ready to perform a linear regression. Equation (15.17) becomes

$$\varepsilon_{t,0} + \phi_{1,0} x_{1,t} + \theta_{1,0} x_{2,t} = \phi_1 x_{1,t} + \theta_1 x_{2,t} + \varepsilon_t \tag{15.28}$$

Equation (15.28) is a linear regression equation, and ordinary least squares can be used to estimate ϕ_1 and θ_1. If these estimates of ϕ_1 and θ_1 are significantly different from the first guesses $\phi_{1,0}$ and $\theta_{1,0}$, then they are used as *new* first guesses, and the *entire process is repeated* all over again, to yield *new* estimates for ϕ_1 and θ_1. Again, if the change is significant, then the process is repeated. Hopefully, the estimates for ϕ_1 and θ_1 will converge after a few iterations, but we have no guarantee of this, nor, in fact, do we even have a guarantee that the process will converge *at all*. (If the estimation process fails to converge at all, it should be started again using a new and different initial guess for the parameters.)

15.2 DIAGNOSTIC CHECKING

After a time-series model has been specified and its parameters have been estimated, a check must be made to test whether or not the original specification was correct. This process of diagnostic checking usually involves two steps. First, the autocorrelation function for the "simulated series" (i.e., the time series generated by the model) can be compared with the sample autocorrelation function of the original series. If the two autocorrelation functions seem very different (and we offer no quantitative measure of just how different that is), some doubt may be cast on the validity of the model and a respecification may be in order. If the two autocorrelation functions are not markedly different (and this will most often be the case), then a quantitative analysis can be made of the *residuals* generated by the model.

Remember that we have assumed that the random error terms ε_t in the actual process are normally distributed and *independent of each other*. Then if the model has been specified correctly, the *residuals* $\hat{\varepsilon}_t$ (which are *estimates* of the unobservable error terms) should have close to the same properties. In particular, we would expect the residuals to be *nearly uncorrelated* with each other, so that a *sample autocorrelation function* of the residuals would be close to 0 for displacement $k \geq 1$.

Recall that the residuals of the model are simply

$$\hat{\varepsilon}_t = \hat{\theta}^{-1}(B)\hat{\phi}(B)w_t \tag{15.29}$$

These residuals should be nearly uncorrelated if the model has been correctly specified. Let us denote the sample autocorrelation function (for displacement k) of the residuals as $\hat{r}_k$. It is calculated by

$$\hat{r}_k = \frac{\sum_t \hat{\varepsilon}_t \hat{\varepsilon}_{t-k}}{\sum_t \hat{\varepsilon}_t^2} \tag{15.30}$$

It turns out that a very convenient test, based on some statistical results obtained by Box and Pierce, can be applied to this sample autocorrelation function.[10] *If the model is correctly specified*, then for large displacements k (for example, $k > 5$ for low-order models) *the residual autocorrelations $\hat{r}_k$ are themselves uncorrelated, normally distributed random variables with mean 0 and variance* $1/T$, where T is the number of observations in the time series. This fact makes it possible to devise a simple diagnostic test.

---

[10] G. E. P. Box and D. A. Pierce, "Distribution of Residual Autocorrelations in Autoregressive-Integrated Moving Average Time Series Models," *Journal of the American Statistical Association*, vol. 65, December 1970.

Consider the statistic R composed of the first K residual autocorrelations $\hat{r}_1, \ldots, \hat{r}_K$:[11]

$$R = T \sum_{k=1}^{K} \hat{r}_k^2 \qquad (15.31)$$

This statistic is a sum of squared independent normal random variables, each with mean 0 and variance $1/T$, and is therefore itself approximately distributed as *chi-square* (see Appendix 2.1). We say "approximately" because the first few autocorrelations r_1, r_2, etc., will have a variance slightly less than $1/T$, and may themselves be correlated. Box and Pierce demonstrate that the approximation is quite close, and that the statistic R will be distributed as $\chi^2(K - p - q)$, i.e., chi-square with $K - p - q$ degrees of freedom. Therefore, a statistical hypothesis test of model accuracy can be performed by comparing the observed value of R with the appropriate points from a chi-square table.

Suppose, for example, that we have specified an ARMA(1,1) model for a series w_t, that the model has been estimated, and that the statistic R is calculated to be 31.5 with $K = 20$. From a chi-square table we see that the 10 percent point for $K - p - q = 18$ degrees of freedom is 26.0, and the 5 percent point is 28.9. Thus the statistic R is too large and we can reject the model, since the probability that the residuals are not white noise is at least 95 percent. Suppose that a new model, ARMA(2,2), is specified and estimated, and the statistic R is now 22.0, again with $K = 20$. From the chi-square table we see that the 10 percent point for 16 degrees of freedom is 23.5. Thus we need not accept the hypothesis that the residuals are nonwhite, and this second model would be acceptable.[12] To determine the "best" specification, we might want to specify and estimate some other ARMA models to see whether a lower chi-square statistic can be obtained.

If the calculated value of R is between the 10 percent and 5 percent points of the chi-square tail, some doubt would be thrown on the model. At the very least a second test should be applied. This second test would involve observing the individual values of $\hat{r}_k$ for all k between, say, $K/4$ and K, e.g., between $k = 5$ and $k = 20$. Since these $\hat{r}_k$ are normal with variance $1/T$, we can test to see if they are all within two or three standard deviations from their means of 0. If several of the r_k are larger than $2/\sqrt{T}$ (two standard deviations of the normal variable), evidence exists that the model is misspecified. In addition the evidence might suggest how the model should be respecified. For example, if for an ARMA(2,1) model $\hat{r}_3$ is very much larger than $2/\sqrt{T}$, this would indicate that

---

[11] For low-order models. K equal to 15 or 20 is certainly sufficient.

[12] Note that this chi-square test is a "weak" hypothesis test. A value of R below the 10 percent point on the chi-square distribution indicates that it is not necessary to accept the hypothesis that the residuals are nonwhite, since the probability that the hypothesis is true is less than 90 percent. It is thus only an *indirect* test of the hypothesis that the residuals are white.

the model should be respecified with the inclusion of a third-order moving average term.

In constructing a time-series model one often estimates several alternative specifications. It may be the case that two or more specifications pass the diagnostic checks described above. In this case additional tests must be used to determine the "best" specification. One test is to compare the "simulated series" (i.e., the time series generated by the model) for each specification with the original series. The specification that yields the smallest RMS simulation error would then be retained.[13] However, unless one specification has a markedly lower RMS error, we suggest retaining all the specifications (that pass the diagnostic checks) and choosing among them based on their *forecasting* performance. The generation and evaluation of forecasts from a time-series model is discussed in the next chapter.

Example 15.2   Interest Rate

In the last two chapters we began analyzing two different time series. The first series contained quarterly data for the interest rate on 4–6 month commercial paper from the beginning of 1947 to the second quarter of 1972, and the second consisted of monthly data for hog production in the United States from the beginning of 1960 to the end of 1967. Let us now estimate some alternative ARIMA models for these time series.

Review the sample autocorrelation functions in Figs. 13.12, 13.14, and 13.16 for the interest rate series undifferenced, differenced once, and differenced twice. Recall that we suggested that these autocorrelation functions indicate that the series is second-order homogeneous nonstationary. In addition, in Chapter 14 we suggested that ARIMA(2,2,2) or ARIMA(4,2,2) might be appropriate specifications for a model of the series. Suppose, however, that one judged the autocorrelation function of the *undifferenced* series to be stationary, and indicative of a first-order autoregressive model. Since the autocorrelation function declines geometrically from a value of $\rho_1 = .9$, some indication of an ARIMA(1,0,0) model with $\phi_1 \approx .9$ does exist. For this reason we estimated the ARIMA(1,0,0) model, with the following results:

ARIMA(1,0,0)

$$(1 - .9607B)y_t = .1783 + \varepsilon_t \tag{15.32}$$

$$R^2 = .939 \qquad \chi^2(1,20) = 37.38$$

---

[13] Calculation of the RMS simulation error is discussed in Chapter 10.

Note that while the R^2 of Eq. (15.32) is high, one should not be misled into thinking that the equation is necessarily a good one. Remember that the R^2 measures fit in terms of the dependent variable of the regression, which in this case is a level variable. A more revealing statistic is the chi-square, which is equal to 37.38. With 19 degrees of freedom (20 lags minus one estimated parameter), this value is above the critical 5 percent level, so that we may conclude that the residuals from the ARIMA(1,0,0) model are autocorrelated. Thus, we must turn to a homogeneous nonstationary model for our interest rate series.

We next estimate the ARIMA(2,2,2) and ARIMA(4,2,2) models that we suggested earlier. The results are shown below:

ARIMA(2,2,2)

$$(1 - .2604B + .3019B^2)\Delta^2 y_t = -.0008 + (1 - .4563B - .5434B^2)\varepsilon_t \quad (15.33)$$

$$R^2 = .114 \qquad \chi^2(4,20) = 15.12$$

ARIMA(4,2,2)

$$(1 - .1675B + .1867B^2 + .0915B^3 - .2100B^4)\Delta^2 y_t = -.0008$$

$$+ (1 - .3627B - .6372B^2)\varepsilon_t \quad (15.34)$$

$$R^2 = .101 \qquad \chi^2(6,20) = 13.63$$

Note that both models have approximately the same statistical fit. The R^2's are low, but that is merely reflective of the fact that the dependent variable has been differenced twice. (If the R^2's were calculated in terms of the *undifferenced* variable y_t, their values would be approximately .95.) Both models have about the same chi-square statistic (they are both significant at the 5 percent level), so that in each case we may conclude that the residuals are not autocorrelated. In practice, sets of forecasts should be produced using both models, so that their performance can be compared. We will produce forecasts using the (4,2,2) model in the next chapter.

Example 15.3 Hog Production

Let us now turn to the series for monthly hog production. Recall from the last chapter that we suggested that an appropriate model for the series might be

$$(1 - \phi_1 B - \phi_2 B^2 - \phi_3 B^3)(1 - B)(1 - B^{12})y_t = \varepsilon_t$$

This model was estimated over the period January 1960 to December 1967, with the results as shown below:

$$(1 + .6681B + .2015B^2 - .1298B^3)(1 - B)(1 - B^{12})y_t = .0014 + \varepsilon_t \qquad (15.35)$$

$$R^2 = .365 \qquad \chi^2(3,20) = 12.83$$

The model is acceptable, and will be used to forecast in the next chapter. The reader might wonder, however, whether another model specification might provide a better fit to the data. Perhaps, for example, the addition of moving average terms would improve the model. To test this, we estimated a model that includes first- and second-order moving average terms:

$$(1 + .6626B + .3945B^2 - .0179B^3)(1 - B)(1 - B)^{12}y_t$$

$$= .0015 + (1 + .0168B - .2191B^2)\varepsilon_t \qquad (15.36)$$

$$R^2 = .349 \qquad \chi^2(5,20) = 13.01$$

Inclusion of the moving average terms results in a slightly lower value for the R^2. Of greater importance, however, is the fact that the estimated values of ϕ_1, ϕ_2, and ϕ_3 add up to a number greater than 1. The result is a nonstationary model for a series that we believe to be stationary. We would thus reject this model, and retain the model of Eq. (15.35).

Exercises

15.1 Following the example in section 15.1.4, show how the estimation of ϕ_1, ϕ_2, and θ_1 for an ARMA(2,1) model would be carried out. Go through the steps of the Taylor series expansion, show how the data series are generated, and indicate how the linear regressions are performed.

15.2 Suppose that an ARMA(0,2) model has been estimated for a time series that has been generated by an ARMA(1,2) process.

(1) How would the diagnostic test indicate that the model has been misspecified?
(2) What will the residual autocorrelations $\hat{r}_k$ look like? What characteristics of these autocorrelations might indicate that ARMA(1,2) is a more correct specification?

15.3 Repeat Exercise 15.2 for an ARMA(0,2) model estimated for a time series that has been generated by an ARMA(2,3) process.

APPENDIX 15 / INITIALIZATION OF THE TIME SERIES

We saw in section 15.1.1 that the sum-of-squares function $S(\phi, \theta)$ and thus the likelihood function $L(\phi, \theta, \sigma_\varepsilon)$ are conditional on the past unobservable values of w_t and ε_t. For this reason the least-squares estimates will depend on the choice of values that we use for w_0, w_{-1}, ..., etc. We suggested using unconditional expected values of w_0, ..., w_{-p+1} and for ε_0, ..., ε_{-q+1}, i.e., setting them all equal to 0.

A procedure also exists for finding *conditional expected values* for w_0, ..., w_{-p+1}, i.e., values that are conditional on the *observed* values of w_1, ..., w_T and the *estimated* values of ε_1, ..., ε_T. Essentially one can *initially* set w_0, ..., w_{-p+1} and ε_0, ..., ε_{-q+1} to 0, estimate the ARMA model by minimizing $S(\phi, \theta)$ conditional on these 0 values, and then *backcast* the model to generate new values for w_0, ..., w_{-p+1}. Since the differenced series w_t is stationary, the ARMA process of Eq. (15.1) can be turned around in time; i.e., it is equivalent (statistically so in a large sample) to the process

$$\phi(F)w_t = \theta(F)\varepsilon_t \qquad (A15.1)$$

where F is the *forward lag operator*:

$$Fw_t = w_{t+1}$$

$$F^2 w_t = w_{t+2}$$

and so forth, and $\phi(\ )$ and $\theta(\ )$ are the same polynomials as in (15.1). Thus (A15.1) can be written as

$$w_t = \phi^{-1}(F)\theta(F)\varepsilon_t \qquad (A15.2)$$

and can be used to solve for $\hat{w}_0$, $\hat{w}_{-1}$, ..., $\hat{w}_{-p+1}$ in terms of the estimated values of ε_1, ..., ε_T. These estimated values are the residuals formed by subtracting the actual series for w_t from the predicted series generated by the initially estimated ARMA model. We can obtain *new* least-squares estimates for ϕ and θ by minimizing $S(\phi, \theta, \sigma_\varepsilon)$ *conditional* on $w_0 = \hat{w}_0$, $w_1 = \hat{w}_1$, etc. A new round of estimates for $\hat{w}_0$, $\hat{w}_1$, ..., $\hat{w}_{-p+1}$ can then be computed from (A15.2), and the process repeated until the estimates converge, i.e., until $\hat{\phi}$ and $\hat{\theta}$ stop changing in value. We have no guarantee, unfortunately, that this process will converge. If it does not, one may be forced to fix $\hat{w}_0$, $\hat{w}_1$, ..., $\hat{w}_{-p+1}$ at their initial estimates.

The determination of conditional expected values for the series w_0, ..., w_{-p+1} is difficult, and usually involves a good deal of computation. Thus it is reasonable to ask whether or not our estimates of ϕ and θ will be very sensitive to this initialization of the series. The answer depends on the length of the observed time series that is to be modeled, and, in particular, the length of the series relative to the values of p and q. If the time series is long relative to p and q, then the conditional sum-of-squares function will be nearly equal to the unconditional sum-of-squares function, and our estimates of ϕ and θ will be very insensitive to the initialization process. In this case one can simply set all the initial values to 0. If the time series is short (relative to p and q), then some gain in efficiency would probably result from the use of conditional expected values of $w_0, \ldots, w_{-p+1}$, but we cannot determine how large this gain in efficiency would be. Our knowledge of the statistical properties of the parameter estimates is based on asymptotical results, i.e., on large samples. Unfortunately the small-sample properties of the estimates are not known.

Usually one would not want to model a time series as an ARMA process anyway unless a reasonably large number of observations are available (e.g., more than 50). Otherwise it is unlikely that one could obtain a reasonable statistical fit for the model and the model will be of limited value for forecasting. Furthermore, many of the ARMA models that one would construct in economic or business applications are of low order (i.e., p and q are not more than 2 or 3). In this case the initialization of the series will usually not be a problem, and one can simply set all the initial values equal to 0. We suggest this practice, and we apply it to all the numerical examples in this chapter and the next.

16

Once a time-series model has been estimated and its original specification has been checked, it can be used for forecasting. In this chapter we explain how one can use the general ARIMA model

$$\phi(B)\Delta^d y_t = \theta(B)\varepsilon_t \qquad (16.1)$$

to obtain a forecast of y_t for period $T + l$ (that is, l periods ahead, with $l \geq 1$). We denote this forecast by $\hat{y}_T(l)$, and call it the *origin-T forecast for lead time l*. We assume for now that the true parameters of the model are known, and examine the properties both of the forecast and of the forecast error. Later we will see how imperfect knowledge of the true parameter values increases the forecast error.

We begin this chapter by discussing the basis for making forecasts, after which we go through the steps of actually computing a forecast. Then we discuss the nature of forecast errors, showing how forecast confidence intervals can be computed. In order to give the reader an understanding of the characteristics of time-series forecasts, we examine in detail the properties of the forecasts of some simple ARIMA models. Finally, we present two examples in which we generate forecasts for an interest rate and for hog production using the time-series models estimated at the end of the last chapter. In discussing these examples we attempt to give the reader some feeling for the strengths and weaknesses of time-series forecasts.

FORECASTING WITH TIME-SERIES MODELS

16.1   MINIMUM MEAN SQUARE ERROR FORECAST

Our objective in forecasting is to predict future values of a time series subject to as little error as possible. For this reason we consider the "optimum" forecast to be that forecast which has the *minimum mean square forecast error*. Since the forecast error is a random variable, we minimize the *expected value*. Thus we wish to choose our forecast $\hat{y}_T(l)$ so that $E[e_T{}^2(l)] = E\{[y_{T+l} - \hat{y}_T(l)]^2\}$ is minimized.[1] We show that this forecast is given by the *conditional expectation* of y_{T+l}, that is, by

$$\hat{y}_T(l) = E[y_{T+l} | y_T, y_{T-1}, \ldots, y_1] \tag{16.2}$$

To prove that the minimum mean square error forecast is given by Eq. (16.2), we begin by rewriting the ARIMA model in Eq. (16.1) above as

$$\phi(B)(1 - B)^d y_t = \theta(B)\varepsilon_t \tag{16.3}$$

since $\Delta = (1 - B)$, as explained in Chapter 14. Therefore,

$$y_t = \phi^{-1}(B)(1 - B)^{-d}\theta(B)\varepsilon_t$$

$$= \psi(B)\varepsilon_t = \sum_{j=0}^{\infty} \psi_j \varepsilon_{t-j} \tag{16.4}$$

Here we have expressed the ARIMA model as a purely moving average process of infinite order.[2] Then

$$y_{T+l} = \psi_0 \varepsilon_{T+l} + \psi_1 \varepsilon_{T+l-1} + \cdots + \psi_l \varepsilon_T + \psi_{l+1} \varepsilon_{T-1} + \cdots$$

$$= \psi_0 \varepsilon_{T+l} + \psi_1 \varepsilon_{T+l-1} + \cdots + \psi_{l-1} \varepsilon_{T+1} + \sum_{j=0}^{\infty} \psi_{l+j} \varepsilon_{T-j} \tag{16.5}$$

In Eq. (16.5) we have divided the infinite sum into two parts, the second part beginning with the term $\psi_l \varepsilon_T$, and thus describing information up to and including time period T.

Of course the forecast $\hat{y}_T(l)$ can be based only on information available up to time T. Our objective is to compare this forecast with the actual value y_{T+l} as expressed in Eq. (16.5). To do so, we write the forecast as a weighted sum

---

[1] In this way, "mean square forecast error" refers to the *variance* of the forecast error.

[2] Any ARIMA process can be equivalently expressed as purely moving average or as purely autoregressive. We could have, for example, rewritten Eq. (16.3) as $\phi(B)(1 - B)^d \theta^{-1}(B)y_t = \varepsilon_t$, or $\xi(B)y_t = \varepsilon_t$. This is a purely autoregressive process of infinite order. The reason that we do not originally specify the ARIMA process as purely autoregressive or purely moving average (of infinite order) is that we would then have an infinite number of parameters to estimate.

of those error terms *which we can estimate*, namely, ε_T, ε_{T-1}, ... Then, the desired forecast is

$$\hat{y}_T(l) = \sum_{j=0}^{\infty} \psi_{l+j}^* \varepsilon_{T-j} \tag{16.6}$$

where the weights ψ_{l+j}^* are to be chosen optimally so as *to minimize the mean square forecast error*. We can now write an expression for the forecast error, $e_T(l)$, using Eqs. (16.5) and (16.6):

$$e_T(l)' = y_{T+l} - \hat{y}_T(l) = \psi_0 \varepsilon_{T+l} + \psi_1 \varepsilon_{T+l-1} + \cdots + \psi_{l-1} \varepsilon_{T+1}$$

$$+ \sum_{j=0}^{\infty} (\psi_{l+j} - \psi_{l+j}^*) \varepsilon_{T-j} \tag{16.7}$$

Since by assumption $E[\varepsilon_i \varepsilon_j] = 0$ for $i \neq j$, the mean square forecast error is

$$E[e_T^2(l)] = (\psi_0^2 + \psi_1^2 + \cdots + \psi_{l-1}^2)\sigma_\varepsilon^2 + \sum_{j=0}^{\infty} (\psi_{l+j} - \psi_{l+j}^*)^2 \sigma_\varepsilon^2 \tag{16.8}$$

Clearly this expression is minimized by setting the "optimum" weights ψ_{l+j}^* equal to the true weights ψ_{l+j}, for $j = 0, 1, \ldots$. But then our optimum forecast $\hat{y}_T(l)$ is just the conditional expectation of y_{T+l}. This can be seen by taking the conditional expectation of y_{T+l} in Eq. (16.5). The expected values of $\varepsilon_{T+l}, \ldots,$ ε_{T+1} are all 0, while the expected values of ε_T, ε_{T-1}, ..., are just the actual observed errors, i.e., the residuals from the estimated equation. Thus we have

$$\hat{y}_T(l) = \sum_{j=0}^{\infty} \psi_{l+j} \hat{\varepsilon}_{T-j} = E[y_{T+l} | y_T, \ldots, y_1] \tag{16.9}$$

This provides the basic principle for calculating forecasts from our ARIMA models. Now we apply this principle to the actual computation of forecasts.

16.2 COMPUTING A FORECAST

The actual computation of the forecast $\hat{y}_T(l)$ can be done recursively using the estimated ARIMA model. This involves first computing a forecast one period ahead, using this forecast to compute a forecast two periods ahead, and continuing until the l-period forecast has been reached. Let us write the ARIMA(p,d,q) model as

$$w_t = \phi_1 w_{t-1} + \cdots + \phi_p w_{t-p} + \varepsilon_t - \theta_1 \varepsilon_{t-1} - \cdots - \theta_q \varepsilon_{t-q} + \delta \tag{16.10}$$

with
$$y_t = \Sigma^d w_t \tag{16.11}$$

To compute the forecast $\hat{y}_T(l)$, we begin by computing the *one-period* forecast of w_t, $\hat{w}_T(1)$. To do so, we write Eq. (16.10) with the time period modified:

$$w_{T+1} = \phi_1 w_T + \cdots + \phi_p w_{T-p+1} + \varepsilon_{T+1} - \theta_1 \varepsilon_T - \cdots - \theta_q \varepsilon_{T-q+1} + \delta \qquad (16.12)$$

We then calculate our forecast $\hat{w}_T(1)$ by taking the conditional expected value of w_{T+1} in Eq. (16.12):

$$\hat{w}_T(1) = E[w_{T+1} | w_T, \ldots] = \phi_1 w_T + \cdots + \phi_p w_{T-p+1}$$

$$- \theta_1 \hat{\varepsilon}_T - \cdots - \theta_q \hat{\varepsilon}_{T-q+1} + \delta \qquad (16.13)$$

where the $\hat{\varepsilon}_T$, $\hat{\varepsilon}_{T-1}$, etc., are observed residuals. Note that the expected value of ε_{T+1} is 0. Now using the one-period forecast $\hat{w}_T(1)$, we can obtain the *two-period forecast* $\hat{w}_T(2)$:

$$\hat{w}_T(2) = E[w_{T+2} | w_T, \ldots]$$

$$= \phi_1 \hat{w}_T(1) + \phi_2 w_T + \cdots + \phi_p w_{T-p+2} - \theta_2 \hat{\varepsilon}_T - \cdots - \theta_q \hat{\varepsilon}_{T-q+2} + \delta$$
$$(16.14)$$

The two-period forecast is then used to produce the three-period forecast, and so on, until the l-period forecast $\hat{w}_T(l)$ is reached:

$$\hat{w}_T(l) = \phi_1 \hat{w}_T(l-1) + \cdots + \phi_l w_T + \cdots + \phi_p w_{T-p+l}$$

$$- \theta_1 \hat{\varepsilon}_T - \cdots - \theta_q \hat{\varepsilon}_{T-q+l} + \delta \qquad (16.15)$$

Note that if $l > p$ and $l > q$, then this forecast will be

$$\hat{w}_T(l) = \phi_1 \hat{w}_T(l-1) + \cdots + \phi_p \hat{w}_T(l-p) \qquad (16.16)$$

Once the differenced series w_t has been forecasted, a forecast can be obtained for the original series y_t simply by applying the summation operator to w_t, i.e., by summing w_t d times. Suppose, for example, that $d = 1$. Then our l-period forecast of y_t would be given by

$$\hat{y}_T(l) = y_T + \hat{w}_T(1) + \hat{w}_T(2) + \cdots + \hat{w}_T(l) \qquad (16.17)$$

On the other hand, if the model for y_t were ARIMA with $d = 2$, then the l-period forecast $\hat{y}_T(l)$ would be given by

$$\hat{y}_T(l) = y_T + [\Delta y_T + \hat{w}_T(1)] + [\Delta y_T + \hat{w}_T(1) + \hat{w}_T(2)] + \cdots$$

$$+ [\Delta y_T + \hat{w}_T(1) + \cdots + \hat{w}_T(l)]$$

$$= y_T + l\Delta y_T + l\hat{w}_T(1) + (l - 1)\hat{w}_T(2) + \cdots + \hat{w}_T(l) \qquad (16.18)$$

Here the summation operator has been applied twice.[3] The procedure is similar for larger values of d.

16.3 THE FORECAST ERROR

As we saw before, if we express the ARIMA model as a purely moving average process of infinite order, the forecast error l periods ahead is given by

$$e_T(l) = y_{T+l} - \hat{y}_T(l) = \psi_0 \varepsilon_{T+l} + \psi_1 \varepsilon_{T+l-1} + \cdots + \psi_{l-1}\varepsilon_{T+1} \qquad (16.19)$$

Remember that the weights ψ_j are determined from

$$\psi(B) = \phi^{-1}(B)(1 - B)^{-d}\theta(B) \qquad (16.20)$$

We assume that the model parameters $\phi_1, \ldots, \phi_p$ and $\theta_1, \ldots, \theta_q$ are known exactly, and therefore the weights $\psi_0, \psi_1, \ldots,$ are also known exactly. In this case the *variance* of the forecast error is given by

$$E[e_T{}^2(l)] = (\psi_0{}^2 + \psi_1{}^2 + \cdots + \psi_{l-1}^2)\sigma_\varepsilon{}^2 \qquad (16.21)$$

Therefore, the algebraic form for the forecast error variance depends on the particular ARIMA specification that has been adopted. In the next section we examine the forecast error in more detail for some simple ARIMA models. For now, however, there are two things that the reader should observe.

First, we know from the definition of $\psi(B)$ above that $\psi_0 = 1$.[4] Therefore, for *any* ARIMA specification, we know that the forecast error *one period* ahead is just

$$e_T(1) = \varepsilon_{T+1} \qquad (16.22)$$

---

[3] The reader may wish to review the use of the summation operator as described in Chapter 14.

[4] Remember that the ARIMA model (with 0 mean) is $w_t = \phi_1 w_{t-1} + \cdots + \phi_p w_{t-p} + \varepsilon_t - \theta_1 \varepsilon_{t-1} - \cdots - \theta_q \varepsilon_{t-q}$. The only unlagged term on the right-hand side is ε_t (which has a weight of 1). Thus ψ_0 must equal 1 in Eq. (16.4).

and this has variance σ_ε^2. Thus the forecast error variance one period ahead is always the variance of the error term.

Second, we must keep in mind the fact that our calculation of the forecast error was based on the assumption that we knew the parameter values $\phi_1, \ldots, \phi_p$ and $\theta_1, \ldots, \theta_q$ with certainty, i.e., that we had obtained perfect estimates of the parameter values. Needless to say, this is never the case. The parameters are estimated via a nonlinear least-squares regression, and, as in any least-squares regression, the estimates are random variables with means and variances. Therefore the *actual* forecast error variance will be *larger* than the variance calculated above. To determine exactly *how much larger*, we must know the variances (or standard errors) of the parameter estimates in the ARIMA model. Because the parameters are estimated nonlinearly, however, the variances of their estimates are difficult to determine. The best we could do, in fact, would be to calculate standard errors for the parameter estimates based on the *last iteration* of the nonlinear estimation procedure.[5] In other words, we could take the ordinary least-squares regression from the last iteration, calculate the residuals of that linearized equation, and obtain standard errors in the manner discussed in Chapter 6. The residuals from this linearization could also be used to calculate an estimate of the variance σ_ε^2.

The difficulty here is that the meaning of the standard errors for the linearization in the last (or any particular) iteration is somewhat limited—certainly they are not "true" estimates of the actual standard errors for the parameter values. As a practical matter, one has the choice of using these standard errors in the calculation of the forecast error variance, or ignoring them and simply calculating the forecast error variance based on Eq. (16.21) above.

16.4 FORECAST CONFIDENCE INTERVALS

We base our forecast confidence intervals on the assumption that the parameter values are known. However, these confidence intervals will be overly optimistic if the standard errors for the parameter estimates based on the last iteration are large (e.g., if the corresponding t statistics are less than 5). When generating forecasts from a linear single-equation regression model (in Chapter 6), we calculated confidence intervals which accounted for errors due to imperfect knowledge of the model's parameter values. However, this becomes rather difficult to do in the case of a time-series model, because the model is nonlinear in the parameters.

Before we can calculate a confidence interval for our forecast, we need an estimate $\hat{\sigma}_\varepsilon^2$ for the variance of the disturbance term. This estimate would logi-

---

[5] Assuming that the procedure is based on repeated linearizations of the nonlinear model. As we mentioned in section 7.5, there exist other approaches to nonlinear estimation.

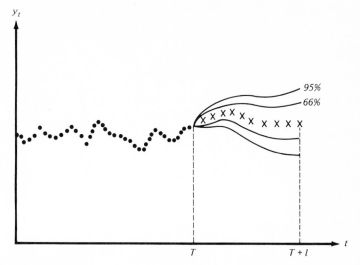

FIGURE 16.1
Forecasts and confidence intervals for a stationary ARMA process.

cally be based on the sum of squared residuals $S(\hat{\phi}, \hat{\theta})$ obtained after final estimates of the parameters have been obtained:

$$\hat{\sigma}_\varepsilon^2 = \frac{S(\hat{\phi}, \hat{\theta})}{T - p - q} = \frac{\sum_{t=1}^{T} \hat{\varepsilon}_t^2}{T - p - q} \tag{16.23}$$

Here $T - p - q$ is the number of degrees of freedom in the linear regression. We see from Eq. (16.21) and the fact that $\psi_0 = 1$ that a *confidence interval of n standard deviations* around a forecast l periods ahead would be given by

$$C_n = \hat{y}_T(l) \pm n\left(1 + \sum_{j=1}^{l-1} \psi_j^2\right)^{1/2} \hat{\sigma}_\varepsilon \tag{16.24}$$

As expected, this interval gets larger as the lead time l becomes larger, although the exact pattern depends on the weights ψ_j.

Forecasts of y_t, together with a typical 66 percent confidence interval ($n = 1$) and 95 percent confidence interval ($n = 2$), are shown for a hypothetical ARMA model ($d = 0$) in Fig. 16.1. Note that the forecasts (denoted by $\times$'s) first are increasing but then decline to the constant mean level of the series. We know that the forecast will approach the mean of the series as the lead time l becomes large because the process is stationary. The confidence intervals, of course, increase as the forecast lead time becomes longer.

16.5 PROPERTIES OF ARIMA FORECASTS

We now examine the properties of the forecasts derived from some simple ARIMA models. In all the cases that follow we assume that the parameters of the particular ARIMA model are known with certainty.

The AR(1) Process

Let us begin with the stationary first-order autoregressive process, AR(1):

$$y_t = \phi_1 y_{t-1} + \delta + \varepsilon_t \tag{16.25}$$

For this process the one-period forecast is

$$\hat{y}_T(1) = E[y_{T+1} | y_T, \dots, y_1]$$

$$= \phi_1 y_T + \delta \tag{16.26}$$

Similarly,
$$\hat{y}_T(2) = \phi_1 \hat{y}_T(1) + \delta$$

$$= \phi_1^2 y_T + (\phi_1 + 1)\delta \tag{16.27}$$

And the *l*-period forecast is

$$\hat{y}_T(l) = \phi_1^l y_T + (\phi_1^{l-1} + \phi_1^{l-2} + \cdots + \phi_1 + 1)\delta \tag{16.28}$$

Note that in the limit as *l* becomes large, the forecast converges to the value

$$\lim_{l \to \infty} \hat{y}_T(l) = \delta \sum_{j=0}^{\infty} \phi_1^j = \frac{\delta}{1 - \phi_1} = \mu_y \tag{16.29}$$

We see, then, that the forecast tends to the mean of the series as *l* becomes large [recall Eq. (14.23) for the mean of the AR(1) process]. Of course this is not surprising, since the series is stationary. As the lead time *l* becomes very large, there is essentially no useful information in recent values of the time series, y_T, y_{T-1}, etc., that can be used to "adjust" the forecast away from the mean value. Thus for a very large lead time the best forecast is the stationary mean of the series.

Let us now calculate the forecast error for this process. The forecast error *l* periods ahead is given by

$$e_T(l) = y_{T+l} - \hat{y}_T(l)$$

$$= \phi_1 y_{T+l-1} + \delta + \varepsilon_{T+l} - \hat{y}_T(l)$$

$$= \phi_1^2 y_{T+l-2} + (\phi_1 + 1)\delta + \varepsilon_{T+l} + \phi_1 \varepsilon_{T+l-1} - \hat{y}_T(l)$$

$$\vdots$$

$$= \phi_1^l y_T + (\phi_1^{l-1} + \phi_1^{l-2} + \cdots + \phi_1 + 1)\delta$$

$$+ \varepsilon_{T+l} + \phi_1 \varepsilon_{T+l-1} + \cdots + \phi_1^{l-1} \varepsilon_{T+1} - \hat{y}_T(l)$$

Now substituting Eq. (16.28) for $\hat{y}_T(l)$, we get

$$e_T(l) = \varepsilon_{T+l} + \phi_1\varepsilon_{T+l-1} + \cdots + \phi_1^{l-1}\varepsilon_{T+1} \qquad (16.30)$$

which has a variance

$$E[e_T^2(l)] = (1 + \phi_1^2 + \phi_1^4 + \cdots + \phi_1^{2l-2})\sigma_\varepsilon^2 \qquad (16.31)$$

Note that this forecast error variance increases (nonlinearly) as l becomes larger.

The MA(1) Process

Now let us examine the simple first-order moving average process, MA(1):

$$y_t = \delta + \varepsilon_t - \theta_1\varepsilon_{t-1} \qquad (16.32)$$

The one-period forecast for this process is

$$\hat{y}_T(1) = E[y_{T+1}|y_T, \ldots, y_1]$$

$$= \delta - \theta_1\hat{\varepsilon}_T \qquad (16.33)$$

where $\hat{\varepsilon}_T$ is the actual residual from the current (and most recent) observation. On the other hand, the l-period forecast, for $l > 1$, is just

$$\hat{y}_T(l) = E[y_{T+l}|y_T, \ldots, y_1] = E[\delta + \varepsilon_{T+l} - \theta_1\varepsilon_{T+l-1}]$$

$$= \delta \qquad (16.34)$$

This is also as expected, since the process MA(1) has a "memory" of only one period. Thus recent data are of no help in making a forecast two or more periods ahead, and the best forecast is the mean of the series, δ.

The variance of the forecast error for MA(1) is σ_ε^2 for the one-period forecast, and for the l-period forecast, $l > 1$, it is given by

$$E[e_T^2(l)] = E\{[y_{T+l} - \hat{y}_T(l)]^2\}$$

$$= E[(\varepsilon_{T+l} - \theta_1\varepsilon_{T+l-1})^2] = (1 + \theta_1^2)\sigma_\varepsilon^2 \qquad (16.35)$$

Thus the forecast error variance is the same for a forecast two periods ahead, three periods ahead, etc. The forecast confidence intervals would appear as shown in Fig. 16.2.

The ARMA(1,1) Process

Let us now calculate and examine the forecasts generated by the simplest mixed autoregressive-moving average process, ARMA(1,1):

$$y_t = \phi_1 y_{t-1} + \delta + \varepsilon_t - \theta_1\varepsilon_{t-1} \qquad (16.36)$$

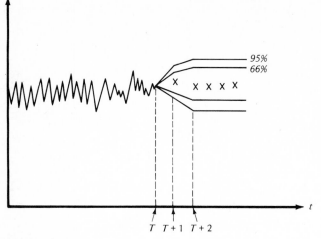

FIGURE 16.2
Forecasts and confidence intervals for an MA(1) process.

The one-period forecast for the ARMA(1,1) model is given by

$$\hat{y}_T(1) = E[\phi_1 y_T + \delta + \varepsilon_{T+1} - \theta_1 \varepsilon_T]$$

$$= \phi_1 y_T + \delta - \theta_1 \hat{\varepsilon}_T \tag{16.37}$$

The two-period forecast is

$$\hat{y}_T(2) = E[\phi_1 y_{T+1} + \delta + \varepsilon_{T+2} - \theta_1 \varepsilon_{T+1}]$$

$$= \phi_1 \hat{y}_T(1) + \delta$$

$$= \phi_1{}^2 y_T + (\phi_1 + 1)\delta - \phi_1 \theta_1 \hat{\varepsilon}_T \tag{16.38}$$

Finally, the l-period forecast is

$$\hat{y}_T(l) = \phi_1 \hat{y}_T(l - 1) + \delta$$

$$= \phi_1{}^l y_T + (\phi_1^{l-1} + \cdots + \phi_1 + 1)\delta - \phi_1^{l-1}\theta_1 \hat{\varepsilon}_T \tag{16.39}$$

Note that the limiting value of the forecast as l becomes large is again the mean of the series:

$$\lim_{l \to \infty} \hat{y}_T(l) = \frac{\delta}{1 - \phi_1} = \mu_y \tag{16.40}$$

Examining these forecasts for different lead times, we see that the current disturbance (i.e., the current measured residual $\hat{\varepsilon}_T$) helps to determine the one-period forecast, and in turn serves as a starting point from which the remainder of the forecast profile, which is autoregressive in character, decays toward the mean $\delta/(1 - \phi_1)$.

The fact that forecasts from ARMA models approach the (constant) mean value of the series as the lead time becomes large indicates an important limitation of these models. As we will see in the examples in this chapter and the next, time-series models are useful largely for short-term forecasting. If one is interested in a long forecasting horizon, then a structural econometric model is likely to be a more useful tool.

The ARI(1,1,0) Process

Now we examine a simple nonstationary process, the integrated autoregressive process ARI(1,1,0):

$$w_t = \phi_1 w_{t-1} + \delta + \varepsilon_t \tag{16.41}$$

with
$$w_t = \Delta y_t = y_t - y_{t-1} \tag{16.42}$$

Forecasts for y_t are related to forecasts of the differenced series w_t as follows:

$$\hat{y}_T(1) = y_T + \hat{w}_T(1) \tag{16.43}$$

and
$$\hat{y}_T(l) = y_T + \hat{w}_T(1) + \cdots + \hat{w}_T(l) \tag{16.44}$$

Since the differenced process w_t is AR(1), its forecasts are given by

$$\hat{w}_T(l) = \phi_1{}^l w_T + (\phi_1^{l-1} + \phi_1^{l-2} + \cdots + \phi_1 + 1)\delta$$
$$= \phi_1{}^l y_T - \phi_1{}^l y_{T-1} + (\phi_1^{l-1} + \cdots + \phi_1 + 1)\delta \tag{16.45}$$

Then the one-period forecast for y_t is

$$\hat{y}_T(1) = y_T + \phi_1(y_T - y_{T-1}) + \delta$$
$$= (1 + \phi_1)y_T - \phi_1 y_{T-1} + \delta \tag{16.46}$$

The two-period forecast for y_t is

$$\hat{y}_T(2) = y_T + \hat{w}_T(1) + \hat{w}_T(2)$$
$$= \hat{y}_T(1) + \hat{w}_T(2)$$
$$= \hat{y}_T(1) + \phi_1{}^2 w_T + (\phi_1 + 1)\delta$$
$$= (1 + \phi_1 + \phi_1{}^2)y_T - (\phi_1 + \phi_1{}^2)y_{T-1} + (\phi_1 + 1)\delta + \delta \tag{16.47}$$

FIGURE 16.3
Hypothetical forecasts for an ARI(1,1,0) process.

A more instructive way to look at this forecast, however, is in terms of its *changes*. Since

$$\hat{w}_T(2) = \phi_1 \hat{w}_T(1) + \delta \tag{16.48}$$

we can write the forecast $\hat{y}_T(2)$ as

$$\hat{y}_T(2) = \hat{y}_T(1) + \phi_1 \hat{w}_T(1) + \delta \tag{16.49}$$

Similarly, $$\hat{y}_T(l) = \hat{y}_T(l-1) + \phi_1 \hat{w}_T(l-1) + \delta \tag{16.50}$$

Now let us examine the properties of this forecast. Since w_t is an AR(1) process, we know from Eq. (16.29) that

$$\lim_{l \to \infty} \hat{w}_T(l) = \frac{\delta}{1 - \phi_1} \tag{16.51}$$

Thus as the forecast horizon l becomes large, the forecast profile approaches a straight line with slope $\delta/(1 - \phi_1)$. In other words, as the horizon becomes large, the forecast becomes dominated by the *deterministic drift* of the process. For a short forecast horizon this would not be so. It might have been the case,

FIGURE 16.4
Adaptive nature of ARI(1,1,0) forecast.

for example, that the last few differences w_T, w_{T-1}, w_{T-2} were negative (i.e., the series had been decreasing in the recent past), although δ was positive so that the series had an overall upward drift. In this case the short-term forecasts $\hat{w}_T(1)$ and $\hat{w}_T(2)$ might be negative, even though $\hat{w}_T(l)$ would tend toward $\delta/(1 - \phi_1)$ as l became larger. The forecasts for y_t, then, would first be decreasing, but then would *change direction*, ultimately approaching a straight line with slope $\delta/(1 - \phi_1)$. This hypothetical ARI(1,1,0) forecast is shown graphically in Fig. 16.3.

One thing that becomes immediately clear about ARIMA forecasts is that they are *adaptive*. As can be seen from Fig. 16.3, the forecast makes use of the most recent data, and "adapts" accordingly. Another example of the adaptive nature of ARIMA forecasts is shown in Fig. 16.4. This process is also ARI(1,1,0), and is identical to the process in Fig. 16.3, for $t \leq T$. The ×'s in Fig. 16.4 represent the forecasts made at time T. Now suppose that the series *increases* in periods $T + 1$, $T + 2$, and $T + 3$, and a *new* set of forecasts is made in period $T + 3$. These forecasts are denoted by ○'s, and as can be seen in Fig. 16.4, they first *increase* and then *decrease*. Ultimately they will also approach a drift line. This new drift line will have the same slope as before, but will be slightly higher as a result of the new data points. What we observe, then, is that the forecast has "adapted" to the new data that became available in periods $T + 1$, $T + 2$, and $T + 3$. Notice that the values of this forecast for a long lead time have adapted as well.

Confidence Intervals for the ARI(1,1,0) Forecast

We now calculate the forecast error and its variance for the ARI(1,1,0) process, so that we may obtain a forecast confidence interval. As we will see, the forecast confidence interval for y_t is related to the forecast confidence interval for the differenced series, w_t.

We begin with the forecast error for the one-period forecast, $y_T(1)$:

$$e_T(1) = y_{T+1} - \hat{y}_T(1)$$

$$= y_T + w_{T+1} - y_T - \hat{w}_T(1)$$

$$= w_{T+1} - \hat{w}_T(1) = \varepsilon_{T+1} \tag{16.52}$$

which has a variance σ_ε^2. The two-period forecast error is given by

$$e_T(2) = y_{T+2} - \hat{y}_T(2)$$

$$= y_T + w_{T+1} + w_{T+2} - y_T - \hat{w}_T(1) - \hat{w}_T(2)$$

$$= [w_{T+1} - \hat{w}_T(1)] + [w_{T+2} - \hat{w}_T(2)]$$

$$= (1 + \phi_1)\varepsilon_{T+1} + \varepsilon_{T+2} \tag{16.53}$$

and this has a variance

$$E[e_T{}^2(2)] = \sigma_\varepsilon^2[(1 + \phi_1)^2 + 1] \tag{16.54}$$

Note that this forecast error (and its variance) is "cumulative"; i.e., it is equal to the two-period error for $\hat{w}_T(2)$ in *addition* to the one-period error for $\hat{w}_T(1)$. Thus the error in $\hat{y}_T(2)$ is an *accumulation* of the errors in $\hat{w}_T(1)$ and in $\hat{w}_T(2)$. Now observe this cumulative phenomenon in the *l*-period forecast:

$$e_T(l) = [w_{T+1} - \hat{w}_T(1)] + [w_{T+2} - \hat{w}_T(2)] + \cdots + [w_{T+l} - \hat{w}_T(l)]$$

$$= \varepsilon_{T+1} + (\varepsilon_{T+2} + \phi_1\varepsilon_{T+1}) + \cdots + (\varepsilon_{T+l} + \phi_1\varepsilon_{T+l-1} + \cdots + \phi_1^{l-1}\varepsilon_{T+1})$$

$$= (1 + \phi_1 + \phi_1^2 + \cdots + \phi_1^{l-1})\varepsilon_{T+1} + (1 + \phi_1 + \cdots + \phi_1^{l-2})\varepsilon_{T+2}$$

$$+ \cdots + (1 + \phi_1)\varepsilon_{T+l-1} + \varepsilon_{T+l}$$

$$= \sum_{i=1}^{l} \varepsilon_{T+i} \sum_{j=0}^{l-i} \phi_1{}^j \tag{16.55}$$

FIGURE 16.5
Confidence interval for $\hat{w}_T(l)$ for ARI(1,1,0) process.

and this has a variance

$$E[e_T{}^2(l)] = \sigma_\varepsilon{}^2 \sum_{i=1}^{l} \left(\sum_{j=0}^{l-i} \phi_1{}^j \right)^2 \tag{16.56}$$

Thus the error in $\hat{y}_T(l)$ is an accumulation of errors in $\hat{w}_T(1)$, $\hat{w}_T(2)$, ..., $\hat{w}_T(l)$. This can be seen graphically in Figs. 16.5 and 16.6, which compare confidence intervals for forecasts of the differenced series w_t with confidence intervals for forecasts of y_t. Note the relationship between the forecasts of the differenced series w_t and the forecasts of y_t. w_{T-2} and w_{T-1} are decreasing, and w_T is negative, so that $\hat{w}_T(1)$ and $\hat{w}_T(2)$ are also negative [$\hat{y}_T(1)$ and $\hat{y}_T(2)$ are decreasing], $\hat{w}_T(3)$, $\hat{w}_T(4)$, etc., are positive [$\hat{y}_T(3)$ is larger than $\hat{y}_T(2)$], and finally $\hat{w}_T(l)$ approaches the mean $\delta/(1 - \phi_1)$ as l becomes large [so that $\hat{y}_T(l)$ approaches the drift line]. Observe that the confidence interval for $\hat{y}_T(l)$ grows rapidly, since it must account for the accumulation of forecast errors in the differenced series.

We have examined some of the properties of the forecasts of only the simplest of ARIMA models, but some of our conclusions apply to more complicated (i.e., higher-order) ARIMA models. In particular we should observe that a moving average model of order q has a "memory" of only q periods, so that the observed data will affect the forecast only if the lead time l is less than q. An autoregressive model has a memory of infinite length, so that all past observations will have some effect on the forecast, even if the lead time l is long. But although all past observations have *some* effect on the forecast, only more recent observations will have a large effect. Thus even with autoregressive (or mixed autoregressive-moving average) models, past observations have little effect on the forecast if the lead time is long. The conclusion, then, is that ARIMA models are best suited to *short-term forecasting*, i.e., forecasting with a lead time l not much longer than $p + q$.

y_t

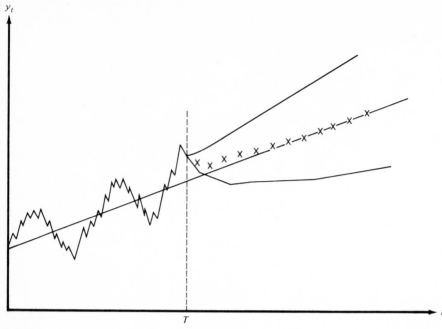

FIGURE 16.6
Confidence interval for $\hat{y}_T(l)$ for ARI(1,1,0) process.

16.6 TWO EXAMPLES

In the last chapter we estimated ARIMA models for two time series; we found that the first series, which consisted of quarterly data for the interest rate on 4–6 month commercial paper, could be represented using an ARIMA(4,2,2) model. The estimated version of that model is

$$(1 - .1675B + .1867B^2 + .0915B^3 - .2100B^4)\,\Delta^2 y_t$$

$$= -.0008 + (1 - .3627B - .6372B^2)\varepsilon_t \qquad (15.34)$$

The second time series consisted of data on monthly hog production in the United States, which we represented by applying an ARIMA(3,1,0) model to a twelfth-differencing of the original series. The estimated version of that model is

$$(1 + .6681B + .2015B^2 - .1298B^3)(1 - B)(1 - B^{12})y_t = .0014 + \varepsilon_t \qquad (15.35)$$

Recall that the twelfth-differencing $(1 - B^{12})$ accounts for seasonal (annual) cycles in the data. We now generate forecasts of the interest rate and hog production using these two ARIMA models.

Example 16.1   Interest Rate Forecast

Recall that the ARIMA model for the interest rate was estimated using data that ran through the second quarter of 1972. In this example we generate two *ex post* forecasts that cover the end of the estimation period. The forecasts are presented in terms of the twice-differenced stationary series, and compared with the actual data.

A 10-period *ex post* forecast (from 1970–1 to 1972–2) is shown in Figs. 16.7 and 16.8, a 6-period forecast (1971–1 to 1972–2) is shown in Figs. 16.9 and 16.10, and a 7-period forecast that begins in 1972–2 and ends in 1973–4 is shown in Figs. 16.11 and 16.12. Note that in all these figures we are examining a series that has been differenced twice; i.e., we are examining a forecast of the second-difference of the interest rate variable, rather than the level of the variable itself.

An evaluation of the model's forecast is somewhat difficult because the period over which we have forecasted was one of considerable fluctuation in interest rates. What we do see, however, is that the ARIMA model captures trends, but fails to predict sharp turns. This is characteristic of forecasts generated by time-series models. Nonetheless, the usefulness of this particular ARIMA model as a forecasting tool can be seriously evaluated only in comparison with other available forecasting tools. In the case of a short-term interest rate, particularly during a period when interest rates were fluctuating considerably, one might

FIGURE 16.7
ARIMA(4,2,2)—Ten-period forecast of interest rate.

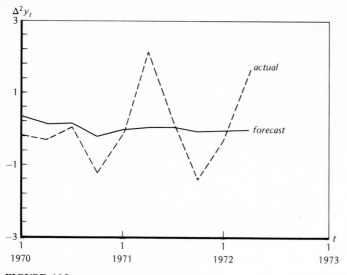

FIGURE 16.8
ARIMA(4,2,2)—Ten-period forecast (enlarged).

FIGURE 16.9
ARIMA(4,2,2)—Six-period forecast of interest rate.

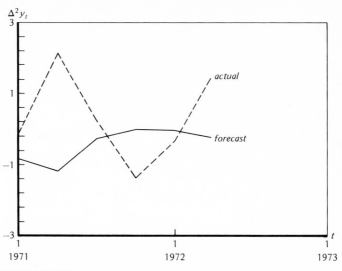

FIGURE 16.10
ARIMA(4,2,2)—Six-period forecast (enlarged).

FIGURE 16.11
ARIMA(4,2,2)—Forecast to end of 1973 of interest rate.

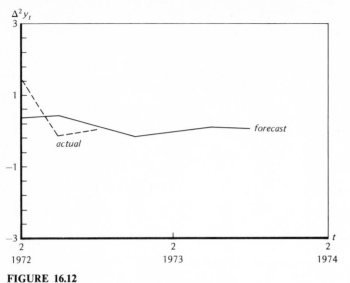

FIGURE 16.12
ARIMA(4,2,2)—Forecast to end of 1973 (enlarged).

expect a structural regression model to show a better forecasting performance than a time-series model. (In the next chapter we will demonstrate how a time-series model can be combined with a regression model to improve the forecast of interest rates.)

Example 16.2   Hog Production Forecast

Recall that the ARIMA model for hog production in Eq. (15.35) was estimated using data from the beginning of 1960 to the end of 1967. We generate our forecast out over a 2-year horizon, beginning in January 1968 and ending in January 1970. Since data on hog production are available for this period, we can compare the 25 months of forecasted production with the actual data.

The forecasted and actual series for hog production are shown in Fig. 16.13. The reader can observe that our model has generated forecasts which are quite accurate. The model not only correctly forecasts changing trends in the series, but also picks up the broad seasonal cycle (as it should, since the model includes a twelfth-difference of the series to explain seasonality). Usually the forecast is within 10 or 15 percent of the actual series, and reproduces most of the turning points in the actual series. This model would be quite acceptable as a forecasting tool. Unlike our interest rate example, hog production can probably be forecasted better using a time-series model than by using a single-equation regression model. The reason for this is that the economics of hog production are rather complicated, and cannot be represented easily by a single

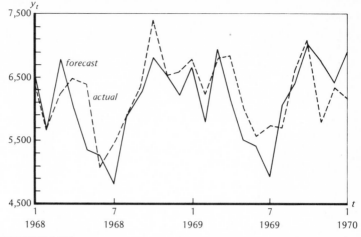

FIGURE 16.13
Two-year (25-month) forecast of hog production. Time bounds: January 1968 to January 1970.

structural equation. Although hog production could probably be modeled rather well by a multi-equation simulation model, constructing such a model would probably be rather difficult and time-consuming. The time-series model, on the other hand, can be constructed easily and quickly, and does a reasonable job of forecasting.

In the next chapter we will look at some other examples of time-series models as applied to problems in economic and business forecasting. In each case we will go through the complete process of specifying, estimating, and checking an ARIMA model, and will then use the model to produce forecasts. Hopefully, this will provide the reader with more of a "feeling" for the properties and characteristics of time-series models and forecasts.

Exercises

16.1 Write the equation that determines the forecast $\hat{y}_T(l)$ in terms of $\hat{w}_T(1)$, $\hat{w}_T(2)$, ..., for a third-order homogeneous nonstationary process; i.e., derive the equivalent of Eq. (16.18) for an ARIMA model with $d = 3$.

16.2 Does it seem reasonable that for any ARIMA specification the forecast error variance one period ahead is always the variance of the error term? Offer an intuitive explanation for why Eq. (16.22) must always hold.

16.3 Derive expressions for the one-period, two-period, and three-period forecasts, $\hat{y}_T(1)$, $\hat{y}_T(2)$, and $\hat{y}_T(3)$, for the second-order moving average process MA(2). What are the variances of the errors for these forecasts? What is the variance of the error for the l-period forecast, with $l > 3$?

16.4 Derive expressions for the one-period, two-period, and three-period forecasts for the second-order autoregressive process AR(2). What are the error variances of these forecasts?

16.5 Repeat Exercise 16.4 for the ARMA(2,1) process.

16.6 Suppose that a particular nonstationary time series y_t can be modeled as a stochastic process that is ARIMA(1,1,1).

(1) How would you calculate the autocorrelation functions for y_t and its differences and use them to verify that ARIMA(1,1,1) is a proper specification for y_t?

(2) How would you estimate the parameters of this ARIMA model?

(3) Once you have estimated the model's parameters, how would you forecast y_t one period ahead? Express this one-period forecast, $\hat{y}_t(1)$, as a function of observable data. In what sense is this forecast "adaptive"?

(4) How would you calculate the standard error of the one-period forecast $\hat{y}_t(1)$ *assuming that the parameters of the model are known perfectly*? Note that this is analogous to calculating the standard error of a regression forecast under the assumption that the coefficients β are known perfectly.

(5) What will be the *difference* between the l-period forecast $\hat{y}_t(l)$ and the $(l + 1)$-period forecast $\hat{y}_t(l + 1)$ *when l is very large*?

17

EXAMPLES OF TIME-SERIES APPLICATIONS

In this chapter we construct some simple time-series models for economic variables and examine their properties. We hope to demonstrate, through examples, how an analyst can decide what specification to use for a time-series model, how to estimate the model, and finally how to check the model and use it for forecasting. In addition, we would like to acquaint the reader with the usefulness of time-series models in applied forecasting problems. We will see that time-series models can be used in forecasting applications not only by themselves, but also in combination with regression models.

We have seen that econometric model building is as much an art as it is a science. Even when constructing a simple single-equation econometric model, one must make judgments as to which explanatory variables should and should not be included, how the statistical fit of the model should be interpreted, and how useful the resulting model is for forecasting or explanation purposes. In building a regression model for predicting interest rates, for example, there might be many explanatory variables (with and without time lags) that could be justified on theoretical grounds and thus included in the model. The analyst must decide which of those variables to include, and there are usually no well-defined rules for doing so. Also, the evaluation of the model's predictive performance is not straightforward. One can calculate confidence intervals for predictions of the dependent variable based on the assumption that the independent variables will be known with certainty, but these confidence intervals assume that the structural relationship will be stable over the forecasting period. Since this may not be the case, the analyst must make a judgment as to the applicability of the model to forecasting.

The situation is very much the same with time-series models. It is usually not obvious what the proper specification for an ARIMA model should be. For example, if one looks at the autocorrelation functions for a short-term interest rate and its differences, it may not be clear whether the model should be ARIMA(4,0,2), ARIMA(2,2,2), or some other specification. In general, many different specifications might be reasonable for a single time series and its autocorrelation function, so that sound judgment must be used. As in the regression case, one will often specify and estimate more than one ARIMA model, and check each of them individually. In general, the usefulness of an ARIMA model for forecasting purposes is difficult to ascertain. While confidence intervals can be determined for the model's forecasts, one must still decide whether any significant structural change in the determination of the variable under study might occur, and thus alter the future movement of the time series.

In this chapter we consider the application of time-series analysis to several forecasting problems. We begin with a model for an aggregate economic variable, nonfarm inventory investment, and then turn to a model for forecasting seasonal telephone data. One might argue that inventory investment can be better explained by a structural econometric model, but such a model can be difficult and time-consuming to build. The seasonal telephone data that we examine are cyclical, highly fluctuating, and difficult to explain using a structural econometric model, so that a time-series model provides a natural vehicle for forecasting.

As a final application, we show in two examples how it is possible to combine a time-series model with a structural econometric model. To do so, we first construct a regression model, and then develop a time-series model for the regression residuals (i.e., for the unexplained noise terms). If used with proper care, the combined regression-time-series model can provide an extremely effective forecasting tool.

17.1   REVIEW OF THE MODELING PROCESS

Let us briefly review the steps that one takes in constructing, evaluating, and using time-series models. One begins with the *specification* of the model. This involves a decision as to the degree of homogeneity in the time series, i.e., how many times the time series must be differenced before a stationary series results. The decision is made by looking at the autocorrelation functions for the time series and its differences. (We have seen, however, that the correct degree of homogeneity is not always obvious.) After the degree of homogeneity has been specified, the orders of the moving average and the autoregressive parts of the model must be determined. In other words, values for p and q must be chosen for the ARMA model that will be used to represent the differenced series.

Once a model (or a group of models) has been specified, it must then be *estimated*. If the number of observations in the time series is large relative to the order of the model, then this estimation process involves a straightforward nonlinear regression. In such cases, the initialization of the time series can be ignored when performing the estimation.

After the model has been estimated, one must then perform a *diagnostic check* on it. This usually involves looking at the autocorrelation function of the residuals from the estimated model (i.e., the series determined by subtracting the actual series from the estimated series). A simple chi-square test can be performed to determine whether or not the residuals are themselves uncorrelated.

If the model passes the diagnostic check, it must then be *evaluated*. The model may pass a diagnostic check but have a very poor statistical fit, and this would seriously limit its usefulness for forecasting. If the model's estimated parameters have large standard errors, then the standard error of forecast will be increased. Unfortunately, the evaluation of the model is complicated by the fact that a nonlinear estimation has been performed. As a result the standard statistics of fit (i.e., R^2, t statistics, etc.) have meaning only in the context of the last linearization in the iterative estimation process. Nonetheless, even if a model passes a diagnostic check on its residuals, an R^2 near 0 would indicate that the model is of very limited use for forecasting purposes. A useful rule of thumb is to drop from the equation those terms whose coefficients have t statistics that are small (e.g., below 1). Often, one might want to respecify and reestimate a model, with the hope that the new version will also pass the diagnostic check, while yielding a better statistical fit.

After the model has been both checked and evaluated, it should be *analyzed*. The analysis of the model should be made so as to provide a better understanding of its forecasting properties. One method of analysis is to perform an *historical simulation* of the model beginning at different points in time, i.e., to simulate the model over the historic time period, but beginning at different instants of time. In addition, one can perform an *ex post forecast*, comparing the forecast to actual data to evaluate its performance. The analysis of the model can help the researcher decide how far into the future the model can be used for forecasting. This is extremely important, particularly if a time-series model is to be used in conjunction with a structural econometric model. Typically, the time-series model will provide a better forecast over the very short term, but the structural econometric model will provide a better forecast over the longer term.

17.2 MODELS OF ECONOMIC VARIABLES—INVENTORY INVESTMENT

In this section we construct and examine some time-series models for the level of nonfarm inventory investment. This variable is difficult to explain and forecast using structural econometric models, so that the construction of an ARIMA model seems appropriate.

We construct our models using quarterly data beginning in 1946 and ending

FIGURE 17.1
Nonfarm inventory investment.

in the second quarter of 1972. The time series is shown in Fig. 17.1, and its sample autocorrelation function is shown in Fig. 17.2. Note that the time series seems stationary, since there are no long-run trends either upward or downward. The autocorrelation function also exhibits (at least roughly) the properties of a stationary series. Its highest value (for a nonzero displacement lag) is .7 (at $k = 1$), and after a displacement lag of three or four it quickly goes down to values that are between $\pm.2$.

Before deciding on a stationary specification for the model, we choose to difference the time series and examine the autocorrelation functions of the

FIGURE 17.2
Nonfarm inventory investment—sample autocorrelation function.

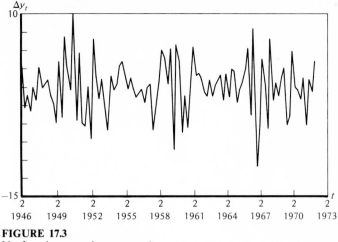

FIGURE 17.3
Nonfarm inventory investment: Δy_t.

series that result. A first-difference of the series is shown in Fig. 17.3, and the corresponding autocorrelation function is shown in Fig. 17.4. Note that the autocorrelation function drops immediately to a value of $-.5$, and then oscillates, without any apparent damping, between values of $\pm.3$. The autocorrelation function has few clear-cut patterns, making it difficult to specify an ARIMA model.

The time series is differenced a second time, and the resulting series and its autocorrelation function are shown in Figs. 17.5 and 17.6. This autocorrelation function also lacks definitive qualities that would make an ARIMA specification

FIGURE 17.4
Nonfarm inventory investment: autocorrelation function of Δy_t.

FIGURE 17.5
Nonfarm inventory investment: $\Delta^2 y_t$.

possible, and exhibits no more stationarity than does the autocorrelation function for the undifferenced series in Fig. 17.2. It would probably be most logical to assume that our time series is stationary, i.e., to use a value of $d = 0$ in our ARIMA model. We do this, but for purposes of comparison we also specify and estimate one or two models using a value of $d = 2$ (i.e., differencing the series twice).

Let us begin with a stationary specification. Looking at the autocorrelation function in Fig. 17.2 closely, we see that it begins to decay exponentially after about two or three displacement lags. It would thus be reasonable to specify

FIGURE 17.6
Nonfarm inventory investment: autocorrelation function of $\Delta^2 y_t$.

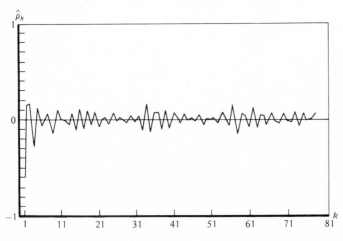

the moving average portion of the model as second order. The autoregressive portion of the model is somewhat more difficult to specify, since the autocorrelation function seems to exhibit oscillations with a period of about eight lags. Since these oscillations are somewhat damped, we might ignore them and specify the autoregressive portion of the model as first or second order. On the other hand, we could take them into account using a fourth-order autoregressive specification (which could have generated the observed oscillations). A fourth-order autoregressive specification would also be reasonable, since it would help account for any annual cycles in the original time series. Thus, there are at least three specifications that could be candidates for our ARIMA model: (1,0,2), (2,0,2), and (4,0,2). We estimate all three models and then compare them.

Upon reexamining the autocorrelation function in Fig. 17.6 for the twice-differenced series, we note that the autocorrelation function is a damped sinusoid after the second displacement lag. Thus, it appears that a moving average specification of second order would be appropriate. The autoregressive portion of the model could be specified as either second or fourth order; to be complete, we will estimate ARIMA models that are (2,2,2) and (4,2,2).

All five ARIMA models were estimated, with the results as shown in Eqs. (17.1) to (17.5) below. In each equation, the R^2 is shown, but its usefulness is limited because of the nature of the estimation process. After each model was estimated, a residual series was formed by subtracting the series predicted by the model from the actual time series. An autocorrelation function was then calculated for the residual series, after which a chi-square statistic was determined [see Eq. (15.40)] from the first 20 values of the autocorrelation function. The results are as follows:

ARIMA(1,0,2)

$$(1 - .6330B)y_t = 1.6055 + (1 - .0677B + .2880B^2)\varepsilon_t \qquad (17.1)$$

$$R^2 = .399 \qquad \chi^2(3,20) = 14.77$$

ARIMA(2,0,2)

$$(1 - .8824B + .2686B^2)y_t = 1.685 + (1 - .3015B + .4280B^2)\varepsilon_t \qquad (17.2)$$

$$R^2 = .519 \qquad \chi^2(4,20) = 14.01$$

ARIMA(4,0,2)

$$(1 - .2622B - .2554B^2 - .1991B^3 + .2473B^4)y_t$$

$$= 2.333 + (1 + .3632B + .1822B^2)\varepsilon_t \qquad (17.3)$$

$$R^2 = .236 \qquad \chi^2(6,20) = 13.97$$

ARIMA(2,2,2)

$$(1 + .8938B + .2603B^2)\Delta^2 y_t = -.0175 + (1 - .380B - .620B^2)\varepsilon_t \quad (17.4)$$

$$R^2 = .523 \qquad \chi^2(4,20) = 24.55$$

ARIMA(4,2,2)

$$(1 + .7478B + .1695B^2 + .0317B^3 + .1848B^4)\Delta^2 y_t$$

$$= -.0166 + (1 - .480B - .520B^2)\varepsilon_t \quad (17.5)$$

$$R^2 = .459 \qquad \chi^2(6,20) = 22.38$$

Remember that the chi-square test is a test of the hypothesis that the residuals are not white noise, i.e., that they are correlated with each other. Since the statistic is a measure of correlation among the residuals, we would expect (if the model is correctly specified) it to be as small as possible. Based on this chi-square test alone, we may eliminate the two models (2,2,2) and (4,2,2). Consider, for example, the ARIMA(4,2,2) model. The chi-square statistic has 14 degrees of freedom (20 lags minus 6 estimated parameters) and a value of 22.38, falling above the 10 percent point (21.1) on the distribution (so that the probability that the residuals are not white noise is 90 percent). On the other hand, all three stationary ARIMA models have chi-square statistics that are low enough to fall at about the 50 percent point on the distribution. Thus, we were correct in our initial hypothesis that a stationary specification would have been most appropriate for the model.

FIGURE 17.7
ARIMA(4,0,2) model—residual series.

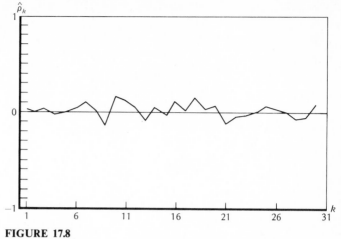

FIGURE 17.8
Autocorrelation function of ARIMA(4,0,2) residuals.

For purposes of comparison, we retain the ARIMA(2,0,2) and the ARIMA(4,0,2) models, and examine their forecasting properties. The residual series for the ARIMA(4,0,2) model and the autocorrelation function of the residuals are shown in Figs. 17.7 and 17.8. The reader can observe that the autocorrelation function has small values for most displacement lags, and no prominent peaks that would suggest the addition of more autoregressive or moving average terms. We have used this ARIMA(4,0,2) model to produce a 10-period forecast, beginning in the first quarter of 1970 and ending in the

FIGURE 17.9
ARIMA(4,0,2)—Ten-period forecast.

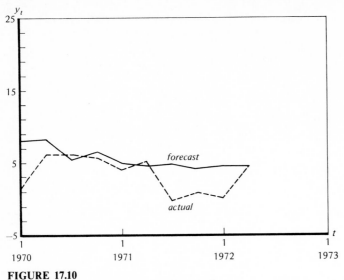

FIGURE 17.10
ARIMA(4,0,2)—Ten-period forecast (enlarged).

second quarter of 1972. The forecasted series is shown (in comparison with the actual series) in Figs. 17.9 and 17.10. Note that the ARIMA model predicted that the level of inventory investment in the first quarter of 1970 would be close to its mean value, thus failing to predict the sharp downturn in inventory investment that occurred in that period. The model does, however, predict a

FIGURE 17.11
ARIMA(4,0,2)—Six-period forecast.

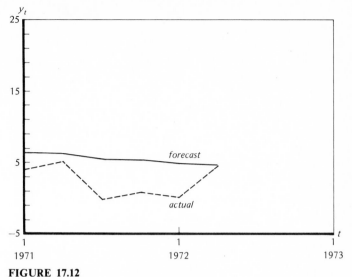

FIGURE 17.12
ARIMA(4,0,2)—Six-period forecast (enlarged).

gradual decline over the entire 10 periods. The forecast is rather close to the actual performance of inventory investment during the last three quarters of 1970 and the first two quarters of 1971, but it fails to predict the sharp drop in inventory investment during the last two quarters of 1971 and the first quarter of 1972.

Would the model have predicted the downturn in inventory investment during the second half of 1971 if we had begun the forecast at a later date? To answer this question, let us examine the six-period forecast that begins in the first quarter of 1971 and ends in the second quarter of 1972. This forecast is shown in Figs. 17.11 and 17.12. What we find is that the six-period forecast is not very different from the 10-period forecast; i.e., it also predicts a gradual decline in inventory investment, but fails to predict the sharp downturn that actually occurred. This is not very surprising, since the original model was specified in an attempt to capture the overall trends and cycles in the original time series. Thus we should expect its predictive power to be limited largely to overall trends and cycles. (Had the inventory downturn at the end of 1971 been cyclical—which it was not—the time-series model probably would have captured it.)

A seven-period forecast, beginning in the second quarter of 1972 and ending in the fourth quarter of 1973, is shown in Figs. 17.13 and 17.14. Data on the actual time series were available only through the fourth quarter of 1972, but this is sufficient to allow us to observe again that the ARIMA forecast only replicates overall trends in the series, and thus fails to predict the upturn in inventory investment that took place at the end of 1972.

FIGURE 17.13
ARIMA(4,0,2)—Forecast to 1974.

For comparison, forecasts were also produced using the ARIMA(2,0,2) model: 10-period forecasts (1970–1 to 1972–2) are shown in Figs. 17.15 and 17.16; 6-period forecasts (1971–1 to 1972–2) are shown in Figs. 17.17 and 17.18; and 7-period forecasts running through the end of 1973 are shown in Figs. 17.19 and 17.20. We observe that the ARIMA(2,0,2) model is a better predictor in the short term (two or three periods), but less able to predict longer-run trends.

FIGURE 17.14
ARIMA(4,0,2)—Forecast to 1974 (enlarged).

FIGURE 17.15
ARIMA(2,0,2)—Ten-period forecast.

The 10-period ARIMA(2,0,2) forecast does, for example, predict the sharp downturn in the beginning of 1970, but its predictive power after the second quarter of 1970 is no better than that of the ARIMA(4,0,2) model [although its overall performance over 10 periods is slightly better—the root-mean-square forecast error is 2.25 versus 2.43 for the (4,0,2) model].[1]

FIGURE 17.16
ARIMA(2,0,2)—Ten-period forecast (enlarged).

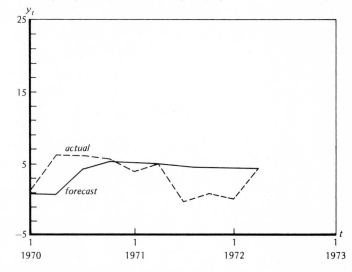

---

[1] The root-mean-square error is defined and explained in Chapter 10.

FIGURE 17.17
ARIMA(2,0,2)—Six-period forecast.

FIGURE 17.18
ARIMA(2,0,2)—Six-period forecast (enlarged).

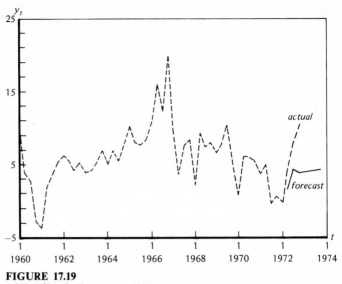

FIGURE 17.19
ARIMA(2,0,2)—forecast to 1974.

FIGURE 17.20
ARIMA(2,0,2)—forecast to 1974 (enlarged).

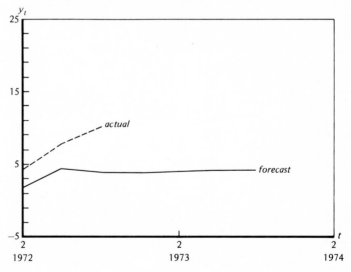

Would the ARIMA(2,0,2) model be a better choice for actual use in forecasting? The answer to this question would probably be yes, particularly if the model were going to be used for short-term forecasts (i.e., two or three periods). The decision as to which model should be used would be made by comparing the forecasting performance of both models over recent years. If the reader if fact makes this comparison, he/she would probably choose the (2,0,2) model, at least for short-term forecasting purposes.

The inability of both our ARIMA models to predict sharp downturns and upturns in inventory investment limits their value for forecasting. But before they are discarded as forecasting tools, they must be compared with alternative forecasting tools that are available. Many single-equation and multi-equation regression models have been constructed to forecast inventory investment, some with a performance not much better than that of our simple ARIMA model. Because inventory investment is dependent on several other macroeconomic variables—which are themselves dependent on inventory investment—it can probably best be explained and forecasted using a complete simultaneous equation macroeconometric model. Such a model, however, is time-consuming and costly to build, so that a time-series model might provide an economical forecasting alternative.[2]

17.3   FORECASTING SEASONAL TELEPHONE DATA

A recent article by H. E. Thompson and G. C. Tiao provides an interesting case study for the application of time-series analysis.[3] In the study forecasting models were constructed for the inward and outward station movements of the Wisconsin Telephone Company using monthly data from January 1951 to October 1966. The inward station movement in a given month is the sum of residence and business telephone installations, while the outward station movement consists of removals and disconnects of telephones. The problem of obtaining forecasts of station movements is rather important to the telephone industry, since these forecasts are used as fundamental inputs to both short- and long-term company planning. The difference between inward and outward station movements represents the net increase (or decrease) of telephones in

---

[2] There have been several studies made recently of time-series models as a forecasting alternative to large-scale econometric models of the macroeconomy. The more interesting and illuminating studies include C. R. Nelson, "The Prediction Performance of the FRB-MIT-PENN Model of the U.S. Economy," *American Economic Review*, vol. 62, December 1972; and T. H. Naylor, T. G. Seaks, and D. W. Wichern, "Box-Jenkins Methods: An Alternative to Econometric Models," *International Statistical Review*, vol. 40, no. 2, 1972. In both these studies the authors found that time-series models can often provide better forecasts of macroeconomic variables than do some of the better-known large econometric models. It is hard to say whether this should be taken as a compliment to time-series analysis, or a comment on the state of the art of macroeconometric modeling! A more detailed discussion (including examples) of the use of time-series models for macroeconomic forecasting is given in C. R. Nelson, *Applied Time Series Analysis* (San Francisco: Holden-Day, 1973).

[3] H. E. Thompson and G. C. Tiao, "Analysis of Telephone Data: A Case Study of Forecasting Seasonal Time Series," *Bell Journal of Economics and Management Science*, vol. 2, no. 2, Autumn 1971.

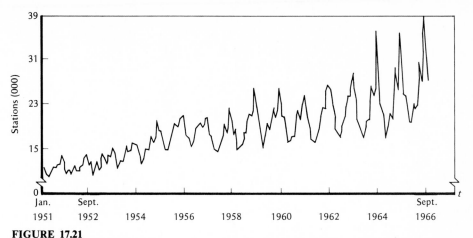

FIGURE 17.21
Monthly inward station movements, January 1951 to October 1966. (*Source: Bell Journal of Economics and Management Science.*)

service, so that an expected positive difference would lead to a sequence of capital expenditures. Underestimating the difference might create a shortage in the supply of telephones and associated facilities, while overestimating it would result in a premature expansion of facilities and thus added cost to the company.

The data used by Thompson and Tiao for inward and outward station movements are shown in Figs. 17.21 and 17.22. The data show a very distinct seasonal pattern, with a peak and a trough reached each year. Note that the level of each series tends to increase over time, and that the variance of the data tends to increase as the level increases. In order to reduce this dependence of the variance on the level, the authors applied a logarithmic transformation to both series. Thus, the analysis that follows is given in terms of transformed log data. (Logarithmic transformations are often used in time-series analysis as a means of removing growth over time of the variance of the data.)

The methodology for time-series analysis can easily be applied to seasonal series. In fact we treated seasonality earlier when we constructed a time-series model for hog production.[4] It is reasonable to expect a seasonal pattern in station movements, i.e., similarities in observations of the same month in different years. Thus, we would expect observations 12 periods apart to be highly correlated (as was the case in our hog production example). We can express this seasonal relationship with the simple autoregressive model

$$(1 - \phi^* B^{12})y_t = e_t \tag{17.6}$$

---

[4] For a detailed treatment of seasonal time-series models, see G. E. P. Box, G. M. Jenkins, and D. W. Bacon, "Models for Forecasting Seasonal and Non-Seasonal Time Series," in *Spectral Analysis of Time Series* (New York: Wiley, 1967), and C. R. Nelson, *Applied Time Series Analysis* (San Francisco: Holden-Day, 1973), chap. 7.

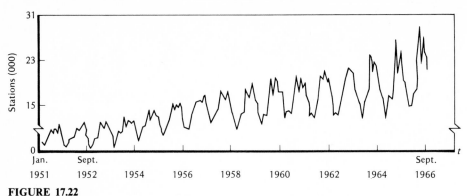

FIGURE 17.22
Monthly outward station movements, January 1951 to October 1966 (y_t). (*Source: Bell Journal of Economics and Management Science.*)

where e_t is a random shock. While this equation explains observations "between years," observations in successive months may also be dependent. This dependence might be represented by a second autoregressive model:

$$(1 - \phi B)e_t = \varepsilon_t \tag{17.7}$$

where ε_t is a random shock. Equation (17.6) can be substituted into (17.7) to eliminate e_t:

$$(1 - \phi^* B^{12})(1 - \phi B)y_t = \varepsilon_t \tag{17.8}$$

or $$y_t - \phi y_{t-1} - \phi^* y_{t-12} + \phi\phi^* y_{t-13} = \varepsilon_t \tag{17.9}$$

Equation (17.9) is a simple autoregressive model. It serves to describe, however, both seasonal and nonseasonal dependence between observations.[5]

In this case study we present Thompson and Tiao's model of the log outward series. The reader interested in the rest of their results may refer to the original paper. Our purpose is simply to demonstrate how a seasonal time-series model might be constructed.

We represent the logarithm of monthly outward station movements by the variable y_t. The sample autocorrelation function of y_t is shown in Fig. 17.23.

---

[5] This equation can be generalized to yield a class of models for seasonal series:

$$\phi_{p_1}^*(B^{12})\phi_p(B)(1 - B^{12})^{d_1}(1 - B)^d(y_t - \mu) = \theta_q(B)\varepsilon_t$$

where $\phi_{p_1}^*(B^{12})$ is a polynomial in B^{12} of order p_1, and $\phi_p(B)$ is a polynomial of order p. The parameters $\phi_1^*, \ldots, \phi_{p_1}^*$ can be called seasonal autoregressive parameters. In the preliminary model-building stage, particular attention is given to peaks in the sample autocorrelation functions which occur at multiples of 12 lags. Generally, differencing 12 periods apart (one or more times) is needed when ρ_k is persistently large for $k = 12, 24, 36, \ldots$.

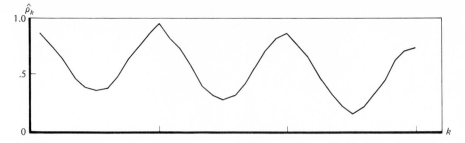

FIGURE 17.23
Sample autocorrelation function of y_t. (*Source: Bell Journal of Economics and Management Science.*)

Note that this autocorrelation function peaks at $k = 12$, 24, and 36, which is not surprising in view of the seasonal pattern in the data. We thus calculate 12-period differences in the series, and call this new series w_t:

$$w_t = (1 - B^{12})y_t \tag{17.10}$$

The sample autocorrelation function for w_t is shown in Fig. 17.24. Note that the seasonal dependence between years has been removed, and the magnitude of the autocorrelations has been dampened considerably. Also, note that this autocorrelation function has peaks at every third lag, thus suggesting the autoregressive model[6]

$$(1 - \phi_3 B^3)w_t = \varepsilon_t \tag{17.11}$$

FIGURE 17.24
Sample autocorrelation function for w_t. (*Source: Bell Journal of Economics and Management Science.*)

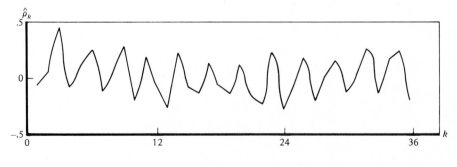

---

[6] Cycles every third period could also be generated by a second-order autoregressive model (with the proper parameter values). The authors may have tested a second-order model and found Eq. (17.11) to be preferable. In general, however, if a distinct peak occurs in the autocorrelation function at every nth lag, we suggest including an nth-order autoregressive term in the specification of the ARIMA model.

FIGURE 17.25
Forecasts of log outward series for the 36 months, November 1966 to October 1969, made in
October 1966. (*Source: Bell Journal of Economics and Management Science.*)

Thompson and Tiao fitted a third-order autoregressive model to the series w_t,
and then calculated the autocorrelation function for the residuals of this model.
They found peaks at $k = 9$, 12, and 13, suggesting the addition of three moving
average parameters. Thus, their final ARIMA model for y_t was of the form

$$(1 - \phi_3 B^3)(1 - \phi_{12} B^{12})y_t = (1 - \theta_9 B^9 - \theta_{12} B^{12} - \theta_{13} B^{13})\varepsilon_t \quad (17.12)$$

The five parameters ϕ_3, ϕ_{12}, θ_9, θ_{12}, and θ_{13} were estimated, and the resulting
model was used to forecast the log outward series for the 36 months from
November 1966 to October 1969. The forecast, together with the 95 percent
confidence interval, is shown in Fig. 17.25.

Note that the model does a rather good job of forecasting outward station
movements, even over a period of 36 months. In fact, the model seems to
perform considerably better than did our models of the level of inventory investment. The reason for this is that the telephone data used in Thompson and
Tiao's study were particularly amenable to time-series analysis. Time-series
analysis works best when a persistent pattern (seasonal or otherwise) exists in
the data, and such a pattern is present in the telephone data.

17.4 COMBINING REGRESSION ANALYSIS WITH A TIME-SERIES MODEL—A SHORT-TERM INTEREST RATE FORECAST

At the end of Chapter 15 we estimated a time-series model for a short-term
interest rate. Although we used the model to produce a forecast in Chapter 16,
we suggested that a better forecast could have been obtained by using a single-
equation structural regression model (as in Chapter 6). Now, let us see how

time-series analysis and regression analysis can be combined to produce a better forecast than would be possible through the use of either of these techniques alone.

Suppose that one would like to forecast the variable y_t using a regression model. Presumably such a model would include all those independent variables that could provide an explanation for movements in y_t but that are not themselves collinear. Let us suppose, for example, that the best regression model contains two independent variables, x_1 and x_2, as follows:

$$y_t = a_0 + a_1 x_{1t} + a_2 x_{2t} + \varepsilon_t \tag{17.13}$$

This equation has an implicit additive error term that accounts for *unexplained* variance in y_t; i.e., it accounts for that part of the variance of y_t that is not explained by x_1 and x_2. The equation can be estimated, and an R^2 will result which (unless by some chance y_t is perfectly correlated with the independent variables) will be less than 1. The equation can then be used to forecast y_t. As we saw in Chapter 6, one source of forecast error would come from the additive noise term whose future values cannot be predicted.

By subtracting the estimated values of y_t from the actual values, we can calculate a residual series u_t which represents unexplained movements in y_t, i.e., pure noise. One effective application of time-series analysis is to construct an ARIMA model for the residual series u_t of the regression. We would then substitute the ARIMA model for the implicit error term in the original regression equation. When using the equation to forecast y_t, we would also be able to make a forecast of the error term ε_t using the ARIMA model. The ARIMA model provides some information as to what future values of ε_t are likely to be; i.e., it helps "explain" the unexplained variance in the regression equation. The combined regression-time-series model is

$$y_t = a_0 + a_1 x_{1t} + a_2 x_{2t} + \phi^{-1}(B)\theta(B)\eta_t \tag{17.14}$$

where η_t is a normally distributed error term which may have a different variance from ε_t. This model is likely to provide much better forecasts than the regression equation (17.13) alone, or a time-series model alone, since it includes a structural (economic) explanation of that part of the variance of y_t that can be explained structurally, and a time-series "explanation" of that part of the variance of y_t that cannot be explained structurally.[7]

---

[7] The reader should be aware that the technique described here is a generalization of the technique described in Chapter 6 in the section on forecasting with regression models having serially correlated errors. If possible, one should estimate the parameters a_0, a_1, and a_2 of the structural regression equation and the parameters ϕ and θ of the time-series model *simultaneously*. This presents a difficult computational problem, however, and is therefore often not done.

As an example, let us construct a model to forecast, on a monthly basis, the interest rate on 3-month Treasury bills. We begin by examining the regression model that was developed for that interest rate in Chapter 6. The regression equation related the interest rate R to disposable income YD, a moving sum of changes in the money supply M, and a moving sum of monthly inflation rates $\Delta P/P$ (note that the time unit is 1 month):

$$R = -3.662 + .053\text{YD} - .280(\Delta M + \Delta M_{-1} + \Delta M_{-2})$$
$$(-9.45) \quad (14.76) \quad\;\; (-6.13)$$

$$+ 104.38 \left(\frac{\Delta P}{P} + \frac{\Delta P_{-1}}{P_{-1}} + \frac{\Delta P_{-2}}{P_{-2}}\right) \tag{17.15}$$
$$ (5.23)$$

$$R^2 = .853 \qquad \text{SER} = .552 \qquad F = 271.9 \qquad \text{DW} = .24$$

A historical simulation of the regression model was performed over the 24-month period January 1968 to January 1970 and is shown in Fig. 17.26. That simulation had an RMS (root-mean-square) error of .542 (the mean value of the interest rate over the period was 6.138). Next, the regression model was used to produce an *ex post* forecast of the interest rate over the 6-month period January 1970 to June 1970, and the results are shown in Fig. 17.27. The RMS error for this forecast was .750 (the actual series had a mean value in this period of 6.943).

We now attempt to improve upon the forecasting performance of this model

FIGURE 17.26
Historical simulation of Eq. (17.15). Time bounds: January 1968 to January 1970.

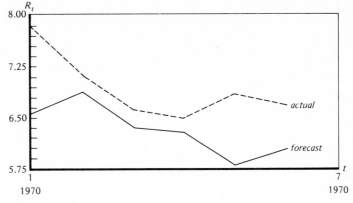

FIGURE 17.27
Ex post interest rate forecast using Eq. (17.15). Time bounds: January 1970 to June 1970.

by constructing and applying a time-series model to the residual series. Autocorrelation functions are shown in Figs. 17.28 and 17.29 for the series of regression residuals undifferenced and differenced once. The reader can observe that the autocorrelation function for the undifferenced series has the properties that one would expect for a stationary time series, so that differencing the series one or more times is unnecessary to create a stationary series. The autocorrelation function appears to be autoregressive, since it decays exponentially, and also has some cyclical characteristics. This suggests the use of three models: ARIMA(2,0,0), ARIMA(4,0,0), and ARIMA(8,0,0). The estimation

FIGURE 17.28
Autocorrelation function of residual series u_t.

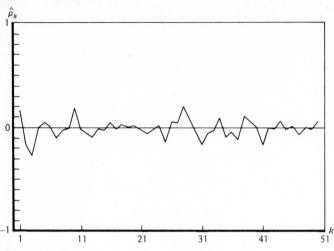

FIGURE 17.29
Autocorrelation function of residual series first-differenced (Δu_t).

results for these three models are shown in Eqs. (17.16), (17.17), and (17.18) below, together with R^2, chi-square statistics, and t statistics:

ARIMA(2,0,0)

$$u_t = .0066 + 1.036u_{t-1} - .238u_{t-2} + \eta_t \qquad (17.16)$$
$$\quad (.24) \quad (9.50) \qquad (-2.09)$$

$$R^2 = .670 \qquad \chi^2(2,22) = 16.25$$

ARIMA(4,0,0)

$$u_t = .0143 + 1.028u_{t-1} - .180u_{t-2} - .290u_{t-3} + .324u_{t-4} + \eta_t \quad (17.17)$$
$$\quad (.53) \quad (9.52) \qquad (-1.16) \quad (-1.87) \quad (2.87)$$

$$R^2 = .701 \qquad \chi^2(4,24) = 11.99$$

ARIMA(8,0,0)

$$u_t = .019 + 1.014u_{t-1} - .140u_{t-2} - .344u_{t-3} + .283u_{t-4}$$
$$\quad (.70) \quad (8.81) \qquad (-.85) \quad (-2.10) \quad (1.69)$$

$$+ .131u_{t-5} - .117u_{t-6} - .075u_{t-7} + .171u_{t-8} + \eta_t \qquad (17.18)$$
$$\quad (.77) \qquad (-.69) \qquad (-.43) \qquad (1.39)$$

$$R^2 = .712 \qquad \chi^2(8,28) = 11.25$$

FIGURE 17.30
Historical simulation of residual series using ARIMA model. Time bounds:
January 1968 to January 1970.

Because the models do not contain moving average terms, a linear regression
can be used to estimate them, and the t statistics and R^2 retain their usual
meaning. The resulting statistics seem to indicate that the ARIMA(4,0,0) model
is most favorable. High-order terms in the eighth-order model are largely
insignificant, and the second-order model has a lower R^2 and higher chi-square
statistic. We therefore use the (4,0,0) model for forecasting.

Before we combine this ARIMA model with the regression model from
Eq. (17.15) above, let us see how well it forecasts the residual series. In Fig. 17.30
we present a historical simulation of the residual series using the ARIMA
model over the period 1968 to 1970, as well as the actual series. The reader
can observe that the model tracks the actual series fairly closely. In Fig. 17.31,
we use the ARIMA model to produce an *ex ante* forecast of the residuals
over the time period January 1970 to January 1972. Since the regression equation
was estimated only through the end of 1969, we do not have an actual residual
series with which to compare this forecasted series, but we can observe the
characteristics of the ARIMA forecast. Notice that the forecasted series drops off,
increases slightly, and then goes toward 0 as the time horizon expands outward.
An autoregressive model has an infinite memory, but the farther out in time one
goes, the less influence past events have on our forecast, and the closer to 0 (the
mean value of the residuals u_t) our forecast becomes.

We can now combine the ARIMA(4,0,0) model with our regression model
and use the combined model to produce forecasts of the interest rate. First,
we performed a historical simulation of the interest rate using the combined
regression-time-series model over the period January 1968 to January 1970.
These results are shown in Fig. 17.32, where one can observe that the simulated

FIGURE 17.31
Ex ante forecast of residual series using ARIMA model. Time bounds:
January 1970 to January 1972.

series is much closer to the actual series than was the case when the regression model was used alone. In fact, the RMS simulation error has now been reduced by almost half—to a value of .269. A 6-month *ex post* forecast, from January 1970 to June 1970, using the combined regression-time-series model is shown in Fig. 17.33. Once again the reader can observe that the forecast is closer to the actual series than was the case with the regression model alone. Again, the RMS forecast error has been reduced by a factor of almost 2, to a value of .340. This increase in forecasting accuracy gives an illustration of the usefulness of this application of time-series analysis.

FIGURE 17.32
Historical simulation of interest rate using combined regression-time-series model. Time bounds: January 1968 to January 1970.

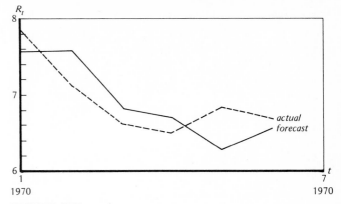

FIGURE 17.33

Ex post forecast of interest rate using combined regression-time-series model. Time bounds: January 1970 to June 1970.

17.5 COMBINING REGRESSION ANALYSIS WITH A TIME-SERIES MODEL—FORECASTING SHORT-TERM SAVINGS DEPOSIT FLOWS

We now examine a second example of an application of time-series analysis in combination with regression analysis. This example, based on a study by R. S. Ludwig,[8] involves a forecast of the monthly flow of deposits into Massachusetts mutual savings banks. As in the last example, a regression model is first constructed (to explain deposit flows), and then a time-series model is developed to "explain" the residual series (i.e., the error term) in the regression equation.

We begin with a regression equation that provides a structural explanation for mutual savings deposit flows. Ludwig used the ratio of deposit flows S to personal wealth W as the dependent variable, and chose monthly Massachusetts personal income as a proxy variable for wealth. He found that his best regression equation included three explanatory variables: the effective percentage return (including dividends) on mutual savings deposits r_{ms}, the interest rate on 3-month Treasury bills r_m, and the ratio of the previous month's stock of mutual savings deposits A_{-1} to the wealth variable. His equation, estimated using monthly data for the state of Massachusetts over the period February 1968 to June 1973, is

$$\frac{S}{W} = \underset{(1.89)}{.16} + \underset{(2.98)}{.019r_{ms}} - \underset{(-5.27)}{.011r_m} - \underset{(-2.23)}{.032} \frac{A_{-1}}{W} \tag{17.19}$$

$$R^2 = .41 \qquad \text{SER} = .016 \qquad F = 14.42 \qquad \text{DW} = 1.55$$

---

[8] R. S. Ludwig, "Forecasting Short-Term Savings Deposit Flows: An Application of Time Series Models and a Regional Analysis," unpublished Master's thesis. Sloan School of Management, M.I.T., June 1974.

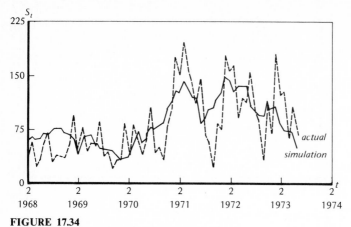

FIGURE 17.34
Historical simulation of Eq. (17.19) for deposit flows.

As one would expect, there is a positive relationship between savings deposit flows and the effective percentage return on deposits. The interest rate on 3-month Treasury bills, used as a market rate of interest, represents the return on competing risk-free investment alternatives for savings, and thus should have a negative impact on savings deposit flows. Finally, the negative relationship between deposit flows and the stock of deposits represents a stock adjustment effect; savings deposits should be proportional to that part of personal wealth that has not already been placed in a savings bank, that is,

$$S_t = A_t - A_{t-1} = a(W_t - A_{t-1}) \tag{17.20}$$

so that

$$\frac{S_t}{W_t} = a - a\frac{A_{t-1}}{W_t} \tag{17.21}$$

A historical simulation of Eq. (17.19) is shown in Fig. 17.34, and an *ex post* forecast of the equation over the period July 1973 to October 1973 is shown in Fig. 17.35. The historical simulation has a root-mean-square *percent* error of 75.1, and the *ex post* forecast has a root-mean-square percent error of 157.[9] The reader can observe that the simulation tracks the general movement of the series, but leaves much of the variance unexplained. The regression model does well in forecasting deposit flows in July 1973, but fails to capture the strong downward trend in deposits in August of that year.

Let us now see how to improve the forecast by constructing a time-series

---

[9] The root-mean-square percent error is defined and explained in Chapter 10.

FIGURE 17.35
Ex post forecast of Eq. (17.19) for deposit flows.

model for the residual series of the regression equation. The sample auto-correlation function for the residual series is shown in Fig. 17.36. The reader can observe that high-order correlations damp toward 0, so that the residual series can be considered stationary. The autocorrelation function does, however, contain peaks at monthly lags which are multiples of 12, indicating annual seasonality. In Fig. 17.37 we show the sample autocorrelation function for a series which is a 12-month difference of the original residual series, i.e., for the series $(1 - B^{12})u_t$. This autocorrelation function has a damped sinusoidal shape which is indicative of a purely autoregressive process of order 2 or greater.

FIGURE 17.36
Autocorrelation function of residuals u_t from Eq. (17.19).

FIGURE 17.37
Autocorrelation function of 12-month difference of residuals, $(1 - B^{12})u_t$.

Ludwig estimated a variety of autoregressive models for this residual series, and found the best model to be of the form

$$(1 - \phi_{12} B^{12})(1 - \phi_1 B - \phi_2 B^2 - \phi_3 B^3 - \phi_4 B^4 - \phi_5 B^5 - \phi_6 B^6)u_t = \eta_t$$
$$(17.22)$$

which in its expanded and estimated form is

$$(1 - .736B - .025B^2 - .055B^3 - .009B^4 + .310B^5 - .128B^6 - .782B^{12} + .532B^{13}$$

$$+ .081B^{14} + .125B^{15} - .213B^{16} - .103B^{17} - .060B^{18})u_t = \eta_t \qquad (17.23)$$

$$R^2 = .78 \qquad \chi^2 = 14.5$$

A historical simulation of the time-series model alone is shown in Fig. 17.38. The reader can observe that the residual series is reproduced closely.

Now the time-series model for the residual series can be combined with the regression model of Eq. (17.19). An historical simulation of the combined regression-time-series model is shown in Fig. 17.39. The reader can observe that savings deposits are tracked much more closely than was the case before. Indeed, the root-mean-square percent error has been reduced by a factor of more than 3, to 29.3.

Finally, an *ex post* forecast of savings flows is made using the combined regression-time-series model, again for the 4-month period July 1973 to October

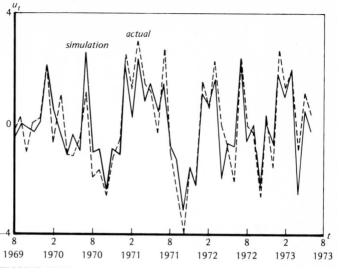

FIGURE 17.38
Historical simulation of time-series model for residuals.

FIGURE 17.39
Historical simulation of combined regression-time-series model for savings
deposit flows.

FIGURE 17.40
Ex post forecast of savings deposit flows using combined regression-time-series model.

1973. This forecast, shown in Fig. 17.40, is closer to the actual data than was the case when the regression model alone was used. (The root-mean-square percent error has been reduced from 157 to 118.) Although the forecast does not capture the extent of the downturn in savings deposit flows in August 1973, it does predict general movements in the variable.

STATISTICAL TABLES

Table 1
STANDARDIZED NORMAL DISTRIBUTION

z	.00	.01	.02	.03	.04	.05	.06	.07	.08	.09
0.0	.5000	.4960	.4920	.4880	.4840	.4801	.4761	.4721	.4681	.4641
0.1	.4602	.4562	.4522	.4483	.4443	.4404	.4364	.4325	.4686	.4247
0.2	.4207	.4168	.4129	.4090	.4052	.4013	.3974	.3936	.3897	.3859
0.3	.3821	.3873	.3745	.3707	.3669	.3632	.3594	.3557	.3520	.3483
0.4	.3446	.3409	.3372	.3336	.3300	.3264	.3228	.3192	.3156	.3121
0.5	.3085	.3050	.3015	.2981	.2946	.2912	.2877	.2843	.2810	.2776
0.6	.2743	.2709	.2676	.2643	.2611	.2578	.2546	.2514	.2483	.2451
0.7	.2420	.2389	.2358	.2327	.2296	.2266	.2236	.2206	.2217	.2148
0.8	.2119	.2090	.2061	.2033	.2005	.1977	.1949	.1922	.1894	.1867
0.9	.1841	.1814	.1788	.1762	.1736	.1711	.1685	.1660	.1635	.1611
1.0	.1587	.1562	.1539	.1515	.1492	.1469	.1446	.1423	.1401	.1379
1.1	.1357	.1335	.1314	.1292	.1271	.1251	.1230	.1210	.1190	.1170
1.2	.1151	.1131	.1112	.1093	.1075	.1056	.1038	.1020	.1003	.0985
1.3	.0968	.0951	.0934	.0918	.0901	.0885	.0869	.0853	.0838	.0823
1.4	.0808	.0793	.0778	.0764	.0749	.0735	.0721	.0708	.0694	.0681
1.5	.0668	.0655	.0643	.0630	.0618	.0606	.0594	.0582	.0571	.0559
1.6	.0548	.0537	.0526	.0516	.0505	.0495	.0485	.0475	.0465	.0455
1.7	.0446	.0436	.0427	.0418	.0409	.0401	.0392	.0384	.0375	.0367
1.8	.0359	.0351	.0344	.0366	.0329	.0322	.0314	.0307	.0301	.0294
1.9	.0287	.0281	.0274	.0268	.0262	.0256	.0250	.0244	.0239	.0233
2.0	.0228	.0222	.0217	.0212	.0207	.0202	.0197	.0192	.0188	.0183
2.1	.0179	.0174	.0170	.0166	.0162	.0158	.0154	.0150	.0146	.0143
2.2	.0139	.0136	.0132	.0129	.0125	.0122	.0119	.0116	.0113	.0110
2.3	.0107	.0104	.0102	.0099	.0096	.0094	.0091	.0089	.0087	.0084
2.4	.0082	.0080	.0078	.0075	.0073	.0071	.0069	.0068	.0066	.0064
2.5	.0062	.0060	.0059	.0057	.0055	.0054	.0052	.0051	.0049	.0048
2.6	.0047	.0045	.0044	.0043	.0041	.0040	.0039	.0038	.0037	.0036
2.7	.0035	.0034	.0033	.0032	.0031	.0030	.0029	.0028	.0027	.0026
2.8	.0026	.0025	.0024	.0023	.0023	.0022	.0021	.0020	.0020	.0019
2.9	.0019	.0018	.0018	.0017	.0016	.0016	.0015	.0015	.0014	.0014
3.0	.0013	.0013	.0013	.0012	.0012	.0011	.0011	.0010	.0011	.0010

The table plots the cumulative probability $Z \geq z$.

Source: Produced from Edward J. Kane, *Economic Statistics and Econometrics: An Introduction to Quantitative Economics*, New York: Harper & Row, Publishers, 1968.

Table 2
PERCENTILES OF THE χ^2 DISTRIBUTION

df	Percent									
	0.5	1	2.5	5	10	90	95	97.5	99	99.5
1	0.000039	0.00016	0.00098	0.0039	0.0158	2.71	3.84	5.02	6.63	7.88
2	0.0100	0.0201	0.0506	0.1026	0.2107	4.61	5.99	7.38	9.21	10.60
3	0.0717	0.115	0.216	0.352	0.584	6.25	7.81	9.35	11.34	12.84
4	0.207	0.297	0.484	0.711	1.064	7.78	9.49	11.14	13.28	14.86
5	0.412	0.554	0.831	1.15	1.61	9.24	11.07	12.83	15.09	16.75
6	0.676	0.872	1.24	1.64	2.20	10.64	12.59	14.45	16.81	18.55
7	0.989	1.24	1.69	2.17	2.83	12.02	14.07	16.01	18.48	20.28
8	1.34	1.65	2.18	2.73	3.49	13.36	15.51	17.53	20.09	21.96
9	1.73	2.09	2.70	3.33	4.17	14.68	16.92	19.02	21.67	23.59
10	2.16	2.56	3.25	3.94	4.87	15.99	18.31	20.48	23.21	25.19
11	2.60	3.05	3.82	4.57	5.58	17.28	19.68	21.92	24.73	26.76
12	3.07	3.57	4.40	5.23	6.30	18.55	21.03	23.34	26.22	28.30
13	3.57	4.11	5.01	5.89	7.04	19.81	22.36	24.74	27.69	29.82
14	4.07	4.66	5.63	6.57	7.79	21.06	23.68	26.12	29.14	31.32
15	4.60	5.23	6.26	7.26	8.55	22.31	25.00	27.49	30.58	32.80
16	5.14	5.81	6.91	7.96	9.31	23.54	26.30	28.85	32.00	34.27
18	6.26	7.01	8.23	9.39	10.86	25.99	28.87	31.53	34.81	37.16
20	7.43	8.26	9.59	10.85	12.44	28.41	31.41	34.17	37.57	40.00
24	9.89	10.86	12.40	13.85	15.66	33.20	36.42	39.36	42.98	45.56
30	13.79	14.95	16.79	18.49	20.60	40.26	43.77	47.98	50.89	53.67
40	20.71	22.16	24.43	26.51	29.05	51.81	55.76	59.34	63.69	66.77
60	35.53	37.48	40.48	43.19	46.46	74.40	79.08	83.30	88.38	91.95
120	83.85	86.92	91.58	95.70	100.62	140.23	146.57	152.21	158.95	163.64

Source: Reprinted with permission from W. J. Dixon and F. J. Massey, Jr., *Introduction to Statistical Analysis*, third edition, McGraw-Hill, 1969.

Table 3
PERCENTILES OF THE t DISTRIBUTION

df	$t_{0.60}$	$t_{0.70}$	$t_{0.80}$	$t_{0.90}$	$t_{0.95}$	$t_{0.975}$	$t_{0.99}$	$t_{0.995}$
1	0.325	0.727	1.376	3.078	6.314	12.706	31.821	63.657
2	0.289	0.617	1.061	1.886	2.920	4.303	6.965	9.925
3	0.277	0.584	0.978	1.638	2.353	3.182	4.541	5.841
4	0.271	0.569	0.941	1.533	2.132	2.776	3.747	4.604
5	0.267	0.559	0.920	1.476	2.015	2.571	3.365	4.032
6	0.265	0.553	0.906	1.440	1.943	2.447	3.143	3.707
7	0.263	0.549	0.896	1.415	1.895	2.365	2.998	3.499
8	0.262	0.546	0.889	1.397	1.860	2.306	2.896	3.355
9	0.261	0.543	0.883	1.383	1.833	2.262	2.821	3.250
10	0.260	0.542	0.879	1.372	1.812	2.228	2.764	3.169
11	0.260	0.540	0.876	1.363	1.796	2.201	2.718	3.106
12	0.259	0.539	0.873	1.356	1.782	2.179	2.681	3.055
13	0.259	0.538	0.870	1.350	1.771	2.160	2.650	3.012
14	0.258	0.537	0.868	1.345	1.761	2.145	2.624	2.977
15	0.258	0.536	0.866	1.341	1.753	2.131	2.602	2.947
16	0.258	0.535	0.865	1.337	1.746	2.120	2.583	2.921
17	0.257	0.534	0.863	1.333	1.740	2.110	2.567	2.898
18	0.257	0.534	0.862	1.330	1.734	2.101	2.552	2.878
19	0.257	0.533	0.861	1.328	1.729	2.093	2.539	2.861
20	0.257	0.533	0.860	1.325	1.725	2.086	2.528	2.845
21	0.257	0.532	0.859	1.323	1.721	2.080	2.518	2.831
22	0.256	0.532	0.858	1.321	1.717	2.074	2.508	2.819
23	0.256	0.532	0.858	1.319	1.714	2.069	2.500	2.807
24	0.256	0.531	0.857	1.318	1.711	2.064	2.492	2.797
25	0.256	0.531	0.856	1.316	1.708	2.060	2.485	2.787
26	0.256	0.531	0.856	1.315	1.706	2.056	2.479	2.779
27	0.256	0.531	0.855	1.314	1.703	2.052	2.473	2.771
28	0.256	0.530	0.855	1.313	1.701	2.048	2.467	2.763
29	0.256	0.530	0.854	1.311	1.699	2.045	2.462	2.756
30	0.256	0.530	0.854	1.310	1.697	2.042	2.457	2.750
40	0.255	0.529	0.851	1.303	1.684	2.021	2.423	2.704
60	0.254	0.527	0.848	1.296	1.671	2.000	2.390	2.660
120	0.254	0.526	0.845	1.289	1.658	1.980	2.358	2.617
∞	0.253	0.524	0.842	1.282	1.645	1.960	2.326	2.576

Source: Obtained from Table III of Fisher and Yates, *Statistical Tables for Biological, Agricultural and Medical Research*, with the permission of the authors and publishers, Oliver & Boyd, Ltd., Edinburgh.

Table 4a
F DISTRIBUTION, 5 PERCENT SIGNIFICANCE

	Degrees of freedom for numerator																		
	1	2	3	4	5	6	7	8	9	10	12	15	20	24	30	40	60	120	∞
1	161	200	216	225	230	234	237	239	241	242	244	246	248	249	250	251	252	253	254
2	18.5	19.0	19.2	19.2	19.3	19.3	19.4	19.4	19.4	19.4	19.4	19.4	19.5	19.5	19.5	19.5	19.5	19.5	19.5
3	10.1	9.55	9.28	9.12	9.01	8.94	8.89	8.85	8.81	8.79	8.74	8.70	8.66	8.64	8.62	8.59	8.57	8.55	8.53
4	7.71	6.94	6.59	6.39	6.26	6.16	6.09	6.04	6.00	5.96	5.91	5.86	5.80	5.77	5.75	5.72	5.69	5.66	5.63
5	6.61	5.79	5.41	5.19	5.05	4.95	4.88	4.82	4.77	4.74	4.68	4.62	4.56	4.53	4.50	4.46	4.43	4.40	4.37
6	5.99	5.14	4.76	4.53	4.39	4.28	4.21	4.15	4.10	4.06	4.00	3.94	3.87	3.84	3.81	3.77	3.74	3.70	3.67
7	5.59	4.74	4.35	4.12	3.97	3.87	3.79	3.73	3.68	3.64	3.57	3.51	3.44	3.41	3.38	3.34	3.30	3.27	3.23
8	5.32	4.46	4.07	3.84	3.69	3.58	3.50	3.44	3.39	3.35	3.28	3.22	3.15	3.12	3.08	3.04	3.01	2.97	2.93
9	5.12	4.26	3.86	3.63	3.48	3.37	3.29	3.23	3.18	3.14	3.07	3.01	2.94	2.90	2.86	2.83	2.79	2.75	2.71
10	4.96	4.10	3.71	3.48	3.33	3.22	3.14	3.07	3.02	2.98	2.91	2.85	2.77	2.74	2.70	2.66	2.62	2.58	2.54
11	4.84	3.98	3.59	3.36	3.20	3.09	3.01	2.95	2.90	2.85	2.79	2.72	2.65	2.61	2.57	2.53	2.49	2.45	2.40
12	4.75	3.89	3.49	3.26	3.11	3.00	2.91	2.85	2.80	2.75	2.69	2.62	2.54	2.51	2.47	2.43	2.38	2.34	2.30
13	4.67	3.81	3.41	3.18	3.03	2.92	2.83	2.77	2.71	2.67	2.60	2.53	2.46	2.42	2.38	2.34	2.30	2.25	2.21
14	4.60	3.74	3.34	3.11	2.96	2.85	2.76	2.70	2.65	2.60	2.53	2.46	2.39	2.35	2.31	2.27	2.22	2.18	2.13
15	4.54	3.68	3.29	3.06	2.90	2.79	2.71	2.64	2.59	2.54	2.48	2.40	2.33	2.29	2.25	2.20	2.16	2.11	2.07
16	4.49	3.63	3.24	3.01	2.85	2.74	2.66	2.59	2.54	2.49	2.42	2.35	2.28	2.24	2.19	2.15	2.11	2.06	2.01
17	4.45	3.59	3.20	2.96	2.81	2.70	2.61	2.55	2.48	2.45	2.38	2.31	2.23	2.19	2.15	2.10	2.06	2.01	1.96
18	4.41	3.55	3.16	2.93	2.77	2.66	2.58	2.51	2.46	2.41	2.34	2.27	2.19	2.15	2.11	2.06	2.02	1.97	1.92
19	4.38	3.52	3.13	2.90	2.74	2.63	2.54	2.48	2.42	2.39	2.31	2.23	2.16	2.11	2.07	2.03	1.98	1.93	1.88
20	4.35	3.49	3.10	2.87	2.71	2.60	2.51	2.45	2.39	2.35	2.28	2.20	2.12	2.08	2.04	1.99	1.95	1.90	1.84
21	4.32	3.47	3.07	2.84	2.68	2.57	2.49	2.42	2.37	2.32	2.25	2.18	2.10	2.05	2.01	1.96	1.92	1.87	1.81
22	4.30	3.44	3.05	2.82	2.66	2.55	2.46	2.40	2.34	2.30	2.23	2.15	2.07	2.03	1.98	1.94	1.89	1.84	1.78
23	4.28	3.42	3.03	2.80	2.64	2.53	2.44	2.37	2.32	2.27	2.20	2.13	2.05	2.01	1.96	1.91	1.86	1.81	1.76
24	4.26	3.40	3.01	2.78	2.62	2.51	2.42	2.36	2.30	2.25	2.18	2.11	2.03	1.98	1.94	1.89	1.84	1.79	1.73
25	4.24	3.39	2.99	2.76	2.60	2.49	2.40	2.34	2.28	2.24	2.16	2.09	2.01	1.96	1.92	1.87	1.82	1.77	1.71
30	4.17	3.32	2.92	2.69	2.53	2.42	2.33	2.27	2.21	2.16	2.09	2.01	1.93	1.89	1.84	1.79	1.74	1.68	1.62
40	4.08	3.23	2.84	2.61	2.45	2.34	2.25	2.18	2.12	2.08	2.00	1.92	1.84	1.79	1.74	1.69	1.64	1.58	1.51
60	4.00	3.15	2.76	2.53	2.37	2.25	2.17	2.10	2.04	1.99	1.92	1.84	1.75	1.70	1.65	1.59	1.53	1.47	1.39
120	3.92	3.07	2.68	2.45	2.29	2.18	2.09	2.02	1.96	1.91	1.83	1.75	1.66	1.61	1.55	1.50	1.43	1.35	1.25
∞	3.84	3.00	2.60	2.37	2.21	2.10	2.01	1.94	1.88	1.83	1.75	1.67	1.57	1.52	1.46	1.39	1.32	1.22	1.00

Degrees of freedom for denominator

Source: Reproduced with the permission of the Biometrika Trustees from M. Merrington, C. M. Thompson, "Tables of percentage points of the inverted beta (F) distribution," *Biometrika*, vol. 33, p. 73, 1943.

Table 4b

F DISTRIBUTION, 1 PERCENT SIGNIFICANCE

	Degrees of freedom for numerator																		
	1	2	3	4	5	6	7	8	9	10	12	15	20	24	30	40	60	120	∞
1	4,052	5,000	5,403	5,625	5,746	5,859	5,928	5,982	6,023	6,056	6,106	6,157	6,209	6,235	6,261	6,287	6,313	6,339	6,366
2	98.5	99.0	99.2	99.2	99.3	99.3	99.4	99.4	99.4	99.4	99.4	99.4	99.4	99.5	99.5	99.5	99.5	99.5	99.5
3	34.1	30.8	29.5	28.7	28.2	27.9	27.7	27.5	27.3	27.2	27.1	26.9	26.7	26.6	26.5	26.4	26.3	26.2	26.1
4	21.2	18.0	16.7	16.0	15.5	15.2	15.0	14.8	14.7	14.5	14.4	14.2	14.0	13.9	13.8	13.7	13.7	13.6	13.5
5	16.3	13.3	12.1	11.4	11.0	10.7	10.5	10.3	10.2	10.1	9.89	9.72	9.55	9.47	9.38	9.29	9.20	9.11	9.02
6	13.7	10.9	9.78	9.15	8.75	8.47	8.26	8.10	7.98	7.87	7.72	7.56	7.40	7.31	7.23	7.14	7.06	6.97	6.88
7	12.2	9.55	8.45	7.85	7.46	7.19	6.99	6.84	6.72	6.62	6.47	6.31	6.16	6.07	5.99	5.91	5.82	5.74	5.65
8	11.3	8.65	7.59	7.01	6.63	6.37	6.18	6.03	5.91	5.81	5.67	5.52	5.36	5.28	5.20	5.12	5.03	4.95	4.86
9	10.6	8.02	6.99	6.42	6.06	5.80	5.61	5.47	5.35	5.26	5.11	4.96	4.81	4.73	4.65	4.57	4.48	4.40	4.31
10	10.0	7.56	6.55	5.99	5.64	5.39	5.20	5.06	4.94	4.85	4.71	4.56	4.41	4.33	4.25	4.17	4.08	4.00	3.91
11	9.65	7.21	6.22	5.67	5.32	5.07	4.89	4.74	4.63	4.54	4.40	4.25	4.10	4.02	3.94	3.86	3.78	3.69	3.60
12	9.33	6.93	5.95	5.41	5.06	4.82	4.64	4.50	4.39	4.30	4.16	4.01	3.86	3.78	3.70	3.62	3.54	3.45	3.36
13	9.07	6.70	5.74	5.21	4.86	4.62	4.44	4.30	4.19	4.10	3.96	3.82	3.66	3.59	3.51	3.43	3.34	3.25	3.17
14	8.86	6.51	5.56	5.04	4.70	4.46	4.28	4.14	4.03	3.94	3.80	3.66	3.51	3.43	3.35	3.27	3.18	3.09	3.00
15	8.68	6.36	5.42	4.89	4.56	4.32	4.14	4.00	3.89	3.80	3.67	3.52	3.37	3.29	3.21	3.13	3.05	2.96	2.87
16	8.53	6.23	5.29	4.77	4.44	4.20	4.03	3.89	3.78	3.69	3.55	3.41	3.26	3.18	3.10	3.02	2.93	2.84	2.75
17	8.40	6.11	5.19	4.67	4.34	4.10	3.93	3.79	3.68	3.59	3.46	3.31	3.16	3.08	3.00	2.92	2.83	2.75	2.65
18	8.29	6.01	5.09	4.58	4.25	4.01	3.84	3.71	3.60	3.51	3.37	3.23	3.08	3.00	2.92	2.84	2.75	2.66	2.57
19	8.19	5.93	5.01	4.50	4.17	3.94	3.77	3.63	3.52	3.43	3.30	3.15	3.00	2.92	2.84	2.76	2.67	2.58	2.49
20	8.10	5.85	4.94	4.43	4.10	3.87	3.70	3.56	3.46	3.37	3.23	3.09	2.94	2.86	2.78	2.68	2.61	2.52	2.42
21	8.02	5.78	4.87	4.37	4.04	3.81	3.64	3.51	3.40	3.31	3.17	3.03	2.88	2.80	2.72	2.64	2.55	2.46	2.36
22	7.95	5.72	4.82	4.31	3.99	3.76	3.59	3.45	3.35	3.26	3.12	2.98	2.83	2.75	2.67	2.58	2.50	2.40	2.31
23	7.88	5.66	4.76	4.26	3.94	3.71	3.54	3.41	3.30	3.21	3.07	2.93	2.78	2.70	2.62	2.54	2.45	2.35	2.26
24	7.82	5.61	4.72	4.22	3.90	3.67	3.50	3.36	3.26	3.17	3.03	2.89	2.74	2.66	2.58	2.49	2.40	2.31	2.21
25	7.77	5.57	4.68	4.18	3.86	3.63	3.46	3.32	3.22	3.13	2.99	2.85	2.70	2.62	2.53	2.45	2.36	2.27	2.17
30	7.56	5.39	4.51	4.02	3.70	3.47	3.30	3.17	3.07	2.98	2.84	2.70	2.55	2.47	2.30	2.39	2.21	2.11	2.01
40	7.31	5.18	4.31	3.83	3.51	3.29	3.12	2.99	2.89	2.80	2.66	2.52	2.37	2.29	2.20	2.11	2.02	1.92	1.80
60	7.08	4.98	4.13	3.65	3.34	3.12	2.95	2.82	2.72	2.63	2.50	2.35	2.20	2.12	2.03	1.94	1.84	1.73	1.60
120	6.85	4.79	3.95	3.48	3.17	2.96	2.79	2.66	2.56	2.47	2.34	2.19	2.03	1.94	1.86	1.76	1.66	1.53	1.38
∞	6.63	4.61	3.78	3.32	3.02	2.80	2.64	2.51	2.41	2.32	2.18	2.04	1.88	1.79	1.70	1.59	1.47	1.32	1.00

Degrees of freedom for denominator

Table 5

5 PERCENT SIGNIFICANCE POINTS OF d_l AND d_u

n	$k = 1$		$k = 2$		$k = 3$		$k = 4$		$k = 5$	
	d_l	d_u	d_l	d_u	d_l	d_u	d_l	d_u	d_l	d_u
15	0.95	1.23	0.83	1.40	0.71	1.61	0.59	1.84	0.48	2.09
16	0.98	1.24	0.86	1.40	0.75	1.59	0.64	1.80	0.53	2.03
17	1.01	1.25	0.90	1.40	0.79	1.58	0.68	1.77	0.57	1.98
18	1.03	1.26	0.93	1.40	0.82	1.56	0.72	1.74	0.62	1.93
19	1.06	1.28	0.96	1.41	0.86	1.55	0.76	1.73	0.66	1.90
20	1.08	1.28	0.99	1.41	0.89	1.55	0.79	1.72	0.70	1.87
21	1.10	1.30	1.01	1.41	0.92	1.54	0.83	1.69	0.73	1.84
22	1.12	1.31	1.04	1.42	0.95	1.54	0.86	1.68	0.77	1.82
23	1.14	1.32	1.06	1.42	0.97	1.54	0.89	1.67	0.80	1.80
24	1.16	1.33	1.08	1.43	1.00	1.54	0.91	1.66	0.83	1.79
25	1.18	1.34	1.10	1.43	1.02	1.54	0.94	1.65	0.86	1.77
26	1.19	1.35	1.12	1.44	1.04	1.54	0.96	1.65	0.88	1.76
27	1.21	1.36	1.13	1.44	1.06	1.54	0.99	1.64	0.91	1.75
28	1.22	1.37	1.15	1.45	1.08	1.54	1.01	1.64	0.93	1.74
29	1.24	1.38	1.17	1.45	1.10	1.54	1.03	1.63	0.96	1.73
30	1.25	1.38	1.18	1.46	1.12	1.54	1.05	1.63	0.98	1.73
31	1.26	1.39	1.20	1.47	1.13	1.55	1.07	1.63	1.00	1.72
32	1.27	1.40	1.21	1.47	1.15	1.55	1.08	1.63	1.02	1.71
33	1.28	1.41	1.22	1.48	1.16	1.55	1.10	1.63	1.04	1.71
34	1.29	1.41	1.24	1.48	1.17	1.55	1.12	1.63	1.06	1.70
35	1.30	1.42	1.25	1.48	1.19	1.55	1.13	1.63	1.07	1.70
36	1.31	1.43	1.26	1.49	1.20	1.56	1.15	1.63	1.09	1.70
37	1.32	1.43	1.27	1.49	1.21	1.56	1.16	1.62	1.10	1.70
38	1.33	1.44	1.28	1.50	1.23	1.56	1.17	1.62	1.12	1.70
39	1.34	1.44	1.29	1.50	1.24	1.56	1.19	1.63	1.13	1.69
40	1.35	1.45	1.30	1.51	1.25	1.57	1.20	1.63	1.15	1.69
45	1.39	1.48	1.34	1.53	1.30	1.58	1.25	1.63	1.21	1.69
50	1.42	1.50	1.38	1.54	1.34	1.59	1.30	1.64	1.26	1.69
55	1.45	1.52	1.41	1.56	1.37	1.60	1.33	1.64	1.30	1.69
60	1.47	1.54	1.44	1.57	1.40	1.61	1.37	1.65	1.33	1.69
65	1.49	1.55	1.46	1.59	1.43	1.63	1.40	1.66	1.36	1.69
70	1.51	1.57	1.48	1.60	1.45	1.63	1.42	1.66	1.39	1.70
75	1.53	1.58	1.50	1.61	1.47	1.64	1.45	1.67	1.42	1.70
80	1.54	1.59	1.52	1.63	1.49	1.65	1.47	1.67	1.44	1.70
85	1.56	1.60	1.53	1.63	1.51	1.66	1.49	1.68	1.46	1.71
90	1.57	1.61	1.55	1.64	1.53	1.66	1.50	1.69	1.48	1.71
95	1.58	1.62	1.56	1.65	1.54	1.67	1.52	1.69	1.50	1.71
100	1.59	1.63	1.57	1.65	1.55	1.67	1.53	1.70	1.51	1.72

Source: Reprinted with permission from J. Durbin and G. S. Watson, "Testing for Serial Correlation in Least Squares Regression," *Biometrika*, vol. 38 (1951), pp. 159–177.

SOLUTIONS TO SELECTED PROBLEMS

1.1 (1) The regression line is $Y = 0.17 + 1.72X$.

(2) The slope tells us that on average a \$1 million increase in the quantity of money will lead to a \$1.72 million increase in national income. Interpreted literally, the intercept tells us that if the money supply fell to zero, national income would be \$1.17 million. However, since no observations were available for values of X near zero, we cannot place any reliance on such an interpretation.

(3) We would set the money supply at \$6.3 million.

1.3 (1) The slope will be reduced by a factor of 10, and the intercept will remain unchanged.

(2) To evaluate the effects of the transformation on the slope and intercept, substitute the equations describing the transformed variables into the least-squares estimators:

$$\hat{b}^* = \frac{\sum (X_i^* - \bar{X}^*)(Y_i^* - \bar{Y}^*)}{\sum (X_i^* - \bar{X}^*)^2} \qquad \hat{a}^* = \bar{Y}^* - \hat{b}^*\bar{X}^*$$

(The student should check that $\bar{Y}^* = c_1 + c_2\bar{Y}$ and $\bar{X}^* = d_1 + d_2\bar{X}$.) After some elementary algebra, it follows that

$$\hat{b}^* = (c_2/d_2)\hat{b} \qquad \hat{a}^* = [c_1 - (c_2 d_1/d_2)\hat{b}] + c_2\hat{a}$$

1.4 The least-squares intercept and slope are both undefined. When all independent variable observations are identical $\sum x_i^2$ equals zero. Since there is no change in the independent variable (in the sample), it is impossible to tell how the dependent variable would respond to a change in the independent variable.

2.1 $s^2 = .14$ and $t_c = 2.3$. Therefore, the 95 percent confidence interval for the intercept is

$$1.17 \pm 2.3\sqrt{(.14/8)} = 1.17 \pm .30$$

The 95 percent confidence interval for the slope is

$$1.72 \pm 2.3\sqrt{(.14/8.8)} = 1.72 \pm .29$$

Yes, you can reject the null hypothesis in both cases.

2.4 $R^2 = \hat{b}^2 \sum x_i^2 / \sum y_i^2$. If $R^2 = 1$, $\hat{b}^2 = \sum y_i^2 / \sum x_i^2$. But, by construction, $\hat{b} = \sum x_i y_i / \sum x_i^2$. Therefore, $\sum x_i^2 = (\sum x_i y_i)^2 / \sum y_i^2$ and $\hat{b} = \sum y_i^2 / \sum x_i y_i = 1/\hat{B}$.

2.8 $\sum x_i \hat{\varepsilon}_i = \sum x_i(y_i - \hat{\beta} x_i) = \sum x_i y_i - \hat{\beta} \sum x_i^2$. But, $\hat{\beta} = \sum x_i y_i / \sum x_i^2$. Therefore, $\sum x_i \hat{\varepsilon}_i = \hat{\beta} \sum x_i^2 - \hat{\beta} \sum x_i^2 = 0$.

2.9 Using data in deviations form, $y_i^* = a_2 y_i$ and $x_i^* = b_2 x_i$ (since $Y^* = a_1 + a_2 Y$, $X^* = b_1 + b_2 X$). Then, using transformed data

$$(R^*)^2 = \frac{\hat{\beta}^{*2} \sum x_i^{*2}}{\sum y_i^{*2}}$$

But from Ex. 1.3, $\hat{\beta}^{*2} = (a_2/b_2)^2 \hat{\beta}^2$. Substituting, we find that $(R^*)^2 = R^2$.

2.11 (1) B is the slope of the straight line passing through the points $(\overline{X}_1, \overline{Y}_1)$ and $(\overline{X}_2, \overline{Y}_2)$. Dividing the data into two groups is sufficient to allow for the fitting of a straight line, which yields an estimate of the slope.

(2) B does not equal $\hat{\beta}$, but it is an unbiased estimator of β. To prove this, utilize the original model to calculate that

$$\overline{Y}_1 = \alpha + \beta \overline{X}_1 + \overline{\varepsilon}_1 \qquad \text{and} \qquad \overline{Y}_2 = \alpha + \beta \overline{X}_2 + \overline{\varepsilon}_2.$$

Then,
$$E(\overline{Y}_2 - \overline{Y}_1) = \beta(\overline{X}_2 - \overline{X}_1)$$

and
$$E(B) = E(\overline{Y}_2 - \overline{Y}_1)/(\overline{X}_2 - \overline{X}_1) = \beta.$$

(3) We know that $\text{Var}(B) \geq \text{Var}(\hat{\beta})$ from the Gauss-Markov theorem which states that $\hat{\beta}$ is the *best* linear unbiased estimator of β. (It is easy to show that B is a linear estimator.) In this particular case, it is possible to show that $\text{Var}(B) = .157\sigma^2$, while $\text{Var}(\hat{\beta}) = .115\sigma^2$.

3.1 *a.* Let $Z_i = Y_i - X_{2i}$; then by substitution into Eqs. (3.6), (3.7), and (3.8), we find that

$$\hat{\beta}'_2 = \hat{\beta}_2 - \frac{(\sum x_{2i}^2 \sum x_{3i}^2) - (\sum x_{2i} x_{3i})^2}{(\sum x_{2i}^2)(\sum x_{3i}^2) - (\sum x_{2i} x_{3i})^2} = \hat{\beta}_2 - 1$$

Likewise $\hat{\beta}'_3 = \hat{\beta}_3$ and $\hat{\beta}'_1 = \overline{Y} - \overline{X}_2 - \hat{\beta}_2 \overline{X}_2 + \overline{X}_2 - \hat{\beta}_3 \overline{X}_3 = \hat{\beta}_1$.

b. In model (1),

$$\hat{\varepsilon}_i = Y_i - \hat{\beta}_1 - \hat{\beta}_2 X_{2i} - \hat{\beta}_3 X_{3i}$$

In model (2),

$$\hat{\varepsilon}_i' = Y_i - X_{2i} - \hat{\beta}_1' - \hat{\beta}_2' X_{2i} - \hat{\beta}_3' X_{3i}$$

$$= Y_i - X_{2i} - \hat{\beta}_1 - \hat{\beta}_2 + X_{2i} - \hat{\beta}_3' X_{3i} = \hat{\varepsilon}_i$$

c. $R^2 = 1 - \sum \hat{\varepsilon}_i^2 / \sum (Y_i - \bar{Y})^2$ in model (1); and $R'^2 = 1 - \sum \hat{\varepsilon}_i'^2 / \sum (Z_i - \bar{Z})^2$ in model (2). Since the regression residuals are identical, the relationship between R^2 and R'^2 will depend directly on the relationship between the variance of Y and the variance of Z.

3.3
$$\beta_2 = \frac{\partial \log Y}{\partial \log X_2} = \frac{(1/Y)\, dY}{(1/X_2)\, dX_2} = \frac{dY}{dX_2} \cdot \frac{X_2}{Y_2}$$

Thus, $\hat{\beta}_2$ provides an estimate of the elasticity of Y with respect to X_2. The analogous result holds for $\hat{\beta}_3$. These elasticities are constant because the least-squares slope estimates are constant.

3.5 From the regression $X_{2i} = \alpha_1 + \alpha_2 X_{3i} + \varepsilon_i'$, the residuals are $\hat{\varepsilon}_i' = X_{2i} - \hat{\alpha}_1 - \hat{\alpha}_2 X_{3i}$. Substituting into the regression $Y_i = \beta_1' + \beta_2' \hat{\varepsilon}_i + \beta_3' X_{3i} + \varepsilon_i^*$, we find that $Y_i = (\beta_1' + \beta_2' \hat{\alpha}_1) + \beta_2' X_{2i} + (\beta_3' - \beta_2' \hat{\alpha}_2) X_{3i} + \varepsilon_i^*$. Comparing this with the original regression makes it clear that $\hat{\beta}_2' = \hat{\beta}_2$. The intuition behind this result lies in the fact that $\hat{\varepsilon}_i$ measures the portion of X_{2i} which is uncorrelated with X_{3i}.

3.7 Each beta coefficient will equal the corresponding regression parameter.

3.10 In the two-variable model,

$$\hat{\beta}^* = \hat{\beta}\frac{s_X}{s_Y} = \left|\frac{\sum x_i y_i}{\sum x_i^2}\right|\left|\frac{\sum x_i^2}{\sum y_i^2}\right|^{1/2} = \frac{\sum x_i y_i}{(\sum x_i^2)^{1/2}(\sum y_i^2)^{1/2}} = r_{XY}$$

4.2 Yes, we might expect that the error terms associated with communities with high educational expenditures would have larger variances than the error terms associated with communities with low educational expenditures. The Goldfeld-Quandt test might be more useful than Bartlett's test because there is no natural way to group the data so as to estimate sample error variances. To use the Goldfeld-Quandt test we might order the observations by level of median income in the community.

4.4 In cross-section studies there is usually no natural sequence to the data. In such a case, there is no reason to expect that errors associated with different observations will be correlated. However, serial correlation may be present if, for example, observations are geographically related. In a regional model of economic growth or a metropolitan model of local government behavior, errors corresponding to geographically related units of observation may be correlated.

5.1 Measurement of error in the dependent variable results in increased error variance, but as long as the measurement error is uncorrelated with the independent variable, parameter estimates will be unbiased and consistent. When an independent variable is measured with error, however, the measurement error will be correlated with the independent variable, causing parameter estimates to be biased and inconsistent.

5.3
$$\hat{\beta} = \sum y_i z_i / \sum z_i^2 = \beta \sum x_i z_i / \sum z_i^2 + \sum z_i \varepsilon_i / \sum z_i^2$$

If z is an instrument, the second term will approach zero as the sample size gets large, but the first term will approach β only when $\sum x_i z_i / \sum z_i^2$ approaches 1.

5.7 Ordinary least squares will yield biased and inconsistent estimates of the parameters in the first equation. Indirect least squares, instrumental variables, and two-stage least squares all yield biased but consistent parameter estimates (there are two possible estimates for each parameter in the indirect least-squares case). However, two-stage least-squares estimation is more efficient than either indirect least squares or instrumental variables. This regression of Y on Z_1 and Z_2 will not yield estimates of either parameter in the first equation.

6.3 At least two explanations could be offered. First, one could argue that the narrowly defined money stock (currency plus demand deposits) used in the model is not the appropriate variable to explain interest rates, and that the broadly defined money stock (including time deposits as well) should be used instead. Time deposits in fact did increase much more rapidly in the second half of 1970 than did demand deposits, so that use of the broadly defined money stock in the model would probably have resulted in a better forecast during that period. A second argument that could be made is that the time relationship between the interest rate and income, the money stock, and the inflation rate is not a linear one as specified in the model, and a nonlinear specification would forecast the downturn more closely.

7.2
$$\beta_2^* = \sum x_{2i} y_i / \sum x_{2i}^2 = \beta_2 + \beta_3 \sum x_{2i}^3 / \sum x_{2i}^2$$

Therefore, the specification bias is equal to $\beta_3 \sum x_{2i}^3 / \sum x_{2i}^2$. Thus, the slope coefficient will be biased upward when $\beta_3 \sum x_{2i}^3$ is positive, and biased downward when $\beta_3 \sum x_{2i}^3$ is negative.

7.5 From Eq. (3.8)

$$\hat{\beta}_3^* = \frac{(\sum x_{3i} y_i)(\sum x_{2i}^2) - (\sum x_{2i} y_i)(\sum x_{2i} x_{3i})}{(\sum x_{2i}^2)(\sum x_{3i}^2) - (\sum x_{2i} x_{3i})^2}$$

Substituting for $y_i = \beta_2 x_{2i} + \varepsilon_i$ and taking expected values, we get

$$E(\hat{\beta}_3^*) = \frac{\beta_2(\sum x_{2i} x_{3i})(\sum x_{2i}^2) - (\sum x_{2i}^2)(\sum x_{2i} x_{3i})}{(\sum x_{2i}^2)(\sum x_{3i}^2) - (\sum x_{2i} x_{3i})^2}$$

$$+ \frac{E(\sum x_{3i} \varepsilon_i)(\sum x_{2i}^2) - E(\sum x_{2i} \varepsilon_i)(\sum x_{2i} x_{3i})}{(\sum x_{2i}^2)(\sum x_{3i}^2) - (\sum x_{2i} x_{3i})^2} = 0$$

7.8 Using time as an instrument, $\hat{X}_T = \hat{\alpha}_1 + \hat{\alpha}_2 T$ and $\hat{X}_t = X_t$; $t = 1, 2, \ldots,$ $T - 1$ where $\hat{\alpha}_2 = \sum x_t t / \sum t^2$. The least-squares slope estimate is $\hat{\beta} = \sum \hat{x}_t y_t / \sum \hat{x}_t^2$. Now, substituting $y_t = \beta \hat{x}_t + \beta(x_t - \hat{x}_t) + \varepsilon_t$ we get

$$\hat{\beta} = \beta + \beta \sum \hat{x}_t(x_t - \hat{x}_t)/\sum \hat{x}_t^2 + \frac{\sum \hat{x}_t \varepsilon_t}{\sum \hat{x}_t^2}$$

$$\text{plim } \hat{\beta} = \beta + \beta \text{ plim} \left[\frac{\hat{x}_T(x_T - \hat{x}_T)}{\sum \hat{x}_t^2} \right] + \text{plim} \left[\frac{\sum \hat{x}_t \varepsilon_t}{\sum \hat{x}_t^2} \right] = \beta$$

if time is a proper instrument. However, if the error term is serially correlated, time t and the error will be correlated, and the consistency of $\hat{\beta}$ will disappear.

7.9 The appropriate test statistic is

$$F_{N-1, NT-N-1} = \frac{(\text{ESS}_1 - \text{ESS}_2)/(N - 1)}{(\text{ESS}_2)/(NT - N - 1)}$$

where ESS_1 = residual sum of squares using ordinary least squares
ESS_2 = residual sum of squares using cross-section dummies

7.13 Using a second-degree polynomial specification, we assume that

$$W_i = C_0 + C_1 i + C_2 i^2 \qquad i = 0, 1, 2, 3$$

Substituting into the original specification, we get

$$Y_t = \alpha + \beta C_0 X_t + \beta(C_0 + C_1 + C_2)X_{t-1} + \beta(C_0 + 2C_1 + 4C_2)X_{t-2}$$

$$+ \beta(C_0 + 3C_1 + 9C_2)X_{t-3} + \varepsilon_t$$

and combining terms,

$$Y_t = \alpha + \beta C_0(X_t + X_{t-1} + X_{t-2} + X_{t-3})$$

$$+ \beta C_1(X_{t-1} + 2X_{t-2} + 3X_{t-3})$$

$$+ \beta C_2(X_{t-1} + 4X_{t-2} + 9X_{t-3}) + \varepsilon_t$$

which can be estimated using ordinary least squares if there are no endpoint restrictions. If the tail and the head are set equal to zero, then $W_{-1} = C_0 - C_1 + C_2 = 0$ and $W_4 = C_0 + 4C_1 + 16C_2 = 0$. Solving we find that $C_1 = -3C_2$ and $C_0 = -4C_2$. Then we may rewrite the original equation to be estimated by eliminating C_0 and C_1

$$Y_t = \alpha - \beta C_2 (4X_t + 6X_{t-1} + 6X_{t-2} + 4X_{t-3}) + \varepsilon_t$$

Using least squares we can estimate one of the lag weights, and by substitution we can determine the remaining two.

7.15
$$S = \sum_{t=1}^{T} [C_t - a_0 - a_1 YD_t^{a_2}]^2$$

The normal equations are

$$\sum_{t=1}^{T} [C_t - a_0 - a_1 YD_t^{a_2}] = 0$$

$$\sum_{t=1}^{T} YD_t^{a_2} [C_t - a_0 - a_1 YD_t^{a_2}] = 0$$

$$\sum_{t=1}^{T} YD_t^{a_2} \log YD_t [C_t - a_0 - a_1 YD_t^{a_2}] = 0$$

Solution of these equations for a_0, a_1, and a_2 would typically require a computer algorithm that iteratively linearizes the normal equations around values for the parameters. Thus this direct optimization method of estimation can be computationally more expensive than the iterative linearization method suggested in section 7.5.1.

8.1 There is a *unique* error variance associated with each observation on X_i and Y_i. It is impossible to obtain an estimate of each error variance from a single residual observation.

8.2 All coefficients will be doubled. This suggests that the estimated least-squares parameters are meaningful only relative to the magnitude of the other parameters and to the units of the dependent variable.

8.5 Assume that there exists an index Z_i, a linear function of the attributes of the ith community, which measures the probability that a community will default. Associated with each community is a normally distributed random variable Z_i^* which determines the cut-off point between default and nondefault. Then, the probit estimation procedure is appropriate for estimating the probability that a community will default. The probit model will yield predicted probabilities that lie within the 0–1 interval, but it does necessitate a nonlinear estimation procedure.

8.7 The regression line is $\hat{Y} = 1/2 + 3/8X$, $R^2 = .75$, and the number of correct classifications is five.

9.2 Let G = number of predetermined variables in the system

G_1 = number of predetermined variables in the equation being considered

H = number of endogenous variables in the system

H_1 = number of endogenous variables in the equation being considered

The first form of the order condition is equivalent to the following:

$$G - G_1 \geq H_1 - 1$$

The second form of the order condition is equivalent to

$$(G - G_1) + (H - H_1) \geq H - 1$$

Subtracting $(H - H_1)$ from both sides of the second condition yields the first.

9.4 There are four endogenous variables and three predetermined variables in the system. Thus, according to the order condition a necessary condition for identifiability is that the number of excluded predetermined variables be three or more. According to this criterion the first equation is just identified, while the second and third equations are unidentified. The first equation can be estimated by using two-stage least squares.

9.6 Write the model equations as $y_1 = \alpha x + u_1$ and $y_2 = \beta x + u_2$ with $\sigma_{12} = \text{cov}(u_1, u_2) = 0$. Then the derivation follows as in the text, except that $z^* = x^*$. Thus, Eqs. (9.36) and (9.37) simplify as follows:

$$\hat{\alpha} = \left(\frac{1}{C}\right)(A\sigma_1^2 \sum x^2) \qquad \hat{\beta} = \left(\frac{1}{C}\right)(B\sigma_2^2 \sum x^2)$$

$$A = \sigma_2^2 \sum xy_1 \qquad B = \sigma_1^2 \sum xy_2 \qquad C = \sigma_1^2\sigma_2^2 \left(\sum x^2\right)^2$$

Substituting, we find that $\hat{\alpha} = \sum xy_1 \sum x^2$ and $\hat{\beta} = \sum xy_2 \sum x^2$, both of which are the ordinary least-squares parameter estimates.

10.1 The RMS error is usually a better performance criterion when the variable of interest exhibits fluctuations and turning points—if the simulated series misses a turning point in the actual series, one would like to penalize heavily for the larger error that results. The mean absolute error might be preferred if the variable of interest exhibits a steady trend, in which case the concern is only how far above or below the actual trend line is the simulated series. Since we most often construct models to explain fluctuations in economic variables, the RMS error is the standard statistic calculated in most computer simulation programs.

10.3 The underprediction of GNP is largely the result of the inability of the model to predict turning points in the interest rate, combined with a negative error in the estimated propensity to consume resulting in a general underprediction of consumption. In the historical simulation consumption is usually below the actual series. (Consumption and GNP are close to the actual series in 1970–71 because of a positive error in simulated investment, resulting in turn from large negative errors in the simulated interest rate in 1969–70.) Observe in the *ex post* forecast that the interest rate is overpredicted in 1972 so that investment is underpredicted in 1973. Consumption is underpredicted throughout the *ex post* forecast. The result is an underprediction of GNP.

11.2 (1) The fundamental dynamic equation for the model is given by

$$Y_t - (a_2 + b_2 a_2)Y_{t-1} + b_2 a_2 Y_{t-2} = a_1 + b_1 + G_t$$

so that the characteristic equation is

$$\lambda^2 - (a_2 + b_2 a_2)\lambda + b_2 a_2 = 0$$

The characteristic roots are therefore

$$\lambda_1, \lambda_2 = \frac{a_2 + b_2 a_2}{2} \pm 1/2\sqrt{(a_2 + b_2 a_2)^2 - 4b_2 a_2}$$

(2) The solution will oscillate if the characteristic roots are complex, i.e., if $4b_2 a_2 > (a_2 + b_2 a_2)^2$. The solution will explode if the roots are greater than 1 in magnitude. The type of solution will depend on a_2 and b_2 as follows:

$a_2 > \dfrac{4b_2}{(1 + b_2)^2}$, $b_2 < 1$ stable, nonoscillatory solution

$a_2 > \dfrac{4b_2}{(1 + b_2)^2}$, $b_2 > 1$ explosive, nonoscillatory solution

$\dfrac{1}{b_2} < a_2 < \dfrac{4b_2}{(1 + b_2)^2}$ explosive, oscillatory solution

$a_2 < \dfrac{1}{b_2}$ stable, oscillatory solution (damped cycles)

12.1 The wage-price dummy variable appears directly in the inflation rate and wage rate equations; and by setting the dummy equal to 1, the inflation and wage rates will be forced down. The only link between wages and prices and the real sector (consumption, investment, and GNP) is through interest rates. Interest rates in the model are *nominal* rates; the *real* rate of interest (determined by money demand-supply equilibrium) is the nominal rate minus the inflation rate. Thus a drop in the inflation rate results in a drop in interest rates, which in turn stimulates residential, and to some extent nonresidential, investment. The net effect on GNP, however, is positive but small.

12.5 (1) An increase in the support price will result in an increase in the amount of leaf pledged under the support program, from Eqs. (12.42) and (12.43). This in turn results in a drop in SQNET, the ratio of inventory stock to sales, which produces an increase in the actual leaf price as producers try to raise the inventory-sales ratio back to its desired level—see Eqs. (12.37) and (12.39). Finally, this increase in price results in an increase in the dollar value of producing acreage, an increase in the amount of acreage planted, and an increase in production [see Eqs. (12.31) through (12.36)].

(2) An increase in the government acreage allotment AL results in an increase in underage [from Eqs. (12.34) and (12.35)]. In Eq. (12.36) observe that the increase in underage has a negative effect on acreage planted, but the increase in the allotment has a direct positive effect. The net effect is positive: a 1-acre increase in AL results in an increase of $1 - .016 = .984$ acres planted. Thus production increases. This will raise the inventory-sales ratio, however, so that the actual leaf price will fall.

12.7 To use the financial simulation model to determine the breakeven point for sales, make earnings before tax (EBT) an exogenous input parameter, and rewrite the equations for operating income (OI) and EBT in Block I of the model as follows:

Replace the third equation (for OI) with:

$$SALES = OI + CGS + OC$$

Replace the seventh equation (for EBT) with:

$$OI = EBT + INT + DEP$$

To determine the breakeven point for sales, simulate the new model setting EBT equal to zero.

13.2 Observe from the derivation of Eq. (13.20) that if an *actual* value of y_{T+1} is available, the forecast $\hat{y}_{T+2}$ will take this data point into account. The forecast will then be

$$\hat{y}_{T+2} = \alpha \sum_{\tau=0}^{\infty} (1-\alpha)^{\tau} y_{T-\tau+1}$$

rather than as given by Eq. (13.20).

13.4 We know that the process given by Eq. (13.30) is nonstationary since its mean and variance increase indefinitely. It is first-order homogeneous since

$$w_t = \Delta y_t = d + \varepsilon_t$$

This process has a constant mean d and a constant variance σ_ε^2, and is stationary.

14.1 The variance and covariances for the MA(3) process are

$$\gamma_0 = \sigma_\varepsilon^2(1 + \theta_1^2 + \theta_2^2 + \theta_3^2)$$

$$\gamma_1 = \sigma_\varepsilon^2(-\theta_1 + \theta_2\theta_1 + \theta_3\theta_2)$$

$$\gamma_2 = \sigma_\varepsilon^2(-\theta_2 + \theta_3\theta_1)$$

$$\gamma_3 = -\theta_3\sigma_\varepsilon^2$$

$$\gamma_k = 0, \quad k > 3$$

14.2 Observe in Fig. 14.2 that y_t tends to be positively correlated with adjacent values; for example, a positive value is more likely to be preceded and followed by a positive value than by a negative value. The correlation, however, does not extend more than one period out, so that the realization appears very "noisy." A realization of the process

$$y_t = 1 + \varepsilon_t - .8\varepsilon_{t-1}$$

would show negative correlations between adjacent values, so that a positive value of y_t would be more likely to be followed by a negative value.

14.4
$$\rho_1 = \frac{\phi_1}{1-\phi_2} - \frac{\theta_1(1 - \phi_1^2\phi_2 - \phi_1^2 - \phi_2)}{(1-\phi_2)^2(1 - 2\phi_1\theta_1 + \theta_1^2) - 2\phi_1\phi_2\theta_1(1-\phi_2)}$$

$$\rho_2 = \phi_2 + \phi_1\rho_1$$

$$\rho_3 = \phi_1\rho_2 + \phi_2\rho_1$$

14.6
$$y_t = \sum w_t, \quad \text{so } E[y_t] = \sum E[w_t]$$

$$E[w_t] = 1/(1 - .9) = 10$$

then

$$E[y_t] = 10t$$

15.2 (1) This misspecification will result in residuals that are autocorrelated. The diagnostic check described in Section 15.2 can be used, and the statistic R is likely to be above the 10 percent point on the chi-square distribution.

(2) Let us assume that the parameters of the process are known with certainty. Write the true ARMA(1,2) process as

$$\varepsilon_t = y_t - \phi_1 y_{t-1} + \theta_1 \varepsilon_{t-1} + \theta_2 \varepsilon_{t-2}$$

and write the ARMA(0,2) model as

$$\tilde{\varepsilon}_t = y_t + \theta_1 \varepsilon_{t-1} + \theta_2 \varepsilon_{t-2}$$

The error term for the model is thus related to the error term for the true process by

$$\tilde{\varepsilon}_t = \varepsilon_t - \phi_1 y_{t-1}$$

The error term $\tilde{\varepsilon}_t$ will therefore be autocorrelated

$$E[\tilde{\varepsilon}_t \tilde{\varepsilon}_{t-1}] = E[(\varepsilon_t - \phi_1 y_{t-1})(\varepsilon_{t-1} - \phi_1 y_{t-2})] = \phi_1 \sigma_\varepsilon^2 + \phi_1^2 \gamma_1$$

where γ_1 is the covariance (for displacement 1) of the true process ARMA(1,2). Generally $\phi_1^2 \gamma_1$ will be much smaller than $\phi_1 \sigma_\varepsilon^2$, so that we may write

$$E[\tilde{\varepsilon}_t \tilde{\varepsilon}_{t-1}] \simeq \phi_1 \sigma_\varepsilon^2$$

Similarly $E[\tilde{\varepsilon}_t \tilde{\varepsilon}_{t-2}] \simeq \phi_1^2 \sigma_\varepsilon^2$, and so on. Thus the residual autocorrelations for the ARMA(0,2) model will look like those for a *first-order autoregressive process*, and this would indicate that ARMA(1,2) is a more correct specification.

16.2 Reexamine Eqs. (16.10) and (16.11) for the ARIMA(p,d,q) model. Note that in making a forecast one period ahead, the only missing information is the value of the error term ε_t in the next period, i.e., the value of ε_{T+1}

(the values of w_T, w_{T-1}, ..., ε_T, ε_{T-1}, ... are all known, assuming that the parameters of the model are known). Therefore the forecast error variance for the one-period forecast should simply be the variance of ε_t.

16.4 The one-period, two-period, and three-period forecasts for the AR(2) process are

$$\hat{y}_T(1) = \phi_1 y_T + \phi_2 y_{T-1} + \delta$$

$$\hat{y}_T(2) = \phi_1 \hat{y}_T(1) + \phi_2 y_T + \delta$$

$$= (\phi_1^2 + \phi_2)y_T + \phi_1\phi_2 y_{T-1} + (1 + \phi_1)\delta$$

$$\hat{y}_T(3) = (\phi_1^3 + 2\phi_1\phi_2)y_T + (\phi_1^2\phi_2 + \phi_2^2)y_{T-1} + (1 + \phi_1 + \phi_1^2 + \phi_2)\delta$$

These forecasts have error variances

$$E[e_T^2(1)] = \sigma_\varepsilon^2$$

$$E[e_T^2(2)] = (1 + \phi_1^2)\sigma_\varepsilon^2$$

$$E[e_T^2(3)] = [1 + \phi_1^4 + \phi_1^2(1 + 2\phi_2) + \phi_2^2]\sigma_\varepsilon^2$$

AUTHOR INDEX

Afifi, A. A., 197n.
Aigner, D., 58n., 72n.
Aitchison, A., 258n.
Allen, R. G. D., 338n.
Almon, S., 220
Andersen, L. C., 348
Ando, A., 370n.
Anstrom, K., 361n.
Anthonyson, R. B., 402n.

Bacon, D. W., 535n.
Baily, M. N., 394n.
Balestra, P., 206n.
Bartlett, M. S., 438n.
Baumol, W. J., 310n., 338n., 340n.
Berkson, J., 249n.
Boschan, C., 320n.
Bowen, W. G., 82n.
Box, G. E. P., 419, 438n., 460n., 477n., 478n.,
    490, 535n.
Brehm, C. T., 238, 283
Brewer, G. D., 308n., 334n.
Brunner, K., 348n.
Brunner, R. D., 308n., 334n.

Cacappolo, G. J., 308n.
Carlson, K. M., 348
Chaudry, M. A., 308n.
Choucri, N., 308n.
Chow, G. C., 192, 205n., 287n., 343n., 346n.
Cochrane, D., 111n.
Cooper, J. P., 402n.
Cootner, P. H., 394n., 432n.
Corbo, V., 230n.
Cox, D. R., 249n., 250
Crecine, J. P., 334n.

Dagenais, M. G., 197n.
Davis, B. E., 308n.
Dean, J., 77n.

Dhrymes, P. J., 60n., 212n., 217n., 320n.
Domencich, T., 238n., 247n., 250
Draper, N., 71n., 227n.
Duesenberry, J., 150n., 278n.
Duggal, V. G., 370n.
Durbin, J., 113n.
Dutton, J. M., 334n.

Eisner, M., 228n., 230n.
Elashoff, R. M., 197n.
Elliott, J. W., 308n.
Evans, M. K., 320n., 371n.

Fair, R. C., 147n., 278n., 329n., 331n.
Fama, E. F., 432n.
Farrar, D. E., 68n.
Feldstein, M., 177n.
Finegan, T. A., 82n.
Finney, D. J., 245n.
Fisher, F. M., 205n., 273n., 278n., 394n.
Forrester, J. W., 334n.
Fox, K., 346n.
Freund, J. E., 49n.
Fromm, G., 150n., 278n., 313n.

Geisel, M. S., 217n.
Gilbert, R. F., 282n.
Glasser, M., 199n.
Glauber, R. R., 68n.
Goldberger, A., 86n., 155n., 172n., 306n., 347n.
Goldfeld, S., 104n., 105n., 230n.
Graybill, F. A., 49n.
Grenander, U., 478n.
Griffen, J. M., 394n.
Griliches, Z., 212n., 217n.

Haitovsky, Y., 197n., 320n.
Heller, P., 209n.
Hickman, B., 320n.
Hildreth, G., 112n.

569

SUBJECT INDEX